Decision analysis is a technology designed to help individuals and organizations make wise inferences and decisions. It synthesizes ideas from economics, statistics, psychology, operations research, and other disciplines. A great deal of behavioral research is relevant to decision analysis: behavioral scientists have both suggested easy and natural ways to describe and quantify problems and shown the kinds of errors to which unaided intuitive judgments can lead. This long-awaited book offers the first integrative presentation of the principles of decision analysis in a behavioral context.

The authors break new ground on a variety of technical topics – sensitivity analysis, the value–utility distinction, multistage inference, attitudes toward risk – and attempt to make intuitive sense out of what has been treated in the literature as endemic biases and other errors of human judgment.

The technical content of *Decision Analysis and Behavioral Research* will be especially useful to professionals in decision analysis and in cognitive psychology; the book will be required reading for advanced students in programs ranging from business to the behavioral and social sciences to medicine. Its more general ideas, especially those on problem structuring, will be important to a broad range of scientists interested in decision making, and to people who make major decisions themselves. Those interested in artificial intelligence will find it the easiest to understand presentation of hierarchical Bayesian inference available.

Decision analysis and behavioral research

Decision analysis and behavioral research

DETLOF VON WINTERFELDT

*Institute of Safety and Systems Management
and Social Science Research Institute
University of Southern California*

WARD EDWARDS

*Social Science Research Institute
University of Southern California*

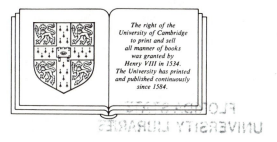

The right of the
University of Cambridge
to print and sell
all manner of books
was granted by
Henry VIII in 1534.
The University has printed
and published continuously
since 1584.

CAMBRIDGE UNIVERSITY PRESS

*Cambridge
London   New York   New Rochelle
Melbourne   Sydney*

Published by the Press Syndicate of the University of Cambridge
The Pitt Building, Trumpington Street, Cambridge CB2 1RP
32 East 57th Street, New York, NY 10022, USA
10 Stamford Road, Oakleigh, Melbourne 3166, Australia

First published 1986

Printed in the United States of America

Library of Congress Cataloging-in-Publication Data
Winterfeldt, Detlof von
Decision analysis and behavioral research.
1. Decision-making – Research.   2. Statistical
decision. 3. Psychology – Research.   4. Psychometrics.
5. Psychophysics. I. Edwards, Ward. II. Title.
BF441.V66   1986   153.8′3   85–31393

British Library Cataloguing in Publication Data
Winterfeldt, Detlof von
Decision analysis and behavioral research.
1. Decision-making
I. Title   II. Edwards, Ward
658.4′0354   HD30.23

ISBN 0 521 25308 X hard covers
ISBN 0 521 27304 8 paperback

This work was in part supported by Department of the Navy Contract N00014-79-C-0529
issued by the Office of Naval Research. The U.S. government has a royalty-free license
throughout the world in all copyrightable material contained herein.

To

Leonard J. Savage
Professor of Statistics, Yale University

and

S. Smith Stevens
Professor of Psychology, Harvard University

Both were forceful advocates in the 1950s and 1960s of lines of thought with deep historical roots that they transformed, updated, and made useful. We hope both would have seen in this book a coherent set of intellectual technologies derived from their very different ideas.

Contents

Preface   xi

**1 Basic concepts of decision analysis and their relation to
      behavior**   **1**
1.1. Introduction   1
1.2. The central topics of decision analysis   4
1.3. Rationality and expected quantities   18
1.4. Other purposes of decision-analytic procedures   22
1.5. Decision aids, artificial intelligence, and other aspects of
      intellectual technology   23

2 Structuring for decision analysis   **26**
2.1. The structuring problem   26
2.2. Identifying the problem   29
2.3. Developing an overall analytic structure   32
2.4. Structuring value trees   36
2.5. Structuring probabilistic inference problems   45
2.6. Advances in structuring research   55

3 Decision trees   **63**
3.1. Introduction   63
3.2. How to build a decision tree   66
3.3. One-stage decision tree calculus   72
3.4. Multistage decision tree calculus   76
3.5. Value of information   82
3.6. Epilogue   86

4 Uncertainty and its measurement   **90**
4.1. Fundamentals   90
4.2. Other representations of uncertainty   98
4.3. Randomness, exchangeability, and independence   105
4.4. Probability assessment   107
4.5. Eliciting judgments of uncertainty from people   112

4.6.   Extremeness, proper scoring rules, and calibration   122
4.7.   Debiasing   131
4.8.   Group probability assessments   133

5   Elementary inference: Bayesian statistics   **137**
5.1.   Introduction   137
5.2.   Principles of Bayesian statistics   138
5.3.   A smattering of Bayesian distribution theory   147
5.4.   Hypothesis testing and related decisions   153
5.5.   Present state of Bayesian statistics   161

6   Inference   **163**
6.1.   Introduction: scenarios, inference, and explanations   163
6.2.   The Reverend Bayes meets the ungodly inference   170
6.3.   Formal multistage inference structures   176
6.4.   Generic structures, dependencies, and types of evidence 192
6.5.   Behavioral results and lessons for application   200

7   Value and utility measurement   **205**
7.1.   Basic issues in value and utility measurement   205
7.2.   Methods of unidimensional value and utility measurement 215
7.3.   Value measurement   226
7.4.   Utility measurement   241
7.5.   Implications for decision-analytic practice   257

8   Multiattribute utility theory: examples and techniques **259**
8.1.   Introduction to MAUT   259
8.2.   The simple multiattribute rating technique   278
8.3.   Indifference techniques for value measurement   287
8.4.   Indifference techniques for utility measurement   298
8.5.   Implications for decision-analytic practice   308

9   Theoretical foundations of value and utility measurement **314**
9.1.   Measurement theories of value and utility   314
9.2.   Theoretical foundations of single-attribute value and utility
       measurement   317
9.3.   Theoretical foundations of multiattribute value and utility
       measurement   326
9.4.   Qualitative model tests and consistency checks   341
9.5.   Implications for decision-analytic practice   350

10 Experiments on value and utility measurement   **351**
10.1. Introduction: experiments are relevant   351
10.2. Numbers in the head?   351

Contents   ix

10.3. Consistency and reliability of value and utility judgments   355
10.4. Experimental validation of multiattribute utility structures   362
10.5. Bets, money, and the fate of static models in a changing
       world   369
10.6. Implications for decision-analytic practice   383

11 Sensitivity analysis and flat maxima   **387**
11.1. Introduction: now that you have the numbers . . .   387
11.2. Dominance   388
11.3. Ideas for sensitivity analysis   399
11.4. Flat maxima in EV models   420
11.5. Flat maxima in MAUT models   436
11.6. Implications of the insensitivity of decision-analytic
       models   444

12 Applications and pitfalls of decision analysis   **448**
12.1. Introduction   448
12.2. Applications to diagnostic and prediction problems   448
12.3. Applications to evaluation problems   462
12.4. Applications to decisions under uncertainty   499
12.5. Pitfalls of decision analysis: examples and lessons   517

13 Cognitive illusions   **530**
13.1. Messages of despair, confidence, and help   530
13.2. Cognitive illusions in probability and inference:
       conservatism   533
13.3. Other classes of cognitive illusions   544
13.4. Reflections on cognitive illusions   550

14 Some idiosyncratic history and guesses about things to come   **560**
14.1. Introduction   560
14.2. Background: pre–World War II   561
14.3. 1944–1954   561
14.4. 1954–1963   564
14.5. 1963–1971   566
14.6. 1971–1979   568
14.7. A glimpse of the future: a research agenda for decision
       analysis   569

References   575
Author index   595
Subject index   600

Preface

This book has taken five years to write, and the task has changed our views. When we started, we considered ourselves to be fairly orthodox decision analysts with backgrounds in psychology. As researchers, we were concerned with improving the tools of decision analysis. As practitioners, we applied those tools. In both roles, we were acutely aware of the enormous importance of two psychological traditions: psychophysics and human engineering. Psychophysics is the science of numerical subjectivity. Decision analysts routinely address problems to which psychophysical tools are relevant, often without knowing much about those tools. The most trivial lesson of human engineering is to design tasks mercifully, so that they will be easy to perform. Decision analysts do this less often than they should.

Behavioral decision theory might be expected to link decision-analytic practice with its psychological roots. On the whole, it has not done so. Behavioral decision theory, like decision analysis, got its unknowing start in 1947, with the publication of the second edition of von Neumann and Morgenstern's *Theory of Games and Economic Behavior,* a book its authors considered to be primarily a contribution to economic theory. Crucial differences in agenda among three different audiences led to important divergences in the impact of that book. From the perspectives of economics and of statistics, it used elegant mathematical tools to extend the domain of the classical idea that decision makers either do or should choose the option that maximizes utility to decisions in risky situations and to games against hostile opponents. Decision analysis emerged as some researchers and practitioners, often coming from statistics or operations research, brought an explicitly prescriptive agenda to the same set of ideas. They developed tools intended to help decision makers do what economists often assume they are already doing. That, we now know, is a challenging task. Psychologists, whose most fundamental agenda has typically been that of describing and understanding actual individual behavior, soon began to find in experiments that their respondents, working without tools, did not behave as the prescriptive rules said they should. Thus, the same ideas combined with three different agendas to produce three different ways of looking at decisions. The decision-analytic perspective is unique in aspiring to combine prescriptiveness with practicality.

Some psychologists have prescriptive agendas. Many do not. The message of a vigorous psychological tradition of research on human intellectual limitations and their organizational consequences often seems to be that even under the best circumstances human intellectual performance is not very good. A frequently encountered implication is: discard the errant human being and use a computer instead. But the thrust of decision analysts and many others with prescriptive agendas is to see that the requirements for good human performance are met, rather than to regret human limitations and seek to automate the intellectual task. We value appropriate automation of intellectual tasks. But we know from experience that many intellectual tasks cannot be done well without a great deal of human participation. And there are many more instances than we might like in which the hope of automating such tasks has motivated large expenditures with little or no useful result.

We believe that decision analysts and psychologists interested in cognitive problems have much to gain from each other. Decision analysts can learn from psychophysicists how vulnerable the process of producing subjective numbers is to response mode and framing effects. Behavioral decision theorists can learn from decision analysts how well human beings can perform difficult intellectual tasks, given time, help, and tools. Cognitive psychologists can help decision analysts to see what kinds of tools are most helpful.

Our primary agenda is that of decision analysts: unabashedly prescriptive. But much that is prescriptively useful can be found in the work of many cognitive psychologists, especially that of behavioral decision theorists. We see far more unity than divergence between these points of view and believe that more unity can exist than exists now. So, combining our descriptive with our prescriptive agendas, we have tried to write about the unity we see – and in the process to enhance it.

As we wrote, we found ourselves facing problems for which conventional decision-analytic solutions seemed inadequate and pondering conclusions about human cognitive limitations that seemed to us overdrawn. Both kinds of confrontations between received ideas and perceived realities drove us, often unwillingly, to face the problems afresh, for ourselves. As a result, this book contains some unorthodox treatments of standard topics in decision analysis.

One novel treatment has to do with complex inference. Studies of several real-world inference problems have convinced us that simple one- or two-stage Bayesian formulations do not come close to matching their complexity. Rudimentary approaches to building complex inference structures and constructing Bayesian models for them have been devised, mostly by Professor David A. Schum. We summarize what little we know about complex Bayesian inference. We do not offer a technology built around those ideas, though work toward that end is in progress.

A second novel treatment has to do with the value–utility distinction. In decision-analytic tradition, value is typically a transformation (which may be linear) on some physical scale, and utility is a further transformation on value, intended to take into account the decision maker's attitude toward risk. We found ourselves uncomfortable with this distinction on both formal and experimental grounds – and became more and more uncomfortable with it as the book progressed. By now, only vestiges of the idea remain in our thoughts and recommendations. Though we recognize that attitudes toward risk are observable and important, we prefer to think about them in ways other than as visible evidence of the value–utility distinction.

A third novel treatment has to do with the conflict between a traditional economic definition of value or utility as a function of total economic assets and the fact, derived from both experimentation and decision-analytic practice, that decisions are made in relation to a reference point. As we thought hard about it, we came to realize that the reference point is simply the non-occurrence of the transaction at hand. We are embedded in flows of transactions of various kinds; the way we evaluate transactions under consideration is much more limited than accounting for all these flows. One advantage of this line of thought is that it makes behaving as though you have various attitudes toward risk, all of them of course relative to a reference point, not only understandable but even normatively appropriate. Your attitude toward risk depends, and should depend, on the transaction stream into which the transaction you are currently considering will be assimilated, if made.

A fourth novel treatment has to do with cognitive illusions. This topic gave us more trouble than any other in the book, and the chapter with that title was revised many more times than any other. We are very grateful to Baruch Fischhoff, Sarah Lichtenstein, Paul Slovic, and Amos Tversky for patient and tolerant willingness to advise us through effort after effort, until we finally found a point of view with which, at least for now, we are satisfied.

Two thoughts are central to our current view. Much of the standard literature treats cognitive illusions as having to do with probability and, to a lesser extent, with utility effects. People simply make mistakes in probability assessments and in maximizing utility. It was enormously helpful, though very difficult, for us to realize that these mistakes are no different in character from other kinds of familiar and less familiar mistakes in which relatively casual thought violates formal rules. In the end, we found it most helpful to think about mental arithmetic, primarily because of the seamless gradation of problem difficulty to which it gives rise. This enabled us to discover at least four different meanings of the word *intuition* and to recognize the roles that education and tools play in helping us to avoid errors. We educate young people to do arithmetic correctly; we do not educate them to assess probabilities, to make Bayesian inferences, or to maximize utility.

A fifth treatment that was novel to us, though we believe it to be familiar to some practitioners, has to do with sensitivity analysis. Our main ideas here are, first, that dominance can play a very useful and important role in sensitivity analysis and, second, that a principle we call the flat maximum often implies that, once dominance has done as much as it can, not much is left to do. We also introduce a helpful distinction between sensitivity analysis for the analyst and sensitivity analysis for the client.

There are other new lines of thought scattered through the book, but this summary may be enough to whet your appetite.

But can you read the book? We hope so. Our two primary intended audiences are mature decision scientists and first-year graduate students in a wide variety of disciplines. Though we have been unable to banish symbols and equations completely, we have tried to keep them at a minimum and to provide verbal explanations wherever they do appear. Only two chapters seem to us difficult to read. One, Chapter 9, on the theory of multiattribute utility, is not crucial to someone who wants to understand ideas and apply them, though it is crucial for justifying them. The other, Chapter 11, on sensitivity analysis, is just plain hard. Nonetheless, even a nonmathematical graduate student can work through it, though the going will be slow. We simply do not know how to make it easier.

The book makes liberal use of examples, both imaginary and real. We have attempted to provide an explicit, easy-to-understand example of every topic we discuss. So if the arguments raise issues or make intellectual difficulties for you, just be a bit patient; perhaps the example will make things clearer.

The real examples are drawn from the somewhat scanty published literature of decision-analytic cases. Chapter 12 is devoted to applications. Most of the applications we discuss are government- rather than business-oriented. This reflects both our backgrounds, which are primarily in government decision making, and the published literature. As far as we can judge, this should make no difference to the business-oriented reader, since the tools and types of problem are essentially the same; the main difference is that many governmental problems are very complex, so that it is not as easy as it might be in a business application to identify either the decision maker or the quantity the decision should maximize.

We are intellectually indebted to many people. Our dedication to L. J. Savage and S. S. Stevens acknowledges one kind of debt – very direct in Edwards's case, since he learned from extensive personal interaction with both. Our chapter on history acknowledges other intellectual debts: to C. H. Coombs, Ronald A. Howard, and Howard Raiffa. Extremely helpful critiques of parts of the book were made by Thomas Eppel, Baruch Fischhoff, Ralph Keeney, and Howard Kunreuther. Not explicitly acknowledged elsewhere is the intellectual debt that von Winterfeldt owes to Ralph Keeney, whose Ph.D. in derisive footnotes, like his book, taught us what to avoid.

We are also greatly indebted to Martin A. Tolcott, Robert Sasmor, and Stephen J. Andreole. They provided funding that covered part of the cost of writing the book. They also won our permanent gratitude with their tolerance and understanding as due dates came and went. Somehow they never doubted that the book would someday be finished – which shows them wiser than us.

Mary Stepp and Judith Webb were invaluable in typing, keeping things straight, and not letting pressure get them down. Mary Sears also shared the typing. Patrick Henry was the utility infielder for the book, searching out references, helping with a few analyses, and generally doing what needed to be done. We thank them all.

The preparation of this book was supported by the Office of Naval Research under Contract N00014-79-C-0529, with cosponsorship by the Army Research Institute. Other supporters included the University of Southern California, the Wood Kalb Foundation, and the Defense Advanced Research Projects Agency. We are grateful. The views and conclusions expressed in this book are those of the authors and should not be taken as representing those of the U.S. government or any of its agencies.

D. v. W.
W. E.

1 Basic concepts of decision analysis and their relation to behavior

1.1. Introduction

This book is about how to make hard decisions well. Decision making is usually trivial, either because the topic is trivial or because the best option is obvious or both. You may not care much whether you have dessert after dinner. You may care a great deal about whether to borrow money from a bank, but if one bank charges 9% interest and another charges 10%, you will have no trouble recognizing that you will be better off paying less interest. Accident statistics probably do not deter you from driving to the local shopping center. We would love to own an ocean-going racing yacht apiece – but only if you insist that all your friends buy this book can you make our decision about whether to buy a yacht for each of us nontrivial.

Hard decisions

Occasionally all of us must make complex, confusing, and stressful decisions. Perhaps you must decide whether to have an operation. Perhaps the 9% loan requires a greater down payment. You must select among investment options in spite of uncertainties about interest rates, stock values, and market trends. (If that is not your case this year, wait until next year.) If you want and can afford one but not both, should you get that yacht or a private airplane?

   If you are a business or government executive or a politician, the same issues come up on a far grander scale. Except in unusual circumstances, you are deciding for others as well as for yourself. Should the United States deploy the MX missile? Should your company borrow money in order to buy out a competitor? What plants should it build, and where should they be located? How much benefit cutting and tax raising should Congress do to keep the Medicare system solvent?

What this book is about: rationality

This book is about a set of formal models, semiformal techniques for interacting with people, and bits of lore and craft that are collectively called deci-

1

sion analysis. Their goal is to structure and simplify the task of making hard decisions as well and as easily as the nature of the decisions permits. These techniques all depend heavily on human judgments of many kinds. Therefore, the book also dwells on research, mostly psychological, about how and how well people make such judgments and about how they can be helped to make them. Explicitly, this book is intended to help people be rational in making inferences and decisions.

Today, few people are willing to commit themselves firmly to the goal of rationality, and even fewer are willing to claim that the goal is attainable. We do both, and should explain what we mean.

The notion of rationality is clearly prescriptive: in any version, it explicitly says that some thoughts and actions are appropriate and others are not. But one can easily distinguish two kinds of prescriptions. One has to do with ends or goals or moral imperatives: "Thou shalt not steal." A quite different kind of prescription has to do with selecting ways of thinking and acting to serve your ends or goals or moral imperatives, whatever they may be, as well as the environment permits: "If you want to minimize the cost of your plane ticket for your upcoming trip to Helsinki, go to travel agent A; she is expert about discount fares and very helpful in arranging for them." One of several reasons for the unfashionableness of the notion of rationality is the failure to distinguish between rationality in the selection of ends and rationality in the selection of means.

This book is almost entirely about the latter. The word *almost* in the preceding sentence appeared for the first time in the last draft of this chapter. It conveys a dilemma in our thinking. In applications of decision analysis we often find ourselves suggesting ends to decision makers. For example, we often suggest that the political ramifications of a decision be considered in evaluating its consequences; in our experience, decision makers too often ignore this slippery issue and are bitten by it after the decision is made. Sometimes we encourage decision makers to be open and explicit about selfish values and motives. In almost all applications we have felt that decision makers benefited from clarification of all their values, socially acceptable or not, insofar as they were related to evaluating the decision to be made.

Yes, decision analysis focuses on instrumental values. But in the process it helps decision makers think about and clarify the values here called "ends" as well.

We must set explicit ground rules for distinguishing wise from foolish prescriptions. A common but subtle and often misused idea is that decisions, and so rules for decision making, should be evaluated on the basis of their results. But good decisions can lead to bad outcomes; bad decisions can lead to good outcomes. You are probably wise enough not to buy insurance against damage to your old and rusty car – but you may wish you had done so if you hit a tree and damage it severely. We don't advise you to stake your last $100 on a single number at the roulette table. But if you win . . .

People like to kid themselves. Good luck is habitually seen as good management, and misfortune as the result of frivolous or stupid decisions. This book, like all other treatments of decision analysis, draws a hard-and-fast dividing line: the quality of decisions really means the quality of the processes by which they are made, and that can be evaluated only on the basis of information available before their outcomes occur or become certain. Rational decisions are made and must be evaluated with foresight, not hindsight. Arguments that link the outcomes of decisions to their evaluation are, of course, indispensable. For decisions the outcomes of which are certain, those arguments are direct. For decisions made under uncertainty (the usual case), they are subtle and do not apply to any single decision.

Two messages

As a whole, the book has two main messages. One is that rationality of inference and rationality of decision are attainable goals. If you face a difficult problem of either kind, you will find in this book some technologies for dealing with it, along with references to literature in which these tools are presented in more detail and from a variety of viewpoints. Throughout the book, *technology* means any collection of orderly and useful techniques.

The second message is that the technologies needed to attain rationality are more often than not demanding to learn and difficult to use. We ourselves use elements of decision analysis (e.g., probability estimates) daily but perform full analyses to facilitate or to check on personal decisions only once or twice per year. The cost of systematic, careful thought using formally appropriate tools is high enough that even experts do not routinely or casually incur it. Casual thought suggests that careful analysis is worthwhile when the stakes are high. More thought makes clear that high stakes are necessary, but not sufficient. Careful analysis is justified when the stakes are high *and* the inference or decision is intellectually difficult or insecure.

Structure of the book

The technology of decision analysis includes elicitation techniques for obtaining numbers bearing on the merits of well-defined options and mathematical tools for using those numbers to make decisions. If that were all, it would be useful far less often than it is. However, at least in our experience, the more common starting point for a decision analysis is not the question "Which is preferable, option A or option B?" but rather "This situation is intolerable. The goals I want to attain conflict with one another, and no sensible ideas occur to me about how to proceed. What shall I do?" The second starting point implies a series of structuring and invention problems; they are the topic of Chapters 2 and 3. Quite often, by the time the problem is adequately structured, little or no further analysis is needed.

If further analysis is needed, it is focused on either or both of two topics:

the values the decision should serve and the degree of certainty with which the effectiveness of the available actions in serving those values can be predicted. Chapter 4 presents the fundamentals of uncertainty measurement, Chapter 5 introduces the topic of inference by dealing with the special and simple cases with which statistical inference is concerned, and Chapter 6 deals with the broader topic of inference in general. Chapters 7 and 8 present the technology of value and utility measurement. Chapter 9 presents the theory on which Chapters 7 and 8 rest. Chapter 10 relates the content of Chapters 7, 8, and 9 to behavioral research bearing both on how well value and utility measurement work (and how to improve them) and on the degree to which the fundamental ideas have descriptive as well as prescriptive usefulness. Chapter 11 is essentially about what one does with the numbers that measure uncertainty and value or utility after they are available. Chapter 12 discusses applications. That statement is a little misleading; examples of applications are liberally scattered throughout the book. Chapter 13 deals with what has become a major topic of behavioral research: the ability of human beings to perform intuitively some of the intellectual tasks that are defined in the book, especially Chapters 4 and 5, as tasks that have to be performed somehow. That theme is also touched on in Chapter 4, and in the utility domain is the topic of Chapter 10. Finally, Chapter 14 grew out of our frustration at the difficulties of understanding the history of decision analysis. It presents a brief history of the topic since 1944 and as much perspective as we have about where decision-analytic thought is going. Among books on decision analysis, this one differs from others in two main ways: its emphasis on the intertwining of formal analysis and behavioral research, and its primary attention to governmental rather than business examples.

1.2. The central topics of decision analysis

Decision analysis is particularly useful for coping with two recurrent complexities of decision making: uncertainty and multiple objectives.

Uncertainty

Uncertainty hardly needs an introduction. "If I only knew" and "If I had only known" are common pre- and postdecisional complaints about the vagaries of nature (or enemies) that contribute to the vulnerability of our decisions.

We cope with uncertainty irrationally by ignoring it, or by worrying. We cope with it rationally in numerous ways. We make quantitative analyses of its bases. We collect evidence to reduce it. We hedge against unfavorable outcomes, perhaps trading off payoff against uncertainty. Doing such things well constitutes the expertise of many professionals. Reliability engineers and risk analysts make numerical assessments of the probabilities of failure of complex systems in order to identify and eliminate weak components. Forecasters of rain, sales, or knockouts reduce uncertainties by collecting and processing information and by communicating their expert interpretation of it. Insurers do little to change the chances that you will have an automobile accident. But in return for your premiums, they make the consequences of doing so bearable. Portfolio analysts and investment counselors expertly trade off uncertainties against potential profits and losses.

Decision analysts do all of these things in order to cope with uncertainty, but their emphasis is on trading off uncertainties against various value aspects of the outcomes in an effort to arrive at a rational choice.

The commonness of "If only I had known" feelings invites the equally common error that the way to make good decisions is to eliminate uncertainties. Though that is normally pleasant and sometimes appropriate, good decisions must often be made in the face of unreduced or irreducible uncertainties. The issue is one of balancing uncertainties and outcomes. The decision whether to buy a 50 : 50 chance of winning $1,000 or winning nothing may be more or less difficult, depending on price. The decision is equally easy at $1 and at $999. But would you pay $300? Would you pay $500? Good decisions balance uncertainties and outcomes in accordance with the judgments and preferences of the decision maker. Decisions do, and should, depend on outcomes and probabilities, on stakes and odds, on values and uncertainties.

The theme of Chapter 4 is the explicit measurement of uncertainties. The tool we, like other decision analysts, invoke for the purpose is probability – more specifically, the Bayesian approach to probability. The heart of that approach is the notion that probabilities are numerical measures of opinions about the uncertainties of propositions. Chapter 4 spells out the idea and hints at some of the controversies surrounding it. Chapters 5 and 6 are concerned with the revision of such opinions in the light of new evidence, in statistical and nonstatistical contexts respectively.

Multiple conflicting objectives

Decision analysis is also especially concerned with multiple conflicting objectives. Almost any important decision engages multiple values. Often these go together; the shortest route from A to B is usually the fastest. But when they do, you are scarcely aware that you have to make a decision. The tough problems arise when, within the set of options you have, doing well on one value requires that you do poorly on another. The marketplace makes such requirements for trade-offs abundant. When you buy a car, you must make trade-offs among speed, handling characteristics, comfort, prestige, price, and other things. If one manufacturer did better than the others on all of these, the rest would be out of business. When choosing a site for a new plant, a manager must consider, for example, road access, geological criteria, environmental impact, the populations of the surrounding communities. Rarely does luck offer an option that is simultaneously best on them all.

Trade-offs are judgments. They depend on the decision maker's assessment of the relative desirability of the available options on each dimension and on his or her feelings about the relative importance of these dimensions. A safety-conscious driver may want as much metal as possible to be located between the driver's seat and a potential intruding object. A racing enthusiast, eager for quick acceleration and lively handling, may regard the weight of that metal as undesirable. The president of a utility company may consider the costs of scrubbing emissions from the smokestack of a coal-fired power plant not worth the resulting marginal reductions in air pollution. Environmentalist pickets around the plant may disagree.

Trade-offs are personal; there can be no objective or universal rules for making them. But that process can be made simpler and better by methods known as multiattribute utility techniques, or technology, or theory (MAUT, in any case). Typically these techniques first require the decision maker to rate the options on each value dimension or attribute separately. Next he or she assigns relative weights to the value dimensions that express the trade-offs among attributes. Ratings and weights must then be aggregated by means of some formal model that generates an overall evaluation of each option.

Chapters 7 through 10 detail both the mathematical logic and the clinical details of measuring values and/or utilities, in both single-dimensional and multidimensional approaches. Such measures may themselves embody trade-offs among multiple objectives and in any case are needed as inputs to the process of rationally balancing uncertainties and outcomes.

Other complexities

Almost every important decision affects the interests of *multiple stakeholders;* many involve them actively in the decision process. Different participants in the decision process may formulate the problem differently in that they consider different options and objectives. They may also differ in assessments of uncertainties, in evaluations of outcomes on any single attribute, and in trade-offs among attributes. The risks, costs, and benefits of decision outcomes may be distributed inequitably among stakeholders. This may require difficult judgments about the relative importance of the affected groups.

Decisions may have *far-reaching consequences.* The time span to be considered may be years, or even generations. The environment in which decisions must be made is typically *dynamic.* The decision maker may know that it will change but have no idea how or when. Preparing for the unforeseen and being able to adapt effectively may distinguish a good manager from a poor one.

Having made three obsequious bows to multiple stakeholders, far-reaching consequences, and dynamic decision environments, we shall do a quick about-face and try to ignore them as resolutely as we can manage for the remainder of the book. (We will not totally succeed.) We have bitten off quite enough by focusing on uncertainties and multiple objectives. They are the main topics of decision analysis, and addressing them adequately will more than exhaust our competence and your patience.

Instrumental rationality is attainable

The discussion so far has suggested a very simple view of decision analysis. It begins either with frustration resulting from a sense that something must be done and a lack of ideas about what to do or with a proposed set of alternative ideas about what to do. If the former is the case, the first step is to move to the latter. Once a set of options is available, the next step is to determine what values should be served in the process of selecting among them. The next step is to specify the extent to which each option serves each relevant value. The answer to this question is almost always uncertain because the result of taking an option usually depends on events not under the decision maker's control. Sometimes, but by no means always, such uncertainties are important enough to require explicit representation in the analysis. If so, the various possible outcomes of each action must be represented in some orderly way, and the linkage of each to the relevant values must be determined. In addition, the uncertainty about the outcome of each possible action must be measured. Sometimes these uncertainties may be so important that actions intended to reduce them are useful preliminaries to final action. These information-gathering actions produce evidence that changes the probabilities that measure uncertainty by a process called fallible inference. With or without the benefit of uncertainty-reducing information, the numbers representing linkage between options and values must be appropriately aggregated across values and then combined with numbers representing uncertainty (if any) to lead to a tentative choice of an option. The detailed characteristics of that choice and of its close competitors are then typically studied more carefully by a process called sensitivity analysis, which may leave original analysis and conclusions unchanged or may lead to further thought. Finally, the chosen option is implemented – or, more often, recommended for implementation.

The preceding, fairly succinct paragraph summarized the content of decision analysis and so of this book. Implementing its steps can be easy or hard or impossible. To introduce some ideas that later chapters elaborate and to offer at least a smidgen of intuition about what instrumental rationality is, we examine two examples of real, personal implementations – one trivial and one concerned with a life-or-death decision.

An example of dominance

Your nephew, a studious young composer, age 24, has just arrived to do graduate work at your university and is staying with you until he finds a place of his own. He drives your car to his evening class, which ends at 10 p.m. At 4 a.m. you wake up and discover that he is not yet home.

First, you invent some hypotheses. He may have been in an automobile accident; he may have been robbed, attacked, or involved in some other event that left him in a hospital or police station; he may have stayed over-night with friends; or he may be enjoying some big-city night life.

Your second task is to invent options. One is to roll over and go back to sleep. The only other that occurs to you is to call someone. The alternatives are the police, the university security office, or both. But the nephew is highly responsible; if he had been in an accident or robbery, he would have called. The only reason for his not calling would be an incapacitating injury. But in that case, those dealing with the problem would have looked in his wallet, found his home number, and called his mother, and his mother would have called you. On any hypothesis involving catastrophe that you could learn about with a phone call, you would already have been informed. The most plausible alternative hypothesis is that your nephew has found some form of late-night diversion. In either case, calling someone would do no good and would interfere with sleep.

If option A is at least as good as option B for any state of the world, and definitely better for at least one state, option A is said to (strictly) *dominate* option B, and option B should be discarded. Dominance is perhaps the simplest and most persuasive rule that rational choice should not violate. In this example, rolling over and going back to sleep dominates other options.

Then your wife wakes up, makes the same discovery, and urges action. Now dominance no longer exists. Since domestic harmony is a more important value than either sleep or avoidance of unnecessary 4 a.m. phone calls, you call – with the expected negative results.

The example illustrates, twice, the fact that structuring a decision problem often solves it and that neither numbers nor arithmetic are necessarily needed. Such solutions at the structuring stage are especially satisfying, because they are convincing and the logic that makes them so is simple.

An example of a more complete decision analysis

The next example uses all the tools of decision analysis with which this book is concerned except inference. It too is real.

A sedentary academic remained intellectually productive until the age of 78 in spite of two known small strokes and various other effects of athero-

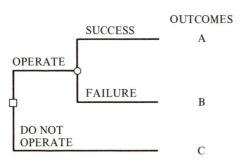

Figure 1.1. Decision tree representation of the decision about whether to have carotid artery surgery. Outcomes: A, avoidance of diminution of mental capacity; B, death on the operating table; C, progressive diminution of mental capacity.

sclerosis. He faced the consequences of severe atherosclerotic obstruction of both carotid arteries, which constitute the major blood supply to the brain. These consequences normally include progressively diminishing mental capacity; the blood supply to the brain is impaired, and multiple strokes, most so minor that neither victim nor family members know they have happened, destroy an ever-increasing amount of brain tissue. The patient's view of this future was heavily influenced by the fact that his father had died of the same disease, after a harrowing 7-year period of progressively increasing mental impairment.

The alternative to conservative medical treatment was carotid artery surgery, which essentially reams out the obstructions and restores the blood supply to the brain. A major uncertainty was whether the patient could survive the surgery, since other arteries, including those that supply blood to the heart, were obstructed as well. His regular doctors considered survival sufficiently unlikely that they were unwilling to try the operation. However, a distinguished surgeon in another city who had played a major role in developing carotid artery surgery was willing to undertake it.

The patient's decision, of course, was whether to proceed. No formal analysis was made, but the informal thinking done before the operation is relatively easy to translate into one. A simple diagram representing the alternative decisions and possible outcomes is shown in Figure 1.1. (Such diagrams are called decision trees. More about them appears in Chapter 3.) The outcome of no surgery is assumed to be progressive diminution of mental capability with probability 1. The outcomes of surgery are assumed to be avoidance of that diminution with some probability and death in surgery as the other possibility.

The next step is to identify the values relevant to the outcomes of the decision. As the problem was posed, three seemed relevant: avoidance of diminution of mental capacity, prolongation of life, and avoidance of the costs and inconveniences of major surgery. Arbitrarily assigning a utility or

Table 1.1. *First outcome by value matrix for the carotid artery surgery decision*

	Value		
Outcome	Avoidance of progressive mental diminution	Prolongation of life	Avoidance of medical costs and inconveniences
A: Successful operation	80	100	0
B: Failed operation	100	0	0
C: No operation	0	90	100

subjective value (we need not distinguish these two concepts here) of 100 to the best possible outcome and of 0 to the worst possible outcome on each dimension, we can express the relevant values in a simple matrix (Table 1.1). Inspection of Table 1.1 reveals a most important fact. Confining attention to the values of death in surgery and no operation, we find that the former is preferable to the latter if avoidance of diminution of mental capacity is considered more important than the combination of prolongation of life and avoidance of the costs and inconveniences of surgery. Since there was little doubt that this statement correctly described the patient's values, there was little point in a more detailed analysis (e.g., one that sought a measure of the probability that the surgery would be successful).

The patient traveled to the remote city, and the operation was performed. The following day the patient had a heart attack. For a period of 2 weeks those in charge of the surgical service insisted on keeping him marginally alive with torturous life-sustaining procedures, before a united family finally succeeded in forcing them to let him die. (In fairness to the surgeons, we should note that the reward for failure to use the methods here described as torturous may be a grateful family, but also may be a malpractice suit or even a murder charge.)

No more dramatic evidence of the inadequacy of the analysis presented in Figure 1.1 and Table 1.1 could possibly be found; the actual sequence of events and the key values that ultimately controlled what happened do not appear in either. To search for a better analysis ex post facto seems a futile exercise in hindsight, but is not.

The first step toward a better analysis is to identify a larger set of possible outcomes. Though the treatment of the possible outcomes of the no-operation action is crude, improving it is unlikely to change its basic structure, since the main issue for that option is simply the rate at which deterioration will occur. The important improvement needed is to recognize that the alternative to surgical success is not necessarily immediate death. Other possible outcomes include torturous treatment leading to eventual full recovery

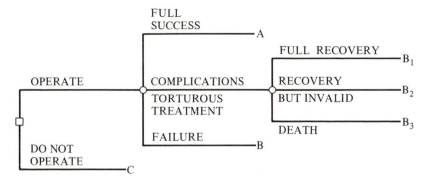

Figure 1.2. Better decision tree for the decision about whether to have carotid artery surgery. Outcomes: A, B, C, as in Figure 1.1; B_1, full recovery after complications and torturous treatment; B_2, recovery but with permanent physical disability after complications and torturous treatment; B_3, death after complications and torturous treatment.

Table 1.2. *Outcomes, values, and impact assessment for the restructured surgery problem*

	Life expectancy	Quality of life	Torture	Cost/inconvenience
A	Long	Good	None	Some
B	None	None	None	Some
B_1	Fairly long	Fairly good	Much	Much
B_2	Medium	Very poor	Much	Much
B_3	None	None	Much	Much
C	Fairly long	Very poor	None	None

(B_1); torturous treatment leading to recovery, but with major cardiac impairment (B_2); and torturous treatment leading to eventual death (B_3). Figure 1.2 displays the revised decision tree. Another improvement on the previous analysis can be produced by thinking about the relevant values more carefully. First, note that the new decision tree suggests that the values be separated into two classes: (1) the cost, inconvenience, and possible torture produced by the process of having the operation and by its immediate consequences and (2) values on which extended life after the operation should be evaluated (length and quality of life). Table 1.2 summarizes the impacts of the six outcomes with respect to the four value dimensions.

The evaluation of the outcomes on the dimensions "Life expectancy" and "Quality of life" presented us with an interpretation problem. Over the relevant range of life expectancies, this decision maker would have wished to maximize life expectancy if quality of life were reasonably high. But for several forms of low quality of life he would have felt that less life expectancy was preferable to more. He would have been horrified by the conse-

Table 1.3. *Values assigned to outcomes in the carotid surgery decision*

	Value dimension			
Outcome	Quality-adjusted life expectancy	Torture/ pain	Cost/ inconvenience	Aggregate utility
Successful operation (A)	100	100	50	95
Death on table (B)	0	100	50	35
Full recovery after torture (B$_1$)	80	0	0	48
Recovery as cardiac cripple after torture (B$_2$)	−30	0	0	−18
Death after torture (B$_3$)	0	0	0	0
No operation (C)	−20	100	100	28
Weights	.6	.3	.1	

quences of a prolonged life associated with severe mental deterioration and the need for constant care. He would also have been horrified, probably more so, by the thought of becoming so severely impaired, for example as a cardiac cripple, that he could not work and would require constant care from his loved ones. In short, whether prolongation of life would have seemed good or bad to him would have depended on the quality of that life.

We captured that effect in Table 1.3, which combines these dimensions. We treated the longest reasonably healthy life as having a utility of 100 and immediate death as having a utility of 0. But we assigned negative utility to life expectancy as a cardiac cripple and to life expectancy of the kind the patient's father had experienced.

The extent of medical costs and inconveniences will obviously be greater for any scenario that includes torturous treatments than for those that do not. Moreover, the 100 assigned to this dimension for the no-operation option does not mean that that option would not have implied medical costs – quite possibly large ones. It only means that, for the decision at hand, that outcome is preferable to any outcome of having the operation on that value dimension. Fine discriminations on that dimension are not worth bothering with in view of the very low weight assigned to it by the decision maker.

Inspection of the raw values in Table 1.3 produces no obvious conclusions. The meaning of these numbers, unlike that of those in Table 1.1, depends in some detail on the relative importance of each dimension. The simplest way to represent relative importance and to work with a set of numbers like these is to assign a weight to each value dimension, using for convenience the convention that weights sum to 1, and then calculate weighted averages over the relevant values for each possible outcome. In principle, the weights should be chosen by the decision maker. Since he is not available to make the needed judgments, we have chosen a set of weights that, we believe, have some resemblance to the ones he might have chosen. This approach to value measurement is an instance of MAUT, mentioned earlier.

Given weights, the values on the separate dimensions can be aggregated to give values for each possible outcome of the decision. For the weight set presented, those aggregated values are also displayed in Table 1.3. In a qualitative way, these assessments of outcomes make sense. The two that imply avoidance of mental deterioration and continued life are best. Immediate death is preferable to a life of progressive mental impairment. Torturous treatments followed by a life of cardiac impairment is worst of all.

Tentatively accepting these weights, one could assess the probabilities of each of the possible outcomes of the operation and then conclude whether it was sensible to have the operation or not. But the crucial implication of Table 1.3 is that torturous treatments should be allowed only if the likelihood of eventual full recovery is very high – which in such cases it is not. Since the imposition of torturous treatments is to some extent controllable by the surgeons, the obvious implication is that a course of action that either prevented their use entirely or severely limited their duration would have been extremely appropriate. Indeed, the availability of such an act would have produced a situation much like that of Table 1.1, in which the decision to have the operation is preferable to the decision not to have it for almost any set of weights that seem consistent with the values of this decision maker. Table 1.3, if it had been available at the time, would have provided a strong incentive to negotiate with the surgical team before deciding whether to proceed and, if that team were composed of reasonable surgeons, would have made the design of an option fine-tuned to the decision maker's values relatively easy to work out. How easy such an option would have been to implement would have depended on applicable state laws and enforcement procedures, on the mores of the hospital, and perhaps on other variables. In any case, exploration of the issue with the surgical team before deciding to proceed with surgery would clearly have been a better option than the ones actually considered.

Suppose that such discussions were fruitless, so that Table 1.3 in fact summarizes the situation. Suppose further that the weights included in the table adequately capture the decision maker's values. Should he choose to be operated on or not? The answer clearly depends both on the probability that the operation would lead to the kinds of events here called torturous treatments and on the probability of eventual recovery if they should occur. To simplify calculations, assume that all three outcomes that involve torture are equally likely. Then the indifference equation describing the decision becomes

$$85P(A) + 25P(B) = 18. \tag{1.1}$$

If, for example, $P(A) = P(B)$, the implication is that the operation should be undertaken if $P(A) > .164$. If $P(B) = 0$, the operation should be undertaken if $P(A) > .212$. The reason for this somewhat surprising outcome is obvious from Table 1.3. All outcomes except for two of the three involving torture are better than the outcome of doing nothing. Thus, the judgment that dominated thought about the inadequate analysis represented by Table 1.1 also dominates thought about Table 1.3.

It is inconceivable that the surgical team would have been willing to proceed with the operation had they regarded outcomes leading to torturous treatments as having a probability even as high as 1/3 or if they had not considered $P(A)$ to be greater than $P(B)$. Given that set of assessments, operating is clearly preferable to not operating over any of a quite wide set of assessments of the probabilities of the three outcomes involving torturous treatments. As this chapter has already emphasized, decisions must be evaluated prospectively, not retrospectively. Good decisions can lead to bad outcomes. This one did.

This discussion has assumed throughout that the decision maker was the patient and consequently that his values should control the decision. The first of these statements is true, but it does not clearly imply the second. The issue of multiple stakeholders with inconsistent values, though important in this example, is too complex to discuss here and, indeed, is dealt with only glancingly in this book. It is a focus of much current research in decision analysis.

The observant reader may be wondering by now what logic organizes this chapter. Under the heading "Instrumental rationality is attainable" we have discussed two examples. In the first of two options, first one and then the other is taken, and both choices are defended as rational. In the second, an obviously inadequate analysis is used as the basis for a decision. The outcome of that decision leads to a better analysis, which in turn leads to the same decision. Are we seriously proposing either of these as examples of rationality attained?

Not exactly; not exactly not. The point of these examples has been to illustrate more carefully than we would know how to do otherwise the limitations of the notion of instrumental rationality. The first illustrates how completely the notion depends on the situation and on the values it engages. A change in the situation leading to a change in what values are relevant will frequently lead to a change in assessment of what action is best. The second example makes the same point, but in addition emphasizes the degree to which an assessment of instrumental rationality depends on the knowledge about the situation on which that assessment depends and how the entire analysis can easily change as that knowledge changes.

Yet the task of specifying what values are relevant, of structuring what the options are, and of defining the relation between options and outcomes is all part of what decision analysts call *structuring the problem*. Unfortu-

Table 1.4. *Classification of models with examples*

Classification	Model of		
	People	Environments	Tasks
Descriptive	Prospect theory	Water pollution dispersion model	Organizational satisficing in pollution control
Normative	SEU	Balance model of ecosystem	SEU model for water pollution control

Note: SEU denotes subjectively expected utility to be described in Section 1.3. Prospect theory will be discussed in chapter 10.

nately, decision problems are structured by art, not algorithm. Instrumental rationality is meaningful only within a specified problem structure, and the prescriptions to which it leads can be expected to change in response to changes in that structure. The assertion that rationality is attainable, then, simply means that if you know what your problem is, what your options are, and what values bear on their merits, you can make assessments and then do arithmetic that will lead you to an instrumentally rational act. These statements imply that structuring the problem is by far the most important step in decision analysis. Chapters 2 and 3 discuss structuring explicitly, but in a more general sense the entire book focuses more on structuring than on anything else, not only by the liberal use of examples, but also by frequent explorations of the structuring implications of assessment and computational procedures and consequences. The point is probably clearest in Chapter 11, which is formally about sensitivity analysis but really about how to use the results of sensitivity analyses to restructure problems, preferably to the point at which you are quite confident that the conclusions you have reached are not at all sensitive to the input assumptions or numbers.

Some distinctions among models

Decision analysts combine many different models in their task of helping people make decisions. These models can be distinguished by their topics and by whether they are descriptive or normative. The topics include modeling people's behavior, modeling the environments in which people act, and modeling the tasks people face in these environments. Descriptive models describe people, environments, or tasks; normative models prescribe actions for people (or machines) in tasks and specify conditions that environments should be in. Table 1.4 summarizes these distinctions and provides examples.

Models of people

Considering for the moment only people, a normative model or theory is a set of rules specifying what individuals or groups should do. A normative model for decision making, then, specifies what decisions you should make. The set of normative decision-theoretic models together with the techniques for applying them are usually called *decision analysis.* A descriptive model attempts to predict what people *do* do; a descriptive model of decision making predicts what decision you in fact will make. Almost all of the familiar psychological models or theories are descriptive, not normative. The set of descriptive decision-theoretic models is called *behavioral decision theory.*

This distinction between normative and descriptive models is much less clear-cut than it sounds. For example, a normative model of decision making will predict correctly the behavior of anyone who is willing and able to apply that model in making decisions. The larger and more important the decision, the more likely is the decision maker to calculate carefully the potential consequences of each act and so try to make the normatively correct decision. Moreover, descriptive considerations have changed the content of normative models of decision making over the years. The earliest normative model of decision making in effect attempted to prescribe not only how one should go about implementing one's value system, but also to some extent what that value system should be. Such prescriptions turned out to be so different from the actual behavior of reasonable people that the content of the normative model was reexamined and much of the prescription of values was removed. Contemporary normative models for decision making are little more than sets of rules designed to ensure that acts will be coherent or internally consistent with one another in the pursuit of whatever goals the decision maker may have. Nevertheless, this requirement of coherence or internal consistency is a very strong one, so strong that no one seems able to satisfy it fully.

Every descriptive model in psychology actually contains two parts. One is a description of the environment and task facing the organism; the other is a description of the basic response tendencies the organism brings to that environment and task. The interplay of these two kinds of descriptions produces detailed predictions about the behavior of the organism in the situation. Often, perhaps usually, the description of the environment and of the task is very much more sophisticated than is the description of the response tendencies the organism brings to that environment and task. The predictive success of many descriptive models in psychology depends, not on the effectiveness of their description of the organism, but on the effectiveness of their description of the environment. Since normative models of decision making are descriptions of an environment and of a task with few assumptions about the response tendencies the organism brings with it, they are incomplete descriptive models. Yet they provide most of the intellectual substance that descriptive models need. It is relatively simple to add to these normative models assumptions about the way people behave in response to decision-making tasks and come up with sophisticated predictions about what people will actually do. This is especially so because people very often attempt to do the best they can in a decision-making task; that is, people attempt to behave as a normative model would prescribe. From this point of view, a normative model is simply an incomplete descriptive model.

Another and quite different class of normative models of people is popular among economists, who find the notion of rationality helpful. Nowadays few economists, if any, would believe that such ideas are descriptively appropriate. But they provide the basis for sophisticated mathematical analyses that can be combined with appropriate data-gathering tools to model large-scale economic phenomena. From our point of view, such models are really more models of tasks than models of people. Such usefulness as they seem to have arises because they are good models of tasks.

Models of environments

Few major decisions about, for example, far-reaching energy or social security policies could be made without sophisticated models of the environment. Such models are produced by many brands of scientist, especially economists and operations researchers. We consider them indispensable inputs to the decision problems to which they relate.

Models of the problem environment (or, perhaps more generally, of the system the decision maker can influence), like economic trend analysis, population growth models, and pollution dispersion models, can be purely predictive or descriptive of the behavior of the system. Normative environmental models embody explicit or implicit values; they aim at optimizing the state of the modeled environment. Ecological models that imply that the stability of a particular ecology is desirable have this normative flavor.

Since models of the environment are essential inputs to every decision process concerned with modelable environments, they are abundant and come from many sources, including operations research, econometrics, management science, computer science, and others.

Models of tasks

Models of tasks, like those so common in operations research, always start with assumptions about the quantities to be maximized and can be no more valid than those assumptions. They are therefore much more likely to be relevant to repetitive tasks than to unique ones. Concern with repetitive decisions typically resides much lower in the administrative hierarchy of any organization than does concern with unique decisions. Consequently, we do not expect top-level managers to be automated out of existence, even if their subordinates have been.

Task-analytic models of *unique* decision tasks must mediate between the relevant information provided in part by appropriate environmental models and the characteristics and needs of the human decision makers (who often are also sources of relevant input information). The generic name for this kind of task analysis is decision analysis.

Decision analysis is not descriptive either of people or of environments and describes only parts of tasks. It is most fundamentally prescriptive. That is, it attempts to facilitate wise decision making by contributing to the orderly elicitation of judgments and to orderly thought processes relating inputs to choices. Such prescriptive models build the bridge between models of environments and models of people.

The mix of models of people, tasks, and environments depends entirely on the problem. A fault tree or a spread sheet is a model of an environment. The prescriptions that emerge from those models are occasionally so compelling that little human input is required. Most bargaining and negotiation problems are entirely human. The environment may define constraints, but not options. In such cases, the options normally grow out of the interaction between the underlying long-range goals of stakeholder groups and the environmental constraints. Labor–management bargaining is an obvious example. For a decision analyst, such problems are less interesting than are problems in which the environment is significantly constraining but not absolutely decisive. Plant-siting problems, research program evaluations, and weapons system procurements are examples.

This book is concerned throughout with the interweaving of normative and descriptive models of decision processes. But its primary emphasis is on normative rather than descriptive models, since normative models are more profound and explicit than descriptive models and form the basis from which descriptive models depart.

1.3. Rationality and expected quantities

The literature offers perhaps 20 or 30 criteria by which a rational decision, given a well-structured decision problem, can be distinguished from an irrational one. Each, considered separately, is claimed to be a rule that no one would willingly violate when the stakes are high. Unfortunately, some of them contradict others. You have already encountered one of the most important of them: the principle of dominance. We will not examine such rules in detail here. Instead we will state without proof the decision rule to which this book is committed: maximization of expected utility. For a thorough axiomatic treatment of it see Savage (1954).

Expectations and subjectively expected utilities

We begin by introducing the idea of an expectation. This idea, a fundamental concept of probability theory, is nothing other than a weighted average.

Consider the following bet. You will throw a fair coin three times. If it comes up heads all three times, we will pay you $1.00. If it fails to come up heads all three times, you will pay us $0.15. What is the average payment to you on each trial, over a large number of trials, of that bet? Clearly, it is larger than −$0.15 and smaller than +$1.00. The payoffs should be weighted by the probability of obtaining each; such a weighted average is called an expectation. In this example the quantities being averaged are values, and so the average is called an expected value. To calculate the expected value of that bet, we need use only a little probability theory to find that the probability of three heads coming up in three tosses of an unbiased coin is $\frac{1}{2} \times \frac{1}{2} \times \frac{1}{2} = \frac{1}{8}$; the probability of not getting three heads must therefore be 1 $- \frac{1}{8} = \frac{7}{8}$. The expected value of the bet, then, is $\frac{1}{8}(+\$1.00) + \frac{7}{8}(-\$0.15) =$ −$0.00625. On the average, you would lose $\frac{5}{8}$ of a cent every time you played the bet.

More formally, the expected value, abbreviated EV, of a bet can be written

$$EV = p_1v_1 + p_2v_2 + p_3v_3 + \cdots + p_nv_n. \tag{1.2}$$

Or, more compactly, the same value can be written

$$EV = \sum_{i=1}^{n} p_iv_i. \tag{1.3}$$

Equation 1.3 introduces some useful ideas and notation. The "world," meaning the environment relevant to the consequences of the action the EV of which is being calculated, is conceived of as being partitioned into n different *states*. These states are mutually exclusive, and the set of n of them is exhaustive; that is, exactly one of them will happen, or *obtain*. Of course, p_i is the probability that state i will turn out to be the one that obtains, and v_i is the payoff (which may be negative) that will accrue to the decision maker if it does. Not all expectations are EVs. The expectation of any kind of quantity involved in a betlike situation can be calculated. We shall be concerned primarily with expected utilities rather than EVs. An expected utility is calculated in exactly the same way as any other expectation, but the quantities being averaged are utilities rather than objective quantities such as number of dollars, bushels of wheat, kisses, or ice cream cones. Such quantities are called *subjectively expected utilities* (SEUs).

This book assumes that the *only* rational decision rule is that, among the options available, you should choose the one with the largest SEU. This view is called the SEU model.

We hate acronyms. Yet the concepts of *expected value* and *subjectively expected utility* appear so frequently in this book, both in equations and in the text, that we feel we have no choice but to adopt a policy and stick with it. Since these concepts are abbreviated as EV and SEU in every equation in which they appear, we think it simple and consistent to use the same abbreviations in the text.

Numerical subjectivity

The SEU model embodies a fundamental principle. Both the utilities and the probabilities that enter into it are numbers, but they are inherently subjective in the sense that you and your colleagues might disagree about them and would often have no way of resolving any such disagreement. The fundamental principle might be called *numerical subjectivity,* the idea that subjective judgments are often most useful if expressed as numbers. For reasons we do not fully understand, numerical subjectivity can produce considerable discomfort and resistance among those not used to it. We suspect this is because people are taught in school that numbers are precise, know from experience that judgments are rarely precise, and so hesitate to express judgments in a way that carries an aura of spurious precision. Judgments indeed are seldom precise – but the precision of numbers is illusory. Almost all numbers that describe the physical world, as well as those that describe judgments, are imprecise to some degree. When it is important to do so, one can describe the extent of that imprecision by using more numbers. Very often, quite imprecise numbers can lead to firm and unequivocal conclusions. The advantage of numerical subjectivity is simply that expressing judgments in numerical form makes it easy to use arithmetical tools to aggregate them. The aggregation of various kinds of judgments is the essential step in every meaningful decision.

Although we shall often use bets as examples, the SEU model applies to all kinds of choices. Utility is in some decisions closely related to nonfinancial variables: the probability of survival, fuel remaining, palatability of food – any dimension or combination of dimensions that has value for you.

Unique and repeated decisions

An appropriate counterargument to our advocacy of the SEU model would be, for the bet mentioned above, "I am certainly not going to lose $\frac{5}{8}$ cent if I take the bet. I will either win \$1.00 or lose 15 cents. What does this calculated $-\frac{5}{8}$ cent have to do with my choice?" The argument is deep and deserves considerable respect.

Our answer to it is as follows. Suppose that you were going to play the identical bet 1,000 times. The expected loss from doing so would be 1,000 times the expected loss from the single play: −\$6.25. Although that exact loss would not be realized, some number quite close to it would be. Under such circumstances, you would not for a moment consider committing yourself to the 1,000 bets.

But we are talking about a policy for making decisions. It makes no difference whatever whether you apply that policy to 1,000 identical decisions or to 1,000 decisions of varying character. Maximization of EV, or generally of SEU, is the optimal policy.

Ruin and quasi ruin

An important exception to that principle sometimes confuses the issue. If the bet were favorable but random fluctuations could cause you to lose so much that you could no longer afford to play, the argument about the optimality of maximizing EV would not apply. Formally, this is known as the *gambler's ruin problem,* and a substantial literature examines it. For one discussion see Feller (1968).

The real problem of gambler's ruin seldom arises in that form – though it can. An important concept that does arise often is that of quasi ruin – losses, either of money or of other things of value, so great that they leave the loser in no position to continue to function more or less as before. Of course, such major losses are not only distressing in themselves; they also force changes of life style that serve many of your values ill. The unpleasant consequences of quasi ruin are always multidimensional, but the experience is unpleasant on virtually every dimension. So we modify our prescriptive rule: maximize SEU, as long as the potential losses from doing so do not reach the point of quasi ruin.

Quasi ruin is a subjective concept. We consider it wise to make the changes of life style that one chooses to call quasi ruin relatively large. A decision maker who defines almost any loss as quasi ruin will be unwilling to face possible losses and so will be unable to accept even highly favorable risky options. We speculate that one difference between entrepreneurs and wage earners is that entrepreneurs have learned to set what might be called the threshold of quasi ruin quite a long way beneath the present status quo, while wage earners have not.

Rationality and human behavior

We have already commented on the intertwining of normative and descriptive thinking in decision theory and in this book. If the SEU model is a prescriptively appropriate model of rational behavior, how well does it do as a model of real behavior?

This formulation of the question is naive; what is "real" behavior? Some people want to maximize SEU, especially when the stakes are high, and therefore do so. This typically requires some decision-analytic knowledge and some computational support. Studies of unaided human decision making (e.g., Goodman, Saltzman, Edwards, and Krantz, 1979) show that even the idea that people maximize EV approximates choices among gambles in a casino quite well. However, experimental psychologists can create stimuli and situations in which naive and unaided subjects exhibit systematic and persistent deviations from EV and SEU. In fact, studies of this kind have dominated the behavioral decision theory literature (for reviews see, e.g., Einhorn and Hogarth, 1981; Pitz and Sachs, 1984; Slovic, Fischhoff, and

Lichtenstein, 1977). As a description of the decisions of naive, unaided decision makers, SEU maximization is a reasonable global approximation but is clearly wrong in many details. The ways in which it is wrong can be viewed as clues to the characteristics of human information processing (see Chapters 10 and 13).

Such topics intrigue experimental psychologists. For a decision analyst interested in normative issues, the question of how naive, unaided decision makers behave is of less concern. Their respondents are not unaided and may not be naive. Decision analysts want their clients to accept the SEU model as an appropriate tool for arriving at prescriptions. Some of the elicitation methods they use require the assumption that the judgments on which they are based obey the SEU model, though it is easy to design an entire decision analysis that never needs to make that assumption. These issues are complex and controversial; they recur throughout the book, especially in Chapters 10 and 13.

1.4. Other purposes of decision-analytic procedures

In spite of its name and these examples, decision analysis serves many purposes other than that of directly helping people or organizations to make decisions. One of these is *identifying or reformulating options*. An example is the acceptable risk problem of nuclear power generation. This is often phrased as the question of nuclear engineering: how safe should the design of a nuclear power plant be in order to ensure that the residual risk is acceptable? Fischhoff, Lichtenstein, Slovic, Derby, and Keeney (1981) present a lucid analysis that reformulates this acceptable risk problem as one of choosing among technological options and trading off risks and benefits.

Another purpose of decision analysis is *defining objectives*. Keeney (1975), for example, performed a decision analysis for a private firm in which he identified the structure of its corporate objectives. Miller (1969) developed a complex value tree for evaluating transportation systems. Keeney, Renn, and von Winterfeldt (1985) developed Germany's energy objectives from interviews with leading representatives of major interest groups. The point is that the decision focus of the analysis together with a rough structure of options and objectives often helps the decision maker(s) to solve the problem without further numerical analysis. We presented a trivial example of this kind in our discussion of the missing nephew above.

If the problem involves multiple stakeholders or multiple decision-making organizations, yet another purpose of decision analysis is to *provide a common language for communication and to pinpoint agreements and disagreements*. In intelligence analysis, Kelly and Peterson (1971) used Bayesian inference structures and the language of probabilities, partly for communicating uncertainty; von Winterfeldt and Rios (1980) used value tree structures to elucidate the conflicts between opposing groups in the nuclear debate. Edwards (1980) used multiattribute utility procedures to aid conflicting groups in the Los Angeles school desegregation case to evaluate alternative desegregation plans. Gardiner and Edwards (1975) studied differences among various pro- and antidevelopment factions in decisions of the California Coastal Commission. Gardiner and Edwards (1975) and Aschenbrenner and Kasubek (1978) found that the structures and numerical assessments of decision analysis often produce surprising agreement and help people substantially to understand disagreements among conflicting groups.

These purposes of decision analysis are conprehensive in the sense that they try to address the whole problem – either in a full analysis or in some structuring activity. In many instances decision analysts can usefully address a small part of the decision problem, for example a probability assessment problem, the construction of a subjective value scale, or aiding probabilistic inference. *Quantification of subjective variables* – probabilities and values – can in itself be very useful, even if the further analysis is left to non-decision-analytic procedures or to the intuition of the decision maker. Miller, Kaplan, and Edwards (1967, 1969), for example, used a simple value scale construction technique to assess the worth of military targets. This value assessment was an important input into a complex optimal dispatching model. Keeney and Lamont (1979) developed a simple model and technique to quantify probabilities of earthquakes and resulting landslides.

Complex probabilistic inference is another activity in which decision analysis is useful. Kelly and Peterson (1971) provide a number of examples of the use of probabilistic inference models for intelligence analysis. Schum and Martin (1982) examine formal aids for legal inference. Such models are based on hierarchical inference structures (see Kelly and Barclay, 1973; Schum, 1980; and Chapter 6 of this book) that link observable events (e.g., intelligence reports) to hypotheses (e.g., whether an enemy country is preparing an attack). The outputs are probability distributions over relevant hypotheses. Decisions are then made by policy makers on the basis of such probabilities, either with or without further decision analysis. Bayesian prediction of oil spill accidents, probability assignment to nuclear risks, and weather forecasting are other examples in which the probabilistic inference part of decision analysis is useful alone.

The *development of value-relevant indices* is frequently useful. An example is the multiattribute index of medical underservedness developed by Gustafson and Holloway (1975). That index heavily affects where new hospitals can be built with federal funds. Another example is O'Connor's (1972) indices of water quality.

1.5. Decision aids, artificial intelligence, and other aspects of intellectual technology

The computer revolution has led to a speedup in the potentially revolutionary changes now going on in the way intellectual work is done. The ideas of decision analysis presented in this book are deeply relevant to these changes. An obvious form of relevance is the concept of decision aids. Military decision makers, medical decision makers, and some business decision makers are eager to have computers help them with their intellectual tasks. The problem is: how?

A very simple and common approach is to organize the information the decision maker needs in such a way that it is accessible and easy to understand. This is the fundamental idea underlying *management information systems.* Such systems can be very sophisticated and helpful, but incorporate very few decision-analytic ideas.

The idea has a serious limitation. The major problem of most decision makers is less one of organizing the relevant information than one of figuring out what it means and what relevance it has to the decision at hand. Such systems offer little help with that kind of task.

An outgrowth of the notion of management information systems and of this deficiency has been the currently in vogue notion of *decision support systems.* A decision support system is a management information system that also has some processing capability designed to help the decision maker use the information. A common form of such processing capability is the ability to ask "What if . . .?" questions about possible courses of action and quickly receive answers from the computer. How helpful such a capability is depends on the problem at hand. It seems to be quite helpful in some business decision contexts because it informs the decision maker of the long-range consequences of the available options.

The most interesting kinds of decision aids currently being designed for use by decision makers without analytic aids attempt to do more of the decision maker's intellectual work than either of the above. Many of these aids make use of techniques from a field called *artificial intelligence,* which has been in existence for a long time but has started to be useful in real applications only recently. The original goal of research on artificial intelligence was to reproduce various aspects of human thought by means of computer programs. This goal, though still a major theme of research in artificial intelligence, has been supplemented by the goal of usefulness. Currently the most useful computer systems using ideas drawn from research on artificial intelligence for aiding decisions are *expert systems.* An expert system is a computer program that exploits the judgments previously made by an expert in the task at hand. These judgments, which may be in the form of numbers or in the form of production rules that tell the computer what to do next in a given situation, can provide both expertise and procedural advice that a decision maker may find helpful.

This book is not oriented toward decision aids; its main concern is with the intellectual tasks required for decision making. But someone familiar with research on artificial intelligence, and in particular with work on expert systems, can easily see many places in which elicitation procedures applied ahead of time can produce structures and numbers that can reside in a computer program, to make or help make decisions that are repetitive or are needed quickly.

A more mundane kind of decision-analytic decision aid is one that helps the analyst by performing number elicitations, computations, sensitivity analyses, or other aspects of the decision-analytic task. Many such programs exist, and more are being developed. As stand-alone decision aids they have a serious deficiency: they are too general purpose and consequently too difficult for one not sophisticated about decision analysis to use. A major, though unattained goal of decision aid design is to combine generality of purpose with enough user-friendliness that the decision analyst need not be present when the aid is used. Although that is not the topic of this book, many of the ideas discussed might be helpful especially to those oriented toward simplification of decision-analytic procedures.

Research on decision aids is very lively these days. Ten years from now, a book intended to facilitate the making of real decisions, as this one is, might well have to focus on the properties and uses of decision aids.

2   Structuring for decision analysis

2.1. The structuring problem

Three phases of structuring

Textbook examples of decision problems usually come neatly structured, with options, objectives, and uncertainties prespecified. In the experience of most decision analysts, structuring problems and identifying options and objectives are the most difficult parts of most problems. As initially presented, many problems do not offer an opportunity for choice among options. The most common initial condition is a set of often vague values, typically inconsistent with one another, and a sense of perplexity about how to find a sensible course of action that at least partially serves them all. In such cases the first and most important step in structuring must be to translate the problem into a set of alternatives and values, options and objectives. A later important step often is to identify uncertainties about the outcomes of the available options and to think about acts that may help to reduce some of these uncertainties or allow the decision maker to hedge against them.

This chapter is concerned mainly with the initial tasks of identifying options and objectives. After presenting some general ideas about problem structuring, we present a tool for structuring objectives: value trees. We have much less to say about inventing or structuring options. We also present some tools for structuring uncertainties: event trees, fault trees, and inference trees. In Chapter 3 we introduce decision trees, which structure uncertainties as sequences of decisions and subsequent events.

Value trees, event trees, inference trees, and decision trees are the major structuring tools of decision analysis. However, building trees is itself a fairly specific structuring activity. To see structuring in a broader perspective, it is useful to think of it as a three-step sequence of tasks:

1   Identify the problem, develop an overall analytic structure, and formalize parts of it. In the first phase the following questions are answered. What is the nature of the problem and its environment? Who is the decision maker? What are the decision maker's values? What are the generic classes of

options? What groups are affected by the decision? What is the purpose of the analysis? At this stage only rough formal relations are created. Simple matrices of options by objectives and lists of impact categories and uncertainties are typical products.

2   Pick the appropriate subset from the bag of tricks spelled out in this book (plus others we have omitted). Is uncertainty the key problem, or are conflicting values more important? Is it worthwhile to model parts of the problem with non-decision-analytic techniques like linear programming or simulation models? How can different part models be combined creatively? The analyst answers these questions by choosing one or more generic analytic structures (e.g., multiattribute utility, hierarchical inference, or signal detection). It is useful, however, to avoid an early commitment to traditional analytic structures and to explore alternatives in some detail.

3   Refine the elements and relations within the generic analytic structures identified in the second step.

Although these three steps are reasonably distinct, the intellectual work behind them is extremely recursive. The analyst should expect to go through each several times – and indeed should worry about whether the problem has been thought through carefully enough if it is has not been restructured at least once or twice. A good way of checking an initial structure is to make some preliminary numerical assessments and run through some rough calculations. For example, if the first step is a matrix of options by objectives, the analyst should try to rank-order the options under each objective. Often the results produce insights for restructuring and simplification.

The analyst should be relatively certain that the current structure is reasonably acceptable before eliciting numbers in detail. Only a well-defined and acceptable structure will provide a feeling for what numbers are important and require refined assessment. Moreover, number elicitation is expensive, time-consuming, and irksome for the sponsor. It is unpleasant as well as wasteful to elicit numbers that later seem irrelevant.

Multiple alternative problem formulations

Our advice to look carefully at various problem formulations before working hard on one is persuasive but may be hard to implement. How does one take a confusing, messy, ill-defined problem and impose not one but several structures on it?

To offer an example and highlight some problems, we report an early postdoctoral decision analysis one of us (von Winterfeldt) faced and considers flawed. (For an Edwards boo-boo, see Chapter 12.) This example will be carried on throughout this book, from problem definition (this section) to choosing an analytic structure (Section 2.3) to modeling and analysis (Chapter 12).

In 1971, the United Kingdom passed the Prevention of Oil Pollution Act. It prohibited all intentional oil pollution from fixed offshore installations. Growing oil development in the North Sea made this act obsolete, since offshore oil platforms must discharge oily water in the course of their routine operations. The Petroleums and Pipelines Act of 1975 allowed exemptions from the no-discharge rule of 1971, provided that offshore oil operators use "best practicable" means to reduce the oil content in the discharge water. Exemptions were to be granted by the staff of the Petroleum Engineering Division (PED) of the Department of Energy. In order to streamline and justify the exemption rules, the PED decided to set chronic oil discharge standards achievable by best practicable technology.

While working at the International Institute for Systems Analysis, von Winterfeldt took on an analysis of this regulatory problem. An easy formulation of the problem was: what should the standard be? A simple structure of the decision problem looks like this. The decision alternatives are standards (admissible oil content in water at the emission point) together with some specific application and enforcement rules. The decision-making organization is the PED, and the objectives are to minimize the impact of oil pollution by economically reasonable means. This problem structure invites the relatively straightforward application of multiattribute utility techniques to trade off environmental and economic impacts, possibly considering their uncertainties.

After numerous visits to regulatory agencies, oil platforms, and other relevant stakeholder locations, von Winterfeldt concluded that a simple decision-analytic structure would not work easily, since in practice standard setting engages the conflicting interests of multiple decision makers. In this case, at least three groups were involved: the regulator (PED), the industry (the multinational oil companies), and the potential victims of pollution (fishermen). An alternative structure linked these three decision-making organizations in a formal interaction. Separate decision-analytic models for each group considered group-specific options, objectives, and concerns about events. By considering one group's action to be another group's event, it was possible to link the models. We present more details later in Section 2.3.

Although this structure seemed more realistic for the standard-setting situation than a formulation that treated the regulator as the only decision maker, the problem invited speculation that standard setting was not the real issue. Most previous UK regulations painfully avoided numerical standards. Environmental regulations in the United Kingdom tend to be local and specific to circumstances and usually treat the environmental carrying capacity, rather than absolute or marginal pollution levels, as the limiting factor. So why did the United Kingdom choose to set numerical oil pollution standards?

Two factors seem to have contributed. First, Norway, the other major oil producer, was at the time considering numerical standards of its own. Second, several countries in the European Community had for some time pressured the United Kingdom to help clean up the North Sea, a resource shared by eight countries. One member country used the standard-setting issue to improve its bargaining position in an unrelated subcommittee in the community, rather than treating it as an independent issue. Such facts lead to a fundamentally different interpretation of the decision problem. The problem is determining how to satisfy other European Community countries in the push for a clean North Sea, while maintaining the United Kingdom's own flexible energy and environmental policy. This formulation implies that the PED is not the key decision maker and that technical debates over the best standard have only incidental importance. A wide variety of political and technical options become relevant, requiring another, more complex problem structure. The problem could conceivably be interpreted as a European Community–United Kingdom bargaining situation in which the role of decision analysis would be to define alternative bargaining postures and to explore the impacts of various positions on future negotiations about matters unrelated to oil.

The three-actor formulation of the decision problem led to a rather successful technical publication (von Winterfeldt, 1982) but to no change in any stakeholder's behavior. The criterion that an analysis is successful only if it is used is both extremely stringent and surprisingly hard to interpret. In this instance, most reasonable interpretations indicate that this criterion was not fulfilled. Whether the criterion *could* have been satisfied given the circumstances, in particular the outside origin of the study and the extremely political nature of what seem to be the central issues of a more apropos analysis, is another question; we doubt it.

This example shows that a seemingly simple decision problem can be viewed in several ways and that the problem definition strongly shapes the initial structuring of the analysis. It also shows that it may be dangerous to select a given structure (e.g., a multiattribute evaluation of standards) too quickly, before exploring alternative problem definitions and corresponding analytic structures. Such neglect can lead to the most common pitfall of analysis: producing a sophisticated solution to the wrong problem.

2.2. Identifying the problem

Becoming educated about the problem environment

Problems that lead an organization or individual to seek outside help are almost always difficult, substantively and organizationally. The worst frustrations an analyst encounters are likely to occur early in the process of discovering the nature of the problem. The initial contact person, typically a member of the analysis or program staff of the client organization, is eagerly explaining what the problem is, and the analyst finds that each sentence contains two or three unfamiliar words. Usually, they are the crucial ones.

At a minimum, the analyst must understand two things: the vocabulary of the problem area and the structure of the employing organization. We attempt, if at all possible, to get internal memoranda and other written materials and also an organization chart before the first interview. But rapid learning during early interviews is crucial.

As the analyst's expertise develops, it is often useful to understate it. Comments of the form "Mr. A. told me that oil discharges should be continuously monitored, but I didn't understand why. Can you explain it?" are much better than comments like "Mr. A. told me that oil discharges should be continuously monitored, but you seem to be telling me that intermittent sampling is enough. Why do the two of you disagree?" Both questions yield the same information, but the latter can easily cause later problems with both respondents.

The requirement that the analyst learn quickly has had several consequences. One is that, as decision analysis has become more successful, analysts specializing in specific classes of problems and specific organizational settings have emerged. These specialists can familiarize themselves with the details of the problem with greater speed than other analysts. This trend is likely to continue in decision analysis, as it has in other forms of operations research. Another is that generic problem structures are both inevitable and useful; we return to the point at the end of this chapter.

Identifying the decision makers and their values

One task the analyst must face in interacting with any client is to figure out who the client is. Virtually all clients are organizations. The contact person is full of lore about how the organization works. Is there a boss? Sometimes yes, sometimes no. The real boss may not be the one who formally approves decisions. Or the boss role may be partitioned. Invariably the boss delegates decision-making power, and invariably he or she retains some degree of ex post facto evaluative (and perhaps veto) power over the result.

Although the analyst will, later in the structuring process, elicit in detail the values related to the specific decision problem at hand, early clarity about the overall objectives of the client organization is essential. Superficial definitions of an organization's function are inherent in its mission statement and organization chart. Ford makes cars; the Environmental Protection Agency polices the environment. But Ford's organizational style and goals are different from those of General Motors, Chrysler, or (especially) Nissan. Every organization's personality is unique.

A myth to watch out for is that a single value dominates all others. This myth is more common in corporations than in government agencies, since corporation executives are so often taught in business schools that corporations exist to make money. Though no entity, corporate or individual, is averse to making money, no value structure is that simple. Instead, the corporate myth that profit is the goal serves as a useful structuring tool for much more complex corporate objectives: maximizing market share, meeting future demand, reducing unnecessary overhead costs, upgrading the quality of personnel and of production processes and products, and even enhancing corporate flexibility. If you encounter this myth or any other similar oversimplification of values, it is usually easy to endorse it and elicit the real values that lie beneath it. Myths could not exist if they prevented effective interaction with the realities underneath.

Identifying the unscratched itch

Usually you have been called in because the organization has a problem and believes you can help. It is very common for an analyst to discover that the organization does not know what its problem is. We like to say that it has an unscratched itch.

Perhaps the most useful task during early exploration is to hunt for the decision. Almost always there is one, or more. Contact people usually know what it is, though they may have different perspectives on what the relevant options and values are. Often, if the problem is not brand new, a helpful question is: how did they deal with this problem in the past, and why won't that method still work? The corresponding question for new problems is: if they were to rely only on internal resources, what would they do, and how well would they fare?

Once the analyst can get the contact person and key others in the organization to agree on what the decision is and to agree that the job is to work on it or some aspect of or input to it, half the structuring is done.

Defining the purpose of the analysis

The analyst and the relevant people in the organization have identified the decision or decisions to be made – and all have breathed a sigh of relief. Now the analyst's task is to help the organization make that decision as well as it can, right? Often dead wrong.

1. The organization may not be in a position to make the decision. The Central Intelligence Agency needs decision-analytic help badly but (according to its rules) makes no decisions; it merely provides well-structured information to remote decision makers. Such problems are typically, but not always, diagnostic. They may require hypothesis invention.

2. To make decisions, a list of options must exist. The real problem may be producing that list. If a dominant option emerges during the decision structuring, the decision problem may vanish, with or without the analyst's help.

3. The task may be, not to make a decision, but to design and install a decision-making mechanism or procedure. The rules for picking the winner or winners in a competitive situation must usually be in place before the competition starts. Such problems are typically evaluative.

4. Time pressure or other constraints may make it necessary to complete all analysis before the decision problem arises. Crisis management is the most

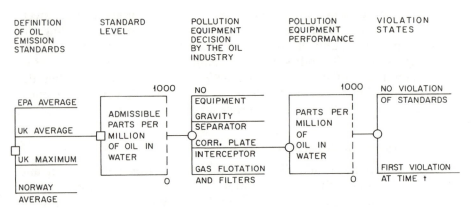

Figure 2.1. Deep decision tree. (*Source:* von Winterfeldt, 1980b.)

common example. The analyst must substitute scenarios about the future for information about the real decision problem and must package the output either as rapid, easy-to-use decision aids, often in the form of consoles interacting with computer programs, or as system design for the quick-response system, or, ideally, both.

5   Decision makers do and should resist the idea that machines or computational procedures should or can replace them. By definition, a decision maker is the person who takes the blame if the decision leads to a distressing outcome. So he or she must feel and should insist on feeling that that responsibility is deserved. The output of any decision-analytic procedure is at best an input to a decision. It is almost never the only one.

6   The decision may already have been made or may be made independently while the analyst is working on the problem. A common and quite legitimate purpose of analysis is to justify decisions ex post facto. The only constraint that situation places on the analyst is to ensure that the analysis is honestly reported and that elements of it that might argue against what was done are not distorted or suppressed. This is not always easy. In such a situation, measures that protect analyst and client are urgent.

This list of alternatives to making a decision states or implies some other purposes an analysis may serve. We do not intend to imply that decision analyses never lead to decisions. Chapter 12 of this book presents a few examples of analyses that have done so: Keeney and Raiffa (1976), Bell, Keeney, and Raiffa (1977), and Howard, Matheson, and Miller (1976) present many more.

2.3. Developing an overall analytic structure

To discuss the second step of structuring, the development of an overall analytic structure, we take a more careful look at von Winterfeldt's oil pollution problem.

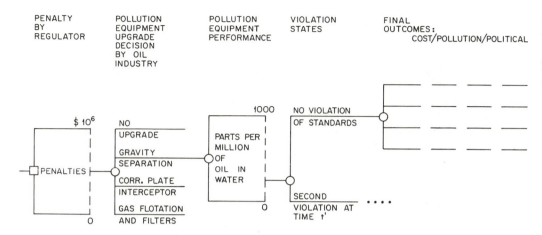

An evolving structure for standard setting

Recall that von Winterfeldt finally decided to accept the "choice among emission standards" formulation of the chronic oil pollution problem. The next step was to choose a generalizable and tractable analytic structure for this problem. The overall question was: using the decision-analytic format, how can standard-setting problems best be formulated in a model specific enough to capture the main features of particular standard-setting problems and general enough to be applied to a variety of such problems? In other words, what is a generic decision-analytic structure for standard setting?

Since the regulator or regulatory agency was presumed to be the main client for such models, the initial structuring focused on regulatory alternatives and objectives. One structure was a wide but shallow alternative tree that included a variety of regulatory options: emission standards, ambient standards, direct intervention, and others. Given an appropriate tree of regulatory objectives, one could conceivably perform a decision analysis by evaluating each alternative with a simple MAUT procedure, assessing the costs of meeting standards against the risk reduction achieved.

This simple traditional structure seemed inappropriate. Regulators seldom have to evaluate such a wide range of alternatives, and this formulation does not capture the interaction between the regulators and the regulated. Also, regulators care a great deal about monitoring and implementation of standards, a topic to which a variety of detailed technical issues not well addressed by a simple MAUT structure are relevant.

The second structure was a narrow but deep decision tree (Figure 2.1). In addition to the regulator's alternatives, this tree includes the responses of the industry to the standard, the possible detection of standards violations, and subsequent sanctions. The structure is aimed at fine-tuning the regulator's definitions of the standard level (maximum emission, etc.) and at monitoring and sanction schemes, as well as at assessing environmental impacts.

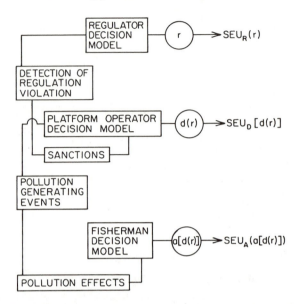

Figure 2.2. Three-decision-maker model. Here, *r* is the regulator's decision, *d(r)* the operator's decision, and *a[d(r)]* the fishermen's decision.

The structure is specific about the regulatory alternatives, but by considering industry responses to be random events and by leaving out responses of environmental groups, it fails to address a major concern of regulatory decision making.

The third structure was the three-decision-maker model mentioned at the beginning of this chapter, in which the regulator, the platform operator, and the fishermen are represented by separate decision-analytic models (see von Winterfeldt, 1978). A model links the regulator's decision to the operator model by considering the possible detection of violations and sanction schemes. These are options for the regulator and external events for the operator. An event tree of pollution-generating events and effects links the operator's decisions to the fishermen model (Figure 2.2).

The model works as follows. The regulator's alternatives are treated as exogenous events, that is, independent variables. The platform operator's response to the regulator's chosen set of regulations is to minimize expected investment, operation, and detection costs or to maximize equivalent SEUs. Finally, the fishermen are assumed to maximize their SEUs conditional on the regulator's and the developer's decisions. At this point the model stops. The structure cannot choose an optimal act, since it does not treat utilities accruing to the three actors as being measured on the same scale. But it can identify and eliminate dominated options, a process called Pareto analysis in contexts like this. This often greatly simplifies and structures the decision problem that remains.

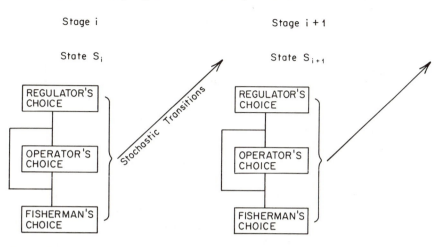

Figure 2.3. Structure of a multistage game-theoretic model. (*Source:* von Winterfeldt, 1980b.)

The final structure considered was a game-theoretic extension of the three-decision-maker model. The structure of the game-theoretic model is presented in Figure 2.3. This model explicitly treats the standard-setting process as dynamic and considers all feedbacks. In addition, transitions from one stage to another are probabilistic. Höpfinger and von Winterfeldt (1979) applied a seven-stage version of the model in a pilot study.

The game-theoretic model overcomes the criticisms of the static decision-analytic model but gives up the possibility of fine-tuning and detailed modeling of trade-offs and probabilities. Detailed provisions for these would have made running the model impossible. Therefore, linear utility functions and simple transition probability structures have to be assumed.

Matching problems and structures

After the research team had designed these alternative structures, they wondered which could best be applied to the oil pollution standard-setting problem. Three criteria came to mind. The structures should be (1) simple, (2) descriptive of the problem environment, and (3) amenable to further modeling and analysis, or manageable.

Simplicity is required because the decision makers and experts should be able to understand inputs, process, and outputs. Complex optimization models or dynamic simulation models often do not affect decisions because the decision maker does not understand them. At the other extreme, over-simplification can lead to dismissal of the model if concerns important to the decision maker or experts are overlooked.

A problem description must, of course, capture the analyst's (and, with luck, the decision maker's) intuitions about the important aspects of the problem, including values, structures, and other features of the organization and processes, entities, and phenomena that specify its environment.

The third criterion, manageability, is simplicity of another kind. A problem structure that requires judgments from decision makers or experts that are too numerous or too difficult is useless. So is one that requires excessively tedious or expensive computation or that does not mesh with the user's needs. The existence of any of these deficiencies invites restructuring of the analytic model.

In the present example, the investigators decided to use the three-decision-maker one-stage model as a prototype structure. A formal application is described in Chapter 12. Regulators considered the model meaningful and insight producing. But analysts and regulators agreed that the static character of the model and the lack of feedback loops required improvements.

2.4. Structuring value trees

We now turn to a review of more familiar territory – structuring ideas and tools appropriate after the basic analytic structure has been identified. We start with evaluation, because in our experience it is both most common and most important.

An example

Routine forecasts of regional electricity supply and demand predict a sizable gap in 15 years. Regional utility companies probably will not be able to deliver enough current to meet demand reliably unless they increase production capacity.

Suppose that preliminary studies of possible supply alternatives have led a particular supplier to the conclusion that the only feasible short-term solution is to build an additional plant to generate about 2,000 megawatts. The board of directors asks for a study comparing the two most attractive options: a coal-fired plant and a nuclear plant. The board stresses that legal and political uncertainties make it essential that the evaluation of these supply options be comprehensive and that it include social and environmental considerations as well as direct costs and benefits.

Structuring this evaluation problem consists of defining and organizing the values, objectives, and attributes on which the two options should be compared. What are the major objectives and concerns of the utility company? What attributes differentiate the coal and the nuclear options? How can these attributes be measured? And how are attributes, objectives, and values related?

Figure 2.4 presents typical answers to these questions in the form of a value tree. The top layer of the tree contains very general, and sometimes

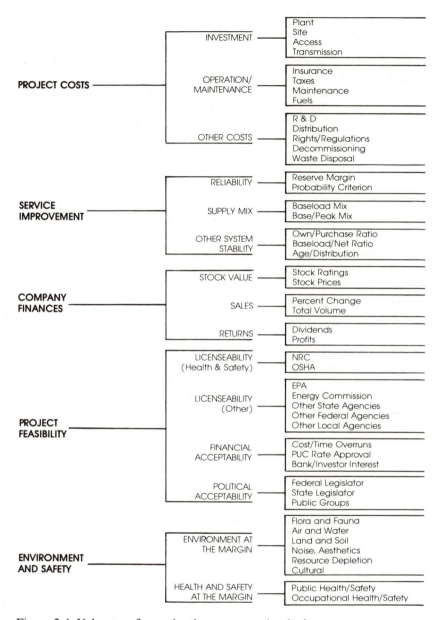

Figure 2.4. Value tree for evaluating energy technologies.

vague, values. The values become more specific in the lower layers of the tree. The word *site* is a condensation of "Minimize site acquisition costs"; the term *reserve margin* stands for "Maximize the amount by which the total production capacity of the system including the new plant will exceed expected peak-hour demand 15 years from now." The twigs (bottom branches) of the value tree are not included. They consist of operationalizations of the last branches. For example, the branch *investment cost* could be operationalized as "annualized capital costs for plant construction computed over a 30-year lifetime." *Air pollution* could be operationalized by means of several different pollution indices. One might be "average of three density samples of ambient air concentration of sulfur dioxide two miles from the plant, averaged over 30 consecutive days of plant operations."

We use value trees in most evaluative contexts. Before we can explain how to build them, we must define some language.

Some definitions

Values are abstractions that help organize and guide preferences. They are most often expressed as statements of desired states, positive intentions, or preferred directions. The actions or objects of value may be such diverse things as social policies, marketing strategies, or individual consumer choices. The "evaluator" is not necessarily an individual, but can be an organization, a firm, or society as a whole.

In general, we write of *value dimensions* or *attributes,* implying that they are continuous variables. Some individuals and organizations prefer to speak or write of *goals,* which seem to us to dichotomize continua. The word *objective* is ambiguous; the dictionary comes close to equating it with *goal,* but the literature sometimes uses it to mean what we mean by *value dimension.* Since we are interested in trade-offs, we prefer language implying the continuous formulation of attributes to any that implies absence of continuity – even in cases where attributes are discontinuous or dichotomous. *Benefits* are attractive value dimensions; *costs* are unattractive ones; neither are necessarily measured in dollars.

What we call a value tree Keeney and Raiffa (1976) call an objectives hierarchy, but they treat objectives as typically continuous. Thus, our thought is fully consistent with theirs, though our language is not.

In Chapter 7 we discuss our views about the distinction, traditional in decision analysis, between value and utility. Since we strongly question the usefulness of that distinction, we frequently use the neutral term *location measure* to describe the relative value or utility of a particular object on a value dimension.

How to build a value tree: top-down approach

The analytic, or top-down, approach to building value trees has been discussed in detail by Keeney and Raiffa (1976), Mannheim and Hall (1968), and Miller (1970). It starts from an explication of the evaluators' most general values relevant to the problem. The analyst begins by asking the eval-

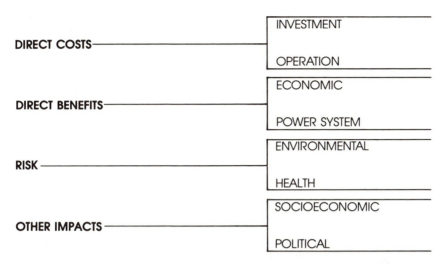

Figure 2.5. Upper layers of a value tree for evaluating energy technologies.

uators to state the relevant general values. A public utility commissioner who is examining the coal versus nuclear options for adding electrical capacity may, for example, differ somewhat from the utility company executive and list the following top-level values:

> Investment costs
> Operations costs
> Economic benefits
> Power systems benefits
> Environmental impacts
> Health impacts
> Socioeconomic impacts
> Political impacts

It is wise to start structuring values with such a list of initial categories rather than with one or two overgeneral value categories (e.g., "the good life"). Sometimes, however, lists such as the one above can be grouped under meaningful supervalues. Figure 2.5 shows an example.

Next the analyst asks the evaluators to explain what the initial value categories mean by using more specific value dimensions. The analyst can help by suggesting various meanings and by probing the evaluators' suggestions. It may be useful to partition the value "cost of a site" in the above example into investment and operational costs, short-term and long-term costs, and so on. The analyst should check the following:

1   Does the subdivision really help explain the meaning of the general value category, or are they value dimensions related in some other way (e.g., functional relation, means–ends relation)?

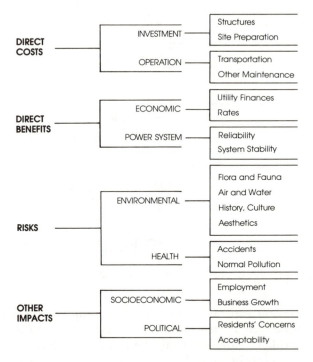

Figure 2.6. Refinement of a value tree for evaluating energy technologies.

2   Is the proposed subordinate value dimension unique to the superordinate value being explicated, or is it linked to others?
3   Is the list of value dimensions exhaustive?
4   Are some value dimensions redundant or partially redundant?

Ideally, the relationship between the lower level dimensions and a higher dimension is hierarchical and directed (by 1), avoids cross-links with other higher level value categories (by 2), and creates an exhaustive (by 3) and nonredundant (by 4) list of explanatory value dimensions. This ideal is often hard to attain; deviations from it are not devastating. But obvious failures of any of these tests invite the analyst to attempt an improved disaggregation.

Figure 2.6 puts together segments of the first three levels of the value tree for the power-plant-siting decision. The top layer regroups the initial list of value categories. The lower layers disaggregate the left-hand values.

The same procedure applies to lower levels of the value tree. Usually the analyst proceeds with one value category first until reaching the twigs. For example, the analyst and evaluators may decide on the following disaggregation of investment cost:

    Land acquisition costs
    Road access costs

Differential transmission line costs
Land refill and reshaping costs
Differential plant costs

This level is sufficiently well defined that the attributes seem measurable. In other value categories further disaggregation may be necessary to arrive at operationalizable or judgable attributes. One of us built a value tree with 6 layers and 144 twigs. Such trees are quite bushy.

When should the analyst stop disaggregating? The usual answer is: When the dimensions at the lowest level are measurable, operationalizable, or easy to assess judgmentally. Sometimes quantifying a value dimension is easy. Various monetary measures exist for investment cost. Sometimes further disaggregation does not lead to quantification. An example is aesthetics, often an important subdimension of the environmental impact of a decision. Even more specific dimensions such as visual aesthetics, odor, and noise seem unmeasurable. But, in our view, the direct judgment of such attributes is a measurement procedure like any other. Faithful representation of an inherently subjective value structure, not objectivity, is the goal of structuring value trees. Chapter 7 gives a technical description of constructing and using appropriate judgmental scales for attribute location measures.

How to build a value tree: bottom-up approach

Humphreys and Humphreys (1975) and Humphreys and Wishuda (1980) have examined the bottom-up, or synthetic, approach. The analytic approach to structuring value trees begins with the question, What general value categories does the evaluator consider important to the problem? In contrast, the synthetic approach begins with the question, What characteristics distinguish the objects of evaluation? The idea is to identify value-relevant characteristics and to synthesize them in order to obtain higher order values.

The synthetic approach begins with a very large list of aspects, characteristics, or indicators of the outcomes of the options under consideration. Exhaustiveness is the initial goal; logical consistency and redundancy do not matter. Attributes, value dimensions, and values can be mixed with indicators and impact variables characterizing evaluation objects. One way to start is by listing the good and bad aspects of each alternative. For example, one site for a power plant may have good road access and may be located far from the nearest earthquake fault, but it may be close to a park and require much earth moving. Such characteristics are then redefined and regrouped into value-relevant attributes that distinguish the evaluation objects. The access road, for example, is a positive characteristic because it eliminates the need for expensive road construction. The underlying attribute is therefore road construction cost. Distance from an earthquake fault is valuable because it reduces the risk of structural damage to the plant with possible pollution. An underlying attribute could be earthquake risks.

Often the analyst can draw on previous comparisons of the evaluation objects. In the coal versus nuclear case, for example, past cost–benefit and risk–benefit studies and studies of health effects and costs of power generation can be examined to create an initial list of attributes and quantifiable measures.

In selecting or defining value-relevant attributes from such lists, the analyst should have in mind the following questions:

1	Does the evaluator have meaningful preferences for different degrees of an attribute?
2	Can the alternatives be distinguished on the basis of that attribute?
3	Are evaluations of some attributes dependent on other attribute values?
4	Are some attributes highly correlated?

The first question determines whether an attribute is value relevant. Sulfur dioxide pollution, for example, may appear on the initial list for comparing alternative power plants, but the evaluator may find it hard to say much more about sulfur dioxide levels than "less is better." The real preferences may concern the health effects of sulfur dioxide, which are related to pollution levels in complicated ways. Distance from a population center may not be a good attribute for evaluating sites for a power plant, because long distance can be both good (for environmental reasons) and bad (because of power loss from transmission lines).

The second question determines whether the attribute is relevant to the evaluation. If all possible options score the same on a given attribute, that attribute is irrelevant and should not be included in the list. It is important to think imaginatively about the possible options. Otherwise an attribute may be deleted that would, in fact, be important if new alternatives were generated. For example, if all possible sites for a power plant have an excellent cooling water supply, that attribute should not be used to compare them. But a new site might be superior in terms of all other attributes and have an inferior cooling water supply.

The third and fourth questions cover two kinds of dependencies among attributes: judgmental and environmental. The distinction is important; we shall make it as clear as we can.

Two attributes are called *judgmentally dependent* if the evaluation of an alternative with respect to one attribute depends on how the alternative performs with respect to the other. For example, in judging the quality of a rifle, accuracy and maximum range are two important attributes. Yet if a rifle is very inaccurate, one may not care about its range. Consequently the evaluation of the relative benefits of range depends on the relative accuracy of the rifle. A more dramatic instance of judgmental dependency occurs in the evaluation of the outcomes of surgery with respect to life expectancy and quality of life. Normally one would prefer more of both. However, if the result of an operation is the deterioration of the quality of life to an intolerable level, one might actually wish to reverse one's preference for greater life expectancy. The analyst can sometimes eliminate judgmental dependencies by restructuring the attribute set.

Two attributes may be judgmentally independent but still *environmentally correlated.* For a manufacturing plant, cost of production and cost of distribution might be an example if the decision has to do with production volume, since it presumably costs more to ship more units. Note that the same two dimensions might be uncorrelated if the decision concerns where to locate a plant having a specified capacity. Or the sign of the correlation might be reversed; consider a decision about whether to locate a plant producing for the U.S. market in the United States or Taiwan. In general, one can ignore environmental correlations in constructing a value tree, unless they indicate redundancy.

Once an appropriate set of initial attributes exists, the analyst and evaluator can group subsets of these attributes to form higher order values. A group of attributes should represent a common higher level value. Aggregation and synthesis can be based on various rationales. For example, costs, risks, and benefits may be an appropriate set of higher order values. An alternative higher level structure might consist of health impacts, economic impacts, and environmental impacts. It is sometimes useful to build a value tree in the analytic mode and another in the synthetic mode and then to synthesize the two to produce a final set of values, attributes, and measures.

Checking and pruning the tree

Keeney and Raiffa (1976) propose the following criteria for examining the objectives and attributes in a tree:

> Completeness
> Operationality
> Decomposability
> Absence of redundancy
> Minimum size

Completeness requires that all relevant values be included in the superstructure of the tree and that the substructure completely define the higher level values. Operationality requires that the lowest level values or attributes be meaningful and assessable. Decomposability means that the attributes can be analyzed one or two at a time, that is, that they are judgmentally independent. Absence of redundancy means that no two attributes or values mean the same thing. Minimum size requirement refers to the necessity of keeping the number of attributes small enough to manage. These requirements conflict. Operationality often requires further decomposition, thus increasing the number of attributes. Completeness may lead to redundancy, since true value independence is often an unattainable ideal.

We too have a checklist, closely related to Keeney and Raiffa's:

1   Does the value tree repeat subobjectives and attributes? The subordinate values may be redundant and unnecessary.
2   Can the decision maker think of any value-relevant aspect of the options that has not been captured? If so, the tree may not be complete.
3   Are the attributes highly correlated across options? If so, they may be redundant.
4   Can the options be located on each attribute easily? If not, the attribute may be ill-defined.
5   Can the decision maker or experts think of "good" and "bad" scenarios for each objective and value dimension in the hierarchy? If not, the dimension may not be value relevant.
6   Can the decision maker think of preferences for several levels of an attribute independently of the levels in other attributes? If not, the dimension may not be judgmentally independent.
7   Are there some easy rules for aggregating attribute measures (e.g., combining various dollar costs by summation)? If so, the breakdown may be unnecessary.

The quality of a tree may be clear only after assessment of the numerical values and weights. One can usually remove difficulties in such assessments by restructuring the parts of the tree that produce the problem. In an apartment evaluation problem, for example, two attributes may be distance from campus and facilities for transportation to campus. The importance of transportation facilities clearly depends on the distance from campus. These attributes can be collapsed into, say, accessibility of the campus.

In other cases one can remove such interactions by adding attributes. Keeney (1980) gives the example of a value tree including benefits to person A and to person B as two attributes. If the decision maker cares about equitable distribution of benefits, the result is a judgmental dependency. A way to deal with it is to define yet another dimension: equity of the distribution of benefits accruing to A and B.

Attributes are easiest to think about if either more is preferred to less or less is preferred to more. Sometimes an attribute may have an ideal point other than the upper or lower end. Such nonmonotone preferences can often be removed by redefinition of objectives or attributes. Consider, for example, distance from the office in a house or apartment evaluation problem. There may be an optimal distance, because the neighborhood next to the office is too industrialized or smoggy but the decision maker likes short commutes. Distance from the office can be redefined as two monotone attributes: travel time and pleasant living environment.

The use of value trees

In theory, the use of value trees for evaluating options is straightforward: the analyst simply uses the operational attributes (twigs), obtains estimates of how the options perform on these attributes, converts these estimates to utilities, weights the attributes, and carries out the appropriate calculations to generate an overall evaluation of the options.

In practice, this approach has difficulties:

1   There may be too many twigs to carry out a sensible evaluation.
2   Some branches of the tree may be irrelevant because the options do not differ in their performance on them.
3   Higher level branches of the tree may be more meaningful than the twigs to the decision maker.

Because of these difficulties, value trees are most often used as background material in the development of attribute sets for the formal evaluation. They also facilitate the process of ensuring that the final set of attributes actually captures all the relevant and useful values. In Keeney's (1980) evaluation of pumped storage sites, for example, a rather complex value tree containing 14 lower level twigs was used to develop a simple set of four attributes. All other twigs were eliminated either because they were captured by the four attributes considered as proxies or because they did not differentiate among the options.

A second purpose of value trees is to identify the appropriate level of abstraction at which it is useful to carry out the evaluation. Simplicity and the ease of the judgmental task must be balanced against the operationality of the attributes. If higher level branches are used for the evaluation, the lower level twigs may still be helpful in formulating scales or in setting up measurement procedures.

A third purpose of value trees is to communicate concisely the entire spectrum of values and concerns of the decision maker about the issue at hand. Even if the final evaluation makes use of only parts of the tree or involves higher branch levels and ignores twigs, the whole tree should be presented in order to put the concrete evaluation in perspective.

Having built the value tree and having identified the appropriate attributes, the analyst often uses a matrix of options by attributes as a comprehensive display of the evaluation structure. The matrix then becomes an input into the multiattribute evaluation described in Chapter 8.

2.5. Structuring probabilistic inference problems

Examples and introduction

In this section we describe structures for relating hypotheses, data, events, and information in probabilistic settings. The fundamental intellectual tool of inference is a set of scenarios, or stories. Scenarios are composed of events, some observed, others initially unobserved but observable, and others never observed. Some of the unobserved and/or unobservable ones come in clusters; the concept of a disease is a familiar example. Unobserved events can be simple or can themselves comprise a complex scenario. Either

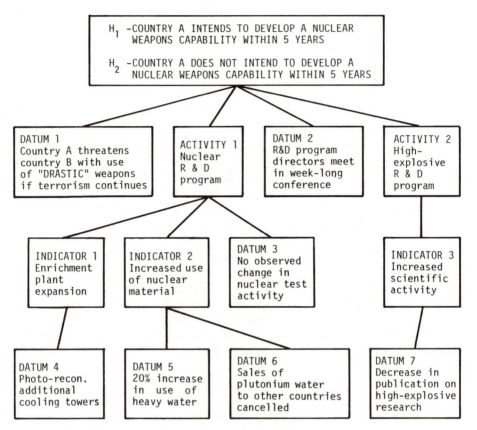

Figure 2.7. Example of an inference tree. (Reprinted with permission of Decisions and Designs, Inc., from Barclay, Brown, Kelly, Peterson, Phillips, & Selvidge, 1977.)

way, we call them hypotheses. Invariably, the function of an inferential process is to infer unobserved events from observed ones. Such inferences are normally fallible, since more than one set of unobserved events is usually consistent with actual observations. Assessing the probabilities of competing hypotheses is the purpose of inference.

The sequential structure of a scenario is not directly represented in probabilistic inference, though it plays a major role in the definition of hypotheses and in the task of linking data to them. Inference problems are often structured as *inference trees;* Figure 2.7 presents an example from Barclay et al. (1977). At the top of such a tree are the hypotheses to which probabilities are to be attached. At the bottom are data. In between are unobserved events in the scenarios that fulfill the role of hypotheses with respect to the data beneath them and the role of data with respect to the hypotheses above them. The problem of assessing probabilities for the top events in such trees is common in risk analysis (see McCormick, 1981). *Event trees*

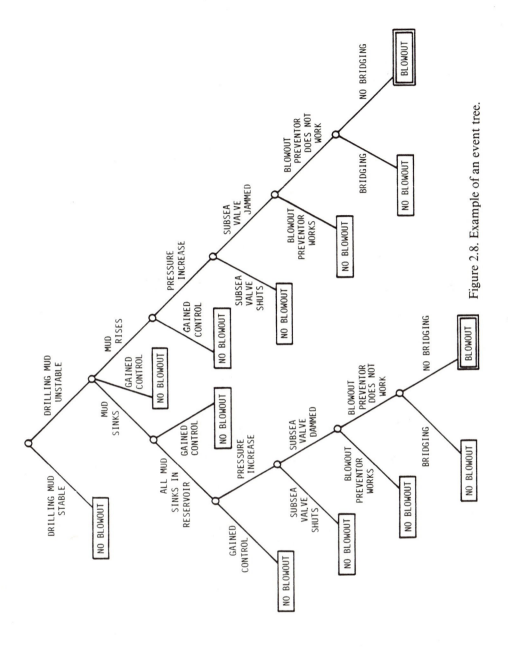

Figure 2.8. Example of an event tree.

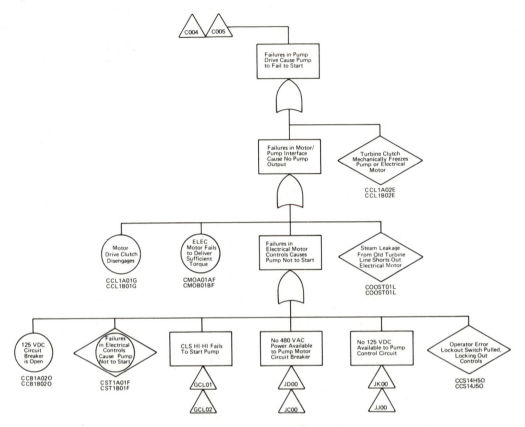

Figure 2.9. Example of a fault tree. (*Source:* U.S. Nuclear Regulatory Commission, 1975.)

frequently model such event sequences. Figure 2.8 shows how a workover on an oil rig may result in a blowout. Finally, *fault trees* are often used in mechanics and engineering to trace the cause of a problem. Figure 2.9 shows a fault tree of possible causes of a nuclear power plant failure. Although inference trees, event trees, and fault trees have different relational logics, they all require a structure that allows probability assessments (priors, likelihoods, etc.; see Chapter 6) on each of the branches.

Inference trees

The need for inference trees arises in statistical explanations if the observable data are logically far removed from the hypotheses or states about which inferences are to be made. L. D. Phillips (personal communication, 1982) described an insurance example, an inference problem in which the data are observations by an underwriter about a ship. The observations

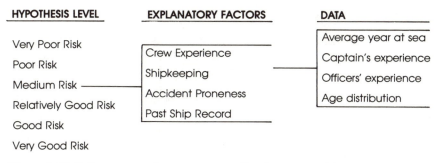

HYPOTHESIS LEVEL	EXPLANATORY FACTORS	DATA
Very Poor Risk		Average year at sea
Poor Risk	Crew Experience	Captain's experience
Medium Risk	Shipkeeping	Officers' experience
Relatively Good Risk	Accident Proneness	Age distribution
Good Risk	Past Ship Record	
Very Good Risk		

Figure 2.10. Inference tree for assessment of an insurance risk.

include the age of the ship, its size, accident record, crew experience, quality of management, and others. On the basis of these observations, the insurance underwriter has to determine the risk category into which this ship falls. To facilitate the process, Phillips defined explanatory factors that connect data and hypotheses. One factor, for example, could be shipkeeping, data related to the cleanliness and orderliness of the ship and its operations. Figure 2.10 shows the structure of the inference tree.

Examples of real and complex inference trees are rare. One reason is that such trees are often unmanageable and require too many conditional (branch probability) assessments. Even in the insurance case, Phillips was unable to model the conditional probabilities between the datum level and the factor level, since too many probabilities would have been required.

To build an inference tree, begin by listing the hypotheses or states about which inferences should be made. Next define intermediate factors, events, or aggregate data that bear on the probability of the hypotheses or states. Then disaggregate further through various levels of detail down to specific and unequivocal data. In the simplest case (as in the insurance underwriting example) all intermediate levels bear on all higher levels in the tree.

Intelligence analysis provides examples of more complex inference trees. Consider the hypothesis that the Soviet Union is preparing to attack Iran from Afghanistan. The data include satellite pictures, spy reports, and political analysis. An actual datum could be a report by a spy who overheard a conversation between two Russian officers in Kabul in which one officer stated, "The Ayatolla will soon get it." In this case intermediate explanatory levels would include troop concentrations at the border, troop movements in Siberia, and political instability in the Politburo.

Any hierarchy of data, explanatory events, and hypotheses that links its elements without loops or interconnections is an inference tree. All levels of any inference tree except the data at the bottom are uncertain. In a *single-chain tree,* the simplest kind of inference tree, a single datum is related through one or more explanatory variables to the ultimate hypotheses. The datum might be a radiograph, the intermediate hypotheses might be

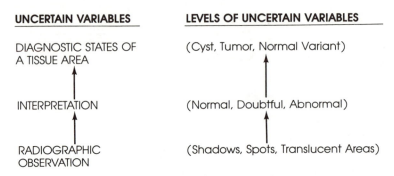

Figure 2.11. Example of a single-chain inference tree.

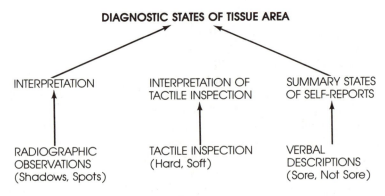

Figure 2.12. Example of a multichain inference tree.

whether a spot on it is normal or abnormal, and the final state might be whether it indicates a tumor, a cyst, or a normal variant. This simple tree is shown in Figure 2.11.

Gettys and Willke (1969) studied another simple tree, one combining several single-chain trees. Several data can be entered into such a tree. Each datum is linked to a *separate* intermediate event level, and all intermediate event levels are linked to the same hypothesis sets. Figure 2.12 shows an extension of the example in Figure 2.11. We have added two more data sources: tactile inspections and self-reports. The intermediate levels are the actual states (hardened vs. soft and sore vs. not sore). The final state is again the tumor–cyst–normal distinction. Phillips's insurance tree is another example of this simple structure.

Another structure dealing with multiple data is the last we present here – though Chapter 6 considers more complex structures. Consider again the medical diagnosis example. Instead of one radiograph, the radiologist may have taken three from different positions. And instead of simply examining the surface area for possibly hardened tissue, the patient may have reported

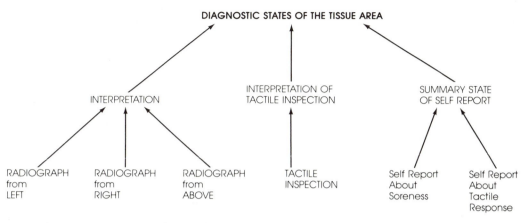

Figure 2.13. Example of a multichain tree with multiple data.

whether or not the area was sore and how the tissue responded to self-examination. This structure is shown in Figure 2.13.

Naturally, trees can become much more complex, as in Barclay et al. (1977). All such trees have a common structure: each variable (datum, event, etc.) has one and only one intermediate successor (next higher level); all paths must lead to the final hypotheses; all paths must fan down from the hypothesis level in a tree form without loops (see Kelly and Barclay, 1973; Schum, 1980; and Chapter 6).

We have little experience in structuring inference trees. Typically, one starts by defining the two end points: the top – the hypothesis variable; and the bottom – the observables, the data. One usually constructs intermediate levels by two procedures: clustering data beneath variables that help explain them and disaggregating hypotheses into subhypotheses. These processes are not unlike the analytic and synthetic approaches to building value trees. Structuring a tree fails if complex interdependencies exist. Constructing inference trees that justify the independence assumptions needed to make them analytically tractable is an art. Often the logic of structuring itself creates the required independence relations. The most serious difficulty in building inference trees is that they soon become unmanageable; in Phillips's insurance example a full three-level analysis would have required more than 900 assessments of conditional likelihoods! Unless models can be used to simplify or shorten such assessments, even relatively simple trees may become unwieldy.

A useful way to simplify complicated inference structures is to combine groups of relevant data into aggregate indices. An example of such an index is the familiar grade point average, an unweighted linear combination of individual grades. This compression is useful for many predictive purposes (e.g., undergraduate grade point average is a predictor of graduate grade

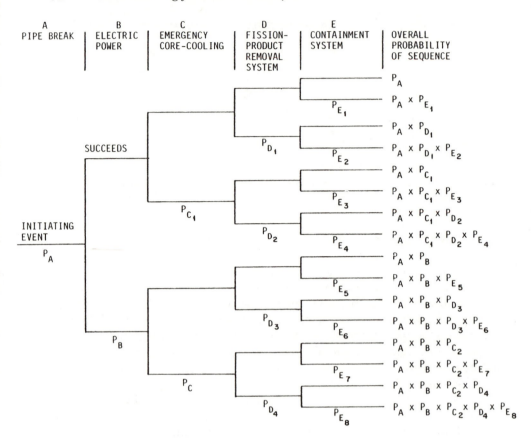

Figure 2.14. Event tree for a nuclear power plant failure. (*Source:* U.S. Nuclear Regulatory Commission, 1975.)

point average). The trade-off between the resulting simplicity and the loss of interdependencies among the components that enter into the index depends on the precision required, the purpose, and the tastes of the modeler.

Event trees and fault trees

The logic of event trees is quite simple. The first node is an *initiating event*. From there, several paths lead to a set of possible *final events.* In the blowout example above, the initiating event was the loss of drilling mud stability. The final events were occurrence or no occurrence of a blowout. The logic of building the paths between starting and final events is straightforward: all relevant events intermediate in time between start and finish are included. As usual, the tree may not have loops.

Figure 2.14 shows a segment of an event tree for a nuclear reactor failure that may cause a loss-of-coolant accident. The upper branch of each node in the tree indicates the success of a given system (from A through E); the lower branch indicates failure. The worst possible case, the loss-of-coolant accident, occurs if all systems (A through E) fail. The joint probability of this accident sequence is indicated at the bottom twig as the product of all branch probabilities.

The first crucial assumption in event trees is the independence of individual events from others. In this example we assume that the probability of failure of the emergency cooling system is independent of a previous pipe break and independent of a subsequent failure of the containment system. Common-mode failures are the most typical violations of this independence assumption. We can relax the assumption somewhat by allowing dependencies on previous events, at the cost of a considerable increase in the assessment and calculation effort.

In structuring event trees, one should include all possible failure modes. That is hard to do. In the near meltdown at the Brown's Ferry nuclear plant in Alabama, the initiating event was a fire in the electrical system, accidentally set by an electrician who was searching for air leaks with a lit candle. The fire spread rapidly because the electrical insulation material was not fireproof. Such anomalies are difficult to capture in an event tree analysis.

Fault trees invert the logic of event trees. They begin with an accident or failure and trace the possible causes of that failure. Figure 2.15 is a very simple fault tree for the failure "Car won't start" (see Fischhoff, Slovic, and Lichtenstein, 1978). Figure 2.16 is a segment of a fault tree for a loss-of-coolant accident (LOCA) in a nuclear power plant. Fault trees have two types of nodes. The first is the "and" node, which indicates that all lower level events must occur before the higher level event can occur. The probability of the higher level event is then the product of the individual probabilities of the lower level events (provided that these are independent). The "or" node indicates that the occurrence of any event connected to it from the next lower level is sufficient to cause the event that names the node. For exclusive events the sum of individual event probabilities is the probability of the next higher event. Assessments and calculations are easy, for fault trees as for trees of other kinds, only if appropriate independence assumptions hold. Since fault trees are inverted event trees, we need say little more about how to construct them. As with event trees, the most common difficulty in constructing fault trees is covering all possible causes.

Fischhoff et al. (1978) showed subjects the fault tree in Figure 2.15 and asked them to assign probabilities to the various categories, including the catchall category "other problems." Another group of subjects was shown half the tree, subsuming three categories under "other problems." Student subjects and professional mechanics attached much too high a probability to the failure modes shown and too little to the "other problems" category.

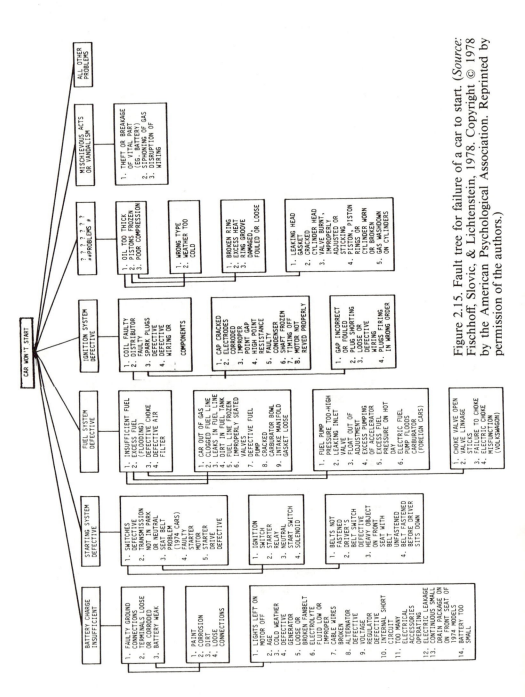

Figure 2.15. Fault tree for failure of a car to start. (*Source:* Fischhoff, Slovic, & Lichtenstein, 1978. Copyright © 1978 by the American Psychological Association. Reprinted by permission of the authors.)

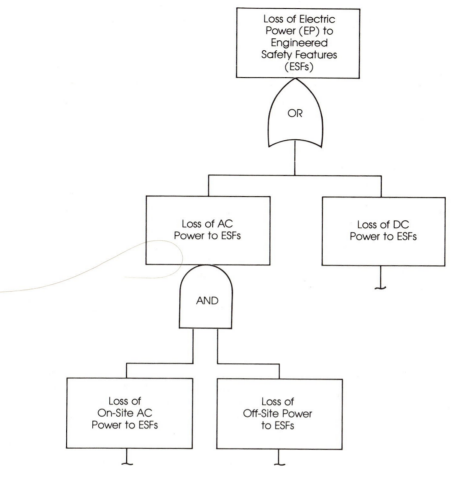

Figure 2.16. Fault tree for a nuclear power plant failure. (*Source:* U.S. Nuclear Regulatory Commission, 1975.)

Fischhoff et al. concluded that people are often ignorant of what they do not know and too confident of having captured all failure modes after insufficient analysis.

2.6. Advances in structuring research

Option invention and hypothesis invention

Before you can develop decision trees, value trees, or inference trees you must be able, at least tentatively, to answer two questions: what can be done by, and to, the decision maker(s)? The first question requires that you inventory the options available and often invent new ones. The second question requires that you figure out, for each option, what the environment, the world, the opposition, chance, or anything else over which the decision makers have no control may do to affect the outcome of the option.

The growing literature on option invention marries decision analysis and creative thinking. Pearl (1977) and Pearl, Leal, and Saleh (1980), for example, used means–end analysis in artificial intelligence as a starting point for a methodology for option generation. The idea of means–end analysis is to define a problem as a difference between a desired goal state and the status quo. Subproblems are defined by the dimensions on which the status quo falls short of the goal state. One solves the problem dimension by dimension by inventing actions sequentially that reduce the difference between the status quo and the goal state.

Pitz, Sachs, and Heerboth (1980) tested a version of the means–end analysis idea in a behavioral study. All subjects generated as many reasonable alternatives as possible in a decision problem. Three groups generated alternatives that satisfied the list of objectives (attributes) one at a time, two at a time, or all simultaneously. Two groups saw example alternatives (either categorized or randomly displayed), one group was told to think of possible objectives relevant to the decision problem, and one group was told just to generate alternatives. Although the mean group differences were small, single-attribute maximizers tended to produce more alternatives and the multiple-attribute maximizers fewer alternatives than did other subjects.

Research on hypothesis or event generation is in a similar state of infancy. Gettys, Mehle, Baca, Fisher, and Manning (1979) and Gettys, Fisher, and Mehle (1978) conducted a series of experiments to test subjects' ability to generate and judge hypotheses. In one example, subjects provided a list of hypotheses about which state was described by a list of characteristics. In another example, subjects generated hypotheses about a student's major based on a list of courses the student had taken. In both experiments the subjects performed relatively poorly. They did not generate a large enough set of hypotheses and were overconfident that their set included the true hypothesis. Fischhoff et al. (1978) examined hypothesis generation about car failures, with similar results. Both experiments used essentially a recall paradigm in which hypothesis sets are known to the experimenter and could be known to the subject. Creative hypothesis generation has unfortunately not been studied much.

Recent approaches to structuring aids

Influence diagrams are a relatively recent development in decision-analytic structuring (see Howard and Matheson, 1980; Miller, Merkhofer, Howard, Matheson, and Rice, 1976). Influence diagrams present a graphic picture of the interactions of decision and random variables in a decision model with-

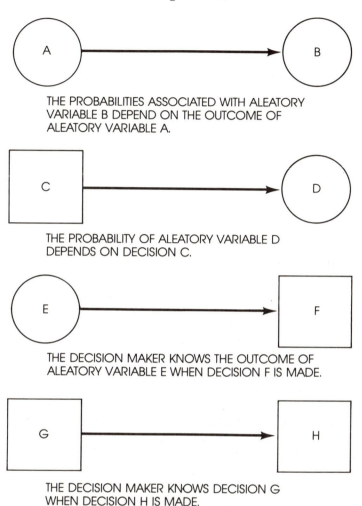

THE PROBABILITIES ASSOCIATED WITH ALEATORY
VARIABLE B DEPEND ON THE OUTCOME OF
ALEATORY VARIABLE A.

THE PROBABILITY OF ALEATORY VARIABLE D
DEPENDS ON DECISION C.

THE DECISION MAKER KNOWS THE OUTCOME OF
ALEATORY VARIABLE E WHEN DECISION F IS MADE.

THE DECISION MAKER KNOWS DECISION G
WHEN DECISION H IS MADE.

Figure 2.17. Types of influence relations. (*Source:* Howard & Matheson, 1980.)

out superimposing a decision or event tree structure. Howard and Matheson (1980) distinguish between deterministic and probabilistic influence relations. An example of a deterministic influence is the relation between price, demand, and product introduction. A decision variable (price) may "influence" a state variable (demand) and thus influence the final state (successful introduction of a new product into a market). The probabilistic influence relation is very similar to the interpretation "changes the probability of " or "changes the outcome of." For example, an information variable (seismic observations) may influence a decision variable (drill or not), which finally influences the final event variable (strike or no strike). Figure 2.17 presents

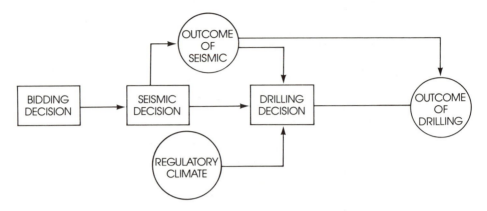

Figure 2.18. Example of an influence diagram.

the definitions in influence diagrams and Figure 2.18 presents an influence diagram version of the oil-drilling example.

At present, influence diagrams are considered a simplification of decision trees. They are useful as initial cognitive maps of a decision problem. Given certain independence assumptions (see Howard and Matheson, 1980), influence diagrams can be turned into decision trees and numerically analyzed in the usual manner.

Several computer programs have been developed to aid decision makers or experts in structuring decision problems. Some of these are discussed in Kelly (1978) and Humphreys and Wishuda (1980). These aids typically rely on empty structuring concepts (decision trees, value trees, inference trees, or influence diagrams), and they guide the decision maker or expert in the analytic formulation of his or her problem. Special aids include (1) OPINT for moderately complex problems that can easily be formulated into a decision tree or matrix structure, (2) the decision triangle aid for sequential decision problems with a focus on changing probabilities, and (3) EVAL for multiattribute utility problems (Kelly, 1978).

MAUD (Humphreys, and Wishuda, 1980) is an especially interesting computer aid for structuring evaluation problems. It interactively elicits attributes for evaluation by asking the decision maker to make similarity–dissimilarity judgments among triples of alternatives. For example, in a job evaluation problem, MAUD first asks the decision maker to list his or her alternatives. Then it picks randomly three job options and asks the decision maker, "In what way does job A differ from jobs B and C?" MAUD then uses the dissimilarity dimensions as attributes in a MAUT analysis. MAUD also has the capacity to restructure attributes based on redundancy and intercorrelations.

EXPERT CHOICE is a computer program based on Saaty's analytic hierarchy process (AHP) and developed by Decision Support Systems, Inc. (see

Saaty, 1980). The AHP is an evaluation procedure that is somewhat similar to the multiattribute procedures discussed in Chapter 8. EXPERT CHOICE allows the analyst to structure value trees ("analytic hierarchies" in Saaty's terminology), to obtain various graphic displays of their substructures, and to carry out numerical evaluation.

We have highlighted MAUD and EXPERT CHOICE because of their structuring capabilities. Numerous other decision analysis software packages are available, and many more are under development. Most of these, however, are more useful for formal evaluation and analysis than for problem structuring.

Most computer aids turn the fundamentally empty structures of decision trees, value trees, and inference trees into more operational, computerized elicitation tools, without adding specifics relevant to the problem at hand and already known by the computer. There are clear advantages to such an approach: a wide range of applicability, flexibility, user involvement, speed, limited training, and feedback, to name only a few. It also reduces the demands on the decision analyst's time.

There is, of course, the other extreme: the prestructured, precanned, problem-specific version of decision analysis applicable to problems that occur repeatedly with little variation. A military example is the SURVAV model of Decisions and Designs, Inc. (Kelly, 1978), which aids the selection of routes for ships that will help them avoid detection by satellites. Such a structure and model can routinely be implemented with almost no additional training. In turn it sacrifices generalizability.

Neither extreme is totally satisfactory. With empty general structures one must consider each problem from scratch. Substantive specific structures have limited generalizability. The middle ground of problem-driven but still generalizable structures and models has not yet been filled.

Generic problem classes

One approach to generating generalizable structures is to build a taxonomy synthetically by generalizing substantive problem features that distinguish one problem from another. Rather than analytically dividing the universe of problems, this approach begins with the questions, What is special about this particular problem? How is it different from others? What other problems are substantively similar in the sense of containing similar elements, having similar relations, or requiring similar solution operations? Such an inductive approach may eventually lead to the definition of *generic problem classes,* for which decision-analytic structures can be developed. Some generic classes have been investigated in the decision-analytic literature.

Facility siting is clearly a typical decision problem. Keeney and other decision analysts have investigated this problem in much detail and in a variety of contexts (see the examples in Keeney and Raiffa, 1976). Indeed,

Table 2.1. *Steps in the decision analysis siting procedure*

---

1. Identifying candidate sites
Selecting the region of interest
Choosing screening criteria
Determining candidate areas
Initial site visits

2. Specifying objectives and attributes of the siting study
Specifying general concerns and relevant interest groups
Determining the objectives
Defining measures of effectiveness (attributes) for each objective

3. Describing possible site impacts
Quantifying impacts in terms of attributes
Quantifying uncertainty, using probability distributions
Assessing judgments of experts
Collecting data and updating estimates

4. Evaluating site impacts
Determining the functional form of the multiattribute utility function
Assessing the single attribute utility functions
Assessing the value tradeoffs and the multiattribute utility functions

5. Analyzing and comparing candidate sites
Verifying the appropriateness of the decision analysis assumptions
Integrating the previous information to evaluate alternatives
Conducting a sensitivity analysis with respect to preferences and impact inputs
Reappraising assumptions made in the analysis

Source: Keeney (1980)

Keeney (1980) has published a book on the problem of energy facility siting. Table 2.1 presents his five steps; note that they combine problem definition with methodology. A typical feature of siting problems is sequential screening from candidate areas to possible sites, to a preferred set, to final site-specific evaluations. Another feature is that they are multiattribute evaluation problems with common generic classes of objectives: investment and operating cost, economic benefits, environmental impacts, social impacts, and political considerations. Also, the process of organizing, collecting, and evaluating information is similar in many siting decisions. Keeney's prototypical structure for facility-siting decisions simply assembles the generalizable features of past applications.

Contingency planning is another recurring problem. Decisions and Designs, Inc., has addressed this problem in the military context, but it is also relevant to planning for action in the case of disasters such as liquefied natural gas plant explosions or blowouts from oil platforms. Generic properties that characterize contingency planning include strong central control by executive bodies, the requirement that numerous decisions be made simultaneously, the fact that major events can drastically change the focus of the problem, rapid influx of no-cost or low-cost information, and organizational problems that may impede information flows and actions. At first glance, decision trees seem to be natural models for contingency planning. But a generic structure would need special characteristics not found in many decision trees. For example, the model structure should allow rapid changes due to unforeseeable events. It should be able to update its information base quickly but should not overstress the value of information, since most information is free. It should be able to fine-tune its actions essentially instantaneously in response to rapidly changing input information.

Budget allocation to competing programs is another typical problem. In many problems such as this, different programs attempt to pursue similar objectives, and the merit of the program mix is at least as important as the direct benefits of single programs. Budgeting decisions allocate a single continuous decision variable subject to a total budget constraint. Typically, budget allocation problems also have semipermeable constraints on suballocations to major budget elements and must take implicit or explicit commitments carried over from previous years very seriously indeed. MAUT is a natural structure for budget allocation decisions, since it easily handles program evaluation (see Edwards, Guttentag, and Snapper, 1975; Edwards and Newman, 1982). But neither the evaluation of alternative program mixes nor the constrained and continuous characteristics of budgets are appropriately addressed by simple MAUs. A generic decision-analytic structure would aim at evaluating the mix of programs funded at particular levels.

As our previous discussion illustrated, *regulation* presents a class of decision problems that have a number of recurrent themes. Three generic groups are involved (regulators, regulated, beneficiaries of regulation). Monitoring and sanction schemes are important. Those regulated and the beneficiaries of regulation usually have opposing objectives. The objectives of the regulator are usually highly political. In a previous discussion we examined the specific regulation problem of standard setting and suggested prototypical decision-analytic structures for it. A decision-analytic structure for regulation in general would have many features of the standards model.

This list could be extended to include private investment decisions, product mix selection, resource development, diagnostic problems, social conflict resolution, and others. But the four examples suffice to demonstrate how prototypical decision-analytic structuring can be approached in general. In our opinion, such an approach to structuring will be at least as useful for the implementation of decision analysis as computerization of decision models. Generic decision-analytic structures are transferable; that is their technical advantage. More important, they enable decision analysts to be knowledgeable and concerned about problems. We find unappealing the too frequently encountered methods expert, looking for problems that can be made to fit methods on hand by lopping off some goals here, stretching some assumptions there, and distorting intuition and common sense everywhere. Decision analysts can, should, and occasionally do do better.

3   Decision trees

3.1. Introduction

The concept of decision trees

The outcome of a decision often depends not only on the option chosen but also on external events not under the decision maker's control. In part for that reason, it may be useful to consider sequences of decisions, in which the action taken at a later point depends both on the decision maker's earlier action and on the nature of subsequent events. Often the analyst can make the initial decision easier by structuring the sequences of possible external events and actions consequent to each external event. Such a representation is called a decision tree. Later in the chapter we examine when and why one might represent a decision problem with a decision tree and explore the intellectual difficulties of deciding how extensive that representation should be. First, consider some examples.

Figure 3.1 presents a very simple decision tree. The problem is whether to pay a $300 annual premium for collision insurance with a $200 deductible to cover a car worth $10,000. Obviously, you are insuring against all kinds of possibilities, ranging from any accident causing $200 worth of damage to the car to one that destroys it totally. Since that set of possibilities is inconveniently large, you choose to consider only no accident and the two extreme accidents: one that causes $200 worth of damage and one that totals the car. (A more sophisticated analysis certainly would include at least one intermediate accident.)

Figure 3.2 presents a more complex tree. The decision problem is whether an exploration and production company should bid on an offshore oil-drilling lease. The bid may be accepted or rejected by the government agency offering the lease. Before making the final decision to drill, but after the bid is accepted, the company can perform seismic tests of the lease area. After studying the results of the test it can decide whether to drill an exploration well. Finally, the exploration may be dry or may result in a strike of unknown size. Outcomes are oil production volumes of various sizes.

Any path through a decision tree can, without loss of generality, be

63

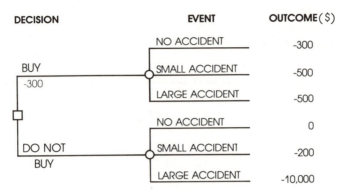

Figure 3.1. Decision tree for an insurance example.

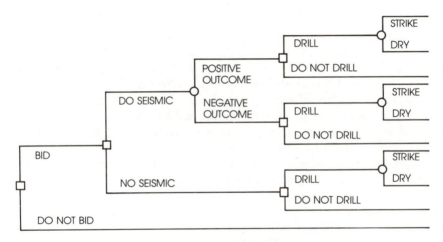

Figure 3.2. Decision tree for an oil-drilling example.

thought of as an alternating sequence of actions by a decision maker and events in the environment. If A is an action by you and E an environmental event, then any path through the tree will have the form $A_i, E_p, A_j, E_q, A_k, E_r, \ldots$. Each chance node is usually represented by a circle in a decision tree; each decision node by a square. Events fan out from circles, decisions from squares. By convention, the tree extends from left to right. At the tips of the tree (the rightmost nodes) are outcomes that describe where a specific act–event sequence will lead. Outcomes can be very specific, like dollar amounts lost or won, but they can also be complex scenarios.

In the following sections we describe how to build such trees and how to do some simple analyses with them. Fortunately, our description can be brief, since Behn and Vaupel (1982) have already provided an excellent introduction to decision trees, *Quick Analysis for Busy Decision Makers*.

This highly readable book explains how to structure decision trees, assess probabilities and utilities, and carry out the appropriate calculations. It follows the more formal expositions of Raiffa and Schlaifer (1961), Raiffa (1968), Brown, Kahr and Peterson (1974), and Holloway (1979).

Purposes of decision trees

The main purpose of decision trees is scenario preparation. By specifying in detail the complex interactions between the decision maker and the environment, a decision tree compactly represents a set of scenarios; any path from left to right through the tree constitutes a scenario. Scenarios would, of course, be completely unnecessary if the decision maker knew for certain the consequences of each available action.

By specifying an (in principle) exhaustive set of scenarios consequent to each possible action, a decision tree facilitates evaluation of the action. In the absence of uncertainty, it should be possible to evaluate the unique outcomes of each action directly. Given uncertainty, decision trees permit an indirect evaluation of each action by specifying each of its possible outcomes, contingent on act–event sequences. A test of the usefulness of a decision tree, then, is whether the evaluation of its final outcomes is substantially easier than direct evaluation of actions or their immediate outcomes.

Another purpose of decision trees is action invention in the light of uncertainty. A period of head scratching, more formally called option invention, typically precedes any formal decision. Decision trees guide option invention in two important ways. The first is the invention of information-gathering options, which help sort out which events are likely to occur, before final actions are taken. The second is the invention of hedging options, which do reasonably well against all event contingencies.

Analysts, especially beginners, often confuse the thought-facilitating function of scenarios, and so of decision trees, with their simulation function. A realistic portrayal of act–event sequences may be an excellent simulation of future events, but it may in fact be a very poor representation for the purpose of decision making. Realistic simulation unfortunately often leads to bushy messes. For decision analysis, the main function of decision trees is simplification for evaluation.

Instrumental outcomes and bushy messes: a philosophical interlude

The most important outcome of a decision, in almost every case, is the opportunity to make more decisions. Most decisions therefore have instrumental outcomes. We shall illustrate the point with a situation involving money, since money is purely instrumental. You must choose what to buy. Suppose you buy gasoline. Then you must choose where to drive using that gasoline. Suppose you choose to go to lunch. Then you must select a restaurant. And so on. From this rather Olympian perspective, decision processes never really end. They do not end even with your death, since in making your will and managing your affairs you produce effects that far outlast you.

Realistic portrayals of such never-ending decision processes would produce an unmanageably complex tree – a bushy mess, as decision analysts say. A natural means of reducing the bushy mess to manageable size is illustrated in Figure 3.1: let the decision problem and the uncertainties you face suggest where to cut the tree. In this example, cutting at the point where the insurance-buying decision and its possible outcomes terminates seems quite natural; the introduction of considerations about how you will use (or pay) the money seems to add rather than reduce uncertainties.

Few real-life decision problems are that kind to the struggling analyst. Pruning decision trees is an important practical problem in almost every case. We shall examine some ideas for approaching it in the next section – but we warn you in advance that they are not really adequate to the problem they address.

If the consequences of a decision extend to your death or beyond, the point at which you cut each branch of the tree growing from that decision will inevitably be arbitrary. This means that the idea of an outcome is also arbitrary. *Outcome* is simply a name applied to the end point at which you cut a branch of the tree. Outcomes are essentially fictions, though indispensable ones; the truth is that life goes on after the outcome occurs.

The remainder of this chapter, abandoning philosophy, will blithely read as though outcomes were realities rather than fictional representations of indefinitely extended futures.

3.2. How to build a decision tree

A sample problem

We mentioned earlier that structuring a problem typically begins, not with a decision tree, but with a vague problem formulation or with the identification or generation of some rough options and spelling out the main objectives for choosing among the options. Thus, it is always useful to structure options and objectives in a matrix before building a decision tree.

Consider a decision one of us (von Winterfeldt) once had to make, namely, whether to file suit for damages in a car accident:

I was driving to work at the University of Southern California's Social Science Research Institute.[1] Just before turning into the campus I stopped behind a car waiting for the red light to change. About two seconds after I stopped, the rear end of my car was hit by another car, and my car was pushed into the car in front of me. The police took a report, and the situa-

---

[1] The material written in the first person was drafted by von Winterfeldt.

Table 3.1. *Initial alternatives* × *objectives matrix in the uninsured motorist problem*

Alternative	Cost	Recovered money	Hassle	Knowledge	Revenge	Social empathy
Sue	About $200	?	Much	Much	Much	None
Don't sue	$0	$0	Little	Little	None	Much

tion seemed simple enough. No serious injuries had occurred, but my car was severely damaged. Unfortunately, Billy J., the woman who had caused the accident, was an uninsured motorist.[2] I had no collision insurance and thus faced the loss of the value of my car, about $2,000. I was furious over Billy J.'s irresponsibility in driving without insurance, at the state of California for letting drivers get away with being uninsured, and at myself for not having obtained collision coverage. (My regret about not having bought collision insurance later subsided. Decision analysis had taught me that that decision was right – I just had to live with the outcome.)

Decision analysis had also taught me to lay out my alternatives and objectives, and a decision tree, before taking any important actions. The problem I faced was, of course, whether to go through an arduous, time- and money-consuming lawsuit with uncertain returns or to write the car off as a loss.

The problem was not just monetary. I had mixed feelings about suing. Billy J. was poor, and though I resented her irresponsibility in not carrying insurance I also recognized that insurance premiums are high; perhaps she could not afford them. Los Angeles does not offer public transportation, so what is a poor person to do? The court case intrigued me, nonetheless. I knew little about the U.S. legal system and wanted to learn more. Being involved in a case of my own seemed like an excellent chance to do that.

These thoughts generated the matrix of alternatives by objectives shown in Table 3.1. Perhaps the most interesting aspect of this matrix is that only one of the twelve cells is truly uncertain: the cell indicating recovered money.

I did some very crude subjective sensitivity analysis and concluded that "hassle" would cancel out "knowledge," and "revenge" would cancel out "social empathy." I also felt that "cost" and "recovered money" could be combined into "net monetary return" without explicit consideration of time. In effect, this turned the problem into a single-dimensional (monetary) outcome problem under uncertainty.

With this structure in mind, I went to a lawyer and asked him, "Are the chances of winning this case larger than your legal fees divided by two thou-

---

[2] The names were changed, as were some relatively minor details of the case for the purpose of this presentation.

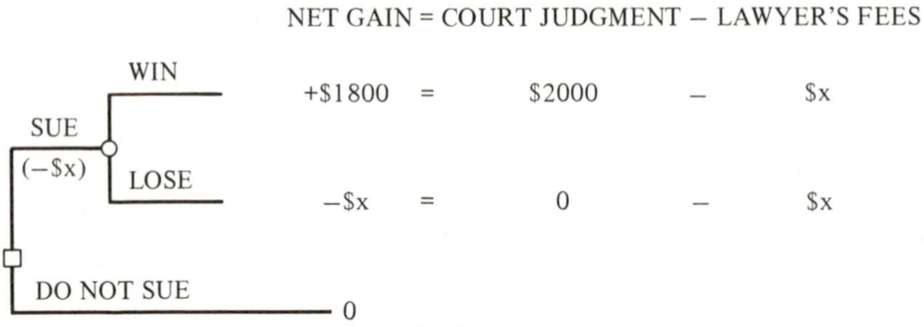

NET GAIN = COURT JUDGMENT − LAWYER'S FEES

Figure 3.3. Decision tree formulation of the uninsured motorist problem.

sand dollars?" The question was derived from the decision tree displayed in Figure 3.3. If x is the legal fee, I would lose x dollars if I sued and lost. If, however, I sued and won, I assumed I would receive $2,000 (the value of the car) minus the legal fee x. Since not suing has zero outcome in either case, a risk-neutral decision maker would apply the following decision rule: sue if

$$EV(\text{sue}) = P(\text{win})(2,000 - x) + [1 - P(\text{win})](-x) > 0. \qquad (3.1)$$

The question I posed to my lawyer was a straightforward translation of that equation into language relevant to the case, since Equation (3.1) implies that I should sue if

$$P(\text{win}) > x/2,000. \qquad (3.2)$$

My lawyer's response was that (1) his legal fees would be $200, and (2) my chance of winning would be much higher than 200/2000, or 1/10. Being an aspiring decision analyst, I took that as sufficient reason to ask him to file a suit.

I had made several mistakes, some or all of which I could have avoided had I spent more time building a decision tree. First, I had not determined in sufficient detail what the term *fees* meant. I understood *fees* to mean the total cost of the proceedings from filing the suit to collecting the money. My lawyer, as it turned out, had a somewhat different understanding. Some months later, before going to court, he wrote me that the $200 had been an "initial modest retainer."

Second, I had not determined in sufficient detail what *winning* meant. I had equated *winning* with obtaining a judgment of $2,000 and collecting it. But obviously there are differences among (1) obtaining a judgment, (2) obtaining a financial award, and (3) collecting that award.

Third, I had not paid enough attention to what information would and would not be relevant in the trial. I thought the case would be open and shut. I carefully collected police reports, estimates of the value of my car, and statements about its status as a wreck, thinking they would be sufficient information to make my case. I later learned that I needed to present different and more costly information from eyewitnesses.

These mistakes should haunt me. In retrospect, I believe I made the wrong decision – not because of an unfavorable outcome, but rather because of a poorly structured problem. I had made my decision on the basis of a tree that looked like the one in Figure 3.3. I later recognized that a much more appropriate tree would have looked like that in Figure 3.4. In between these two trees lies a great deal of structuring, sensitivity analysis, and soul searching, all of which I could have done before deciding to sue. The difference is that the tree in Figure 3.3 clearly shows that suing is the highest EV action, but that in Figure 3.4 implies the opposite. This chapter presents various examples of trees and calculations that lie between those in Figures 3.3 and 3.4. At the end, it returns to reality and tells you about the actual path I took through the tree in Figure 3.4.

Structuring a decision tree

Since a decision tree represents the interaction between decisions and environmental states and events, its construction relies heavily on the expertise of the decision maker and his or her advisers. It is customary, but not necessary, to begin with a set of options at the first node of a decision tree. Moving to the right from each option, the decision maker and/or experts must list the events that may occur and that affect either the probabilities of future events or the desirability of the final states or outcomes.

A matrix of alternatives by objectives is, in a sense, the most radically pruned tree. In the decision about whether to sue Billy J., that matrix turned out to be very simple (see Table 3.1 or the decision tree in Figure 3.3).

The tree in Figure 3.3 includes two uncertainties, one major and one minor. The major uncertainty concerns winning or losing the case and about collecting money won, if any. The minor uncertainty concerns the legal fees. Should I have taken the $200 estimate for granted? What other costs would be involved? What would be the upper limit of possible fees? $300? $500? Even $1,000?

I had recognized the major uncertainty and dealt with it in Figure 3.3. My mistake was that I had equated "winning" with obtaining $2,000, which was high but probably not preposterous for the purposes of sensitivity analysis. Even if "winning" had meant only $1,000, the EV rule would still have favored suing. A more important mistake was that I had underestimated the sequential accrual of legal fees.

Had I focused on identifying events that would control the amount of money I would recover, I would certainly have included:

> More legal fees
> Different types of judgments

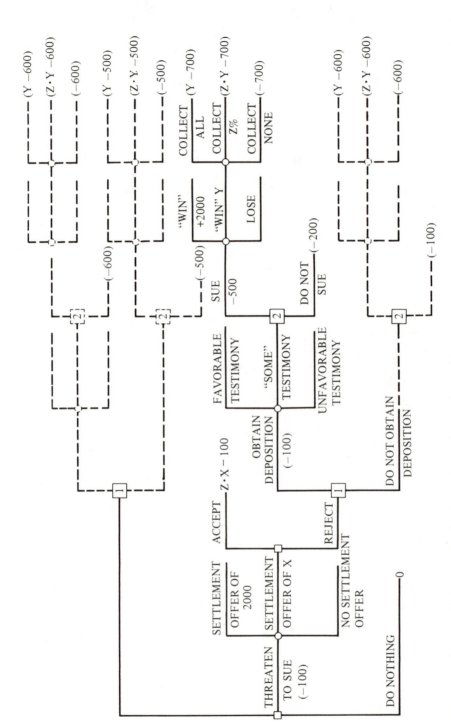

Figure 3.4. Improved decision tree for the uninsured motorist problem.

The difference between the amount of a judgment and the amount
collectable

As with any other decision tree, I should have searched for act–event
sequences that would have allowed a relatively firm evaluation of the final
outcome of each sequence.

Decision trees can include two types of uncertain variables: events and
information variables. Events are states of nature or things that can happen
to you and thereby change the outcomes of your decision directly. Information variables do not directly influence outcomes, but they can change
the probabilities of the events in a tree. Often one must decide whether to
purchase information, and that decision can be explicitly included in a decision tree.

In my case against Billy J., I "bought" information about her employment status. That information cost very little and turned out to be positive
(she was employed as a waitress), thereby influencing the probability distribution over the amount I could collect. I also could have bought information by obtaining a deposition from an eyewitness. That information
would have been more costly but could have affected my assessment of the
probability of winning the case.

How do you decide whether to include an information-buying option as
an explicit branch in a tree? As a general rule, the information must be both
valuable (i.e., must have a high potential for changing subsequent probabilities) and expensive.

Most information is cheap relative to the stakes involved in a decision
tree. I did not include the information variable "Billy J.'s employment status" as a chance branch in Figure 3.4, simply because it cost my lawyer
merely a telephone call to determine it. The rule for collecting cheap information is rather simple: do so. If you must select an order in which to collect
items or if you could collect so many items that doing so would become
expensive, a simple rule also obtains: choose first those items of information
that have the largest potential impact on event probabilities.

In Figure 3.4 the decision to obtain a deposition from an eyewitness was
included as an information-buying act. Later sections of this chapter spell
out the procedures for evaluating the value of such information. For now it
is sufficient to say that the act of buying information is treated as any other
act in a decision tree, and the information is treated formally as an event.

Pruning and knowing where to stop

Every decision tree terminates at its right-hand side in a set of nodes labeled
"outcomes." In Figures 3.3 and 3.4 the outcomes were monetary returns or
losses from the decision to sue or not to sue. But should the tree really stop
with these outcomes? Losing my case and additional legal fees would have
meant continued hardship for me, difficulties in paying off my new car loan,

much frustration and anger. Although that outcome would not have been ruinous, it might have led to several changes in my life. Thus, the question was where the decision tree should end.

A decision such as this is known as "pruning the decision tree." In most artificial examples, it is easy. A decision tree built around monetary gambles typically treats payoffs as outcomes, without considering how the money paid off will later be spent. But the art of pruning real-life decision trees is ill-understood and subject to few guidelines. Some obvious rules are (1) exploit the work of others, (2) disaggregate high-probability branches, and (3) make judgments easy.

Most decision problems that we know of are generic, in the sense that you decide on strategy rather than on detail. In so doing, you exploit the expertise and prior decisions of others. If you must decide, say, whether to have a laminectomy (removal of a spinal disc), you will surely delegate to the surgeon decisions about which surgical procedure to follow, how much of the disc to remove, and so on. The surgeon may have previously asked you to make decisions (e.g., whether to undergo straight disc removal or the spinal fusion operation that unites two vertebrae), but you delegate much of the detailed decision making. Similarly, you delegate to the anesthetist the choice of sequence and dosages of analgesics and anesthetics. All these exploitations of the generic properties of acts and events depend on using the actions and expertise of others to avoid complexity. Only in this way can any complex decision be rendered tractable.

A reasonable second rule is that the tree should extend to the right farther from chance nodes having relatively high probability of occurrence than from chance nodes having lower probability of occurrence, since the parts of the tree rightward of the high probability are more likely to be reached than others and therefore further analysis of them is more likely to be useful.

The preceding discussion was built around the notion that everything the decision maker thinks about should be kept simple. For example, it should be easy for the decision maker to express preferences or utilities about outcomes. The only reason to draw a decision tree is the hope that the points at its far right will be easier to evaluate than the point of origin at its left. This suggests a helpful rule: stop disaggregating (i.e., prune the tree) if the decision maker can comfortably express preferences among final states.

A final note: if you cannot draw the decision tree on a single sheet of paper, complete with labels for all the nodes, it is probably too big.

3.3. One-stage decision tree calculus

The simplest tree

We return to *von Winterfeldt* v. *Billy J.* I could have made much progress by asking my lawyer some simple questions about additional legal fees. I believe that the answer would have been somewhere between $200 (if we

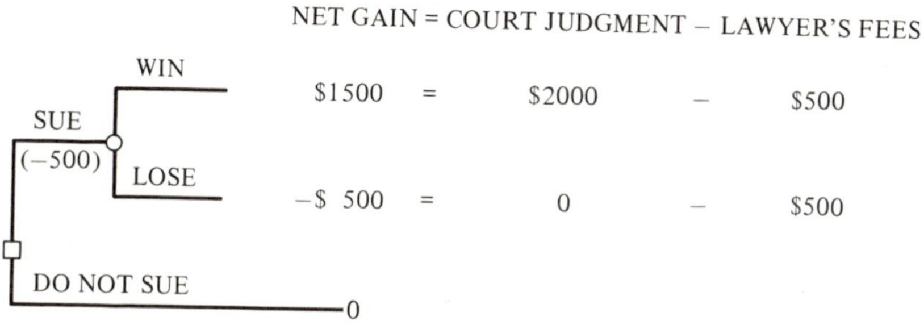

NET GAIN = COURT JUDGMENT – LAWYER'S FEES

Figure 3.5. Decision tree for the uninsured motorist problem using "best guess" for legal costs.

settled out of court) and $1,000 (if we lost and perhaps faced a countersuit). Working with a best guess or expected fee of $500 changes Figure 3.3 slightly (see Figure 3.5).

As a general rule, costs that occur as a direct result of a decision (here the decision to sue) are written in parentheses under that decision. The tips are the final outcomes minus these costs. With $500 legal fees and the very simple structure, the decision tree calculus is trivial. Just determine EV(sue) and EV(don't sue) and choose the decision with higher EV:

$$EV(\text{sue}) = P(\text{win})(\$1,500) + P(\text{lose})(-\$500),$$
$$EV(\text{don't sue}) = 0. \qquad (3.3)$$

At the time of the decision, my lawyer and I believed that my chances of winning were fairly good, around .7. The EV calculations showed that I certainly should sue, since EV(sue) = $900. To be sure, I could determine the break-even probability of winning, that is, the minimal winning probability P^* that would make suing worthwhile:

$$EV(\text{sue}) = P^*(\text{win})(\$1,500) + [1 - P^*(\text{win})](-\$500) \qquad (3.4)$$
$$= EV(\text{don't sue}) = 0, \qquad (3.5)$$
$$P^*(\text{win}) = 500/2,000 = 1/4.$$

Even this conservative analysis indicated I should sue.

Multiple outcomes

An analyst would worry about the simplification in the dichotomy of winning versus losing and would suggest a first extension of the tree in Figure 3.5 in which multiple events would be considered, ranging from total victory to total loss. The analyst would argue that, though I would most likely get some money out of this case, it would be unlikely that I would receive as much as $2,000 and, worse yet, there would be a very small chance of my being responsible for the damages to Billy J.'s car, which were relatively minor ($500) and which I would probably have to pay out of my pocket to avoid increased insurance rates.

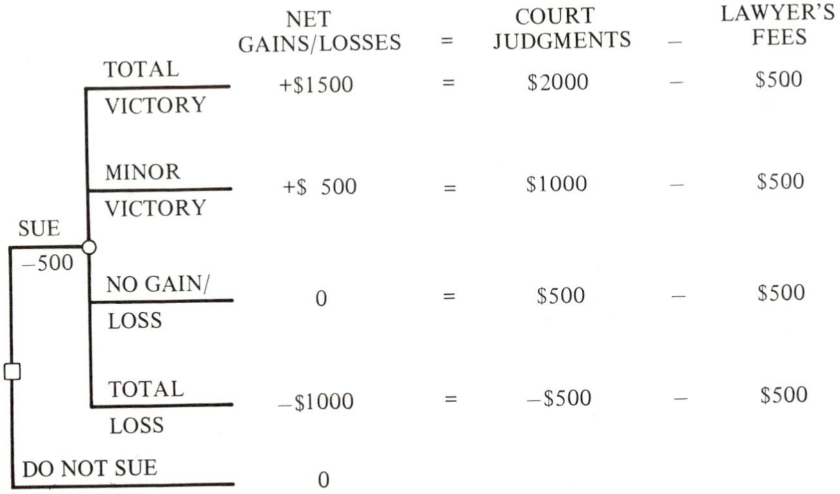

	NET GAINS/LOSSES	=	COURT JUDGMENTS	−	LAWYER'S FEES
TOTAL VICTORY	+$1500	=	$2000	−	$500
MINOR VICTORY	+$ 500	=	$1000	−	$500
NO GAIN/ LOSS	0	=	$500	−	$500
TOTAL LOSS	−$1000	=	−$500	−	$500
DO NOT SUE	0				

SUE −500

Figure 3.6. Multiple-outcome complication of the uninsured motorist problem.

An analyst might suggest the following outcome categories: total victory, minor victory, no gain/loss, total loss, and the associated outcomes, as represented in Figure 3.6. As before, the net gains/losses column was created by subtracting $500 from the possible court award.

The relative chances are still skewed toward the positive side:

$$P(\text{total victory}) = .20,$$
$$P(\text{minor victory}) = .60,$$
$$P(\text{no gain/loss}) = .15,$$
$$P(\text{total loss}) = .05.$$

The EVs of suing versus not suing are

$$EV(\text{sue}) = .20(\$1{,}500) + .60(\$500) + .15(0) + .05(-\$1{,}000)$$
$$= \$300 + \$300 - \$0 - \$50 \tag{3.6}$$
$$= \$550,$$
$$EV(\text{don't sue}) = 0. \tag{3.7}$$

Thus, the refined analysis confirmed my inclination to sue, but not as strongly as the first extreme outcome analysis.

The generalized one-stage tree

One-stage trees have one decision node followed by a chance node after each possible act and ending with an outcome. Figure 3.7 schematically illus-

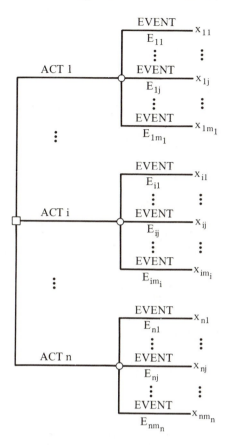

Figure 3.7. Generalized one-stage decision tree.

trates a general version of such a tree. In our example we calculated the value of each act a_i as

$$EV(a_i) = \sum_{j=1}^{m_i} P(E_{ij})x_{ij},$$ (3.8)

where $P(E_{ij})$ is the probability of E_{ij}. In general, we would calculate the SEU of each act a_i as

$$SEU(a_i) = \sum_{j=1}^{m_i} P(E_{ij})u(x_{ij}),$$ (3.9)

where $u(x_{ij})$ is the utility of outcome x_{ij}. Clearly, the decision maker should select the act that maximizes EV or SEU.

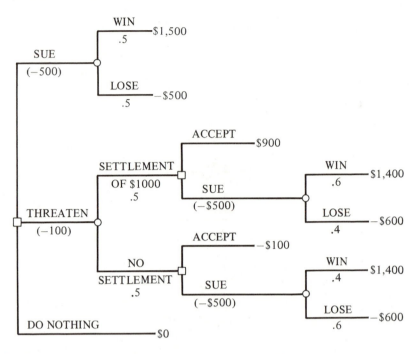

Figure 3.8. Multistage tree for the uninsured motorist problem.

3.4. Multistage decision tree calculus

Example of "averaging out and folding back"

The above one-stage tree expanded the possible events and outcomes to provide boundaries on the actual net returns. Similarly, one can expand the possible actions. A very natural expansion in this case is to fill the middle ground between filing a suit and not filing a suit. I could first threaten to sue and offer to consider proposals for settlement and wait for the response. Conditional on the response, I could then either settle or proceed as if I faced the situation described by Figure 3.5. The structure of this extended tree is shown in Figure 3.8, which retains the simple event–outcome structure of Figure 3.5.

Figure 3.8 has two interesting properties. First, total costs have changed. The cost of first threatening, then suing is split. Having a lawyer write a letter to Billy J. will cost $100. If Billy J. and I agree on a settlement, I will not have to pay any other lawyer's fee. Only if no settlement occurs and I decide to sue after all will an additional fee of $500 be due.

Second, by threatening, I can actually learn about the probabilities. If Billy J. offers a settlement, I will infer that she believes her case is not very strong and my assessment of my chances of winning may increase. If she

refuses to settle, I may infer that she believes she has a strong case (for whatever reasons) and that therefore my chances of winning may be less than I
had previously thought they were. Either way, the wording of her response
may influence my assessment of my chances of winning. Thus, threatening
is, among other things, an information-buying act, which costs $100 and has
the potential of changing the subsequent probabilities somewhat.

Clearly, after threatening and receiving either an offer to settle or a refusal
to settle, I have the choice of suing or not suing. My decision will depend
on the size of the offer of settlement. If it is $1,500 I obviously should accept,
but amounts lower than that are disputable.

I know the net dollar amounts at the tips of the decision tree. I must
assess, however, the probabilities of settlement versus no settlement and, in
addition, reconstruct the conditional probabilities of winning or losing after
Billy J.'s response. Remembering the results of the multiple-outcome analysis, which indicated that winning the full amount of $2,000 was relatively
unlikely (.2) and that winning a medium amount was relatively likely (.6), I
decide to carry out a conservative analysis and assign a probability of .6 to
winning given that a settlement is offered, and a probability of .4 if a settlement is refused. This creates the following conditional probabilities:

$$P(\text{win} \mid \text{settlement offer}) = .6,$$
$$P(\text{lose} \mid \text{settlement offer}) = .4,$$
$$P(\text{win} \mid \text{no settlement offer}) = .4,$$
$$P(\text{lose} \mid \text{no settlement offer}) = .6.$$
$$(3.10)$$

In addition, I think that there is about an even chance that Billy J. will make
an offer to settle for $1,000:

$$P(\text{settlement offer}) = .5,$$
$$P(\text{no settlement offer}) = .5.$$
$$(3.11)$$

Notice that the choices of these probabilities are not totally arbitrary since

$$P(\text{win}) = P(\text{win} \mid \text{settlement offer})P(\text{settlement offer})$$
$$+ P(\text{win} \mid \text{no settlement offer})P(\text{no settlement offer}).$$
$$(3.12)$$

Next I "average out and fold back" the decision tree. This procedure
begins at the tips of the tree, all of which emerge from a chance node (if one
end branch were a decision node, the branches that have lower values or
utilities attached to them would simply be removed; hence the tips of decision trees are always chance branches).

First, I take the EVs of all the final chance nodes. For example, the EV of
suing right away (without first threatening) is $500, that of suing after a set-
tlement offer has been made is $600, and that of suing after a settlement has
been rejected is $200. In all other cases, the outcomes are certain. Next, I
inspect a pruned tree, in which the EV of each twig chance node is substituted for the gamble. In other words, I construct a tree in which I assume

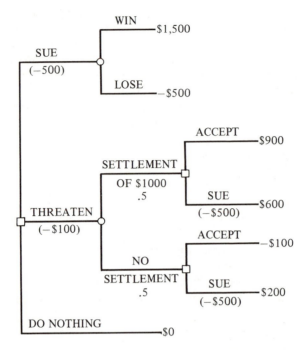

Figure 3.9. Folding back the tree by substituting EVs for twig chance nodes.

that I am sure to obtain the EV of a chance node if I should arrive at it. This tree (Figure 3.9) clearly suggests how I should act after the offer or refusal to settle: accept the $1,000 settlement offer but sue if no settlement is offered. Thus, I can cancel two branches of the tree, which leaves a simplified one-stage tree of the form displayed in Figure 3.10.

This tree can be solved simply by taking EVs:

$$EV(\text{sue}) = .5(\$1,500) + .5(-\$500) = \$500,$$
$$EV(\text{threaten}) = .5(\$900) + .5(\$200) = \$550,$$ (3.13)
$$EV(\text{do nothing}) = \$0.$$

According to this calculation, I should first threaten to sue and subsequently decide whether in fact to sue on the basis of the possible settlement offer.

Multiple and continuous events

Let us consider one more complication of the decision tree in Figure 3.5 by including the fact that the amount that can be collected is often different from the amount specified by a judgment. Figure 3.11 represents a step in that direction by considering five different outcomes of the court trial. It is

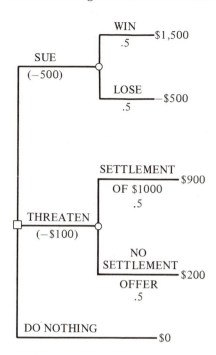

Figure 3.10. Folded-back tree for the uninsured motorist problem.

relatively easy, although computationally tedious, to consider many possible outcomes and to incorporate multiple stages of events. Figure 3.11 gives an example of the initial "suing" branch of the original tree, which is expanded to cover several judgments and several possible outcomes of the collection effort. The total EV of suing can be calculated by first calculating the EVs at the tips of the tree (as indicated in Figure 3.11) and then substituting them at the next branch. Note that here two event branches are connected directly, so we need not fold back. The total is calculated as follows:

$$EV(\text{suing}) = .1(\$700) + .2(\$500) + .4(\$350) + .2(\$0) + .1(-\$1000)$$
$$= \$210. \tag{3.14}$$

Writing out and calculating decision trees in the format of Figure 3.11 is rather tedious. Often it is useful to construct continuous events and their corresponding probability distributions or density functions. Figure 3.12 schematically shows a decision tree with continuous outcomes.

When solving trees like those in Figure 3.12, we must know the forms of the probability distributions and make appropriate assumptions about conditional independencies or, alternatively, model dependencies among parameters of the distribution. We might consider, for example, normal dis-

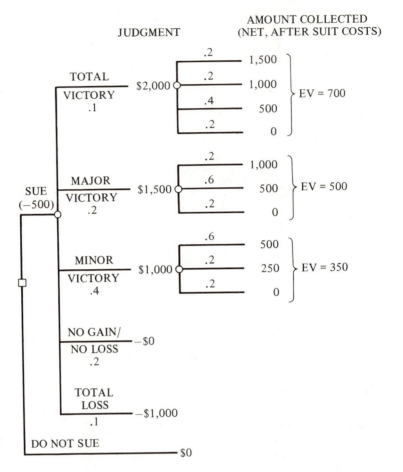

Figure 3.11. Decision tree with multiple judgments and collection amounts.

tributions to simplify the assessment tasks and the calculations. Further-more, we could assume that, independent of the amount of the judgment, the percentage collected is also normal, with a mean of 50% and a standard deviation of 20%. For an EV maximizer, we can substitute for any particular assumed judgment the value of 50% as the assumed equivalent amount and subsequently substitute the expected value of the distribution of judgments divided by 2 as the EV of suing (i.e., $250).

It is more interesting to conditionalize the probability distributions on percentages of the amount of judgments and, in the case of the threatening decision, on a settlement offer. For example, if Billy J. offers $1,500, both the probability of a favorable judgment and the probability of a higher per-centage of collection might increase. In Chapter 5 we discuss how such con-

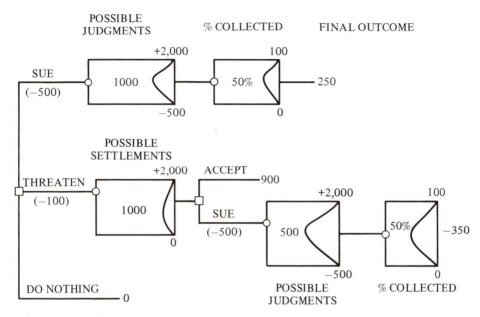

Figure 3.12. Decision tree with continuous events. (Numbers in boxes represent average estimates.)

ditional probability distributions can be constructed and how calculations can be derived from them.

Generalized multistage decision tree

Figure 3.13 shows a cut through a general multistage decision tree. Trees can become infinitely more complex, but we can show all the necessary calculations for more complex trees in this simplified version. In this tree we have n initial acts, n_i events following act a_i, n_{ij} acts following event E_{ij}, and n_{ijk} final events F_{ijk}, followed by outcomes x_{ijkl}.

The general formula for calculating the EV of act a_i is

$$EV(a_i) = \sum_{j=1}^{n_i} P(E_{ij}) \max_{k} \left\{ \sum_{l=1}^{n_{ijk}} P(F_{ijk})x_{ijkl} \right\}. \tag{3.15}$$

This is simply the formal expression of the averaging and folding back operations already illustrated. Reading the equation from right to left, first the EVs are taken at the final event nodes. Then the act is found that maximizes EV, and the maximum EVs are substituted into the next equation, which calculates the EV of the maxima. We can solve any more complex form of decision tree simply by repeatedly using this averaging out and folding back logic.

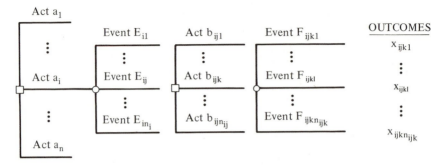

Figure 3.13. Cut through a general multistage decision tree.

3.5. Value of information

EV of perfect information

How much should I pay a clairvoyant who offers to tell me unambiguously whether I will win or lose my suit? Consider the simplest formulation of Figure 3.5. Obviously, if the clairvoyant tells me that I will win (and I believe in clairvoyants) I should sue and thus be assured of $1,500. If, however, the clairvoyant tells me that I will lose, I should not sue and stay with the status quo. In the absence of any further information about the chances of winning versus losing, I probably will consider the clairvoyant's report to have the same likelihood of favoring winning as my own feeling. Thus, the EV of acting with the clairvoyant's perfect information is

$$EV(\text{act with perfect information}) = P(\text{win})(\$1,500) \\ + [1 - P(\text{win})](0). \tag{3.16}$$

My initial assessment of p was .7, so the EV of acting with perfect information is $1,050 as opposed to the EV of acting without further information, which was $900. The difference between the EV of acting with perfect information and the EV of acting without is called the EV of perfect information. In my case, EV of perfect information is $150. I should therefore be willing to pay this amount to a clairvoyant.

Notice that the EV of perfect information increases as the uncertainty about the clairvoyant's prediction increases. If I consider winning and losing to be equally likely, the following EVs are appropriate:

$$EV(\text{act without perfect information}) = .5(\$1,500) \\ + .5(-\$500) = \$500, \tag{3.17}$$

$$EV(\text{act with perfect information}) = .5(\$1,500) + .5(\$0) = \$750, \tag{3.18}$$

so that the EV of perfect information would be $250.

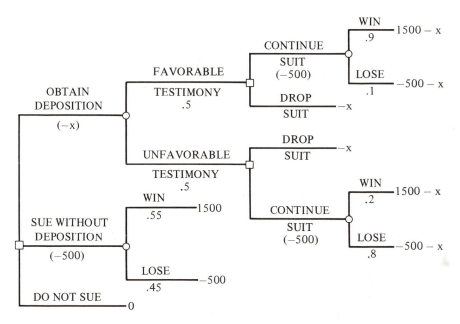

Figure 3.14. Structure for obtaining information from a witness in the uninsured motorist problem.

EV of sample information

Information is seldom perfect. A seismic investigation may give an oil engineer some idea about the size of a reservoir, but substantial uncertainties may remain. An X ray reduces only some of the uncertainties about the existence of a malignant tumor.

In my court case a possible source of unreliable information would be an eyewitness, the woman who drove the car into which my car was pushed. Her name was Yolanda, and I had obtained her address from the police report. Unfortunately, I did not know what she had seen and how she would testify. There was a reasonable chance that she would testify against me. I could obtain a deposition, at a relatively minor cost, to find out whether her testimony would favor my case. If it was favorable, I could use it in the court case and increase my chances of winning. If it were unfavorable, I could decide to drop the case or sue without Yolanda's testimony and hope that Billy J.'s lawyer would not subpoena this witness. Figure 3.14 introduces the structure of this problem.

On the basis of this structure I would estimate that my probability of winning would increase dramatically, say to .9, if the deposition clearly favored my case. If the deposition were unfavorable, however, I would assess my chances of winning as no more than .2. Finally, the chances would be about even that the deposition would in fact be favorable.

OUTCOMES

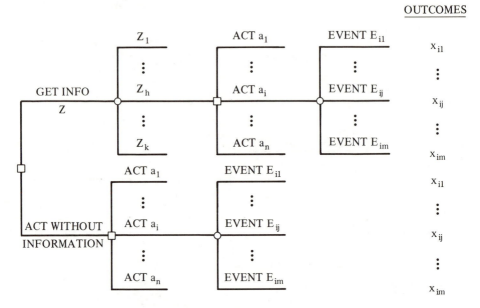

Figure 3.15. Structure of the EV of sample information problem.

The process of solving this problem is similar to the averaging out and folding back process I used to analyze the decision of whether to threaten first or sue directly. Let us assume for the moment that $x = 0$; that is, the deposition can be obtained without cost. In that case it seems only reasonable to obtain it, because the EV of acting with information is clearly larger than the EV of acting without information.

Using the normal averaging out and folding back technique, we first calculate the EVs of suing, provided that the report is favorable versus not favorable:

$$EV(\text{sue} \mid \text{favorable report}) = .9(\$1,500) + .1(-\$500) = \$1,300, \quad (3.19)$$
$$EV(\text{sue} \mid \text{unfavorable report}) = .2(\$1,500) + .8(-\$500) = -\$100. \quad (3.20)$$

Thus, since the deposition does not cost anything, I should sue if the report is favorable and not sue if it is unfavorable. Substituting the respective EVs (1,300 and 0) in the decision box of Figure 3.14 and taking EVs over the report, we obtain

$$EV(\text{obtain deposition}) = .5(\$1,300) + .5(0) = \$650, \quad (3.21)$$
$$EV(\text{sue without deposition}) = \$600. \quad (3.22)$$

Thus, our calculation shows that there is a positive EV of sample information of $50. In other words, I should be willing to pay up to $50 to obtain the deposition.

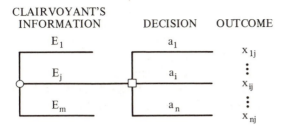

Figure 3.16. Structure for calculating the EV of perfect information.

General structure for calculating the EV of information

Figure 3.15 shows a diagram of a typical value of information problem in which the upper branch uses the information and the lower branch does not use it. Only the conditional probabilities, given the information, change. From the diagram it is straightforward to calculate the EV of acting with sample information Z versus the EV of acting without the information:

$$EV(\text{act with } Z) = \sum_{h=1}^{k} P(Z_h) \max_{i} \left[\sum_{j=1}^{m} P(E_{ij} | Z_h) x_{ij} \right], \qquad (3.23)$$

$$EV(\text{act without } Z) = \max_{i} \left[\sum_{j=1}^{m} P(E_{ij}) x_{ij} \right]. \qquad (3.24)$$

The EV of sample information is simply the difference between the EV of acting with and without it.

The general structure of calculating the EV of perfect information is shown in Figure 3.16. The principle is that, rather than calculate the EV of perfect information, one takes the expectations of the maximum values that can be obtained by choosing the appropriate act, given the clairvoyant's event. The formula for calculating the EV *with* perfect information is

$$EV(\text{act with perfect information}) = \sum_{j=1}^{n} P(E_{ij}) \max_{i} \{x_{ij}\}. \qquad (3.25)$$

The EV of perfect information is

$$EVPI = -EV(\text{act with perfect information})$$
$$EV(\text{act without perfect information})$$
$$= \sum_{j=1}^{n} P(E_{ij}) \max_{i} \{x_{ij}\} - \max_{i} \left[\sum_{j=1}^{n} P(E_{ij}) x_{ij} \right]. \qquad (3.26)$$

3.6. Epilogue

Before I tell you how the case against Billy J. ended, let us use the techniques sketched in the previous sections to solve the decision tree in Figure 3.4, which now seems like a reasonable representation of this decision problem. In it we assessed the cost of the deposition to be $100; x is the amount of the settlement offer; y the amount of the judgment; and z the percentage collected.

Let us work our way backward through this tree. First, we have to resolve the uncertainty about the collectible percentage of a possible judgment. Since I had information about Billy J.'s employment status, I thought I had a fairly good chance of collecting about 50% of the judgment. Substituting this best guess at the last chance node of the tree generates collectible estimates of $0.50y - 600$ in case I sued directly with the deposition; $0.50y - 500$ if I sued directly without the deposition; $0.50y - 700$ if I threatened first, obtained the deposition, and subsequently sued; and finally, $0.50y - 600$ if I threatened first and then sued without the deposition. The likely amounts of the judgment y differ in these cases, of course, since the witness's testimony would substantially influence the judge.

If the deposition is favorable, I expect a judgment of $1,500 and clearly should sue. If the deposition is unfavorable, I expect a judgment of $0. If the deposition is ambiguous, I expect a judgment of $800, the same amount I would expect without the deposition. Notice that I have intuitively carried out my EV calculations. To simplify matters I have also assumed that a possible settlement offer does not affect the subsequent probabilities of winning or losing and that the percentage of the collectable amount if a settlement is reached is 50% of the settlement offer. With these assumptions I can simplify my tree by averaging out and rolling it back to the tree displayed in Figure 3.17.

Let us examine first the branches subsequent to the resolution of the uncertainty about the deposition. If the testimony in the deposition is favorable, I clearly should sue, since I expect to gain more from suing than from not suing. Similarly, if the deposition contains unfavorable testimony, I should definitely not sue, since suing would cost an additional $500 and produce a zero return. I should also not sue in case of "iffy" testimony, since the expected cost of suing is $100 higher than the cost of not suing.

In Figure 3.18 the tree is rolled back one more layer to the point where I have to decide whether to obtain the deposition. This process involves averaging out the uncertainty over the deposition using as outcomes the results of the test decision made after each of the three states of the deposition. Assuming that the probability is .6 for favorable testimony, .2 for "iffy" testimony, and .2 for unfavorable testimony, we can calculate the expected values at the tips of the tree in Figure 3.18.

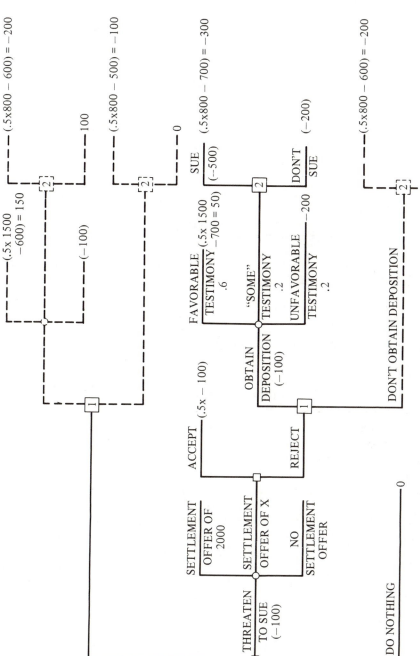

Figure 3.17. Decision tree folded back to the decision about whether to sue.

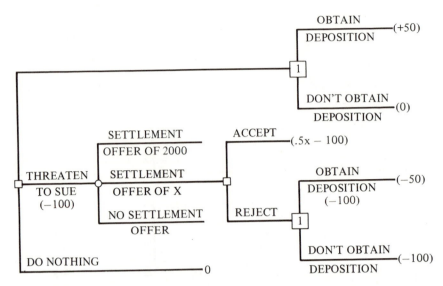

Figure 3.18. Decision tree folded back to the decision about whether to obtain a deposition.

According to this rolled-back tree, the "do nothing" branch is dominated by suing without first threatening to sue. If I decide to sue without first threatening, I should definitely obtain a deposition and act in accordance with the result of the deposition. However, my net EV of this action is surprisingly small – so small that I probably would start worrying again about the other, nonmonetary aspects of the decision. More important, the tree shows the power of the threatening decision versus suing without threatening. Even if my expectation of obtaining a settlement offer is $300, it would give me a net EV of $0.5 × 300 − 100, which is just equal to the EV of obtaining a deposition without threatening. Therefore, I should threaten first if my expectation of a settlement offer is larger than $300.

Having threatened, I should accept any offer over $100. Therefore, after threatening, I should accept less than the amount I would have to expect to make it best for me to threaten in the first place. This is a sophisticated version of the "sunk cost" phenomenon. After having spent $100, I cannot go back and recoup the expected $50 of the act of obtaining a deposition without threatening. Only if the settlement offer is less than $100 should I obtain the deposition. Note that I would not decide to sue without the deposition.

Let us return to reality. I expected a settlement offer of at least $500, and I threatened first, which is exactly what the tree suggests. Initially I did not receive a settlement offer, and my lawyer proceeded to file a suit without taking the deposition first. That was a minor mistake according to the tree. A major mistake occurred just before the court case began and I had already spent $600 on the case (for threatening and filing the suit). Just before the trial Billy J.'s lawyer offered a settlement of $800, an event not anticipated in the tree, at least not that late. However, from a quick inspection of the end branches of the tree in Figure 3.4 it is clear that the EV of continuing the suit would be less than $800, and I therefore should accept that offer. But after losing a car valued at $2,000 and after paying my lawyer $600, I forgot everything I knew about decision analysis. I was not about to give up!

I rejected the offer and continued the suit. I won the case but the judgment was low ($1,000). I collected $400 over a period of 5 years from Billy J., of which my lawyer consumed another $100. After 10 years I wrote off the remaining $600 as a loss and swore never again to enter a lawsuit without first building a couple of decision trees.

4   Uncertainty and its measurement

4.1. Fundamentals

Concepts of probability

Consider the following seven propositions:

1.   Take a coin from your pocket or purse. You are about to flip it. It will come up heads.
2.   Count off decimal digits of pi, moving rightward from the decimal point. The 100,000th one is a 7.
3.   The first decimal digit of pi to the right of the decimal point is a 1.
4.   There are more than 10,000 telephones in Addis Ababa, Ethiopia.
5.   The 20th president of the United States was a Republican.
6.   The president of the United States who is inaugurated in 1989 will be a Democrat.
7.   The numbers 87, 83, 85, 92, and 89 were obtained by us by random sampling from a normally distributed population with a mean of 80 and a standard deviation of 1.

All but three of these examples are propositions about which we expect you to be uncertain. We expect you to be uncertain because we are uncertain ourselves about all of them except 3 and 7 (actually, we cheated by looking up the answer to 5 but were uncertain when we wrote the question down). Each proposition was chosen to illustrate a broad class of uncertainties. Thus, 1 is a conventional example of a random event; 2 and 3 are the results of a deterministic computation, differing only in that we are familiar with 3 but not 2; 4 is a present asserted fact; 5 is a past asserted fact; 6 is a prediction, or future asserted fact; and 7 is a past asserted fact of a special kind dear to statisticians.

You and we have information bearing on all of these propositions, as you do for any other meaningful proposition you can formulate. A convention based on the symmetry of a coin applies to proposition 1. If you take any large contiguous collection of digits from pi, the ratio of the frequencies of appearance of any two decimal digits will be close to 1. Addis Ababa is the capital city of a very poor, not highly developed country. The 20th president must have taken office some time after the Civil War; the Republican party

90

was very successful then. We won't list the data you have bearing on 6. Of course, we know how we got the numbers in 7. You may consider it unlikely that we sampled randomly from any distribution. If we did, it seems unlikely that we would have obtained five numbers this far from the mean of a tight symmetric distribution, all on the same side.

On the basis of these and other items of information, you surely have opinions about the truth of each proposition. Note that it is the proposition, not the event, about which you have an opinion. The coin will come up either heads or tails, depending on some complex physics. Whatever the 100,000th decimal digit of pi is, it has been that from the beginning of time and will be that until the end of time. Similarly for the first decimal digit, but you probably know what the first one is. The number of telephones in Addis Ababa and the identity of our 20th president are facts; so is our method of obtaining the five numbers. The party affiliation of the president who will be inaugurated in 1989 will become a fact then. Uncertainty is a property of your knowledge about these events, not of the events themselves.

We assert that

1   all uncertainties are inherently of the same kind;
2   probabilities are useful numbers with which to measure uncertainties;
3   probabilities are personal degrees of belief about uncertain events.

These assertions place us firmly on one side of a controversy about what probabilities represent. We must explore the issues to some extent, though of course we cannot do justice to their mathematical or philosophical depth.

In a very important sense, everyone agrees about what a probability is. It is a number between zero and 1, inclusive. These numbers obey several laws, all of which are derived from the simple rule that the sum of the probabilities assigned to mutually exclusive events, one of which must happen, is 1. The argument arises not over what these mathematical properties are but over the rules we should use in relating them to our observations of the real world. Three kinds of observations are related to such numbers: relative frequencies, logical arguments, and personal judgments of likelihoods. Each could be and has been proposed to be the fundamental source of rules relating probabilities to real-world events.

Relative frequencies

If a coin is flipped a large number of times, the difference between the number of heads and the number of tails increases with the number of flips. It is very unlikely that that difference will ever be 0 for a fair coin after, say, 10 or more flips. But it is very likely indeed that the ratio of the number of heads to the total number of flips will, for a fair coin, be very close to .5. For excellent but highly technical reasons, that ratio itself cannot be thought of as the probability that the coin will fall heads. But one viewpoint about how to relate probabilities to observations defines the probability of a coin's falling heads as the limit that the ratio of heads to total tosses approaches as the number of tosses increases without limit (i.e., approaches infinity). From this viewpoint, the ratio of heads to total tosses for a finite number of tosses, though not the probability, is what is called an unbiased estimator (i.e., a good though fallible guess) of that probability.

With this conception of probability, most uncertainties that people experience cannot be described by means of probabilities. Examples 2, 3, 4, and 5 in the list of propositions at the beginning of this chapter illustrate the point. Moreover, it may be quite difficult to determine whether a particular relative frequency is an appropriate estimator of a probability. The coin toss is the textbook example of relative frequencies. But how should the coin be tossed? The successive tosses should be made under "substantially identical" conditions. But the conditions cannot be absolutely identical, or the coin would come up the same way every time. How much variation in tossing procedure from one toss to another is permissible? Would you be comfortable with an estimate that the probability of heads is .5 if the data on which the estimate is based were 50 heads followed by 50 tails? If you agree with us that the answer to such questions must be arbitrary and subjective, the frequentistic conception of probability loses most of its "objective" character. But the frequentistic position does not specify further what "substantially identical" means. Finally, the frequentistic position would almost never lead you to estimate that the probability of getting heads in tossing a coin is 1/2. In any reasonably long finite sequence of tosses, the relative frequency of heads will almost certainly not be 1/2; moreover, it will vary from one occasion to another and from one coin to the next. But the best frequentistic estimate of a probability is the observed relative frequency, so frequentists are stuck with estimates like 521/1,000 or 5,187/10,000 – unless they are wise enough to ignore or (preferably) not collect relative frequencies when they have a better basis for probabilistic judgment, as they do for symmetric coins.

Symmetry and necessary views

Some mathematicians have attempted to treat probability as a branch of logic and have argued that at least some probabilities are logically necessary. Such views hinge on various versions of the notion that some partitions are sufficiently symmetric that all elements of the partition should be considered equally likely. For example, even with biased coins, the probability of flipping first heads and then tails is equal to the probability of flipping first tails and then heads. There must be something of at least psychological importance in this idea, since one of our major industries is built around it. Every popular form of gambling except betting on contests of strength or skill depends on devices like shuffled cards, perfectly cubical dice, or symmetrically laid out roulette wheels. All such devices make use of visible symmetry to support the idea that the symmetric elements are equally likely. This conception of probability seems to us more reasonable than the frequentistic conception, but it too is of very limited applicability and, when applicable, is very difficult to distinguish from the personalistic view.

The personalistic view

You might be willing to say "Heads coming up on the next flip of this coin has a probability 1/2" if and only if you would as soon guess heads as not, even if there were some important reward for being right. Your verbal statement of probability and your choices among gambles are devices whereby you can report your opinion about the coin. Such consistent opinions, we think, are the essence of probability. Your opinions about a coin can, of course, differ from your neighbor's – hence the "personal" in the term *personal probability*. Any probability should in principle be indexed with the name of the person, or people, whose opinion it describes; that indexing is usually suppressed unless there is a special reason to expect that people will disagree.

The personalistic approach permits just as meaningful a discussion of the probability of a unique event as of the probability of a repeatable event – if any event can appropriately be called repeatable. Your probability that the next toss of a coin will be heads, your probability that the next president of the United States will be a Democrat, your probability that the next child born in your family will be a boy, your probability that the last child to be born to one of us was a boy, and your probability that the 200th decimal digit of pi is a 7 – all of these probabilities are the same kind of quantity, though they vary widely in the degree to which relevant relative frequencies can be defined. From this point of view, then, all uncertainties can appropriately be measured using probabilities. However, not all numerical opinions about uncertain events are probabilities; opinions, to be treated as probabilities, must be consistent.

The personal approach to probability does not imply that "your guess is as good as mine" about what a probability is. Although your initial opinion about the future behavior of a coin, or about any other uncertain hypothesis, may differ radically from your neighbor's, your opinion and his or hers will ordinarily be so transformed by a series of relevant observations as to become nearly indistinguishable. This approximate merging of initially divergent opinions is, as some people see it, one reason that inferences from relative frequencies and other such data are considered "objective." Personal probabilities are sometimes dismissed by the argument that scientific or other knowledge cannot be mere opinion. But obviously no sharp lines separate the conjecture that many human cancers are caused by viruses, the opinion that many are caused by smoking, and the knowledge that many have been caused by radiation.

The point of view that probabilities are measures of uncertainties is often called Bayesian, for the rather inadequate reason that those who hold it often find Bayes's theorem useful. Bayes's theorem, a totally uncontroversial consequence of the fact that probabilities sum to 1, is a mathematical formalization of the process of learning from experience. Its inputs are a set of opinions about how likely the elements of a partition are, conditional on a given state of information, and some numbers that describe the relation of a datum or data to those hypotheses. Its outputs are a set of revised opinions, modified to include the impact of the datum or data as well as the prior information. Chapter 5 presents mathematical details.

A significant controversy has existed in statistics, and to some extent still does, between Bayesian and non-Bayesian approaches. As far as we can tell, the fundamental intellectual difference leading to the controversy is between the frequentistic and the personal approaches to probability. These points of view lead to dramatically different practical conclusions about how to perform statistical inferences. Though Chapter 5 gives a brief overview, we suggest that interested readers consult such sources as Edwards, Lindman, and Savage (1963) and Phillips (1973) for details.

Measurement of personal probability

Personal or subjective or judgmental probabilities can be measured by two fundamentally different procedures. The first involves simply asking someone who should know (in principle, the decision maker; often, an expert to whose expertise the decision maker wishes to defer) to judge the probabilities of the relevant events. The second also entails asking someone to make judgments, but these are judgments or decisions from which probabilities can be inferred. Both procedures have adequate formal justification; both in practice can lead to good results.

Lest we be misunderstood, we should make clear that the formal mathematical model called probability theory, stripped of the linkage to the real world implicit in our assertion that we wish to use it to model uncertainty, can be used to model other things instead. It can, for example, be used to model limits of relative frequencies. It can also, as in atomic physics, be used to model the kind of physical property implicit in the Heisenberg principle of uncertainty, which takes expectations rather than events as primitives. But the topic of this chapter is uncertainty, not probability theory.

Events, outcomes, and uncertain variables

The formulation of the propositions about which people are uncertain should be unambiguous. This simply means that, for each proposition to which a probability is to be attached, it should be possible to imagine a set of observations that will increase that probability to 1. (The same idea applies to probability distributions over continuous variables, but we would have to use slightly more fussy language to express it precisely.) We usually use the word *outcome* to describe the kind of observation that would raise

some probability to 1 and reduce the probabilities of alternative propositions to 0. For example, the proposition "It will rain tomorrow in Los Angeles" is ambiguous, because it fails to specify the area (Los Angeles County,
Los Angeles City, or Greater Los Angeles) and the meaning of "rain." Consequently it would be hard to determine whether the proposition was true
after observing that .02 inch of precipitation occurred in Palos Verdes. The
proposition "At least one-hundredth of an inch of rainwater will be found
in the downtown Los Angeles rain gauge at tomorrow's first observation"
fulfills the criterion of unambiguity.

Ambiguity can arise in another way. The events whose occurrence is contemplated in an uncertain proposition belong to a set of possible events that
could be contemplated. In order for useful probabilities to be attached to
propositions about events, this set must include all possible events, their
unions and intersections, and the null and certain events. Ambiguous event
formulations sometimes leave out possible events. Proposition 6 in our initial list proposed that the next U.S. president will be a Democrat. The most
natural alternative is that he or she will be a Republican. However, it is
possible, although unlikely, that the next president will be from an independent party. Often, the inclusion of a "catchall" event is necessary to make
sure that all possible events are included.

A logically satisfactory description of a topic about which we are uncertain would include an appropriate collection of contemplated events, their
unions, intersections, negations, and so on. Some topics about which we are
uncertain are numerical, like propositions 2, 3, 4, and 7. When events take
numerical form, one can specify the possible partitions, unions, and intersections by using simple arithmetic to form new events or by defining limits
and boundaries in numerical terms. When contemplating the uncertain variable "maximum temperature in downtown Los Angeles tomorrow," one
can construct the events "less than 70°F" or "more than 80°F" or "between
70 and 80°F."

Probabilities are numbers between 0 and 1 attached to propositions about
which we are uncertain. Zero means that the contemplated event is impossible; 1 means that it is certain. The crucial rule that such assignments of
numbers must obey is that the probability of any combination of mutually
exclusive events must be the sum of the probabilities of its component
events. This rule, along with a few others linked to it, ensures that probabilities behave in an orderly way both in appropriate kinds of formal arithmetic and in response to the acquisition of new information about the
events.

Additivity

The additivity requirement of the preceding paragraph can be expressed in
symbols as follows:

$$p(A \cup B) = p(A) + p(B). \tag{4.1}$$

The usefulness of probability as a measure of uncertainty derives from this property. But the property is so demanding that no real person's real opinions can fully comply with it. Our approach to dealing with the fact is to admit it and to try to devise ways of helping real people to do as well as possible in structuring their opinions so that they obey all the elaborate implications of the additivity property. Others take other tacks, all of which have in common the denial of the additivity of probability. Zadeh (1978), in fuzzy set theory, proposes that

$$P(A \cup B) = \max\{P(A), P(B)\}. \tag{4.2}$$

This leads to a quite different and far less general representation of order relations and uncertainty; Zadeh applies it primarily to rather vague verbal representations like "John is somewhat taller than Jim." Cohen (1977) uses the same alternative to the additivity property that Zadeh does but proposes a numerical system for representing uncertainties that is in other ways quite different. Shafer (1976) proposes yet another nonprobabilistic representation of uncertainty. Shafer's representation can be thought of as a generalization of the notion of probability, since it can be reduced to probability itself by requiring additivity. These approaches give up power for presumed realism in representing how people think and consequently presumed greater ease of use. We are very much concerned with usefulness but believe that probabilities with the additivity property have thoroughly established their utility. Our goal, therefore, is to help people use conventional probabilities well.

Conditionality

All probabilities are conditional. Formally, any set of events can be partitioned into subsets, and a probability is a measure assigned to a subset. Sometimes the assertion to which a probability is assigned carefully defines the set being partitioned. For example: "This bookbag contains fifty red and fifty blue poker chips, well mixed. One of us will select one by reaching in blindly and grabbing the first one his hand encounters. It will be red." More often, the assertion omits most of the information that would specify the set being partitioned. For example: "The next person I [Edwards] will see will be at least six feet tall." The chance that that statement is true depends on such issues as where I am and what the likely sequences of events that might lead to my seeing someone are. (As it happens, the probability is very high as I write that the next person I see will be my wife, who is well under six feet tall, so the probability of the statement being true is quite small.) Whether the conditioning information is explicit, implicit, or unspecified, it always exists. Since probabilities model beliefs or opinions, the most important kind of conditioning has to do with the information available to you at the time you assess the probability. Rules for changing probabilities as new information becomes available are described in the next chapter.

It may be slightly unclear intuitively that conditionalization on information is equivalent to specification of the set being partitioned to define a probability. To understand it, simply note that the relevant set includes not only the events about which probability statements are made, but also other events (such as those that might provide information). In principle, such a set is very large, since it includes all possible items of information that may bear on the probabilities of interest. Fortunately, one almost never needs to enumerate the elements of the set.

Since the notation of conditional probability is a nuisance to use, we shall avoid it except when we want to specify some particular conditionalization.

Relation to relative frequencies

Virtually everything said so far has been severely at variance with what most people learn about probabilities. Textbooks teach that probabilities have to do with repeatable sets of events and that they describe events rather than opinions about propositions or statements. Often a probability is defined as the limit that the ratio of occurrences of an event to occurrences of an ensemble of events approaches as the size of the ensemble increases without limit. (To be technically complete, we would have to say more about the characteristics of the ensemble.) Of the list of events with which this chapter started, none are repeatable, and only 1 and 7 can easily be thought of as members of an ensemble. Can unique events have probabilities?

Since people can obviously reach enough agreement about such events to base substantial bets or other decisions on that agreement, a definition of probability that makes that agreement nonsensical seems to us to be nonsense. Many probabilists would agree. Sometimes, therefore, authors distinguish "objective" probabilities, which are limits of relative frequencies (or something similar but fancier for nondiscrete events), from numbers that are sometimes called "subjective" probabilities and sometimes called "degrees of belief" and that fit the description of probability we have given.

We see no point in multiplying the kinds of probability we must talk about, and we know of no decision problems in which probabilities are useful but our description of them does not fit their use. This book is not the place to argue the point at length.

But we have an obvious obligation to give an account of how, from this viewpoint, we treat relative frequencies. Actually, we have already given it in very brief form. An observation is an item of information that changes a probability. Moreover, the nature of that change is approximately the same as any frequentist would wish to make. Consider an attempt to estimate the probability that a thumbtack, tossed in the air, will land with its point sticking straight up. If a frequentist has observed it do so r times in N tosses, and N is reasonably large, he or she is usually willing to take r/N as the estimate of the probability.

We would prefer $(r + 1)/(N + 2)$, which, for N of reasonable size and r

not too close to 0 or *N,* is just about indistinguishable from r/N. Our reason for the preference is buried in the mathematics of beta distributions and grows out of the fact that we already know something about the thumbtack before the first toss: that it can, in fact, land point up or down. To grasp this intuitively without descending into mathematics, simply notice that for small *N*, *r* may be 0, in which case the estimator $0/N = 0$ makes one uncomfortable, while the estimator $1/(N + 2)$ at least implies that the tack *could* land with its point straight up.

4.2. Other representations of uncertainty

The metric for measuring uncertainty called probability is by far most familiar to scientists – so much so that the fact that it has competitors, especially among nonscientists, is sometimes overlooked.

Words

The most familiar and important competitor of probability is verbal communication about uncertainty. "It seems unlikely that it will rain tomorrow." "I'm almost sure this chapter will require at least two rewrites." (It actually required six.)

Words are by far the most common means of informing others about your opinions – and most languages offer an abundance of words to express degrees of uncertainty. The trouble with them, of course, is that they are vague. Sherman Kent (1964), the Grand Old Man of U.S. intelligence analysis at one time, was so concerned with the fact that almost all intelligence documents contained ambiguous verbal reports of uncertainty that he proposed a set of rules for translating probabilities into words. Barclay et al. (1977, pp. 67–8) reported a study performed by NATO intelligence analysts. NATO officers experienced with intelligence publications saw sentences like "It is highly likely that the Soviets will invade Czechoslovakia" and judged the implied probability. Figure 4.1 shows the result. Points are judgments; the shaded areas represent the ranges of uncertainty that Kent proposed for each phrase. Obviously, even within communities in which this kind of communication is both routine and important, its results are not precise. Similar results have been reported by Beyth-Marom (1982).

We are fairly confident that Kent's proposal wouldn't work. Intelligence analysts in his day did not have probabilities at their disposal. They started and ended with verbal labels. So we are unsure how they could have exploited the kind of additional precision for which Kent asked. Perhaps that is why his proposal never caught on.

Why are words so much more appealing than numbers? Exactly because they are vague, we believe. People incorrectly associate numbers with precision. Seldom if ever is an unaided intuition about uncertainty precise.

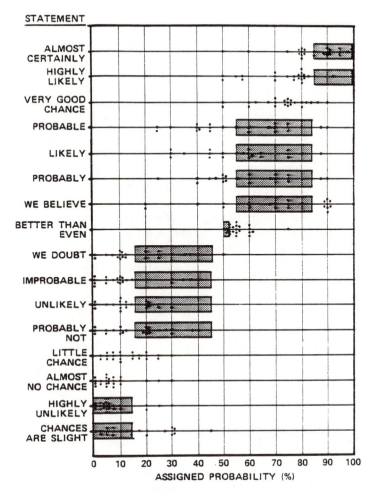

Figure 4.1. Relation between probabilities and verbal expressions. The shaded areas indicate Kent's (1964) proposal for matching words and probabilities. (Reprinted with permission of Decisions and Designs, Inc., from Barclay, Brown, Kelly, Peterson, Phillips, & Selvidge, 1977.)

But probabilities are neither inherently precise nor inherently the opposite. Suppose we now assert that the probability that we will revise this chapter at least twice is .92. How would you prove us wrong? We felt more comfortable with the number after the second revision than we did while initially drafting the chapter – but there would be no way to evaluate that statement taken alone any more stringently than that.

A second reason for using words is that precision about uncertainty is not always necessary. If no decision is to be based on the assessment, communication about uncertainty simply reports a state of mind. But suppose you must decide whether to undergo surgery and the surgeon says, "My experience with this operation in the past has been excellent. People almost never die on the table, and recovery usually takes a week. In a month, you'll be as good as new." How useful would it be to replace the verbal statements of uncertainty in that quote with numbers? The answer varies somewhat with the statement. The final sentence is clearly misleading about uncertainties; a number would have made clearer that the probability of being as good as new is less than 1. But the other uncertainties might as well remain in verbal form, simply because the numerical form, without other numbers, is useless information. We do not defend the quote. We would prefer to see the uncertainties in numerical form, even if we didn't have an explicit use for the numbers. But we are by no means sure that a layperson would share our preference.

A final reason for avoiding numbers is that they invite the collection of data, which is always a nuisance. If the surgeon wanted to substitute a number, or preferably a set of them, for "People almost never die on the table," he or she would feel compelled to keep careful records and do a fairly complex analysis. Bad statistical procedures can easily be hidden behind verbal statements of uncertainty.

We ourselves press our physicians for such numerical statements and tend to trust those who can give them to us more than we trust those who cannot. We think that good performance as a statistician accompanies good performance in other respects.

Odds

A common nonscientific numerical representation of uncertainty is odds. The word is both singular and plural but usually takes a plural verb. If the probability of an assertion is p, then the odds that the assertion is correct are $p/(1 - p)$, and the odds against it are $(1 - p)/p$. Odds are commonly used in gambling because of their very direct relationship with fair bets. Suppose you think a particular horse has probability 1/3 of winning the race. The fair odds would then be 2 : 1 against it. (That number can be written as 2 : 1, or 2/1, or 2. An odds is a ratio. If the denominator is not stated explicitly, it is always 1.) The betting procedure at the race track is as follows. You make a bet S. If you win, S is returned, and in addition you receive an amount of winnings W. If you lose, you lose S.

For the bet to be fair, its EV must be zero. In other words,

$$\tfrac{2}{3}(-S) + \tfrac{1}{3}(W) = 0.$$

A little algebra will show you that the ratio of W to S must be 2 : 1 in order for the above equation to hold. Obviously, if the track offers better than 2 : 1 odds on that horse (i.e., W is more than twice S), then from your point of view the bet is favorable. If W is less than twice S, the bet is unfavorable.

The direct estimation of odds, either as numbers or on a logarithmic scale, has been frequently used in research on uncertainty, though not often in applied work. In applied work, it is sometimes inconvenient, since one is often interested in the probabilities, not just of A and $\bar{A}$ ($\bar{A}$ means the assertion that A did not or will not occur), but of a set of more than two mutually exclusive events. For such a set, it is not obvious which event to use as the denominator of an odds. One possibility is to ask the respondent to assess the odds of A against $\bar{A}$, B against $\bar{B}$, and so on. This invites incoherent assessments – incoherent in the sense that the probabilities of the exhaustive set of mutually exclusive events do not sum to 1. Another possibility is to choose one of the events as the denominator of all odds ratios. If one of the assertions is a catchall intended to produce exhaustiveness ("none of the above"), it is sometimes natural to use it as the denominator of a set of odds ratios. If the same denominator is used for each of a set of odds ratios, no set of numbers can be formally incoherent.

Conversion from odds back to probabilities is simple. If Ω is an odds, then

$$p = \Omega/(1 + \Omega) \tag{4.3}$$

and

$$1 - p = 1/(1 + \Omega) \tag{4.4}$$

for the case in which only an event and its complement are considered. If you are dealing with an exhaustive set of N mutually exclusive assertions and your respondent has assessed odds for the first $N - 1$ of them, using the Nth in the denominator of each odds ratio, then

$$\sum_{i=1}^{N-1} \Omega_i = \sum_{i=1}^{N-1} \frac{P(E_i)}{P(E_N)} = \frac{1 - P(E_N)}{P(E_N)} . \tag{4.5}$$

The sum on the left is known, so the equation can be solved for $P(E_N)$ as follows:

$$P(E_N) = \frac{1}{1 + \sum_{i=1}^{n-1} \Omega_i} . \tag{4.6}$$

Then

$$P(E_i) = \Omega_i P(E_N). \tag{4.7}$$

Log odds

The logarithm of an odds, $\log[p/(1 - p)] = \log p - \log(1 - p)$, is a useful representation of uncertainty, both formally and intuitively. Its formal usefulness is tightly linked to Bayes's theorem, so we reserve our discussion of it for the next chapter. Its intuitive usefulness arises from the fact that it ranges from minus to plus infinity, with $p = 1 - p = .5$ corresponding to 0. The scale is symmetric. Moreover, it tightens up in the middle, near 0, and spreads out both ends, relative to probability, but not nearly so much as does the odds scale above 1 : 1. This is a valuable property that makes it difficult for anyone to assert that a probability is 1 or 0 – and that is a good thing. If you say that an assertion has probability 0, you are saying that you would be willing to stake (i.e., stand to lose) your entire current fortune, your prospects for future income, your house, your car, and everything else you can control if the event specified in the assertion occurs, against a penny that you win if it does not. Not only are you willing to do so, but you are eager, because you know that you have infinitely the better side of the bet! Few propositions in life justify such certainty.

The usual way to use log odds as a scale on which to assess uncertainties is to prepare such a scale but to label the lines on it with the corresponding odds or probabilities or both. Figure 4.2 shows such a scale.

As numerical representations of uncertainty, odds are peculiar numbers. Their asymmetry implies that one should always assess them with the less likely assertion in the denominator. Log odds are better. They are symmetric. Both odds and log odds have an intuitive advantage over probabilities in dealing with extremes of the probability scale. No one can intuit the difference between .001 and .0001 or between .999 and .9999. Both the odds scale and the log odds scale spread these differences out, though the odds scale does so only above 1 : 1. In our view, the odds scale spreads them too much, the probability scale spreads them far too little, and the log odds scale is not bad.

Continuity

We must pause a moment to make our language more convenient. So far we have been careful to specify that a probability always refers to an assertion, not to the event that the assertion is about. That statement is as true of continuous as of discrete events, but it is verbally less convenient to implement. If λ is a continuous numerical variable, the statement that λ is 10 or less is an assertion like any other. But it is inconvenient to write about continuous probability distributions in that careful a way; it requires clumsy statements like "Consider the function that expresses, for all possible values of λ, how likely you consider it to be that λ has that value or less. What is the value of that function at $\lambda = 10$?" So from here on, we shall use phrases like "the probability that λ is no greater than 10" as verbal shorthand for clumsier phrases like "the probability that the statement 'λ is no greater than 10' is true."

Continuous distributions over some unknown quantity are typically presented in one of two forms. Most familiar is the plot of probability density

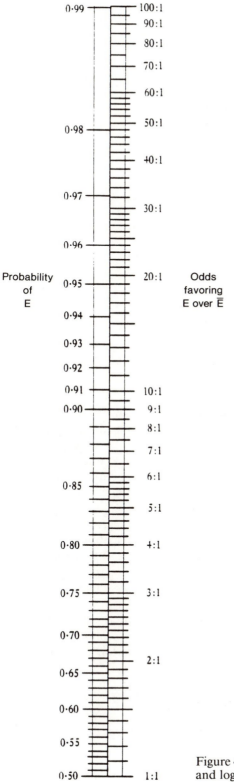

Probability of E

Odds favoring E over Ē

Figure 4.2. Relation between probabilities, odds, and log odds.

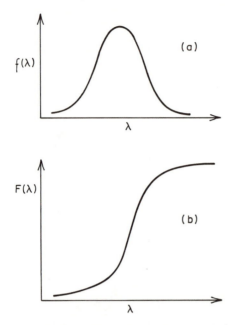

Figure 4.3. Probability density (a) and cumulative probability distribution (b) of a continuous random variable.

represented, for example, for the normal distribution by Figure 4.3a. The key requirement for a probability density function is that the area under it integrate to 1. It is useful to remember that a probability density is not a probability. In particular, probability densities may be and often are greater than 1. For a normal distribution, for example, the probability density at the mean will be equal to 1 if $\sigma = 1/\sqrt{2\pi}$. If σ is smaller than that, the density at the mean will be greater than 1.

The cumulative distribution function is simply the integral of the density function up to a point λ. The y axis of any cumulative distribution function, such as that in Figure 4.3b, is the probability (*not* probability density) that the true value of λ is less than or equal to the point on the λ axis being plotted. Since probabilities are much more intuitively understandable than are probability densities, most methods for eliciting distributions over continuous variables ask questions that in effect seek to elicit cumulative distribution functions. This has an unfortunate side effect. Since cumulative distribution functions are the integrals of density functions, it is difficult visually to detect differences between them that would be obvious in the corresponding density functions. For example, it is extremely easy to recognize skewness by inspecting a density function but hard to recognize it by inspecting a cumulative distribution function. This insensitivity property, of course, translates directly into insensitivity of elicited numbers.

4.3. Randomness, exchangeability, and independence

Randomness

We have done well to get this far into a chapter on probability having used the word *random* only three times. Though the notion of a random variable is well-defined mathematically, it is difficult to translate that definition into observables, from our point of view. A random variable is one that takes on any of a well-defined set of numerical values with specified probabilities; these probabilities sum to 1 over the various possible values. A set of random numbers, for example, is a set of values of a random variable. These values are produced by a random data-generating process.

Unfortunately, we cannot observe the randomness of a variable or a set of numbers directly – and, except in artificial cases, we cannot observe the data-generating process at all. Consequently, the definitions of the preceding paragraph are difficult to apply.

We frequently speak of random sampling. One wants to sample randomly so that the resulting numbers can be considered the product of a random data-generating process. Most of the time, a random sampler wants to treat all elements of the sample space, or set of all possible values of the random variable, as equally likely (or perhaps equally likely within strata) to be sampled. This is typically accomplished by the use of a random number table. The numbers in such tables are produced by completely deterministic methods into which randomness does not enter at all. An easy and fairly good way to produce six-digit random numbers uniformly distributed between 0 and 1 is to apply the equation

$$r_{n+1} = \text{FRC}(9821r_n + .211327),$$

beginning with an arbitrary positive decimal number r_n and recursively generating r_{n+1}; FRC is the operation of discarding all digits to the left of the decimal point. More complex but equally deterministic equations are used to prepare random number tables because the physical operations that correspond to our intuitions about randomness are prohibitively expensive to perform often enough to produce a large table and because the results of performing these physical operations are almost never random enough.

The statement at the end of the preceding paragraph should give you pause. If a random sample is any sample produced by a random data-generating process, how can one be not random enough? Intuition suggests the obvious answer: if you were to obtain 100 successive numbers from an ordinary random number table and found that 75 of them were odd, you would probably reject them and take another set from somewhere else in the table. More complex and sophisticated versions of this kind of test are used to evaluate procedures, physical or mathematical, for producing random numbers. The physical ones virtually always flunk such tests, unless they are dependent on such processes as radioactive decay. Determinate mathematical processes that pass such tests are not too hard to develop; they are the basis for random number tables. Random sampling is almost always done by linking the sampling process to successive numbers drawn from a random number table – and inspected before use to make sure that they do not have uncomfortable properties such as highly skewed distributions.

The purpose of these exercises obviously is to justify conventional (usually uniform) assignment of probabilities. The point of this discussion is that such conventional assignments depend on a complex judgment, which is guided by but is not identical to objective mathematical properties and procedures. Of the seven examples with which this chapter started, only one (7) involves a random variable.

Exchangeability

You should call a set of events exchangeable if you consider each pair of events to have the same probability of occurrence as any other pair, identical except for temporal order, each triple to be the same as any other triple, identical except for temporal order, and so on. For example, suppose that you are sampling without replacement from a bookbag containing five red and five blue poker chips. You might feel that the probability that the first three chips will be red, blue, and blue, P(RBB), is equal to P(BRB), which is equal to P(BBR). Similarly, you might feel that P(RBB) = P(BRB) = P(BBR) for the 8th, 9th, and 10th samples; all three might in this case be 0 if you had exhausted the supply of one color during the first seven draws. Clearly P(RBB) for the first three draws will not be equal to P(RBB) for the last three. If, however, for a fixed history you regard the three orders as equally likely, and similarly for all fixed histories and sequences of possible events, then you regard the events as exchangeable. Note that exchangeability is a judgment. Also note that exchangeability does not imply conditional independence (defined below), which is a stronger property.

The great importance of exchangeability for Bayesians is that data can be conveniently summarized if they are exchangeable, because the property allows you to ignore the order in which the data occurred. Such summaries as "I sampled from the bookbag ten times, and got seven red poker chips and three blue ones" would be improper if the events were not considered exchangeable. This is the first mention in this book of the *sufficiency principle*. Roughly speaking, this principle means that a small set of numbers fully describes the observation for all inferential purposes. This principle fails in hierarchical inference (see Chapter 6).

Independence and conditional independence

Two events are defined to be independent if the probability of their joint occurrence is the product of the probabilities of each separately. Interesting data are almost never independent, because the inferential impact of one changes your opinion about the probability of the next. Two events are conditionally independent if, for each hypothesis you are considering about the data-generating process, you would consider the events to be independent if the hypothesis were known to be true. Formally, consider two data D and E and two hypotheses H_1 and H_2. The definition of independence would require that

$$P(D \cap E) = P(D)P(E), \qquad (4.8)$$

which is equivalent to saying that

$$P(D \mid E) = P(D), \qquad (4.9)$$

where the symbol $P(D \mid E)$ stands for the probability of D given the occurrence (or truth) of E.

The definition of conditional independence would require that

$$P(D \cap E \mid H_i) = P(D \mid H_i)P(E \mid H_i). \qquad (4.10)$$

for both i. Similarly, conditional independence can be formulated as

$$P(D \mid E; H_i) = P(D \mid H_i). \qquad (4.11)$$

In the bookbag example above, the events are conditionally (but not unconditionally) independent if you are sampling with replacement from a particular bookbag, but do not know what is in it. If you are sampling without replacement, the data are not conditionally independent. Either way, they are exchangeable. Conditional independence implies exchangeability, though not vice versa; for many purposes the two properties are equivalent.

We have gone into this much detail about rather technical ideas because the Bayesian treatment of these ideas is so different from non-Bayesian treatments. Bayesians apply probabilities to all uncertainties, not only to those produced by the operation of random data-generating processes. They therefore need to know when economical descriptions of evidence are appropriate. The answer is: when the data are exchangeable. The most common criterion of exchangeability is conditional independence. Data that are meaningfully related to an inference problem cannot be (unconditionally) independent.

4.4. Probability assessment

If we plan to use numerical representations of uncertainty, we must first know what they are. If probabilities are beliefs, they must be the beliefs of someone. So we must identify and select suitable elicitation procedures for that person.

The topic can be naturally divided into two subtopics. One is methods of probability assessment conceived as methods of eliciting direct probability judgments from people. The other is methods of probability assessment conceived as methods of making simple judgments that enable us to calculate the numbers we want. Most simple judgments that permit such calculations are judgments of probability based on one version or another of the idea that the members of some elementary set of events are all equally likely. In the special case of estimation of probabilities from statistics already collected, assumptions of equal likelihood are combined with other assumptions (e.g., stationarity).

We discuss the methods that incorporate equiprobability assumptions leading to calculations first because they are far more common than direct judgmental assessments.

Intuition versus computations

The main reason for assessing probabilities is to use them in calculations. The results of those calculations are often other probabilities. Intuition and calculation may conflict. Then what?

Consider an example. If we ask for the probability that, of a group of 23 people selected on any basis other than birthdays, at least 2 will have the same birthday, you may well scratch your head. The event seems unlikely, but most people will have a hard time intuiting a number and presumably will want to supplement intuition with arithmetic. The probability that at least 2 people will have the same birthday is 1 minus the probability that no 2 will have the same birthday. That suggests a way of getting at the problem. Start by picking a person from the 23 – any person. Since only that person has been considered, he or she cannot have the same birthday as anyone else already considered, so the probability that that person introduces a new date to the list of birthdays is 1. Now pick a second person. The probability that that person introduces a new date to the list of birthdays is 364/365. The probability that the third person will do the same thing is 363/365 – and so on, for 20 more probabilities. Since all 23 of these events are independent of one another, we obtain their joint probability by multiplying them together – inconvenient to do by hand but easy with a programmable calculator: the product is .4931. (If you want to verify this exact number, you have to know that it takes leap years into account.) In conclusion, the probability that at least 2 people in a group of 23 people will have the same birthday is greater than .5. With 46 people, the probability is .95.

This is an old chestnut of probability theory. We chose it to illustrate the problems we encounter when intuition and arithmetic disagree. Are you willing to be guided by the arithmetic, even if it conflicts with your intuition? In this case, you would be wise to say yes – but only because the assumptions that make the arithmetic reasonable are easy to check. There are only two. One is that the basis on which you picked these 23 people has nothing to do with birthdays. This justifies treating the events as independent and so multiplying their probabilities. The other is that people are equally likely to be born on any day of the year. This assumption is known to be false; its incorrectness simply increases the probability that birthdays will coincide. If you still feel uncomfortable, you can make an additional check by trying it out in a few classrooms; that kind of experience is rapidly educative to intuition. Generally, a conflict between arithmetic (or statistical information) and intuition should lead you to think very hard about what causes the conflict. In this case, it is fairly easy to see that you didn't appreciate how rapidly the product of a set of numbers all a bit less than 1 decreases from 1. In many cases, you may want to conclude that an assumption behind the calculation, or the use of the statistic, was violated; you may prefer to trust your judgment rather than a calculation or a set of statistics. Or you may want to combine the two; wait for the next chapter in that case.

The point of the preceding discussion, of course, is that computations are good aids to intuition, but poor substitutes for it. Sometimes, as in the birthday example, you may be willing to trust the arithmetic enough to let it serve as proxy for your judgment. But there is no law of probability that requires you to do so, and it is often a poor idea.

Still, intuition is fallible. Among families of six children, three girls and three boys, which of the following birth orders is most likely: BBBGGG, BGBGBG, or BGBBGG? If your intuition answers the third, as data from Kahneman and Tversky (1972b) would lead you to expect, you have a problem. Do you think the sperm that fertilizes a later egg is somehow affected by the identity of its successful predecessors? If you do not, then all sequences of three Bs and three Gs will seem equally likely to you. If you want your judgments to be consistent with one another, you should revise either your judgment about how much knowledge a sperm has about its predecessors or else your intuitions about birth orders.

Ultimately, we argue, you should accept your intuitions but only after you have sought both arguments and data that might influence them. As this section illustrates, unaided intuition can lead to mistakes. We know of no substitute for hard thinking about difficult problems, and we consider it fortunate that conflict between arithmetic or data and intuition so often signals the need for it.

Conventions as a basis for probability assessments

Some probabilities are assigned by convention. The most familiar convention is that which assigns .5 to both heads and tails of any coin. Probabilities assigned by convention appear more often in such elementary expositions of probabilistic thinking as this than in real applications. They are not the same as the equiprobability assumptions used in many empirical sciences.

We have already illustrated probabilities by convention twice without labeling them as such. In the birthday example, we ignored the specific date on which each birthday falls; we adopted instead the useful convention that all birthdays are equally likely, so that the probability that two people selected in a way that has nothing to do with birthdays have the same birthday would be 1/365 if there were no leap years. Similarly, in the birth sequence example, we could have added to the basic example the statement that the sequence BBBBBB is as likely as any sequence involving three boys and three girls. This statement is known to be false; it would be true only if the ratio of boys born to girls born were exactly 1 : 1, whereas in fact more girls than boys are born. Nevertheless, the discrepancy is so small that the convention that treats the probability of each sex as 1/2 is adequate for almost every problem. (Note that the example of birth sequence for families of three boys and three girls is unaffected by what the actual birth probabilities are; the example would work equally well if boys were nine times as likely to be born as girls.)

The concept of probability by convention was long ago, and incorrectly, elevated to a rule for the assessment of probabilities called the principle of insufficient reason: if there is no basis for judging one member of an exhaustive set of mutually exclusive events to be more likely than another, they should be treated as equally probable. This rule, which would greatly simplify many probability assessments if only it worked, leads to many paradoxes. The most striking of these result from transformations of numerical uncertain variables. Assume, for example, that you know only that the percentage of gin in a gin and tonic mix is between 25 and 75%. Using the principle of insufficient reason, you might assign equal probability densities of 1/50 for each of the percentages of gin between 25 and 75%. But would it not make equal sense to consider the ratio of gin to tonic as the random variable? This ratio would vary between 1/3 and 3. Again you could use the principle of insufficient reason and assign equal densities of 1/2.67 to each ratio between 1/3 and 3. According to the first definition you would consider the two propositions (1) "The drink contains more gin than tonic," and (2) "The drink contains more tonic than gin" to be equally likely. However, using the second definition you would consider (1) to be three times as likely as (2).

Statistics as a basis for probability assessments

By far the most common practical procedure for assessing probabilities is to collect a large enough set of observations and then to use a relative frequency. This procedure is tedious – but the existence of empirical science testifies to its success.

The collection of statistics can pose several practical problems. Useful relative frequencies are always conditional. We made the point implicitly in commenting on the kind of information the doctor would need in order to justify a statement that "people almost never die on the table" during a particular operation. To make statistical information about that operation useful, it would have to be conditioned on the age and physical condition of the patient, complications, experience of the surgeon at the time of the operation, any changes in technique introduced over time, and probably many other things. The desire to condition on relevant variables conflicts with the desire to have a sufficiently large number of observations in each cell of the resulting contingency table that the relative frequencies will be stable. Much of the art of data collection consists exactly of choosing conditionalizations properly, so that the individual data cells will be both useful and different from one another.

But such conditionalizations complicate a problem that would exist in any case: before entering an observation into a contingency table, we must know in which cell it belongs. This problem will not impress the theoreticians of probability, but the practical users of relative frequencies in, for example, social statistics will recognize it with pain. Even calling neonates male or female is occasionally hard or impossible to do.

The use of statistics depends on two assumptions. The first is stationarity, the assumption that the future will be like the past, so that past data are relevant to prediction. Stationarity is a property, not of the world, but of how we think about it. The most intellectually demanding problem of collecting statistics is to find a way of thinking about their topic that permits the world that generates them to look stationary. Sometimes we do this by conditionalizing; the racehorse's win–loss record depends on whether the tract was muddy or dry. Sometimes we do it by admitting that the world changes but asserting that the change is slow, so that we can deal with nonstationarity by discarding old data every now and then. Mortality tables, for example, are periodically updated to keep track of changes in mortality statistics caused by such nonstationary processes as the development of modern medicine. A particularly interesting case is time series analysis. In time series analysis data are considered to have a stationary data-generating function that produces changing data over time.

Too often we don't worry about nonstationarity – or we may worry about it but be unable to do much. Pollsters trying to predict an election outcome often face the latter problem; voting decisions may change in the week between the last poll and the election. There are two practical excuses for ignoring nonstationarity. One is that we are hard put to find an alternative. The other is that such procedures bite us much less often and less severely than would procedures based on intuition alone.

The second assumption underlying the use of statistics is that a new case about which we wish to make a prediction is like the cases from which we are predicting. The .400 hitter has probability .4 of getting a hit this time up. Most often, this is a version of an equiprobability assumption; the probabilities of the dependent variables of interest within the cell defined by the relevant conditionalizations are the same for the new case as for those already observed.

Occasionally, we may use statistics to determine the parameters of a model and in turn use the model to predict new instances. That procedure still depends on the assumption of equiprobability for the cases treated as equivalent for fitting the model but need not assume equiprobability for the new cases being predicted, unless the same parameter values are used to predict more than one case.

4.5. Eliciting judgments of uncertainty from people

We have examined all the crutches we know about that enable those who work with probabilities to dodge the fact that numerical measures of uncertainty are opinions. Now we must face the question of how to obtain judgments of such opinions.

Like any other form of systematic extraction of numerical judgments from people, uncertainty elicitation is a branch of psychophysics. Stevens (1951) identifies seven kinds of judgments with which psychophysics is concerned; three are directly related to uncertainty elicitation. They are equality (Are two events considered equally likely?), order (Is event A considered more or less likely than event B?), and stimulus rating (How likely is event A, rated on a 0 to 1 scale of probabilities?). Of these, the first and third are commonly used in probability elicitation. Order judgments are not common but appear from time to time in methods that are not common. Two other kinds of judgment from Stevens's list, equality of intervals and equality of ratios, are unused, perhaps because uncertainty has several different numerical representations.

A sobering quote from Stevens (1951, p. 43) helps set the stage: "The reason for the traditional emphasis on method in psychophysics is simple enough: responses of organisms vary from moment to moment. Forced to take time samples of a fluctuating process, we find ourselves thrown on the tender mercies of statistical procedures whenever we try to draw stable conclusions. It is a frustrating business. And in order to temper their frustration the psychophysicists have elaborated subtle measures that try to transcend the inconstancy of the mercurial response." The frustration is familiar to those who elicit numbers that represent uncertainty, though we usually attribute inconsistency to nontemporal forms of human cussedness rather than to temporal fluctuation and try to deal with it by asking for convergent judgments from one respondent and enforcing consistency among them, rather than by following the statistical procedures Stevens had in mind.

Like other psychophysicists, those who elicit probabilities or other measures of uncertainty are blessed in one way. No probability assessment (except 0 or 1) can be shown to be wrong directly. Methods for showing that such numbers are biased or inappropriate do exist but are tedious, contentious, inapplicable to single instances or small ensembles, and rather rarely used. Even the temporal inconsistency that Stevens mentioned will not be available if the questions are sufficiently memorable that the response given on the first asking will be recalled at the second asking. In no way is this situation worse for judgments of certainty than for judgments of loudness; in fact, in many ways it is better.

Getting situation and stimuli right

If a numerical measure of uncertainty is an opinion, it characterizes a person as well as an event; we want to elicit from the right person. Who is that? Some people answer, "The decision maker" – and responsible decision analysts blush. Few significant decisions are made by one decision maker unassisted. If the decision maker is not a group, the individual in that role may well want expert help. On any significant topic, more than one expert is likely to exist, and we do not know which one or ones to ask or what to do with the answers if we get more than one. We examine some approaches to using more than one assessment later. By the way, both theory and evidence teach us to use more than one respondent whenever we can.

Assessing uncertainties that may control significant decisions is serious business and should be done in the right atmosphere. The analyst should work either one on one or in a small group. The analyst should avoid taking too much control of the situation and instead aim at helping the respondents to do a good job. Classroom settings are inappropriate. The respondent should feel relaxed, not challenged, but should take the task seriously. Of course, he or she should understand the techniques to be used, as much as time and other limits permit. The analyst should point out that there are no right or wrong answers and that revisions will and should occur in the process of assessment.

The respondent cannot hope to do a good job unless the quantity to be assessed is clearly defined. It is perhaps most important to make any conditionalities that enter into the assessment explicit. If an assessment of the probability that the German mark will increase in value against the dollar tomorrow implicitly assumes that the relevant exchange rate is the closing rate at the New York currency exchange, this should be said explicitly. Spetzler and Staël von Holstein (1975) suggest a simple test: a clairvoyant should be able to specify the outcome without asking additional questions for clarification. Since formally the events over which a probability distribution is assessed must be exhaustive, another test is to make sure that the respondent can specify what they are. Often it is convenient to exclude some of them (e.g., multiple diseases when symptom–disease relations are being considered); such exclusions are conditionalities of which the respondent should be clearly aware. A closely related practical suggestion is: never ask a respondent for an estimate of the likelihood of an event without also asking about its complement or complements.

Good elicitation practice is never to rely on only one way of asking. Instead, ask the same or related questions in various ways, looking for inconsistencies. If you find some, be glad. They can be fed back to the respondent, who must then be asked to think some more in order to eliminate them. Anything that promotes hard thinking and insight helps.

Another way of promoting inconsistent judgments is to turn uncertainties into imputed decisions, either by using them to specify hypothetical gambles or by applying them to the real decision problem at hand. Inconsistencies thus produced can also stimulate thought.

Finally, if the task of uncertainty assessment is routine for the respondent, methods based on feeding back scores obtained from proper scoring rules or calibration data will help. We describe these two tools for evaluating ensembles of probability assessments later.

We recognize some idealism in this set of prescriptions. Time, respondent impatience, or cost may not permit their execution. If they do, the enhanced accuracy may not be worthwhile. A very high degree of accuracy in uncertainty assessment is frequently not worthwhile if such assessments are used only as guides to thought rather than as numerical inputs to decisions or if the decision is insensitive to the numbers used. We give this advice for two purposes: to specify standards of skilled performance for an analyst and to provide a checklist against which to assess the conditions of experimental studies that conclude that respondents do a poor job of uncertainty assessment. We are not very impressed with evidence that performance is poor unless the analyst went to great pains to try to help the respondent do well.

Response modes for discrete events

Of numerous variables in eliciting response modes that could be used for taxonomizing, three seem especially important to use a priori: whether the method applies to discrete or continuous variables, whether events are directly judged or evaluated as parts of gambles, and whether the method uses the respondent to judge indifference or to provide direct numerical estimates. Unfortunately, the resulting taxonomy isn't clean; the methods are distinct in theory, but the differences often vanish in practice. We need examples to make the point, so we return to it after a bit of discussion.

We confine ourselves to the case of two discrete events, H and $\overline{H}$; if the discussion does not clearly generalize to the case of more events, we explain what the problem is. The most obvious way to find out what someone thinks about the probability of H is simply to ask. It is unwise to consider only H (though it is often done). It is better to ask for both $P(H)$ and $P(\overline{H})$, even though these must sum to 1. This is just about imperative for cases involving more than two events and is, in any case, a good idea if it can be used to encourage the respondent to think hard about H. Because a standard finding (reviewed, e.g., in Lichtenstein, Fischhoff, and Phillips, 1982; Slovic, Fischhoff, and Lichtenstein, 1977) is that people assess $P(H)$ as too high whenever it is not tiny, such thinking is important. We have already explained why probability is an awkward metric for uncertainty and why we like log odds. Several studies comparing probability with log odds revealed that the latter is frequently preferable (see, e.g., Fujii, 1967; Phillips and Edwards, 1966; and a review of various probability elicitation experiments by Goodman, 1972). However, for the technically trained, probabilities are sometimes more natural and familiar. When Lusted et al. (1980) allowed emergency room physicians with only brief training to choose between the two modes, about 65% of them chose probabilities. Log odds are preferable to probabilities when probabilities are very small or very large; we return to very small probabilities later.

Weaker direct assessment methods could be used. Stillwell, Seaver, and Schwartz (1981; see also Wallsten and Budescu, 1983) draw on the psychophysical literature for a set of possibilities: paired comparisons, ranking, sorting, ordinal rating, and fractionation. We know of little evidence from sensory psychophysics to convince us that these procedures are preferable to direct numerical estimation, but of course they could be. Most of them require much more respondent effort, make strong psychometric assumptions, or both.

Equality judgments for assessing probabilities typically require the use of reference events that can be finely adjusted, the probabilities of which are known by convention. A frequently used reference event is a probability wheel, which is a wheel having a red and a green segment with a spinner over it (see, e.g., Spetzler and Stäel von Holstein, 1975). The respondent is asked if he or she thinks that the event under consideration is more or less likely than the event of obtaining green in a spin of the probability wheel. Then the percentage of green showing on the probability wheel is varied until the respondent is indifferent.

This illustrates one reason for the inadequacy of our taxonomic distinctions. The judgments are hypothetical, and the respondent may recognize them to be disguised assessments of the proportion of green showing on the wheel. So such procedures are only marginally different from numerical estimation.

For discrete events, elicitation methods using gambles as stimuli and the SEU model as a means of calculating probabilities can be quite distinct from those based on direct numerical estimation. A pervasive problem of any such model-based method has to do with whether the underlying utility scale for the commodity used in the gamble (almost always money) is known. For a few of the methods, it doesn't matter; for others, it does. When it does matter, a convenient approach is to assume utility linear with money. This may bother theoreticians, but it doesn't bother us. For modest amounts of money (and imaginary gambles), the amount of deviation from linearity is likely to be trivial.

The first instance of such a procedure, now of only historical importance, was proposed by Ramsey (1931) and implemented with some difficulty by Davidson, Suppes, and Siegel (1957). Ramsey's idea was to identify first a subjectively 50 : 50 event. For such an event, the respondent should be indifferent between winning $\$X$ if E occurs and losing $\$Y$ if it does not, and the same bet with roles of E and $\overline{E}$ reversed. Using that event, one can measure the utility of money. Given the utility scale, any probability can be measured. If, for example, you win money worth 100 utiles to you if some event F (not the subjectively 50 : 50 event E) occurs, and no utility changes happen otherwise, then the utility of the amount of money that you would regard as just as attractive as that bet is 100 times the probability of F. This procedure is of historical importance only because of its first half, the search for the subjectively 50 : 50 ("ethically neutral" in Ramsey's language) event.

The second half, ignoring utility considerations and using money directly, is a standard and straightforward procedure. One can do it either directly by asking the respondent to estimate the certainty equivalent of the gamble, or indirectly by varying the certain amount and zeroing in on the equivalence point.

Consider the bet "You win ten dollars if it rains tomorrow, nothing if it does not rain." Compare that with a certain gift of $\$5$. Obviously, if you are fairly sure that it will rain, you will prefer the bet over the $\$5$. On the other hand, if you think rain is unlikely, you will take the sure thing. By varying the sure amount and asking whether the respondent prefers the sure thing or the bet, the analyst can usually pinpoint a range in which the respondent switches from the sure thing to the bet. For example, a respondent who is quite certain that it will rain tomorrow may prefer the bet up to a sure thing of $\$8$ but prefer the sure thing at $\$9$. The analyst should point out that the switch occurred and ask whether the preference is easier to state at $\$8$ or at $\$9$. If it is more difficult at $\$9$, the indifference point is probably closer to $\$9$ than to $\$8$. Through such questions the analyst can lead the respondent to his or her indifference point.

Let us assume that in the example the indifference point is $\$9$. Then the EV calculations would suggest that

$$9 = P(E)10 + [1 - P(E)](0), \qquad (4.12)$$

or

$$P(E) = 9/10. \qquad (4.13)$$

The EV assumption can, of course, be replaced by the SEU assumption. In that case utilities have to be found first and the dollar values above have to be replaced by utiles.

This SEU-based procedure is open to two criticisms. One is that it assumes the validity of the EV or SEU model as descriptive of human behavior; psychologists have been debating this for more than 30 years. (For successive reviews, see Edwards, 1954d, 1961; Becker and McClintock,

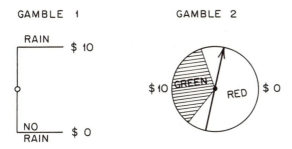

Figure 4.4. Illustration of an SEU-based reference gamble method for eliciting probabilities.

1967; Rapoport and Wallsten, 1972; Slovic et al., 1977; Einhorn and Hogarth, 1981; Pitz and Sachs, 1984.) Another, dearer to the hearts of contemporary decision analysts, is that it compares a gamble with a sure thing. If people have what the literature calls attitudes toward risk, meaning that they either dislike or like gambling, those attitudes can cause a problem.

A possible solution to the problem of attitudes toward risk is to make all the choices available to the respondent risky. The most obvious way to do this is to use reference events like the probability wheel. The technique is identical to that described above: find a setting of the wheel such that the respondent is indifferent between a specified gamble on E or on one color of the wheel.

For example, consider the choices illustrated in Figure 4.4. You can place either one of two bets. The first bet involves the event "It will rain tomorrow," which has unknown probability. If it rains, you will receive $10; otherwise you will receive nothing. Alternatively you can bet on the gamble represented by the wheel. If the pointer stops on the "green" area, you will receive $10; otherwise nothing. If you prefer the wheel with the shaded area presented in the figure, the analyst will reduce that area until you are indifferent between betting on rain and betting on the wheel. Since the probability of the "green" area is known by convention and since the SEU model implies that

$$P(\text{rain})u(10) + P(\text{no rain})u(0) = P(\text{green})u(10) + P(\text{red})u(0), \quad (4.14)$$

it follows that $P(\text{rain})$ must be equal to the known probability $P(\text{green})$.

Assessments based on the SEU model have been much favored by theoreticians, who argue that a choice among bets, even if imaginary, is more realistic than a numerical subjective assessment (see, e.g., Savage, 1954). This premise is widely accepted in the decision-analytic literature. But while those procedures are formulated as a question about gambles and indifference points, most respondents are quick to realize that they are being asked to give an estimate that is a multiple of the probability of E, especially if, as is appropriate, the elicitor makes that point to help the respondent understand the task.

We have just summarized the principles of three probability assessment procedures:

1   Direct numerical estimation
2   Procedures based on equality judgments among events with known and unknown probability
3   Procedures based on the SEU assumption

Esoteric minds can imagine other possibilities. Perhaps the most important arises from the concept of proper scoring rules, described below. Since such rules assign scores that make it optimal to assess probabilities properly, extracts from a table of such scores could be listed as an orderly array of bets. The probability corresponding to the most preferred bet would be the estimated probability (assuming linear utilities).

Response modes for continuous distributions

The analogue of making direct numerical estimates for continuous distributions is providing estimates of selected probability densities and smoothing a curve or drawing a probability density directly. In practice this can be done only by highly experienced experts who know both the subject matter of the uncertain variable for which a density is constructed and the theory and mechanics of probability density functions.

More commonly, one assesses continuous distributions by making them discrete. In the direct numerical estimation method, the assessor provides the respondent with selected values of the uncertain variable and asks him or her to state the probability that the true value is above or below the selected values. The probabilities that the true value is below should increase as the selected value increases and thus provide points for a plot of a cumulative probability distribution. Usually such distributions are drawn into the assessments by freehand smoothing or curve fitting. Alternatively the analyst can attempt to construct a probability distribution over segments of the uncertain variable.

Consider, for example, the task of estimating next year's inflation rate. A respondent may think that it will be slightly higher than this year's rate; a best first guess may be 6%. Next it is useful to get a feeling for the extremes of the range of possible values. The analyst asks the respondent to provide a lower and upper estimate such that he or she is absolutely certain that the true inflation rate will fall in between. These values should be probed and pushed, since experimental evidence indicates that they are often too close to the best estimate.

Having established a best guess and the range, the analyst then can provide some equidistant values and ask the respondent to assign probabilities that the true inflation rate will fall in each of the segments. Finally, a density function is smoothed through these estimates.

The construction of cumulative distributions and density functions should be cross-checked for consistency whenever possible. After obtaining a probability plot the analyst should carry out some simple calculations and cross-checks.

The analyst can reverse this process of constructing cumulative probability distributions or density functions by providing the respondent with probabilities and asking him or her to find ranges of values of the uncertain variable such that the true value will fall into these ranges with the prespecified probability. The best known of these procedures is the fractile procedure in which the respondent is asked to find the 1st, 5th, 25th, 50th, 75th, 95th, and 99th fractiles. The 50th fractile is simply the median of the distribution. The respondent must contemplate the task: find a value of the uncertain variable x such that the true value is equally likely to fall below or above it. In estimating next year's inflation rate, the respondent may feel strongly that the true inflation rate is more likely to fall above 6% than below and so realize that the initial best guess estimate lies below the median. By varying the value, the assessor can help the respondent find the approximate median. The zth fractile is found in a similar way: the respondent is asked to find a value such that the probability that the true value falls below the selected one is z%. For the 1st fractile z would be 1%, for the 25th fractile z would be 25%, and so forth. Figure 4.5 illustrates some possible fractile assessments for the task of estimating next year's inflation rate. The lower panel shows the smoothed cumulative probability distribution.

Consistency checks are particularly obvious in the fractile procedure. For example, the analyst can ask the respondent whether it seems equally likely that the true value lies below the 25th fractile, between the 25th and the 50th, between the 50th and the 75th, or above the 75th.

All of the procedures based on the SEU model that were discussed in the section about discrete events can be applied to continuous events after discretization. Moreover, it is frequently useful to probe the extremes of probability distributions by asking questions involving small bets to check whether the certainty with which subjects exclude tails is justified by their choices.

Some sophisticated forms of elicitation apply to special families of distributions. One, applicable only with highly trained and experienced respondents, is to obtain estimates of the parameters of the distribution. For example, in the case of estimating the inflation rate the respondent may have reasons to believe that the distribution is normal with unknown mean and variance. Estimates of these two parameters would specify the complete density function. Such specifications should be cross-checked with some direct probability estimates.

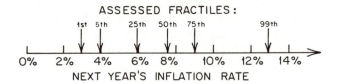

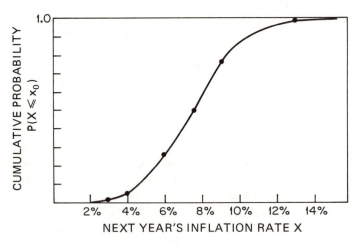

Figure 4.5. Illustration of the fractile method for continuous variables.

The special problem of extreme probabilities

Extremely high or low probabilities (or odds, or log odds) are usually very hard to estimate. Events with extremely high probabilities are seldom of much practical importance; they are typically so common that they can be treated as having a probability of almost 1 without much intellectual or practical loss. But events with extremely low probabilities can be very important indeed. The most common reason is that they may be associated with very large payoffs, positive or negative. What is the probability that a core meltdown will occur within a specified time in a nuclear power plant? That number had better be very low, but we care enormously whether its magnitude is nearer 10^{-6}, 10^{-8}, or 10^{-10}. A second reason for caring about very low probabilities has not acquired significance in applications as yet, but might in the future. Unlike simple inference, hierarchical inference requires (or perhaps we should say would greatly profit from) the assessment of numbers of the form $P(D|H)$, where D is some datum and H a hypothesis to which it is inferentially relevant. In almost any real-world situation $P(D|H)$ is very small indeed, simply because most data, if specified in detail, are quite unlikely relative to their alternatives, no matter what hypothesis is true.

The most common method of assessing very small probabilities is to calculate them from bigger ones. The event tree and fault tree methods discussed in Chapter 3 illustrate the ideas. Opinions about very low probabilities are almost certain to be vague, for the reasons suggested by the preceding paragraph. Availability of instances (see Tversky and Kahneman, 1973) is likely to be crucial to such assessments. In direct experience, such instances are infrequent, and the assessment of probability based on them is likely to be vague and unstable. Secondhand collections of instances (e.g., that provided by the media) have a built-in bias in favor of overestimating the frequency of rare but newsworthy or gossip-worthy events. "Dog Bites Man" isn't news; "Man Bites Dog" is news. Tversky and Kahneman (1973) call this environmental effect together with various cognitive effects "availability biases."

Selvidge (1975) published a paper that deals explicitly with how to elicit probabilities of rare events. She starts with the same emphasis on unambiguous specification of the event that we have already outlined. She also suggests that the assessor should identify mutually exclusive sets of events that might lead to the event in question. This is an adaptation of the fault tree notion. Kahneman and Tversky (1982) have argued persuasively that one will consider an event more likely if one can think of causal chains or scenarios that are likely to lead to its occurrence; Selvidge uses that procedure in structuring the estimation process. Next she asks the respondent to order the uncertainties and then to assign numerical values to them. In the final step, the respondent also judges probabilities within the causal chains, and, as usual, the elicitor looks for inconsistencies and uses them to stimulate thought. For obvious reasons, no one has studied Selvidge's procedure in a context in which external criteria that correspond to the respondent's knowledge are available. We blanch at the requirements of criterion validation research on methods for eliciting very small probabilities. Incidentally, Selvidge uses probabilities as her primary response mode; we would prefer odds on a log scale.

We close our discussion of this topic with an oddball idea we had that didn't make it. Some events, though very unlikely, come from sets with which we have abundant experience – so abundant that initially vague opinions should have had plenty of opportunity to stabilize. How likely do you consider it that you will meet someone 6 feet 8 inches or taller tomorrow? How likely do you consider it that the next time you drive to work you will have an accident? Statistics relevant to such questions are not difficult to find. A list of such events, called marker events, can be assembled and arrayed in likeliness. To assess the probability of an unknown event, the respondent need only insert it into the marker event list at the point such that the next event above it is more likely and the next event below it is less likely; this constitutes a numerical probability estimate if we know the relative frequencies of those two events.

We tried the idea out rather halfheartedly in collaboration with Slovic, Lichtenstein, and Fischhoff. Subjects had trouble getting the marker events themselves into the appropriate order. This probably means that we simply hadn't worked hard enough to get events that provided indicative markers for the assessments. The quality of a person's intuitions depends both on who the person is and how much effort he or she is making. In applications of decision analysis, we usually encounter respondents who are modestly well trained about probabilities and who are given extensive assistance by elicitors who are very well trained. Unfortunately, very little experimentation has been carried out and not many reported real data have been obtained using such conditions. We are stuck with the evidence we have; we regard it as defining lower limits on what is possible.

4.6. Extremeness, proper scoring rules, and calibration

You would like any probability assessment to have two characteristics that are related to the outside world. One is obvious: you would like it to be extreme. An assessment close to 1 or 0 gives far more useful guidance about what to expect, and therefore what to do, than an assessment near .5. In the case of continuous distributions, you would like probability density functions to be as peaked as possible.

The other desirable property of probability assessments is calibration, and it is much subtler than extremeness. You cannot assess the calibration of any single assessment. But if you had a number of probability assessments, all of .6, you would feel more comfortable with them if about 60% of the propositions so assessed turned out to be true and the other 40% turned out to be false than if, say, 10 or 90% turned out to be true. In the case of a continuous distribution over a parameter, you would like the area of the density function between any two cutoff points to correspond to the relative frequency with which the true value of the parameter falls between them.

Calibration and extremeness pull in opposite directions. Consider yourself a weather forecaster who must specify the probability of rain every day in a given city. One way to proceed would be to inspect records, note that it rained last year on 60% of all days in that city, and so make each day's assessment for this year 60%. Such assessments (called climatological in meteorology) will most likely be well calibrated because the percentage of rainy days changes relatively little from year to year. But they will be almost useless because they do not differentiate among days.

The alternative of saying either that it will rain or that it will not rain is better, but not much. It makes no distinction between days on which you think it a bit more likely than not that it will rain and days on which you

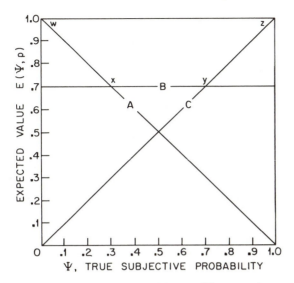

Figure 4.6. A three-act, two-state problem to illustrate the concept of scoring rules.

can see the puddles accumulating in the street while you formulate your forecast.

In order to balance the inward pull of the desire for good calibration against the outward pull of the desire for extremeness, you must use the evidence at hand – which is exactly what weather forecasters do.

Proper scoring rules

The preceding discussion specifies qualitatively the issues of probability assessment but offers little to someone attempting to encourage good assessments or to measure quality. The more quantitative concept of proper scoring rules helps.

A probability estimate is a response, and a response is a probability estimate. Consider a three-act, two-event problem. Figure 4.6 shows the plot of the EVs of the three acts as a function of the probability ψ of event H (event $\overline{H}$ is assumed to have probability $1 - \psi$). These EV functions are straight lines, a property that generalizes to planes in 3-space and hyperplanes in 4-space and above as the number of hypotheses increases. Note that the intersections of any line with the left and right boundaries are the payoffs if that act is chosen and that state obtains.

In this example, act A is best if $P(H)$ is less than $1/3$, act B is best if $P(H)$ is between $1/3$ and $2/3$, and act C is best if $P(H)$ is between $2/3$ and 1. Obviously a choice of A signals your opinion that $P(H)$ is less than $1/3$; a choice of B puts it between $1/3$ and $2/3$; and a choice of C puts it between $2/3$ and

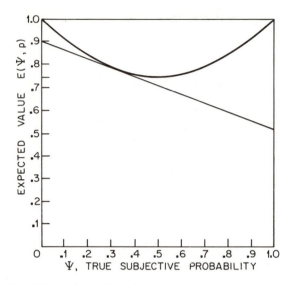

Figure 4.7. Illustration of a strictly proper scoring rule.

1. This example generalizes to any number of hypotheses and to continuous cases. Let us suppose that you have some opinion $P(H)$ about the probability of H. How can we encourage you to state that opinion accurately? Obviously, by offering you a reward for doing so that makes it better to take that action than to take any other. To identify a probability uniquely by observing an act, we must offer you an essentially infinite number of bets, each having the property that it maximizes expected value among the ones that we offer for a different unique probability. By choosing that bet you in essence signal that your probability is equal to the one that turns this bet into an SEU-maximizing choice.

On the surface it may seem difficult to arrange such a list of bets. But consider the convex upper boundary of the graph in Figure 4.6 defined by w, x, y, and z. If it were replaced by a smooth, slightly convex curve, that curve would do the trick.

To construct bets from scoring rules, one simply constructs all tangents to this curve – each tangent defines a bet with outcomes at the points $P(H) = 0$ and $P(H) = 1$. An example is shown in Figure 4.7. It also illustrates why offering all bets defined by the tangents of the convex curve in Figure 4.7 helps identify probabilities: each bet is optimal for one and only one probability. The requirement, called strict convexity, that any such curve must meet is that a straight line tangent to it at any point within the figure must be below it at all other points in the figure. This sounds like, and is, a fairly simple requirement; infinite families of functions fulfill it and its generalization to a larger number of hypotheses. In practice one would, of course, present only a dense subset of all possible bets to the respondent, because it would be too confusing to present continuous versions of bets. Ten to 20 bets spaced throughout the probability range would probably be sufficient.

Such strictly convex functions are known as *strictly proper scoring rules* (Aczel and Pfanzagl, 1966). The curve *w, x, y, z* in Figure 4.6 is a proper scoring rule, but not a strictly proper one. Most discussions of this topic are confined, as this one will be, to strictly proper scoring rules. For convenience, we omit the word *strictly* in what follows.

In applications of scoring rules, the bets are often phrased as if they were direct estimates of the probabilities, and the payoffs are formulated as functions of the probability estimates and the event that in fact occurs. The essential property of such proper scoring rules is that the response of telling the truth must have a greater EV than any other response. By "telling the truth" we mean that the respondent must report an estimate p_i exactly equal to his or her true opinion ψ_i for all i.

To communicate the idea, we present the most obvious scoring rule. Let the event that actually occurs be called E_k, your true probability estimate for it ψ_k, and the verbal (or other) response you give p_k. One obvious and very important scoring rule is the *linear* rule: if $p_k = .25$, pay \$0.25; if $p_k = .75$, pay \$0.75; and so on. In general, one will win $s = p_k$ if event E_k occurs. Is this a proper scoring rule? Intuition, reinforced by a glance at Figure 4.7, suggests that it is not, and mathematics can easily prove that it is not. The EV of the vector of estimates **p** is

$$EV(s) = \sum_{k=1}^{N} \psi_k p_k. \tag{4.15}$$

Intuition might suggest, and it is indeed the case, that you can maximize this EV, not by setting p_i equal to ψ_i for all hypotheses, but rather by selecting the hypothesis that has the largest value of ψ_i, assessing its probability to be 1, and assessing all other probabilities to be zero. That strategy makes sure that the EV of the situation will be equal to the probability of that most likely event; no other strategy can do as well. So the linear scoring rule is not proper.

The two most commonly discussed proper scoring rules are the logarithmic and the quadratic ones. The logarithmic rule assigns a payoff

$$s = c + d \ln p_k, \ c, d > 0 \tag{4.16}$$

to the assessment of p_k for the event E_k that in fact occurs. The quadratic one is quite similar; it assigns

$$s = 2p_k - \sum_{i \neq k} p_i^2. \tag{4.17}$$

Trial and error, or some calculus, will show that both of the discrete proper scoring rules do indeed maximize your score if you set p_i equal to ψ_i for all i. The notion of proper scoring rules generalizes to continuous distributions, though it appears relatively rarely in studies of them. Matheson and Winkler (1976) have proposed something called the ranked scoring rule, which is designed to reward a respondent whose assessment is "close" to the correct answer, while maintaining the defining property of proper scoring rules. Its continuous version is

$$s = - \int_{-\infty}^{t} F(x) \, dx - \int_{t}^{\infty} [1 - F(x)]^2 \, dx, \qquad (4.18)$$

where $F(x)$ is the assessed cumulative distribution and t the true value of x. The calculus required for demonstrating that this continuous version of the rule is strictly proper is quite complicated.

Both the logarithmic and the quadratic scoring rules have significant drawbacks. They share an important one: although the optimal strategy is indeed to set p_i equal to ψ_i, the cost of not doing so is very small for modest deviations and not that high even for large ones. This is an instance of the flat-maximum phenomenon discussed in Chapter 11.

The logarithmic rule has the unique property that its expected value is unaffected by your probability assessments for events other than the one that occurred. Whether this property is attractive depends on context. If you are considering which horse will win a race, the only relationship that one horse typically has to another is that only one can win; in this case, the property might be attractive. But suppose you are assessing the probability that the temperature at noon tomorrow will be between 60 and 70°F, between 70 and 80°F, or between 80 and 90°F. If the true temperature turned out to be 85°F, you might prefer the assessment vector (.2; .3; .4) to (.3; .2; .4) even though you assigned a .4 probability to the truth in both. Unfortunately, neither the logarithmic nor the quadratic rule has this property. You will do best with the quadratic rule if you distribute $1 - p_k$ uniformly over the remaining hypotheses. Epstein's (1969) ranked probability score is designed for cases in which you wish to reward the assessor for near misses. This is a discrete version of the Matheson–Winkler rule.

The logarithmic score has one dramatically unattractive property; in practice the property is so unattractive that the score is seldom used. It is that if you happened to assign probability 0 to the event that in fact occurred, you would lose an infinite amount of money, for any finite value of the constant c. Although you might in practice avoid this property by truncating the possible losses at some suitably large value, the net effect is an ugly rule. When the logarithmic rule has been used, even with truncating, subjects have responded by staying well away from extreme estimates (Fischer, 1982).

The quadratic rule, known in meteorology as the Brier score (Brier, 1950), is used extensively for the evaluation of probabilistic forecasts in meteorology and consequently has received much research attention. Murphy (1973) has looked at a way of partitioning it. First, a collection of responses and scores is partitioned into subcollections such that all the responses in a subcollection are the same. Then an algebraic partitioning of the scores into three parts is possible. One part measures the uncertainty inherent in the events themselves. A second is a measure of calibration (Murphy calls it "variability"). The third is a measure of the assessor's ability to sort the situations into separate categories – that is, to avoid the climatological response already discussed.

The content of this partitioning itself stimulates reflection. How difficult is it to make good probability assessments? This depends on more than calibration; it depends both on the inherent uncertainty of the events to be predicted (maximized if, for kN events to be distributed over N categories, approximately k fall in each category; minimized if they all fall in one category) and on the degree to which information and skill enable the assessor to differentiate among the elements of the set of events. Note that, in this formulation, it is impossible to discriminate the effects of information from the effects of skill. Either provides a basis for making finely differentiated probability assessments, and in the absence of external measures of how definitive the information is, one cannot judge how well it has been used.

Before leaving the topic of scoring rules, we should note that the linear scoring rule, which rewards extreme estimates, is implicitly built into many probability assessment situations. A great deal of research on probability assessment has used what have come to be known as almanac questions. For example, "General Diaz was a famous dictator of which country in the early 1900s, Mexico or Peru?" You are asked to answer the question and then judge a probability that the answer is correct. The answer is Mexico. Would you feel twice as foolish about not having been certain if you had assessed its probability at .6 than if you had assessed it at .8? Then you are using an implicit linear scoring rule, and you will maximize your implicit score over a large collection of such items by always estimating the probability of the most likely answer to be 1. As the example suggests, implicit scoring rules are hard to avoid.

Evidence about calibration

Research evidence about calibration is abundant but singularly hard to make sense of. Lichtenstein et al. (1982) have done an exceptionally good job of reviewing the experimental studies, which reach back all the way to Adams (1954). Most of the numerous experiments they review show excessively high assessments of probabilities over .5. This kind of finding is in apparent conflict with early, unsophisticated work relating subjective to objective probability (reviewed by Edwards, 1954d, 1961) that argues that probabilities are overestimated below about .25 and underestimated above that. Both findings are probably correct; the difference is that most of the calibration studies involved various forms of direct verbal or written numerical judgment, while those reviewed by Edwards inferred probabilities from choices among bets.

An important conclusion from Lichtenstein et al.'s review is that people are much less likely to be overconfident about easy probability judgments than about difficult ones. The way to think of this finding, suggested to us by B. Fischhoff (personal conversation, 1984), is that respondents show insensitivity to their degree of knowledge, thus producing both findings. Pitz (1974) found that very difficult judgments produce the most overconfidence. Lichtenstein and Fischhoff (1977), asking subjects to discriminate between such stimuli as drawings made by Asian or European children, found essentially no calibration at all; virtually any response meant about .5. Using various other stimuli and manipulations that made the discriminations easier, they found much better performance. Indeed, Lichtenstein and Fischhoff (1980) found underconfidence for easy judgments, as have several others. A particularly encouraging finding by Koriat, Lichtenstein, and Fischhoff (1980) is that respondents are less overconfident even with difficult questions if asked to write why the answer they chose might be wrong.

Response modes may help reduce overconfidence, at least in the continuous case. Numerous studies have shown that probability distributions over continuous variables elicited by the fractile method are far too tight (see, e.g., Alpert and Raiffa, 1982; Schäfer and Borcherding, 1973a; for reviews see Lichtenstein, Fischhoff, and Phillips, 1977, 1982). Seaver, von Winterfeldt, and Edwards (1978) used direct probability assessment methods to construct continuous probability distributions and found that overconfidence and excessive tightness vanished.

Expertise helps too, even in experiments. Both Sieber (1974) and Pitz (1974) found good calibration for students taking tests on the subject matter of their courses – about which they might be assumed to be fairly expert. However, Lichtenstein and Fischhoff (1977) found that graduate students in psychology did no better on psychology-related items than on general-knowledge items. Perhaps expertise should be more specific than that.

Yet another conclusion implicit in the literature that Lichtenstein et al. review is that subtle methodological issues may have much to do with how such experiments come out. For example, asking how likely it is that General Diaz was dictator of Mexico rather than Peru is not at all the same as asking for the same information in the form in which we presented the question. The procedure we used above produces higher estimates, so the data suggest.

An encouraging fourth conclusion suggested by some of the studies Lichtenstein et al. review is that training in and experience at probability estimation can improve matters.

Both the fact that easy assessment tasks produce better calibration than difficult ones and the fact that training in probability estimation and experience at it improve performance help to explain other findings. Zlotnick (1968) found relatively good calibration for intelligence analysts; it was hampered primarily by a mild tendency to overestimate the probabilities of occurrence of dire events. The latter finding is widely reported in the literature of assessments made by experts who must make forecasts about events in the expectation that these forecasts will be a basis for action. The standard and plausible interpretation is that it is a by-product of the way job performance is evaluated. An intelligence analyst, or a doctor, would much rather warn of a dire event and later be proven wrong than miss the event in the first place.

Ludke, Stauss, and Gustafson (1977), in a study focused primarily on response modes and featuring the only instance we are aware of in which log log odds, a response mode that seems especially likely to encourage extreme assessments, were used, found relatively high quality of performance in calibration terms as well as others for all response modes studied; the respondents were trained medical personnel answering questions about familiar physiological topics like blood pressure. Lusted et al. (1980), reporting a very large field study of probability assessments by emergency room attending physicians, found generally good calibration except for the warning effect mentioned above. DeSmet, Fryback, and Thornbury (1979) also reported good performance by medical respondents.

But the world's probability assessment championship clearly belongs to weather forecasters. Murphy and Winkler (1974) found average deviations of only .028 from perfect calibration for credible interval temperature forecasts. United States weather forecasters have been making public probabilistic forecasts of rain since 1965. Figure 4.8 from Murphy and Winkler (1977a) shows the calibration data for 24,859 judgments made in Chicago during four years ending in June 1976. The number associated with each point is the number of observations it represents. A. H. Murphy (personal communication, 1983) has reported data that are even better. He believes that forecasters learn to do better with experience, and other data support that belief. Among numerous reasons for the high level of accuracy of weather forecasters are that (1) they make forecasts every day, (2) they get feedback each day about the previous day's forecast, (3) they get Brier score (quadratic proper scoring rule) feedback about their individual performance, and (4) to some extent their Brier scores affect their promotion and pay.

In summary, these data seem to us to argue that substantive expertise improves probability assessment by making the task easy rather than hard. Expertise about probability assessment helps too, probably because the proficient and experienced probability estimator simply has a better understanding of what such estimates mean. Feedback both of outcomes and of

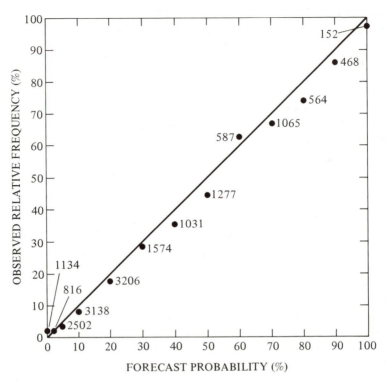

Figure 4.8. Calibration curve for weather forecasters. (*Source:* Murphy & Winkler, 1977a.)

scoring-rule information is helpful. And given these conditions, probability assessors can be expected to do a good job.

But these conditions are rare. In contexts in which they do not obtain and cannot be instituted, can anything be done? Not much. There has been a great deal of discussion about correcting probability estimates after the fact; the general view, with which we concur, is that this would be unwise. For one thing, the information about calibration that would be needed to make such transformations (or to reach the conclusions we summarized above) would be very hard to get. Few forms of research are so demanding of data as is the study of calibration. Individual differences, in the rare cases in which they are reported, seem to be large enough to discourage averaging across respondents. The task of collecting, say, enough instances in which a single person estimated .60 (or, more realistically somewhere between .55 and .65) to find a correction to be associated with that estimate would be formidable indeed, especially since it would have to be done for at least 10 different probability values. An obvious thought is to substitute a function with one or two parameters for a correction to each of a set of probabilities.

Lichtenstein et al. (1977) explored a few such suggestions, but rather halfheartedly; we have heard nothing of them since then. Perhaps most important, there is no good reason to expect a person's tendency to make errors not to change with the kind of experience required to collect such a large amount of data.

4.7. Debiasing

We commented earlier that virtually none of the experimental literature reporting probability estimates conformed to the conditions for eliciting numbers that report uncertainties that we proposed earlier in this chapter and that decision analysts routinely use in practice. Since much of that literature has in various ways argued that people make systematic errors in assessing uncertainties, it is natural to dismiss such studies by saying, "Oh, they didn't do it right." But a number of studies have in fact tried, one by one, some of the ways of improving elicitation procedures explicit or implicit in this chapter. Fischhoff (1982) has written an extraordinarily thoughtful and insightful review of such studies in the context of two frequent experimental findings: the overconfidence we have already discussed and the hindsight biases (Fischhoff, 1975) discussed in Chapter 13.

Consider Table 4.1, taken from Fischhoff (1982). Fischhoff's proposed list of debiasing strategies bears a very close resemblance indeed to the rules for probability estimation we have proposed already and to some that emerged from our discussion of calibration. Fischhoff intended "Offer alternative formulations" to mean the kind of search for inconsistencies in convergent assessments of the same quantity that decision analysts so emphasize. He dwelt on it less than we have. Fischhoff does not discuss significant computational assistance, while decision analysts insist on it. Fischhoff's list is a very serious attempt to examine methodological deficiencies of probability elicitation experiments.

Fischhoff proceeds to review a rather large number of studies that attempt to correct one or another of the faults he lists by means of one or more of the strategies he lists. His review is both detailed and discouraging. Such corrections, at the level of intensity at which they have been tried, on the whole do very little to correct the two biases he examines. The two most effective procedures seem to be to make the task easier (or, equivalently, to enhance the substantive abilities and information the respondent brings to it) and to teach skills in probability estimation. The review seems to us to slight somewhat the earlier literature on effects of response modes.

Fischhoff's summing up is a gem of balanced thought. One point he makes is especially important to the perspective taken by this chapter – and book. We have assumed all along that probability assessments are important enough that one should work hard to get them right. "The relative validity of casual and work-hard laboratory experiments depends upon the real

Table 4.1. *Debiasing methods according to underlying assumption*

Assumption	Strategies
Faulty tasks	
Unfair tasks	Raise stakes
	Clarify instruction/stimuli
	Discourage second-guessing
	Use better response modes
	Ask fewer questions
Misunderstood tasks	Demonstrate alternative goal
	Demonstrate semantic disagreement
	Demonstrate impossibility of task
	Demonstrate overlooked distinction
Faulty judges	
Perfectible individuals	Warn of problem
	Describe problem
	Provide personalized feedback
	Train extensively
Incorrigible individuals	Replace them
	Recalibrate their responses
	Plan on error
Mismatch between judges and task	
Restructuring	Make knowledge explicit
	Search for discrepant information
	Decompose problem
	Consider alternative situations
	Offer alternative formulations
Education	Rely on substantive experts
	Educate from childhood

Source: Fischhoff (1982).

world situations to which their results are to be extrapolated. Each has its place. Understanding the laboratory-world match requires good judgment in characterizing both contexts. For example, work-hard situations are not necessarily synonymous with important situations. People may not work hard on an important problem unless they realize both the centrality of a judgment to the problem's outcome and the potential fallibility of that judgment" (Fischhoff, 1982, p. 441). We have already noted that probability judgments are often not central to important decision problems of which they are a part. And, clearly, the overwhelming majority of our uncertainties bear either on trivial decisions or on no decisions at all. In a sheer numerical sense, instances in which it is important to get the measurement of uncertainty just right are quite rare, and the kinds of uncertainty judgments studied in typical experiments are much more common, though still rare. Our perspective arises from three related points. First, when it is important to do as well as possible, we should know how to do so, both for practical reasons and because the knowledge reflects our deepest understanding of what processes and procedures underlie getting the estimate(s) right. Second, conclusions about limitations on human ability to assess probabilities well abound in the literature. Such conclusions are meaningful only if based either on an exhaustive attempt to assess uncertainties as well as possible or on a specific set of less strenuous circumstances considered common enough to be worth studying in their own right. In the latter case, conclusions about limited human ability must be confined to those circumstances, and good science should lead us to accept Fischhoff's invitation to explore what happens as those circumstances change. Third, attention to methods for assessing probabilities as well as possible is likely to suggest very inexpensive methods of improving much more casual procedures. Good examples include Koriat et al.'s (1980) suggestion to reduce overconfidence by considering why an answer might be wrong and Fischhoff and Slovic's (1980) procedure of encouraging respondents to give answers reflecting complete uncertainty if they are in fact completely uncertain.

4.8. Group probability assessments

By now we have discussed many ideas about how to improve probability assessments. We have recommended structuring the problem carefully, using appropriate interactive elicitation procedures carefully, exploiting inconsistencies, using substantive experts as assessors, providing both scoring-rule and calibration feedback. We left out the question of whether to use group procedures, and if so, how. Seaver (1978) has provided a comprehensive treatment of this topic; we follow it closely.

Perhaps the easiest way to use groups of expert respondents is to collect an assessment from each and then average the assessments. There is an important formal sense in which this is *always* a good idea. The argument is easy to state, but harder to intuit. "Since proper scoring rules are convex functions on the probability simplex, the score of the average of individual probabilities will necessarily be better than the average of the individual's scores" (Seaver, 1978, p. 11). To make this thought intuitive, recall that every proper scoring rule must have the property that, as the assessment gets smaller for the event that actually occurs, the penalty for not having assigned that event a probability of 1.0 increases, not linearly, but faster than that. (This restates the thought that proper scoring rules are convex; see Figure 4.6.) Now, consider estimates of .7, .8, and .9 for the event that occurs. If you average these, the score for the average will be whatever is appropriate to .8. If you score each estimate individually and then average the scores, the score for the .9 estimate will be a bit above the score for the .8 estimate, but the score for the .7 estimate will be considerably below that for the .8 estimate. Consequently, the average of the three scores will be smaller than the score for the .8 estimate. This property is general and underlies much of our thinking about using groups to perform probability assessments.

A number of authors have proposed various complex variations on the idea of simply averaging probability estimates. An obvious idea is to use unequal weights rather than equal weights when averaging judged probabilities. People might weight themselves according to their knowledge of the topic or might weight others in an interacting group; DeGroot (1974) has presented a particularly complex and sophisticated version of the latter idea. Several empirical studies (e.g., Brown, 1973; Staël von Holstein, 1971, 1972; Winkler, 1971) show that weighted linear combinations of individual probabilities are superior to individual assessments as evaluated by scoring rules – but then, we have just argued that they must be. The studies are more than empirical demonstrations of mathematical necessity, however; in most of them only 10% or fewer of the individual subjects outperform the group estimates.

Even more complex procedures for aggregating judgments rest on the idea that one assessor's judgment is an informational input to another assessor, who may wish to revise his or her own judgment accordingly. Dalkey (1975), Morris (1974, 1977), and Winkler (1968) have presented versions of this idea. Such procedures typically involve major increments in mathematical and judgmental complexity over simple averaging. No reason exists for expecting such procedures to lead to better estimates. Experiments by Hogarth (1977), Staël von Holstein (1972), Gough (1974), Rowse, Gustafson, and Ludke (1978) and some others have shown that weighting procedures either make little difference or even (as Hogarth found) slightly reduce performance.

The idea underlying the use of groups to assess probabilities is that different experts have different kinds or items of knowledge, all of which should enter into the estimate. The thought is persuasive, at least to us. But how should the experts be used? Two obvious baseline procedures suggest themselves. One, as implied above, is to assess each respondent's judgment separately and then average the assessments. That procedure has a mathematical edge, but assumes that nothing is to be gained by sharing knowledge and thought among respondents – a very counterintuitive supposition. The other baseline procedure is, roughly, to lock the experts in a room and not let them out until they produce a consensus estimate. Evidence collected by Goodman (1972) and by Staël von Holstein (1971) combines with intuition to argue that, of these two procedures, the latter is mildly preferable. This is particularly true if the feelings of the respondents about the merit of the consensus judgment are important. But theoreticians of group interaction have worried over the years about various kinds of group effects they consider unattractive. Most important to them has been the role of the voice that dominates by virtue either of position or of persuasiveness. A second issue is that of group pressure for conformity.

Dalkey and Helmer (1963) used the Delphi procedure, designed to get rid of these group effects, for the first time in 1951. The applications have been so widespread and diverse that it is now difficult to ascertain just what the "Delphi procedure" means, except that it is somehow different from free-form group discussion. As originally conceived, it was a rather formal procedure in which the group members never met, remaining anonymous. Each member produced an estimate of whatever was of interest (not necessarily a probability or a distribution), along with written arguments for it. In sequential rounds, these arguments were exchanged anonymously, and new estimates were made. Some form of averaging was used to determine final group output after (typically) the third round.

Research-based cases for Delphi over its natural competitor, free-form group discussion, are very hard to make in general; Dalkey (1969) tried to make such a case, but with very weak data. Sackman (1974) concluded that the evidence does not justify the popularity of the method. (For instances of application and discussions of method, see Linstone and Turoff, 1975.)

Van de Ven and Delbecq (1971) proposed the nominal group technique as an alternative both to free-form discussion and to Delphi. Delbecq, Van de Ven, and Gustafson (1975) described the technique as requiring silent judgments in the presence of the group, presentation of all judgments, group discussion, individual reconsideration, and mathematical aggregation of final judgments. This technique, unlike Delphi, requires face-to-face interaction. A few years ago that would have seemed like a clear one-up for Delphi; soon, as teleconferencing develops, that will no longer be the case. Three experiments have compared Delphi, the nominal group technique, and free-form discussion for probability estimation. Gustafson, Shukla, Delbecq, and Walster (1973), seeking likelihood ratio judgments (see Chapter 5), found the nominal group technique best and Delphi worst. Gough (1975) did a similar study asking for probability assessments and also favored the nominal group technique, but very weakly. Fischer (1982) did a study somewhat similar to Gough's and found virtually no difference among the groups.

Seaver (1978), using almanac questions as stimuli, compared averages of individual judgments (weighted and unweighted) with the outputs of Delphi, nominal group technique, free-form discussion, and two other group procedures. The quadratic scoring rule applied to the group outputs was the evaluative criterion. He found that, among the interacting groups, the type of interaction made very little difference to the results. But, more important, he also found that "simple procedures, such as combining individual probability assessments linearly with equal weights, produce group assessments that are as good as or better than those produced by more complicated procedures involving interaction or complex aggregation models. Interaction among the assessors produces only a feeling of satisfaction and not any over-all improvement in the quality of the assessed probabilities" (Seaver, 1978, p. 51). In fact, Seaver's results make a case against group interaction of any kind: "The result of interaction among assessors is quite clear . . . it produces more extreme and less well-calibrated assessments. If all of the members of the group agree . . . , the individual assessments tend to become more extreme. Apparently, subjects treat the information provided by other group members' assessments as somewhat independent of their own information, rather than redundant" (Seaver, 1978, p. 52).

To our minds, the implications are clear. By all means use groups if you can; the mathematical advantages are convincing, and you can, by choosing group members carefully, cover the fields of knowledge relevant to your topic. But don't bother to get the members together, unless group pressures or other social factors make it necessary. Instead, simply elicit the desired uncertainty measures from each member individually, using whatever methods of elicitation fit the problem best, transform the results into probabilities, and average them. The odds seem excellent that, if you do anything more complex, you will simply be wasting your effort.

The only context in which we have any reservations about this conclusion is that of very low probabilities. Here, interactions among kinds of information may be crucial to the formulation of models of the events of interest, and if so, there should be face-to-face discussion of those models. Moreover, for such extreme numbers, we would prefer averaging log odds to averaging probabilities.

5   Elementary inference: Bayesian statistics

5.1. Introduction[1]

Real-world probabilistic inference making is a widespread, mostly undocumented human activity, based primarily on narrative data in nonquantitative form. The development of a mature technology designed to perform it is a major task ahead.

But empirical scientists have faced a rather different kind of inferential task for a long time. Sometimes it is useful to study scientific questions by taking small samples from larger populations, under rules (collectively called *random sampling*) that justify the belief that the samples in some sense are representative of the populations. (Most common rule: every member of the target population is equally likely to be sampled.) The samples may be data generators, such as subjects for psychological experiments or plots of ground for agricultural ones, or data, such as police records.

The ideas of statistics can make few claims of relevance to inference as a general intellectual task, since they are almost always linked to very special procedures such as random sampling. But they are powerful, elegant, intellectually appealing, and very useful to empirical science. This chapter presents a smattering of them. There would be no need to include the topic in this book except that it introduces a few ideas that are useful in nonstatistical inferences as well.

Two schools of thought about statistical inference exist. Loosely, they can be called Bayesian and classical. This chapter takes the Bayesian position. For a thorough discussion of some of the issues involved, see Edwards, Lindman, and Savage (1963). The key difference between the schools lies in the personalistic view of probability presented in Chapter 4. If, as we asserted in that chapter, probabilities describe orderly opinions, it makes sense to ask how likely a hypothesis is in the light of data. The issue that divides Bayesian statisticians from classical ones is simply whether or not that question is meaningful.

---

[1] Large segments of this chapter were liberally adapted from Edwards, Lindman, and Savage (1963). Copyright © by the American Psychological Association. Reproduced by permission of the authors.

Bayes's theorem is an uncontroversial consequence of the definition of conditional probability and the fact that probabilities sum to 1. If probabilities describe orderly opinions, Bayes's theorem describes how such opinions should be revised in the light of new information. This chapter explores a few key ideas needed to carry out such revisions in the very special case of single-stage inference tasks.

We start by explaining Bayes's theorem. Next we explore some characteristics of single-stage inference itself and then look briefly at two special cases of the relation between statistical inference and decision making. We must warn statistically untrained readers that this chapter assumes a great deal, including probability distributions. Nevertheless, those unfamiliar with such ideas may find the chapter worth reading, since its examples are elementary.

5.2. Principles of Bayesian statistics

Bayes's theorem and the revision of opinion in the light of information

The mathematical definition of conditional probability of an event D given another event H is

$$P(D|H) = \frac{P(D \cap H)}{P(H)}, \tag{5.1}$$

unless $P(H) = 0$. The symbol $P(D \cap H)$ means the probability that both D and H will occur. The symbols D and H could stand for anything, but they have been chosen because they are the initial letters of datum and hypothesis.

Since, by definition, $P(H \cap D) = P(D)P(H|D)$, a little algebra applied to Equation 5.1 now leads to one form of Bayes's theorem,

$$P(H|D) = \frac{P(D|H)P(H)}{P(D)}, \tag{5.2}$$

provided that $P(D)$ is not 0.

In Equation 5.2, $P(H)$ is the prior probability of some hypothesis H. Though not written so, it is a conditional probability; all probabilities are really conditional. It is the probability of H conditional on all the information about H you had before learning D. Similarly, $P(H|D)$, the posterior probability of H, is the probability of H conditional on that same background knowledge together with D. Here $P(D|H)$ is formally the probability that the datum D would be observed if the hypothesis H were true. For an exhaustive set of mutually exclusive hypotheses H_i, the $P(D|H_i)$ represent the impact of the datum D on each of the hypotheses. Obtaining the values of $P(D|H)$ for each D and H is the key step in applying Bayes's theorem to any revision of opinion in the light of information. In statistical applications, $P(D|H)$ is typically obtained by computation from a so-called statistical model (like the assumption that a set of observations is normally distributed).

The probability $P(D)$ is usually of little direct interest. It is typically calculated, or eliminated, as follows. The hypothesis H is one of a list, or partition, of mutually exclusive and exhaustive hypotheses H_i. Since the definition of probability requires that $P(D \cap H_i) = P(D|H_i)P(H_i)$ and since

$$\sum_i P(D \cap H_i) = P(D), \tag{5.3}$$

Equation 5.3 implies that

$$P(D) = \sum_i P(D|H_i)P(H_i). \tag{5.4}$$

Equation 5.4 makes a subtle point. Like any other probability, $P(D)$ is conditional; it is, among other things, conditional on the set of hypotheses being considered and will change if they change.

The choice of the partition H is of practical importance but largely arbitrary. For example, tomorrow will be "fair" or "foul," but these two hypotheses can themselves be subdivided and resubdivided. Equation 5.4 is, of course, true for all partitions but is more useful for some than for others. In principle, a partition should always leave room for "some other" possibility. Since it may be difficult to obtain $P(D|H)$ for the hypothesis that "some other possibility" is the true one, one usually handles this catchall hypothesis in part by studying the situation conditionally on denial of the catchall and in part by informally appraising whether any of the explicit hypotheses fit the facts well enough to maintain this denial.

A particularly convenient version of Bayes's theorem for some of the applications to be discussed in this book is the odds–likelihood ratio form. For two hypotheses H_A and H_B and one datum D, Bayes's theorem can be written twice thus:

$$P(H_A|D) = \frac{P(D|H_A)P(H_A)}{P(D)}, \tag{5.5}$$

$$P(H_B|D) = \frac{P(D|H_B)P(H_B)}{P(D)}. \tag{5.6}$$

Dividing Equation 5.5 by 5.6, we obtain

$$\frac{P(H_A|D)}{P(H_B|D)} = \frac{P(D|H_A)P(H_A)}{P(D|H_B)P(H_B)} \tag{5.7}$$

or

$$\Omega_1 = L\Omega_0. \tag{5.8}$$

In Equation 5.8, Ω_0, the prior odds, is simply the ratio of the prior probability of H_A to that of H_B. The same ratio after observation of D is Ω_1; it is called the posterior odds. The ratio $L = P(D|H_A)/P(D|H_B)$ is called the likelihood ratio. The word *odds* here means exactly what it does at the race track, and the notion of likelihood ratio is just what it is in classical statistics. Equation 5.8 is as valid and appropriate a way of writing Bayes's theorem as is Equation 5.2 – and in some applications is considerably more convenient.

Bayes's theorem can be written in many ways. For the purposes of this chapter, we shall frequently be working with continuous rather than discrete observations, and often with continuous rather than discrete prior and posterior distributions. The continuous version of Equation 5.2 is

$$f(\lambda|x) = \frac{g(x|\lambda)f(\lambda)}{g(x)}, \tag{5.9}$$

where $f(\lambda|x)$ is the posterior probability distribution over the parameter λ, given the datum or data represented by x; $g(x|\lambda)$ is the probability distribution of x given λ, typically calculated from a public model of the data-generating process; $f(\lambda)$ is the prior probability distribution over λ; and, as in the discrete case, $g(x) = \int g(x|\lambda')f(\lambda')\,d\lambda'$ is essentially a normalizing function designed to make $f(\lambda|x)$ integrate to 1 over λ. This change of notation in no sense represents any change in thought, and every argument we present here about continuous distributions is equivalent to a comparable argument about discrete distributions.

Problem of prior probabilities

Since $P(D|H)$, the probability of the datum given the hypothesis, is often easy to calculate from a model of the data-generating process, and $P(H|D)$, the probability of the hypothesis given the datum, is usually just what the scientist wants, the reason classical statisticians do not base their procedures on Bayes's theorem lies in $P(H)$, the prior probability of the hypothesis. Since $P(H)$ is a personal probability, is it not likely to be both vague and variable, and subjective to boot, and therefore useless for public scientific purposes?

Yes, prior probabilities often are vague and variable, but they are not necessarily useless on that account (Borel, 1924a,b). The impact of actual vagueness and variability of prior probabilities differs greatly from one problem to another. They frequently have but negligible effect on the conclusions obtained from Bayes's theorem, although utterly unlimited vagueness and variability would have utterly unlimited effect. If observations are precise, in a certain sense, relative to the (continuous or dense) prior distribution on which they bear, then the form and properties of the prior distribution have negligible influence on the posterior distribution. From a practical point of view, then, the untrammeled subjectivity of opinion about a parameter ceases to apply as soon as many data become available. Generally, two people with widely divergent prior opinions but reasonably open minds will be forced into arbitrarily close agreement about future observations by a sufficient amount of data. An advanced mathematical expression of this phenomenon is in Blackwell and Dubins (1962).

Frequently, the data so completely control your posterior opinion that there is no practical need to attend to the details of your prior opinion. For example, headachy and hot, you are convinced that you have a fever but are not sure how high it is. You do not hold the interval 100.5–101°F even two times more probable than the interval 101–101.5°F on the basis of your malaise alone. But now you take your temperature with a thermometer that you strongly believe to be accurate and find yourself willing to give much more than 20 : 1 odds in favor of the half-degree centered at the thermometer reading.

Your prior opinion is rather irrelevant to this useful conclusion but of course not utterly irrelevant. For readings of 85 or 110°F, you would revise your statistical model according to which the thermometer is accurate and correctly used rather than proclaim a medical miracle. A reading of 104°F would be puzzling – too inconsistent with your prior opinion to seem reasonable and yet not obviously absurd. You might try again, perhaps with another thermometer.

Principle of stable estimation

It has long been known that, under suitable circumstances, your actual posterior distribution will be approximately what it would have been had your prior distribution been uniform, that is, described by a constant density. As the fever example suggests, prior distributions need not be, and never really are, completely uniform. To ignore the departures from uniformity, it suffices that your actual prior density change gently in the region favored by the data and not itself too strongly favor some other region.

The overall goal is valid justification for proceeding as though your prior distribution were uniform. Three assumptions implying this justification can be pointed out. First, some region B is highly favored by the data. Second, within B the prior density changes very little. Third, most of the posterior density is concentrated inside B. A more stringent but more easily verified assumption, that the prior density nowhere enormously exceeds its general value in B, may be substituted for the third assumption. (For technical details and formal proofs, see Edwards, Lindman, and Savage, 1963.)

Given the three assumptions, what follows? One way of looking at the implications is to observe that nowhere within B, which has high posterior probability, is the ratio of the approximate posterior density to the actual posterior density much different from 1 and that what happens outside B is not important for our purposes. Again, if the posterior expectation, or average, of some bounded function is of interest, the difference between the expectation under the actual posterior distribution and under the approximating distribution will be small relative to the absolute bound of the function. Finally, the actual posterior probability and the approximate probability of any set of parameter values are nearly equal. In short, the approximation is a good one in several important respects – given the three assumptions. Still, other respects must sometimes be invoked and these may require further assumptions (see, e.g., Lindley, 1961).

Even when assumption 2 is not applicable, a transformation of the parameters of the prior distribution sometimes makes it so. If, for example, your prior distribution assigns about as much probability to the region from 1 to 2 as to the region from 10 to 20, a logarithmic transformation of λ may well make assumption 2 applicable.

Numerically, what can the principle of stable estimation do in the fever–thermometer example? Figure 5.1 is a reasonably plausible numerical picture of the situation. Your prior distribution in your role as invalid has a little bump around 98.6°F, because on other occasions when you have felt out of sorts you have taken your temperature and found it depressingly normal. Still, you really think you have a fever, so most of your density is spread over the region 99.5–104.5°F. It gets rather low at the high end of that interval, since you doubt you could have a fever as high as 104°F without feeling even worse than you do.

The thermometer has a standard deviation of 0.05° and negligible systematic error; this is reasonable for a good clinical thermometer, the systematic error of which should be small compared with the errors of procedure and reading. For convenience and because it is plausible as an approximation, we assume also that the thermometer distributes its errors normally. The indicated reading then lies within a symmetric region 0.1° wide around the true temperature with probability a little less than .7. If the thermometer reading is 101.0°F, we might take the region B to extend from 100.8 to 101.2°F, 4 standard deviations on each side of the observation.

How good should the approximation be before you can feel comfortable about using it? That depends entirely on your purpose. There are purposes for which an approximation of a small probability that is within one order of magnitude of the actual probability is adequate. For others, an error of 1% would be painful. Fortunately, if the approximation is unsatisfactory, it is often possible to improve it as much as seems necessary at the price of collecting additional data, an expedient that often justifies its costs in other ways. In practice, the accuracy of the stable-estimation approximation will seldom be as carefully checked as in the fever example. As individual and collective experience builds up, many applications will properly be judged safe at a glance.

Far from always can your prior distibution be practically neglected. At

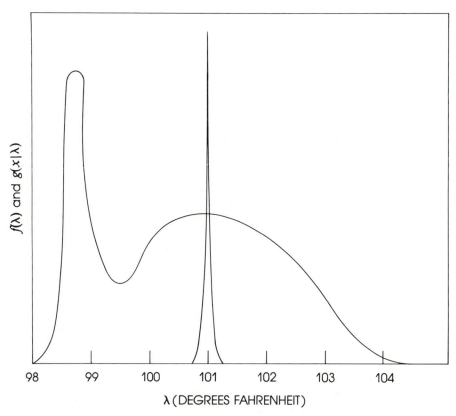

Figure 5.1. $f(\lambda)$ and $g(x|\lambda)$ for the fever–thermometer example. Note that the units on the *y* axis are different for the two functions. (*Source:* Edwards, Lindman, & Savage, 1963. Copyright © 1963 by the American Psychological Association. Reprinted by permission of the authors.)

least five situations in which detailed properties of the prior distribution are crucial occur to us:

1   If you assign exceedingly small prior probabilities to regions of λ for which $g(x|\lambda)$ is relatively large, you in effect express reluctance to believe in values of λ strongly pointed to by the data and thus violate assumption 3, perhaps irreparably. Rare events do occur but should not be permitted to confound us utterly. Also, apparatus and plans can break down and produce data that "prove" preposterous things. Morals conflict in the fable of the Providence man who on a cloudy summer day walked to the post office to return his absurdly low-reading new barometer to Abercrombie and Fitch. His house was flattened by a hurricane in his absence.

2   If you have strong prior reason to believe that λ lies in a region for which $g(x|\lambda)$ is very small, you may be unwilling to be persuaded by the evidence to the contrary and so again may violate assumption 3.

3   If your prior opinion is relatively diffuse, but so are your data, assumption 1 is seriously violated.

4   If observations are expensive and you have a decision to make, it may not pay to collect enough information for the principle of stable estimation to apply.

5   It is sometimes necessary to make decisions about sizable research commitments such as sample size or experimental design while your knowledge is still incomplete. In this case, an extreme instance of the former one, the role of prior opinion is particularly conspicuous.

Whenever you cannot neglect the details of your prior distribution, you have, in effect, no choice but to determine the relevant aspects of it as best you can and use them. Almost always, you will find your prior opinions quite vague, and you may be distressed because your scientific inference or decision has such a labile basis. Perhaps this distress, more than anything else, has discouraged statisticians from using Bayesian ideas all along. To paraphrase de Finetti (1959, p. 19), people noticing difficulties in applying Bayes's theorem remarked, "We see that it is not secure to build on sand. Take away the sand; we shall build on the void." If it were meaningful to ignore prior opinion entirely, it might sometimes be wise to do so, but reflection shows that any policy that pretends to ignore prior opinion is acceptable only insofar as it is actually justified by prior opinion. Some policies recommended under the motif of neutrality, or on the basis of using only the facts, may flagrantly violate even very confused prior opinions and so be unacceptable. The method of stable estimation might casually be described as a procedure for ignoring prior opinion, since its approximate results are acceptable for a wide range of prior opinions. Actually, far from ignoring prior opinion, stable estimation exploits certain well-defined features of prior opinion and is acceptable only insofar as those features are really present.

Likelihood principle

A natural question about Bayes's theorem leads to an important conclusion, the likelihood principle, which was first discovered by classical statisticians (Barnard, 1947; Fisher, 1956).

Two possible experimental outcomes D and D' – not necessarily of the same experiment – can have the same (potential) bearing on your opinion about a partition of events H_i, that is, $P(H_i|D)$ can equal $P(H_i|D')$ for each i. Just when are D and D' thus evidentially equivalent, or of the same import? Analytically, when is

$$P(H_i|D) = \frac{P(D|H_i)P(H_i)}{P(D)}$$
$$= \frac{P(D'|H_i)P(H_i)}{P(D')} = P(H_i|D') \tag{5.10}$$

for each *i*?

Aside from certain academic possibilities [e.g., some of the $P(H_i)$ are 0], Equation 5.10 plainly means that, for some positive constant k and for all i,

$$P(D'|H_i) = kP(D|H_i). \tag{5.11}$$

But Equation 5.11 implies Equation 5.10, from which it was derived, no matter what the initial probabilities $P(H_i)$ are, as is easily seen:

$$
\begin{aligned}
P(D') &= \sum_i P(D'|H_i)P(H_i) \\
&= k \sum_i P(D|H_i)P(H_i) \\
&= kP(D).
\end{aligned}
\tag{5.12}
$$

This conclusion is the likelihood principle: two (potential) data D and D' are of the same import if Equation 5.11 obtains.

Since for the purpose of drawing inferences, $P(D|H_i)$ is, according to the likelihood principle, equivalent to any other sequence obtained from it by multiplication by a positive constant, a name for this class of equivalent sequences is useful, and there is precedent for calling it the likelihood (of the datum D as a function of H_i). The likelihood principle can now be expressed thus: D and D' have the same import if $P(D|H_i)$ and $P(D'|H_i)$ belong to the same likelihood – more idiomatically, if D and D' have the same likelihood.

If, for instance, the partition is twofold, the likelihood to which the pair $[P(D|H_0), P(D|H_1)]$ belongs is plainly the set of pairs of numbers $[a, b]$ such that the fraction a/b is the likelihood ratio $P(D|H_0)/P(D|H_1)$. The use of likelihood ratios in place of pairs of conditional probabilities is thus an application of the likelihood principle.

Of course, the likelihood principle applies to a parameter λ as well as to a partition H_i. The likelihood of x, or the likelihood to which $g(x|\lambda)$ belongs, is the class of all those functions of λ that are proportional to the function $g(x|\lambda)$. Also, conditional densities can replace conditional probabilities in the definition of likelihood ratios.

There is one implication of the likelihood principle that all statisticians seem to accept. It is not appropriate in this chapter to pursue this implication, which might be called the principle of sufficient statistics, very far. One application of sufficient statistics so familiar as almost to escape notice will, however, help clarify the meaning of the likelihood principle. Suppose a sequence of 100 Bernoulli trials is undertaken and 80 failures are recorded. What is the datum, and what is its probability for a given value of the Bernoulli parameter p? We are all perhaps overtrained to reply that the datum is 20 successes out of 100, and its probability, given p, is $\binom{100}{20} p^{20}(1 - p)^{80}$. Yet it seems more correct to say that the datum is this particular sequence of successes and failures, and its probability, given p, is $p^{20}(1 - p)^{80}$. The conventional reply is often more convenient, because it would be costly to transmit the entire sequence of observations. It is permissible, because the two functions $\binom{100}{20} p^{20}(1 - p)^{80}$ and $p^{20}(1 - p)^{80}$ belong to the same likelihood; they differ only by the constant factor $\binom{100}{20}$. The legitimacy of condensing the datum is often expressed by saying that the number of successes in a given number of Bernoulli trials is a sufficient statistic for the sequence of trials. Insofar as the sequence of trials is not altogether accepted as Bernoullian – and it never is – the condensation is not legitimate. The practical experimenter always has some incentive to look over the sequence of data with a view to discovering periodicities, trends, or other departures from Bernoullian expectation. Anyone to whom the sequence is not available, such as the reader of a condensed report or the experimentalist who depends on automatic counters, will have some doubt about the interpretation of the ostensibly sufficient statistic.

Moving on to another application of the likelihood principle, imagine a different Bernoullian experiment in which you continue the trials until 20 successes have accumulated and the 20th success happens to be the 100th trial. It would be conventional and justifiable to report only this fact, ignoring other details of the sequence of trials. The probability that the 20th success will be the 200th trial is, given p, easily seen to be $\binom{99}{19} p^{20}(1 - p)^{80}$. This is exactly one-fifth of the probability of 20 successes in 100 trials, so according to the likelihood principle, the two data have the same import. This conclusion is a trifle more immediate if the data are not condensed, for a specific sequence of 100 trials of which the last is the 20th success has the probability $p^{20}(1 - p)^{80}$ in both experiments. Those who do not accept the likelihood principle believe that the probabilities of sequences that might have occurred, but did not, somehow affect the import of the sequence that did occur.

In general, suppose you collect data of any kind whatsoever – not necessarily Bernoullian, or identically distributed, or independent of one another given the parameter – stopping only when the data thus far collected satisfy some criterion of a sort that is sure to be satisfied sooner or later. Then the import of the sequence of n data actually observed will be exactly as it would be had you planned to take exactly n observations in the first place. It is not even necessary that you stop according to a plan. You may stop when tired, when interrupted by the telephone, when you run out of money, when you have the casual impression that you have enough data to prove your point, and so on. The one proviso is that the moment at which your observation is interrupted must not in itself add anything to the information in the data already at hand. A man who wanted to count lions watering at a certain pool was chased away by lions before he actually saw any of them watering there; in trying to conclude how many times per day lions did water at the pool he would have to remember why his observation was interrupted when it was. We would not have given a facetious example had we been able to think of a serious one. A more technical discussion of the irrelevance of stopping rules to statistical analysis can be found in Raiffa and Schlaifer (1961, pp. 36–42).

This irrelevance of stopping rules to statistical inference restores a simplicity and freedom to experimental design that were lost by classical emphasis on significance level (in the sense of Neyman and Pearson) and on other concepts that are affected by stopping rules. Many experimenters would like to feel free to collect data until they have either conclusively proved their point, conclusively disproved it, or run out of time, money, or patience. The likelihood principle justifies this procedure, as long as Bayesian inferential procedures are used to interpret the result.

The irrelevance of stopping rules is one respect in which Bayesian procedures are more objective than classical ones. Classical procedures insist that the intentions of the experimenter be crucial to the interpretation of data, that 20 successes in 100 observations mean something quite different if the experimenter intended the 20 successes than if he or she intended the 100 observations. According to the likelihood principle, data analysis stands on its own feet. The intentions of the experimenter are irrelevant to the interpretation of the data once collected, though of course they are crucial to the design of experiments.

We must mention an important qualification: the likelihood principle does not apply to the kinds of hierarchically structured inferences that are the topic of Chapter 6. Its loss has major undesirable consequences; we spell them out in that chapter.

5.3. A smattering of Bayesian distribution theory

The mathematical equipment required to turn statistical principles into practical procedures, for Bayesian as well as for traditional statistics, is distribution theory, that is, the theory of specific families of probability distributions. Bayesian distribution theory, concerned with the interrelation among the three main distributions of Bayes's theorem, is in some respects more complicated than classical distribution theory. But the familiar properties of distributions in traditional statistics, and in the theory of probability in general, remain unchanged. To a professional statistician, the additional complication requires little more than a possible shift to a more complicated notation. Chapters 5 through 13 of Raiffa and Schlaifer's (1961) book contain an extensive discussion of distribution theory in Bayesian statistics. As usual, a consumer need not understand in detail the theory on which the methods are based; the manipulative mathematics have already been done.

Conjugate distributions

Suppose you take your temperature at a moment when your prior probability density $f(\lambda)$ is not diffuse with respect to $g(x|\lambda)$, so that the principle of stable estimation does not apply. The determination and application of $f(\lambda|x)$ may then require laborious numerical integrations of arbitrary functions. One way to avoid such labor when appropriate conditions are met is to use conjugate distributions. When a family of prior distributions is so related to all the conditional distributions that can arise in an experiment that the posterior distribution is necessarily in the same family as the prior distributions, the family of prior distributions is said to be conjugate to the experiment. By no means do all experiments have nontrivial conjugate families, but a few ubiquitous kinds do. For example, beta priors over the Bernoulli parameter are conjugate to observations of a Bernoulli process, and normal priors over the mean are conjugate to observations of a normal process with known variance. Several other conjugate pairs are discussed by Raiffa and Schlaifer (1961).

Even when there is a conjugate family of prior distributions, your own prior distribution could fail to be in or even near that family. The distributions of such a family are, however, often versatile enough to accommodate your actual prior opinion, especially when it is a bit hazy. Furthermore, if stable estimation is not quite justifiable, a conjugate prior that approximates your true prior even roughly may be expected to combine with $g(x|\lambda)$ to produce a rather accurate posterior distribution.

If the fit of members of the conjugate family to your true opinion is unsatisfactory, realism may leave no alternative to something as tedious as approximating the continuous distribution by a discrete one with many steps and applying Bayesian logic by brute force. Respect for your real opinion as opposed to some handy stereotype is essential. That is why our discussion of stable estimation specified criteria for deciding when the details of a prior opinion really are negligible.

The problems in which such distribution-theoretic elegance is most useful are called parameter-estimation problems. A parameter is simply a number that specifies a probability distribution. The mean μ and variance σ^2 of a normal distribution are parameters. The bias parameter p of a Bernoulli process is another example. (Parameters are not to be confused with *statistics* like the calculated mean and variance of a sample of measurements. Statistics can be used to *estimate* parameters but are not parameters themselves.)

If one knows the parameters of a distribution, one knows the whole distribution; that is, one could plot for each point of a discrete variable what its probability would be, and one could plot for each point of a continuous variable what its probability density would be.

Often, parameters are uncertain variables. How a pollution cleanup device will function on the average may be unknown, although the distribution of the day-to-day performance is known to be log normal. The average future cost of a stock may be very uncertain, although some experts may assert that the stock price varies according to a normal distribution. Similarly, data may suggest that the occurrence of oil blowouts from offshore oil production platforms follows a Poisson distribution, but the mean of that distribution may be unknown.

An example: normal measurement with variance known

To give a minimal illustration of Bayesian distribution theory, and especially of conjugate families, we discuss briefly, and without the straightforward algebraic details, the normally distributed measurement of known variance. The Bayesian treatment of this problem has much in common with its classical counterpart. As is well known, it is a good approximation to many other problems in statistics.

Three functions enter into the problem of known variance: $f(\mu)$, $g(x|\mu)$, and $f(\mu|x)$. The reciprocal of the variance appears so often in Bayesian calculations that it is convenient to denote $1/\sigma^2$ by h and call h the precision of the measurement. We are therefore dealing with a normal measurement with an unknown mean but known precision h. Suppose your prior distribution is also normal. It has a mean μ_0 and a precision h_0, both known by introspection. There is no necessary relationship between h_0 and h, the precision of the measurement, but in typical worthwhile applications h is substantially greater than h_0. After an observation has been made, you will have a normally distributed posterior opinion, now with mean μ_1 and precision h_1:

$$\mu_1 = \frac{\mu_0 h_0 + xh}{h_0 + h} \tag{5.13}$$

and

$$h_1 = h_0 + h. \tag{5.14}$$

The posterior mean is an average of the prior mean and the observed mean weighted by the precisions. The precision of the posterior mean is the sum of the prior and data precisions. The posterior distribution in this case is the same as would result from the principle of stable estimation if in addition to the datum x, with its precision h, there had been an additional measurement of value μ_0 and precision h_0.

If the prior precision h_0 is very small relative to h, the posterior mean will probably, and the precision will certainly, be nearly equal to the data mean and precision; that is an explicit illustration of the principle of stable estimation. Whether or not that principle applies, the posterior precision will always be at least the larger of the other two precisions; therefore, observation cannot but sharpen opinion here. This conclusion is somewhat special to the example; in general, an observation will occasionally increase rather than dispel doubt.

In applying these formulas to inference based on a large number n of normally distributed observations with average $\bar{x}$ and sample variance s^2, $\bar{x}$ is x and h is n/s^2. Figure 5.2 illustrates both the extent to which the prior distribution can be irrelevant and the rapid narrowing of the posterior distribution as the result of a few normal observations. The top section of the figure shows two prior distributions, one with mean -9 and standard deviation 6 and the other with mean 3 and standard deviation 2. The other four sections show posterior distributions obtained by applying Bayes's theorem to these two priors after samples of size n are taken from a distribution with mean 0 and standard deviation 2. The samples are artificially selected to have exactly the mean 0. After 9 observations, and still more after 16, these markedly different prior distributions have led to almost indistinguishable posterior distributions.

Of course, the prior distribution is never irrelevant if the true parameter happens to fall in a region to which the prior distribution assigns virtually zero probability. A prior distribution that has a region of zero probability is therefore undesirable unless you consider it impossible that the true parameter might fall in that region. Moral: keep the mind open, or at least ajar.

Figure 5.2 shows the typical narrowing of the posterior distribution with successive observations. After 4 observations, the standard deviation of your posterior distribution is less than one-half the standard deviation of a single observation; after 16, less than one-fourth; and so on.

An example: estimating the frequency of oil blowouts

In the following example of Bayesian inference in action, we consider the prediction of a rare event: a blowout on an offshore oil production platform. Specifically, a risk analyst may be concerned with determining the probabilities that zero, one, two, or more blowouts could occur during 1 year of oil production in the North Sea oil fields (Central Unit on Environmental Pollution, 1976a; Council for Environmental Quality, 1974).

Experts generally agree that the probability distribution over the number of oil blowouts depends on the oil volume produced – the more oil produced, the higher is the probability of a blowout in a given time unit. Furthermore, the probability distribution over the number of oil blowouts for a given volume t of oil produced is assumed to be a Poisson distribution,

$$P(n|\lambda, t) = \frac{e^{-\lambda t}(\lambda t)^n}{n!}, \qquad (5.15)$$

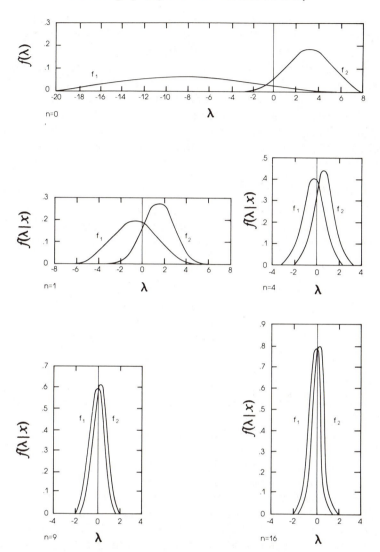

Figure 5.2. Posterior distributions obtained from two normal priors after n normally distributed observations. (*Source:* Edwards, Lindman, & Savage, 1963. Copyright 1963 © by the American Psychological Association. Reprinted by permission of the authors.)

where n is the number of blowouts, λ the rate of blowouts per volume of oil produced (e.g., one blowout for each 100 million tons of oil), and t the volume of oil contemplated in the study (e.g., in the North Sea instance, 200 million tons of oil per year). The expression λt is therefore the expected number of blowouts for the contemplated volume t; in the above example $\lambda t = 2$.

Early in the course of North Sea oil development, a risk analyst will be rather uncertain about λ. Past observations may be helpful, but surely the new case occurs in a different environment and adjustments must be made. In addition, empirical accident rates are based on rather scanty data. Between 1964 and 1975 only 10 major blowouts occurred in the United States, and during this time the oil production volume in the observation area was 518 million tons (U.S. Geological Survey, 1976).

Conjugate distributions offer some help for modeling the uncertainties, both before and after data are generated by experience with the North Sea development. First, a prior gamma distribution is constructed over λ:

$$f(\lambda \mid N, T) = e^{-\lambda T}(\lambda T)^{N-1}T/(N-1)!, \tag{5.16}$$

where N and T are parameters that characterize the uncertainty over λ. Next, we exploit the fact that this gamma prior and the Poisson conditional (Equation 5.15) are conjugate distributions that together produce a gamma posterior:

$$f(\lambda \mid N, T, n, t) = e^{-\lambda(T+t)}[\lambda(T+t)]^{N+n-1}(T+t)/(N+n-1), \tag{5.17}$$

where n is the number of actually observed spills in a time period with oil production volume t. Thus, the gamma prior with parameters N and T becomes a gamma posterior with parameters $T + t$ and $N + n$.

Predictive distributions

Conjugate distributions are only one element in the bag of tricks of Bayesian statistics. Another useful tool is predictive distributions.

To illustrate this concept, Figure 5.3 shows schematically the relations between prior, conditional, and posterior distributions in our oil blowout example. For each parameter λ, there will exist a Poisson distribution over the possible numbers of blowouts. The shape of that conditional distribution will vary with λ, as can be seen by the two examples for $\lambda_1 = 10^{-8}$ and $\lambda_2 = 0.5 \times 10^{-8}$ (assuming again an oil production volume of 200 million, so that $\lambda_1 t = 2$ and $\lambda_2 t = 1$). The figure also illustrates how the prior is transformed into a posterior after the observation of exactly one accident during the production of 200 million tons.

Clearly, even after one observation, much uncertainty remains about λ, and it would be imprudent to make predictions about future accidents based on a fixed value or estimate of it. Instead, the best Bayesian prediction of the distribution of n should be a weighted average of the conditional distribution $P(n \mid \lambda_1)$, weighted by the posterior probability distribution of λ.

Fortunately, for some classes of distributions, predictive distributions have a simple parametric expression. In the above example, the predictive distribution $P(n)$ is, in fact, a negative binomial distribution (see Raiffa and Schlaifer, 1961). Other classes of predictive distribution are discussed in Raiffa and Schlaifer (1961).

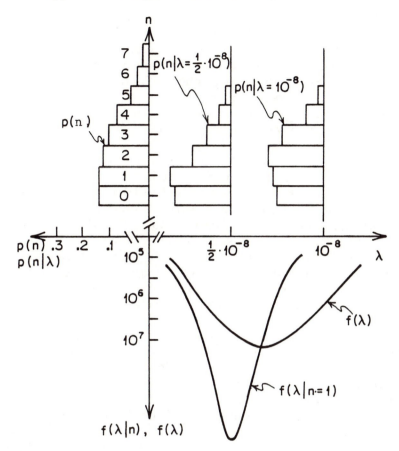

Figure 5.3. Illustration of prior $f(\lambda)$, conditional $P(n|\lambda)$, and predictive $P(n)$.

5.4. Hypothesis testing and related decisions

Simple dichotomy

The topic of hypothesis testing plays a remarkably dominant role in inferential statistics. We speculate that the reason for this dominance lies in the urge, natural to scientists of all kinds, to translate thought, such as statistical inference, into action. Edwards et al. (1963) explore in some detail some of the meanings hypothesis testing has in statistical theory and practice. For the purposes of this chapter, we have chosen the simplest interpretation of the idea. We confine our attention strictly to cases in which two hypotheses A and $\overline{A}$ exist and are considered to be mutually exclusive and exhaustive. Moreover, two courses of action C and $\overline{C}$ are available. Action C is assumed to be clearly preferable if A is correct, and $\overline{C}$ is assumed to be clearly preferable if $\overline{A}$ is correct. Our problem is simply to choose between C and $\overline{C}$ in the face of uncertainty about A and $\overline{A}$.

The problem has two parts. One is to ascertain $P(A)$ and $P(\overline{A}) = 1 - P(A)$. This is a judgmental problem if no data are available, and an inference problem in the presence of data. The other half of the problem is to evaluate the consequences of successes and errors.

Our discussion centers on a strongly intuitive property of all simple dichotomies. If you know that A obtains, you will choose C, and if you know that $\overline{A}$ obtains, you will choose $\overline{C}$. If you are almost certain that A obtains, you will probably also choose C. Remember that you must choose either C or $\overline{C}$. If, perhaps as a result of evidence against it, you become more and more doubtful that A obtains, some point will be reached at which you switch from C to $\overline{C}$. In other words, a critical value of $P(A)$ must exist. If $P(A)$ is above that critical value, you will choose C; if $P(A)$ is below it, you will choose $\overline{C}$. The focus of analysis should therefore be on finding that critical value and discovering on which side of it your $P(A)$ falls. The critical value should, of course, depend on the costs and/or payoffs for the four combinations of action and hypothesis. Since the focus of this chapter is inference rather than decision, we shall ignore the elaborate technical issues that surround those costs and/or payoffs.

From a Bayesian standpoint, part of what "testing" suggests is finding the posterior probability $P(A|D)$ of the hypothesis A in the light of the datum D or, equivalently, finding the posterior odds $\Omega(A|D)$. Equation 5.8 tells us that, in order to find that posterior odds, one should multiply the prior odds by the likelihood ratio $L(A; D)$.

It is useful, at least for exposition, to consider problems in which $L(A; D)$ is entirely public. For example, someone whose word you and we trust might tell us that a die he hands us produces 6s either (A) with frequency 1/6 or ($\overline{A}$) with frequency 1/5. Your initial opinion $\Omega(A)$ might differ radically from ours. But, for you and for us, the likelihood ratio in favor of A on the basis of a 6 is $(1/6)/(1/5)$, or 5/6, and the likelihood ratio in favor of A on the basis of a non-6 is $(5/6)/(4/5)$, or 25/24. Thus, if a 6 appears when the die is rolled, everyone's confidence in A will be diminished slightly; specifically, odds in favor of A will be diminished by 5/6. Similarly, a non-6 will augment $\Omega(A)$ by the factor 25/24.

If such a die could be rolled only once, the resulting evidence $L(A; D)$ would be negligible for almost any purpose; if it could be rolled many times, the evidence would ultimately become definitive. As is implicit in the concept of the not necessarily fair die, if D_1, D_2, D_3, ... are the outcomes of successive rolls, the same function $L(A; D)$ applies to each. Therefore, Equation 5.8 can be applied repeatedly thus:

$$\Omega(A|D_1) = L(A; D_1)\Omega(A),$$
$$\Omega(A|D_2, D_1) = L(A; D_2)\Omega(A|D_1)$$
$$= L(A; D_2)L(A; D_1)\Omega(A), \tag{5.18}$$

$$\Omega(A \,|\, D_n, \ldots, D_1) = L(A; D_n)\Omega(A \,|\, D_{n-1}, D_{n-2}, \ldots, D_1)$$
$$= L(A; D_n)L(A; D_{n-1}) \cdots L(A; D_1)\Omega(A)$$
$$= \prod_{i=1}^{n} L(A; D_i)\Omega(A).$$

This multiplicative composition of likelihood ratios exemplifies an important general principle about observations that are independent given the hypotheses.

For the specific example of the die, if x 6s and y non-6s occur (where of course $x + y = n$), then

$$\Omega(A \,|\, D_n, \ldots, D_1) = \left(\frac{5}{6}\right)^x \left(\frac{25}{24}\right)^y \Omega(A). \tag{5.19}$$

For large n, if A obtains, it is highly probable at the outset that x/n will fall close to $1/6$. Similarly, if A does not obtain, x/n will probably fall close to $1/5$. Thus, if A obtains, the overall likelihood $(5/6)^x(25/24)^y$ will probably be very roughly

$$\left(\frac{5}{6}\right)^{n/6} \left(\frac{25}{24}\right)^{5n/6} = \left[\left(\frac{5}{6}\right)^{1/6} \left(\frac{25}{24}\right)^{5/6}\right]^n$$
$$= (1.00364)^n \tag{5.20}$$
$$= 10^{0.00158n}.$$

By the time n is 1,269, everyone's odds in favor of A will probably be augmented about a hundredfold, if A is in fact true. One who was initially very skeptical of A, say with $\Omega(A)$ about a thousandth, will still be rather skeptical. But only an extreme skeptic will fail to be strongly convinced when n is 6,955 and the overall likelihood ratio in favor of A is about 10 billion.

The arithmetic for $\overline{A}$ is

$$\left[\left(\frac{5}{6}\right)^{1/5} \left(\frac{25}{24}\right)^{4/5}\right]^n = (0.9962)^n = 10^{-0.00165n}. \tag{5.21}$$

So the rate at which evidence accumulates against A, and for $\overline{A}$, when $\overline{A}$ is true is in this case a trifle more than the rate at which it accumulates for A when A is true.

At a given moment, let us suppose, you have to guess whether A or $\overline{A}$ obtains, and you will receive $\$I$ if you guess correctly that A obtains, $\$J$ if you guess correctly that $\overline{A}$ obtains, and nothing otherwise. (No real generality is lost in not assigning four arbitrarily chosen payoffs to the four possible combinations of guess and fact.) The EV of guessing A is $\$I\,P(A)$ and that of guessing $\overline{A}$ is $\$J\,P(\overline{A})$. You will therefore prefer to guess A if and only if $\$I\,P(A)$ exceeds $\$J\,P(\overline{A})$; that is, only if $P(A)$ exceeds $J/(I + J)$. (A more rigorous treatment would replace dollars with utilities.)

Similarly, if you need not make your guess until after you have examined a datum D, you will prefer to guess A if and only if $\Omega(A \,|\, D)$ exceeds J/I.

Putting this together with Equation 5.8, you will prefer to guess *A* if and only if

$$L(A; D) > \frac{J}{I\Omega(A)} = L^*, \tag{5.22}$$

where your critical likelihood ratio L^* is defined by the context.

The importance of Equation 5.22 is that the critical likelihood ratio depends only on the prior odds for *A*, $\Omega(A)$ and on the ratio J/I, which is simply the ratio of the costs of the two possible errors. For any given problem, the prior odds can be taken as a constant. Since the likelihood ratio times the prior odds is the posterior odds, the implication of the argument is that the cutoff in posterior odds (or, equivalently, posterior probabilities) is fixed and depends only on that same ratio J/I. This is the proof of the intuition with which this discussion of simple dichotomy started.

Since prior odds are a constant for any given problem, corresponding to any critical posterior odds is a critical likelihood ratio. Formulations of this fundamental property of simple dichotomy in terms of cutoff odds, cutoff probabilities, or cutoff likelihood ratios are equivalent mathematically but have quite different intuitive meanings. We consider the implications of a cutoff on posterior odds or posterior probabilities to be much clearer than those associated with a cutoff likelihood ratio. Our reason is the intuition with which this discussion of simple dichotomy started: which action you take should depend on how confident you are of the truth of the hypothesis to which that action is appropriate.

Signal detectability theory

One application of the theory of simple dichotomy we have just presented is the detection of signals in noise. The two hypotheses are that a signal is present (*S*) or that it is not (*N*). The actual observations are usually assumed to be generated by processes describable by probability distributions, the means and variances of which depend on whether *S* or *N* obtained (see Tanner and Swets, 1954).

When Van Meter and Middleton (1954) developed the theory of signal detection from the theory of simple dichotomy, they found it convenient to write about *hits,* correct statements that the signal *S* was present, and *false alarms,* or statements that a signal was present when it was not. The latter is one type of error; the former is the denial of the other type of error, and so its probability is simply 1 minus the probability of that error. A plot of the probability of hits against the probability of false alarms is called a receiver operating characteristic (ROC) curve. Figure 5.4 is an example. Here the assumption was made that both signal and noise states generate normal distributions of observations, which differ only in means. The quality of performance is measured by d', the difference between the means, divided by the standard deviation.

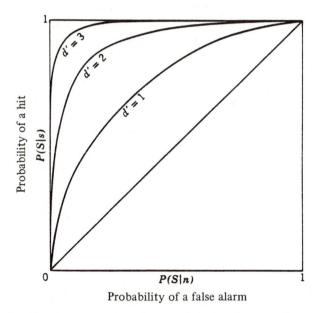

Probability of a false alarm

Figure 5.4. Receiver operating characteristic for three receivers. (*Source:* Green & Swets, 1966. Copyright © John Wiley & Sons, 1966.)

The first thing to notice about Figure 5.4 is that one could attain any point along the 45° diagonal by flipping an appropriately biased coin. Consequently, any real receiver should be able to attain point to the northwest of that line.

Any actual receiver can attain a probability of false alarms of 0 only by denying that signals ever occur, in which case the probability of a hit is also 0. Similarly, the probability of a hit can be made 1 only if a signal is always said to be present, in which case the probability of a false alarm is also 1. Thus, real receivers must be capable of producing the points (0, 0) and (1, 1).

But you would never use a receiver in such a way as to produce either extreme value. Instead, you would tune it so that above some threshold it would in effect say *"S"* and below that threshold it would say *"N."* Depending on the desired trade-off between hits and false alarms, any of a theoretically infinite set of points could be generated. ROC curves are frequently used to describe both mechanical and human capabilities for detecting signals in noise. Tracing them out is empirically tedious, because points must be estimated at various values of the cutoff. Figure 5.4 contains three ROC curves. The one farther to the northwest is clearly preferable to the ones closer to the diagonal, since for any hit rate it gives fewer false alarms, or for any false alarm rate it gives more hits.

The theory of simple dichotomy makes one more very important contribution to Figure 5.4. Borrowing a device from economics, one could conceive of indifference curves in that figure; one would be indifferent between the various combinations of hit rate and false-alarm rate that lay on any one such curve. We know, either from economics or from common sense, that such curves cannot cross one another. Do we know more? Yes. Equation 5.22 tells us that they should be parallel straight lines with slope $J/I\Omega(A)$. To determine how to tune the receiver, all one need do is find the point on the ROC curve tangent to the most northwesterly of the attainable indifference curves and tune the receiver to produce the combination of hit and false-alarm rates specified at that point. Savage (1962, p. 65) comments on this property of simple dichotomy in the statistical context: "The subjectivist's position is more objective than the objectivist's, for the subjectivist finds the range of coherent or reasonable preference patterns much narrower than the objectivist thought it to be. How confusing and dangerous big words are!"

Null hypothesis testing

Next we turn to one other application, this one statistical, of the theory of simple dichotomy. We examine situations in which a very sharp, or null, hypothesis is compared with a rather flat, or diffuse, alternative hypothesis. This short section indicates general strategies of such comparisons. None of the computations or conclusions depends on assumptions about the special initial credibility of the null hypothesis, but a Bayesian will find such computations uninteresting unless a nonnegligible amount of prior probability is concentrated very near the null hypothesis value.

For the continuous cases to be considered in following sections, the hypothesis A is that some parameter λ is in a set that might as well also be called A. For one-dimensional cases in which the hypothesis A is that λ is almost surely negligibly far from some specified value λ_0, the odds in favor of A given the datum D, as in Equation 5.8, are

$$
\begin{aligned}
\Omega(A\,|\,D) &= \frac{P(A\,|\,D)}{P(\overline{A}\,|\,D)}\,\Omega(A) \\
&= \frac{g(D\,|\,\lambda_0)}{\int g(D\,|\,\lambda)f(\lambda\,|\,\overline{A})\,d\lambda}\,\Omega(A) \\
&= L(A;\,D)\Omega(A)
\end{aligned}
\tag{5.23}
$$

Natural generalizations apply to multidimensional cases. The numerator $g(D\,|\,\lambda_0)$ is, in usual applications, public. But the denominator, the probability of D under the alternative hypothesis, depends on the usually far from public prior density under the alternative hypothesis.

Why would the model expressed by Equation 5.23 ever be of interest to anyone? Taken quite literally, the only prior distribution (in the one-dimensional case to which this discussion will be confined) that would justify such a model would be one with a sharp spike of probability (*not* probability density) at exactly λ_0. Though scenarios justifying such a model can be constructed, they are remarkably rare, and we have never come across one in our own research.

The case for such a model as an approximation is much better. Often one has good reason to think that λ may have some specific value λ_0; perhaps that value is optimal or mandated by law or predicted by some physical model in which one has confidence. In such cases, the use of λ_0 as a specific hypothesis, and its negation as an alternative, can make sense.

The cases that lead to classical null hypothesis tests of this kind are frequently unreasonable. The most common of them is the null hypothesis that two different treatments made no difference to λ; that is the application from which the phrase *null hypothesis* originally came. Often that hypothesis is tested in experimental situations in which the experimenter has every reason to believe and hope that one of the treatments will produce an effect quite different from that produced by the other. For example, if two different kinds of fertilizer are applied to otherwise equivalent plots of ground, there should in general be a difference in the amount of corn produced by each plot; if not, the researchers didn't do their biochemistry very well. Such an experiment does *not* provide a Bayesian with a good reason to do the Bayesian version of a classical null hypothesis test. A far more natural Bayesian analysis would try to ascertain how certain we would be of the proposition that the superior fertilizer in this particular experiment would, if widely used, generally produce more corn than the inferior fertilizer.

So Bayesian null hypothesis testing is appropriate only if you happen to have a prior distribution that is generally gentle but has a sharp spike of probability quite close to λ. We shall consider a crude example, adapted from Edwards et al. (1963).

You are, we suppose, an organic chemist, eager to synthesize statistic acid and with a bright and shining new idea about how to do so. You have gone through some complex chemical procedures, and now you have a beaker full of foul-smelling glop. Is it statistic acid? Many years ago, one of Priestley's students, with more passion for precision than imagination, measured the melting point of statistic acid so precisely that you are now willing to take as an article of faith that it is exactly 150°C. By one of the happy accidents that occur only in statistical examples, you have available to you a thermometer that, you know from prior use, produces normally distributed errors with a standard deviation of 1° and no bias. Having failed Experimental Design I in graduate school, you decide to find out whether this is statistic acid by measuring its melting point, once.

From a classical statistical inference point of view, this scenario would justify a classical two-tailed critical ratio test with a standard deviation of 1°. For the moment, suppose the null hypothesis that this is statistic acid is true. Then the probability of a reading of 151.96°C or greater is .025, and the probability of a reading of 152.58°C or greater is .005. (The numbers 1.96 and 2.58 are the .05 and .01 levels of the normal curve for a classical two-tailed test – but here we are looking at only one tail.) Consequently, the probability of a reading between these two values, if this is statistic acid, is .02.

Suppose, to consider a question that is not in the spirit of classical statistical inference, that this is not statistic acid. What then is the probability of a reading in this region? Let us suppose that the melting points of all the other foul-smelling glops you might have gotten instead fall diffusely (and, for the example, *diffusely* means uniformly) from 130 to 170°C, a 40° span. The probability, if your glop is not statistic acid, is then $(152.58 - 151.96)/40 = .62/40 = .0155$.

Startling, isn't it? The probability of a reading in that region is .02 if the glop is statistic acid and only .0155 if it is not. Yet a properly applied classical .05 level critical ratio test would lead you to reject the null hypothesis that this is statistic acid – on the basis of evidence in its favor.

The phenomenon is quite general. Classical procedures are violently biased against the null hypothesis they test – so much so that they easily and often reject them on the basis of evidence favoring them.

The part of the argument that is new to classically trained intuitions is taking seriously the probability of the evidence on the basis of the alternative hypothesis. Actually, the 40° width for the alternative hypothesis is relatively small; a wider spread would make the probability under the alternative hypothesis smaller and so make the effect larger.

Edwards et al. (1963) present an elaborate and detailed exposition of this phenomenon and the various ways in which the numbers in the denominator of Equation 5.23 can be limited. The discussion both establishes the generality and measures the size of this bias against null hypotheses.

Does this argument imply that the experimental literature is full of incorrect .05-level rejections of null hypotheses? We think so. Even some of the .01-level rejections are almost certainly wrong. We tend to be rather confident of the .001-level rejections.

Why have we not encountered numerous instances of scientific disaster resulting from such procedure for discrediting potential truths? One answer is that we have. We tend to lump such consequences under headings of non-replicability and experimental artifact rather than to attribute them to errors of statistical inference – but they are problems nevertheless. Fortunately, most rejections of important hypotheses are based on intellectual as well as statistical grounds. A second answer is that the procedures discredit potential, not actual, truths. We have already argued that classical null hypothesis testing is often applied to situations in which no basis exists for a sharp spike of prior probability at the null value. In the absence of such a spike of prior probability, the null hypothesis is preposterous to start with, and therefore no amount of bias against it can be too great. That argument invites the rather snide question: if the hypothesis is absurd to start with, why bother to test it?

When Bayesians and classicists agree that null hypothesis testing is appropriate, the results of their procedures usually also agree. If the null hypothesis is false, the interocular traumatic test[2] will often suffice to reject it; calculation will serve only to verify clear intuition. If the null hypothesis is true, the interocular traumatic test is unlikely to be of much use in one-dimensional cases but may be helpful in multidimensional ones. In at least 95% of cases when the null hypothesis is true, Bayesian procedures and the classical .05-level test agree. Only in borderline cases do the two lead to conflicting conclusions. The widespread custom of reporting the highest classical significance level from among the conventional ones actually attained would permit an estimate of the frequency of borderline cases in published work; any rejection at the .05 or .01 level is likely to be borderline. Such an estimate of the number of borderline cases may be low, since it is possible that many results not significant at even the .05 level remain unpublished.

5.5. Present state of Bayesian statistics

When the Bayesian point of view became visible in the 1960s, most Bayesians were convinced that in time classical procedures, and especially classical null hypothesis testing, would die out. Although inspection of any current journal of mathematical statistics will reveal that Bayesian thinking is widespread among theoretical statisticians, null hypothesis testing is as common as ever, and most texts and courses in statistics for the various disciplines of science give scant recognition to Bayesian ideas. Bayesian procedures are rare in experimental publications, and even convinced Bayesians have been known to publish classical significance tests. Why?

The Bayesians of the 1960s clearly underestimated the power of human inertia. More important, perhaps, they underestimated the difficulty of making a transition from one form of statistical inference to another. Because of the massive number of classical statistical procedures in experimental journals, graduate students cannot read the literature unless they understand those procedures. The editors of the journals, trained in classical procedures, often insist on them; that is one reason for the inclusion of classical procedures in articles by Bayesians. Our own experience has been that one can always insist that one's paper be refereed by someone who understands Bayesian procedures, but some of our Bayesian friends believe that it isn't worth the trouble.

Perhaps the most important reason for the continued use of classical procedures, however, is that many experimenters, not being professional statisticians, regard statistical inference as a form of number magic that is nec-

---

[2] You know what the evidence means if the conclusion hits you between the eyes.

essary for getting papers published but ancillary to the business of empirical science. Most Bayesians would thoroughly agree that statistical inference is ancillary but would regard number magic of any kind, Bayesian or other, as unnecessary and undesirable. Scientists and statisticians of all persuasions would probably agree that estimation is best when it is stable, and inference is best when it comes from interocular trauma. But not all experimenters are lucky enough to have overwhelming evidence for their conclusions. When delicate inferences must be made, we recommend Bayesian procedures.

It used to be difficult to apply Bayesian procedures because many Bayesian calculations are more complicated than those required in classical inference. However, the recently developed CADA, a package of Bayesian statistical procedures developed by Professor Melvin Novick and available for many kinds of computers, greatly simplifies the task of making Bayesian calculations (see, e.g., Novick, 1973; Isaacs and Novick, 1974). We admire and recommend it.

6　Inference

6.1. Introduction: scenarios, inference, and explanations

In Chapter 5 we discussed statistical inference, a well-developed and useful tool for scientists and others who can create the rigorous conditions required to make the procedures of statistical inference reasonable. These conditions are the following:

1　　　Datum or data and hypotheses are clearly defined and specifiable.
2　　　The inference maker can obtain from somewhere a number, set of numbers, function, or set of functions that link datum or data to hypotheses in quantitative form. These numbers or functions obey the familiar rules of the probability calculus.
3　　　Data are conditionally independent of one another; that is, the answer to the question "How likely is datum D if hypothesis H is true?" remains unchanged as the inference maker learns about data other than D.

We know of no real-world nonscientific contexts in which inferences must be made that fit any one of these three assumptions. With our hearts in our mouths, we therefore set out to explore the general topic of inference, *not* statistical inference. We must warn you that we find this exploration tantalizing and frustrating, and you will too. Useful things can be said, and in this chapter we probably say some of them. But no formal technology useful for real-world inferences yet exists. We include this chapter in the book in part to document that fact and in part because we believe the knowledge base for such technology has been developed very recently. We want to report it in the hope that others more skillful than we will evolve the technology we think is inherent in it.

Recognition of the need for a modern theory of inference, and the technical effort needed to carry it to the point it has reached so far, originated primarily with Professor David A. Schum. In the early 1970s, Schum, like many Bayesians, attempted to increase the complexity of Bayes's theorem in order to match the richness of real inference problems. He soon found himself reading legal texts on evidence, since systematic thinking about inference is more extensive in legal scholarship than in any other publicly available source. He found that thought and writing about legal evidence are enormously rich, structurally and factually. He happily discovered that his own interest in the structure of evidence had long been anticipated by a

163

legal scholar named John Henry Wigmore (1937). Wigmore developed a set of categories for evidentiary structures and a way of diagramming those structures. His purposes were not quantitative, but his structures lent themselves well to quantification. Our treatment in this chapter is based entirely on the work of Schum and his former student, Anne Martin; we add our own thoughts about the relation between scenarios and their decomposition into evidence structures.

The fact that the work of Schum and Martin forms the basis of this chapter and that these writers drew their thought and work from legal sources has heavily influenced our treatment. We have not been ingenious enough to develop nonlegal parallels to the legal examples on which they focused. The literature we know of on inference in medicine is rudimentary in comparison with that on legal inference. We hope, without knowledge, that there is a substantial body of literature on inference in intelligence systems. If there is, we have no access to it; the open literature on the topic is also rudimentary, though fascinating. Consequently, this chapter has the legal flavor that permeates its major sources. There is, of course, a substantial philosophical literature on inference (see, e.g., Cohen, 1977; Shafer, 1976). We have chosen to ignore it, because its main focus is on alternatives to Bayesian formulations, while our concern is the major task of turning those formulations from a formidable batch of equations into a usable technology.

If our bets are well placed, this chapter represents this book's most profound gesture toward future technology. We hope so. But please don't expect us to make it enjoyable.

The importance of scenarios: a trivial example

Simply to make a few points about the problem, we start with a trivial example. It comes from the title of a song popular some years back. Standing next to Joe and Jean, an attractive couple whom we have not met, at a crowded cocktail party, we hear Joe say, "How could you believe me when I said 'I love you!' when you know I've been a liar all my life?" What can we infer about Joe and Jean from this datum?

Obviously, they have been well acquainted for some time; it seems likely that they are lovers. Though we cannot be sure from this datum alone, that Joe ever did tell Jean that he loved her, it seems very likely that he did – not primarily because he says so, but rather because he says so and essentially admits that the statement was a lie. We find it hard to believe that Joe would make such an unflattering statement about himself if any part of it were untrue.

Why does Joe make the statement at all? Presumably because he no longer wishes Jean to believe that he loves her. A scenario that makes sense of the datum is that Joe seduced Jean, partly by telling her that he loved her, and that now he is dumping her – but has a guilty conscience, or he wouldn't bother to explain himself.

The example illustrates what seems to us the fundamental fact about real-world inference. Inferences are about scenarios, or unfolding sequences of events in time. We observe the available bits and pieces of these unfolding events and try to figure out what they imply about what we did not observe. A hypothesis may be a "complete" scenario but is more likely to be an unobserved event embedded in one or more "complete" scenarios. We enclose the word *complete* in quotation marks because, as you will see later, we have no formal guides to the amount of detail to include in either a scenario or a datum, and consequently no scenario can ever be complete.

This invites a fundamental distinction between two kinds of real-world inference tasks. One, just illustrated, consists of taking data and constructing a scenario to fit them. This is the most important kind of inference making – but we know almost nothing about it. The task seems to be entirely psychological. We retrieve past instances of similar events from records or memory, extract from them events that fit together with the data we have, and link them together according to purely subjective rules of coherence in such a way that the data seem very likely given the scenario. If we care and have the opportunity to do so, we may use the scenario to predict other possible observations, and then check to see if the predictions are correct. We might ask a mutual friend about Joe and Jean.

We can say a great deal more about the second, more highly structured situation. Suppose we have data and, not just one, but more than one scenario that may or may not be consistent with them. We want to assess the merits of these scenarios in the light of the data. Recall that the Bayesian formulation of statistical inference has exactly this structure; it requires data and at least two hypotheses that may explain them. Issues of this kind are of great practical importance, since people seem to be quite good at fitting scenarios to data, even though we have no idea how they do it. For example, another scenario about Joe and Jean is that Jean had just asked, "What is that old-fashioned tune the band is playing?" Note that we could readily accept or reject this scenario except that independent information about what the band was playing is absent. Such missing data characterize *all* real-world inferences.

Perhaps the most highly developed public context in which multiple scenarios occur is legal inference. Criminal law mandates at least two hypotheses: guilty and innocent. These two hypotheses can be taken as hypothetical observations to be combined with the real evidence into scenarios. The goal of the prosecution is to construct and make persuasive a scenario that includes one of those hypothetical observations and to discredit the other. The goal of the defense is often the reverse, though formally it need not be.

A complex example

To introduce the key ideas of complex inference, we turn to a complex example of Schum and Martin (1980, 1981). Please study it carefully. Most of this chapter is built around it.

Payne, a 22-year-old white male employed as a service station attendant, lives alone in a garage apartment in southeast Houston. Payne is charged with robbing the apartment of Keith MacMillan, a bachelor airline pilot, who was out of town at the time of the robbery. Articles that Payne allegedly stole include a television set, a stereo set, a camera, and a shotgun. The victim, MacMillan, had engraved an identification number supplied by the police on each of these articles. The robbery occurred on the morning of February 4, 1979, at or about 3 a.m. MacMillan's apartment is located in west Houston near the Galleria. The time of the robbery was verified by several neighbors who were awakened by the sound of a burglar alarm in the victim's apartment.

In Payne's trial, the jury hears testimony and cross-examination from four witnesses, three testifying for the prosecution, one for the defense. The first witness is Oscar Wyatt, a 40-year-old male detective sergeant in the Robbery Investigations Branch of the Houston Police Department; he has 15 years of experience in criminal investigation. Officer Wyatt testifies that he found the victim's television in defendant Payne's apartment at 5:00 p.m. on Monday, February 5, 1979, the day after the robbery. Officer Wyatt had a search warrant at the time of this investigation (a_1).[1]

In later testimony, the defendant Payne states that he had not owned a television set and that he had purchased the one in question from a stranger he encountered in the parking lot of the Gulfgate mall department store at or about 2:30 p.m. on Monday, February 5, 1979, the day after the robbery. On cross-examination, Officer Wyatt testifies that there was no television set other than the one belonging to MacMillan in the defendant's apartment.

The second witness for the prosecution is Richard W. Bolt, a 27-year-old white male police officer in the Robbery Division of the Houston Police Department. He was assigned to assist Officer Wyatt in his investigation of defendant Payne on the day after the robbery. Officer Bolt testifies that he found the victim's stereo set in the trunk of defendant Payne's car at 5:00 p.m. on Monday, February 5, 1979 (b_1).

In later testimony, defendant Payne testifies that he had not owned a stereo set and that he had purchased the set in question from the same stranger he met in the parking lot at Gulfgate mall on February 5, 1979. Payne testifies that he paid the stranger $300 for both the television and the stereo. On cross-examination, both Officers Bolt and Watt testify that they found no stereo equipment other than that belonging to the victim, MacMillan, in the defendant's apartment or car.

The third witness for the prosecution is Emily D. Weston, a white female, age 24, employed as an elementary school teacher in Houston and Payne's former fiancé. She lives in the same apartment complex as the victim MacMillan. Ms. Weston testifies that the defendant Payne visited her at her apartment at 2:00 a.m. on the day of the robbery (which took place around 3:00 a.m.). Ms. Weston says she was certain about the time of Payne's visit since the late movie she was watching on television had just ended. She says Payne had rung her doorbell at 2:00 a.m. and that she had refused to admit him into her apartment. After a short discussion, Payne left, she says (d_1).

---

[1]The symbols following certain statements are later used to characterize testimony in the formal inference structures.

On cross-examination Ms. Weston testifies that she does not know the victim MacMillan even though they live in the same apartment complex, which, she says, contains about 50 units. Ms. Weston, when asked why she broke off the engagement with defendant Payne, testifies that she had become increasingly attached to another man who could offer her a more promising future. She further says that there had been no unpleasantness between her and the defendant after their engagement had been broken.

Hilda P. Grant is the only witness for the defense. Ms. Grant is a 65-year-old white widow who owns the defendant's garage apartment. She lives alone in the house in front of the garage apartment. Ms. Grant testifies that on the day in question, about 3:00 a.m., she was awakened by the defendant as he walked down the sidewalk, beside her bedroom window, toward the garage apartment. She says she could see the defendant Payne clearly since the night light at the rear of the house was on at the time (c_2).

On cross-examination, Ms. Grant admits that she cannot be positive about the time she saw defendant Payne. She says she was awakened by the sound of someone coming down the sidewalk. She looked out of the window and saw the defendant; she did not note the time. After this she went back to sleep and woke up again, at which time she noted that it was 5:30 a.m. She says she thought that she had slept for 2 hours. She admits that the time of her initial awakening could have been as late as 4:30.

That's all the evidence. The prosecution's scenario is obvious. Payne, frustrated by Ms. Weston's rejection of him, tries to see her, presumably to plead his case, but is not allowed in. Aware that his economic insecurity and low status as a service station attendant were partly responsible for that rejection, he turns his attention to obtaining the kinds of goods he can't afford to buy. He breaks into MacMillan's apartment and steals the television and stereo. The story that he bought them in a parking lot is fabricated, and his alibi means nothing because Ms. Grant cannot be precise about the time she saw him.

The defense problem is tougher. No full defense scenario is suggested by the evidence. One part of the defense case must consist in arguing the validity of Ms. Grant's original time estimate; if true or approximately true, it would give the defendant a complete alibi. Another part involves the question of what Payne did between 2:00 a.m., when he left Ms. Weston's apartment, and 3:00 a.m., when the robbery occurred. Was he roaming the corridors of the apartment complex, taking the risk of being seen? An hour of his time is unaccounted for in the prosecution scenario but is easier to account for if Ms. Grant's time estimate is correct, or if Payne woke her before 3:00 a.m. A third part of the defense case is a simple question: if Payne committed the robbery, where are the camera and shotgun that were stolen but not recovered? The prosecution's scenario ignores the question.

Note that it is easy to construct fairly plausible scenarios. We also find it easy to assess their relative plausibilities. If we were on the jury, we would vote to convict. Note also that crucial evidence is missing. Testimony from the individual who sold Payne the television and stereo would be crucial. So would testimony about Payne's location at, say, 2:30 a.m. Such missing evidence characterizes all real-world inference problems. If someone had seen Payne coming out of MacMillan's apartment carrying the television set, the case would not have presented an inference problem and would not appear in this book.

Scenario construction is an exercise in synthesis. But the structure of evidence in most complex real-world situations is such that the synthesis cannot be complete. That is why the defense need not necessarily build a scenario of its own; it can instead simply try to pick holes in the scenario built by the prosecution. Inconsistent or inconvenient or missing evidence is explained away, attacked as untrustworthy, ignored, or somehow shoehorned into the scenario. We gave illustrations of all four mechanisms. Payne's assertion that he bought the stereo and television is explained away as a lie. Ms. Grant's alibi evidence is attacked as untrustworthy. The fact that the camera and shotgun were not found is ignored. The time difference between 2:00 a.m. and 3:00 a.m. is shoehorned into the scenario, perhaps with some assertion that Payne roamed the corridors in a frenzy of despair.

Now let us start structuring the inference problem. Figure 6.1 presents a diagrammatic analysis of the Payne case. This structure suggests various thoughts. For example, although the impact of Wyatt's and Bolt's testimony is jointly greater than the impact of either alone would be, the testimonies are redundant to some degree. (Technically, this is an instance of cumulative redundancy.) The testimony of Grant to some degree contradicts that of Weston, though the extent of the contradiction is diminished by the shakiness of Grant's statement about time.

Let us take a deep breath and try to embody the structure of this case in a set of equations based on the odds – likelihood ratio version of Bayes's theorem presented in Chapter 5. Since the likelihood ratios contain all the information about the diagnostic impacts of the testimony, appropriate Bayesian equations would define the following likelihood ratios and conditional likelihood ratios:

$$L(a_1) = \frac{P(a_1 | H_1)}{P(a_1 | H_2)}, \tag{6.1}$$

$$L(b_1 | a_1) = \frac{P(b_1 | H_1, a_1)}{P(b_1 | H_2, a_1)}, \tag{6.2}$$

$$L(d_1) = \frac{P(d_1 | H_1)}{P(d_1 | H_2)}, \tag{6.3}$$

$$L(c_2 | d_1) = \frac{P(c_2 | H_1, d_1)}{P(c_2 | H_2, d_1)}. \tag{6.4}$$

The posterior odds favoring "guilty" would then be

$$\frac{P(H_1 | a_1, b_1, c_2, d_1)}{P(H_2 | a_1, b_1, c_2, d_1)} = L(a_1)L(b_1 | a_1)L(d_1)L(c_2 | d_1)\frac{P(H_1)}{P(H_2)}. \tag{6.5}$$

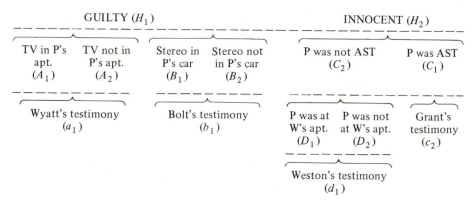

Figure 6.1. Formal representation of the inference structure in the Payne example. Testimonies or hypotheses with a subscript 1 point toward guilt (H_1). Capital letters denote hypotheses; lower-case letters, testimony (AST, at the scene and time of the crime; P, the defendant Payne; W, the witness Weston).

Writing out the likelihood ratio equations is a true chore; fortunately, it has been done for us in this case by Schum. Table 6.1 summarizes the result.

Table 6.1 is, we believe, an adequate summary of the result of decomposing the case into its evidentiary elements. In principle, it invites implementation. Simply ask the jury members to estimate the numbers called for in the table, do the arithmetic, and plug the resulting numbers back into Equations 6.1 through 6.5, and you have the posterior odds for Payne's guilt. Then you need only decide whether those posterior odds are or are not sufficient to justify convicting him. The logical structure of this question is exactly that of the treatment of simple dichotomy in Chapter 5.

But no one does inference this way. Why not? First, 25 numerical judgments are required to carry out this program, and all seem insecure and difficult. Second, we have specified the structure of the problem for the jury in Figure 6.1; in general a jury would not have such help – if it is help, which could very easily be questioned.

But in fact Schum and Martin (1980, 1981), using this case and others like it, tried exactly this divide-and-conquer procedure, found that it is feasible with naive respondents, and even found some reasons to believe that it may be better than other procedures for performing such inferences. Specifically, they compared full decomposition, whereby the respondents estimated all 25 numbers, which were then aggregated by mathematical tools, with a procedure in which the respondents assessed posterior odds directly, and with yet another involving partial decomposition, whereby the respondents assessed the four likelihood ratios of Equations 6.1 through 6.4 and the prior odds, which were then aggregated by means of Equation 6.5.

In this, as in other real-world inference tasks, there is no answer to the

Table 6.1. *Equations for likelihood ratios in the robbery case against Payne*

$$L(a_1) = \frac{P(A_1|H_1) + \left[\dfrac{P(a_1|A_1)}{P(a_1|A_2)} - 1\right]^{-1}}{P(A_1|H_2) + \left[\dfrac{P(a_1|A_1)}{P(a_1|A_2)} - 1\right]^{-1}}$$

$$L(b_1|a_1) = \frac{K_1[P(B_1|A_1, H_1) - P(B_1|A_2, H_1)] + P(B_1|A_2, H_1) + \left[\dfrac{P(b_1|B_1)}{P(b_1|B_2)} - 1\right]^{-1}}{K_2[P(B_1|A_1, H_2) - P(B_1|A_2, H_2)] + P(B_1|A_2, H_2) + \left[\dfrac{P(b_1|B_1)}{P(b_1|B_2)} - 1\right]^{-1}}$$

where

$$K_i = P(A_1|a_1, H_i) = \frac{P(A_1|H_i)P(a_1|A_1)}{P(A_1|H_i)[P(a_1|A_1) - P(a_2|A_1) + P(a_2|A_2)]}$$

$$L(d_1) = \frac{P(C_1|H_1)[P(D_1|C_1, H_1) - P(D_1|C_2, H_1)] + P(D_1|C_2, H_1) + \left[\dfrac{P(d_1|D_1)}{P(d_1|D_2)} - 1\right]^{-1}}{P(C_1|H_2)[P(D_1|C_1, H_2) - P(D_1|C_2, H_2)] + P(D_1|C_2, H_2) + \left[\dfrac{P(d_1|D_1)}{P(d_1|D_2)} - 1\right]^{-1}}$$

$$L(c_2|d_1) = \frac{T_1 + \left[\dfrac{P(c_2|C_1)}{P(c_2|C_2)} - 1\right]^{-1}}{T_2 + \left[\dfrac{P(c_2|C_1)}{P(c_2)|C_2)} - 1\right]^{-1}}$$

where

$$T_i = \frac{P(c_1|H_i)\left\{P(D_1|C_1, H_i) + \left[\dfrac{P(d_1|D_1)}{P(d_1|D_2)} - 1\right]^{-1}\right\}}{P(c_1|H_i)[P(D_1|C_1, H_i) - P(D_1|C_2, H_i)] + P(D_1|C_2, H_i) + \dfrac{P(d_1|D_1)}{P(d_1|D_2)}}$$

question: what is the true posterior odds? Consequently, no direct evaluation of results is possible. But various indirect questions can be asked. Schum and Martin found that full decomposition provided an assessment that was more sensitive to redundancies and other subtleties of the situation and evidence than was partial decomposition and that partial decomposition was more sensitive than holistic judgment.

6.2. The Reverend Bayes meets the ungodly inference

The spirit of decision analysis is the spirit of divide and conquer, of piece-by-piece analysis of the relevant kinds of information and thought, followed by reintegration using quantitative methods. We shall explore the usefulness of this spirit to problems of complex inference.

This is an ambitious program, guaranteed to be full of difficulties. A scenario is worthless unless it makes sense as a whole; we are proposing to take it apart, to treat the data one by one, in emotional isolation from the coherent story or stories in which they so naturally nestle. We call that isolation emotional, because we shall argue that the important structure of scenarios is in fact retained and represented, partly in the development of the inference structure and partly in the assessments it calls for.

Some problems with scenarios

We shall confront a few of the difficulties before embarking on the program. Sequence is a crucial aspect of any scenario. Consider three scenarios, all realistic. "They met, fell in love, and got married." "They met, got married, and fell in love." "They married, met, and fell in love." The first is a normal scenario in the United States. The second is rare in the contemporary United States but describes many upper-class European marriages of a century ago. The third, implying either marriage by proxy or a first meeting at the altar, fits an earlier European tradition, especially among royalty, as well as some contemporary Asiatic customs.

Such sequential effects can be represented in inference problem structuring. Thus, the sequence in which events occur may itself be an explicit datum. "After Mr. X was hired as our night warehouseman, we started to notice that major appliances were missing from the warehouse. We had never had any trouble before." That would be acceptable testimony in a grand theft case against Mr. X, though obviously far from enough to convict him. Such evidence would have a direct probative impact on the hypothesis that Mr. X had a hand in the thefts. Without the "We had never had any trouble before," it would not.

A subtler problem is that of missing or negative data. We have already argued that missing data are simply a fact of life; you never know everything you would like to know. Scenarios are devices for filling in holes. The real subtlety lies in negative data. The most illustrious example comes from Doyle's (1892) story "Silver Blaze." Reviewing evidence in a murder investigation with Scotland Yard Inspector Gregory, Sherlock Holmes responds to Gregory's question about whether he should note any other items of information bearing on the case:

> "[I would wish to draw your attention] to the curious incident of the dog in the nighttime."
> "The dog did nothing in the nighttime."
> "That was the curious incident," remarked Sherlock Holmes.

It later turns out that the dog did nothing because the nefarious act, a horse theft, was carried out by the dog's master.

The example illustrates the diagnostic value of the nonoccurrence of events. Simple Bayesian mathematics shows that such effects must be abundant. Suppose $P(D|H) > P(D|\overline{H})$, and consequently D is evidence in favor of H. Then it is logically necessary, as a result of the additivity of probabilities, that $P(\overline{D}|H) < P(\overline{D}|\overline{H})$. If D is diagnostic, $\overline{D}$ must be diagnostic also, and in the opposite direction.

Holmes noticed $\overline{D}$. Often, we fail to imitate his acumen and lose the diagnostic content of nonoccurrences. Indeed, a real dilemma in the design of information-gathering systems is knowing exactly how to recognize and gather for processing the diagnostically relevant nonoccurrences.

We offer no solutions to the dog-in-the-nighttime problem, as we choose to label it. We note that it is simply a special instance of the broader missing-data problem we have already discussed. We also note that most values of $P(D|H)$ are quite small for any D and H. Consequently, $P(D|H)/P(D|\overline{H})$ may be very large, while $P(\overline{D}|H)/P(\overline{D}|\overline{H})$ may be extremely close to 1 and consequently not costly to neglect. The problem becomes more complex when the possible observations are not dichotomous, but the principle remains the same.

Finally, scenarios lend themselves to coherent, orderly, and even emotionally compelling presentation. From our point of view, that is exactly what is wrong with them. The inner logic of the coherent, sequentially organized, humanly plausible story becomes much more important than the shreds of actual evidence around which the story has been built. Most fiction makes more sense than most factual stories. Motives can be simple, not conflicting. Technical inconveniences can be swept away. (The Baker Street Irregulars, a lively and successful society with chapters in many U.S. cities, devotes some of its time to making elaborate, tortuous efforts to explain away or reconcile the numerous factual impossibilities Doyle built into his Sherlock Holmes stories. But only scholars on a spree are likely to be that meticulous.) Scenarios are essentially fictions constrained only by the available facts. The existence of courts, intelligence agencies, and diagnostic clinics suggests that, when the issues at stake are important enough to justify close examination of scenarios, the scenarios rarely turn out to be simple or as unequivocally linked with the available data as one would like.

We therefore think that the formal and intellectual complexity of formal structures that link data with hypotheses is worth their high costs. We hope for a technology that will replace the facile scenario generation that is now our normal mode of inference. But only pieces of that technology are identifiable, and none of it is up and running.

Independence and conditional independence

In Chapter 5 we played a sneaky trick on you, and it is time to explain and undo it. In all of our discussions of inference, we avoided careful examination of the topic of dependent data. We thus avoided two related issues that we must now face. The fundamental issue is that of forms of nonindependence. Another issue, derived from the first, is very practical: what to do with old data.

Formally, two data are defined as independent of one another if knowledge about one does not change your opinion about the likelihood of the other. In symbols, D_1 and D_2 are independent if

$$P(D_1) = P(D_1|D_2) \quad \text{and} \quad P(D_2) = P(D_2|D_1).$$

This definition of independence is also a definition of irrelevance to inference. No two data can be independent of one another if both are relevant to any variety of inference process. The reason is obvious. In order to be relevant to discrimination between H_1 and H_2, for example, $P(D_1|H_1) \neq P(D_1|H_2)$, and similarly for D_2. Let us suppose that D_2 is very likely if H_2 is true and very unlikely if H_1 is true. This means that, the more likely you consider H_1 to be, the less likely you think it is that you will observe D_2. Now if D_1, which strongly favors H_1, comes along, your judgmental assessment of $P(D_2)$ necessarily goes down.

Classical statisticians tend not to be as explicit as they might be about this obvious fact, simply because they usually deal with $P(D_i)$ in a manner that makes the probability implicitly conditional on the truth of the null hypothesis and do not bother to calculate $P(D_i)$ conditional on the alternative hypothesis.

Bayesians, aware of the fact that independence means irrelevance, are interested in conditional independence: D_1 is conditionally independent of D_2 if and only if $P(D_1|H_i, D_2) = P(D_1|H_i)$ for all i, and similarly for D_2. So far we are only making explicit what has been implicit throughout these chapters and indeed was stated in this chapter with reference to conditional independence.

A function of random sampling and the other devices of experimental design is to provide the intellectual underpinnings for the assumption of conditional independence. Why is that assumption so important? Because if it (or at least its close relative *exchangeability*, discussed in Chapter 4) is not appropriate, the likelihood principle and the intimately related sufficiency principle, both discussed in Chapter 5, do not apply. Of the many painful practical consequences of the failure of these two related principles, we highlight one here.

If inferences are based on conditionally independent data, then once a given set of data has been used for all its inferential purposes, it can be ignored, even discarded; the probability distribution posterior to inclusion of those data summarizes all they can tell us about the inference problem at hand. In contexts in which potential conditional dependencies may exist, this is untrue. If we have received and processed D_1, we cannot thereafter ignore it if $P(D_2|H_i, D_1)$ may not be equal to $P(D_2|H_i)$. Instead, we must either wait to process D_1 until we have D_2 in hand, or else make proper adjustments for the impact of D_1 when we get around to processing D_2.

Either way, we must keep track of D_1 until D_2 comes along. Generally, any sequence of possibly conditionally nonindependent data must be treated as a single datum or a related batch of data. This is like the assertion that such data form a scenario and that the emergent characteristics of the scenario not latent in any single datum cannot be ignored.

To understand more clearly what the issues may be when conditional independence is not a tenable assumption, consider a case in which we try to infer the sex of someone, knowing his (H_1) or her (H_2) height and weight. Among both men and women, height and weight are related, and consequently the assumption of conditional independence of these data is obviously wrong. Let us call height e and weight d, and examine the specific case in which $e = 6.4$ feet and $d = 175$ pounds. Bayes's theorem becomes

$$P(H_1|6.0, 175) = \frac{P(6.0, 175|H_1)P(H_1)}{P(6.0, 175|H_1)P(H_1) + P(6.0, 175|H_2)P(H_2)}, \qquad (6.6)$$

$$= \frac{P(6.0|H_1)P(175|H_1, 6.0)P(H_1)}{P(6.0|H_1)P(175|H_1, 6.0)P(H_1) + P(6.0|H_2)P(175|H_2, 6.0)P(H_2)}, \qquad (6.7)$$

or

$$= \frac{P(175|H_1)P(6.0|H_1, 175)P(H)_1}{P(175|H_1)P(6.0|H_1, 175)P(H_1) + P(175|H_2)P(6.0|H_2, 175)P(H)_2}. \qquad (6.8)$$

Which of the three formulas to use depends on whether one knows the joint distribution of height and weight for the male and female subpopulations or the conditional distribution of height given weight or of weight given height. The latter distributions can often be inferred from linear-regression-type approaches, making suitable normality assumptions.

The general case involving all conditional dependencies can be written out by expanding

$$P(d_1, d_2, \ldots, d_k, \ldots, d_m|H_i). \qquad (6.9)$$

This expansion can be done in any sequence observing the necessary dependencies, for example, as

$$\begin{aligned} P(d_1 - d_m|H_i) = {} & P(d_1|H_i)P(d_2|H_i, d_1)P(d_3|H_i, d_1, d_2) \\ & \times P(d_4|H_i, d_1, d_2, d_3) \cdots \\ & \times P(d_k|H_i, d_1, d_2, \ldots, d_{k-1}) \cdots \\ & \times P(d_m|H_i, d_1, d_2, \ldots, d_{m-1}). \end{aligned} \qquad (6.10)$$

This order of expansion can, of course, be reversed or mixed, depending on the convenience to the analyst and the availability of data. For example, it could be reversed as

$$\begin{aligned} P(d_1, d_2, \ldots, d_m|H_i) = {} & P(d_m|H_i)P(d_{m-1}|H_i, d_m) \\ & \times P(d_{m-2}|H_i, d_{m-1}, d_m) \cdots P(d_1|H_i, d_2, d_3, \ldots, d_m). \end{aligned} \qquad (6.11)$$

Naturally, expressions like these quickly become messy computationally, but, more important, the kinds of data necessary for such refined assessments of conditional probabilities are frequently unavailable, and judgments, which are already difficult to make with one conditionality, are impossible to make with two or more. If a hierarchical inference problem therefore involves conditional dependence, it is often more useful to restructure the data set than to expand the equation. The conditionally dependent data can be combined into subsets, which themselves are conditionally independent of one another. In other cases intermediate hypotheses can be constructed such that data are independent conditional on these hypotheses. If conditional dependence cannot be totally avoided, consideration of first-order dependencies (ignoring second and higher orders) often provides reasonable approximations (see, e.g., Fryback, 1974).

Failure of likelihood and sufficiency principles

We pointed out earlier that the likelihood principle, explained in Chapter 5, does not necessarily apply to hierarchical inference. This is because, in multistage inferences, the rareness of an event expressed by $P(D|H)$ can affect its probative value. The likelihood principle would, of course, say that $P(D|H)$ does not matter, as long as $P(D|H_1)/P(D|H_2)$ remains constant.

Unfortunately, rareness is closely related to the degree of detail of a scenario. When is a scenario sufficiently detailed? Intuitively, we would answer (1) when all data known to the scenarist have been included, (2) when the hypothesis of interest has been included, and (3) when enough additional unobserved or unobservable events have been incorporated so that the scenario, considered as a narrative, hangs together. The thrust of our comments above means that we can hope for only such intuitive guidance; formal answers are not and will not be available. It is interesting that the rules of procedure in California criminal court cases specify that information about prior arrests and convictions is not legitimate for inclusion in the evaluation of guilt or innocence, though such evidence might be used, for example, to show that the accused was an expert at the method of burglary in the Payne case. However, such evidence is admissible in the penalty phase of cases when the issue is not one of diagnosis but one of decision. We do not anticipate that formal answers to questions about how much detail is enough will ever exist.

When is a datum sufficiently specified? Consider the case of Ms. Weston's testimony in the Payne case. She testified that Payne left her apartment at 2:00 a.m. and gave good reason for that precision. But suppose, with equally good reason, she had testified that he had left sometime after 1:55 a.m. and before 2:05 a.m. and that she had no idea when it was within that interval. Ignore for the moment any doubts this might raise in your mind about her credibility; assume both possible items of testimony equally credible. Given the other facts of the case, they are utterly equivalent in their implications concerning Payne's guilt. Yet the second formulation is inherently much more likely than the first, simply because Payne is more likely to have left at some time within an interval than at exactly one moment of that interval – quite independently of his guilt or innocence. This is the kind of effect the likelihood principle of Bayesian statistical inference allows us to ignore. But the datum here is part of a hierarchical structure, and the specificity attached to it affects $P(D|H)$, even though it is entirely irrelevant to diagnosis.

Again, common sense fills in where formal rules fail. Though our logical argument that the second testimony would lead to a higher value of $P(D|H)$ than the first seems impeccable to us, we would expect human assessors to ignore it. They would make judgments about a statement of the form "Payne was, according to Weston, in the apartment complex at around 2:00 a.m., and the crime occurred at 3:00 a.m." for either item of testimony.

6.3. Formal multistage inference structures

An overview

In Chapter 3 we described some basic inference structures. In this section we examine several classes of structures, model classes that have been developed for these structures. After this overview, we discuss some special cases of inference structures in more detail.

Inference structures can typically be represented by *inference trees* like the one in Figure 6.1. In an inference tree, final hypotheses, intermediate hypotheses, and data are represented in a treelike form. The simplest tree, involving a one-stage inference from a single datum that can assume two values, is shown in Figure 6.2. A much more complex tree, involving several stages, multiple data, and multiple hypotheses, is shown in Figure 6.3.

We indicate hypotheses and intermediate states by capital letters. Sub-hypotheses are indexed with a number. In a single chain a lower level hypothesis indexed by a number favors the upper level hypotheses indexed by the same number. For example, D_1 favors C_1, which favors B_1, which favors H_1. Small letters refer to data. Frequently, data are a report of the next level of the tree. For instance, d_1 reports the occurrence of D_1. Thus, our notation invites a direct analogy between the lowest and second-lowest level of the tree.

The first general distinction we will make when talking about such inference structures is that between a *single stage* of inference and *multiple stages*. Single-stage inference is direct inference from data to hypotheses. The direct testimony of a witness who observed the defendant commit a crime creates a single-stage inference problem. Figure 6.2 is an abstract version of such a problem. Multiple stages, in contrast, require several intermediate stages of the reasoning chain as, for example, in Figure 6.1.

Next we distinguish *single-chain* from *multiple-chain* inferences. A sin-

Figure 6.2. Simple inference structure.

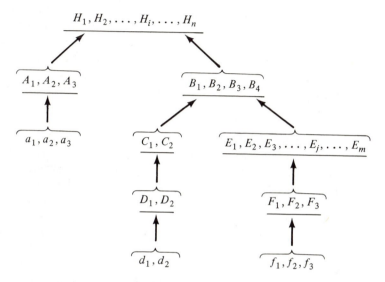

Figure 6.3. Complex inference structure.

gle-chain inference begins with a set of data, goes up through several layers
of hypotheses, and ends with the final hypothesis set. Causal inferences are
frequently single chain. More commonly, we find multiple chains, in which
inference from various sources come together to form the basis for the
appropriate revision of the hypotheses in question.

Data, intermediate hypotheses, and final hypotheses can be *dual*-valued,
multiple-valued, or even *continuous* variables. If you want to make inferences about the sex of someone on the basis of the color of his or her hair,
you combine multiple-valued data (blond, brown, brunette, etc.) with a
dual-valued hypotheses set (male, female). If you make an inference about
the height of a person on the basis of his or her weight, you combine continuous data with continuous hypotheses.

In addition to these formal distinctions among inference structures, substantive distinctions related to the type of data available and their relevance
to the inference problem are also useful. The first substantive distinction is
between *mainframe data and hypotheses* and *ancillary data and hypotheses*.

Mainframe elements are directly represented in the inference tree and form the basis of the inferential argument. Ancillary data and hypotheses strengthen or weaken the probabilistic links in the mainframe, but they are frequently not considered directly as elements of the tree. In the Payne case, for example, the time between Payne's visit at Weston's apartment and the occurrence of the crime (1 hour) is a datum that somewhat weakens the inference from Weston's testimony without ever appearing in the tree. Similarly, the fact that two stolen items were not found in Payne's car or apartment weakens the impact of the officers' testimony. As these examples illustrate, the inclusion or noninclusion of possibly relevant evidence in a data structure is a matter of choice, not perception. If Payne had had a better defense attorney, these two points would have been raised at his trial, and so Figure 6.1 would have been more complex.

Schum (1980) makes some further distinctions about data patterns and their overall impact. According to Schum, data can be *contradictory, corroboratively redundant,* or *cumulatively redundant* – as well, of course, as *nonredundant.* Schum and Martin (1981) exploit the fact that these four categories, combined with the level at which the interaction or absence thereof appears in an inferential hierarchy, produce a taxonomy of possible patterns of evidence. This taxonomy has 14 categories, the simplest of which is "direct testimonial assertion, zero order" (the traditional Bayesian case). Most complex are the mixed-order cases, in which interactions among data do or do not occur at various levels of removal from the top-level hypotheses of interest. We speculate that these 14 categories of evidential structures can be thought of as the building blocks of a very general theory of evidence. In other words, we speculate that any inferential structure, no matter how complex, can be decomposed into various combinations of these 14 elements. Moreover, since these 14 patterns include all kinds of dependencies among items of evidence, each block should be conditionally independent of every other block. In that sense (if our speculation is correct), Schum and Martin have accomplished the extraordinary feat of providing a comprehensive taxonomy of inferential structures applicable to all possible instances of human (or machine) inference.

But we can't prove it, and they make no such claims.

Single-chain, two-stage discrete inferences

The following adaptation of the infamous bookbag and poker chip paradigm (see, e.g., Phillips and Edwards, 1966) is a contrived example of a two-stage inference structure. In one postal bag you have 70% "pink" packages and 30% "white" packages. In the other postal bag the percentages of pink and white packages are reversed. The packages look the same but differ in content. The pink packages contain 80% red letters and 20% white letters. The white packages contain 80% white letters and only 20% red ones. Assume you first choose one of the two bags at random, then you draw one package out of that bag, and finally you draw five letters from that package randomly and with replacement. You observe then that the sample contains four red letters and one white letter. What is the probability that you chose the predominantly pink bag?

To formulate this problem, let

H_i = hypotheses that the bag contains predominantly pink packages (H_1) versus white packages (H_2),

D_j = the intermediate hypotheses that the observed sample of letters was drawn from a pink package (D_1 versus from a white package (D_2),

d_1 = the number of red letters in the sample.

The formal structure of this problem as shown in Figure 6.4 requires solution of

$$P(H_i|d_1) = \frac{P(d_1|H_1)P(H_1)}{\sum_{i=1,2} P(d_1|H_i)P(H_i)} \tag{6.12}$$

or, equivalently,

$$\Omega_1 = \frac{P(H_1|d_1)}{P(H_2|d_1)} = \frac{P(d_1|H_1)P(H_1)}{P(d_1|H_2)P(H_2)} = L(d_1)\Omega_0. \tag{6.13}$$

The problem with this formulation is that neither the conditional probabilities $P(d_1|H_i)$ nor the likelihood ratio $L(d_1)$ is readily available, since the data are one step removed from the H_i.

We can, however, break down the inference into two steps, by first determining $P(D_j|d_1)$ and then considering $P(H_i|D_j)$, with $P(H_i|d_1)$ simply being the weighted average:

$$P(H_i|d_1) = \sum_{j=1,2} P(H_i|D_j)P(D_j|d_1). \tag{6.14}$$

In our example, the first terms $P(H_i|D_j)$ are calculated by

$$P(H_i|D_j) = \frac{P(D_j|H_i)P(H_i)}{\sum_{i=1,2} P(D_j|H_i)P(H_i)}. \tag{6.15}$$

The second terms also follow from the simple one-stage treatment of Bayes's theorem:

$$P(D_j|d_1) = \frac{P(d_1|D_j)P(D_j)}{\sum_{j=1,2} P(d_1|D_j)P(D_j)}. \tag{6.16}$$

The only problem in this formula is $P(D_j)$, which we have to calculate from

$$P(D_j) = \sum_{i=1,2} P(D_j|H_i)P(H_i). \tag{6.17}$$

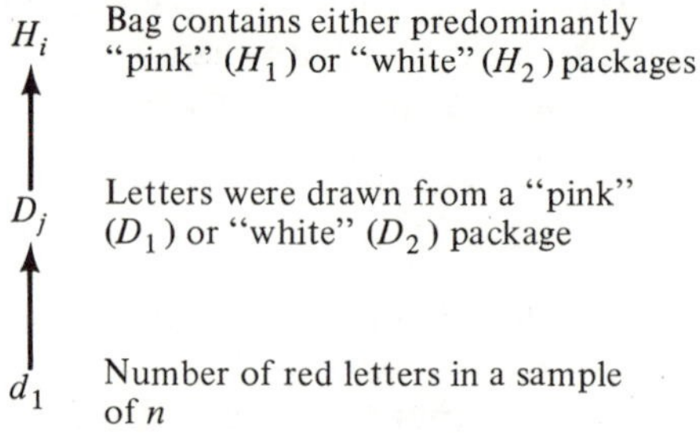

H_i — Bag contains either predominantly "pink" (H_1) or "white" (H_2) packages

D_j — Letters were drawn from a "pink" (D_1) or "white" (D_2) package

d_1 — Number of red letters in a sample of n

Figure 6.4. Structure of the two-stage postal bag problem.

The next step simply requires substitution of Equations 6.15 and 6.16 into Equation 6.14. We obtain

$$P(H_i|d_1) = \sum_{j=1,2} \frac{P(D_j|H_i)P(H_i)}{\sum_{i=1,2} P(D_j|H_i)P(H_i)} \frac{P(d_1|D_j)P(D_j)}{\sum_{j=1,2} P(d_1|D_j)P(D_j)} \tag{6.18}$$

or

$$P(H_i|d_1) = \sum_{j=1,2} \frac{P(D_j|H_i)P(d_1|D_j)P(H_i)}{\sum_{j=1,2} P(d_1|D_j) \sum_{i=1,2} P(D_j|H_i)P(H_i)} \tag{6.19}$$

or

$$P(H_i|d_1) = \sum_{j=1,2} \frac{P(d_1|D_j)P(D_j|H_i)}{P(d_1)} P(H_i). \tag{6.20}$$

All the numbers required to use Equation 6.19 were included in the original problem statement. Using them, we find that $P(H_i|d_1) = .69$; that is, the probability that the postal bag consists of predominantly pink packages increased somewhat. Equation 6.20 is already in its most general form, except for the specific meaning of d_1, which can be replaced by some generic d_k, $k = 1, \ldots, m$, which would characterize the possible realizations of the datum. This form of Bayes's theorem was first written out by Gettys and Willke (1969), who called it the modified Bayes's theorem (MBT). It makes an important, often useful simplifying assumption. It assumes, as in our contrived example, that d_1 is directly informative only about D_j, not about H_i. If, for example one knew that D_1 were true, d_1 would have no relevance to the inferential task. This eliminates the need for terms of the form $P(d_1|D_j, H_i)$ – at a significant cost in generality.

Schum and DuCharme (1971) used similar calculations to generate the two-stage version of the odds–likelihood ratio form of Bayes's theorem. We derive this version from MBT, but point out that both can be derived independently (see also Schaefer and Borcherding, 1973a).

$$\frac{P(H_1 \mid d_k)}{P(H_2 \mid d_k)} = \frac{\displaystyle\sum_{j=1,2} \frac{P(d_k \mid D_j)P(D_j \mid H_1)}{P(d_k)} P(H_1)}{\displaystyle\sum_{j=1,2} \frac{P(d_k \mid D_j)P(D_j \mid H_2)}{P(d_k)} P(H_2)} \tag{6.21}$$

$$= \frac{\displaystyle\sum_{j=1,2} P(d_k \mid D_j)P(D_j \mid H_1)P(H_1)}{\displaystyle\sum_{j=1,2} P(d_k \mid D_j)P(D_j \mid H_2)P(H_2)} \tag{6.22}$$

$$\frac{P(H_1 \mid d_k)}{P(H_2 \mid d_k)} = L(d_k)\Omega_0.$$

Schum (1980) calls the term $L(d_k)$ the *adjusted likelihood ratio*. Several versions of this ratio are instructive. Since

$$P(D_2 \mid H_i) = 1 - P(D_1 \mid H_i), \tag{6.23}$$

we can rewrite

$$L(d_k) = \frac{P(d_k \mid D_1)P(D_1 \mid H_1) + P(d_k \mid D_2)[1 - P(D_1 \mid H_1)]}{P(d_k \mid D_1)P(D_1 \mid H_2) + P(d_k \mid D_2)[1 - P(D_1 \mid H_2)]} \tag{6.24}$$

or

$$L(d_k) = \frac{P(D_1 \mid H_1)[P(d_k \mid D_1) - P(d_k \mid D_2)] + P(d_k \mid D_2)}{P(D_1 \mid H_2)[P(d_k \mid D_1) - P(d_k \mid D_2)] + p(d_k \mid D_2)}. \tag{6.25}$$

Equation 6.25 shows why the likelihood ratio is referred to as "adjusted." If observation d_k were perfectly diagnostic about D_j, then $P(d_k \mid D_j)$ would be either 0 or 1. Assuming $P(d_1 \mid D_1) = 1$, $P(d_1 \mid D_2) = 0$, perfect second-stage diagnosticity means that

$$L(d_1) = \frac{P(D_1 \mid H_1)}{P(D_1 \mid H_2)} = L(D_1), \tag{6.26}$$

that is, the adjusted likelihood ratio would be identical to the likelihood ratio of D_1. This likelihood ratio is "degraded" or adjusted by the imperfection of the report d_k, that is, its inability to tell us with certainty whether D_1 or D_2 is true. Notice that we cannot simply modify $L(D_1)$ by multiplication or by degrading the term linearly. The degradation of this likelihood ratio depends on the relative probabilities $P(d_k \mid D_j)$ as well as on the rareness of the intermediate hypotheses $P(D_j \mid H_i)$. This fact naturally complicates the calculations considerably.

To introduce a more intuitive version of the adjusted likelihood ratio formula, we shall provide a legal example with the same formal structure as the bookbag and poker chip example. Here H_1 and H_2 are the two hypotheses "Defendant X committed the crime" and "Defendant X did not commit the crime"; D_1 and D_2 are the intermediate hypotheses "Defendant X was at the scene of the crime" and "Defendant X was not at the scene of the crime"; finally d_1 and d_2 are the two reports "Witness Y reported seeing defendant X at the scene of the crime" and "Witness Y reported not seeing defendant X at the scene of the crime." In this formulation the conditional probabilities $P(d_k|D_j)$ have a rather natural meaning: $P(d_1|D_1)$ is a "hit" report (i.e., the witness correctly identified a significant event); $P(d_2|D_1)$ is a "miss" (i.e., the witness failed to report the significant event). Similarly, $P(d_1|D_2)$ is a false-alarm probability, and $P(d_2|D_2)$ signals a correct rejection. The terms are borrowed from signal detection theory (SDT) and they have exactly the same meaning in this type of problem as they have in SDT (see Green and Swets, 1966).

The hit, false-alarm, miss, and correct-rejection rates are important ingredients in the adjusted likelihood ratio formula. They are related to the credibility of the witness. A perfectly credible witness would have a hit probability of 1 and a correct-rejection probability of 1. Note that we can determine in this problem all requisite probabilities from the hit probability $h = P(d_1|D_1)$ and the false-alarm probability $f = P(d_1|D_2)$ alone, since $P(d_2|D_1) = 1 - P(d_1|D_1)$ and $P(d_2|D_2) = 1 - P(d_1|D_2)$. Using this notation and assuming $h \neq f$ and d_1 being reported, we can write Equation 6.25 as

$$L(d_1) = \frac{P(D_1|H_1)(h - f) + f}{P(D_1|H_2)(h - f) + f} \tag{6.27}$$

or

$$L(d_1) = \frac{P(D_1|H_1) + [(h/f - 1]^{-1}}{P(D_1|H_2) + [(h/f - 1]^{-1}} . \tag{6.28}$$

Equation 6.28 is interesting, because it clearly shows that the multistage likelihood ratios are not linearly degraded single-stage likelihood ratios; their adjustments depend in subtle ways on hits and false-alarm rates. The one-stage likelihood ratio $L(D_1)$ would suffer no degradation as h approaches 1 or f approaches 0. The higher the ratio of hits to false alarms, the smaller is the added "degradation term" $[(h/f) - 1]^{-1}$ and therefore the lower is the overall degradation of the likelihood ratio $L(D_1)$. Thus, we find a subtle dependence of the degradation of links at higher stages on the credibility of the report made in the lower stage in this type of inference problem.

Obviously, the adjusted likelihood ratio $L(d_i)$ also depends on the inferential value of the event being reported, that is, on $P(D_j|H_i)$. However, the adjusted likelihood ratio must include information that goes beyond the information contained in the likelihood ratio $L(D_1)$. Adjustment will occur differently depending on the absolute size of the conditionals $P(D_j|H_i)$. In other words, we need to preserve information about the *rareness* of the intermediate events. (This can be considered an example or a consequence of the failure of the likelihood principle in multistage inference.)

In our legal example, the notion that both the rareness of the intermediate event and the credibility of the source are relevant to inference seems self-evident. Assume that the location of the crime is defendant X's apartment building and that D_1 means that the defendant was at the scene of the crime, H_1 that he committed it. Then we can assume that simply by the general facts of life $P(D_1|H_1)$ is very high (say, .9), but also that $P(D_1|H_2)$ will be high (say, .45). Thus, if we know that the defendant was at the apartment building at the time of the crime (D_1), we can infer $L(D_1) = 2$. A witness report of D_1 might be unreliable, characterized by, say, a ratio h/f of 5. Solving Equation 6.28 with these numbers yields $L(d_1) = 1.6$, a reasonable degradation from the original value 2, which could be used if the witness were perfectly credible.

Now let us assume that the location of the crime is quite a distance from the defendant's apartment. This would tend to make both $P(D_1|H_1)$ and $P(D_1|H_2)$ much less likely. Let us assume that the respective likelihoods are .09 and .045, thus maintaining the same likelihood ratio for D_1. Using the identical values of h and f for the witness, we obtain an adjusted likelihood ratio of 1.15, which is a substantially stronger degradation.

This is a nontrivial finding. It says that the strength of hierarchical inference as expressed in adjusted likelihood ratios depends not only on the inferential strength of a particular stage of inference (as expressed in the likelihood ratio at that level), but also on the rareness of the conditional events at that level and the source credibility terms.

As if matters were not complicated enough, we should point out that we made some heroic independence assumptions when writing out Equations 6.18 through 6.28. In particular, we assumed that

$$P(d_k|D_j, H_i) = P(d_k|D_j) \quad \text{for } i, j, k = 1, 2 \tag{6.29}$$

and

$$P(D_j|H_i, d_k) = P(D_j|H_i) \quad \text{for } i, j, k = 1, 2. \tag{6.30}$$

Let us defend the more reasonable of these assumptions, using as a backdrop the legal example with the notation introduced on p. 181. Consider $i, j = 1$, for example. Is it reasonable to assume that the probability of the defendant being at the scene of the crime, given that he actually did not commit the crime, is independent of the report of the witness? More simply put, do we learn anything about the D–H relationship from the report of the witness that we do not actually know from knowing H_2? Probably not, and therefore the independence assumption makes sense. This statement can frequently be generalized: it is often the case that knowledge of the truth of higher level hypotheses in an inference tree makes knowledge at lower levels of that tree irrelevant; that is, the conditional probabilities at a higher level are independent of knowledge about lower level hypotheses or data. This was the assumption to which we called attention in discussing MBT.

We can make the same thought much more intuitive by translating it back into words in a legal context. Suppose D_j is what lawyers call a fact-at-issue, that is, an assertion that would bear materially on the guilt or inno-cence of the defendant but about which our information is fallible. It is often reasonable, as in the case of Payne, to assume that our evidence about the fact-at-issue is unaffected by whether or not the defendant is guilty or inno-cent. Nothing in the structure of the story of Payne as we originally told it would suggest that either Weston or Grant cared enough about Payne's guilt or innocence that one might want to discount the testimony of either because of its relationship to that judgment.

We could, of course, modify the story a little and thereby destroy the con-ditions that permit us to make this independence assumption. Suppose we can prove that, contrary to Weston's testimony, the breakup of the engage-ment between Payne and Weston was acrimonious. Suppose that Payne had been pestering Weston ever since it occurred and that the 2:00 a.m. visit was one more occasion of harassment. Now we might suppose that Weston would be glad to have Payne go to jail (and thus be gone from her life) and might slant her testimony that way. This new scenario implies a dependence between Weston's testimony and the hypothesis of guilt, resulting from the fact that Payne was becoming an intolerable nuisance.

The complications of such scenarios can boggle the mind. Whether Wes-ton would, for example, shade her information about when Payne visited her to put him at the scene of the crime only an hour before it occurred when (let us say) it was actually 2 hours would depend not only on how seriously Weston took her oath, but also on her speculation about what other infor-mation might be available to the prosecution and/or defense; she surely would not want to be caught perjuring herself. If she were relatively law abiding and concerned with justice, whether she shared her information might also be related to her assessment of the likelihood that Payne was guilty; she might be more willing to offer incriminating testimony if she were already convinced of his guilt than she would otherwise be. Similarly, Grant might believe, as some do, that police do not arrest without good cause. Too upright to perjure herself, she might nevertheless have been unduly vague about the time she saw Payne (perhaps she looked at her bedside clock-radio and saw that it was 3:00 a.m.). All of these are examples in which minor changes of scenario would make independence assumptions that are embod-ied in Table 6.1 quite inappropriate.

Independence assumptions and inferential structures imply and are implied by scenarios and are essentially diagrammatic representations of them. We believe, without much evidence, that any scenario can be concep-tually represented by an inference tree with appropriate patterns of depen-dencies and absences thereof. We suppose that the key missing element of the technology of inference is a set of rules and procedures that specify how to translate scenarios into structural representations. The scenario repre-sents sequence as such; the structural representation represents sequence as nature and values of failures of conditional independence. Given the structural representations, their translation into Bayesian algorithmic form is straightforward, though tedious. Thus, we find that in inference, as we shall later find in utility assessment, the task left to the artistry of the practitioner rather than to technology is structuring.

Our example of the dependence of Weston's testimony on payoff considerations is, we think, a rather general problem of complex inference. The neat distinction between inferential and evaluative issues that is a bedrock of the formal structure of decision analysis breaks down here. Those who face the practical problem of making real systems for inference and decision work recognize this and devise essentially ad hoc schemes to minimize the breakdown. In the legal case, laws against perjury are an obvious example; separation between the guilt-or-innocence phase and the penalty phase of major trials is another. The distinctions among diagnosis, evaluation, and decision that are built into decision analysis are also built into every real-world decision context we know about.

So far we have discussed only two-stage inference structures in which the states at each level are binary (the general hypotheses H and the intermediate hypotheses D) and the data d can assume only two values. Generalization to multiple levels of data, events, and hypotheses is straightforward, however, as indicated in the generic formula 6.20, which in fact does not depend on the assumption (except for the limits of the summation) and in which $j = 1, \ldots, m$ and $i = 1, \ldots, n$ can easily be assumed.

Rather than spell out these multiple-level cases in more detail, we shall immediately generalize to continuous states for all levels of the single-chain, two-stage inference problem.

Single-chain, two-stage continuous inferences

As it turns out, the insights to be gained from the continuous structures are somewhat limited, and we can therefore restrict ourselves to a detailed discussion of a single case.

Consider the intelligence problem of estimating the maximum range R of a new missile developed by an enemy country. Assume that a major source of information about the range is the weight of the missile W. Weight and maximum range are intimately linked for a given power source, and since weight is easier to infer, analysts attempt to establish the weight first. An intelligence analysis reports the weight to be w on the basis of photographs, measurements of the size of the missile, and estimates of its component weights and payload. Clearly, w is only an unreliable report about W, and W is only an unreliable indicator of R. The structure of this problem is a very simple, single-chain, two-stage inference with continuous variables at each stage (Figure 6.5). For the purpose of illustration we assume that all distributions involved in this problem are normal.

The formal representation of the problem can be expressed by the follow-

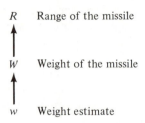

R   Range of the missile

W   Weight of the missile

w   Weight estimate

Figure 6.5. Structure of a simple intelligence system problem.

ing conditional probability density of R, after observing w,

$$f(R|w) = \int_W f(R|W)f(W|w) \, dW, \tag{6.31}$$

where $f(\cdot)$ are the respective conditional probability density functions. Since

$$f(R|W) = \frac{f(W|R)f(R)}{f(W)} \tag{6.32}$$

and

$$f(W|w) = \frac{f(w|W)f(W)}{f(w)}, \tag{6.33}$$

Equation 6.31 can be rewritten as

$$f(R|w) = \int_W f(R) \frac{f(W|R)f(w|W)}{f(w)} \, dW, \tag{6.34}$$

where

$$f(w) = \int_W f(w|W)f(W) \, dW.$$

Finally, for any two estimates R_1 and R_2, we can write out the likelihood ratio version of Equation 6.31 as

$$\frac{f(R_1|w)}{f(R_2|w)} = \frac{f(R_1)}{f(R_2)} \frac{\int_W f(W|R_1)f(w|W) \, dW}{\int_W f(W|R_2)f(w|W) \, dW}. \tag{6.35}$$

The first thing to note about this formulation is that it is by no means obvious which of the three formulas (6.31, 6.34, or 6.35) should be used. Equation 6.31 is relatively straightforward and has a certain intuitive appeal in decomposing the inference task in two steps: first estimating the "true weight" given the observed weight and subsequently estimating the relationship between weight and maximum range. Curiously, Equation 6.31 does not require an estimate of a prior probability distribution for R. That estimate is implicit in the conditionals required for assessing the possible density functions $f(R|W)$.

Equation 6.34 would require us to estimate the inverse conditionals $f(W|R)$, $f(w|W)$, the prior probability $f(R)$, and the prior probability of either w or W. The procedure requires the assessment of more relations than does one based on Equation 6.35. Moreover, some of the relations are less intuitive than those required by Equation 6.31. In particular, assessing the conditional $f(W|R)$ is less intuitive than assessing $f(R|W)$. However, the relation $f(w|W)$ is somewhat more intuitive than the relation $f(W|w)$.

Finally, the likelihood ratio form in Equation 6.35 has the advantage of requiring less assessment effort than Equations 6.31 and 6.34. However, it requires assessment of the complete likelihood functions $f(W|R_1)$ and $f(W|R_2)$, neither of which may be easily intuited, even by experts. Finally, an assessment of the odds as between R_1 and R_2 is much less informative than a full posterior distribution over R; those odds are simply the ratio of the ordinates of that posterior distribution at those two points.

We discussed these possible forms and their uses to make the point that the same basic inference structure can usually be represented by various formally equivalent versions of Bayes's theorem, each breaking the tasks down somewhat differently. The formulas vary in the degree to which they decompose the task, in the assumptions required for the decomposition, and in the ease with which the assessment is carried out. It is almost an article of faith among many Bayesians that decomposition should be as detailed as possible and that likelihood ratios and odds should be used wherever possible. Our example suggests that that may not always be the best strategy.

In fact, in this example we would probably prefer assessment in the form of Equation 6.31. This could proceed as follows. Assuming normal distributions and normal conditionals, we would first assess the *family* of conditional distributions $f(W|w)$ as a function of w. For example, one might reasonably expect that w is an unbiased estimate with variance that is independent of the size of W. Thus, the conditionals could be modeled by

$$f(W|w) \sim \text{Normal}(\mu = w; \sigma_w). \tag{6.36}$$

Next, we assess the uncertainties about the range as a function of weight. Again, we might assume that the conditionals $f(R|W)$ are normal with a mean that is a linear function of W and constant standard deviation σ_R. Formally,

$$f(R|W) \sim \text{Normal}(\mu_R = kW; \sigma_R). \tag{6.37}$$

These are all the ingredients we need. The rest is a result of simple distribution theory (see, e.g., DeGroot, 1970; Raiffa and Schlaifer, 1961). The general integral of the product of two normal distributions can be written as follows:

$$f(R \mid w) = \int_W \left\{ \left[\frac{1}{\sqrt{2\pi}\sigma_R} \exp\left[\frac{-(R - kw)^2}{2\sigma_R^2} \right] \right] \frac{1}{\sqrt{2\pi}\sigma} \exp\left[\frac{-(W - w)^2}{2\sigma_w^2} \right] \right\} dW$$

(6.38)

which is solved as

$$f(R \mid w) = \frac{1}{\sqrt{2\pi} \sqrt{\sigma_R^2 + \sigma_w^2}} \exp\left[\frac{-(R - kw)^2}{2(\sigma_R^2 + \sigma_w^2)} \right].$$

(6.39)

In other words, we obtain, as a posterior over R given the observation w, a normal distribution with mean kw and standard deviation $\sqrt{\sigma_R^2 + \sigma_w^2}$.

Multiple-chain, multiple-stage discrete inference

To introduce the multiple-chain complexity, we turn again to the legal Payne case. Leaving aside the police testimony for a moment, we consider here only the testimony of witnesses Weston and Grant. Weston's is the basis for an inference at the next higher level about whether Payne was indeed at Weston's apartment (D_1) or was not (D_2), which in turn allows an inference to be made about whether Payne was indeed at the scene at the time of the crime (C_1; we call that idea AST) or was not (C_2). Finally, establishing whether Payne was AST has inferential value for the assessment of whether Payne committed the crime (H_1). This chain is a three-stage, single-chain inference structure with dichotomous states or variables.

We add to this chain a conditionally dependent chain, that of Ms. Grant's alibi testimony that Payne was at his apartment, away from the scene of the crime (c_2). This testimony must be considered jointly with Ms. Weston's in order to infer whether Payne truly was AST (C_1) or was not (C_2), which is then relevant though not decisive in inferring Payne's guilt or innocence.

This last inference structure combines two two-stage, single-chain dichotomous structures of the sort discussed in the previous sections. Together they are linked to a multiple-chain (actually, dual-chain), multiple-stage mixed inference structure. For convenience we display that structure again in Figure 6.6.

In addition to the various dependencies *within* each chain, we have to consider dependencies *across* chains when writing out the Bayesian equations. In particular, we have to consider the credibility of Ms. Grant's testimony c_2 given that Ms. Weston testified d_1. These statements contradict one another. Ms. Weston's testimony makes guilt more likely; Ms. Grant's makes it less likely.

We develop the Bayesian formula for Ms. Weston's testimony first. Con-

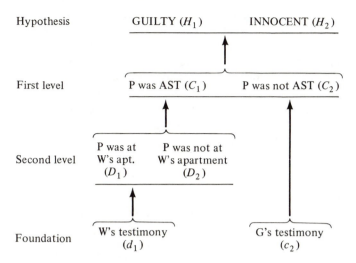

Figure 6.6. Multiple-chain, multiple-stage inference structure: the case against Payne.

sidering all dependencies, we can simply expand the chain

$$P(H_i|d_1) = \sum_{k=1,2} \sum_{j=1,2} P(H_i|C_j, D_k, d_1)P(C_j|D_k, d_1; H_i)P(D_k|d_1; H_i, C_j),$$

$$(6.40)$$

where the elements after the semicolon are the "additional" elements on which the conditional probability may depend, other than the conditioning elements.

Before examining the structure of this equation in more detail, we consider the possible dependencies or independencies. First, does the inferential impact of C (knowledge of whether or not the defendant was AST) on H depend on d or D? This is unlikely, because if we knew that Payne was AST, Weston's testimony would not change our conditional probability $P(H_i|C_1)$. Similarly, if we knew that Payne was not AST, that is, if we had alibi information, $P(H_2|C_2) = 1$ independently of all other testimony. Therefore, $P(H_i|C_j, D_k, d_1) = P(H_i|C_j)$.

Next consider the second term of Equation 6.40. Does knowing whether the defendant is guilty change the conditional probabilities $P(C_j|D_k)$? It is indeed the case that knowledge of H enhances the inferential link between C and D, because if Payne is guilty, he must have been AST. On the other hand, d_1 does not add anything to knowing that D_1 or D_2 was true. Therefore,

$$P(C_j|D_k; H_i, d_1) = P(C_j|D_k; H_i). \qquad (6.41)$$

Finally, consider the credibility-related link $P(D_k|d_1; H_i, C_j)$. This term may depend on H_i, since the witness may be more or less eager to tell the truth depending on whether she has the knowledge that the defendant committed the crime and whether she likes him or holds a grudge against him. For example, if she holds a grudge, she may then be biased toward a false alarm. If the defendant did not commit the crime, however, the witness may be more likely to produce a miss. To keep the example simple, we shall ignore this possible dependency and assume that the credibility of the witness is unaffected by whether or not the defendant committed the crime. We will similarly discard the dependence of $P(D_k | d_1; H_i, C_j)$ on C_j. Therefore, we assume that

$$P(D_k | d_1; H_i, C_j) = P(D_k | d_1). \tag{6.42}$$

Therefore, our total equation simplifies to

$$P(H_i | d_1) = \sum_{k=1,2} \sum_{j=1,2} P(H_i | C_j) P(C_j | D_k; H_i) P(D_k | d_1). \tag{6.43}$$

Using Bayes's theorem in each of the conditionals, we obtain

$$P(H_i | d_1) = \sum_{k=1,2} \sum_{j=1,2} \frac{P(C_j | H_i) P(H_i)}{P(C_j)} \frac{P(D_k | C_j; H_i) P(C_j)}{P(D_k)} \frac{P(d_1 | D_k) P(D_k)}{P(d_1)}. \tag{6.44}$$

Forming the odds–likelihood ratio and canceling terms generates

$$\frac{P(H_1 | d_1)}{P(H_2 | d_1)} = \frac{P(H_1)}{P(H_2)} \frac{\sum_k \sum_j P(C_j | H_1) P(D_k | C_j; H_1) P(d_1 | D_k)}{\sum_k \sum_j P(C_j | H_2) P(D_k | C_j; H_2) P(d_1 | D_k)}. \tag{6.45}$$

Setting $P(d_1 | D_1) = h$ (for hit) and $P(d_1 | D_2) = f$ (for false alarm), we can extract the complete adjusted likelihood ratio describing the diagnostic impact of Weston's testimony:

$$L(d_1) = \frac{P(C_1 | H_1)[P(D_1 | C_1; H_1) - P(D_1 | C_2; H_1)] + P(D_1 | C_2; H_1) + [(h/f) - 1]^{-1}}{P(C_1 | H_2)[P(D_1 | C_1; H_2) - P(D_1 | C_2; H_2)] + P(D_1 | C_2; H_2) + [(h/f) - 1]^{-1}}, \tag{6.46}$$

which, you may recall, is identical to the third equation of Table 6.1, which was part of our initial "shock therapy."

The interesting feature of this likelihood ratio, besides those already discussed in the section on two-stage, single-chain inference structures, is that the inferential value of Weston's testimony can be degraded by high probabilities $P(D_1 | C_2, H_i)$. In other words, if it is likely that the defendant was at Weston's apartment, even if he was not AST, the impact of Weston's testimony would be substantially lower. This is, of course, a desirable feature. For example, if Payne could show that he had knocked at Weston's door each night for the last month at 2 a.m., $P(D_1|C_2; H_i)$ would be substantially higher, and Weston's testimony would be worth less.

Now let us examine Grant's testimony, which is identical in structure to our simple two-stage inference. However, now we have to consider the possibility that the impact of Grant's testimony may depend on Weston's testimony. For example, had Weston's testimony not contradicted Grant's, Grant's testimony might indeed have had more evidentiary impact.

Let us first simply write out Grant's equations assuming that Weston did not testify:

$$P(H_i|c_2) = \sum_{j=1,2} P(H_i|C_j; c_2)P(C_j|c_2; H_i). \tag{6.47}$$

In this case it is relatively straightforward to assume

$$P(H_i|C_j; c_2) = P(H_i|C_j) \tag{6.48}$$

and

$$P(C_j|c_2; H_i) = P(C_j|c_2). \tag{6.49}$$

In other words, knowledge of Grant's testimony does not add anything once one knows whether or not Payne was AST. Similarly, knowledge of guilt does not change the credibility ingredients of Grant's testimony.

Using Bayes's theorem on the simplified terms yields

$$P(H_i|c_2) = \sum_{j=1,2} \frac{P(C_j|H_i)P(H_i)}{P(C_j)} \frac{P(c_2|C_j)P(C_j)}{P(c_2)}. \tag{6.50}$$

In odds–likelihood ratio form this equation reduces to

$$\frac{P(H_1|c_2)}{P(H_2|c_2)} = \frac{P(H_1)}{P(H_2)} \frac{\sum\limits_{j=1,2} P(C_j|H_1)P(c_2|C_j)}{\sum\limits_{j=1,2} P(C_j|H_2)P(c_2|C_j)}. \tag{6.51}$$

Defining $P(c_2|C_1) = m$ (for miss) and $P(c_2|C_2) = c$ (for correct rejection), we can extract the adjusted likelihood ratio from Equation 6.51 as

$$L(c_2) = \frac{P(C_1|H_1) + [(m/c) - 1]^{-1}}{P(C_1|H_2) + [(m/c) - 1]^{-1}}. \tag{6.52}$$

If, in contrast, the inferential impact of Grant's testimony is considered conditional on d_1, Weston's testimony, the picture becomes much more complicated. In fact, it is so complicated that we will give only the final equation here:

$$L(c_2|d_1) = \frac{T_1 + [(m/c) - 1]^{-1}}{T_2 + [(m/c) - 1]^{-1}}, \tag{6.53}$$

where

$$T_i = P(C_1|H_i, d_1)$$

$$= \frac{P(c_1|H_i)\{P(D_1|C_1; H_i) + [(h/f) - 1]^{-1}\}}{P(c_1|H_i)[P(D_1|C_1; H_i) - P(D_1|C_1; H_i)] + P(D_1|C_2; H_i) + [(h/f) - 1]^{-1}}$$

(6.54)

for $i = 1, 2$. Thus, we can see that the conditionality of Grant's testimony on Weston's testimony changes $P(C_j|H_i)$ to $P(C_j|H_i, d_1)$, which in turn depends on such things as Weston's credibility (h and f) and the strength of the inferential linkages in Weston's chain.

Using these likelihood ratios, it is straightforward to determine the combined impact of Weston's and Grant's testimony on the odds of guilt or innocence:

$$\Omega_1(d_1, c_2) = \frac{P(H_1|d_1, c_2)}{P(H_2|d_1, c_2)} = L(d_1)L(c_2|d_1)\Omega_0.$$

(6.55)

6.4. Generic structures, dependencies, and types of evidence

Schum's generic structures

If you are like us, you probably have begun to despair at this point. The structures have become too complex, the formulas virtually unmanageable, and the task of eliciting the inputs into the Bayesian models seemingly prohibitive.

Some small comfort is offered by Schum and Martin's work on generic structures (see, e.g., Schum, 1980; Schum and Martin, 1980, 1981, 1982). This work should facilitate the construction of appropriate inference trees and guide the search for dependencies. Furthermore, Martin (1980) has developed a general-purpose algorithm for generating Bayes's formulas for virtually any structure involving multiple stages and multiple chains as long as the dependencies are not too unwieldy. In addition, Schum (1977a,b, 1979a,b, 1981a,b) and Schum and Martin (1980, 1981, 1982) have provided interpretive discussions of the subtle dependency issues that can be detected and analyzed within special structures and, in the case of legal problems, special types of testimony.

In this section we first describe some generic structures that form the building blocks of inference theory. Combinations of these structures should allow one to construct any complex inference structure. All of these structures concern the main frame of the inferential argument, and supporting structures that strengthen or weaken certain inferential links may have to be added to this main frame.

First, we consider the classes of single-chain structures, which Schum also calls simple inference structures. Such single-chain structures vary only in the number of stages of the chain or, put differently, in the remoteness of the testimony from the hypothesis under consideration. Single-stage structures are frequently called *direct testimonial structures* because, in the legal case, they typically consist of a witness testifying to the guilt or innocence of a defendant. In such a one-stage inference, the main issue is whether the witness can be believed. If the witness is perfectly credible, his or her testimony establishes the truth of the hypothesis under consideration unequivocally.

The nature of the simple two-stage inference structure has already been discussed at some length. It typically occurs when a witness testifies that some event D_j occurred, which is probabilistically linked to the hypotheses H_i under consideration. The foundation of this structure is again the credibility of the witness, and the inferential links in the second stage concern the relationship between, say, circumstantial or alibi evidence and the hypotheses at hand.

Schum and Martin (1981) point out that alibi testimony is a special case, since it involves a peculiar probability chain linking D with H. Let D_1 be the event that the defendant was AST. This datum does not establish unequivocally whether the defendant indeed committed the crime. But the opposite datum D_2, that the defendant was *not* AST, establishes unequivocally that the defendant did not commit the crime. Alibi testimony is of further interest, since it may involve testimony from friends or enemies who, knowing that the defendant committed the crime, testify about whether he or she was AST. This creates subtle opportunities for dependencies of credibility-related issues on the truth of the hypotheses.

The three-stage single-chain inference structure involves testimony about the occurrence of an event, which in turn is circumstantial about the occurrence of another event, which itself bears on the main hypotheses under consideration. Testimony about opportunities or about means are examples of such structures. Schum and Martin (1981) mention as an example the testimony that the defendant, accused of stealing property from the house of a friend, had the key to the house. If true, this fact is circumstantial evidence that the defendant actually used the key to enter the house, and this in turn is circumstantial evidence that the defendant stole the property while in the house. Another type of three-stage inference involves hearsay. The witness might testify that he was told by another person that the defendant had confessed the crime to him. The testimony allows the inference that the other person actually said that, which in turn leads one to infer that the defendant actually confessed, which in turn is evidence that the defendant actually committed the crime. All links may be considered weak, and this is why hearsay evidence is often not admitted in court.

The four-stage inference structure is about as remote as inferences, particularly in legal contexts, can get. Instances in which three levels of reasoning are interspersed between the testimony and the hypotheses under consideration include testimony about character or motive and trace evidence (Schum and Martin, 1980). First, consider an example of motivational testimony. A witness may testify that the defendant had severe financial problems (f_1). This testimony allows an inference that the defendant actually had financial problems (F_1), which may have motivated him to rob a bank (D_1), which he may have done (H_1).

Trace evidence is typical of the often minute work of police officers and intelligence analysts. A detective may testify that a piece of cloth was found in front of the house that was allegedly robbed by the defendant (f_1). This in turn allows an inference to be made that the piece of cloth was actually found in front of the house (F_1), which in turn invites an inference about whether the piece was from clothing belonging to the defendant (E_1), which in turn invites an inference about her presence at the scene of the crime (D_1), which in turn bears on the hypothesis that she committed it (H_1).

The last example shows that remoteness does not necessarily mean the argument is weak. Each link in the remote chain of argument can in fact be strong, so that the overall probative value of the testimony can be strong. However, in many cases remoteness results in reduced impacts, as exemplified in the hearsay and motivational chains.

Next we turn to multiple chains, where the issues of dependencies become more crucial. The main rules for classifying multichain inference structures according to Schum and Martin (1981) and Schum (1980) depend on how the testimonies "mix." They differentiate four types of inference structures: contradictory testimony, corroboratively redundant testimony, cumulatively redundant testimony, and cumulatively nonredundant testimony.

Closely following the discussions in Schum (1980) and Schum and Martin (1981), we shall briefly discuss and illustrate the nature of these structures. *Contradictory testimony* involves two or more witnesses contradicting each other when testifying about the same event. In the two-stage case, witness 1 may testify that she saw the defendant at the scene and the time of the crime (d_1), while witness 2 testifies that he saw the defendant somewhere else at that time (d_2). The joint impact of these two assertions may cancel, if the credibilities of both witnesses (h and f) are equal, or the net impact may favor one or the other, depending on the strength of credibilities.

Corroboratively redundant testimony refers to instances in which two or more witnesses report the same event. For example, witness 1 may report that he saw the defendant carrying the gun with which the victim was murdered on the night the murder occurred. This testimony allows the inference to be made that the defendant actually carried the gun and, furthermore, that the defendant committed the murder. Now assume that, after witness 1, witness 2 testifies to exactly the same observation. If you have utter faith in the first witness, the second testimony will not change your likelihood ratio and that second testimony is therefore completely redundant. If, however, you consider both witnesses somewhat unreliable, you may benefit from their agreeing testimony about the same fact-at-issue.

Schum and Martin give the following example of *cumulatively redundant testimony,* which concerns the case of witnesses testifying about related matters. Let e_1 be testimony that the defendant's car was AST, which may (E_1) or may not (E_2) be true. Given that the car was AST (E_1), one might infer that the defendant too was AST (D_1), which in turn might lead one to believe that the defendant committed the crime (H_1). Now consider an additional piece of testimony: e'_1 is testimony from a tire expert that the tire marks of the defendant's car were found at the scene of the crime. This testimony can be true (E'_1) or not (E'_2), leading one to make inferences very similar to those generated by the testimony about the car being at the scene of the crime. Clearly, the value of the additional testimony depends on the value of the prior testimony about the car itself. If the witness testifying to the presence of the car was perfectly reliable, the testimony about the tire tracks would be perfectly redundant, because it would add nothing of inferential value. If, however, both items of testimony were somewhat unreliable, they could strengthen one another. Thus, the cumulative effect could be positive but not equal to the sum of its parts. Cumulatively redundant testimony is distinguished from corroboratively redundant testimony in that the cumulative case does not require that the testimony be about the same fact-in-issue.

The *cumulatively nonredundant* inference structure is similar to the one just described, but with dependence removed. For example, one witness might testify that the defendant's car was AST, and another might report finding the defendant's raincoat in the victim's apartment. Both items of testimony increase the probability that the defendant was AST, but they seem conditionally independent of one another.

No real inference problem comes neatly packaged, identifying itself as belonging to one of these structures. Most structures are mixed, multistage, multichain structures with many dependencies. However, Schum and Martin found that the above-described structures are reasonably *generic.* All real structures are, in fact, simple concatenations of part structures that take one or another of these forms.

Dependencies, redundancies, and special characteristics of reasoning chains

This section follows the treatment of Schum and Martin (1982) very closely, mainly because the arguments they make are based on a mathematical investigation of the subtleties of Bayesian inference structures that goes far beyond that of this chapter. The conclusions derived by Schum and Martin are conclusions from many sensitivity analyses within formalized Bayesian inference models. We will skip the formalities and merely discuss their conclusions.

Of particular importance in the discussion of inference structures are the credibility-related issues that form the foundation of testimony. If one believes that the hit probability and the false-alarm probability of a witness are about equal, the testimony may be of little value. A perfectly credible witness, having a hit probability approaching 1 and a false-alarm probability approaching 0, would produce testimony that has undegraded inferential value. Although the extremes of credibility are relatively easy to characterize, it is not a straightforward matter to define the middle ground of credibility or, for that matter, to define credibility directly in terms of hit and false-alarm rates. As early as 1971 Schum and DuCharme argued that neither hits, false alarms, misses, not correct-rejection rates are good indicators of witness credibility. A perfectly incredible witness, who has a hit rate of 0 and a false-alarm rate of 1, is as good an information source as a perfectly credible one. One could use testimony from such a witness in formal inference simply by reversing it and applying its full strength.

The point of this kind of analysis is that the witness is not simply an information source. Rather, the witness is a decision maker embedded in a social situation in which the decisions have meaningful consequences.

But the cost–payoff structure appropriate to most forms of human testimony includes not only the social consequences of the specific items of testimony, but also the social consequences of the act of testifying. We are all taught that it is socially desirable not to lie; our legal system enforces that principle with laws against perjury. The rules of evidence permit various forms of testimony the function of which is to impeach the witness, that is, to suggest or prove that a witness is lying. So the cost–payoff structure that controls witness behavior includes not only the social consequences of the trial, but also the social consequences of the witness's behavior during the trial.

Issues of credibility are thus of three kinds. One simply has to do with what the witness knows and is explicitly modeled by the numbers that go into any Bayesian calculation. Another has to do with a witness's personal motives, aside from knowledge. Courtroom law and procedure alike are designed to encourage the belief that the witness will tell "the truth, the whole truth, and nothing but the truth" insofar as he or she knows it. To the degree that these procedures work, witness motives become irrelevant. A third has to do with the fact that any witness, like any other signal detection apparatus, is fallible. The extent of this fallibility is, in principle, discovered in court, especially during cross-examination. To some degree it enters into prosecution and defense scenarios. Unfortunately, the rules of evidence are not well designed to encourage the reporting of fallibility. A witness who volunteers information about the extent of his or her certainty is in trouble. Stating "I thought I saw Mr. Payne under the lamplight, but the night was very dark and my eyesight isn't as good as it used to be" would be a good way for Ms. Grant to let herself in for several hours of unpleasant cross-examination. The system of handling testimonial evidence in court is designed to reduce, not enhance, the usefulness of such evidence in reaching noncategorical conclusions.

The point of this discussion is that an implicit model of witness as decision maker underlies the treatment of witness as information source that we have implied by our summarization of testimony as probabilities. That is indeed the image of the witness built into the legal system and enforced by the system. For those reasons, we work with it. But in nonjudicial contexts (e.g., intelligence analysis) and in some judicial ones, the fact that the witness is also a decision maker is essential for competent analysis of testimony. In the treatment presented in this chapter, the interpreter of evidence is assumed to take witness-as-decision-maker considerations into account when assessing the probabilities that reflect the import of testimony.

Next we turn to the subtle properties of dependencies and redundancies in inference problems. The main distinction between redundancies is between the case where two or more witnesses testify to the fact-in-issue or event and the case in which one or more witnesses testify to facts that are obviously dependent. The first case is exemplified by two witnesses, both of whom testify to having seen the defendant AST. If the first witness is perfectly believable, the testimony of the second is totally redundant, adding nothing to the inferential value of the first testimony. If both witnesses are less than fully credible, the testimony of each enhances that of the other. Sequencing obviously matters, and the impact of the second witness is always smaller than that of the first.

Two different but related events may be redundant for two different reasons. The first is that the events are redundant *in general.* For example, suppose one witness testifies to the height of a suspect, another to his weight. Since weight is highly correlated with height over all possible suspects, the testimony about weight has a smaller impact after the height testimony than before the testimony. A more drastic example of this sort of redundancy was presented in the case of observing a car and its tire marks. The second reason for such redundancies is more complicated, considering the conditional dependencies of two events *given* the truth of particular hypotheses.

Redundancy has a simple formal definition in Schum's adjusted likelihood ratios. Roughly speaking, one would like to express the extent to which the likelihood ratio of testimony about event F is "degraded" by the knowledge of testimony about event E. A simple formula expressing the redundancy between two events E and F is

$$R_{\text{cum}} = 1 - \frac{\log L(F|E)}{\log L(F)} \tag{6.56}$$

Clearly, if $L(F|E)$ were equal to $L(F)$, then R would be 0. If, however, $L(F|E)$ were 1 and therefore log $L(F|E)$ were 0, then R would be at its maximum, 1.

The following factors influence redundancy, according to Schum and Martin:

> The redundancy of the events testified as expressed
> The credibility of the witnesses testifying to the events
> The rarity of the events
> The number of reasoning stages between the testimonies and the facts-at-issue

Corroborative redundancy of the event under consideration is always 1, as can be seen from the following adaptation of the redundancy formula:

$$R_{corr} = 1 - \frac{\log L(E|E)}{\log L(E)} \tag{6.57}$$

Therefore, corroborative redundancy of the testimonies is influenced only by the three last factors above.

Schum and Martin point out a number of interesting results of analyzing adjusted likelihood ratios in a single inference chain. Two are of particular importance here. The first is that the inference chain does not necessarily lead to a transitive argument. In other words if all *individual* inference stages favor a particular hypothesis (e.g., guilt) when looked at separately, the combined effect need not always favor the same hypothesis. Such intransitivities are, of course, possible only if there are conditional dependencies between events in the same chain.

Another interesting finding refers to the rarity of events and the weak links in an inference chain. It was pointed out earlier that rarity does play a part, because rare events are easier to "degrade" with unreliable testimony than are frequent events. In addition, the analysis of rare events in inference chains indicates that the inferential impact of the complete chain is degraded to a greater extent if rare events occur at the top of the chain than if they occur at the bottom.

Intuition tells us that weak links in chains should be more damaging at the bottom of the chain than at the top because we tend to discount a string of reasoning if even its foundation is not solid. The analysis of adjusted likelihood ratios shows, however, that the location of a weak link does not matter as long as the events or hypotheses in the chain are conditionally independent. In that case the overall strength of the argument (in terms of the adjusted likelihood ratio) can never be larger than the size of the likelihood ratio of the weakest link.

Some special types of testimony

Several interesting types of testimony deserve special attention. The first is hearsay testimony about statements made by others. In other words, information is passed through several hands before being reported. In intelligence analysis this is a common structure. In medical diagnosis it is rare. In legal cases it is frequently prohibited.

Hearsay evidence is interesting because it involves credibility issues at each transmission. Each person who presumably passed on the information may have lied. Fortunately, the adjusted likelihood ratios for hearsay problems are recursive and relatively straightforward. Consider the simple case of witness 1 testifying, d'_1, that he was told by person 2 that an event D_1 occurred. Call person 2's statement d_1 and the hypotheses under consideration H_1 and H_2. Obviously a hearsay inference should depend on both the credibility-related hit and false-alarm rates of witness 1, h' and f', and that of person 2, h and f. If hearsay evidence goes through another hand (d''_1), this formula can be expanded in a recursive manner. Martin (1980) writes out one such equation for four stages of hearsay evidence.

Another special type of evidence is equivocal evidence, which is characterized by witnesses adding to their testimony subtleties of the form "but I am not really sure" or "I don't remember well." A related form is "sandbagging," the withholding of information that a witness may have. The extreme of that is silence, or nonproduction of evidence. In all of these cases intuition would suggest that the testimony be discounted and perhaps disregarded. However, formal analysis of the adjusted likelihood ratios indicates that situations exist in which withholding of information can in fact have inferential value. However, to attach inferential value to such information, we must know something about the witness other than his or her testimony. In particular we must know something about the witness's bias or motivation and/or payoff structure. For example, if a witness is likely to have been AST and in addition is a good friend of the defendant and, when asked whether he has seen the defendant AST, responds, "I don't recall," this testimony may in fact provide reasons to revise upward the probability that the defendant was AST.

A final type of inference structure concerns opportunity and alibi testimony. The asymmetry of the conditional probabilities in these cases is of particular interest. If the alibi testimony was completely credible, the probability that the defendant could have committed the crime is 0. Similarly, if the defendant had no opportunity to commit the crime for some other reason, perfect credibility leads to a zero posterior probability of H_1. Schum and Martin have discovered some subtle effects in alibi and opportunity testimony that depend strongly on the conditional dependencies introduced and on the payoff structure of the witnesses.

6.5. Behavioral results and lessons for application

Early behavioral findings

Almost all early experimental studies on Bayesian inference structures examined the one-stage single-chain structure. In the 1960s the literature was dominated by nonhierarchical analysis, frequently using the bookbag and poker chip paradigm of Bayesian inference tasks (for summaries of this literature, see Edwards, 1968; Slovic and Lichtenstein, 1971). The general finding of these studies was that people make conservative inferences. That is, if left to their intuition, they provide estimates of posterior probabilities or posterior odds that are substantially less extreme than those calculated from Bayes's theorem.

This led Edwards and his collaborators to suggest techniques for aiding people in the performance of probabilistic inference tasks. In 1968, they introduced a technique called PIP (Edwards, Phillips, Hays, & Goodman, 1968), in which subjects decomposed a Bayesian inference task into assessment of likelihood ratios and prior odds and the posterior odds were then calculated from the subjects' inputs. The technique was not a great success in the real world, perhaps because it addressed only a very small proportion of the difficulties people have with complex inference tasks and because that proportion may have been an artificial one. In other words, the complexity that PIP addressed was very small compared with the complexity of real-world inference problems.

In the early 1970s psychologists learned about multistage extensions of Bayes's theorem and quickly adapted the bookbag and poker chip paradigm to multistage versions of it. In fact, all multistage experiments at that time involved relatively contrived examples of two-stage, single-chain inference problems, similar to the postal bag problem described in Section 6.2. Most of these studies revealed that, compared with the calculated right answer available in these artificial contexts, subjects' revisions of opinion were *radical* (e.g., Gettys, Kelly, and Peterson, 1973; Peterson, 1973; Schum, DuCharme, and DePitts, 1973; Snapper and Fryback, 1971). Some researchers concluded that subjects assumed the truth of the testimony or report of a datum.

Psychologists involved in Bayesian research did not spend much time pondering the puzzle posed by conservative single-stage inference and radical multistage inference. Instead they mounted a more fundamental attack, arguing that people's intuitive way of processing probabilistic information does not resemble Bayesian models at all. This research generated a number of phenomena that we call *cognitive illusions* concerning people's judgments in single-stage and multistage inference tasks. This research is discussed in Chapter 13. For the purposes of this section it is perhaps useful to say that neither the very early research or the studies of cognitive illusions have had much impact on recent attempts to create inference structures as aids in probabilistic information processing.

Schum and Martin's experiment

In an attempt to understand how people make judgments in complex inference structures, Schum and Martin (1980, 1981) studied a series of complex legal inference problems. They were particularly interested in the way people deviate from the appropriate Bayesian models and in devising techniques or task decomposition for solving such inference tasks efficiently. Schum and Martin constructed 12 separate felony cases of the form presented in the introduction of this chapter (in fact, the case of Payne was used in their experiment).

The subjects were given several blocks of information related to the construction of the mainframe evidence. In addition they were given several pieces of information that provided ancillary evidence about the strength of the inferential relationships.

The subjects then provided probability or likelihood ratio assessments in three different ways. First was a so-called zero decomposition task (ZDT), in which the subjects simply gave a likelihood ratio for all the information they had received about the case. Each subject made one such judgment for each of the 12 cases.

In the partial decomposition task (PDT) the subjects were asked to provide likelihood ratios for each of the chains in the structure separately. If there was a link or conditional dependency between chains, the subjects were asked to consider the conditioning item when judging likelihood ratios. The purpose of instruction was to highlight dependencies and thereby generate conditional likelihood ratios. A perfectly Bayesian subject would provide a ZDT likelihood ratio equal to the product of the PDT likelihood ratios.

The complete decomposition task (CDT) partitioned the inference structure into its lowest level pieces. In other words, the subjects were asked to make all the judgments required in the formal expressions for likelihood ratios. Conditioning and dependencies were pointed out to them. The aggregate likelihood ratio could be computed simply by means of the appropriate likelihood ratio formula.

Schum and Martin first analyzed the directional consistency of the three assessment methods by checking whether the three techniques favored the same hypothesis (guilt or innocence). The directional consistency was only moderate. All three tasks agreed in about 50% of the responses; ZDT and PDT agreed in 55%, ZDT and CDT in 65%, and PDT and CDT in 76% of the judgments.

Another kind of consistency measure is agreement across subjects in the direction and force of the inference. PDT fared best when the overall ranking of the probative value of the 12 cases was compared across subjects. On the basis of individual item agreements, the complete task decomposition produced the best agreement among subjects.

Perhaps the most interesting results of these studies were those of a fine-grain analysis of the influence of contradictory or redundant items or chains in the partial and the complete decomposition tasks. In the partial decomposition task the subjects frequently did not appropriately consider the prior contradictory testimony when assessing a likelihood ratio. They either ignored the contradictory testimony or adjusted the new likelihood ratio to make it agree with the direction of the contradictory testimony. In the complete decomposition task, however, the fine-grain nature of the assessments required generated responses that were in directional agreement with the contradictory nature of the testimonies.

When testimonies were redundant, the subjects tended to "double count" in the partial decomposition condition. That is, they treated the two redundant pieces of evidence as virtually independent. The effect was much smaller in the complete task decomposition.

In conclusion, the complete task decomposition produced substantially more consistency, both convergent and across subjects, and in a fine-grain analysis it produced better directional responsiveness to redundancies and dependencies.

Application to real-world inference problems

The early experimental literature provides little guidance to the structuring and decomposition of complex inference tasks, simply because the kinds of tasks it addresses are much too simple. The experiment by Schum and Martin suggests that a reasonable amount of decomposition may improve the performance of people when judging complex inferences. *Reasonable* is perhaps the key word here. Even in simpler inference structures, the complete task decomposition requires an inordinate number of assessments and, though it reduces the "mental aggregation" burden of the respondent, may impose an enormous elicitation burden.

Inference theory aids the process of making inferences in three ways. First it enables one to translate an inference problem into a formal inference structure, that is, to separate the mainframe from the ancillary evidence and logically connect the evidence items into an inference tree. Inference trees are not unique, as we pointed out earlier. In fact, the timing of evidence is important, and even if evidence comes in a natural stream, the way it is considered in the model can be important for simplifying the task. Sometimes it is possible to restructure an inference tree, simplify it, or remove redundancies and contradictions. In the research reported here there are few rules for carrying out such structuring activities. In multiattribute utility theory this type of research has received increasing attention (see, e.g., Keeney, Renn and von Winterfeldt, 1985), and as a result rules have been devised for generating "good" value trees. Good value trees have few dependencies, allow value-relevant measurement to be made, and are small. Similarly, rules for constructing "good" inference trees, for removing dependencies and making possible the simple assessment of probabilities, may evolve from research on inference theory.

Second, once an inference tree is constructed, the theoretical and empirical research discussed above can help to identify weak links and dependencies. At this stage it is not necessary to make probability assessments, but rather to point out problems to those who have to make the judgments. For example, an inference structure may make intelligence analysts aware of redundant or contradictory information and thus help them to integrate the available evidence.

Finally, inference theory aids in the actual assessment of inputs to an inference structure. Apparently people can make decomposed judgments reasonably well and avoid the fallacies that occur when more holistic inferences are made. At this stage the analyst should probably be flexible with respect to the judgments respondents are required to make. For example, there is no Bayesian doctrine that the judgments have to be conditional probabilities "pointed downward," that is, of the type $P(D|H)$, rather than $P(H|D)$. As the missile range example showed, in some instances the inference chain can easily put together upward-oriented inference judgments. There are many ways to write inference formulas. Each defines an admissible task decomposition. The analyst should examine each formula to find the one that allows a simple task decomposition and requires the least demanding judgments.

This discussion would be incomplete without some mention of the major obstacles to implementing the ideas of formal inference systems. One obstacle is inherent in the imprecise notion of scenarios, data, and hypotheses. The task of defining and linking data and hypotheses in the form of alternative scenarios will, for the time being at least, remain an art. Of particular importance is the problem of the missing datum. We see no tools whatsoever that would have helped Sherlock Holmes overcome the "dog in the nighttime" problem. Creativity, openness, and the awareness that missing data can be relevant are helpful, but they are a far cry from being inference tools.

The failure of the likelihood and sufficiency principles poses another serious problem in the development of a technology of inference making. The key questions are: how detailed should a datum be, and how certain must one be about an intermediate hypothesis linkage before it can safely be ignored? We have no answer to the first question; we can only suggest that one follow common sense. Close scrutiny of the adjusted likelihood ratio equations sometimes helps to answer the second question. As usual, the answer is complex and depends on the rareness of D given H as well as on the reliability features of the report d and the diagnostic impact of D. Equations like 6.20 and 6.25 help – a little.

Finally the problems of dependencies and redundancies make the inference task difficult. Schum and Martin have led us a long way toward solving these problems, but much formal and empirical work lies ahead.

7   Value and utility measurement

7.1. Basic issues in value and utility measurement

This is the first of four chapters addressing evaluation problems in decision analysis. Most evaluation problems involve multiple attributes, and therefore one of the first steps is to structure values, value trees, attributes, and matrices that link alternatives with attributes. The next step, the construction of single-attribute value or utility functions, is described in this chapter. In addition, this chapter covers problems in which a single attribute or dimension dominates but uncertainty makes the choice difficult. Some investment decisions are of this nature. Chapter 8 is the multiattribute extension. It assumes that value or utility functions have been constructed for all attributes by methods described in this chapter and addresses the problem of weighting attributes and aggregating values or utilities across attributes. After these two expository chapters, we shall discuss the theoretical foundation of value and utility measurement in Chapter 9 and present some empirical results about how people perform in these tasks in Chapter 10.

Two examples and motivation for single-attribute utility

Miller, Kaplan, and Edwards (1967, 1969) examined a classical military dispatching problem, in which a Tactical Command Direct Air Support Center receives requests for close air support. Aircraft are limited in number, so those making dispatching decisions must consider the value of each target, the probability of success in attacking the target, and the number of aircraft that remain available for future, possibly more valuable missions. To improve dispatching decisions, Miller et al. developed JUDGE (judged utility decision generator), in which numerical evaluations of the targets and probabilities of mission success are inputs into a dispatching model that maximizes expected utility. The probability side of the model and the optimization process are described in their papers. Here we are concerned with the elicitation of a numerical value index for potential targets.

On the basis of a combat scenario, Miller et al. asked air force officers familiar with tactical air warfare to make value judgments about possible

205

targets in hypothetical dispatching requests. Value considerations were to include the reduction of the target's threat potential as well as the destruction of valuable enemy hardware. Table 7.1 presents illustrative descriptions of targets. Target A was chosen as a standard because the experimenters expected it to fall roughly in the middle of the range of target values. It was arbitrarily assigned a target value of 100. Respondents were told this and were also told to assign a target value of 0 to an imaginary utterly worthless target. These two fixed points defined the scale on which target values were judged; the scale, of course, had no formal upper bound. In our example, target B would have considerably less value than A since it involves only light artillery. It might be assigned a value of 35. For each incoming request the respondent was merely to judge the relative value of the target. Functions relating probability of destroying each target to number of aircraft dispatched were provided externally. The dispatching model that was a part of JUDGE then determined the optimal number of aircraft to be dispatched (including none) by maximizing expected target value. JUDGE was shown to be considerably superior to a simulation of the then-current system and to a minimal "first come first served" system.

This example illustrates the use of a simple rating method for quantifying the value of a decision outcome as a numerical input into a complex expected value optimization model. The need for value judgments arose because the outcomes were relatively complex and did not have a value-relevant numerical description. (Multiattribute utility techniques could have been used as an alternative [see Chapter 8], but Miller et al. did not know about them at the time JUDGE was developed.)

The following example is quite different. Here the problem is to choose among gambles for money. Money provides a convenient objective scale, but this scale may not properly reflect the decision maker's feelings about gambles (see Chapter 1). Consider the somewhat contrived example of Mary J., who has just won $300 in a game show. The host gives Mary an option: she can either quit now and keep the $300, or forfeit the $300 and instead accept a gamble:

Win $1,000	with probability .20,	
Win $500	with probability .30,	$EV = 380$
Win $100	with probability .30,	
Win nothing	with probability .20.	

Mary is in conflict. The idea of winning $1,000 is attractive, but she cannot ignore the danger of losing all she has just won. She indicates that if she had won $350 she would definitely keep the money, but if she had won $250 she would go for the gamble. Since the EV of the gamble is $380, Mary is not an EV maximizer. But let us assume that Mary maximizes SEU (Chapter 1).

One way to solve Mary's problem is to construct a utility function over

Table 7.1. *Example stimuli for the JUDGE simulation experiment*

Target A	Coordinates: T 1019	Location: Sadao
Reported by: 2nd and 3rd brigades, advanced elements		Time: 0900
Description: Advanced elements under attack by enemy tank platoon; attack consists of five tanks, type unknown, with 150-mm guns and heavy machine guns mounted		
Target B	Coordinates: S 1118	Location: Tonar
Reported by: 4th brigade, advanced elements		Time: 1400
Description: Regrouping elements under light artillery fire, source unknown		

Source: Miller, Kaplan, & Edwards (1967).

money and determine whether the SEU of the gamble is smaller or larger than the utility of $300. We might proceed as follows. Since the range of dollar outcomes is between $1,000 and 0, we can arbitrarily assign the following utilities:

$$u(1,000) = 100, \qquad (7.1)$$
$$u(0) = 0. \qquad (7.2)$$

Next we ask Mary to consider the following gamble:

Win $1,000 with probability p,
Win $0 with probability $1 - p$.

Mary says that at $p = .70$ she would feel indifferent between receiving $500 for sure and playing the gamble. This judgment implies the equation

$$u(500) = .70u(1,000) + .30u(0) = 70. \qquad (7.3)$$

Next, we ask her to consider the above gamble again. How high would p have to be to make her indifferent between playing the gamble and receiving $100 for sure? Let us say this value is $p = .20$. Therefore,

$$u(100) = .20u(1,000) + .80u(0) = 20.$$

Finally, we repeat the question for $300, and get the answer $p = .50$. Therefore,

$$u(300) = .50u(1,000) + .50u(0) = 50. \qquad (7.4)$$

These utilities and a smoothed utility function are shown in Figure 7.1.

Since we have now assigned utilities to all dollar amounts under consideration, we can solve Mary's problem by comparing the utility of $300 with the SEU of the original gamble:

$$u(300) = 50, \qquad (7.5)$$
$$SEU(G) = .20u(1,000) + .30u(500) + .30u(100) + .20u(0)$$
$$= 47. \qquad (7.6)$$

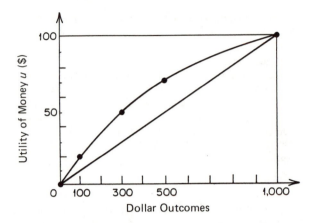

Figure 7.1. Mary J.'s utility function.

$$SEU(300) = 50 \qquad\qquad SEU(G) = 47$$

Since the utility of $300 is larger than the SEU of the gamble, Mary should keep the sure amount and forfeit the gamble. Naturally this conclusion is conditional on two assumptions: that Mary is an SEU maximizer and that her indifference probabilities are indeed accurate.

These two examples span a wide range of problems, evaluation objects, elicitation techniques, and purposes of value and utility measurement. In this chapter we cover the ground between these two extremes for a single scale for value or utility measurement. This scale may reflect an overall evaluation of objects, or it may be a partial evaluation of a particular aspect of an object. For example, an overall intuitive evaluation of job alternatives on a numerical scale from 0 to 100 is covered by this chapter, as is the construction of a scale for the value of an aesthetic impact. In the next chapter, on multiattribute utility measurement, we discuss how to disaggregate overall evaluations into parts and how to aggregate these part evaluations.

Two watershed issues dominate the thinking and choices of those who have worked on utility measurement. Since we have strong views about both, we had better start by presenting the issues and stating our views.

The status of reports of subjective quantities

Decision theorists and analysts of all persuasions would agree that, at least in principle, people presented with objects A and B can meaningfully say whether they prefer A to B, or B to A, or whether they are indifferent. Experimentally oriented psychologists would argue that, in fact, the indifference judgment is never, or almost never, made. But they have no reluctance about varying the attractiveness of A, observing that this variation produces a block of As that is uniformly preferred to B and another block that is uniformly disliked relative to B and then using some interpolation technique to find an indifference point in the region between those two blocks. As von Neumann and Morgenstern showed, if A and B can be gambles, and if certain relatively technical axioms that are required to make such expressions of preference hang together intellectually are satisfied, then such preferences alone are enough to make it possible to represent the underlying mental structure as a cardinal (interval scale) utility function.

Some theorists and practitioners want to stop at that. Others, mainly those with backgrounds in psychology, go farther. They argue that people can communicate not only about preference, but also about strength of preference. Such communication, if possible, greatly enriches the vocabulary of responses available to us in discovering utilities and consequently makes the measurement of utility much easier. We take this view ourselves.

To see where you stand on this question, consider the following scenario. You are employed by a company whose majestic probity is matched only by the ease and frequency with which it fouls up its paper work. Christmas is approaching. Normally, the company does not give Christmas bonuses, but one day you receive letter 1. It says, "Because of your exceptionally diligent and successful efforts during the past year, we have decided to depart from our usual practices and award you a Christmas bonus of $100." The following day, you get letter 2. It says, "We deeply apologize for a typographical error in yesterday's letter. The amount of your Christmas bonus will be $500." The day after that, letter 3 says, "We goofed again! Please accept our embarrassed apologies. The amount of your Christmas bonus will be $10,000." And in due course they pay you the $10,000.

Let us, somewhat artificially, assume that you fully believed each letter until the next one came, and let us forget about the disgust you would probably feel about working for a company capable of such clerical incompetence. Consider only how you would feel about the amounts of the bonuses. Presumably each would please you, and you would be more pleased by 3 than by 2, and by 2 than by 1. Can you make a meaningful comparison of the intensities of those feelings? Is, for example, the following statement a representative description of your feelings? "Bonus 1 was pleasant to receive. Bonus 2 was somewhat more so. But Bonus 3 really delighted me; the change in my feelings from 2 to 3 was much greater than the change in my feelings from 1 to 2."

If you find this statement meaningful, you agree with us that you can make judgments of strength of preference – in the example so far, ordinal ones. Strength of preference is a subjective magnitude, like many others. The name for the discipline that studies, among other things, judgments of subjective magnitude is psychophysics. Psychophysicists routinely collect judgments of loudness, pitch, brightness, and the like; from our viewpoint, strength of preference is no different from these.

How sophisticated can such judgments be? We started with the most primitive useful judgment, that of order. If you can make order judgments, and those judgments are themselves orderly, we can trick you into making judgments of equality of differences. If, for example, we wanted to find out what magnitude of bonus in letter 3 would increase your feeling of pleasure over letter 2 as much as 2 did over 1, we might try various bonuses in 3. It might turn out that a $510 bonus 3 would be very little more attractive than a $500 bonus 2, and that a $5,000 bonus 3 would be so much more attractive than a $500 bonus 2 that you would still consider the increase in attractiveness from 2 to 3 to be greater than that from 1 to 2. By decreasing the $5,000, we can zero in on some value such that you can no longer tell which interval is larger. That value need not be precise; psychophysicists can tell you how to interpolate within a set of such judgments to find an indifference point.

A more difficult step is the one to ratio judgments. Is the difference between 3 and 2 (in attractiveness, not money) more than twice as much as the difference between 2 and 1? We ourselves have no trouble answering this question yes; if you can answer it (it makes no difference whether your answer is yes or no), you can make difference or ratio judgments of attractiveness.

The last step takes us to stimulus ratings. Let us define the attractiveness of bonus 1 as 0 and the attractiveness of bonus 3 as 100. On that scale, how attractive is bonus 2? You may find that question hard to answer. If so, start by asking if 90 would be an appropriate answer. For us, the answer to that question is no. Would 2 be an appropriate answer? For this question, that judgment is difficult, because 2 comes close to being an appropriate rating, but it is a bit too low. Again, by trying out various numbers we believe we can come up with one that expresses our feelings well enough.

We find the preceding argument so convincing a demonstration that you can indeed judge strengths of preference, and we are so well aware of the simplifications that such judgments produce in obtaining measures of utility, that we are compelled to ask why many deeply respected theorists either deny the possibility of such judgments or refuse to use them in decision-analytic procedures. Their writings give us almost no help at all in answering this question. Although the issue has been latent in the literature since 1947 and explicit in the psychological part of the literature since about 1965, it has never been stated as bluntly as we have stated it here, and most authors have simply taken their positions about it for granted, without much explanation.

The possible reasons, and our reactions to them, are as follows:

1. *Lack of axiomatic and formal justification for procedures based on strength of preference.* Historically, this is certainly true, since all the early axiomatizations assumed only preference and indifference judgments. Though true, it is unconvincing. Axiomatizations of strength-of-preference judgments are not difficult to produce; see Krantz, Luce, Suppes, and Tversky (1971) and Dyer and Sarin (1979) for examples.

2. *Preference for minimalism.* This, we think, is in fact the explanation. If preference and indifference are enough, why bother with more? The

answer, of course, is: because it greatly simplifies the work. But that answer, strongly attractive to those with engineering-type minds that tend toward applied work, is far less attractive to formalists – and the literature we are considering has been dominated by formalists.

3. *Inaccuracy or untrustworthiness of procedures based on strength-of-preference judgments.* If judgments of preference and indifference were far more precise than judgments based on strength of preference, a practical case could be made for using only the former. We have heard such arguments made informally, though we have not seen them in print. The question is obviously empirical, not formal, and so should be answered by evidence rather than argument. In Chapter 10 we review such evidence as exists and conclude that judgments based on strength of preference are not inferior in either reliability or validity to judgments based on preference itself; if anything, it is the other way around.

4. *Face validity.* Because we are trying either to predict or to prescribe preferences, we should use preference to do so. This is a familiar and understandable bias – but we can see no formal justification for it. Its premise is questionable; the prediction and prescription of preferences represent only one of the purposes a decision analysis may serve. But even if the premise is granted, surely one should use whatever tools work for either purpose. A question about whether tools based on strength-of-preference judgment work turns this argument into argument 3.

We speculate that the real idea underlying argument 4 is that preferences are objective and observable, whereas strengths of preference are not. We disagree. Data consisting of verbal statements about how choices would be made, such as decision analysts often collect, can be used to infer underlying hypothetical structures that may or may not predict choice behavior. How well either kind does so is an empirical question; the evidence we know suggests that both do well. Data obtained by actually observing choices may or may not have such properties as transitivity; such properties are needed to infer utilities and cannot be checked from field observations. In more general terms, we can see no basis for considering one kind of behavior to be more objective than another. Our purpose is to infer underlying structures from observed behavior; we care about whether the behavior is orderly and whether the inferred structures are useful.

This issue interacts with the next, to which we now turn.

Riskless events and the value–utility distinction

Conventional decision-analytic theories and procedures distinguish between riskless and risky events. Each of the three bonuses in the preceding example represents a traditionally riskless event, and each is conceived as having a subjective value, to be elicited by some appropriate means.

Not all objects are sure things; in this discussion we call anything that is not a sure thing a gamble. For example, consider an event that has probability p, such as drawing a red ball from an urn that has p% balls and $(100 - p)$% blue ones. If the ball is red, you receive $1,000; if it is blue you receive nothing.

Gambles have utilities, just as any other object does; that was von Neumann and Morgenstern's great insight. We can calculate the utility of the gamble by assuming that the utility of receiving nothing is 0, that the utility of receiving $1,000 is 1, and that you behave in a way that maximizes SEU. (The latter is, even in this simple context, a strong and dubious assumption about unaided and casual choices. But this discussion is not concerned with that; for its duration we assume the model to be descriptively true.) On those assumptions, the utility of the gamble is also p.

Suppose you own the gamble and are asked to name the least amount for which you will sell it. It depends on p, of course. If $p = .5$, the EV of the gamble is $500. But you might be willing to sell it for $300, because you would rather have $300 for sure than perhaps end up with nothing. If so, you are called risk averse. Since people can also be risk seeking, a more general statement would be that you have a nonneutral attitude toward risk.

Suppose that Figure 7.1 represents your utility function for money over the region from $0 to $1,000 gained over your present position. Then your aversion to risk would be explained by the shape of that utility function. Note that the function is concave, as risk-averse utility functions are, and that the utility of $300 is exactly .5, the same as the utility of the bet. If Figure 7.1 is an accurate representation of your situation, then for any bet whose outcomes lie within the $0 to $1,000 interval, you will be willing to sell the bet for less than its EV.

But we might try to find out how desirable a $1,000 gain is to you in other ways. If you believe, as we do, that people can make interval and ratio judgments about differences in attractiveness, you could simply answer, "How much gain is half as attractive as a gain of one thousand dollars?" and other questions like it, and we could construct from your answers a function relating the attractiveness of various amounts gained to those amounts. Even if you do not believe that people can make such judgments, complex procedures to be described later in this chapter can be followed to construct functions relating the attractiveness of money (or anything else) to its amount. The important point here is that these methods do not depend on bets.

Will such procedures lead to the same utility function that led you to sell bets for less than their EV? The evidence is scanty and equivocal, but the argument is standard that they will not. So functions relating attractiveness to amount obtained by methods not based on gambles, often called value functions, are assumed to be different from such functions obtained by methods based on gambles, often called utility functions, because utility functions incorporate risk attitudes while value functions do not.

Note that gambles have appeared in this discussion in two different roles: as objects to be evaluated and as elements of an elicitation method. Conventional wisdom says that elicitation methods based on gambles lead to utility functions rather than value functions and that utility functions rather than value functions are needed to prescribe behavior with respect to risky options. If, therefore, you are dealing with uncertain prospects, as you are in many decision problems, you should elicit utilities by means of gamble-based procedures and should use them in all subsequent calculations. If you are willing to think of the options you deal with as sure things, you can work with value functions instead. A fairly small literature examines the logical relationships between value functions and utility functions; severe limitations constrain those relationships, and only a few possibilities exist, one of which is that they are the same (see Barron, von Winterfeldt, and Fischer, 1984; Dyer and Sarin, 1979; Sarin, 1982).

In our opinion, the distinction between value and utility is spurious, because (1) there are no sure things, and therefore values that are attached to presumably "riskless" outcomes are in fact attached to gambles; (2) risk aversion can frequently be explained by marginally decreasing value functions and/or by regret attributes of a value function; (3) repetitive choices tend to eliminate risk aversion, and an argument can be made that all choices in life are repetitive; (4) error and method variance within value and utility measurement procedures overshadow to a great extent the subtle distinctions that one may extract from the theoretical differences. We elaborate these assertions in the following paragraphs.

1. We have written of receiving $1,000, or some lesser amount, as though this were a terminal event. But it is not. After receiving the $1,000, you will do something with it. What? You probably don't know; you might start by putting it in your money market fund, where it will earn interest at some rate of which you are uncertain, until you withdraw it at some uncertain future date. The same argument applies to most other objects. A television set will do little but take up space in your living room unless you turn it on. When you do, what will you watch? Even if you can answer that, how well will you like what you see? The point is that every outcome (except perhaps those that involve direct consumption) is one event in an endless temporal chain of events. You never think of the chain, unless prodded by semiphilosophical discussions like this. But most of the elements in that chain are uncertain, unless your life is very unlike ours. The value of the $1,000 or the television set is really the value of those future events made possible by the current one – and you cannot know for sure what those events will be.

Next, consider the following proposition. The strength of preference of one gamble over another should not depend on events for which the two gambles have identical outcomes. (This is a strong version of Savage's sure-thing principle; see also Sarin, 1982.) To illustrate the idea, consider two bets:

A   30% chance to win $1,000,
            5% chance to lose $X,
            65% chance that no money changes hands;
B   60% chance to win $200,
            5% chance to lose $X,
            35% chance that no money changes hands.

Perhaps you prefer A to B. For us, and perhaps for you, the strength of that preference is unaffected by the value of $X; it could be $5, $100, or $1,000. Note that the value of being committed to the situation of choosing A or B depends strongly on $X; we are considering only the comparison of the two gambles.

This assumption is less than innocuous, but it seems hardly more sweeping than the original sure-thing principle (see Chapter 9 or Savage, 1954). Together with some technical assumptions, it implies that the value of a gamble must equal the expectation of the values of its possible outcomes. This in turns leads to the conclusion that value and utility functions must be identical. (For a formal version of this line of reasoning, see Sarin, 1982.)

2. The fact that risk aversion is not always what it appears to be is indicated by the following example of a subject's choices among gambles for various commodities (see von Winterfeldt, 1980a). This subject exhibited risk neutrality when faced with 50 : 50 gambles for money and gasoline. But when asked for the certainty equivalent of a gamble in which she would receive 10 pounds of beef with probability .5 and nothing otherwise, she gave a certainty equivalent of 3 pounds, indicating risk aversion. She did not change her assessment when questioned but explained her behavior as follows. Though she always preferred more ground beef over less, the marginal increase in her appreciation for ground beef was virtually zero after 6 pounds of ground beef. In other words, her *value* function increased up to about 6 pounds and then increased very little or not at all. She looked at the 10-pound outcome about as if it were only 6 pounds. Consequently, her certainty equivalent of 3 pounds did indeed indicate risk neutrality, not in amounts of beef, but rather in the value of such amounts.

This example illustrates that in many cases a value function constructed with strength-of-preference judgments, possibly considering regret or other attributes of gambles, will capture the essence of what is usually called risk aversion.

3. Risk aversion often appears in unique choices but disappears in repetitive choices. For example, when presented with a one-time chance of winning $110 with probability .50 or losing $100 with probability .50, many respondents refuse to gamble, indicating risk aversion. However, if that gamble were to be played 1,000 times, chances are very good that the winnings would be in the neighborhood of $5,000, which is the EV of the gamble multiplied by 1,000. In repeated choices, therefore, it would appear rea-

sonable to accept the gamble. As a general rule, respondents can usually be induced to buy or sell a gamble at a price near or equal to its EV if the gamble is played many times over. Thus, in repetitive choices people act as EV maximizers, while they seem risk averse in unique choices. To justify this difference, people argue that the repetitive-choice problem creates a completely new choice among decision rules rather than among unique decisions.

As we pointed out in the introduction, the distinction between unique and repetitive choices is, however, far from being clear-cut. Excluding ruin and quasi-ruin situations, most choices people make in their lives can be framed as gambles for valuable outcomes. Thus, most choices are very similar in structure, if not in outcome. Framing all choices as repetitive lends substantial normative appeal to being risk neutral in the sense that the certainty equivalent for each gamble should be equal to its expected value.

4. It is an unfortunate fact of life that utility and value functions are never constructed without error. Recent experiments (e.g., Griffin and von Winterfeldt, 1984; Hershey and Schoemaker, 1983) suggest that the errors introduced by different procedures for eliciting utility functions (e.g., the variable probability method vs. the variable certainty equivalent method; see Section 7.4) may be relatively sizable when compared with the error introduced by trying to match a utility function by strength-of-preference procedures. To put it differently, one might not do much better predicting one utility function from another one than one would predicting a utility function from a value function.

The conclusion of our four assertions is that for theoretical, psychological, and practical reasons the distinctions between utility and value are spurious. This conclusion is at odds with much of the current literature on the topic. For that reason, we decided to start this discussion with a forceful presentation of our own views. In the remainder of the chapter, and in the two that follow, we will respect the views of the authors whose work we report and preserve the distinctions that seem important to them. At any points at which the practical consequences of their views differ from the practical consequences of our own, we will point out the fact. Otherwise, we will simply report the literature as it is, though we cannot guarantee that our biases won't peep through.

7.2. Methods of unidimensional value and utility measurement

Any model or technique for measuring values and utilities is simply a set of prerequisites and rules for assigning numbers to valuable objects. These prerequisites and rules may be as complicated as a measurement axiom system or as simple as a set of instructions about how to construct a rating scale. In all models and techniques human judgment is a major ingredient. The main issues in value and utility measurement are concerned with constructing scales and eliciting responses to stimuli, areas that are typically stressed in psychophysics and psychological scaling (Baird and Noma, 1978; Coombs, 1964; Torgerson, 1958). These issues include the influence of stimulus presentation, the effects of response modes and scales, context effects, scaling artifacts, and errors and biases in judgment. They have been thoroughly studied in classical psychophysics, which established the laws that relate sensory stimuli to subjective perceptions of these stimuli.

Many of the methods of stimulus presentation, the response modes, and the scales used today in value and utility measurement have their roots in psychophysics. For example, the controversy between direct magnitude estimation and indirect choice or indifference methods is the classical counterpart to the issue discussed above of the difference between indifference methods and numerical estimation methods of value and utility assessment. In spite of these obvious parallels, decision analysts have largely ignored psychophysics and its lessons.

Psychophysical perspective

In measurement theories, the *objects* and *relations* are considered primitives for measurement. In SEU theory these objects are gambles and the relation is preference. In difference measurement the objects are pairs of outcomes and the relation is strength of preference. Few measurement theories include a psychological definition of these objects and relations, let alone a precise operationalization. Often, the substantive examples of objects and relations cover a wide range of psychological interpretations. In Krantz et al. (1971), for example, strength of preference is equated with difference in value, and operationalizations include willingness to pay in exchanges and simple ratings of strength of preference.

Psychophysics and psychological scaling take such operationalizations very seriously. Research in these fields focuses on the nature of stimuli (= objects) and response modes (= relations) and on the empirical laws relating stimuli to responses. From these laws inferences are made about the functional relations between stimulus attributes and the mental correlates they produce in a human observer. Although psychophysics has traditionally been concerned with physical stimuli and attributes, more recently psychological scaling has been extended to nonphysical attributes such as aesthetics or severity of a crime. The methodological aspects of this extended research in psychophysics and psychological scaling are usually simply referred to as *scaling*. When we stress the term *psychophysics,* we do so to acknowledge the historical source of the scaling literature.

Three major topics of psychophysics are of direct relevance to value and utility measurement:

> Scales inferred from choices versus direct estimates
> Errors in measurement
> Stimuli, response modes, and context effects

In a typical choice experiment a respondent chooses among a limited set of response alternatives on the basis of a stimulus or stimuli. A very simple example is loudness measurement by means of paired comparisons. The respondent simply names the member of each pair of auditory inputs he or she considers louder. Choice experiments fit nicely into measurement theories in which preference and indifference are the judgmental relations. Notice, for example, that in principle the construction of Mary J.'s utility function requires only choices, that is, preference and indifference judgments.

In value and utility measurement the most common procedures are indifference methods, in which respondents match two stimuli or pairs of stimuli to meet a specified indifference relation. For example, a respondent may be asked to select an amount of money such that he or she would just be indifferent between receiving that amount as a gift and receiving a lottery with a 50% chance of winning $100 and a 50% chance of winning nothing. Alternatively, a respondent may be asked to compare a gift of $50 with a gamble with unspecified probability of winning $100 or nothing. By varying the probability of winning, the analyst can change the attractiveness of the gamble and find the probability at which the respondent would be indifferent between the gamble and the sure thing. These two techniques are commonly used for utility elicitation. They are called the *variable certainty equivalent method* and the *variable probability method*.

When strengths of preferences are being assessed, one must compare two pairs of stimuli. For example, when judging the attractiveness of alternative targets for tomorrow's air strike, a respondent may be asked to consider pairs A and B versus pairs C and D. The respondent is then asked to vary target C such that it is preferred over target D with a strength of preference (degree of attractiveness) that is equal to the strength of preference of A over B. Procedures that require such matching of strengths of preferences are the so-called difference standard sequence method and the bisection method.

Often the analyst can facilitate the establishment of indifference judgments by beginning with simple questions. For example, most respondents would prefer a certain gift of $80 over a 50% chance of winning $100 and $0 otherwise. Similarly most respondents would prefer the 50% chance of $100 versus zero over a certain gift of $20. Having established this pattern of preferences, the analyst then points out to the respondent that the choice or preference switched from the sure thing to the gamble and that therefore a sure amount between $20 and $80 should exist at which the switch occurs. This sure amount would be the matching or indifference point.

Indifference procedures assume that indifference points can be determined exactly. In practice this assumption is never satisfied. Some psychological choice theories have therefore relaxed the postulate of strict indifference or preference and instead assume that choices and preferences are governed by probabilistic processes. Thurstone (1927) proposed the earliest versions of probabilistic choice models. More recent probabilistic models are described in Luce (1959) and Luce and Suppes (1965).

Deterministic and probabilistic choice, preference, and indifference methods for value and utility measurement have their roots in formal measurement theories. In contrast, the numerical estimation methods originated in classical psychophysics (Fechner, 1860). Stevens (e.g., 1935, 1936, 1951) was one of their most persuasive advocates. These methods require respondents to make quantitative judgments about stimuli or relations between stimuli. For example, a respondent may be asked to rate the attractiveness of a target on a numerical scale, as in JUDGE. Similarly, a respondent may state how much more he or she prefers target A over target B when comparing both to target C.

These two judgments exemplify the two most important numerical estimation methods: direct rating and ratio estimation. In utility measurement these techniques require the subject to consider at least three stimuli: two stimuli that provide end points or anchors and one that is used to elicit the numerical judgment. In direct rating, the anchors are usually a "bad," or least preferred, stimulus that is arbitrarily assigned a value of 0 and a "good," or most preferred, stimulus that is arbitrarily assigned a value of 100. In ratio estimation, the two anchors are a "bad," or status quo, anchor and a reference stimulus with a fixed strength-of-preference relation. The strength of preferences for all other pairs of stimuli can then be numerically expressed in terms of ratios of the standard strength of preference.

The distinction between choice or preference and direct numerical estimation is deep and divisive, as our earlier discussion showed. Two reviews of the scaling literature (Ekman and Sjoberg, 1965; Zinnes, 1969) express fundamentally opposite views. After attacking concepts underlying choice theory, Ekman and Sjoberg (1965) concluded, "Should the choice theorist agree to this [criticism], he would perhaps feel, as we sometimes do, that the concept of choice should as far as possible be avoided in psychological theorizing." Four years later in a review of the same name, Zinnes (1969) replied, "Unlike the previous review by Ekman and Sjoberg, the theme of this review is that scaling theory should be a theory of choice." This persistent controversy in psychological scaling inevitably appears in utility measurement, too. Predictably, those who draw their methods from measurement theories favor choice (preference or indifference) methods. In contrast, psychologists with a background in psychophysics and psychological scaling argue for direct estimation methods.

In applied work, the distinctions tend to become blurred or to disappear. One of the reasons is that well-designed indifference methods can frequently be turned into numerical estimation methods. Consider the task of estimating indifference probabilities that make a sure thing indifferent with a gamble. Are you expressing preferences and indifferences, or are you in fact providing a direct estimate of a probability? Conversely, analysts using direct numerical estimation methods frequently check the results of these methods with preference and indifference questions. For example, after rating the attractiveness of a target on a 0 to 100 scale, an analyst is likely to check whether the respondent truly feels that the strength of preference between a target rated at 50 and the 0 anchor is equal to the strength of preference of the 100 anchor over the target rated at 50. The use of graphic displays and numerical features of the stimulus frequently makes it impossible to tell whether the procedure used is, in fact, a numerical elicitation method or an indifference method.

The second relevant topic of psychophysics is the ubiquity of error in human judgment. Deterministic measurement theories are based on the idealized assumption of errorless preference and indifference judgments. In practice, measurement theorists acknowledge error, and they usually treat it as inconsistency and cope with it by forcing consistency or fitting consistent models to judgmental data. Psychophysical and psychological scaling methods attempt to take human error explicitly into account. Choice theories incorporate errors in probabilistic models of choice (Luce, 1959). In probabilistic utility models (Luce and Suppes, 1965), preferences are assumed to be governed by random processes – either in the utilities themselves or in the response mechanisms. Such models specify how to calculate the probability that object A is preferred over object B as a function of utility and value parameters and of individual difference parameters. They can accommodate only some patterns of probabilities of choice and so can be falsified by evidence.

Direct estimation approaches treat error by statistical means. Rather than incorporating error in the preference or choice model, as probabilistic choice models do, such approaches consider respondents to be imperfect, without modeling the imperfections. Error thus becomes a problem of data analysis. Regression and other number-fitting techniques are applied to discern the underlying model through the noisy estimates. In value measurement, for example, a set of direct rating judgments may be used to fit an exponential value function with simple regression techniques.

Probabilistic choice theorists rely on an explicit *model* of error and require an estimate of probabilities of choice or of preference. They have difficulty in estimating error from respondents' impoverished choice or preference responses. For example, to construct utility for 5 objects within the Bradley–Terry–Luce model (Luce and Suppes, 1965) 10 pair comparisons would have to be repeated at least 100 times each to arrive at stable estimates of probabilities of preference. And it is quite doubtful that such repetitions could be considered independent trials. In the practice of utility and value measurement these estimation problems prove insurmountable, and consequently probabilistic utility models have found no practical use.

We believe that forced consistency helps to reduce error, but what remains has to be dealt with. The most practical way to deal with error is to treat it as a property of inevitably noisy data and to use statistical techniques to estimate the underlying parameters of value and utility functions. It also helps to carry out sensitivity analysis to determine whether error matters.

The final psychophysical theme relevant to value and utility measurement is the persistent effects of stimuli (contexts, serial characteristics, etc.) and response modes on judgments. Psychophysical investigations of sensory stimuli have uncovered a number of such effects that apply directly to value and utility measurement. A review article, for example, describes evidence for six scaling biases (Poulton, 1979) in direct estimation methods. Examples are centering effects (subjects like to use the middle of a given scale) and spacing effects (subjects like to space responses equally over the whole scale, no matter what the anchoring points are). Other effects arise from anchoring and adjustment processes in subjects' response to value and utility questions, from the context of previous or simultaneously presented stimuli, from numerical versus nonnumerical presentation of stimuli, and so on. We doubt that consistency checks and forced consistency procedures eliminate such effects. We believe that the existence of such effects requires that the analyst pay very careful attention to the human engineering of stimulus presentations and response modes. In our description of elicitation techniques we therefore discuss possible stimulus presentation and response mode effects and advocate procedures and techniques that seem least susceptible to such effects.

Objects, scales, values, and utilities

Most methods and theories of value and utility measurement attach value and utility numbers directly to evaluation objects. In JUDGE, for example, a value index was directly attached to military targets. In the risky-choice problem of Mary J., a utility index was attached to monetary outcomes. Though such a direct approach is entirely feasible, we find it useful to break down the process of value and utility measurement into four steps. The first three steps have clear interpretations. The interpretation of the fourth step depends on whether you agree with us about the meaninglessness of the distinction between value and utility.

1   *Definitions of objects.* The objects to which values or utilities are to be attached must be carefully defined.
2   *Scale construction.* When it makes sense to do so, a scale is selected or constructed that represents some natural quantitative attribute of the evaluation objects. This makes sense if the objects are, for example, apartments varying in distance from the office. Often such quantitative scales are not readily available or are too remotely related to the values of the decision maker to be useful. In that case qualitative scales should be constructed that carefully define the attribute, its end points, and perhaps some intermediate marker points by means of verbal descriptions. Often, it is useful to associate numbers with qualitative descriptions that are at least ordinally

related to the decision maker's preferences for the levels of the qualitative scale.

3   *Construction of a value function.* The "natural" scale, if there is one, is converted to a value scale by means of judgments of relative value or preference strength. If step 2 has been skipped, for whatever reason, step 3 works directly with the objects of evaluation rather than with the physical scale on which they have been arrayed.

4   *Gamble-based elicitations.* For those who take the value–utility distinction seriously, this step transforms the values that are the output of step 3 into utilities. For those who, like us, do not take that distinction seriously, this is simply a different set of elicitation methods intended to provide consistency checks on the output of step 3.

Figure 7.2 illustrates these steps for evaluations of apartments with respect to their distance from the office. The objects (apartments, here treated as locations) are first arrayed on the natural distance scale. Next a value function is constructed over distance, which ought to reflect the decision maker's relative preference for different levels of that attribute. Finally, the value function is checked or transformed into a utility function.

Let us consider each of these steps separately, assuming that the identification of evaluation objects is completed (although this is not a trivial task in itself). In our example, we consider alternative locations of apartments described presumably as space coordinates or area description (downtown, in the San Fernando Valley, etc.). Such descriptions are seldom value relevant. Our purpose in the first step is to express the objects in value-relevant terms that can be measured. In this example, the concern is with the distance from the office; we assume that the decision maker finds long drives to and from the office tiring and stressful. Thus, driving time or driving distance is more relevant than area descriptions. The choice of a natural scale should depend on the detailed circumstances of the evaluation. If the decision maker had a helicopter, for example, a better measure might be aerial distance. If public transportation were available, a better measure might be travel time. In both cases "better" means more relevant to the values and concerns of the decision maker. The relevance of a natural scale is quite simple: if the decision maker feels that the numbers on the scale properly reflect his or her strength of preference among objects on the value attribute, the scale is relevant.

Sometimes no natural scale captures important values. An example, for many of us, is the aesthetic appeal of the layout of an apartment. This example is illuminating because the layout itself can obviously be described by a set of numbers. Perhaps architects know enough about layouts to translate them directly into natural scales. But most of us do not. Consequently, we are most likely to skip step 2, ignore the physical measurements that describe layout, and simply judge the aesthetic appeal of the layout of each apartment we are considering. We can use various psychological scaling techniques to help us. For example, we might evaluate the layouts of a set

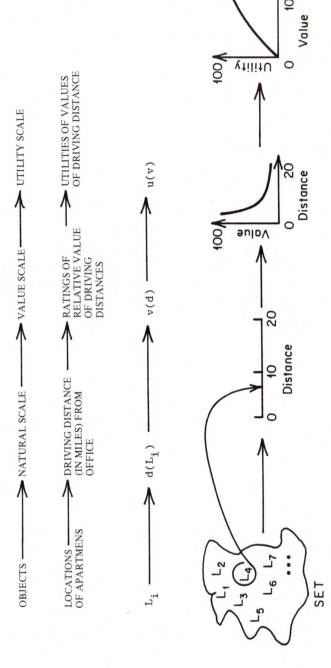

Figure 7.2. The four steps needed to construct value and utility functions.

of apartments, array them in order of aesthetic merit, and then deal with a new apartment by saying that it is worse than D but better than E. Or we might get someone we consider more expert about aesthetics than we ourselves are to lay out such a scale for us and then use it in the same way.

Ideally, either the selection or construction of a natural scale should produce a quantitative or qualitative scale that coincides with the decision maker's preference. Unfortunately, even a cleverly chosen natural scale is sometimes not a fully satisfactory value scale. Although natural scales and value scales are often monotonically related, that relation may not be linear. And sometimes the relevant natural scale actually turns out to be non-monotone in value. The amount of sugar in a cup of coffee or the racial mix in a classroom are two examples.

In such cases a value scale must be constructed. A value scale is created by judgments of the relative desirability of the levels of the natural scale. In our apartment location example, it is clear that distance from the office in miles does not properly reflect the decision maker's preferences. Distance in minutes of driving time is better, but not good enough. The decrease in value from 0 to 5 minutes is relatively large since it includes the step from not driving at all to driving a few minutes. But an additional 5 minutes added to a 30-minute drive may not have such a great impact. The shape of the value function in Figure 7.2 illustrates that relation. (This, like many other cases that produce nonlinear value or utility functions, seems to us to be a multiattribute problem forced into a single-attribute mold. Curvilinear value or utility functions invite that interpretation.)

We now turn from values to utilities. In our example, the decision maker may consider 10 minutes of driving time to the office to be halfway between 0 and 30 minutes, because the displeasure of having to drive at all is substantial. Now consider the following question. Which would you prefer, an apartment with 10 minutes of driving time or a 50 : 50 gamble between two apartments, one of which has 0 minutes of driving time and the other of which has 30 minutes? The decision maker may reject the gamble, even though its SEU (expressed in terms of the value function, not time) is larger than the SEU assigned to the sure thing. There is nothing wrong with that choice. If you like the distinction between values and utilities, it implies that the utility of 10 minutes of driving time is larger than the value of 10 minutes. If you prefer other explanations of risk aversion, you may instead conclude that the decision maker is willing to pay a little in SEU in order not to have to endure the moments of uncertainty until the coin toss (or whatever) that implements the 50 : 50 gamble occurs and the uncertainty is resolved. For some respondents in some situations, such questions can lead to systematically nonlinear functions relating value to utility; we have illustrated the possibility in Figure 7.2. Such research evidence as we know of indicates that the shape of these nonlinearities varies both from person to person and from one decision context to another; in particular, people who are risk averse in contexts in which the worst outcome is breaking even are often risk seeking in contexts in which the best outcome is breaking even (see Edwards, 1953, 1954a,b).

Most practical elicitations of value and utility avoid a full four-step decomposition. The simplest shortcut is to find a convenient natural scale that expresses value-relevant differences and then use this scale directly. The decibel scale for sound intensity is very close to most value-relevant considerations about noise impacts; engineers routinely use it to make decisions about noise acceptability. The construction of a natural scale is often omitted. As in JUDGE, such an omission is often necessary; no natural scale of the objects captures the values and concerns of the decision maker. Utility theorists often leave out value scale construction, because their main interest is to construct and use a utility function for the computation of SEUs. Figure 7.3 illustrates some of these shortcuts.

A taxonomy of techniques

We shall categorize the available value and utility measurement techniques by the stimuli used and the response judgments required. Stimuli can be either riskless outcomes or gambles. Riskless outcomes are used in value measurement, while gambles are used in utility measurement techniques. Judgments can either be indifference judgments or direct numerical judgments. Table 7.2 lists the main value and utility measurement techniques in this 2 × 2 array. In a later section of this chapter we describe each of these techniques in detail.

Direct rating, ratio estimation, category estimation, and curve drawing are versions of the numerical estimation methods in which respondents are presented with some anchored scale and asked to rate or otherwise numerically estimate the attractiveness of the stimulus relative to the anchors. Difference standard sequences and bisection techniques are based on the notion of strength of preference or value difference. Both require that stimuli be densely spaced and that it be possible to vary them in very small steps. In the difference standard sequence method the respondent identifies a sequence of stimuli that are equally spaced in value. For example, stimuli a, b, c, d, ... are found such that the strength of preference of a over b is equal to the strength of preference of b over c, which in turn is equal to the strength of preference of c over d, and so on. In the bisection technique a most preferred stimulus and a least preferred stimulus are identified, and subsequently a midpoint stimulus is found that is equidistant in value from both extremes.

The variable probability and variable certainty equivalent techniques are indifference methods in which a sure thing (a so-called certainty equivalent) is matched to a gamble, either by varying the probabilities of the gamble or by adjusting the certainty equivalent. No equivalent of the numerical estimation methods exists in the case of utility measurement.

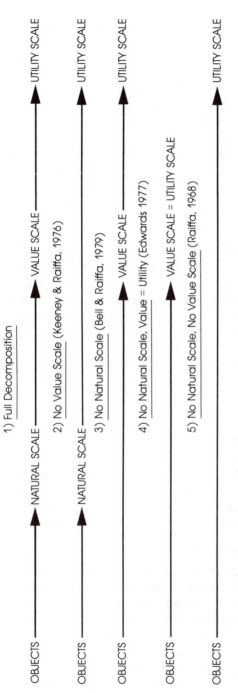

Figure 7.3. Schematic representation of shortcuts in value and utility measurement.

Table 7.2. *Taxonomy of value and utility measurement techniques*

Judgments required	Stimuli	
	Riskless outcomes	Gambles
Numerical estimation	Direct rating	N.A.
	Category estimation	
	Ratio estimation	
	Curve drawing	
Indifference	Difference standard sequence	Variable probability method
	Bisection	Variable certainty equivalent method

Note: N.A. denotes not applicable.

Though the variety of techniques is sometimes confusing to the beginning decision analyst, it is fair to say that the two main techniques used in current decision-analytic practice are direct rating techniques and the variable probability method. The emphasis on these techniques has little theoretical justification; it seems instead to be a result of convention and experience. We shall spend some time explaining and illustrating all the techniques listed in Table 7.2. At the end of this chapter we shall return to the questions of selecting techniques in decision-analytic practice.

7.3. Value measurement

Numerical estimation methods

Perhaps the most important and most widely used numerical estimation method is direct rating. In the JUDGE example, we illustrated it but did not describe the actual process. We shall first present a detailed example of the direct rating method and subsequently present some variations of it, including category estimation, ratio estimation, and curve drawing.

Direct rating technique: an example

A fresh M.D. with an exceedingly distinguished record, having completed internship and residency, considers a number of positions as an assistant professor of surgery. One of her major concerns is the location of the university hospital. She believes that location is important because of proximity to relatives and friends, climate, culture, entertainment possibilities, pollution, and other factors. Although she has many reasons to prefer one location over another, she thinks that she can make rather firm judgments about her relative strength of preference between any two given locations. She would like to quantify that strength of preference in a value function as an input into a further analysis of her job selection problem. For the purposes of this example we shall ignore other attributes entering into the problem.

The location alternatives are:

1 Ann Arbor
2 Boston
3 Chicago
4 Los Angeles
5 San Francisco

The analyst first asks the decision maker to select the worst and the best city, considering all aspects that may make a city better or worse than another but ignoring other attributes of the job selection problem (e.g., the fact that the job in Boston has higher prestige or is better paid). Her responses are

> Worst: Chicago
> Best: San Francisco

At this point it is important to explore the reasons for these judgments. For example, she may feel that Chicago is worst because it is too big, too noisy, too cold, and so on. She likes San Francisco because it is smaller, warmer, and offers the cultural life of a big city but is not plagued by the congestion and pollution that often go hand in hand with large size. These more specific values define the qualitative meaning of the underlying value scale. If location turned out to be decisive in the choice, it might be useful later to spell them out in detail and evaluate the best options on each, using the methods of Chapter 8. In any case, the analyst should spend some time on this step. It might be helpful to ask the decision maker which U.S. city she would consider the worst and which she would consider ideal. Gary, Indiana, and Berkeley, respectively, might be her answers, in line with the above reasoning.

After the meaning of the scale has been clarified, and other cities are ranked between the two extremes, the decision maker may want to reconsider her choices of extremes. For example, when trying to place Ann Arbor she may find that both Ann Arbor and Chicago are bad. The climate is similar, and though Ann Arbor is certainly pleasant and small and has little pollution, it is also dull and has fewer entertainment opportunities than a big city. The analyst should encourage such self-exploration and should avoid forcing consistency with previous judgments, since at this stage of the analysis the meaning of the scale can still change. Let us assume that the decision maker finally puts Ann Arbor at the bottom of the list. She then ranks the cities as follows:

1 San Francisco
2 Boston
3 Los Angeles
4 Chicago
5 Ann Arbor

During the process of ranking, the decision maker also explores how sure she is about her preferences and reasons for their strengths. For example, she is certain that San Francisco offers almost everything she wants and that Boston is not even close because of the climate. Los Angeles and Chicago are close to one another in many respects, but Los Angeles wins out because of the climate and the ocean. Ann Arbor is last for different reasons but is close to Chicago. And there is a sizable gap between Boston and the remaining three.

The purpose of the following steps is to translate this qualitative information into a quantitative value scale. A simple procedure is a numerical rating on a scale such as the one in Figure 7.4. The scale has two anchors: the worst alternative (Ann Arbor) is rated 0, and the best (San Francisco) is rated 100. The upper numerical end point is arbitrary. The lower one is also, unless ratio judgments are to be used. The remaining three cities are rated in between. The decision maker is instructed to consider carefully the *relative value* of the locations and then rate the remaining cities in such a way that the *relative spacing* between cities reflects the strength of her preferences for one city over another. We assume that she tentatively assigns ratings to the three cities as in Figure 7.4b.

The analyst can now perform a number of consistency checks. First, the relative ratings can be cross-checked against one another. For example, the analyst may ask whether the value steps AA–LA, LA–BO, and BO–SF are about equal, as indicated in the ratings. If not, adjustments should be made. Next, the analyst and decision maker should explore more complex questions such as: Is the difference between Chicago and Los Angeles truly smaller than that between Los Angeles and Boston? Perhaps the decision maker feels that Los Angeles and Boston are, in fact, closer in value than Chicago and Los Angeles. This judgment may lead to a revision, as in Figure 7.4c. Finally, the analyst can ask her to rate a few cities not in the original list. Such ratings could refine and enrich the original scale. For example, it may be useful to find a midpoint between Ann Arbor and San Francisco. After some hard thinking the decision maker may find that San Diego is a reasonable midpoint. Again, checks can be performed to determine whether San Diego is preferred to Los Angeles and Boston is preferred to San Diego, as Figure 7.4c indicates.

The scale construction process stops when the decision maker is comfortable with the assessments. The assessments need not be refined to the last digit. Instead it is important that the relative spacings make sense and that the scale has meaning for the decision maker. If she has trouble placing cities on the scale because the meaning shifts from one intercity comparison to another, it may be useful to decompose the scale further (e.g., into such attributes as proximities to relatives and climate; see also Chapter 8). Finally, the meaning of the scale and the justifications of the values of cities on the scale should be recorded for further reference.

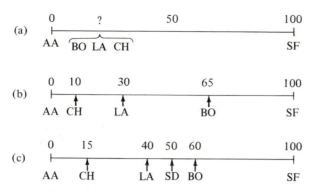

Figure 7.4. Construction of a simple value scale. (a) Creating end points; (b) rating cities in between; (c) rerating after consistency checks and placing a midpoint. AA, Ann Arbor; BO, Boston; LA, Los Angeles; CH, Chicago; SD, San Diego; SF, San Francisco.

Variations of numerical estimation techniques

A variation of the direct rating technique can be used whenever a natural numerical scale exists. An example is rating the value of the size of a home. First, the worst and the best levels of the scale are identified and arbitrarily assigned values of 0 and 100, respectively. For size of home, the end points may be 1,300 sq ft and 2,500 sq ft, respectively. The square footage of all other homes under consideration is then rated in between. Sometimes it is preferable to disassociate the evaluation object from the evaluation of attribute levels. In the case of evaluating home sizes, for example, one might ask the respondent directly to rate different levels of square footage without association to particular homes. The respondent is instructed to consider carefully the relative difference in value as reflected on the numerical scale. Whether a graphic scale is used is a matter of convenience. An example without a graphic aid is the following rating:

$$
\begin{aligned}
v(1,300) &= 0 && \text{(arbitrary assignment),}\\
v(1,700) &= 45 && \text{(judgment, relative to arbitrary assignment),}\\
v(2,000) &= 75 && \text{(judgment, relative to arbitrary assignment),}\\
v(2,100) &= 80 && \text{(judgment, relative to arbitrary assignment),}\\
v(2,300) &= 100 && \text{(arbitrary assignment).}
\end{aligned}
$$

A visual curvilinear fit is shown in Figure 7.5. In this example the end points were chosen to be the actual lowest and highest areas in the set of alternatives. What would happen if homes with 1,200 sq ft and 2,500 sq ft were added to that set? This would require changes in scaling that would be somewhat inconvenient. Although the relative spacing of the original alternatives would not change, the new points would have to be put into per-

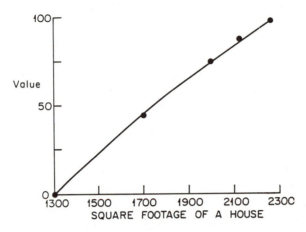

Figure 7.5. Example of a value function.

spective. This could be done in either of two ways. One would be extrapolation.

To extrapolate, the decision maker simply judges how far the new points are from the extremes in the spacing of the given scale. If, for example, 2,500 sq ft is about as much better than 2,300 sq ft as 2,300 sq ft is better than 2,100 sq. ft, the additional value must be 15, according to the previously established scale. Similarly, if the reduction in value from the already small 1,300 sq ft to the 1,200 sq ft is considered appreciable, then the step may be half as much as that from 1,700 to 1,300 sq ft (which on the value scale was 45/2). Consequently, the new sizes would be assigned values of $v(1,200) = -22.5$ and $v(2,500) = +115$, respectively.

Alternatively, the new extreme points (1,200 and 2,500 sq ft) could be given the new values 0 and 100, and two points in between (e.g., 1,700 and 2,000 sq ft) would have to be rerated. Assume that $v(2,000) = 80$ and $v(1,700) = 60$ on that new scale. That information is sufficient to rescale all other alternatives.

The two examples show that changing the scale can be somewhat cumbersome. Therefore, we find it useful to choose end points very likely to include any possible future alternatives. One way to do so is to consider the *available* rather than the *actual* range. An alternative is to use the *acceptable* range, that is, the range of objects that one would be willing to consider. For example, a family of four is unlikely to consider homes with less than 1,000 sq ft and may not be able to afford a home with more than 2,500 sq ft. Finally, it may be possible to consider the theoretically *feasible* range of objects. We discourage such a wide range, however, because most actual objects will lie close to one another in the middle of that range and discrimination among them will be difficult. Figure 7.6 shows the relationship between actual, acceptable, available, and feasible ranges.

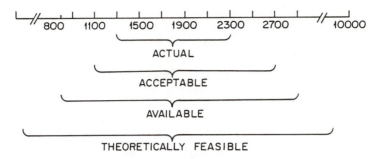

Figure 7.6. Possible choices of end points.

The rating method – with or without a graphic aid – is probably the simplest and most commonly used numerical estimation method for value measurement. Two variations are the *category estimation method* (Torgerson, 1958, calls this method the method of equal-appearing intervals) and the *ratio estimation method.* In category estimation, the possible responses of the decision maker are reduced to a finite number of categories. For example, when judging job locations, the decision maker may be given the following category scale:

Very bad   – – – – – – –   Very good
location   −3 −2 −1   0 +1 +2 + 3   location

The decision maker is instructed to sort possible job locations so that the adjacent categories are considered equally spaced in value. The categorization of the scale makes the task somewhat simpler, but fine distinctions may get lost, unless the number of categories is increased. Another characteristic of this category estimation technique is the loose use of qualitatively defined end points. In most applications of the procedure (e.g., attitude measurement) this is necessary because end points vary across subjects and might overly constrain the responses.

Category estimates are easier to make than simple ratings; ratio estimates are more demanding. In ratio estimation, one stimulus (e.g., a job) is presented as a standard, and the respondent is asked to compare all other stimuli (jobs) with that standard. For each, the respondent is then asked to state how much more or less valuable that job offer is than the standard, in a ratio sense. This judgment assumes a well-understood point of 0 value. The ratio method is described in Torgerson (1958) and Baird and Noma (1978). Ratio measurement instructions make sense in value measurement only if the decision maker compares increments or losses with a standard (which could, e.g., be the present job). If such a standard does not exist, it must be created arbitrarily or ratios of value differences must be compared.

When working with very sophisticated and formally trained respondents, the analyst has yet another option for value measurement: direct selection of functional forms of value curves from a given set or *drawing of such curves* or lines. O'Connor (1973) used this procedure to create value curves for various attributes of water pollution. His respondents were environmental modelers and biologists who were familiar with such functions. Of course, such curve selection or curve-drawing procedures can be used only if the underlying attribute has a numerical scale.

Indifference methods

In the numerical estimation methods the respondents are asked to make direct estimates of strengths of preferences on a numerical scale. In the indifference methods pairs of evaluation objects are varied until a match is established in their respective strengths of preference. In our example of the M.D.'s evaluation of employment locations, we attempted to find a city that was halfway in value between the two anchors, Ann Arbor and San Francisco. Thus, implicitly, we were using an indifference method: by varying cities, we determined a city (San Diego) with a perceived value just midway between the worst (Ann Arbor) and the best (San Francisco). Thus, we would assume that the respondent's strength of preference for San Diego over Ann Arbor should be the same as that for San Francisco over San Diego. This notion of matching strengths of preferences is formalized in the difference standard sequence and bisection methods.

Difference standard sequences

You are planning a Caribbean cruise but wonder whether you should spend 1, 2, or 3 weeks on the boat. To clarify your preferences for length of time on the cruise, you develop a value function over that attribute. One week sounds fine, the second week is all right, but the marginal value of additional time decreases drastically after that. The first step in constructing a value function for time on a cruise ship is to define a zero level and a unit level. The zero level should be the least preferred level, in this case 0 days. The strength of preference of the unit level over the zero level should be small but large enough to be meaningful. One hour would be too small, since it is unclear how to judge the attractiveness of 1 hour on a cruise ship relative to the time periods of 1 to 4 weeks that are being examined. For reasons that will become clear shortly, a general rule of thumb is that the unit stimulus should be located at about one-fifth to one-tenth of the range of the available alternatives. In our example, we choose $x = 3$ days as a unit stimulus.

Next, we arbitrarily define the values of $x_0 = 0$ and $x_1 = 3$ days as

$$v(0) = 0,$$
$$v(3) = 1.$$

Any other assignments would be appropriate as long as the ordering of the v's preserved the ordering of the preference. The remaining task is to find

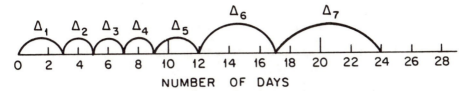

Figure 7.7. Use of the difference standard sequence technique for constructing a value function for time spent on a cruise ship.

time periods x_2, x_3, x_4, etc., such that the increments in strength of preference from x_i to x_{i+1} are equal. This sequence of stimuli that are equally spaced in value is called a standard sequence (see Krantz et al., 1971). Since this standard sequence is built on the notion of strengths of preferences and value differences, we call it a difference standard sequence.

The following hypothetical construction of such a standard sequence is illustrated in Figure 7.7. First pick a time x_2 such that the increase in strength of preference produced by lengthening the cruise from $x_1 = 3$ days to $x_2 = ?$ days is just equal to the increase in strength of preference produced by lengthening it from 0 days to 3 days. Contemplate this question for a moment. Are the first 3 days more or less enjoyable than the next 3 days? Since the first 3 days involve getting accustomed to the cruise, settling down, and so on, the fourth, fifth, and sixth days may each be more enjoyable since you begin to relax and are able to take full advantage of all the facilities on the boat. To make things simple, let us assume that the first 3 days are just as enjoyable as the next 2 days. In the form of an indifference equation, where (x_i, x_{i+1}) means the step from x_i to x_{i+1} days and $\sim$ indicates indifference (judged to have identical differences in value),

$$(x_0, x_1) = (0, 3) \sim (3, 5) = (x_1, x_2). \tag{7.7}$$

Now, once you have settled, your enjoyment for each additional day may stay constant for some time, say for the next 4 days. Thus, we have

$$(x_1, x_2) = (3, 5) \sim (5, 7) = (x_2, x_3) \tag{7.8}$$

and

$$(x_2, x_3) = (5, 7) \sim (7, 9) = (x_3, x_4). \tag{7.9}$$

But now you start to get bored. After 9 days each additional day begins to be less enjoyable. Technically, you show marginally decreasing value. In order to maintain a sequence of days that are equally spaced in strength of preference, you will have to compensate for this marginal decrease in value by increasing the days you add. For example, you may feel that after the ninth day, it takes 3 days (instead of 2) to add the same amount of pleasure, that is,

$$(x_3, x_4) = (7, 9) \overset{\circ}{\sim} (9, 12) = (x_4, x_5). \tag{7.10}$$

After the 12th day, it may take 5 days to generate an equal increase in strength of preferences; thus,

$$(x_4, x_5) = (9, 12) \overset{\circ}{\sim} (12, 17) = (x_5, x_6). \tag{7.11}$$

And, finally, you feel that after 17 days additional days bring hardly any increase in pleasure. It would take a large number of additional days to match the strength of preference between 17 and 12 days, say another week:

$$(x_5, x_6) = (12, 17) \overset{\circ}{\sim} (17, 24) = (x_6, x_7). \tag{7.12}$$

It is easy to confirm that $x_0, x_1, x_2, \ldots, x_7$ is a standard sequence, that is,

$$(x_0, x_1) \overset{\circ}{\sim} (x_i, x_{i+1}) \tag{7.13}$$

for all $i = 1, \ldots, 6$. The only assumption for this indifference equation is transitivity of the relation $\overset{\circ}{\sim}$.

Given other regularity assumptions that are formally expressed in the theory of difference measurement (see Chapter 9), we can now make numerical value assignments based on this standard sequence. Since all value steps from x_i to x_{i+1} are equal,

$$v(x_{i+1}) - v(x_i) = k \tag{7.14}$$

for all i. Furthermore, since

$$v(x_1) - v(x_0) = 1, \tag{7.15}$$

it follows that

$$v(x_{i+1}) - v(x_i) = 1 \tag{7.16}$$

and

$$v(x_i) = i. \tag{7.17}$$

Figure 7.8 is a plot of the resulting value function.

Having obtained fixed values for the points x_i in the standard squence, we can approximate the remaining values by interpolation. Notice that this function has the desired property: it initially accelerates, indicating marginally increasing enjoyment of the trip, and later sharply decelerates, indicating boredom.

To construct a standard sequence it is not necessary to have an underlying numerical scale, but the objects of evaluation must be numerous and densely spaced in value. For example, it would be possible to create a similar standard sequence for cities by specifying a sequence of locations that are equidistant in their relative attractiveness. The general principle of con-

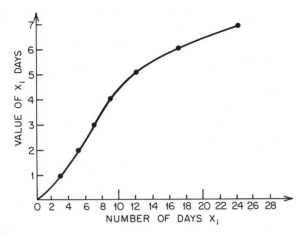

Figure 7.8. Value function obtained by the technique illustrated in Figure 7.7.

structing difference value functions in this manner can be summarized as follows:

1   Pick a starting point and a unit – the zero stimulus x_0 and the unit stimulus x_1.

2   Find a sequence of x_i's such that the indifference equation

$$(x_0, x_1) \overset{\circ}{\sim} (x_i, x_{i+1}) \tag{7.13}$$

holds throughout.

3   Define the value function to be

$$\begin{aligned} v(x_0) &= 0, \\ v(x_1) &= 1, \\ v(x_i) &= i. \end{aligned} \tag{7.18}$$

4   If x is a numerical measure, plot $v(x_i)$ as a function of x_i and interpolate for intermediate values. If x is not a numerical measure, simply list the v values for the standard sequence, and locate the remaining objects by finding their closest x_i's in the standard sequence.

Bisection

In the bisection method (Pfanzagl, 1968; Torgerson, 1958) the respondent is first asked to find the two extreme evaluation objects that span the whole value range. Then the respondent is asked to find an object that is halfway in value between the two extremes. Further subdivision of the scale leads to a refinement of the value function.

To illustrate this procedure, consider the case of an executive of a consulting firm that wants to open a branch office in Los Angeles. We assume that distance from Los Angeles International Airport (LAX) is an important attribute for evaluating alternative sites for the future office. We further assume that average driving time to LAX is an appropriate measure of that concern. Ignoring other attributes for a moment, we shall illustrate the process of constructing a value function over driving time with the bisection method.

First, notice that in this case a numerical measure is available and that more driving time is worse than less. To define the end points of the scale, the executive considers reasonable sites and finds that there are sites near LAX that would require essentially zero driving time. The executive is unwilling to consider sites that are more than 1 hour's driving time from LAX. This specifies a range from 0 minutes to 60 minutes. We arbitrarily assign values of $v(0) = 100$ and $v(60) = 0$ to these end points.

To construct a value function in this range, it is important to ignore the fact that offices with specific driving distances may also have other desirable or undesirable features (e.g., 0-minute driving time also means airport noise). These aspects should be captured in other attributes that are not of concern here. The details of handling this problem of multiple attributes are the topic of Chapter 8. To determine the midpoint value in the range of driving times between 0 and 60 minutes, one might begin with the midpoint on the objective scale and ask whether the executive feels that the displeasure created by the first 30 minutes of driving is equal to the displeasure created by the second 30 minutes. Let us assume that the executive argues that the difference between not driving at all and driving 30 minutes is larger than the difference between driving 30 minutes and 60 minutes. The rationale is that the marginal decrease in value becomes smaller as the time already spent in a car increases. After some probing we find that the bisection point, or the midway point, is 20 minutes; that is, the first 20 minutes are about as bad as the last 40 minutes. This implies that the value of 20 minutes must be halfway between the values of 0 and 60 minutes (Figure 7.9). If we define the midpoint between 0 and 60 minutes as $m_{0,60}$ then

$$v(m_{0,60}) = v(20) = \tfrac{1}{2}v(0) + \tfrac{1}{2}v(60) = 50. \qquad (7.19)$$

Next we find the midpoints between 0 and 20 minutes on one hand and between 20 and 60 minutes on the other. Let us say these are 7.5 and 45 minutes, respectively. Using similar notation, we define $m_{0,20} = 7.5$ and $m_{20,60} = 45$, and we can therefore derive

$$v(m_{0,20}) = v(7.5) = \tfrac{1}{2}v(0) + \tfrac{1}{2}v(20) = 75, \qquad (7.20)$$
$$v(m_{20,60}) = v(35) = \tfrac{1}{2}v(20) + \tfrac{1}{2}v(60) = 35. \qquad (7.21)$$

Additional midpoints can be found to define the value scale more carefully. However, in general three carefully assessed points of the value function should provide sufficient information to smooth a value curve.

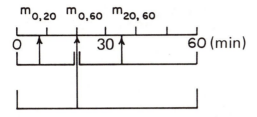

Figure 7.9. Illustration of the bisection method.

Qualitative properties, consistency checks, and curve fitting

Constructing value functions in practical applications involves more than selecting a technique, assessing a few values, and smoothing a curve. In this section we examine some of the skills of value measurement. The first skill is the creation and exploitation of qualitative properties of value scales. Such properties include monotonicity, linearity, concavity, single peakedness, among others. They can be used to restrict severely the shape of the function, even when only a few points have been assessed. The second skill is the detection and resolution of inconsistencies arising from error or from systematic differences between different assessment techniques. The third skill is curve fitting, or the intelligent guess of a functional relationship between a natural scale based on a set of points and qualitative restrictions on the functional form.

Let us consider qualitative scale properties first. If the value dimension has a natural scale, the first question is usually whether value increases or decreases monotonically with it. In other words, is more always better or always worse than less? If so, value is monotonic in the natural scale. If monotonicity is violated, the analyst must explore possible peaks, find out whether the function is single-peaked or multiple-peaked, and so on.

As in our examples of driving times and sizes of apartments, there may be a priori reasons to assume that the value function is concave, convex, or linear. Sometimes these qualitative considerations restrict the shape of the function so much that little more elicitation of actual values is required. We have encountered few if any value functions in research or applications that do not fit one of the cases presented in Figure 7.10.

We go a step farther. We know of few instances in which we would not be able to reformulate an evaluation problem to produce linear or near-linear value functions by carefully selecting or creating a scale. The reason for this is fundamental. A value function is linear in that natural scale that most closely reflects the value concerns to which it is related. If the analyst understands these concerns and if he or she has sufficient flexibility in choosing a

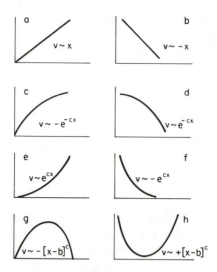

Figure 7.10. Possible shapes of value functions. (The symbol ~ means proportional to.)

natural scale, it makes sense to pick one that is very closely related to the value concerns. To push the idea one step farther, we might argue that an analyst who uncovers extremely curvilinear, single-peaked, or irregular value functions probably has not done the structuring job well.

We and other analysts find more regularity and more linearity in real-world problems and real-world experts than in most experiments. Those who deal with the values and concerns to be quantified in a value function on a regular basis often have already organized their scales in a way that makes it simple to store and process value-relevant information. A natural scale that is linear in value is obviously the most economical device for communicating value-relevant information. This observation leads to the most radical formulation of the linearity argument: values should be linear in appropriate natural scales. Keeney (1981) has offered some interesting thoughts of that kind.

Although the method of exploiting qualitative properties and using simple value functions helps to reduce errors and inconsistencies, it cannot totally eliminate them. We shall be left with judgments that have some undesirable irregularities. Different techniques almost inevitably produce different responses. Rather than finding such differences distressing, we consider them useful for gaining insights into the nature of the value scale and the reasons for technique, stimulus, and response mode effects. Such discrepancies should be carefully examined and resolved through direct interrogation of the respondent or decision maker.

For example, we may find that bisection responses indicate a more curvilinear value function than do rating responses. We can then explore two hypotheses. The rating responses may become artificially linear because of number-matching strategies of the respondent, and bisection methods may produce artificially curvilinear results because of anchoring and adjustment biases. People confronted with such discrepancies often decide that one technique reflects better than others the properties they would like to express in a value scale.

Sometimes, of course, the answer will lie somewhere in the middle. In Chapter 10 we discuss at some length the types of biases and inconsistencies an analyst is likely to find in the types of responses we described here. As usual, the first step toward avoiding such effects is being aware of their existence. The second is using multiple techniques. And the last is exploiting inconsistencies to get the respondent to revise the results.

After reducing the most glaring inconsistencies, the analyst is often left with some error, in the sense that some elicited value points do not have the qualitative properties listed as desirable. If such errors can be attributed mainly to unsystematic differences, the analyst should turn to curve-fitting procedures. Most value scales can be fitted by exponential or polynomial functions. In Figure 7.10 we give some examples that fit the curves presented in the graphs. We use the expression $v \sim f(x)$ to indicate that the function may still have to be linearly transformed in order to match the given set of points.

Besides providing a convenient means of interpolating values at scale points for which no assessments were made, curve fitting allows one to make a parametric analysis of the implications of the decision analysis. By systematically varying the parameters of the curves, one can explore the extent to which a function has to be "stretched" in order to change the initial results of the analysis. Such *sensitivity analyses* can be extremely useful. They either assure both the analyst and the decision maker that the results are robust, or they caution them that they depend crucially on a few sensitive parameters. Good decision analysts use such sensitivity analyses to make conditional statements about the implications of the study.

A version of the assessment of the executive's value function for driving time that exploits qualitative properties and curve fitting might proceed as follows. The analyst begins by providing the executive with the plots in Figure 7.11a and explains that the curves are supposed to express his degree of displeasure about driving to the office. A first assumption might be that the relation is actually linear, but let us assume that the executive argues that the midpoint is lower than 30 minutes, indicating curvilinearity. In particular, his response would indicate that the value of driving 30 minutes must be in the lower quadrant of Figure 7.11b.

The executive's response that the initial 30-minute drive seems more tedious than the added 30 minutes leads the analyst to explore whether the executive feels, in general, that a fixed extra amount of driving time seems

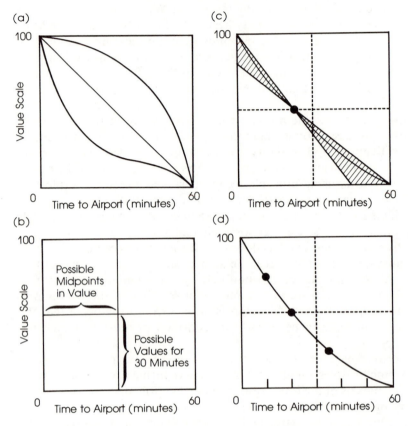

Figure 7.11. Effects of successive restrictions on a value function for driving time to the airport. (a) Possible value functions; (b) implications of nonlinearity; (c) restrictions of value functions by convexity and midpoint; (d) three points on a value function fitted curve.

less tedious after longer initial drives than after shorter ones. Assume that this is the case. "If I have to drive, I get set for the drive and an extra five minutes won't bother me much." This means that identical differences in time should lead to decreasing differences in value. Quantitatively this implies that the curve relating time and value must be *convex*. Convexity and one midpoint of 20 minutes would restrict the value function substantially, as shown in Figure 7.11c. Note that so far we have used only three facts: that the value function decreases monotonically, that it is convex, and that we know its midpoint. Yet we have almost defined it. Let us assume for the moment that the executive gave answers to two additional bisection questions as displayed in Figure 7.11d. Now the analyst can use curve-fitting procedures in order to find a best-fitting value function. For example, the qualitative information and the assessments may suggest an exponential relation. In that case a least squares solution might be the curve depicted in Figure 7.11d.

7.4. Utility measurement

Example: evaluating uncertain job prospects

Many of us have been required to decide whether to accept or reject a job offer while under consideration for another, more attractive job. The dilemma of accepting the sure thing and thus forfeiting the better opportunity versus waiting for the opportunity and risking getting stuck with an inferior job has been well characterized in a set of instructions Fischer (1977) used to elicit a utility function over job alternatives:

Suppose that you have only three job possibilities. The first of these, J_*, is the job which you previously stated was the least desirable of the possible job descriptions. Suppose that you have been offered this job and are free to take as long as you like before making a decision as to whether to accept or reject this offer. The second of your possibilities is J^*, the job which you previously selected as the most desirable of the possible job offers. Assume that you have interviewed for this job and have reasons to believe that you may receive an offer, but you will not know with certainty for several weeks. Finally, let J', the job described on the page of your booklet, be the third possibility. Note that J' is intermediate in value between J^* and J_*. Suppose that you have been offered J' and have been asked to make an immediate decision as to whether to accept or reject it.

This leaves you with two alternatives. First, you may decide to accept J' in which case you forego any chance of obtaining the ideal job, J^*. Second, you may reject J' and await the outcome of the J^* offer. But if the offer does not come through, then you will be forced to accept J_*, the least desirable of the possible jobs. Clearly your decision in this matter will depend upon how likely you think you are to receive the J^* offer. Your task in this portion of the experiment is to specify for each offer, J', a probability p' of receiving the J^* offer, such that you would be indifferent between accepting or rejecting the J' offer [Fischer, 1977, p. 308].

Let us consider a concrete example in which a young Ph.D. has applied for the following five jobs:

J_1 — Research position in an international institute in Europe, 2-year contract, excellent salary, interesting research, no teaching

J_2 — Position for 1 or 2 years at a research institute at his home university, no specific contract, medium salary, interesting research, some teaching

J_3 — Assistant professorship at a very prestigious university, 3-year contract, small salary, heavy teaching load, little research

J_4 — Assistant professorship at a second-rate university, 5-year contract, good salary, medium teaching load, some research

J_5 — Partnership in a small, thriving consultancy firm, 1-year contract, excellent salary, consultancy-type research

The Ph.D.'s preferences are $J_3 > J_5 > J_1 > J_4 > J_2$. The probabilities that the offers will actually be made are as follows:

$$J_1: \quad p_1 = .4,$$
$$J_2: \quad p_2 = 1.0,$$
$$J_3: \quad p_3 = .2,$$
$$J_4: \quad p_4 = .9,$$
$$J_5: \quad p_5 = 1.0.$$

The consultancy firm of J_5 specifies a decision deadline that precedes the date on which the international institute and the universities will say whether they will make their offers. The decision problem can thus be summarized in a decision tree as in Figure 7.12. The problem is this: should the Ph.D. accept the consultancy firm's job offer now or should he reject it and wait? The answer obviously depends on the probabilities (which we know) and the utilities (which we do not know, although we could order the job prospects, if they were certain).

To construct a utility function, the analyst proceeds as follows. First the Ph.D. picks the best and the worst job offer. In this case the best is J_3 and the worst is J_2. Next, the analyst presents the Ph.D. with a series of relatively simple problems. In each of these, the Ph.D. has to compare a gamble with a sure thing. In the gamble he is either offered the best job with probability q_i or he is not offered any of the outside jobs and so has to stay at his home university with probability $1 - q_i$. The sure thing in each gamble is the job offer J_i, where $i = 5$, 1, and 4. Thus, the gambles are somewhat contrived versions of the Ph.D.'s decision to wait. The task of the Ph.D. is to set the probabilities q_i such that he would be just indifferent between the sure offer J_i and the gamble.

For illustration we shall trace the hypothetical thought processes by which the decision maker arrived at $q_5 = .8$ in the first indifference question. He feels that, although the consultancy firm job is very different from the university job, it also is quite attractive. If his chances of getting the university job were excellent (e.g., .99), he would wait for the offer. However, at a probability of .5 he definitely would not like to take the substantial chance of getting stuck at his home university. Therefore, the indifference probability must lie somewhere between .5 and .99.

The Ph.D. feels that the attractiveness of the consultancy job and that of the university job are not extremely far apart. In fact, he might rate them very close on a value scale. But he still would want to have an appreciable probability of getting the university job in order to wait and gamble, because of the regret he would feel if he were to accept the consultancy job and later learn that he could have had the university job if he had waited. After some thought he finally decides that at .9 he would wait, but at .8 he would take the sure thing. When further questioned by the analyst, he recognizes that

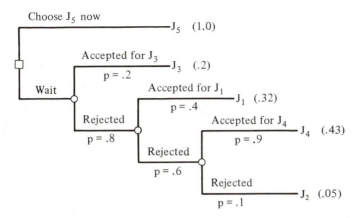

Figure 7.12. Decision tree representation of the job choice problem. Numbers at the tips of the tree are the probabilities of ending up at each tip if the decision maker decides to wait.

he would lower the acceptance probability to .8. Above .8 he would gamble; below .8 he would take the sure thing.

The same process is then repeated for the job offers J_1 and J_4, with the results $q_1 = .6$ and $q_4 = .2$. From the SEU calculus, the analyst can now derive the following utilities:

$$u(J_i) = q_i u(J_3) + (1 - q_i)u(J_2). \qquad (7.22)$$

As usual we set the utility of the worst alternative (J_2) at 0 and that of the best alternative (J_3) at 100. Therefore,

$$u(J_i) = 100q_i. \qquad (7.23)$$

With this example we have just demonstrated the *variable probability method* (also called the indifference lottery method or the basic reference lottery ticket [BRLT] method) and derived the following utilities:

$$
\begin{aligned}
u(J_3) &= 100, \\
u(J_5) &= 80, \\
u(J_1) &= 60, \\
u(J_4) &= 20, \\
u(J_2) &= 0.
\end{aligned}
\qquad (7.24)
$$

Returning to the decision tree of Figure 7.12, we can now easily calculate the SEU of waiting for the better job:

$$
\begin{aligned}
SEU(\text{wait}) &= .05u(J_2) + .43u(J_4) + .32u(J_1) + .2u(J_3) \qquad (7.25)\\
&= 48.
\end{aligned}
$$

Since u (immediate action) $= u(J_s) = 80$, the analysis would suggest that the Ph.D. take the sure thing. Of course, that suggestion should be further explored by sensitivity analysis of both utilities and probabilities.

Example: a utility function over returns from investment

In this section we illustrate the construction of a utility function over a numerical attribute. For the sake of illustration, the decision problem is simplified as follows. We consider an investor who has $10,000 in cash available for a medium-term investment. She wants to maximize her financial return, having in mind a 1-year time horizon. Her investment adviser proposes the following options:

O_1 Buy a bank certificate of deposit at an ensured annual interest rate of 12%.
O_2 Buy stock in a small computer firm. There is a significant chance that the firm will be bought by a large computer firm within a year and that stockholders will be bought out at double the present stock price; there is a smaller chance that the firm's stock value will stay the same and an even smaller chance that the firm will go broke.
O_3 Buy silver, which is expected by some analysts to rise about 25% by the end of the year. However, there is some uncertainty about this increase, and it may be as low as 5% or as high as 45%.

In Figure 7.13 we have plotted the probability distributions over net undiscounted gain after 1 year for each option. Option 1 is the simplest: at a 12% guaranteed annual interest rate, the net gain of a $10,000 investment will be $1,200 *for sure*. For option 2 we consider three scenarios: in the first the firm goes broke within the year and has no residual value. The adviser assigns this scenario a probability of .2. In the second scenario the value of the stock will not change and the firm will not be bought. This scenario has a probability of .3. In the final scenario the buyer purchases the firm and offers to buy the investor out for $20,000. This scenario has a probability of .5. Therefore, option 2 is characterized as follows:

Event	Probability	Net gain
Firm goes bankrupt	.2	− 10,000
Firm remains stable, no purchase	.3	0
Firm is bought	.5	+ 10,000

The silver speculation is characterized as follows. We assume that the probability distribution over an increase in the silver price is normal with a mean of 25% and a standard deviation of 10%. (This does, in fact, allow for a .005 probability that the silver price will actually drop.) From these specifications and the properties of normal distributions we can infer that net gain is also normally distributed with a mean of $2,500 and a standard deviation of $1,000. Figure 7.13 shows the plot of that distribution.

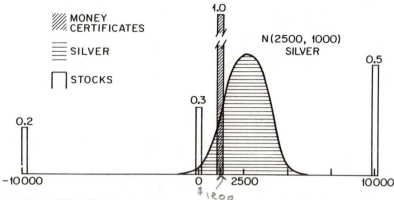

Figure 7.13. Probability distributions over net investment gains for three options.

The EVs of the three options are easy to compute:

$$EV(O_1) = \$1,200; \quad EV(O_2) = \$3,000; \quad EV(O_3) = \$2,500. \quad (7.26)$$

Although these calculations suggest a preference for the stock speculation, the investor is hesitant because of the chance of losing all of her money. Similarly, the (admittedly small) risk of losing money in the silver investment makes her feel uneasy, although the expected gain is larger than the certain gain from buying certificates of deposit. She is willing, however, to accept the axioms of expected utility theory, and an analyst begins to construct a utility function for gains and losses in order to determine her best choice.

The first step in the process of constructing that utility function is to identify the variable over which utility is to be defined. Possible variables are yields, net gain, total final assets, percent profit, among others. We assume for simplicity here that the investor is concerned mainly with net absolute gain or loss.

The second step is to determine the boundaries of the utility function. How large can the possible gain and the possible loss be? The maximum loss is, of course, the invested amount, $10,000. The maximum gain is $10,000 in the case of a successful stock venture. (In principle the silver prices could increase by 500% and yield an even higher gain, but according to our distributional assumption this is extremely unlikely.) We therefore define the following arbitrary boundaries of the utility function u:

$$u(+\$10,000) = 100, \quad (7.27)$$
$$u(-\$10,000) = 0. \quad (7.28)$$

The analyst now constructs the utilities of gains or losses between those boundaries by presenting the investor with a series of simple hypothetical investment options involving only .5 probabilities. These investment options can be described by the notation $(x, \frac{1}{2}, y)$, where x and y are two amounts, positive or negative, and the investor gets x with probability $\frac{1}{2}$, and otherwise gets y. In each case the investor will be asked to provide a certainty equivalent z such that she is indifferent (indicated by a $\sim$ sign) between "playing" $(x, \frac{1}{2}, y)$ and taking a sure gain or loss z. First the investor has to find a certainty equivalent $z_{1/2}$ such that

$$z_{1/2} \sim (+\$10{,}000, \tfrac{1}{2}, -\$10{,}000). \tag{7.29}$$

Beginning with a simple question to bound this certainty equivalent, the analyst asks the investor whether she would prefer to gamble for $\pm \$10{,}000$ or not (i.e., the comparison is between the status quo [0] and the above lottery). Let us assume that the investor declines the gamble because the attraction of the gain does not make up for her aversion to the loss. This implies that

$$z_{1/2} < 0. \tag{7.30}$$

Next the analyst asks the investor whether she would rather take a sure $\$4{,}000$ loss or gamble. The investor does not hesitate: she would gamble. This implies that

$$-\$4{,}000 < z_{1/2} < 0. \tag{7.31}$$

After further probing, the investor finally decides that

$$z_{1/2} = -\$2{,}000. \tag{7.32}$$

From the definition of the utilities of the end points, $-\$10{,}000$ and $+\$10{,}000$, and from SEU theory it now follows that $u(z_{1/2}) = u(-\$2{,}000) = 50$.

Figure 7.14a shows the implication of the end-point utilities, the monotonicity of utility for money, and the one assessment. Already the shape of the utility function has been somewhat confined. Notice also that the utility of $z_{1/2}$ is exactly halfway between the utilities of the extremes. That is, of course, a natural result of our assessment method, which resembles the bisection method for riskless value assessment. As in bisection, the analyst now proceeds by subdividing the utility scale. The following series of indifferences are assessed by the investor in a manner similar to the assessment described for $z_{1/2}$:

$$z_{1/4} \sim (-\$10{,}000, \tfrac{1}{2}, z_{1/2}), \tag{7.33}$$
$$z_{3/4} \sim (z_{1/2}, \tfrac{1}{2}, +\$10{,}000), \tag{7.34}$$

and after these two equations are solved for z,

$$z_{1/8} \sim (-\$10{,}000, \tfrac{1}{2}, z_{1/4}), \tag{7.35}$$
$$z_{3/8} \sim (z_{1/4}, \tfrac{1}{2}, z_{1/2}), \tag{7.36}$$

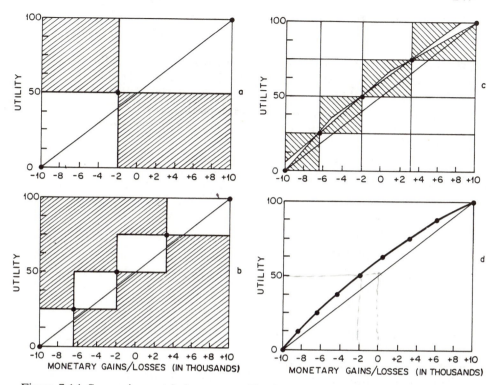

Figure 7.14. Successive restrictions on a utility function. (a), Effects of one point and of knowledge of monotonicity; (b), effects of three points and monotonicity; (c), three points, monotonicity, and concavity; (d), final, smooth curve.

$$z_{5/8} \sim (z_{1/2}, \tfrac{1}{2}, z_{3/4}), \tag{7.37}$$

$$z_{7/8} \sim (z_{3/4}, \tfrac{1}{2}, +\$10{,}000). \tag{7.38}$$

For example, the investor may find that

$$z_{1/4} = -\$6{,}400 \sim (-\$10{,}000, \tfrac{1}{2}, -\$2{,}000) \tag{7.39}$$

and

$$z_{3/4} = +\$3{,}200 \sim (-\$2{,}000, \tfrac{1}{2}, +\$10{,}000).$$

By solving the respective SEU equations, we find that

$$u(-\$6{,}400) = u(z_{1/4}) = 25, \tag{7.40}$$

$$u(+\$3{,}200) = u(z_{3/4}) = 75. \tag{7.41}$$

The additional two assessments imply restrictions on the shape of the utility functions as sketched in Figure 7.14b. From these first three assessments, it appears that the investor's certainty equivalents are always lower than the

EV of the gamble. In other words, if $z \sim (x, \frac{1}{2}, y)$, then

$$z < \tfrac{1}{2}x + \tfrac{1}{2}y. \tag{7.42}$$

The analyst asks the investor whether this will generally be the case. The investor indicates that she generally dislikes to take risks and that, as a result, feels she should get a little more than the straight EV if she does. We have already discussed risk aversion, of which this is an example, and have shown how its interpretation in terms of utility requires a concave utility function.

To keep the discussion brief, we now assume that the investor has provided the following full set of certainty equivalents:

$$
\begin{aligned}
z_{7/8} &= +\$6,000, \\
z_{3/4} &= +\$3,200, \\
z_{5/8} &= +\$400, \\
z_{1/2} &= -\$2,000, \\
z_{3/8} &= -\$4,400, \\
z_{1/4} &= -\$6,400, \\
z_{1/8} &= -\$8,400.
\end{aligned}
\tag{7.43}
$$

These assessments imply the shape of the smoothed utility function indicated in Figure 7.14d, which can now be used to determine the SEUs of the original three investment options.

This is straightforward for the two options with discrete outcomes (options 1 and 2). Option 1 (money certificates) generates a sure net gain of $1,200. The utility of this gain can be read off the curve in Figure 7.15d:

$$u(\$1,200) = 67. \tag{7.44}$$

The unknown utility for option 2 (the stock speculation) is that of $0 (no change). Again reading off of the curve, we find that that utility is 61. Therefore, the SEU of option 2 is

$$
\begin{aligned}
SEU(O_2) &= .2u(-\$10,000) + .3u(\$0) + .5u(+\$10,000) \\
&= .2(0) + .3(61) + .5(100) \tag{7.45} \\
&= 68.
\end{aligned}
$$

The calculation of the SEU for the silver purchase is more difficult, since it has infinitely many outcomes. We use a mathematical trick, by first approximating the utility function in Figure 7.14d with an exponential form $u(x) = ae^{bx} + c$. This function is usually a good approximation for smooth utility functions. In particular, for $a, b < 0$, it approximates concave utility functions like the one in Figure 7.14d. We define the three parameters by solving the equations for the end points $u(-\$10,000)$ and $u(+\$10,000)$, and for the midpoint $u(-\$2,000)$, which yields in approximation:

$$u(x) = 100(1.61 - e^{-(.48/10,000)x}). \tag{7.46}$$

The expectation of this function with respect to a normally distributed random variable can be derived by using tools of mathematical statistics. The expectation E of the function $-e^{-bx}$ can be shown to be

$$E(-e^{-bx}) = -e^{-bm+b^2s^2/2} \tag{7.47}$$

(see Keeney and Raiffa, 1976, Table 4.6), where m and s are the mean and standard deviation of the normal distribution, respectively. In our case the mean is $m = \$2,500$ and the standard deviation $s = \$1,000$. Using these values together with $b = .48/10,000$ we find the resulting SEU of option 3 to be

$$SEU(O_3) = 100E(1.61 - e^{-(.48/10,000)x}) \tag{7.48}$$
$$= 161 + 100E(-e^{-(.48/10,000)x}) = 72.$$

The result of this analysis therefore shows that an SEU-maximizing investor with a utility function as indicated in Figure 7.14d should choose the *silver option,* which has the highest SEU, although the stock option has the highest EV. It is useful to perform sensitivity analyses to check whether the shape of the utility function or the probabilities would make a difference in the final decision. Results are then presented conditional on the assumptions about probabilities and utilities. For example, a result could be formulated as follows. *If* the investor is risk averse with a utility function

$$u(x) = 100(1.61 - e^{-(.48/10,000)x}), \tag{7.49}$$

and *if* the probability assessments of the three options are correct, then the investor should accept the silver option. *If*, in contrast, the investor is risk neutral (i.e., an EV maximizer), she should prefer the stock option given the same probabilities.

An overview of utility measurement techniques

By means of the two examples presented in the preceding sections, we have demonstrated the two basic procedures for eliciting utilities. Because probabilities are varied in the first method to create an indifference between a *given* certainty equivalent and fixed outcomes, this method is also often called the variable probability method. Raiffa (1968) calls this method the basic reference lottery ticket (BRLT), since comparisons always involve the same basic gamble – although the probability of winning varies. In the second example the probabilities were fixed at .5, but the outcomes of the gamble were changed and the certainty equivalent was variable. This method is therefore called the variable certainty equivalent method. Both are indifference methods. We briefly summarize the principles of these two methods and then turn to an interpretation of utility functions and psychophysical issues surrounding the differences and similarities between methods.

The *variable probability method* can be applied to any set of evaluation objects, whether they form a dense set or consist of only a few elements and whether or not they have a natural physical scale. For that reason, <u>many utility theorists favor it.</u> Let $x > y$ stand for "x is preferred to y" and $x \sim y$ for "x is indifferent to y." The principal steps of the variable probability method are as follows:

1   Define the set of evaluation objects X.
2   Select the most and least preferred elements of X; call these x^* and x_*, respectively. (*Note:* If a utility function is to be created over a range of objects arranged on a scale [e.g., the full monetary scale from any low amount to any large amount], set "reasonable" upper and lower bounds that cover most of the range of interest.)
3   Construct a gamble G of the following form,

$$
\begin{array}{cc}
p & x^* \\
1-p & x_*
\end{array}
\tag{7.50}
$$

where p is a variable.

4   Pick any element in X with $x^* > x > x_*$ (by definition of x_* and x^*, this should be true) and compare, for various p,

$$
x \;\begin{array}{c} > \\ \sim \\ < \end{array}\; ?\quad
\begin{array}{cc}
p & x^* \\
1-p & x_*
\end{array}
\tag{7.51}
$$

5   Find the largest p such that the decision maker definitely prefers x to the gamble:

$$
\begin{array}{cc}
\underline{p} & x^* \\
1-\underline{p} & x_*
\end{array}
\tag{7.52}
$$

6   Find the smallest $\overline{p}$ such that the decision maker definitely prefers the gamble

$$
\begin{array}{cc}
\overline{p} & x^* \\
1-\overline{p} & x_*
\end{array}
\tag{7.53}
$$

to x.

7   Point out that the preference switches from a preference for the sure thing at $\underline{p}$ to preference for the gamble at $\overline{p}$. Make sure the decision maker understands the implication that there should be a p_x such that $\underline{p} \le p_x \le \overline{p}$, which produces an indifference between the sure thing x and the gamble. (In other words, p_x makes x a certainty equivalent.)

8   Elicit as precisely as possible the value p_x; that is, establish the indifference

$$x \sim \begin{array}{c} p_x \quad x^* \\ \rule{2cm}{0.4pt} \\ 1 - p_x \quad x_* \end{array} \qquad (7.54)$$

In our experience, subjects in the laboratory after substantial training and decision makers with some familiarity with this task can usually determine the switchover point within a range of .05 of the probability scale. When asked for switchover or indifference probabilities, subjects typically say they are either very close to $\underline{p}$ or $\bar{p}$ or right in the middle.

After steps 1 through 8 have been completed, the utility of x is derived as follows. From the arbitrary definitions of the utilities of the corner points, $u(x^*) = 100$ and $u(x_*) = 0$. From SEU theory,

$$u(x) = p_x u(x^*) + (1 - p_x)u(x_*) = 100p_x. \qquad (7.55)$$

Clearly, $0 \leq p_x \leq 1$, which establishes the bounds of the utility function.

If no natural scale exists and the set of objects is very large, it is useful to select elements in X that are evenly spaced throughout the utility scale. These elements can then be used for scaling the utilities of the remaining elements. For example, if $x_*, x_1, x_2, \ldots, x_i, \ldots, x_9, x^*$ have been assigned utilities of 0, 10, 20, ..., 90, 100, respectively, the analyst can assign a utility to the new element y by simply asking for preferences among x_i and y. If $x_7 < y < x_8$, then $70 < u(y) < 80$. Further precision could be achieved by the creation of more refined indifference gambles.

If there exists a natural scale for X, a common way to select the elements x_i is to space them equally in the natural scale. For example, if the natural scale is monetary gains or losses, with lower bound \$0 and upper bound $+\$1,000$, one would choose \$0, \$100, \$200, ..., \$1,000 as the x_i's. For an illustration, see Figure 7.15. The interpolation of the intermediate utilities can usually be achieved by curve-fitting procedures and by exploiting qualitative properties of utility functions (for an excellent discussion, see Keeney and Raiffa, 1976). In this case a curve $u(x) = ax^b$ was fitted. (Note that the result is a *convex* utility function, indicating a risk-prone decision maker.)

Utility may be nonmonotonically related to the natural scale. An example is the amount of time an individual spends as a passenger on a sightseeing flight in a light aircraft. Figure 7.16 shows how preferences may decrease after increasing for about 2 hours.[1] The procedure for assessing utilities with

---

[1] This example was made up by von Winterfeldt, and Figure 7.16 describes his utilities. Edwards is a light-plane pilot, and a figure expressing his utilities would increase throughout the displayed range.

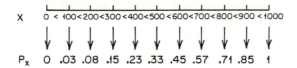

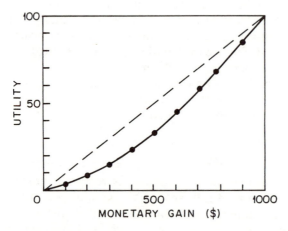

Figure 7.15. Spacing a 7-point utility function <u>for gains</u>. (See text.)

the variable probability method would still be valid, but in this case $x^* =$ 2 hours and there exist *two* x_*'s (0 and an assumed 4 hours). The simplest way to deal with such single-peaked functions is to divide the procedure into two parts: in the first part the utilities between 0 and x^* are elicited, and in the second part the utilities between x^* and 5 hours are elicited. Figure 7.16 shows a hypothetical result. Curve fitting could again be performed with regression methods based on specified function forms (exponential, polynomial, etc.).

In the example, we assume that no ride at all and a 4-hour ride are equally bad, that 2 hours is optimal, and that 1 hour and 3 hours both have utilities of 75. We fit a quadratic utility function. To read off the (dis)utility of a 5-hour ride, one would have to extrapolate. As an alternative, one can extrapolate as follows. Assume that a utility function is constructed between 0 and 4 hours, with the utility specifications as defined above. Now consider the following comparison between a sure 4-hour ride and a gamble for 2 versus 5 hours. The respondent's judgment of an indifference probability p permits us to write

$$u(4) = pu(2) + (1 - p)u(5), \tag{7.56}$$

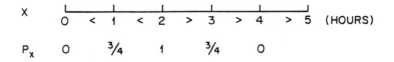

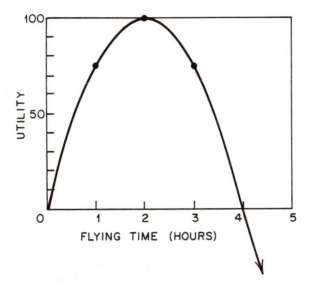

Figure 7.16. Possible utility function for flying time.

which can be solved for $u(5)$:

$$u(5) = -100p/(1 - p). \qquad (7.57)$$

Similarly, utilities can be assigned to any object lying outside the original boundaries of the scale.

The *variable certainty equivalent method* is very much like the bisection #2. method of value scale elicitation (see Section 7.3). It consists of the following steps (see also Keeney and Raiffa, 1976, p. 252):

1   Define the set of evaluation objects X. (*Note:* this set has to be very dense if this procedure is to be followed.)
2   Select $x*$ and x^*, as in the variable probability procedure.
3   Construct a gamble of the following form:

$$\begin{array}{ll} 1/2 & x^* \\ & \\ 1/2 & x* \end{array} \qquad (7.58)$$

4   Select various elements of X and compare

$$x \sim \quad \begin{array}{c} ? \quad 1/2 \quad x^* \\ > \\ < \\ 1/2 \quad x_* \end{array} \tag{7.59}$$

5   Find the largest x such that the decision maker definitely prefers the gamble in

$$\underline{x} < \quad \begin{array}{c} 1/2 \quad x^* \\ \\ 1/2 \quad x_* \end{array} \tag{7.60}$$

6   Find the smallest $\bar{x}$ such that the decision maker definitely prefers the sure thing $\bar{x}$ in

$$\bar{x} > \quad \begin{array}{c} 1/2 \quad x^* \\ \\ 1/2 \quad x_* \end{array} \tag{7.61}$$

7   Point out to the decision maker that the preferences switch from a preference for the gamble at $\underline{x}$ to a preference for the sure thing at $\bar{x}$. Make sure the decision maker understands the implication: there should be an $x_{1/2}$ that causes him or her to be indifferent between the sure thing and the gamble. In other words, $x_{1/2}$ is the certainty equivalent of the gamble.

8   Elicit as precisely as possible the certainty equivalent $x_{1/2}$, that is, establish an indifference between

$$x_{1/2} \sim \quad \begin{array}{c} 1/2 \quad x^* \\ \\ 1/2 \quad x_* \end{array} \tag{7.62}$$

As a rule of thumb, the range between $\underline{x}$ and $\bar{x}$ will be about 5 to 10% of the natural scale values.

After steps 1 through 8 have been completed, the utility of $x_{1/2}$ is derived from the arbitrary definitions of the corner-point utilities $u(x^*) = 100$ and $u(x_*) = 0$ and the SEU assumption:

$$u(x_{1/2}) = \tfrac{1}{2}u(x^*) + \tfrac{1}{2}u(x_*) = 50. \tag{7.63}$$

The same procedure can be used to subdivide the utility scale into equal intervals. If a natural scale exists, three or five points between the corner points are usually sufficient for smoothing a utility function. For seven points the analyst has to determine the certainty equivalents $x_{1/8}, x_{2/8}, \ldots,$

$x_{7/8}$. Since we demonstrated that procedure in the investment example, we will not present any more details at this point.

Qualitative properties, consistency checks, and curve fitting

Since Keeney and Raiffa (1976, pp. 131–218), Raiffa (1968), and Meyer and Pratt (1968) have provided excellent discussions of the "craft" of constructing utility functions, this section is relatively brief.

Risk aversion, risk neutrality, and *risk proneness* are key qualitative properties that preferences among lotteries, or between lotteries and sure things, often exhibit. If interpreted in terms of the shape of the utility function, these properties imply certain functional forms. A decision maker is called risk averse if he or she prefers the expected value of a gamble (as a sure thing) over playing the gamble. Formally, let us assume that the outcomes of a gamble are characterized by a real-valued random variable X (e.g., monetary gains, percent increases in revenue). A gamble can be expressed as a probability distribution P or a probability density function f over that random variable. A decision maker is said to be risk averse if for all probability density functions f (or probability distributions P), the following preference holds,

$$E(x|f) \geq f, \tag{7.64}$$

where $E(x|f)$ refers to the expectation of x with respect to f. Risk aversion has a number of important consequences. First, it implies that the utility of the EV must be larger than the SEU of the gamble. In other words,

$$u[E(x|f)] \geq E[u(x)|f]. \tag{7.65}$$

Second, for increasing utility functions, it implies that the certainty equivalent of a gamble must be smaller than its EV. Since the certainty equivalent is defined as $CE(f)$,

$$E(x|f) \geq CE(f). \tag{7.66}$$

Finally, risk aversion, interpreted as the consequence of a nonlinear one-dimensional utility function, implies that that function is *concave*. Concave utility functions have the following property. All points on a line connecting two points on its graph fall below the utility function. Figure 7.17 gives some examples of concave functions. Formally, for all $x, y, 0 \leq a \leq 1$,

$$au(x) + (1 - a)u(y) \leq u[ax + (1 - a)y]. \tag{7.67}$$

Risk neutrality and risk proneness are defined in analogy to risk aversion. A decision maker is risk neutral if he or she is always indifferent between the expected value of a gamble and the gamble itself. A decision maker is risk prone if he or she always prefers the gamble to its expected value. Risk neutrality implies linear utility functions. Risk proneness, interpreted as a

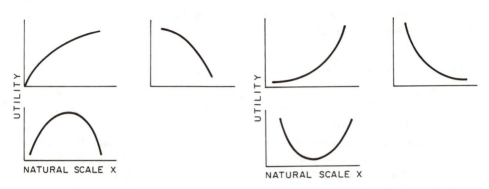

Figure 7.17. Examples of (left) concave utility functions; (right) convex utility functions.

consequence of the shape of a utility function, implies that it is convex. Figure 7.17 shows some examples of convex functions. These concepts have been refined in Pratt (1964), Raiffa (1968), and Keeney and Raiffa (1976) by definitions of risk aversion (proneness) in terms of the derivatives of the utility functions.

The usefulness of such qualitative properties for constructing utility functions should be obvious. Once the analyst has established that a utility function is monotone and that the decision maker always prefers the EV of a gamble over playing the gamble, utility functions are already severely restricted to the shape shown in the upper left corner of Figure 7.17. The assessment of a single utility point further restricts the function to a small range. In Figure 7.18, for example, the utility function was bounded by using monotonicity, risk aversion, and one assessed point, $x_{1/2}$.

So far we have been careful to formulate risk aversion and proneness purely by invoking formal properties of utility functions or by using simple preferences. We could have called risk aversion by any other technical name and still have used the implied properties for restricting utility functions. But those who coined the term *risk aversion* had in mind the psychological interpretation that someone who prefers the EV of a gamble over playing the gamble does not like to take risks. We are uncomfortable with that interpretation, for reasons explained in the introduction to this chapter.

Because of our concerns about a proper psychological interpretation of risk aversion and because of the importance of inconsistencies and errors, we promote the use of multiple convergent procedures for eliciting utility – as we do for the construction of value functions. In particular, we urge analysts to use both riskless and risky procedures simultaneously when assessing a utility function. We also urge them to use both the variable probability method and the certainty equivalent method to check the results against one another. We speculate that formally justified utility elicitation methods

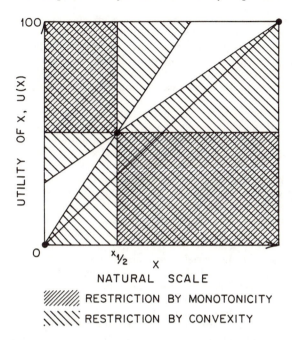

NATURAL SCALE

RESTRICTION BY MONOTONICITY

RESTRICTION BY CONVEXITY

Figure 7.18. Restrictions on a utility function produced by monotonicity and by concavity.

deviate at least as much from one another as the utility methods do from the value scaling methods. Indeed, this is what we imply in our argument that both do or should measure the same thing. This is, of course, an experimental question.

7.5. Implications for decision-analytic practice

You may be rather impatient by now because we have presented a wide variety of methods and you are wondering what to do. Liberally sprinkled throughout this chapter are a number of our own value judgments and hints about what we consider to be useful procedures. We conclude the chapter by summarizing them.

As a decision analyst, you are faced with a problem in which evaluation is important, as it is in all decision problems. What do you do?

1   Structure the problem. Typically, you will find that the evaluation part of it is multiattributed, and you will want to use the methods of Chapter 8. This does not mean, however, that you will not use the methods of this chapter, since they are relevant to the evaluation of each single attribute.

2   Look for a natural scale that is closely related to the decision maker's values, and carefully define its end points. A good scale should be linear or almost linear in value. Often, a trade-off has to be made between the value

relevance of the natural scale and the ease with which alternatives can be measured on it. For example, amounts of pollution can often be measured easily, but the value-relevant issues may have to do with the health effects, which have complicated functional relationships with pollution levels.

3   If you do not find a natural scale, *construct* a scale. This scale can be either qualitative or numerical. In either case, it should suggest a simple relationship to values.

4   Given the scale, either natural or constructed, check for monotonicity of the scale levels and the value levels. If you do not find it, consider restructuring the nonmonotonic scale into two or more monotonic ones.

5   Examine the degree of precision that you (a) need and (b) can hope to get. If you need only approximations, start with linear value functions.

6   If, after taking these steps, you need to assess curvilinear value and utility functions, start with value functions. Go through the steps we have outlined. You will almost certainly want to use order judgments followed by direct ratings rather than anything more complex.

7   For consistency checking, try some gambles. If a dense set of options or a continuous underlying scale is available, use the certainty equivalent method. Otherwise, use the variable probability method. (Inconsistencies invite reassessment of any or all judgments that enter into them.)

8   Do not strive for perfect precision. Quit when you have as much precision as, in both your judgment and that of the decision makers, the problem requires. Rarely will you need to assess more than five points, including the two extremes that define 0 and 100. The rest can be done by curve fitting. For a single-peaked function, you need at most the peak, the two minima, and two more points on each side. Use curve-fitting techniques to fill in as many more points as are needed.

8 Multiattribute utility theory: examples and techniques

8.1. Introduction to MAUT

The methods described in Chapter 7 are likely to fail when the evaluation problem has multiple value dimensions, because intuitive judgments may be exceedingly difficult. When evaluating possible jobs, for example, the decision maker has to consider salary, benefits, location, type of job, colleagues, and promotion prospects, among other things. When evaluating sites for industrial facilities, a manager or board of directors must make complex trade-offs among costs, risks, and benefits. In both instances an overall evaluation seems formidable, especially if the value dimensions are in conflict, as is typically the case with difficult choices. To facilitate value measurement in such complex tasks, multiattribute utility theory (MAUT) was developed.[1] In MAUT the evaluation task is broken down into attributes, and single-attribute evaluations are constructed by means of one of the procedures described in Chapter 7. Then trade-offs among attributes are quantified as importance weights or other scaling factors. Finally, formal models are applied to reaggregate the single-attribute evaluations.

In this chapter we introduce MAUT with two examples. The first example demonstrates the use of a method called SMART (simple multiattribute rating technique; see Edwards, 1977). SMART is the multiattribute extension of the direct rating technique described in Chapter 7. The second example applies an indifference method that is related to the value measurement methods described previously. After providing an overview of MAUT techniques, we describe in detail three classes of techniques: the SMART technique for value measurement, the indifference methods for value measurement, and the lottery-based methods for utility measurement. In the last section of this chapter we give advice on how to choose among techniques in practical applications.

---

[1] Authors have called the tools of complex value measurement MAUT, MAUM, MAUA, and MAU, all referring to the same ideas. The final T may mean technology or theory; M, measurement; A, analysis. Take your pick.

259

An example: evaluating new locations for a drug counseling center[2]

The Drug-Free Center is a private nonprofit contract center that provides counseling for clients sent to it by the city courts as a condition of their parole. It is a walk-in facility with no beds or special space requirements; the center does not give out methadone. It has just lost its lease and must relocate.

The director of the center has screened the spaces to which it might move. All those that are inappropriate because of zoning, excessive neighborhood resistance to the presence of the center, or inability to satisfy such legal requirements as access for the handicapped have been eliminated, as have spaces of the wrong size, price, or location. The city is in a period of economic recession, and so even after this prescreening a substantial number of options are available. Six sites are chosen for serious evaluation. The director must, of course, satisfy the sponsor, the Probation Department, and the courts that the new location is appropriate and must take the needs and wishes of both employees and clients into account. But as a first cut, the director wishes simply to evaluate the sites on the basis of values and judgments of importance that make sense internally to the center.

For this first-cut evaluation the director consults the members of the center staff. Following the ideas of Chapter 2, the director constructs a value tree that expresses the value-relevant objectives and attributes for comparing alternative center locations. The result is shown in Figure 8.1. Since the purpose of the evaluation is to compare quality, cost is omitted. Only at the end of the analysis do we introduce the problem of the quality–cost trade-off.

The numbers attached to the twigs and branches in Figure 8.1 are weights that reflect the relative importance of the attributes for the overall evaluation. These weights were elicited in a two-step process. First, weights were assessed within each of the major branches (A, B, C, and D) to compare the relative importance of the attributes within each branch. For example, the staff members were asked to consider the attributes CA (number and suitability of individual counseling rooms), CB (number and suitability of conference rooms), and CC (suitability of reception and waiting area). Each staff member listed these three attributes in order of their relative importance to their overall suitability for the center's function (C). Assume that there was agreement that the order should be CA–CB–CC. Next each staff member individually assigned relative numerical weights to the three attributes. Several procedures could be used to assign such weights. In this case the staff members simply distributed 100 points over the attributes so that the points reflected the relative "share" of importance. For example, CA, CB, and CC

[2] This section was adapted from W. Edwards and J. R. Newman, *Multiattribute Evaluation.* Copyright © by Sage Publications, Inc. Adapted by permission of Sage Publications, Inc.

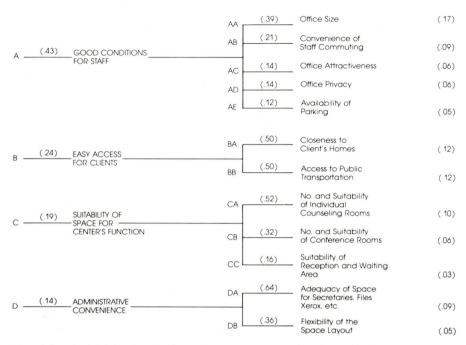

Figure 8.1. Value tree for the Drug-Free Center. (*Source:* Edwards, W., & Newman, J. R., *Multiattribute evaluation.* Copyright © 1982, Sage Publications, Inc. Adapted by permission of Sage Publications, Inc.)

might have been assigned the weights 52, 32, and 16, respectively, by one staff member. These numbers were then normalized to add to 1. The same procedure was followed for the attributes under the remaining branches A, B, and D. Finally, the main branches A, B, C, and D were weighted in the same manner.

Given these assignments, weights on the attribute level were easily obtained by multiplying through the tree. For example, the weight for twig AA (office size) was obtained by multiplying the normalized weight for A (.43) by the normalized weight for AA (.39) to yield .43 × .39 = .17. All the numbers at the right in Figure 8.1 were arrived at by multiplying through the tree.

After individual assessments were made by each staff member, all weights were written on a blackboard, the inevitable individual differences were discussed, and afterward each individual once again produced a set of weights. These still differed, but less so than the first set. The final set was produced by averaging the results of the second weighting; the average values were accepted by the staff as representing its value system.

The director had some reservations about what the staff had produced but kept them to herself, intending to reexamine the issues they raised only if sensitivity analysis showed they made a difference to the overall rankings of sites. She felt that the weights associated with staff comfort issues were too high and those associated with appropriateness to the function of the organization were too low. (Note that she had no serious reservations about the relative weights within each major branch of the value tree; her concern was with the relative weights of the four major branches of the tree. This illustrates the usefulness of organizing lists of twigs into a tree structure for weighting.) She realized, as did the staff, that other stakeholders would also have to be pleased and that the Probation Department and the courts would be much less concerned with staff comfort and much more concerned with suitability for functioning than was the staff. So if the sensitivity analysis showed the final decision to be sensitive to these weights, she planned to elicit some weights from the other stakeholders and combine them with those of the staff.

With a value tree to guide the choice of measures and judgments, the next task was to make detailed assessments of each of the six sites that had survived the initial screening. Such assessments either are or directly lead to the utilities in multiattribute utility measurement.

Inspect Figure 8.1 again. Notice that it lists two kinds of values. Office size is an objective dimension, measurable in square feet. Office attractiveness is a subjective dimension; it can be judged directly. In this example, proximity to public transportation is measured by the distance from the front door of the building to the nearest bus stop. But suppose the sites were in New York. Then both distance to the nearest bus stop and distance to the nearest subway stop would be relevant, and probably the latter would be more important than the former. It would make sense in that case to add another level to the value tree, in which the attribute "proximity to public transportation" would be broken down into those two twigs.

As it happens, all attributes in Figure 8.1 are monotonically increasing; that is, more is better than less. As we explained in Chapter 7, that is not always true.

Figure 8.1 presented the director with a relatively easy value measurement task. Using the procedures described in Chapter 7, she decided to perform the judgments herself. Armed with a tape measure and a notebook, she visited each of the sites, made the relevant measures and counts, and made each of the required value judgments. She used direct rating scales in the case of judgmental attributes (e.g., privacy) and curve-drawing methods in the case of numerical attributes (e.g., office size).

In the case of the judgmental attributes the rating scale was defined to range between 0 and 100. For the attributes with a numerical scale, the director chose end points that reflected a range of plausible alternatives. That is, she did not anchor the scale with the worst and the best of the six alternatives but rather chose "reasonable" anchors. Table 8.1 represents the

Table 8.1. *Values and costs for six sites*

	Site number					
	1	2	3	4	5	6
Attribute label						
AA	90	50	10	50	10	40
AB	50	30	100	10	5	30
AC	30	80	70	10	85	80
AD	90	30	40	10	35	50
AE	10	60	30	10	100	50
BA	30	30	0	50	90	30
BB	70	70	95	50	10	70
CA	10	80	5	50	90	50
CB	60	50	10	10	90	50
CC	50	40	50	10	95	30
DA	10	70	50	90	50	60
DB	0	40	50	95	10	40
Aggregate value	46	53	40	42	49	48
Rental cost ($)	48,000	53,300	54,600	60,600	67,800	53,200
Transformed rental cost	100	73	67	36	0	74

Source: Modified from W. Edwards & J. R. Newman, *Multiattribute evaluation.* Copyright © 1982 by Sage Publications, Inc. Reproduced by permission of Sage Publications, Inc.

location measures of the six sites that survived the initial screening, transformed into the 0 to 100 scale.

The director now had weights provided by her staff and location measures provided either directly by judgment or by calculations based on measurements. Now her task was to aggregate these into measures of the aggregate utility of each site.

We illustrate this aggregation with a simple additive weighted model. This model defines the overall value of a site x (x = 1, 2, . . . , 6) as

$$v(\mathbf{x}) = \sum_{i=1}^{n} w_i v_i(x_i), \qquad (8.1)$$

where $v_i(x_i)$ is the value of site $\mathbf{x}$ on the ith attribute, w_i the importance weight of the ith attribute, and v the value of $\mathbf{x}$.

The results are summarized in the first row below the location measures in Table 8.1. To make a final comparison, the director now plotted rent against value. Figure 8.2 shows the result. Benefits are plotted on the abscissa (horizontal axis); more is better than less. Costs are plotted on the ordinate (vertical axis); since less is better than more, the plot shows high cost at the origin, low cost at the top. Points that are high and to the right

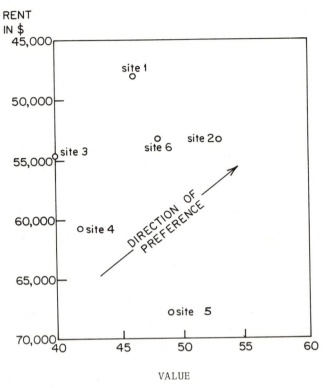

Figure 8.2. Rent vs. value (aggregate benefits) for sites in the Drug-Free Center example.

are preferred to those low and to the left. In abbreviated form, we say that better points lie northeast of worse points, or that northeast is best. We use that scaling convention throughout this chapter.

Without considering how value trades off against cost, the director can infer from Figure 8.2 that she would never choose site 4, since it is more expensive and has less value than site 2. Similarly, sites 3 and 5 are more expensive than site 2 and have less value. They too can be eliminated from consideration. What remains is a tough choice between sites 1 and 2. Site 6, though still in the race, looks like a weak contender, and in fact we eliminate it later. To facilitate the decision, the director contemplates her dollar–value trade-off. Assuming additivity, a trade-off can be characterized by the slope a in the following equation,

$$U(\mathbf{x}) = av(\mathbf{x}) - c(\mathbf{x}), \qquad (8.2)$$

in which $v(\mathbf{x})$ is the value and $c(\mathbf{x})$ the cost. Note that if $v(\mathbf{x})$ and $c(\mathbf{x})$ were both in dollars and a were equal to 1, Equation 8.2 would define aggregate utility in strictly monetary terms. Since $v(\mathbf{x})$ is not in dollars and $c(\mathbf{x})$ is, one

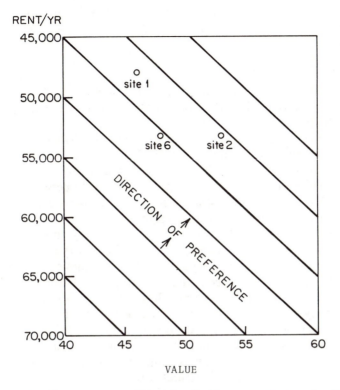

Figure 8.3. Indifference curves (lines) implied by a constant trade-off of $1,000 for one unit of value.

way of interpreting the equation is to say that multiplying $v(x)$ by a translates the units of $v(x)$ into dollars. We ourselves do not find that interpretation useful very often, but it is typically available in contexts such as this in which nonmonetary values trade off against monetary ones. More complex interpretations of the same kind could be made if $c(x)$ were a continuous monotone transformation of dollars.

Consider a set of values of $v(x)$ and $c(x)$ that hold $U(x)$ constant at some value K. Each value of K defines a line in the utility–rent space such that all real or hypothetical points on the line would be considered equally attractive, taking both utility and rent into account. Figure 8.3 illustrates some of these lines. For $a = 1,000$ (the director is willing to pay $1,000 in rent for an increase of one value point), since northeast is best the above trade-off means that the director should choose site 2. If she puts more weight on rent (e.g., $a = 500$), she should choose site 1 instead. Site 6 would never be chosen, since for every conceivable line that goes through its rent–value coordinates either site 1 or site 2 lies northeast of that line. We express this property by saying that sites 1 and 2 *cardinally dominate* site 6.

In Chapter 11 we return to this example to illustrate some tools of sensitivity analysis, the next step in this decision.

An example: evaluating rifles

The previous example was a multiattribute extension of the direct numerical estimation techniques described in Chapter 7. The next example is an extension of the indifference methods.

A military officer was charged with evaluating various rifles that could be included in the standard equipment of NATO soldiers. Three attributes seemed very important for that evaluation: cost, effective range, and weight. Ignoring cost, we shall examine a hypothetical exchange between the military officer and a decision analyst attempting to construct a two-attribute value function over effective range and weight.[3]

First, the analyst and the officer discussed the meaning and the ranges of the two attributes. Weight was defined as the kilogram (kg) weight of the unloaded rifle. The officer was willing to consider rifles that ranged in weight between 3 and 5 kg. Effective range is an interesting combination of the attributes accuracy and range. An analyst may have trouble with these two attributes because they are not independent. A completely inaccurate rifle would be worthless at any range. In standard military definitions that dependency problem has been solved: *range* is defined as maximum distance with a particular degree of accuracy rather than as simply maximum distance. We suspect that similar restructuring of attributes occurs frequently in sophisticated environments.

Our officer was willing to consider effective ranges between 300 and 700 meters (m). From this information the analyst drew Figure 8.4, plotting the abscissa (weight) in descending order to conform with the convention that northeast is best. He also plotted several hypothetical rifles, labeled A through E.

The analyst discussed some direct consequences of this plot for the evaluation of rifles. First note that rifle E would never be chosen if weight and effective range were the only considerations – it is dominated by rifles C and D. However, rifle E could turn out to be particularly cheap, so it is included in the evaluation.

Rifle A is the favorite of all those who worry about effective range but don't think much about the poor soldier who has to carry a heavy load. We speculate that many soldiers would be more likely to pick B. For most reasonable evaluators, the candidates would, of course, be C and D. Those who stress weight would favor D, and those who stress range would favor C.

---

[3] This exchange took place, almost exactly as reported here, in a classroom exercise that was part of a decision analysis course taught by von Winterfeldt to military officers.

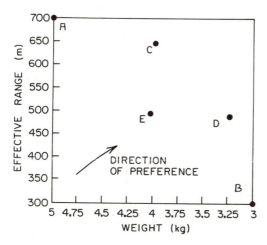

Figure 8.4. Two-dimensional plot of hypothetical rifles that vary on the attributes effective range and weight.

To give the officer a better idea of the trade-off, the analyst constructed a value function $v(m, kg)$ over meters and kilograms. First single-attribute value functions were constructed for effective range $[v_1(m)]$ and weight $[v_2(kg)]$ separately. The analyst assumed that two attributes would combine additively, that is,

$$v(m, kg) = w_1 v_1(m) + w_2 v_2(kg). \tag{8.3}$$

To construct the v_i's and the w_i's, the analyst used an assessment procedure called *dual standard sequence*. He began by choosing an appropriate zero point and an appropriate unit step on both attributes. The officer judged the zero point, the worst possible rifle, to weight 5 kg and have an effective range of 300 m. The analyst defined the unit point on effective range to be 350 m.

With the dual standard sequence procedure one constructs a value scale for weight by laying out a sequence of steps that are equally spaced in value on the weight attribute. The analyst first asked the officer to find a rifle with a 300-m range that was indifferent to the "unit rifle" with a range of 350 m and a weight of 5 kg. If a rifle is described by pairs of numbers (m, kg), then formally the analyst asked the officer to fill in x in the indifference equation

$$(350, 5) \sim (300, x). \tag{8.4}$$

In other words, how great a decrease in weight would add the same value to the worst rifle as a 50-m increase in range? The officer argued that, at such a high initial weight, weight reduction would be fairly important. He thought that an increase in 50-m effective range would be about equivalent

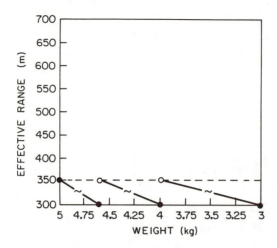

Figure 8.5. Illustration of the standard sequence procedure for constructing a value function for weight.

to a little less than a 0.5-kg decrease in weight, about 0.4 kg. In other words,

$$(350, 5) \sim (300, 4.6).\tag{8.5}$$

This indifference is shown in Figure 8.5, which connects the two points in the plot.

   Next the analyst asked the officer to consider the rifle (350, 4.6) and determine x in the following indifference:

$$(350, 4.6) \sim (300, x).\tag{8.6}$$

In terms of incremental comparisons this is exactly the same question the officer answered before, that is, how much improvement in weight would correspond to an improvement of 50 m in effective range? However, the starting point for that comparison has been systematically moved from the worst weight level, 5 kg, to the next weight level, 4.6 kg, which, sloppily speaking, is 50 m better than 5 kg. Now the analyst asked how much improvement in weight the "50 m better" represented starting from a weight of 4.6 kg. The officer thought that the improvement would now have to be a little more than 0.4 kg, since the starting weight would not be quite as great and therefore the reduction in weight would be somewhat less important. Instead of 0.4 kg, he thought that a 0.6-kg reduction in weight would about match the 50-m increase in range. In other words,

$$(350, 4.6) \sim (300, 4).\tag{8.7}$$

With the 4-kg rifle as the standard, the same incremental question was phrased

$$(350, 4.0) \sim (300, x).\tag{8.8}$$

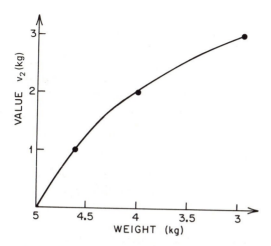

Figure 8.6. Value function for weight.

Using the judgment that the reduction in weight was less and less important as the original weight decreased, the officer assessed this indifference as

$$(350, 4.0) \sim (300, 3.0). \tag{8.9}$$

These three indifferences are plotted in Figure 8.5. They provide three points on a value function for the weight attribute. Each of the weight differences from 5 to 4.6 kg, from 4.6 to 4 kg, and from 4 to 3 kg was worth 50 m of increase in range. In more precise language, the incremental improvements in weight are equally spaced in value because every step in weight was laid off against an equal (unit) step in value on the dimension effective range. (This equal spacing in value depends critically, of course, on the additivity assumption.)

Define the zero point of v_1 at 5 kg and set the unit to correspond to the first value step from 5 to 4.6 kg. It follows that

$$\begin{aligned}
v_2 (5.0) &= 0, \\
v_2 (4.6) &= 1, \\
v_2 (4.0) &= 2, \\
v_2 (3.0) &= 3.
\end{aligned} \tag{8.10}$$

The resulting value function is plotted in Figure 8.6. It indicates that decreases in weight are more valuable for heavy rifles than for light rifles.

Next, the analyst turned to the construction of a value function for the attribute effective range. He followed a similar procedure and picked a hypothetical rifle that was worst on range and one step improved in weight to an arbitrary unit 4.5. He asked the officer how much improvement in range would be needed to match the unit improvement in weight by determining

x in

$$(x, 5) \sim (300, 4.5). \tag{8.11}$$

The officer remembered that $x = 350$ would make it very close to his earlier indifference between (350, 5) and (300, 4.6). But the unit improvement in weight was a little better than the 0.4-kg step in that indifference. He therefore required a slightly larger improvement in range and, after some deliberation, decided that

$$(360, 5) \sim (300, 4.5). \tag{8.12}$$

The analyst repeated the question, but this time starting with a rifle somewhat improved in range; the officer assessed the indifference

$$(x, 5) \sim (360, 4.5). \tag{8.13}$$

He felt that the improvement in range needed to make up for a 0.5-kg improvement in weight would be about the same as before, and therefore $x = 420$ m. This led the analyst to probe whether this was generally true; would the officer always add the same amount of range (60 m) independently of the starting point? The officer's immediate response was that this was probably so, but after some reflection he argued that, once one got into high ranges, it could actually become more important to add a few meters, because the greater range would result in a superb weapon. (This phenomenon is well known to stereo buffs, who consider the last tiny bit of noise reduction to be the most important.)

With this thought in mind, the officer constructed the following indifferences, as shown in Figure 8.7:

$$\begin{aligned}
(420, 5) &\sim (360, 4.5), \\
(480, 5) &\sim (420, 4.5), \\
(540, 5) &\sim (480, 4.5), \\
(590, 5) &\sim (540, 4.5), \\
(630, 5) &\sim (590, 4.5), \\
(660, 5) &\sim (630, 4.5).
\end{aligned} \tag{8.14}$$

Notice that in this sequence the steps in effective range become smaller (from 60 to 30 m), yet they represent equal steps in value. In other words, the marginal value of effective range is, in fact, increasing.

Formally, this can be shown by plotting the value function. As before, we set $v_1(300) = 0$ and $v_1(360) = 1$ and derive the remaining values by exploiting the fact that the series of ranges 300, 360, 420, 540, 590, 630, 660 m is equally spaced in value. Figure 8.8 shows the resulting plot.

The analyst's last task was to construct appropriate weights that matched the two value functions. This was necessary because he picked two unit intervals in the two attributes (350 m and 4.5 kg) that did not produce identical increments in value. Since 4.5 kg seemed to produce a somewhat

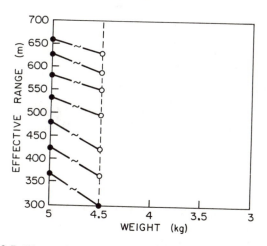

Figure 8.7. Illustration of the standard sequence procedure for constructing a value function for effective range.

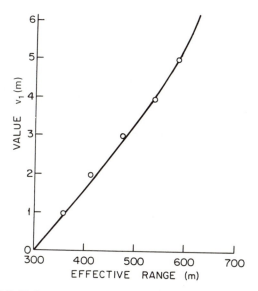

Figure 8.8. Value function for effective range.

smaller increment in value than 350 m, a value of 1 on the value function for range should mean just a little more in the calculation of overall value than a value of 1 on the weight attribute. In order to find the precise weights, we must look at some indifferences between the two attributes. For example, consider

$$(360, 5) \sim (300, 4.5). \tag{8.12}$$

This indifference implies that in the additive value function

$$w_1 v_1(360) + w_2 v_2(5) = w_1 v_1(300) + w_2 v_2(4.5). \tag{8.15}$$

Several values in this equation are known. In fact, the only unknowns are the w_i's and $v_2(4.5)$. By substituting $v_1(300) = 0$, $v_2(5) = 0$, and $v_1(360) = 1$, we find that

$$\frac{w_1}{w_2} = v_2(4.5). \tag{8.16}$$

Inspecting Figure 8.8, we note that $v_2(4.5) = 1.3$. Any two weights that have a ratio of $1.3 : 1$ would be appropriate. A common procedure is to normalize the weights so that they add to 1. In this case

$$w_1 = \frac{1.3}{2.3} = .57, \tag{8.17}$$

$$w_2 = \frac{1}{2.3} = .43,$$

so that the final value function is

$$v(m, kg) = .57v_1(m) + .43v_2(kg). \tag{8.18}$$

This value function implies that the best rifle is C. Note that $C = (650, 4)$ and $D = (500, 3.25)$ and therefore

$$v(C) = v(650, 4) = .57(6.6) + .43(2.00) = 4.6 \tag{8.19}$$

and

$$v(D) = v(500, 3.25) = .57(3.25) + .43(2.75) = 3.0. \tag{8.20}$$

Thus, $v(C) > v(D)$.

An overview of MAUT models and techniques

These examples illustrate two quite distinct approaches to the problem of evaluating complex multiattribute alternatives. Both procedures are mul-tiattribute extensions of the value measurement techniques discussed in Chapter 7 and therefore should technically be called multiattribute *value* measurement techniques. The first procedure, called SMART, builds on the numerical rating technique described in Chapter 7. In fact, the procedures used for constructing single-attribute value functions in SMART are iden-tical to the rating procedure described in that chapter. Following the spirit of direct numerical assessment, SMART often uses direct ratio estimates of the weights assigned to the attributes. In addition SMART assumes a simple additive aggregation rule for trading off the attributes.

SMART is about as simple as multiattribute value or utility measurement gets. The second procedure is much more complicated. It is derived from conjoint measurement theory, which uses dual standard sequences for constructing single-attribute value functions and weights. It is most closely related to the indifference procedures in riskless value measurement (difference measurement and bisection) discussed in Chapter 7.

Though more complicated than SMART, dual standard sequences are far from the most complicated MAUT procedures. First, both SMART and conjoint measurement are concerned only with riskless value measurement, and no gambles are used for elicitation. Versions of multiattribute utility assessment exist that use gambles as stimuli and construct multiattribute versions of *utility* functions using indifference procedures similar to the variable probability and the variable certainty equivalent procedures. Second, both assume an additive model for aggregating single-attribute value functions. Nonadditive aggregation rules have been explored in both riskless and risky contexts.

This chapter covers SMART, conjoint measurement, and the expected utility techniques. Although the multitude of these models and techniques may sometimes create confusion, the unifying themes are clear. All MAUT procedures include the following five steps:

1   Define alternatives and value-relevant attributes.
2   Evaluate each alternative separately on each attribute.
3   Assign relative weights to the attributes.
4   Aggregate the weights of attributes and the single-attribute evaluations of alternatives to obtain an overall evaluation of alternatives.
5   Perform sensitivity analyses and make recommendations.

All approaches are identical in steps 1 and 5, which are discussed elsewhere in this book (Chapters 2 and 11, respectively). The approaches differ in the procedures for single-attribute evaluations (step 2), in the techniques for weighting (step 3), and in the models for aggregation (step 4).

Table 8.2 provides an overview of the main techniques for constructing single-attribute value and utility functions. All but two of these techniques have been described in Chapter 7. The two additional techniques are dual standard sequences and sequential trade-offs. The dual standard sequence technique requires systematic trade-offs to generate sequences of objects that are equally spaced in value along one attribute. In the sequential trade-off technique, one trades off each attribute against a special attribute (like money) in order to find, for each alternative, a hypothetical alternative that is indifferent to it and has constant values in all but the special attribute. A single value function over this special attribute is then sufficient for comparing the alternatives.

Table 8.2. *Taxonomy of techniques for constructing single-attribute value and utility functions*

Judgments required	Stimuli	
	Riskless outcomes	Gambles
Numerical estimation	Direct rating[a] Category estimation[a] Ratio estimation[a] Curve drawing[a]　　　　I	N.A.[b] II
Indifference	Difference standard sequence[a] Bisection[a] Dual standard sequence Sequential trade-off　　　III	Variable probability method[a] Variable certainty equivalent method[a] IV

[a]Described in Chapter 7.
[b]N.A., Not applicable.

Table 8.3. *Taxonomy of techniques for constructing attribute weights*

	Stimuli used	
	Riskless outcomes	Gambles
Numerical estimation	Ranking Direct rating Ratio estimation Swing weights　　　I	N.A.[a] II
Indifference	Cross-attribute indifference Cross-attribute strength of preference　　　III	Variable probability method Variable certainty equivalent method IV

[a]N.A., Not applicable.

Table 8.3 lists the MAUT weighting techniques. The direct numerical estimation methods usually incorporate the concept of attribute importance in order to quantify the relative weight that an attribute carries in the overall determination of value. In the ranking procedure, for example, the respondent is asked to rank the attributes in the order of their importance. In the ratio procedure the respondent directly estimates how much more important an attribute is than the least important one. Direct rating is rarely used as a weighting procedure. A version of it is distribution of 100 points over the attributes so that the number of points assigned to each reflects its relative importance.

Swing weighting does not make use of concept of importance. In this technique the respondent is asked how much an attribute contributes to the overall value of the alternatives relative to other attributes. Typically, the respondent compares alternatives that "swing" between the worst and best levels in each attribute. The respondent estimates which of the swings contributes more in overall value and then assesses the extent to which the value "swings" differ.

Swing weighting is a procedural hybrid derived from an indifference method in which cross-attribute strengths of preference are systematically compared. In this procedure one determines the weights by matching the strength of preference in one attribute to a strength of preference in another. Similarly, cross-attribute indifference methods systematically vary alternatives in two attributes to generate simple equations that can be solved for the attribute weights.

The idea of creating indifferences to generate equations that have simple weighting solutions also appears in the variable probability and variable certainty equivalent methods. In these methods the respondents compare sure things and gambles that have outcomes varying on at least two attributes. The procedures become increasingly complex as one moves from cell I to cell IV in Table 8.3. In cell I simple numerical comparisons among attributes are made; in cell III riskless alternatives are compared that vary on at least two attributes; cell IV involves gambles for outcomes that vary on at least two attributes.

Weights and single-attribute utilities can be aggregated with a variety of models. By far the most frequently used is the weighted additive model,

$$v(\mathbf{x}) = \sum_{i=1}^{n} w_i v_i(x_i), \tag{8.1}$$

where $\mathbf{x}$ is the evaluation object, x_i is its measurement on attribute i, v_i is the single-attribute value function, w_i is the weight of attribute i, v is the overall value of $\mathbf{x}$, and n is the number of attributes. Considerably more complicated in appearance, but about as easy to use, is the multiplicative model

$$v(\mathbf{x}) = \sum_{i=1}^{n} w_i v_i(x_i) + \sum_{i<j} w w_i w_j v_i(x_i) v_j(x_j)$$
$$+ \sum_{i<j<m} w^2 w_i w_j w_m v_i(x_i) v_j(x_j) v_m(x_m)$$
$$+ \cdots + \cdots + w^{n-1} \prod_{i=1}^{n} w_i v_i(x_i). \tag{8.21}$$

Table 8.4. *Models for aggregating single-attribute value functions* (n = 3)

Model	Formula
Additive with linear value function	$v(\mathbf{x}) = w_1 x_1 + w_2 x_2 + w_3 x_3$
Additive	$v(\mathbf{x}) = w_1 v_1(x_1) + w_2 v_2(x_2) + w_3 v_3(x_3)$
Multiplicative (extended)	$v(\mathbf{x}) = w_1 v_1(x_1) + w_2 v_2(x_2) + w_3 v_3(x_3)$ $\quad + w w_1 w_2 v_1(x_1) v_2(x_2)$ $\quad + w w_1 w_3 v_1(x_1) v_3(x_3)$ $\quad + w w_2 w_3 v_2(x_2) v_3(x_3)$ $\quad + w^2 w_1 w_2 w_3 v_1(x_1) v_2(x_2) v_3(x_3)$
Multiplicative (compact)	$1 + w v(\mathbf{x}) = [1 + w w_1 v_1(x_1)]\ [1 + w w_2 v_2(x_2)]$ $[1 + w w_3 v_3(x_3)]$
Multilinear	$v(\mathbf{x}) = w_1 v_1(x_1) + w_2 v_2(x_2) + w_3 v_3(x_3)$ $\quad + w_{1,2} v_1(x_1) v_2(x_2)$ $\quad + w_{1,3} v_1(x_1) v_3(x_3)$ $\quad + w_{2,3} v_2(x_2) v_3(x_3)$ $\quad + w_{1,2,3} v_1(x_1) v_2(x_2) v_3(x_3)$

Notation:
v Overall value function
$\mathbf{x}$ Evaluation object
x_i Measurement (level, degree) of $\mathbf{x}$ on attribute i
v_i Single-attribute value function
w_i Weight of attribute i

In its analytical expansion the multiplicative model seems prohibitive compared to the additive one. Yet it requires only the addition of a single parameter (w), which defines all interaction terms. Therefore, the type of interaction it models is rather constrained, as a more compact form of the multiplicative model (for $w \neq 0$) demonstrates:

$$1 + w v(\mathbf{x}) = \prod_{i=1}^{n} \{1 + w w_i v_i(x_i)\}. \qquad (8.22)$$

For $w = 0$, Equation 8.22 simplifies to the additive form (8.1). In Table 8.4 we have put together some possible functional forms for aggregating single-attribute value or utility functions in the case of three attributes. The common feature of these forms is that they are all simple polynomials (see Krantz, Luce, Suppes, and Tversky, 1971); that is, they are put together by simple multiplication or addition of v_i terms. More general functions,

$$v(\mathbf{x}) = F\{v_1(x_1),\ v_2(x_2),\ \ldots,\ v_n(x_n)\}, \qquad (8.23)$$

Table 8.5. *The three most common combinations of MAUT procedures*

MAUT procedure	Technique for single-attribute values and utilities	Weighting techniques	Aggregation model
SMART	Direct rating	Ratio estimation	Additive
Difference value measurement	Difference standard sequence	Cross-attribute strength of preference	Additive
SEU measurement	Variable probability or certainty equivalent method	Variable probability method	Multiplicative

and functional forms using attribute subsets have been explored in the literature but have so far found little use in applications of MAUT to real-world problems. The functional forms of Table 8.4 have been developed both in the expected utility framework (see Kenney and Raiffa, 1976) and in the riskless difference value measurement framework (Dyer and Sarin, 1979).

In principle it is possible to combine virtually any technique for single-attribute value or utility measurement with any weighting procedure and aggregation model. All possible combinations of our taxonomic elements would create a very large menu of MAUT procedures. Not surprisingly, only a few of these combinations are commonly applied to real-world situations. The first combination, the *SMART procedure,* selects elements that are simple and easily applicable: the direct rating procedure for assessing single-attribute values, ratio estimation for weighting, and additive aggregation. The second combination is based in value measurement theory and emphasizes the use of indifference judgments in measurement. In the multiattribute extension of *difference value measurement,* strength-of-preference judgments are used to construct both single-attribute value functions and weights. It is usually combined with an additive model. Difference value measurement has not been frequently applied in MAUT but is gaining increasing acceptance. The third combination stresses the fact that most options are risky and that procedures should be adequate for the construction of utility functions. The multiattribute versions of *SEU measurement* combine the variable probability or certainty equivalent methods for constructing single-attribute utility functions with the variable probability method for constructing weights. For reasons to be discussed later the multiplicative model is the most commonly used in that paradigm. Table 8.5 summarizes the most common combinations.

8.2. The simple multiattribute rating technique

Origins

Versions of multiattribute value measurement were known as early as 1959, when Adams and Fagot described both the principles of value functions and some assessment procedures based on indifference judgments. Later, Krantz (1964) and Luce and Tukey (1964) provided a thorough formal treatment of additive value functions in the context of conjoint measurement theory. In 1965 Fishburn published a seminal paper in which he formulated the axioms for additive versions of expected utility theory. Pollak (1967) and Keeney (1968) provided an axiomatic basis for multiplicative utility functions in MAUT. By 1968, the theory of MAUT was well in place.

Raiffa (1969) and Edwards (1971) gave MAUT practical respectability. After 10 years of theorizing, these writers in essence said, "It can be done." But their papers were quite different in flavor. Raiffa implicitly advocated the indifference methods and, following his own intellectual heritage, the SEU versions of MAUT. Edwards knew the theory, was frustrated by the complicated measurement and elicitation techniques it seemed to require, and sought simple and robust procedures instead of theoretical soundness and elegance. His solution was SMART, which ignored measurement theory and nonadditivities and instead relied on simple additive models, numerical estimation techniques for eliciting single-attribute values, and ratio estimation of weights. Initially, SMART was justified by its simplicity, later by studies that demonstrated the robustness of additive multiattribute models, and still later by difference measurement, which gave it theoretical support. In the process SMART underwent a number of metamorphoses and today comprises a collection of techniques rather than a single procedure. The main communality among the SMART techniques is their reliance on direct numerical estimation methods. However, more recent versions of SMART – for example, those that make use of sophisticated swing weights with single-attribute curve-drawing procedures – are virtually indistinguishable from difference measurement both behaviorally and theoretically.

The earliest version of SMART consisted of the following 10 steps (see Edwards, 1971, 1977):

1   Identify the organization whose values are to be maximized.
2   Identify the purpose of the value elicitation.
3   Identify the entities (alternatives, objects) that are to be evaluated.
4   Identify the relevant dimensions of value (attributes).
5   Rank the dimensions in order of importance.
6   Make ratio estimates of the relative importance of each attribute relative to the one ranked lowest in importance.
7   Sum the importance weights; divide each by the sum.

8   Measure the relative value of each entity (alternative, object) on each dimension on a scale of 0 to 100.

9   Calculate the overall values using a weighted additive model.

10   Choose the alternative that maximizes the overall value.

In more recent versions of SMART the structuring steps (1–4) have been emphasized. In particular, recognition of the hierarchical nature of structures of objectives and attributes frequently leads to versions of SMART that make use of value trees and hierarchical weighting procedures. Swing weights have become more and more common in SMART. Also, the techniques for constructing single-attribute values have been refined by the use of more sophisticated anchoring methods and by the use of strength-of-preference instructions as a supplement to direct rating.

An application of SMART to coastal zone management

Gardiner (1974) applied an early version of SMART to the evaluation of coastal development plans. He described the problem as follows:

The Coastal Zone Development Act [of California] charged the commissioners of the Region V [Coastal Commission] with evaluating each development request submitted and either approving or disapproving. A major problem results since the Act does not specify just how this very large and difficult evaluation and decision making task is to be accomplished. The permit requests consist of information on many different important dimensions that are specified (at the abstract, conceptual level) by the Act. . . .

Although the Act specifies that certain attributes should be considered, it fails to specify just how they are supposed to enter into the evaluation. Nor does the Act specify how the commissioners are to balance the conflicting interests affected by their decision. In effect, the Act implies that individual commissioners assigned to the Commission will represent the interests of all affected parties with respect to the coastal zone.

Gardiner tried to solve these problems by developing a formal MAUT procedure for evaluating proposals for coastal development. His respondents were individuals involved in coastal zone planning and decision making, including two commissioners. The following dimensions were used for evaluation:

1   Size of the proposed development, measured as the number of square feet of the coastal zone taken up by the development

2   Distance from the mean high-tide line; the location of the nearest edge of the development from the mean high-tide line in feet

3   Density of the development; the number of dwelling units per acre

4   On-site parking facilities; the percentage of cars brought in by the development that would be provided parking spaces

5   Height of the building in feet (17.5 feet per story)

6   Unit rental, measured as the dollar rental per month (on the average), for the development

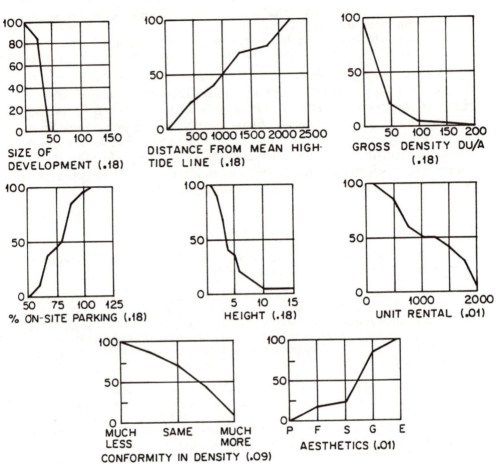

Figure 8.9. Example of value curves and importance weights for permit items for a group 1 subject. (*Source:* Gardiner, 1974.)

7   Conformity with land use in the vicinity; the density of the development relative to the average density of adjacent residential lots (judged directly on a 5-point scale)

8   Aesthetics of the development, measured on a scale from poor to excellent

Note that all these attributes are monotone in value: either more is better or more is worse. This substantially simplifies the single-attribute evaluations. If nonmonotonicities had occurred at this stage, it would probably have been desirable to restructure the attribute set.

To construct value functions with a direct rating technique Gardiner presented his respondents with the worst and the best level on each attribute. For example, in the case of distance from mean high-tide line, worst was 0 yards, best was 3,000 yards. The worst level was assigned a value of 0, and

Table 8.6. *Results of ratio weighing of dimensions to evaluate coastal development permits for Venice, California (for a sample respondent)*

Size	Rank order of importance	Ratio weights	Normalized weights
Distance from mean tide line	Tied for first	180	.178
Gross density	Tied for first	180	.178
Percentage of on-site parking	Tied for first	180	.178
Height	Tied for first	180	.178
Size of development	Tied for first	180	.178
Conformity in density	Second	90	.090
Unit rental	Tied for last	10	.001
Aesthetics	Tied for last	10	.001

Source: Gardiner (1974).

the best was assigned a value of 100. Respondents were then asked to rate the various preselected levels of the attribute between the worst and best level, keeping in mind that the rating should reflect how far in value the level under consideration was from the extremes. Value functions thus derived were plotted, briefly discussed, and revised. The resulting eight value functions for one respondent are shown in Figure 8.9. The respondent's weight is shown underneath each function.

Weights were derived using direct numerical ratio judgments of relative attribute importance. First, the respondents rank-ordered the attributes in importance. Next, they assigned an arbitrary importance of 10 to the least important dimension. Next, they judged how much more important the next dimension was, how much more important the one after that was, and so on. Table 8.6 gives the results for one subject.

These weights were then normalized by

$$w_i = \frac{w_i'}{\sum_{i=1}^{n} w_i'}, \tag{8.24}$$

where w_i' is the unnormalized ratio weight and w_i the normalized weight.

With these inputs, it was possible to evaluate each permit request for coastal development x from each individual's point of view by measuring its performance on each of the eight attributes (x_i), converting these numbers to value numbers [$v_i(x_i)$], and finally aggregating weights and values. For the aggregation step Gardiner used the simple additive model:

$$v(\mathbf{x}) = \sum_{i=1}^{n} w_i v_i(x_i). \tag{8.1}$$

Since the w_i's add to 1 and the v_i's are bounded between 0 and 100, all aggregate values fall between 0 and 100.

Gardiner used this analysis to study disagreements between individuals favoring coastal development and individuals advocating strict conservation. He found that the model produced surprising agreement over a series of permits. He argued that the use of the model in relatively routine cases could substantially improve (and definitely shorten) the commission's evaluation process.

Variations of SMART

Variations of SMART differ in the specific techniques for constructing single-attribute values of the objects under evaluation and in the specific method of weighting.

Three SMART variations exist for constructing single-attribute values. These differ in the degree to which they refine an underlying value scale. In perhaps the crudest version, an attribute is defined in qualitative terms, for example, environmental impact. Next, the alternatives that seem best and worst with respect to that attribute are identified. All other alternatives are rated in between. With this *direct rating technique,* one does not explicitly construct any attribute scale but directly assigns single-attribute values to alternatives.

A first refinement consists of identifying a natural scale that is linear in value and identifying its end points. Cost measured in dollars is an example. If value is linear in the underlying attribute, the analyst's job is done, since the scale directly translates the measurable cost of any alternative into value. Sometimes it is necessary to construct a scale based on qualitative descriptions of the possible levels the attribute can take on. In Gardiner's study, for example, the attribute aesthetics was constructed in this way, with levels of poor, fair, indifferent, good, excellent. Scale construction can be substantially refined by the expansion of such one-word descriptions. In general, one would attempt to construct qualitative descriptions that were equally spaced in value and assign values that preserved that equal spacing. If equal spacing can be assumed for an attribute, one simply categorizes alternatives by levels and assigns each alternative a value for that attribute that corresponds to its level. This procedure closely resembles the category estimation technique. Notice that Gardiner did not assume equal spacing for the attribute aesthetics and instead asked subjects to rate each category in value.

The most refined version of single-attribute value construction in SMART is exemplified by Gardiner's construction of value functions for numerically defined scales like distance from mean high-tide line, gross density, and height. In these cases Gardiner identified a natural scale that was (distance) or was not (density, height) linear in value. In the case of nonlin-

Table 8.7. *Triangular matrix for weight assessment*

Attribute number (= importance rank)	Attribute number considered as standard				
	6	5	4	3	2
1	—	—	—	—	—
2	—	—	—	—	10
3	—	—	—	10	
4	—	—	10		
5	—	10			
6	10				

earities, it is possible to use rating or curve-drawing procedures that define the shape of the value curve over the natural scale.

Which of these three methods should be used is usually dictated by the practical constraints of the problem. Most applications require a mixture of all three. Shortcuts and simplification often suggest the use of direct rating methods, but it may be worthwhile to explore natural scales instead. Well-defined scales, preferably linear in value, are often useful because they allow the analyst to disassociate the task of measuring the location of the alternatives on that scale from the task of value measurement for the scale itself. Such disassociation is particularly helpful when respondents have a strong commitment to one alternative or find it difficult to think of locations in one attribute without considering simultaneous locations in other attributes.

Both examples of SMART demonstrated the use of the ratio weighting technique, and we therefore need not discuss it in detail. However, one aspect of ratio weighting seems worth mentioning. Often, the least important attribute has a very small weight relative to the other attributes. In such a case it may be useful to reiterate the weighting step with another attribute as an anchor. In general, one may consider using each attribute as a standard and construct a complete triangular matrix of weight ratios, as exemplified in Table 8.7. Beginning in the left column, the ratio procedure is carried out using the lowest-ranked attribute (6) as a standard. This attribute is then dropped, and ratio weighting is repeated with the second-lowest attribute as the standard, and so on.

Inconsistencies inevitably arise unless a respondent recognizes and numerically establishes consistency. Inconsistencies are usually resolved by repeated judgments.

When values come in hierarchies, it is often useful to decompose the weighting task by weighting the different levels of the hierarchy separately. Upper level objectives are weighted first by means of the ratio method. Subsequently lower level objectives and attributes are weighted conditional on the upper level. For example, one may consider the relative importance of the risks versus the benefits of offshore oil exploration. That ratio may be $2:1$, resulting in renormalized weights of .67 for risks and .33 for benefits. Next the attributes under risk are weighted relative to their importance in contributing to the overall risks (ignoring benefits). The relative importance weights for these subattributes are again normalized. The final weights for the attribute twigs are then obtained by multiplication of the lower level weights by the upper level weights. The Drug-Free Center site evaluation was an example of that procedure.

Rating and ranking of attribute importance are variations of the ratio estimation procedure. A typical approach to rating consists of asking the respondent to distribute 100 points over the attributes in a way that reflects their relative importance. This constant sum-rating procedure typically produces flatter weight distributions than ratio estimation. Even simpler is rank weighting, in which the respondent ranks the attributes in the order of importance. Let us call these ranks R_i and 1 be the most important and n the least important rank. These ranks can be transformed into normalized weights by several rules (see Stillwell and Edwards, 1979). Among them are the rank reciprocal rule, the rank sum rule, and the rank exponent rule. According to the *rank reciprocal* rule the weight for the ith attribute is calculated as follows:

$$w_i = \frac{1/R_i}{\sum_j 1/R_j}.$$ (8.25)

In the *rank sum* weighting procedure, weights are estimated from

$$w_i = (n + 1 - R_i) \Big/ \sum_{i=1}^{n} R_i.$$ (8.26)

Rank exponent weights were developed to take into account the decision maker's judgments about the dispersion of weights; in some cases all attributes may be very similar in importance; in others they may have a very large dispersion. To adjust, weights are estimated as

$$w_i = (n + 1 - R_i)^z \Big/ \sum_{i=1}^{n} R_i^z,$$ (8.27)

where z is estimated from

$$\frac{w_i}{w_j} = \frac{(n + 1 - R_i)^z}{(n + 1 - R_j)^z}$$ (8.28)

for some convenient pair of attributes – for example, the most and least important. Note that rank exponent weights require one judged number from the respondent in order to specify z. That number could be the ratio w_i/w_j, as we suggest, or could be simply an estimate of w_i for some i, such as the most important one.

All weighting techniques discussed so far explicitly involve the notion of attribute importance. This emphasis on importance has been criticized by various authors (see, e.g., Keeney and Raiffa, 1976), who consider weights to be simple rescaling parameters that are necessary to match the units of one single-attribute value function with the units of another. Since units are dependent on the range of the scale over which the value function is defined, the weight should change when the range of the scale changes. In particular, weights should increase if the range increases and decrease if the range decreases. To see this point, think about evaluating alternative proposals for abating acid rain. Consider the attributes cost of abatement and percentage of trees in the United States that will die as a result of acid rain. Preserving the trees is obviously very important compared with abatement costs if the policies lead to somewhere between 0 and 50% dying trees and all cost relatively little. However, if the range of dying trees is between 0 and 2%, the relative importance of that attribute should decrease, as long as the range of abatement costs stays the same. The problem is that direct judgments of importance may be insensitive to the ranges of the scales under consideration, and thus importance may distort the rescaling of single-attribute value functions. Without explicit consideration of the ranges, a respondent is likely to state, "The danger to U.S. forests is more important than abatement costs." That statement would, of course, be absurd if it turned out that saving three or four trees cost billions of dollars. Do respondents appropriately adjust the importance judgments in relation to the weights? The evidence is mixed (see, e.g., Gabrielli and von Winterfeldt, 1978). This question can obviously be answered by experimental studies, but it has no satisfactory answer as yet.

The preceding discussion illustrates the difficulty of using the concept of importance as a basis for weighting. Your assessment of the relative importance of saving the forests versus pollution abatement costs probably does not come with specific ranges attached. Yet the ranges should strongly control the weights. Those who use the concept of importance because it is intuitively compelling must address that fact. We know of three helpful ideas. First, use the natural ranges that the respondent has in mind – if need be, elicit them first. Second, and most important, be very explicit about the range you are using; make sure the respondent knows what it is and understands the relation between ranges and weights. Third, don't change ranges in midstream. Once you have picked a range that defines 0 and 100, stick with it, even if some new option scores -50 or $+275$ on that attribute because your initial choice of ranges was unwise. An obvious implication of the third point is that in general it is a good idea to pick ranges that are a little too broad rather than a little too narrow.

The preceding discussion obviously applies with more force to contexts in which the scores of the objects of evaluation on the various attributes are unknown at the time weight judgments must be made – a frequent occurrence. But it also applies to contexts in which all objects of evaluation are known ahead of time. The respondent probably has some more or less natural range in mind. Your goal should be to exploit it rather than replace it with the one that happens to characterize the problem at hand. If the range appropriate to the problem at hand is very small (or very large, but that is unlikely) relative to the range the respondent has in mind, use of the respondent's range may result in measurement problems for single-dimensional value functions. But serious violation of that range is sure to create weight elicitation problems.

An alternative solution to the range problem is to give up the notion of importance altogether and use swing weighting instead. In the most common swing-weighting technique, the analyst constructs two hypothetical alternatives. The first has best levels on all attributes; the second has worst levels on all attributes. Let x_i^* be the best level of attribute i and x_{i*} be the worst level on attribute i. Then the (hypothetical) best alternative is defined as $(x_1^*, x_2^*, \ldots, x_3^*, \ldots, x_n^*)$; the (hypothetical) worst alternative is $(x_{1*}, x_{2*}, \ldots, x_i^*, \ldots, x_n^*)$. Next, the decision maker is asked to assume that he or she is stuck with the worst alternative but that *one* attribute can be changed from its worst level x_{i*} to its best level x_i^*. Which one should be changed? After that one is changed, which one should be changed second, third, and so on? Obviously, the order in which the decision maker wants to change attribute levels from worst to best depends on the relative value difference between x_{i*} and x_i^*. The attribute that seems to make the most difference in value should be improved first, the one that has the second greatest impact on value should be improved second, and so on. This process establishes, in a fairly natural way, the rank order of the weights, since it rank-orders the terms

$$v(x_{1*}, x_{2*}, \ldots, x_i^*, \ldots, x_{n*}) - v(x_{1*}, x_{2*}, \ldots, x_{i*}, \ldots, x_{n*}).$$

To see that these terms are really the weights w_i, assume the scaling conventions $v_i(x_{i*}) = 0$ and $v_i(x_i^*) = 1$, together with the convention that the alternative with all the best attribute levels has a value of 1 and the one with all the worst attribute levels has a value of 0:

$$v(x_{1*}, x_{2*}, \ldots, x_i^*, \ldots, x_{n*}) = w_i v_i(x_i^*) + \sum_{j \neq i} w_j v_j(x_{j*}) = w_i. \quad (8.29)$$

To obtain ratio-scale weights from these rank orders, we propose the following procedure. Arbitrarily assign a raw value difference of 100 points to the attribute that was selected first choice for improvement from worst to best. Equally arbitrarily assign a raw value difference of 0 to an attribute (not necessarily in your list of attributes) for which it would make absolutely no (value) difference if one moved it from worst to best. Next, express all other value differences as percentages of 100. Thus, 50% means that the value improvement resulting from moving an attribute from its worst to its best level is half as great as that obtained from moving the attribute chosen first. Finally, renormalize the raw weights thus obtained.

Swing weighting goes a long way toward countering the criticisms of using extraneous and perhaps even distorting importance judgments. In fact, swing weighting coupled with carefully anchored single-attribute value elicitation techniques is virtually indistinguishable from the methods that are formally appropriate in the difference measurement techniques discussed in the next section.

8.3. Indifference techniques for value measurement

Three classes of value measurement techniques rely in one way or another on systematic explorations of indifference judgments or comparisons of strengths of preferences. The first is a straightforward multiattribute extension of *difference measurement*. It is virtually indistinguishable from SMART with swing weights, except that it spells out the axiomatic basis of the theory and makes use of alternative aggregation rules (multiplicative, multilinear) if additivity fails. The second is called *conjoint measurement theory*. Unlike difference measurement, which requires strength-of-preference judgments, conjoint measurement requires only preference and indifference judgments among multiattributed objects. The method used to construct value functions for range and weight in the rifle evaluation problem closely resembles those used in conjoint measurement. As in difference measurement nonadditive forms are available if additivity is grossly violated. The final class of measurement techniques is based on the simple *weak-order* model; it does not make any assumptions about additivity or independence across attributes. Instead, it exploits the assumption of transitive indifferences to trade multiattributed alternatives off sequentially until they become comparable. Trading off all attributes into monetary losses or gains is one such procedure.

Difference value measurement

MAUT difference measurement, as in the single-attribute case of Chapter 7, builds on the notion of relative value or strength of preference. Since it is usually difficult to express such value judgments when evaluation objects vary on several attributes, difference measurement makes various independence assumptions that allow the judgmental task to be broken down into single-attribute evaluations. Two difference models have been suggested for the MAUT case by Dyer and Sarin (1979): additive and multiplicative.

The additive model is of the form

$$v(\mathbf{x}) = \sum_{i=1}^{n} w_i v_i(x_i), \tag{8.1}$$

where $\mathbf{x}$ is a multiattribute evaluation object, x_i is its level in attribute i, v_i is the single-attribute (difference) value function, and w_i is a weight for attribute *i*. As in single-attribute difference measurement, the assumption is that v expresses both the order of preferences among objects of evaluation and the relative strength of preference. The additive form further assumes that the v_i's can be constructed disregarding other attributes. Formally, it introduces a strong independence assumption, which we call *additive differ-ence independence* (ADI). (Dyer and Sarin simply call it difference indepen-dence.) ADI requires that the relative strength of preference between two objects *x* and *y* that have identical fixed levels in some attributes not change when these attributes are fixed at some other level. For example, in the eval-uation of apartments differing only in distance from the beach, the amount of incremental value the decision maker derives from an oceanfront loca-tion over one or two blocks landward should be the same, regardless of rent, size, street noise, or other factors. More formal definitions and possible vio-lations of ADI are examined in Chapter 9.

The actual construction of v and the v_i's and w_i's can be extremely simple if ADI holds. First, single-attribute value functions v_i are constructed by means of the difference standard sequence or bisection procedures described in Chapter 7. Since by ADI a value function for one attribute will be unaf-fected by levels of other attributes, the analyst and decision maker can per-form this task without explicitly mentioning any of these other attributes. For example, in Gardiner's study of coastal developments, ADI allowed respondents to disregard the building height when evaluating distance from mean high tide. If the respondent finds the task of making such single-attrib-ute judgments difficult or impossible without considering other attributes, ADI may be violated. For example, when judging the benefits of distance to the beach in an apartment evaluation, it may be important to know whether beach access is available.

Comparisons of several different pairs of stimuli are constructed by means of the difference standard sequence method or the bisection method described in Chapter 7. The respondents must be aware that the construc-tion is, in principle, over the *i*th attribute, holding the other attribute levels constant. Formally, we could ask respondents to construct a standard sequence by laying out equally spaced x_i, x_i', x_i'', and so on, with the property

$$[(x_{i*}, x_{2*}, \ldots, x_i, \ldots, x_{n*}), (x_{i*}, x_{2*}, \ldots, x_i', \cdot \cdot x_{n*})]$$

$$\underset{\sim}{\circ} [(x_{1*}, x_{2*}, \ldots, x_i', \ldots, x_{m*}), (x_{1*}, x_{2*}, \ldots, x_i'', \ldots, x_{n*})] \qquad (8.30)$$

This complex indifference equation translates verbally into the following. The strength of preference of x_i (holding all other attributes constant at their worst level) over x_i' (holding all other attributes constant at their worst level) is equal to the strength of preference of x_i' (holding all other attributes con-stant at their worst level) over x_i'' (holding all other attributes constant at their worst level).

In practice, an analyst probably would not bother spelling out the other constant attributes in each indifference judgment. In fact, a straightforward application of the difference standard sequence method described in Chapter 7 for each attribute separately is usually a legitimate process, as long as the additive model is valid. This process generates n single-attribute value functions v_i, which are arbitrarily assigned the end-point values $v_i(x_{i*}) = 0$ and $v_i(x_i^*) = 1$.

Weight assessment is the next step in difference value measurement. It is necessary because we assigned equal end points in value (0 and 1) to each attribute. If we did not weigh the attributes by w_i, we would imply that the increases in strength of preference obtained by moving from the worst to the best level in each attribute were identical for all attributes. This is clearly not always true.

The formally appropriate weighting procedure in difference measurement is very similar to the swing weight procedure, but it does not involve direct numerical estimation. Respondents are asked to compare their relative strengths of preference of x_i^* over x_{i*}, the best over the worst attribute level across attributes. One way to ask this question is to determine whether the respondent would rather change x_i from x_{i*} to x_i^* or x_j from x_{j*} to x_j^*. As in the single-attribute value function elicitation, we assume again that all other attributes are constant, for example, at their worst level x_{i*}. Formally, the analyst asks the respondent to establish a strength-of-preference judgment of the following kind:

$$[(x_i^*, x_{j*}), (x_{i*}, x_{j*})] \overset{?}{\underset{\lessgtr}{}} [(x_{i*}, x_j^*), (x_{i*}, x_{j*})]. \tag{8.31}$$

This complex mathematical sentence can be expressed in words as follows. Consider three evaluation objects identical with one another with respect to all attributes except i and j. Clearly, the one in which attribute i has level x_i^* is preferable to the one in which attribute i has level x_{i*} holding attribute j constant at x_{j*}. The same statement is true for attribute j, holding attribute i constant at x_{i*}. Now consider the relative strength of preference of the object described by x_i^* and x_{j*} over the object described by x_{i*} and x_{j*}. Is that strength of preference greater than, equal to, or smaller than the strength of preference of the object described by x_{i*} and x_j^* over the object described by x_{i*} and x_{j*}? (When you see how many words it takes to translate a mathematical sentence into English, you understand why mathematicians insist on using symbols and why the rest of us have to work so hard to follow them.)

Notice that we did not mention the fact that we held x_k, $k \neq i,j$ constant everywhere; otherwise, the translation would have been even more of a mess. If the decision maker thinks that the step in value from x_{i*} to x_i^* is larger than that from x_{j*} to x_j^*, he or she should say that the strength of preference in the left term of equation 8.31 is larger, otherwise that the strength of preference on the right is larger. If the judgment is that the left-hand difference is larger, the implication is that $w_i > w_j$, as can be seen from the following equation:

$$w_i v_i(x_i^*) + w_j v_j(x_{j*}) - w_i v_i(x_{i*}) - w_j v_j(x_{j*})$$
$$> w_i v_i(x_{i*}) + w_j v_j(x_j^*) - w_i v_i(x_{i*}) - w_j v_j(x_{j*}). \quad (8.32)$$

This simplifies to

$$w_i v_i(x_i^*) > w_j v_j(x_j^*),$$

or

$$w_i > w_j. \quad (8.33)$$

To determine how much larger w_i is than w_j, the analyst reduces x_i^* to some intermediate value x_i', trying values of x_i' until the respondent makes the indifference judgment

$$[(x_i, \ x_{j*}), \ (x_{i*}, \ x_{j*})] \ \overset{\circ}{\sim} \ [(x_{i*}, \ x_j^*),(x_{i*}, \ x_{j*})]. \quad (8.34)$$

This difference then implies

$$w_i v_i(x_i') = w_j v_j(x_j^*) \quad (8.35)$$

or

$$\frac{w_j}{w_i} = v_i(x_i'). \quad (8.36)$$

Any weights w_i and w_j can be used as long as they maintain that ratio. Repetition of this procedure for all pairs of attributes should give the desired results. Indeed, it would give redundant information, since it would give $n(n - 1)/2$ weights, though only $n - 1$ are needed to solve for a full set of weights. Some redundancy is a good idea, since it can be used to find inconsistent judgments. However, it would be very tedious for a respondent to make all $n(n - 1)/2$ difference judgments for $n > 4$.

Let us assume that the analyst constructs $n - 1$ indifference equations like the ones above using the attribute with the least potential increase in strength of preference as a standard (note that it is easy to find that attribute simply by ordering single-attribute strengths of preference). Without loss of generality we can assume that the attribute with the least potential increase in strength of preference is attribute n. The $n - 1$ indifference equations are always solved by lowering the x value in the ith attribute from x_i^* to x_i'. (If it were necessary to reduce x_n^* to produce an indifference, attribute n would have a larger potential value increase than attribute i.) Thus, we can generate $n - 1$ equations of the following form:

$$\frac{w_i}{w_n} = v_i(x_i'). \quad (8.37)$$

Together with the restriction that the w_i's should add to 1, we can solve

$$w_i = \frac{v_i(x_i')}{\sum_{i=1}^{n} v_i(x_i')}. \tag{8.38}$$

These are exactly the weights that enter into equation 8.1.

If the additive difference model fails because of dependencies, the multiplicative model may still be appropriate. The multiplicative model has the following compact form:

$$1 + wv(\mathbf{x}) = \prod_{i=1}^{n}[1 + ww_i v_i(x_i)]. \tag{8.39}$$

Its extensive form is more revealing; it clarifies the (limited) potential for interactions:

$$
\begin{aligned}
v(\mathbf{x}) = & \sum_{i=1}^{n} w_i v_i(x_i) + \sum_{i<j} ww_i w_j v_i(x_i) v_j(x_j) \\
& + \sum_{i<j<m} w^2 w_i w_j w_m v_i(x_i) v_j(x_j) v_m(x_m) \\
& + \cdots + w^{n-1} \prod_{i=1}^{n} w_i v_i(x_i).
\end{aligned} \tag{8.40}
$$

In the preceding complex equation, the first term to the right of the equals sign is the familiar additive form for values, the second term deals with dependencies among pairs of attributes, the third with dependencies among triples of attributes, and so on until the last term deals with interdependencies among the entire attribute set. The format for dealing with interdependencies is simply that the value of each attribute entering into an interaction is multiplied by its weight, this product is multiplied by the single interaction parameter w or by a power of it, and these products are added. As the number of interacting terms increases, the power of w by which the product is multiplied also increases. Of course, if w is 0, this becomes the additive model. Shortly we show that w must lie between -1 and infinity. As $|w|$ becomes larger, the overall interaction among all attributes becomes more heavily weighted. This model makes all interactions depend on a single parameter and so cannot appropriately represent values of the form "A depends greatly on B, but much less on C."

The multiplicative model requires that the ordering of strengths of preferences among pairs of objects that vary only in a subset of attributes not change if the constant levels on the remaining attributes are changed to some other constant levels. As an illustration of this condition, consider any set of objects, and suppose that some attributes have the same physical values for all elements of that set. *Multiplicative difference independence* (MDI; Dyer and Sarin [1979] call this weak difference independence) holds if the only effect of changing a constant attribute from one physical value to another is to shrink or expand the scale of value and to move the elements of the set up or down along it; the crucial point is that the *relative* spacing of the elements in the set remains unchanged. This must hold no matter which attributes are originally constant and then changed to another constant value. You can get a good intuitive grasp of this idea by thinking of looking at the left margin of a page of a book through the zoom lens of a camera. If you move the camera up or down (changing a constant attribute), the position of lines 1, 7, 20, and 50 will seem to move down or up. As you zoom the lens in or out, the spaces between those lines will get bigger or smaller. The sense in which the spaces between those lines appear unchanged as you move the camera and simultaneously zoom in or out is exactly what MDI assumes for values.

It is difficult to give convincing examples in which MDI holds and ADI does not. We'll try. If a system is evaluated on the basis of its reliability and some performance measure, ADI may fail because the evaluator does not care about performance if the reliability is low. However, MDI might hold. For that to be the case, reliability has to act as a multiplicative discounting factor on performance (and vice versa). If the ordering of value differences (not just values) based on performance were the same at various fixed levels of reliability and the ordering of value differences based on reliability were the same based on various fixed levels of performance, MDI would hold. We won't even try to give a convincing example for more than two attributes.

The v_i's and the w_i's for the multiplicative model can be assessed as in the additive model, but because the sum of the w_i's will not equal 1 n equations have to be solved. In addition, the interaction parameter w has to be determined. By setting all $x_i = x_i^*$ and scaling all v_i's so that $v_{i*} = 0$ and $v_i^* = 1$, we observe that

$$1 + w = \prod_{i=1}^{n} (1 + ww_i). \tag{8.41}$$

Keeney and Sicherman (1976) present a computer program to solve for w in such formulas. Why is there no assessment of w? Because the w_i's already express the interaction. Consider the two-dimensional case. Equation 8.41 then becomes

$$1 + w = (1 + ww_1)(1 + ww_2), \tag{8.42}$$

or

$$w = \frac{1 - w_1 - w_2}{w_1 w_2}. \tag{8.43}$$

Since $0 \le w_i \le 1$, formula 8.43 also shows the limits on w:

$$-1 \le w \le \infty.$$

If $w_1 = w_2 = 0$, $w = \infty$; if $w_1 = w_2 = 1$, $w = -1$. Of course, if $w_1 + w_2 = 1$, $w = 0$ and ADI holds.

Before we proceed to the conjoint measurement model we should mention the "true" interactive difference model, the multilinear model, which has no restrictions on the form of the interaction terms:

$$v(\mathbf{x}) = \sum_{i=1}^{n} w_i v_i(x_i) + \sum_{i<1} w_{ij} v_i(x_i) v_j(x_j)$$

$$+ \sum_{i<j<m} w_{ijm} v_i(x_i) v_j(x_j) v_m(x_m) + \cdots + \prod_{i=1}^{n} w_1 \ldots {}_n v_i(x_i).$$

(8.44)

The multilinear model allows any combination of interaction terms and requires a substantially weaker independence assumption: *multilinear difference independence* (MLDI) requires multiplicative difference independence to hold only for *each single* attribute, with all others held fixed. In other words, strengths of preferences in any *single* attribute are unaffected by constant values in other attributes. This allows us to construct single-attribute value functions using simple difference standard sequences. But in order to construct the aggregation model 8.44, we have to assess many interaction parameters w_{ij}, w_{ijk}, and so on. In fact, when the number of attributes exceeds four, the number of the necessary interaction parameters becomes mind boggling, and consequently the necessary assessment task becomes unfeasible.

Nevertheless, the multilinear model can sometimes be useful, when some partial interactions are identified a priori. For example, in a systems evaluation one may find that all attributes satisfy ADI except accuracy and reliability. These two may interact multiplicatively, giving rise to a relatively simple model that adds all the v_k's and adds in addition one interaction term $w v_i v_j$, where v_i and v_j are interpreted as the reliability and accuracy values. Note that this model cannot be expressed as a multiplicative model.

Building multilinear models from additive and multiplicative "building blocks" is sometimes possible or necessary when one is working with a complex value tree. Often the superordinate objectives are independent, but subtle interaction may occur in subsets of attributes under one objective.

Assessment of the v_i's in the multilinear case follows exactly the procedures for the additive and multiplicative cases. Assessment of the interaction parameters follows the procedures used in the multiplicative case in those instances for which we can identify a multiplicative subset.

Conjoint measurement

The rifle evaluation example of the introduction was an illustration of conjoint measurement. Notice that we constructed value functions without ever asking strength-of-preference questions. The procedure used in that example, as in most conjoint measurement applications, did require, however, that attributes be additive. Otherwise the standard sequences constructed by that procedure would depend on the levels of the other attributes.

This additive version of conjoint measurement makes an assumption called *joint independence* (JI). In simple terms JI requires that preferences among objects that vary on only a subset of attributes not depend on the levels of the remaining attributes.

In its *single independence* (SI) version, the assumption is that preferences for objects that vary in *one* attribute only should be unaffected by the other attribute values. The size of an apartment, its location, and its rent could be considered attributes that are SI. You typically prefer less rent, more room, and a better location, no matter what the other attribute values are. In its more general form, JI requires that preferences in *any subset* of attributes be independent of fixed levels in the remaining attributes. For example, when choosing among job offers, your preferences over combinations of salary and staff benefits are likely to be jointly independent of, say, the size of the town in which you work. The most interesting cases of violations of the JI conditions are those in which SI is satisfied. Those violations are typically subtle and hard to find. Suppose you work in a large city and want to rent a farm or an apartment. Your options have the following attribute values:

> Farm (F)–city apartment (A)
> One-hour car ride to work (1 h)–20-minute car ride to work (20 min)
> High-speed transit system nearby (HST)–no high-speed transit system (NHST)

We rank the options as follows, depending on the presence or absence of the high-speed transit system:

(1) (F, 20 min, HST)	(1) (F, 20 min, NHST)
(2) (F, 1 h, HST)	(2) (A, 20 min, NHST)
(3) (A, 20 min, HST)	(3) (F, 1 h, NHST)
(4) (A, 1 h, HST)	(4) (A, 1 h, NHST)

Living on a farm in the country seems very attractive to us, and the long ride to work does not matter much because of the convenience of the high-speed transportation system. With no high-speed transportation system the shorter ride from the apartment outweighs the benefits of living on the farm. This produces a switch in our preferences that violates the JI assumption. Note that we always prefer the farm over the apartment and the shorter ride over the longer ride when other values are held fixed. Since, in addition, we always prefer HST over NHST, we satisfy SI.

The procedure needed to construct an additive value function v within the conjoint measurement framework is called *dual standard sequence* (Krantz et al., 1971) or *saw tooth* (Fishburn, 1967) or *lock step* (Keeney and Raiffa, 1976). Here we briefly summarize the essential idea. The procedure can best be demonstrated in two dimensions; that is, we assume that multiattributed outcomes are of the form (x_1, x_2).

We first pick an arbitrary zero point of the scale, usually the worst conceivable or actual combination of attribute values, say (x_{1*}, x_{2*}), and define

$$v(x_{1*}, x_{2*}) = 0. \tag{8.45}$$

We also pick an arbitrary unit value on the first attribute, say x_1^1. We then construct a standard sequence on attribute 2, that is, a sequence of x_2 that is equally spaced in value. In order to guarantee equally spaced values, we make every increase in attribute 2 equivalent to the standard increase in attribute 1 from x_{1*} to x_1^*; thus, the standard sequence is defined by the following judgments:

$$\begin{aligned}
(x_1^1, x_{2*}) &\sim (x_{1*}, x_2^1), \\
(x_1^1, x_2^1) &\sim (x_{1*}, x_2^2), \\
(x_1^1, x_2^2) &\sim (x_{1*}, x_2^3),
\end{aligned} \tag{8.46}$$

and in general

$$(x_1^1, x_2^{i-1}) \sim (x_{1*}, x_2^i). \tag{8.47}$$

Graphically, this procedure can be represented as shown in Figure 8.10, which also shows the derived value function for attribute 2.

Conjoint measurement has also been developed for the multiplicative case, but unlike the multiplicative–multilinear models of difference measurement, multiplicative conjoint measurement models are truly multiplicative, having zero multipliers and reversals. In fact, reversals are necessary in these models. For example, when judging an operation on the basis of quality of life and life span with and without it, a decision maker may feel inclined to reverse a normal preference for a longer over a shorter life if the quality of life is below a certain level (e.g., if an operation guarantees a subsequent lifetime of constant pain). Such sign reversals could be modeled by a multiplicative conjoint measurement model,

$$f(\mathbf{x}) = \prod_{i=1}^{n} f_i(x_i), \tag{8.48}$$

where the ranges of some f_i could produce negative numbers. (See Krantz et al., 1971, for more information.)

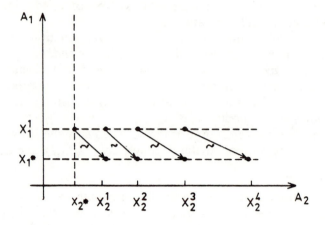

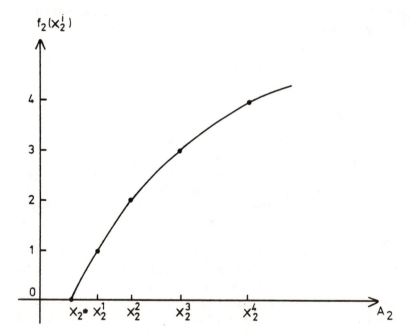

Figure 8.10. Illustration of the dual standard sequence procedure. (*Source:* von Winterfeldt & Fischer, 1975.)

Weak-order model

All models described above make explicit or implicit assumptions about the independence of attributes. The last model we discuss does away with such assumptions but requires very complicated elicitation procedures. This model is called the *weak-order model*. The weak-order model requires only that the decision maker be able to make consistent trade-offs among multiattributed objects.

In practice, a decision maker will, of course, fail to make multiattribute comparisons consistently – otherwise decomposition procedures would not be required at all. But the weak-order model attempts to systematize trade-offs, so that at any given time only relatively simple ones have to be made. Final rank orderings can then be derived by reconcatenation of these trade-offs.

The basic procedure for constructing a value function using the weak-order model consists of the following *trade-off task*. We can construct for each multiattributed outcome an equivalent outcome with specified constant values in all but the ith attribute. In other words, we find for each x and y

$$\mathbf{x} = (x_1, x_2, \ldots, \hat{x}_i, \ldots, x_n) \sim (a_1, a_2, \ldots, \hat{x}_i^1, \ldots, a_n), \tag{8.49}$$
$$\mathbf{y} = (y_1, y_2, \ldots, \hat{y}_i, \ldots, y_n) \sim (a_1, a_2, \ldots, \hat{y}_i^1, \ldots, a_n), \tag{8.50}$$

for some constant values a_j, $j \neq i$. Here and in what follows the superscripts for the values of the trade-off attribute i mean that in the rth trade-off step this attribute value is changed to, say, $\hat{x}_i^r$. After this trade-off, we determine the preference order for attribute i; that is, we construct an order-preserving utility function f_i. This can easily be done for commodities like money. Then the decision maker should prefer $\mathbf{x}$ to $\mathbf{y}$ if and only if

$$f_i(\hat{x}_i^1) \geq f_i(\hat{y}_i^1). \tag{8.51}$$

We can facilitate this trade-off procedure by decomposing it into $n - 1$ steps, as demonstrated in the following example:

$$\begin{aligned}
\mathbf{x} &= (x_1, x_2, \ldots, \hat{x}_i, \ldots, x_n) \\
&\sim (a_1, x_2, \ldots, \hat{x}_i^1, \ldots, x_n) \\
&\sim (a_1, a_2, \ldots, \hat{x}_i^2, \ldots, x_n) \\
&\quad \vdots \\
&\sim (a_1, a_2, \ldots, \hat{x}_i^{n-1}, \ldots, a_n).
\end{aligned} \tag{8.52}$$

After we perform the same sequential trade-off for alternative $\mathbf{y}$, $\mathbf{x}$ would be preferred over $\mathbf{y}$ if and only if

$$f_i(\hat{x}_i^{n-1}) \geq f_i(\hat{y}_i^{n-1}). \tag{8.53}$$

Similar procedures have been described by Keeney and Raiffa (1976) as "pricing out" and by MacCrimmon and Toda (1969) and MacCrimmon and Wehrung (1977) as "indifference curve" procedures.

We should point out that the weak order model is one of the few models applicable when complex interactions exist among attributes. Unfortunately, it is precisely the existence of such complex interactions that makes actual elicitations that use the sequential trade-off method extremely difficult.

8.4. Indifference techniques for utility measurement

An example: the Mexico City airport study

Members of a Mexican planning agency worked with U.S. decision analysts to develop a risky utility model for the evaluation of airport facilities in Mexico City (for detailed reports see, e.g., de Neufville and Keeney, 1972; Keeney, 1973). This study was an analysis of various strategies for expanding Mexico City's airport facilities to accommodate rapid growth and increasingly difficult operating conditions. Two main options were to expand the facilities at Mexico City's present airport (Texcoco) or to develop a completely new facility about 25 miles out of town (Zumpango). In addition, the timing of the construction and development of the airport(s) was considered. The following objectives were developed for the evaluation of these alternatives:

1   Minimize total construction and maintenance *costs.*
2   Provide adequate *capacity* to meet air traffic demands.
3   Minimize the *access time* to the airport.
4   Maximize the *safety* of the system.
5   Minimize the *social disruption* caused by the provision of new airport facilities.
6   Minimize the effects of *noise pollution* due to air traffic.

These were operationalized by the following attributes:

X_1 Total cost in millions of pesos, with suitable discounting
X_2 Practical upper bound on number of aircraft operations per hour
X_3 Access time to and from the airport in minutes, weighted by the number of travelers for each zone in Mexico City
X_4 Number of people killed or seriously injured per aircraft accident
X_5 Number of people displaced by airport development
X_6 Number of people subjected to an unusually high noise level

We will not describe the assessment of the probable impacts of the alternatives on these six attributes, although this was obviously one of the most complicated tasks of the analysis. The results of that part of the analysis were probability distributions for each of the alternatives that completely characterized their impacts.

We turn now to the assessment of the multiattribute utilities. On the basis of axiomatic tests, the analysts concluded that the appropriate model form was multiplicative:

$$1 + ku(\mathbf{x}) = \prod_{i=1}^{6} [1 + kk_i u_i(x_i)], \tag{8.54}$$

where u is the overall utility, the u_i's are conditional single-attribute utility functions, and k and the k_i's are scaling constants. This form is similar to the multiplicative difference function, but it is a von Neumann and Morgenstern utility function suitable for taking expectations over uncertain impacts. The assumptions are therefore somewhat different (see also Section 9.2), and the methods for constructing the u_i's, k, and k_i's differ from those appropriate for the riskless case.

To construct the u_i's the analysts first selected a best and a worst level on each of the attributes, say x_{i*} and x_i^*. For example, the minimum access time was considered to be 12 minutes; the maximum, 90 minutes (see also Table 8.8). The end points of the single-attribute utilities were arbitrarily defined to be 0 and 1, for example,

$$u_3(90) = 0,$$
$$u_3(12) = 1.$$

Next the variable certainty equivalent method described in Section 7.4 was used to construct the single-attribute utility functions between the extreme values. For example, the decision maker considered 60 minutes of travel time to be indifferent to a 50–50 lottery for the extremes, 90 or 12 minutes. Therefore,

$$u_3(60) = \tfrac{1}{2}u_3(12) + \tfrac{1}{2}u_3(90) = \tfrac{1}{2}.$$

A more finely graded utility function for travel time was constructed by further partitioning the attribute set (Figure 8.11). Figure 8.12 shows graphs of the remaining single-attribute utility functions.

The next step was to construct the scaling factors k and the k_i's, which in utility measurement have a somewhat different interpretation from that appropriate to value measurement. Keeney and Raiffa (1976) emphasize that the k_i's are *not* importance weights for attributes but rather are rescaling factors that make single-attribute assessments consistent with overall assessments. In order to construct the k_i's, relatively simple questions suffice. For example, to generate the weight for the travel time attribute the following gamble and sure thing are compared by means of the variable probability method:

$$(x_{1*}, x_{2*}, x_3^*, x_{4*}, x_{5*}, x_{6*}) \begin{array}{c} > \\ \sim \\ < \end{array} \left[\begin{array}{cc} p_3 & \mathbf{x}^* \\ \\ 1 - p_3 & \mathbf{x}_* \end{array} \right. \tag{8.55}$$

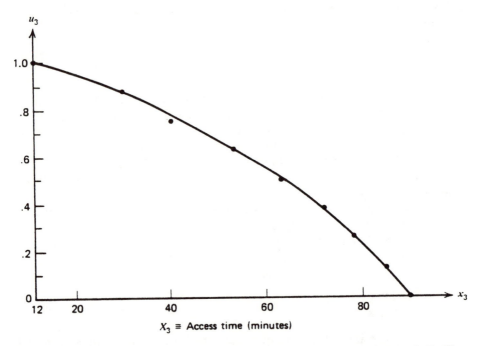

Figure 8.11. Utility function for access time in minutes. (*Source:* Keeney & Raiffa, 1976.)

where x_{i*} is the worst level of the ith attribute, $\mathbf{x}^*$ means an imaginary airport that would be best on all attributes, and $\mathbf{x}_*$ means an equally imaginary airport that would be worst on all attributes. The hypothetical airport on the left of Equation 8.55 has worst levels for all attributes except the third, travel time, and the best level (12 minutes) on it. The analyst varied p_3, the probability of obtaining the airport best on all attributes rather than the one worst on all attributes, until the decision maker was indifferent between the sure thing and the gamble. Clearly, the more significant the change in travel time from 90 minutes to 12 minutes is to the decision maker, the larger p_3 must be to create indifference between the gamble and the sure thing. If travel time were virtually irrelevant to the evaluation, relative to the other differences between $\mathbf{x}_*$ and $\mathbf{x}^*$, p_3 could be tiny.

After a p_i is found such that the respondent is indifferent between the sure thing and the gamble, substitution of the specific values x_{i*} and x_i^* into the multiplicative model and solving the resulting SEU equation gives

$$k_i u_i(x_i^*) = p_i u(\mathbf{x}^*), \tag{8.56}$$
$$k_i = p_i. \tag{8.57}$$

Six such indifference equations resulted in the k_i's presented in Table 8.8. These k_i's represent the relative value of a change in an attribute i from its

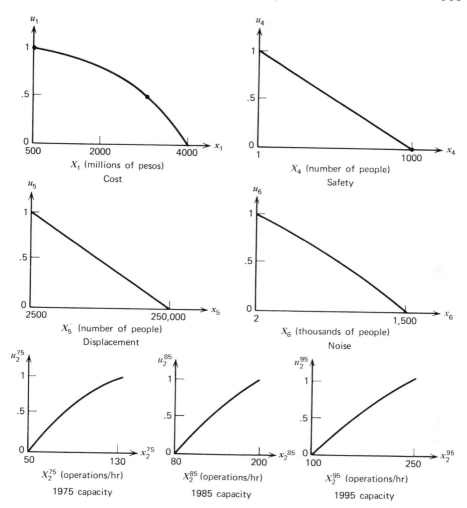

Figure 8.12. Utility functions for the Mexico City airport problem. Note that capacity had three different utility functions, depending on the time horizon. (*Source:* Keeney & Raiffa, 1976.)

worst to its best level on overall utility. If a change is insignificant in terms of overall utility, the respondent should assess only a small indifference probability p_i, because he or she should easily be induced to take the gamble. If the effect of the change in that attribute is, however, substantial, the sure thing may indeed look relatively attractive compared with the optimal option, and a larger indifference probability should be required.

The assessment of the parameter k in the multiplicative model is actually an easy task, since the constraints on the model allow k to be calculated from the k_i's. As Keeney and Raiffa (1976) show, the solution of the multi-

Table 8.8. *Attributes, ranges, and scaling parameter k_i for the multiattribute utility function in the Mexico City airport study*

Attribute	Worst	Best	k_i
X_1: Total cost (millions of pesos)	4,000	500	.48
X_2: Practical capacity in terms of the number of aircraft operations per hours	50	250	.60
X_3: Access time (minutes)	90	12	.10
X_4: Number of people seriously injured or killed per aircraft accident	1,000	1	.35
X_5: Number of people displaced by airport development	250,000	2,500	.18
X_6: Number of people subjected to a high noise level (thousands)	1,500	2	.18

Source: Adapted from Keeney & Raiffa (1976).

plicative model for $x_i = x_i^*$ is simply

$$1 + k = \prod_{i=1}^{6} (1 + kk_i), \tag{8.58}$$

since u and all u_i's are 1. This equation was solved by iterative procedures (see Keeney and Sicherman, 1976), and a value of $k = -.877$ was found. The constraints on the multiplicative model would have allowed k to vary between -1 and $+\infty$.

The final multiplicative model has the form

$$1 + ku(\mathbf{x}) = \prod_{i=1}^{n} [1 + kk_i u_i(x_i)] = 1 - .877u(\mathbf{x})$$
$$= \{1 - .877 [.48u_1(x_1)]\} \{1 - .877 [.60\ u_2(x_2)]\} \tag{8.59}$$
$$\times \{1 - .877 [.10\ u_3(x_3)]\} \{1 - .877 [.35\ u_4(x_4)]\}$$
$$\times \{1 - .877 [.18\ u_5(x_5)]\} \{1 - .877 [.18\ u_6(x_6)]\}.$$

The utility of each alternative $\mathbf{x}$ can now be determined by the following:

1   Reading off its probable impacts on all attributes either as point impacts or as probability distributions
2   Taking expected utilities in each attribute to get a $u_i(x_i)$ for each alternative
3   Plugging these values into Equation 8.59 and solving for u.

Utility measurement techniques

In the following we present the basic multiattribute utility models and scaling techniques illustrated before. Since the book by Keeney and Raiffa (1976) describes these techniques in much detail, we can be brief.

All utility assessment techniques begin, as usual, with the definitions and operationalizations of the set of attributes. Furthermore, we assume that the end points of the attributes have been defined. We should stress again the importance of a careful selection of these end points (see Section 7.3). At the beginning of the numerical assessment, the analyst should have the following inputs:

1   Qualitative descriptions of the value dimensions
2   Operationalizations of the value dimensions in terms of attributes
3   End points x_{i*} and x_i^* that define the worst plausible and best plausible levels of the ith attribute.

In addition we assume that the decision maker or experts can construct for each action (say there are two, a and b) probability distributions $f(\mathbf{x}\,|\,a)$ and $g(\mathbf{x}\,|\,b)$ that assign probabilities to consequences depending on the action taken. Naturally, some of these probability distributions will be degenerate; that is, in cases where there is no uncertainty, $P(\mathbf{x}\,|\,a) = 1$ for some specific value of $\mathbf{x}$. Sometimes we will use f and g to denote two probability distributions generated by different actions and call the set of all such probability distributions F.

Multiattribute SEU theory, like single-attribute SEU theory, makes assumptions that allow preferences among probability distributions f, $g \in F$ to be modeled by the expected utilities of their consequences $\mathbf{x}$. In other words, for all f, $g \in F$,

$$f \succsim g \quad \text{if and only if} \quad SEU(f) \geq SEU(g), \tag{8.60}$$

where $SEU(f)$ denotes the SEU taken with respect to f. For example, when f is the distribution associated with an action a and g is the distribution associated with an action b,

$$SEU(f) = \int f(\mathbf{x}\,|\,a)u(\mathbf{x})\,d\mathbf{x} \tag{8.61}$$

$$SEU(g) = \int g(\mathbf{x}\,|\,b)u(\mathbf{x})\,d\mathbf{x}, \tag{8.62}$$

where $\int$ is a generalized integral.

Direct construction of u, though in principle possible by the methods presented in Chapter 7, can be cumbersome and complex. Instead, multiattribute SEU theory decomposes u into single-attribute u_i's, assesses the u_i's by procedures presented in Chapter 7, and then aggregates according to an appropriate model. In this section, we discuss three models: the additive model, the multiplicative model, and the multilinear model. These models are very similar in structure to the additive, multiplicative, and multilinear difference models. One should keep in mind, however, that the construction procedures and the interpretation differ substantially.

The *additive model* has the form

$$u(\mathbf{x}) = \sum_{i=1}^{n} k_i u_i(x_i), \tag{8.63}$$

where the k_i's are scaling constants. The main assumption behind the additive model has been called marginality (Fishburn, 1965; Raiffa, 1969) and additive independence (Keeney and Raiffa, 1976). To indicate its difference from additive difference independence, we call it *additive expected utility independence,* or AEUI. AEUI requires that acts with identical marginal (single-attribute) probability distributions be equally attractive.

A simple two-dimensional example will illustrate this assumption. Consider that the two attributes are two prizes to be won in a lottery: stereos of various qualities and color television sets of various qualities. Now consider the following two gambles:

	a		**b**	
	Heads	Tails	Heads	Tails
TV	Expensive color TV	Nothing	Expensive color TV	Nothing
Stereo	Expensive stereo	Nothing	Nothing	Expensive stereo

Obviously both gambles have identical marginal probability distributions: they both offer even chances of winning a stereo and winning a color television. Thus, AEUI and the additive model would require that they be equally attractive. This can be shown by a simple calculation:

$$SEU(\mathbf{a}) = \tfrac{1}{2}[k_1 u_1(TV) + k_2 u_2(ST)] + \tfrac{1}{2}[k_1 u_1(0) + k_2 u_2(0)]$$
$$= \tfrac{1}{2}[k_1 u_1(TV) + k_2 u_2(0)] + \tfrac{1}{2}[k_i u_1(0) + k_2 u_2(ST)] = SEU(\mathbf{b}).$$

$$(8.64)$$

But obviously, many people would have a strong preference for gamble **b**, since they would win no matter what happened, while gamble **a** has an all-or-none characteristic. This type of violation of the additive model is called *multiattribute risk aversion,* and we discuss its qualitative nature later.

Let us assume that in another problem with n attributes the analyst and the decision maker are persuaded that AEUI is satisfied. In this case the additive model can be constructed as follows. First, single-attribute utility functions are built by means of the procedures of Chapter 7. Since additivity holds, the other attributes can be set at any constant level in that construction process. For example, assume that the u_i should be constructed. Then all x_j, $j \neq i$, can be set at their worst level x_{j*}. By either the variable probability or the variable certainty equivalent methods described in Section 7.4, u_i can be built. For example, with the variable probability method the decision maker may be asked to find a certainty equivalent $\hat{x}_i$ such that the following gamble and certainty equivalent are indifferent:

$$(x_{1*}, x_{2*}, \ldots, \hat{x}_i, \ldots, x_{n*}) \sim \underset{1-p_i}{\overset{p_i}{\rule{0pt}{0pt}}} \begin{cases} (x_{1*}, x_{2*}, \ldots, x_i^*, \ldots, x_{n*}) \\ (x_{1*}, x_{2*}, \ldots, x_{i*} \ldots, x_{n*}) \end{cases} \tag{8.65}$$

To solve this indifference equation, we arbitrarily set the following corner points of the utility function:

$$u_i(x_{i*}) = 0,$$
$$u_i(x_i^*) = 1,$$
$$u_j(x_{j*}) = 0,$$
$$u_j(x_j^*) = 1.$$

Clearly then, $u_i(\hat{x}_i) = p_i$ in Equation (8.65).

After the construction of the u_i's is the construction of the scaling constants k_i. Although in principle any set of n indifferences (which are not implied by the u_i's) would suffice to solve the equations for the k_i's, the following procedure has the advantage of being mathematically simple. The variable probability method is used to elicit an indifference probability for the following sure thing and gamble:

$$(x_{1*}, x_{2*}, \ldots, x_i^*, \ldots, x_{n*}) \sim \underset{1-p_i}{\overset{p_i}{\rule{0pt}{0pt}}} \begin{cases} (x_1^*, x_2^*, \ldots, x_i^*, \ldots, x_n^*) \\ (x_{1*}, x_{2*}, \ldots, x_{i*}, \ldots, x_{n*}). \end{cases} \tag{8.66}$$

The additive model is used to solve this indifference equation as follows:

$$k_i u_i(x_i^*) = p_i u(\mathbf{x}^*) + (1 - p_i)u(\mathbf{x}_*), \tag{8.67}$$

or

$$k_i = p_i.$$

After all k_i's are available, checks can be made to see whether they add up to 1. This requirement follows simply from the additive model, since

$$u(\mathbf{x}^*) = \sum_{i=1}^{n} k_i u_i(x_i^*) = \sum_{i=1}^{n} k_i = 1. \tag{8.68}$$

If the sum of the k_i's deviates markedly from 1, there is reason to suspect that the additive model has failed. In that case the analyst may wish to explore the less restrictive *multiplicative model:*

$$1 + ku(\mathbf{x}) = \prod_{i=1}^{n} [1 + kk_i u_i(x_i)]. \tag{8.69}$$

This model is structurally similar to the multiplicative difference model, but its utility functions and scaling parameters have a different interpretation here. To distinguish it, we call it the *multiplicative SEU model.* Like the difference model, it can be written out as

$$u(\mathbf{x}) = \sum_{i=1}^{n} k_i u_i(x_i) + \sum_{i<j} kk_i k_j u_i(x_i)u_j(x_j) \tag{8.70}$$

$$+ \sum_{i<j<m} k^2 k_i k_j k_m u_i(x_i)u_j(x_j)u_m(x_m) + \cdots + \prod_{i=1}^{n} k^{n-1} k_i u_i(x_i).$$

The multiplicative independence assumption is considerably weaker than additive independence. According to multiplicative expected utility independence (MEUI), preferences among gambles that have identical, sure consequences in some attributes should be independent of the levels of these sure consequences.

Practically, this means, for example, that certainty equivalents of gambles in one attribute should be the same regardless of the fixed values of other attributes. Naturally, if certainty equivalents can be assessed in subsets of attributes ignoring certain outcomes in other attributes, the assessment task can be substantially simplified.

With some effort we have tried to construct a counterexample for MEUI. Suppose that you, the president of a major corporation, plan to stimulate sales by means of a contest. Your advertising manager, whose expertise is flawless, tells you that either of two contests will produce the same modest increase in sales. One has a spectacular first prize, but the chances that the first prize will be awarded are quite slim. The other has a much more pedestrian first prize, certain to be awarded. You thus face the following actions:

	a		b
	E	$\bar{E}$	Sure
Size of prize awarded	Large	None	Modest
Sales increase	Modest	Modest	Modest

You might prefer to take action **b** over action **a,** since you would avoid the danger of having to pay for the spectacular first prize and explain its cost to your board. But suppose that the sales increase to be expected is not modest, but rather a tripling of sales. Then the actions you face are

	a		b
	E	$\bar{E}$	Sure
Size of prize awarded	Large	None	Modest
Sales increase	Tripling	Tripling	Tripling

In this case you may prefer action **a** to action **b,** perhaps because you can expect no objections from the board members about the cost of the spectacular prize if they are busy congratulating you on your success in tripling sales.

Such a pattern of preferences would violate MEUI. It illustrates what we consider a problem in all such examples. In order to explain the outcome, we extended the scenario so that it brought other consequences of the choice into the picture. A better representation of the problem would take the reaction of the board into account. Most examples of MEUI violation that we know of have such a property; the argument is essentially the same as the one we made when we invoked the regret one feels on losing a gamble to explain multiattribute risk aversion.

If there are no strong reasons to doubt the validity of MEUI, the construction of the multiplicative SEU model is straightforward. The analyst has to go through all the steps involved in the additive model, that is, the construction of the u_i's and the k_i's, in exactly the same way as in the additive case. The parameter k is fully determined by the k_i's, as shown on p. 292.

The form of the *multilinear SEU* model is superficially similar to the expanded version of the multiplicative model:

$$u(\mathbf{x}) = \sum_{i=1}^{n} k_i u_i(x_i) + \sum_{i<j} k_{ij} u_i(x_i) u_j(x_j)$$

$$+ \sum_{i<j<m} k_{ijm} u_i(x_i) u_j(x_j) u_m(x_m) + \cdots + \prod_{i=1}^{n} k_{i...n} u_i(x_i). \tag{8.71}$$

But there is an important distinction: in the multiplicative model *one* interaction parameter k determines the scaling of *all* interaction terms. In the multilinear model these interactions can have different k's. Of course, the assessment of these interaction terms $k_{ij}, k_{ijm}, \ldots$ can be quite cumbersome. For example, in the case of 10 attributes, 1,022 additional scaling factors have to be constructed because there are $\binom{10}{2}$ two-way interactions, $\binom{10}{3}$ three-way interactions, and so on. We will not go into the actual assessment of such terms here but refer you to the extensive treatment in Keeney and Raiffa (1976) instead.

The assumption behind the multilinear SEU model is weaker than that behind the multiplicative model. According to multilinear expected utility independence (MLEUI), preferences among lotteries on a *single* attribute must be independent of sure identical consequences in the other attributes. Note that this assumption does *not* require the consideration of lotteries that have uncertainties in more than one attribute.

Keeney and Raiffa discuss various independence conditions weaker than MEUI, MLEUI, or AEUI that still imply the respective models. These weaker versions of the assumptions can be extremely useful for testing the model and getting a feel for the strength of the assumptions.

8.5. Implications for decision-analytic practice

As in Chapter 7, you feel frustrated by now; you have a multiattribute evaluation problem, and we have offered a menu of methods but haven't told you what to do. The hints scattered throughout this chapter are considerably less clear than they were in Chapter 7. We shall try to compile them here.

Choosing a model

The analyst has a choice among the various model forms described in Table 8.2. We have already argued that the distinction between risky and riskless models is tenuous. In many practical situations, utility and value functions elicited with risky versus riskless methods are hardly distinguishable because of judgmental error and because of stimulus and response mode effects. Studies that have explored differences between risky and riskless utility functions in the MAUT context have not revealed strong effects. Fischer (1977), for example, found high convergence between the procedures and so did Barron, von Winterfeldt, and Fischer (1984).

Our position is this: since there is little *experimental* evidence for drastic differences between risky and riskless utility functions and since there are good *theoretical* arguments that they are identical, the choice between risky and riskless models should be left to the analyst.

Some researchers argue that risky procedures are useful because they make the decision maker think about the decisions in the context of the prevailing uncertainties, and they therefore can help clarify preferences and values (Keeney, 1980). Others have argued that risky models and procedures usually involve rather complex, sometimes awkward questions and are therefore difficult to implement. We prefer simple and flexible procedures in which the preferred model type is chosen to accommodate the decision problem and the decision maker's or expert's natural modes of thought. Furthermore, we encourage checking both risky and riskless models with some questions from the other model type.

The choice of a model form is a little trickier, because none of the models discussed in this chapter have a generalized validity. Most analysts assume or create riskless additivity, at least in the conjoint measurement sense. But riskless interactions obviously depend on the type of stimuli, and the additivity found may simply be the result of luck or clever choice of attributes. One can surely conceive of stimuli for which additivity would be strongly violated (e.g., preferences for seats in a football stadium described by rows and columns). Therefore, the results of studies that support riskless additivity should not be considered evidence that *every* evaluation problem can be modeled with an additive riskless model. We do believe, however, that a clever analyst can structure virtually any evaluation problem so that an additive model is appropriate at least in the sense that riskless additivity assumptions are not grossly violated.

Recent experimental studies that examined risky additivity and the corresponding additive SEU assumption have shown systematic failures of that model. These studies have usually involved very simple stimuli (cigarettes and candy, gasoline and ground beef, jobs) for which riskless additivity surely was valid. Violations of the risky model were probably caused by multiattribute risk aversion, as demonstrated by von Winterfeldt (1980a). In other words, the reasons for violating risky additivity (AEUI) are the same as those for violating single-attribute risk neutrality in value. We would argue then that an analyst should attempt to structure attributes so that they are additive in a riskless sense – and we have not found that to be an exceedingly difficult task. If the decision maker then exhibits multiattribute risk aversion, the arguments for risky additivity and multiattribute risk neutrality should be made. This does not mean that every utility function should be linear; it just means that the transformation from value to utility should be linear. These considerations might lead to the inclusion of new attributes if the decision maker insists on multiattribute risk aversion.

Choosing a single-attribute procedure

A good procedure should

> provide insights into the value problem;
> fit the characteristics of the stimuli;
> fit the characteristics of the decision maker or expert;
> be simple;
> minimize error and artifacts;
> be real, or at least realistic;
> be fast.

Using these criteria, we shall examine the following techniques:

1	Difference standard sequences and bisection
2	Ratings and ratio estimation
3	Curve drawing and selection
4	Variable probability and variable certainty equivalents

Difference standard sequences and bisection are indifference methods that require a densely spaced set of evaluation objects. Therefore, many stimuli may not fit them very well. These methods are inapplicable when stimulus sets are small or have discrete steps. They may suit sophisticated decision makers and experts who tend to think in terms of trade-offs and incremental changes. However, experts who have this ability often prefer the simpler methods of curve drawing or curve selection. Both methods are moderately complicated for numerical scales and may be prohibitively complicated for complex stimuli (multiattribute jobs, apartments, etc.). Whether these methods produce more or less error than others is not known. However, they depend highly on initial assessments (choice of a standard or a midpoint). Subsequent assessments may compound errors made in the initial one. Moreover, they require interpolation, since the objects relevant to the decision are not always included in the indifference responses. Because of the spacing bias, we suspect that both methods lead to spacing of utilities that is too similar to the stimulus scale values – if such a scale exists. These methods can be realistic in some instances. In many cases, however, stimuli have to be artificially enriched, thus creating some unrealistic or even imaginary alternatives. The methods are not extremely time-consuming, although it may take some time for the respondent to become familiar with the task.

Both *rating and ratio estimation methods* are direct numerical judgments. They can be applied to any set of objects and are especially useful if the set is relatively small. If the set becomes prohibitively large, the analyst should select a few representative stimuli that span the value scale. In our experience rating scale methods are very simple and can be used by a wide range of experts, decision makers, and subjects in the laboratory. Ratio estimation of utility has not been very well explored and appears not to match stimuli and decision maker characteristics as well as rating scale methods.

Direct numerical methods have in the past been shown to be reliable, but they may be subject to the response mode and stimulus effects discussed earlier. In particular, spacing, centering, and contraction biases may apply. If a natural scale exists, the respondent may tend simply to match one set of numbers with another one. Anchoring and adjustment problems may occur, but they can be minimized by careful stimulus selection and presentation and by prior scale anchoring. The rating scale method is realistic because it uses only stimuli with which the decision maker is directly concerned. The ratio method scores worse in realism. Rating scale methods are probably the fastest and simplest.

Curve drawing or curve selection should be used only with sophisticated subjects. In addition they can be applied only to a stimuli with a natural underlying scale. Care must be taken that the expert does not simply translate numerical values into another (ill-defined) set of numbers. In order for this method to be useful, properties of curves should be carefully reexamined. For those who are familiar with functions and curves, the method is simple, fast, and realistic. Therefore, we recommend it for sophisticated respondents.

Both the *variable probability* and the *variable certainty equivalent methods* are indifference methods. They suffer from problems similar to those of the standard sequence and bisection methods. However, they may provide more insight into the problem when *real* uncertainty exists in the task. The variable certainty equivalent methods require continuous or dense outcomes. Both may require judgments about hypothetical gambles and can be rather complicated, especially when the outcomes themselves are complex, because the decision maker has to think simultaneously about gambles, values, and probabilities.

We have already cited some evidence that the two methods can produce rather reliable results with relatively little error. Of course, we would expect the errors to increase with increased task complexity and reduced familiarity. Perhaps the biggest problem associated with these methods is realism. In most instances the gambles that have to be created must remain hypothetical. Sometimes they are hard to imagine. Occasionally they may even be inconceivable. If outcomes are essentially riskless, gambles may introduce an unrealistic element into the task.

The time required for the variable probability and variable certainty equivalent methods is probably comparable to that required by the standard sequence and bisection methods. Any of these require more training than direct numerical judgments.

Of course, the analyst should attempt whenever possible to use several techniques rather than rely on a single method. Our suggestion is this: construct the value or utility function first with a direct numerical method and then perform a few checks with an indifference method; finally, explore the implications of possible inconsistencies and produce a coherent set of assessments.

In general, we suggest ratings or curve drawing as a first-cut method. When the task involves uncertainties and when SEU models will be applied later, the checks should be done with the probability or certainty equivalent methods. When the task is riskless, the checks should be done with standard sequences or bisection.

Choosing a weighting procedure

In choosing a weighting procedure, one first asks whether explicit numerical importance assignments should be used. Some authors argue against using the concept of attribute importance because it is essentially extraneous to the value and utility models discussed (see, e.g., Keeney and Raiffa, 1976).

Nevertheless, the concept of importance makes sense to many decision makers because it can be measured in replicable and stable ways, and it thereby can add stability and face validity to the overall model.

Of course, the analyst has to be aware of the danger of distortions. In particular, insensitivity of importance judgments to ranges of alternatives could seriously warp the weights. Usually decision makers and experts have their own plausible set of ranges in mind and probably make their importance judgments on that basis. For example, the fuel economy of a car would probably have received very little importance 20 years ago because the financial difference between an economic car and a noneconomic car was small. Today this difference is big, and the importance of the attribute fuel economy has obviously increased. It might be useful to elicit from the decision maker the plausible ranges on which his or her importance judgments are based. If the standardization of actual alternatives seriously deviates from these plausible ranges, importance judgments should be considered with care.

A final recommendation

In a nutshell, we recommend the following general approach to most MAUT problems:

1   Determine a value tree structure for the problem at hand. If it has more than 20 bottom-level twigs, think again. Can some twigs be restructured or combined into fewer attributes? A good number is 10. Sometimes it may be necessary to define attributes on a higher level of abstraction or define them judgmentally to generate fewer attributes.

2   Before entering the MAUT process, work with the value tree yourself. You can make a very good check of the quality of the attributes by constructing a matrix of alternatives by attributes. Can you rank-order the alternatives in each attribute? Can these rank orders be made independent of other attributes? If you have problems filling out this simple matrix of rank orders, your respondent will probably have considerably more trouble answering more demanding questions. When in doubt, restructure your attributes.

3   Decide which multiattribute aggregation rule to use. Thought experiments are helpful. Usually you will be able to find an attribute set for which an additive rule makes sense. (Your rank orders, your ratings, and your weights in step 2 are independent of other attribute values.) If you find peculiarities in your thought experiments, like "The weight should really depend . . . " or "The ratings depend . . . " see if the multiplicative model might be valid. In practice the additive and the multiplicative models are the only workable ones. Occasionally you may need simple versions of the multilinear model that combine additive and multiplicative building blocks. When anything more complicated occurs, go back to step 1.

4   If the problem permits, assess single-attribute value functions first, using the methods of Chapter 7. Begin with numerical estimation methods, preferably direct rating or curve drawing. Cross-check the results with some simple indifference questions. If your problem does not come with predefined

ranges on the attributes, you may have to spend some time thinking about appropriate end points: plausible ranges are better than feasible or possible ones.

5 Use swing weights or ratio estimation of importance weights with careful instructions to consider attribute ranges. When you are working with the multiplicative model or simple multilinear models, derive the interaction parameters from simple swing weight questions.

6 Use multiple convergent techniques if time permits. Discuss inconsistencies with your respondent. Three kinds of inconsistencies often produce insights: inconsistencies between direct numerical and indifference procedures, inconsistencies between lottery-based and riskless procedures, and inconsistencies between the outputs of a multiattribute procedure and intuitive (holistic) direct evaluations of the alternatives. Be prepared to restructure and return to step 1 even this late in the game. For example, inconsistencies between holistic procedures and decomposed procedures may be due to the omission of an attribute.

9 Theoretical foundations of value and utility measurement

9.1. Measurement theories of value and utility

Introduction

In this chapter we discuss the theoretical foundations of value and utility measurement, describe some techniques for testing the assumptions underlying the theories, and outline some insights about modeling value and utility that follow from the theory.

Most expositions of the theories of value and utility measurement begin by stating the assumptions (or axioms) that underlie a particular value or utility model. For example, transitivity of preference and the sure-thing assumptions are formalized as axioms that must be satisfied in order for the expected utility measurement model to be valid. One then proves the theoretical validity of the model by showing that the axioms are both necessary and sufficient for the model to hold. The theoretically appropriate methods for eliciting value or utility functions within a particular measurement theory are usually hidden in the constructive proofs of the validity of the model.

Seldom if ever, we believe, have theories of value and utility measurement been actually invented in this way. More likely, the inventors of the theories started with the model and a reasonable elicitation procedure and asked themselves, "What are the elementary conditions that must be met in order for this type of model and elicitation procedure to make sense?" Although these elementary conditions are usually phrased as formal axioms, they are nothing but assumptions about the behavior of a respondent in a value or utility construction procedure. For example, when applying the additive difference value model, we would expect that a respondent could assess strengths of preference, that these strengths of preference would be transitive, and that strengths of preference in one attribute would not be affected by values of the alternatives in other attributes. It is easy to see why the model could not be constructed if any of these three assumptions failed: if the respondent could not state strengths of preferences for some pairs of objects, we could not assign value to them; difference standard sequences make transitivity a requirement; and the additivity assumption implies independent single-attribute strengths of preference. Most behaviorally relevant assumptions in measurement theory are "necessary" just in this sense.

314

Wherever possible we shall exploit the fact that axioms are necessary either for the model form (e.g., independence assumptions) or for the elicitation procedure (e.g., transitivity) in value and utility measurement. Usually we shall begin our formal presentation by assuming a particular measurement technique and model, derive the necessary axioms, and when necessary add some sufficient axioms from the literature. The mathematically inclined reader will probably be able to follow the necessity argument that motivates the axioms. We recommend that only mathematically trained readers dig into the references that prove the sufficiency of the representations.

After laying the theoretical foundation of value and utility measurement, we shall try to translate some of the most important assumptions into procedures for detecting model violations. This discussion is meant to sharpen the analyst's eye for places where things might go wrong with a model and provide the analyst with ideas for thought experiments and consistency checks for carrying out actual tests. The key point to keep in mind throughout this discussion is that the assumptions need be *empirically* valid only for the simple judgments and responses required for constructing the model. Of course, they must be *conceptually* valid and thus make sense in the array of intended applications of the model.

An unfortunate truism about measurement-theoretic assumptions is that they will almost certainly be empirically wrong. For an analyst the crucial questions therefore are: what degree of violation should cause concern, and what should one do about gross violations? In the final section we attempt to answer these questions.

Concepts of measurement theory

Modern measurement theory (see Krantz, Luce, Suppes, and Tversky, 1971; Suppes and Zinnes, 1963) makes use of the mathematical theory of ordered algebraic structures such as ordered semigroups, ordered groups, fields, and rings (see, e.g., Fuchs, 1963; Vinogradov, 1969) to prove the feasibility of measurement and to construct scales. First one analyzes an empirical structure of objects to be measured (e.g., stones), their relations (e.g., stone A displaces *more* water than stone B), and their operations (e.g., stones A and B displace *together* as much water as stone C) and states assumptions (axioms) that characterize this empirical structure as an algebraic structure with useful mathematical properties (e.g., transitivity of the relation "displaces more water" and commutativity of the operation "displace together"). Then one identifies a numerical structure containing a subset of the real numbers, with their usual relations (equal to, greater than) and operations (addition, subtraction, multiplication, division), that has the same algebraic structure. Finally, one constructs a function that assigns to each element (e.g., a stone) in the empirical structure a number (e.g., volume) such that the relations and operations in both structures coincide. This function is called a homomorphism. *Measurement, in short, is the construction of a homomorphism between an empirical and a numerical ordered algebraic structure.*

This all sounds rather complicated, but it is really based on very simple ideas. Measurement requires the creation of a rule (function) that assigns numbers to objects. (This is Stevens's [1936] somewhat dated definition of measurement). These numbers should behave in a manner that closely resembles the properties of the objects (their relations and operations). This idea of measurement is very general. One can invent many strange rules and operations and see whether the numbers behave in a way that reflects the physical consequences of the operations. Krantz et al. (1971) describe a rule for length measurement in which a "sum" is defined by the length of a rod forming the hypotenuse of a triangle in which the two sides are the summants.

This is the framework of value and utility measurement. Utility theory distinguishes itself from general measurement theory in three ways:

1   The *objects* to be measured are objects of cost or value (just as stones are objects of extension or mass). In the following, they are called evaluation objects, objects, or alternatives.
2   The *relation* between these evaluation objects is that of preference or strength of preference expressed by or attributed to an individual, group, or organization.
3   The *operations* on these evaluation objects are not directly defined as physical manipulations of the objects (like putting two stones in a water-filled container). Some operations are missing altogether; some are derived from human judgment.

The last two facts mean, of course, that utility theory is quite subjective. The difference in subjectivity between the measurements implied by utility theory and those used in, for example, physical sciences is one of degree, not kind. Even length measurement requires human judgment. The difference between measuring length and measuring utility (and the challenge to measurement theorists) is the need in the latter to create and interpret operations that are not so obvious and directly observable as they are in the former.

Principles of value and utility measurement

The best known theory for constructing value functions is the difference value model based on traditional difference measurement (see Krantz et al., 1971; Suppes and Winet, 1955). The difference value model considers pairs of objects at one time. Such pairs (a, b) are part of a set of objects $X \times X$. The difference value model assumes that the decision maker can express the relative strength of preferences of one object over another in the sense that for all $(a, b), (c, d) \in X \times X$ a judgment can be made as to whether the increase in value obtained by substituting a for b is larger or smaller than the increase in value obtained by substituting c for d. Such strength-of-preference judgments are formalized by the quaternary relation $\overset{\circ}{\succsim}$. Given certain axioms on this relation (e.g., transitivity, monotonicity) there exists a function v setting up a relationship between the objects in X and the real numbers such that

$$(a, b) \overset{\circ}{\succsim} (c, d) \quad \text{if and only if} \quad v(a) - v(b) \geq v(c) - v(d). \tag{9.1}$$

Verbally this statement says that the strength of preference of a over b is at least as large as the strength of preference of c over d if and only if the (numerical) difference in value between a and b is at least as large as the (numerical) difference in value between c and d. An example is the quantification of the degree of displeasure you feel about driving to work as a function of driving time. Obviously, time itself is not a very good measure of your displeasure (negative value). An extra 5 minutes added to an original 1-hour ride may cause you less additional discomfort than an extra 5 minutes added to an original 10-minute ride. That is, the decrease in value caused by changing from 60 to 65 minutes is less than the decrease in value caused by changing from 10 to 15 minutes.

Expected utility theory (von Neumann and Morgenstern, 1947) builds on preferences and indifferences among gambles. No strength-of-preference judgments are introduced. The set of evaluation objects consists of gambles $\mathbf{a} = (a_1, a_2, \ldots, a_i, \ldots, a_n)$, which have an outcome $a_i \in X$ if event E_i occurs with probability $P(E_i)$. A preference relation is defined on the set $\mathbf{A}$ of all gambles; $\mathbf{a} \succsim \mathbf{b}$ means that $\mathbf{a}$ is preferred to or indifferent to $\mathbf{b}$. von Neumann and Morgenstern (1947) and Savage (1954) present axiom systems that specify conditions that permit a utility function to be defined such that for all $\mathbf{a}, \mathbf{b} \in \mathbf{A}$

$$\mathbf{a} \succsim \mathbf{b} \quad \text{if and only if} \quad SEU(\mathbf{a}) \geq SEU(\mathbf{b}). \tag{9.2}$$

The SEU in the case of n events is

$$SEU(\mathbf{a}) = \sum_{i=1}^{n} P(E_i)u(a_i), \qquad a_i \in X. \tag{9.3}$$

Notice that the set of evaluation objects and the relation are fundamentally different from those that appear in the difference measurement case.

9.2. Theoretical foundations of single-attribute value and utility measurement

Difference value measurement

We mentioned in the introduction that value measurement has its roots in the theory of difference measurement. (Pfanzagl's [1968] bisection theory, which is also closely related to difference measurement, is very similar in spirit and concepts – if not in structural assumptions – to difference measurement.) In this section we follow Krantz et al.'s (1971) presentation of positive difference measurement structures to explain the theoretical foundations of rating, bisection, and other methods. But rather than present the theory as a methematical justification for the procedures, we demonstrate how the procedures implicitly assume a theory.

In all procedures judgments are made about *pairs* of objects (e.g., pairs of locations, differences in driving times). Sometimes the idea of an increment (e.g., salary raise) is substituted for such pairs, but an increment is also the difference between the starting point and an end point. In measurement-theoretic terms, the first intuitive notion, therefore, is a set of tuples of objects, $B \subset X \times X$, where X is the set of objects. (A tuple is a fixed number of objects somehow selected from a larger set. In this example, we could have used the word *pairs* instead of *tuples;* in other contexts, tuples might contain three, four, or any fixed number of objects. An *n*-tuple contains n objects. $X \times X$ means that these tuples consist of two objects each, both selected somehow from X.) Next, the procedures require a specific type of response when two pairs of objects, for example, (a, b), $(c, d) \in B$, are presented. That response is a statement about the relative differences in value when the tuples (a, b) and (c, d) are compared. A typical question implicit in any procedure is the following. Is the strength of preference of a over b greater than the strength of preference of c over d? Notice that we have already added a nontrivial assumption here, namely, that the respondent knows which of the two elements in each tuple is preferred. We shall make that assumption explicit by stating that all tuples are ordered such that the first element is preferred to or indifferent to the second. Thus B consists of all such ordered tuples with positive differences. We shall formally express the strength of preference relation as the quaternary relation $\overset{\circ}{\succsim}$ defined on B, where $(a, b) \overset{\circ}{\succsim} (c, d)$ means that the strength of preference of a over b is larger than or equal to the strength of preference of c over d. The primitives for the difference theory therefore consist of the relational system $\langle B, \overset{\circ}{\succsim} \rangle$ (see Suppes and Zinnes, 1963).

In the following paragraphs we inspect the other implicit assumptions that are made when value measurement methods are used, notably the indifference methods (difference standard sequence and bisection). (Assumptions V2 to V4 are illustrated in Figure 9.1.)

V1: *Connectivity.* The first assumption is obviously that the subject can indeed make a judgment when faced with two elements in B. That is, for all (a, b), $(c, d) \in B$,

$$\text{either} \quad (a, b) \overset{\circ}{\succsim} (c, d) \quad \text{or} \quad (c, d) \overset{\circ}{\succsim} (a, b) \quad \text{or both.} \tag{9.4}$$

V2 **TRANSITIVITY**

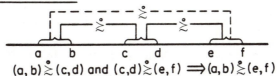

$$(a, b) \overset{\circ}{\succsim} (c, d) \text{ and } (c, d) \overset{\circ}{\succsim} (e, f) \Longrightarrow (a, b) \overset{\circ}{\succsim} (e, f)$$

V3 **SUMMATION**

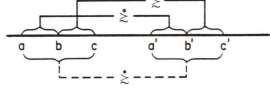

$$(a,b), (b,c) \in B \Longrightarrow (a,c) \overset{\circ}{\succsim} (a,b), (b,c)$$

V4 **CANCELLATION**

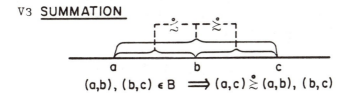

Figure 9.1. Three assumptions of value measurement. Dashed lines indicate implications.

This assumption is called connectivity, and it would be violated if the respondent shrugged and said, "In this case, I really do not know."

V2: *Transitivity*. In the construction and consistency check procedures described above we further assumed that strength of preference is transitive, which can be formally expressed as follows (see Figure 9.1):

When $(a, b) \overset{\circ}{\succsim} (c, d)$ and $(c, d) \overset{\circ}{\succsim} (e, f)$, then $(a, b) \overset{\circ}{\succsim} (e, f)$. (9.5)

Transitivity and connectivity together are often called the *weak-order assumption* – a cornerstone of most measurement theories.

V3: *Summation*. An operation on strengths of preference that might be called *addition* must exist. The result of adding two strengths of preference must be larger than each of the parts. For example, you may prefer scotch to rum and rum to vodka. If so, it seems only natural to require that the strength of preference of the "sum," that is, of scotch over vodka, be larger than either the strength of preference of scotch over rum or that of rum over vodka. Formally, this idea can be expressed as follows (see Figure 9.1):

$$\text{For all} \quad (a, b), (b, c) \in B, (a, c) \overset{\circ}{\succsim} (a, b) \quad \text{and} \quad (a, c) \overset{\circ}{\succsim} (b, c). \tag{9.6}$$

V4: *Cancellation.* This assumption is illustrated in the standard sequence approach of Chapter 7. Naturally, we want to be able to say that jumping three steps in the standard sequence at point *A* leads to the same strength of preference as jumping three steps in the standard sequence at point *B*. A weaker form of the same assumption is the following (see Figure 9.1):

$$\text{If} \quad (a, b) \overset{\circ}{\succsim} (a', b') \quad \text{and} \quad (b, c) \overset{\circ}{\succsim} (b', c'), \quad \text{then} \quad (a, c) \overset{\circ}{\succsim} (a', c'). \tag{9.7}$$

V5: *Solvability.* Obviously, the assumption was made throughout the standard sequence and bisection procedures that objects can be found in *B* that satisfy certain strength-of-preference relations. For example, we assumed that objects can be found that match a given strength of preference or that bisect a given pair of objects. This assumption is called *solvability* because it requires that all strength of preference equations be solvable. The solvability assumption corresponds roughly to the qualitative requirement that the object space be "dense"; that is, that there be no holes in the space.

V6: *Archimedean.* Finally we must assume that bisection and standard sequences can proceed throughout the whole space without "running against" a point of infinite positive or negative value. The Archimedean assumption formalizes this by requiring that a standard sequence not consist of an infinite number of steps and at the same time have a strict (upper or lower) bound in *B*.

If V1 through V6 are satisfied, we call the relational system $\langle B, \overset{\circ}{\succsim} \rangle$ a positive difference structure, and it can be proved that there exists a function v such that for all $(a, b), (c, d) \in B$,

$$(a, b) \overset{\circ}{\succsim} (c, d) \quad \text{if and only if} \quad v(a) - v(b) \geq v(c) - v(d). \tag{9.8}$$

Of course, in practice, axioms V1 through V6 can never be verified, and it is doubtful whether they will be even approximately valid in applied situations. However, they may provide the analyst with insights about the potential *failure* of difference measurement. If there is reason to assume that one of the axioms is systematically violated, difference measurement may not be appropriate.

Of particular importance for this purpose are axioms V1 (connectivity), V5 (solvability), and V6 (no infinite points). Practically, these assumptions will be violated if one of the following holds:

1	The decision maker is very uncertain about his or her strength of preference (violates V1).
2	The decision maker has only discrete and limited options (violates V5).
3	The decision maker finds certain options or consequences extremely unattractive or extremely attractive relative to others (violates V6).

Repeated measures and convergent validation may help make strengths of preference less uncertain. One may think of enriching the option space by adding hypothetical alternatives to it, as is routinely done in indifference methods. To overcome violations of V6, the unattractive options (which would never be chosen) and the extremely attractive option (which is not attainable) may simply be deleted from consideration. Notice that these problems occur only with indifference methods and not with direct numerical methods.

Utility measurement

The variable probability and variable certainty equivalent methods described in Chapter 7 rely heavily on the SEU assumption. The foundations of utility measurement using these two procedures are, in fact, identical with the foundations of SEU theory (although more restricted theories, tailored only to the two procedures, are conceivable). In this section we attempt to reconstruct the axioms of SEU theory (Savage, 1954); (von Neumann and Morgenstern, 1947) by examining the implicit or explicit assumptions underlying utility construction. As an overall framework for reconstructing SEU theory, we use conjoint measurement theory (Krantz, 1964; Krantz et al., 1971; Luce and Tukey, 1964). This theory can lead us – along a somewhat simplified path – to Savage's assumptions.

In both utility construction processes the decision maker expresses *preferences* or *indifferences* among *gambles* and *sure outcomes*. The first step in our theory reconstruction is to define these as primitives. First, we consider a set of outcomes X with typical elements $x, y \in X$. These outcomes are thought of as prizes, gains, or losses. To create gambles, we must define events. We shall assume an exhaustive set of mutually exclusive elementary events, $e_j, j = 1, 2, \ldots, m$. Unions of the e_j's, the certain event, and the null event form the event set E. Events for a particular lottery or gamble are formed by a finite partition of E into set $E_i, i = 1, 2, \ldots, n$. A specific gamble $\mathbf{p}$ can be represented by an n-tuple

$$\mathbf{p} = (x_1, x_2, \ldots, x_i, \ldots, x_n),$$

where x_i is the outcome to be obtained when E_i occurs. The set of all gambles is labeled $\mathbf{P}$ with typical elements $\mathbf{p}, \mathbf{q} \in \mathbf{P}$. Notice that $\mathbf{p}$ could always be represented with the elementary events e_j by assigning identical outcomes

x_i to those elementary events that form the nonelementary event E_i. It is as easy to implement a two-outcome gamble with a die as with a coin; simply assign one outcome to three faces of the die and the other outcome to the other three. We assume that the set of events the experimenter can control is very large and that the experimenter controls probabilities by forming combinations of elementary events. As an illustration, one might think of the e_j's as small segments of a circle on which a random spinner could land and of the E_i's as combinations of these segments (e.g., half the circle).

Finally we define a preference relation $\succsim$ on **P**; $\mathbf{p} \succsim \mathbf{q}$ means that **p** is indifferent or preferred to **q**. Clearly, we can extend $\succsim$ to any pair of elements in X, that is, to any two outcomes, by considering a "gamble" in which an element x is received for all events e_j, that is, for sure. This extension allows us to compare sure things and gambles directly. The primitive can now be summarized as a relational system $\langle \mathbf{P}, \succsim \rangle$ (Suppes and Zinnes, 1963).

This formulation of the primitives of SEU theory already makes some strong assumptions. Luce and Krantz (1971) criticize the formulation, because it assumes that the elementary events are always the same. In many decision situations, the events that control outcomes change according to the option being considered. For example, the uncertainties that control whether you will get from A to B and how much you will enjoy the trip are very different if you choose to fly than they are if you choose to drive. Luce and Krantz developed another formulation of the problem, called conditional expected utility theory, to meet that criticism. We prefer to use the standard Savage-type formulation because it is simpler to explain, and it generalizes – with some stretching – to most situations to which conditional expected utility would apply.

Next, we consider some of the assumptions imposed on $\succsim$ in the construction of u:

U1: *Connectivity.* The first assumption is, of course, that the decision maker can indeed make judgments about preference or indifference when faced with two gambles in **P**. In other words, for all $\mathbf{p}, \mathbf{q} \in \mathbf{P}$ either

$$\mathbf{p} \succsim \mathbf{q} \quad \text{or } \mathbf{q} \succsim \mathbf{p} \quad \text{or both.} \tag{9.9}$$

This assumption is called connectivity. It would be violated if the respondent said, "I really can't make up my mind." Violations of that nature may occur if **p** and **q** are very close in expected utility or are very complex.

U2: *Transitivity.* The construction procedures and consistency checks for building utility functions assume that preferences among gambles are transitive. Formally,

$$\text{when} \quad \mathbf{p} \succsim \mathbf{q} \quad \text{and} \quad \mathbf{q} \succsim \mathbf{r}, \quad \text{then } \mathbf{p} \succsim \mathbf{r}. \tag{9.10}$$

Transitivity is violated if gambles are complex or similar in expected utility.

U3: *Sure thing.* The SEU model is extensively used in construction procedures. When applied to standard gambles, the model is formulated as

$$SEU(\mathbf{p}) = \sum_{i=1}^{n} P(E_i)u(x_i),$$ (9.11)

where $P(E_i)$ is the personal probability that event E_i will occur. We can illuminate one of the "hidden" assumptions of that model by considering the following preferences between the two gambles $\mathbf{p}$ and $\mathbf{q}$ described by

$$\mathbf{p} = (x_1, x_2, \ldots, a_i, \ldots, x_n)$$

and

$$\mathbf{q} = (y_1, y_2, \ldots, a_i, \ldots, y_n).$$

The $\mathbf{p}$ and $\mathbf{q}$ have an identical ith component (a_i); otherwise they are different. Suppose that $\mathbf{p} \succsim \mathbf{q}$. Then, by the SEU formula

$$SEU(\mathbf{p}) = \sum_{j \neq i} P(E_j)u(x_j) + P(E_i)u(a_i) \geq$$
$$SEU(\mathbf{q}) = \sum_{j \neq i} P(E_j)u(y_j) + P(E_i)u(a_i).$$ (9.12)

This inequality is not influenced by $u(a_i)$ or, therefore, by a_i. In other words, if b_i is substituted for a_i, the SEU calculation in Equation 9.12 will still favor $\mathbf{p}$. Consequently, we can infer

$$\mathbf{p}' = (x_1, x_2 \ldots, b_i, \ldots, x_n) \succsim$$ (9.13)
$$\mathbf{q}' = (y_1, y_2, \ldots, b_i, \ldots, y_n).$$

We can now formulate an important necessary condition of SEU theory as follows:

$$(x_1, x_2, \ldots, a_i, \ldots, x_n) \succsim (y_1, y_2, \ldots, a_i, \ldots, y_n)$$
$$\text{if and only if}$$
$$(x_1, x_2, \ldots, b_i, \ldots, x_n) \succsim (y_1, y_2, \ldots, b_i, \ldots, y_n)$$ (9.14)

for all $x_j, a_i, b_i \in X, j \neq i, i = 1, \ldots, n$. This assumption is called the *sure-thing principle* (see Savage, 1954).

The sure-thing principle is *the* cornerstone of SEU theory, and its violation would cast strong doubts on the applicability of the theory.

To get an intuitive grasp of the idea, suppose that when evaluating two investment opportunities, $\mathbf{p}$ and $\mathbf{q}$, you consider three states of the economy: growing, slowing, and slumping; $\mathbf{p}$ is favorable when the economy grows, $\mathbf{q}$ is favorable when the economy slows, but both are equally bad when the economy slumps. Consideration of the probabilities and outcomes leads you to decide on **p.** Now you learn that, although you were right in your probability assessment of an economic slump, you severely underestimated the disastrous effects of a slump on your investments. They are still the same for both investments, but worse than you thought. That information should *not* change your preference for **p.**

U4: *Solvability.* Utility construction procedures rely heavily on "creating" indifferences (or indifference equations) between lotteries by varying outcomes or probabilities. Throughout the construction process, we assume that such indifference equations can be solved. This may require that events be finely graded (in the variable probability procedure) or that outcomes be finely graded (in the certainty equivalent procedure) so that we can always create indifferences. In either case, this assumption is a version of the technical "solvability" axiom in conjoint measurement theory. Without formalizing we note that its application to outcomes requires that for any gamble $\mathbf{p} = (x_1, x_2, \ldots, x_i, \ldots, x_n)$ we must be able to find a $z \in X$ such that $z \sim \mathbf{p}$.

This solvability assumption in essence avoids "holes" in the outcome space. Practically it means that a decision analyst who wishes to use the certainty equivalent procedure must be able to produce finely differentiated reasonable outcomes. An analogous assumption must, of course, be made for events in order for the variable probability procedure to be appropriate.

U5: *Archimedean.* Another technical assumption is sometimes called the Archimedean axiom. The idea of this assumption is to avoid points in the outcome set X that have infinite positive or negative utility. We will not spell out this assumption, but we point out that it rules out ruinous losses.

Axioms U1 through U5 form the basis of what is known as an additive conjoint measurement representation of gambles **p.** Formally, the implication is that there exists a function U and functions u_i such that

$$\mathbf{p} \succsim \mathbf{q} \quad \text{if and only if} \quad U(\mathbf{p}) \geq U(\mathbf{q}), \tag{9.15}$$

where

$$U(\mathbf{p}) = \sum_{i=1}^{n} u_i(x_i).$$

Notice that U1 through U5 provide the necessary additive representation of U but not the full SEU model in which probabilities and utilities are split. In other words, we need an additional assumption that guarantees $u_i = q_i u$, where q_i is interpretable as the probability of E_i. Without formalization, we state verbally the following assumption:

U6: *Equal standard sequence.* Outcomes in event E_i that are equally spaced in utility must also be equally spaced in utility in event E_j, $i \neq j$.

Assumptions U1 through U6 give us the desired result:

$$U(\mathbf{p}) = \sum_{i=1}^{n} P(E_i)u(x_i). \tag{9.16}$$

Moreover, any other function U' satisfying the same conditions U1 through U6 will be related by a positive linear transformation to U. These Us are what we have been calling SEUs throughout the book.

Nobody believes that in practice these six assumptions will be valid. There will always be some unsolvable indifferences; intransitivities will occur; density requirements will be violated. Consequently SEU will almost certainly be violated as a descriptive model. The use of SEU as a prescriptive or normative model, however, puts these axioms in a different light. They suggest ways in which the model might go wrong or in which the decision maker might *want* to disagree with the model. If the decision maker agrees with assumptions U1 through U6 and if the analyst has reason to believe that the decision maker can make judgments satisfying these assumptions at least in the simple tasks required by the utility construction procedures, then the analyst has a solid argument for extrapolating the analysis to more complex options, for which intuitive preferences and indifferences would certainly fail. The assumptions will be violated if one of the following holds:

1   The gambles are too complex and the decision maker simply cannot express preferences or indifferences (violates U1).
2   Utilities depend on events (violates U3 and U6).
3   The set of events or outcomes is not rich enough for the analyst to fine-tune them to solve indifference equations (violates U4).
4   The decision maker finds some alternative or consequence so attractive or unattractive that even very small probabilities cannot reduce their utility or disutility (violates U5).

The first problem can be overcome by a simplification of the comparisons, as is usually done in the case of elicitation procedures. However, this often leads to a loss of realism. To regain solvability, either the event set can be enriched with hypothetical events (e.g., balls drawn from urns, probability wheels, roulette games) or the outcome set can be enriched by hypothetical ones. Neither procedure is totally satisfying because both force decision makers to make hypothetical judgments about lotteries. However, the analyst usually must enrich only one of the two; realism should dictate the choice.

An interesting problem arises when the Archimedean assumption is violated. For example, a decision maker may feel that an option that includes a loss of all savings is intolerable, no matter how small the probability is. Sometimes the analyst can alleviate this so-called ruin problem by demonstrating to the decision makers that they make this kind of decision implicitly all the time; we all gamble with our own (and other people's) lives.

9.3. Theoretical foundations of multiattribute value and utility measurement

In Chapter 8 we presented a variety of MAUT models, including the additive and multiplicative risky and riskless models. The purpose of this section is to provide a somewhat more rigorous description of the assumptions that underlie these models. In the next section we then translate these formal assumptions into more practical tests and checks designed to help the analyst select an appropriate model form.

Multiattribute difference measurement

As in the single-attribute case, the difference model is based on a quaternary strength-of-preference relation $\overset{\circ}{\gtrsim}$ over pairs of objects $X \times X$. The expression $(x, y) \overset{\circ}{\gtrsim} (x', y')$ is interpreted as follows. "The strength of preference of x over y is the same as or larger than the strength of preference of x' over y'." We order x, y, x', y' so that the first element in the tuple is always preferred to the second, that is, so that $x \gtrsim y$ and $x' \gtrsim y'$, and we define the relationship between strength of preference and preference as

$$(x, y) \overset{\circ}{\gtrsim} (x', y) \quad \text{if and only if} \quad x \gtrsim x'. \tag{9.17}$$

In the multiattribute case $\mathbf{X}$ is a product set of attributes X_i, and each $\mathbf{x}$ can be characterized as an n-tuple:

$$\mathbf{x} = (x_1, x_2, \ldots, x_i, \ldots, x_n).$$

The first set of assumptions is related to the definitions of $\mathbf{X} \times \mathbf{X}$ as a positive difference structure and therefore coincides with assumptions V1 through V6 of the single-attribute case.

From these assumptions we can derive the necessary representation of difference measurement:

$$(\mathbf{x}, \mathbf{y}) \overset{\circ}{\gtrsim} (\mathbf{x}', \mathbf{y}') \quad \text{if and only if} \quad v(\mathbf{x}) - v(\mathbf{y}) \geq v(\mathbf{x}') - v(\mathbf{y}'). \tag{9.18}$$

So far, nothing has been said about the decompositions of v over the X_i's. The following three assumptions are necessary and sufficient to generate the three main decomposition forms discussed in Chapter 8: the additive, multiplicative, and multilinear decompositions.

To derive *additive difference independence*, the necessary axiom for the additive decomposition, consider two alternatives that differ only on attribute i:

$$\mathbf{x} = (a_1, a_2, \ldots, x_i, \ldots, a_n),$$
$$\mathbf{y} = (a_1, a_2, \ldots, y_i, \ldots, a_n).$$

As the following calculations show, the value difference between these two alternatives should be determined solely by the levels x_i and y_i:

$$v(\mathbf{x}) - v(\mathbf{y}) = \sum_{j \neq i} w_j v_j(a_j) + w_i v_i(x_i) - \sum_{j \neq i} w_j v_j(a_j) - w_i v_i(y_i)$$

$$= w_i[v_i(x_i) - v_i(y_i)]. \tag{9.19}$$

Now consider $\mathbf{x}'$ and $\mathbf{y}'$, which have the same values x_i and y_i as $\mathbf{x}$ and $\mathbf{y}$ but different constant levels b_j in the other attributes:

$$\mathbf{x}' = (b_1, b_2, \ldots, x_i, \ldots, b_n),$$
$$\mathbf{y}' = (b_1, b_2, \ldots, y_i, \ldots, b_n).$$

It should be clear that

$$v(\mathbf{x}') - v(\mathbf{y}') = w_i[v_i(x_i) - v_i(y_i)] \tag{9.20}$$

and therefore

$$v(\mathbf{x}') - v(\mathbf{y}') = v(\mathbf{x}) - v(\mathbf{y}). \tag{9.21}$$

Consequently, if $\mathbf{x}, \mathbf{y}, \mathbf{x}', \mathbf{y}'$ differ only in the constant attributes, then

$$(\mathbf{x}, \mathbf{y}) \approx (\mathbf{x}', \mathbf{y}'). \tag{9.22}$$

Axiom V7 summarizes this condition, which can also be shown to be sufficient for additivity (see, e.g., Dyer and Sarin, 1979; Krantz et al., 1971).

V7: *Additive difference independence.* For all $i = 1, 2, \ldots, n$, $x_i, y_i \in X_i$; a_j, $b_j \in X_j$, $j \neq i$,

$$[(a_1, a_2, \ldots, x_i, \ldots, a_n); (a_1, a_2, \ldots, y_i, \ldots, a_n)] \tag{9.23}$$
$$\approx [(b_1, b_2, \ldots, x_i, \ldots, b_n); (b_1, b_2, \ldots, y_i, \ldots, b_n)].$$

Figure 9.2 depicts this assumption in graphic form in a two-attribute example. In this case the change in value produced by moving from (x_1, a_2) to (y_1, a_2) should be independent of a_2 and, in particular, should be the same when x_1 and y_1 are compared at b_2.

Behaviorally, additive difference independence means that the strength of preference in a single attribute is unaffected by other constant attributes. In particular, the shape of the value function in a single attribute would be unaffected when constructed at different levels of the other attributes, *and* the weight attached to the value function would remain constant.

Since *multilinear difference independence* is weaker than multiplicative difference independence, we introduce it first. Consider four options $\mathbf{x}, \mathbf{y}$, $\mathbf{x}'$, and $\mathbf{y}'$ that vary only in the ith attribute and have identical elements a_j in the other attributes. Assume further that

$$(\mathbf{x}, \mathbf{y}) \overset{\circ}{\approx} (\mathbf{x}', \mathbf{y}'). \tag{9.24}$$

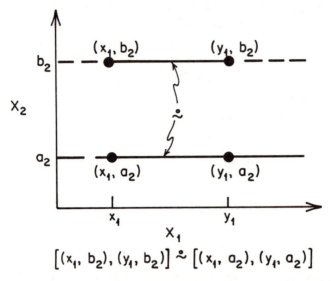

$$\left[(x_1, b_2), (y_1, b_2)\right] \approx \left[(x_1, a_2), (y_1, a_2)\right]$$

Figure 9.2. Graphic representation of additive difference independence in the two-attribute case.

Writing out the multilinear form for x gives

$$v(\mathbf{x}) = z_0 + w_i v_i(x_i) + z_1 w_i v_i(x_i) + z_2 w_i v_i(x_i)$$
$$+ \ldots + z_{n-1} w_i v_i(x_i) = A w_i v_i(x_i) + z_0, \tag{9.25}$$

where the z_j's are constants generated by the terms $w_j v_j(a_j)$, $j \neq i$. Similar terms can be developed for $\mathbf{y}$, $\mathbf{y}'$, $\mathbf{x}'$ to expand the difference inequality

$$v(\mathbf{x}) - v(\mathbf{y}) \geq v(\mathbf{x}') - v(\mathbf{y}') \tag{9.26}$$

as

$$A w_i [v_i(x_i) - v_i(y_i)] \geq A w_i [v_i(x_i') - v_i(y_i')], \tag{9.27}$$

where A is dependent on the constant terms z_j and $A > 0$. Obviously, this inequality should not depend on A. In other words, when any b_j's are to be substituted for all a_j's in the x's and y's, we get

$$B w_i [v_i(x_i) - v_i(y_i)] \geq B w_i [v_i(x_i) - v_i(y_i')] \tag{9.28}$$

with the same direction of the inequality as for the a_j's. Consequently the strength-of-preference relation should be unaffected by switching constant values from a_j to b_j.

This assumption is formalized in the following axiom:

V7′: *Multilinear difference independence.* For all $i = 1, 2, \ldots, n$, a_j, b_j, x_i, y_i, x_i', $y_i' \in X_i$, $j \neq i$,

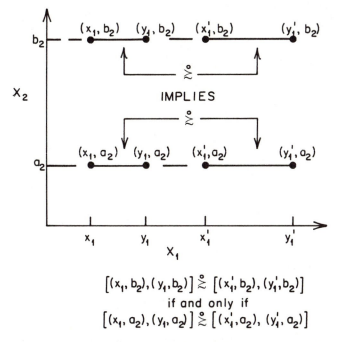

$$[(x_1, b_2),(y_1,b_2)] \overset{\circ}{\gtrsim} [(x_1', b_2), (y_1',b_2)]$$
if and only if
$$[(x_1, a_2),(y_1,a_2)] \overset{\circ}{\gtrsim} [(x_1',a_2), (y_1', a_2)]$$

Figure 9.3. Graphic representation of multilinear difference independence in a two-attribute example.

$$[(a_1, a_2, \ldots, x_i, \ldots, a_n); (a_1, a_2, \ldots, y_i, \ldots, a_n)]$$

$$\overset{\circ}{\gtrsim} [a_1, a_2, \ldots, x_i', \ldots, a_n); (a_1, a_2, \ldots, y_i', \ldots, a_n)]$$

if and only if

$$[(b_1, b_2, \ldots, x_i, \ldots, b_n); (b_1, b_2, \ldots, y_i, \ldots, b_n)]$$

$$\overset{\circ}{\gtrsim} [(b_1, b_2, \ldots, x_i', \ldots, b_n); (b_1, b_2, \ldots, y_i', \ldots, b_n)]. \qquad (9.29)$$

This assumption is graphically depicted in Figure 9.3 for a two-dimensional example. Note that it is considerably weaker than additive difference independence. It requires only that the *relative* strengths of preference in a single attribute be independent of other fixed attribute values. It is therefore possible, and compatible with the multilinear difference model, that the weight w_i of the attribute changes or, in other words, that the relative strength of preferences across attributes changes.

Multiplicative difference independence is a more restricted form of multilinear difference independence, as can be seen from the following considerations. Assume that all attributes vary *except* attribute *i*. For example, let **x**, **y**, **x′**, and **y′** be defined as follows:

$$
\begin{aligned}
\mathbf{x} &= (x_1, x_2, \ldots, a_i, \ldots, x_n),\\
\mathbf{y} &= (y_1, y_2, \ldots, a_i, \ldots, y_n),\\
\mathbf{x'} &= (x_1', x_2', \ldots, a_i, \ldots, x_n'),\\
\mathbf{y'} &= (y_1', y_2', \ldots, a_i, \ldots, y_n').
\end{aligned}
$$

Assume further that

$$(\mathbf{x}, \mathbf{y}) \overset{\circ}{\succsim} (\mathbf{x'}, \mathbf{y'}), \tag{9.30}$$

which implies that

$$v(\mathbf{x}) - v(\mathbf{y}) \geq v(\mathbf{x'}) - v(\mathbf{y'}). \tag{9.26}$$

By substituting the multiplicative model, we observe that

$$1 + wv(\mathbf{x}) = A \prod_{j \neq i} [1 + ww_j v_j(x_j)], \tag{9.31}$$

where $A > 0$ depends on a_i only. Consequently,

$$
\begin{aligned}
&A \left\{ \prod_{j \neq i} [1 + ww_j v_j(x_j)] - \prod_{j \neq 1} [1 + ww_j v_j(y_j)] \right\}\\
&\geq A \left\{ \prod_{j \neq i} [1 + ww_j v_j(x_j')] - \prod_{j \neq i} [1 + ww_j v_j(y_j')] \right\}.
\end{aligned}
\tag{9.32}
$$

Obviously, this inequality should not depend on A. In other words, substituting b_i for a_i everywhere should not change the inequalities and strength-of-preference relation. This assumption is formalized in the following axiom:

V7″: *Multiplicative difference independence.* For all $x_j, y_j, x_j', y_j', a_i, b_i \in X_i$,

$$[(x_1, x_2, \ldots, a_i, \ldots, x_n); (y_1, y_2, \ldots, a_i, \ldots, y_n)]$$

$$\overset{\circ}{\succsim} [(x_1', x_2', \ldots, a_i, \ldots, x_n'); (y_1', y_2', \ldots, a_i, \ldots, y_n')]$$

if and only if

$$[(x_1, x_2, \ldots, b_i, \ldots, x_n); (y_1, y_2, \ldots, b_i, \ldots, y_n)]$$

$$\overset{\circ}{\succsim} [(x_1', x_2', \ldots, b_i, \ldots, x_n'); (y_1', y_2', \ldots, b_i, \ldots, y_n')]. \tag{9.33}$$

Since multiplicative difference independence is different from multilinear difference independence in only three or more dimensions, we cannot easily demonstrate it with a graphic example. However, keep in mind that it is a considerably stronger assumption because it severely constrains cross-attribute trade-offs.

Additive conjoint measurement

Conjoint measurement theory is weaker than difference measurement in that it is based purely on preference relations between elements in **X**. The primitive structure of conjoint measurement is the product set **X** of the attribute X_i and a dual relation $\gtrsim$; $\mathbf{x} \gtrsim \mathbf{y}$ is interpreted as "**x** is preferred to or indifferent to **y**."

The first set of axioms characterizes $\langle \mathbf{X}, \gtrsim \rangle$ as a weak order, which means that $\gtrsim$ is transitive and connected. These two assumptions are clearly necessary for any method of constructing and using conjoint measurement in MAUT:

C1: $\langle X, \gtrsim \rangle$ *is a weak order.* That is, for all $\mathbf{x}, \mathbf{y} \in \mathbf{X}$ either $\mathbf{x} \gtrsim \mathbf{y}$ or $\mathbf{y} \gtrsim \mathbf{x}$ or both and

$$\text{if } \mathbf{x} \gtrsim \mathbf{y} \quad \text{and} \quad \mathbf{y} \gtrsim \mathbf{z}, \quad \text{then } \mathbf{x} \gtrsim \mathbf{z}. \tag{9.34}$$

The second assumption is the technical cornerstone of conjoint measurement theory and it is usually called *joint independence*. To derive joint independence consider the following two options **x** and **y** which have identical elements in attribute *i*,

$$\mathbf{x} = (x_1, x_2, \ldots, a_i, \ldots, x_n),$$
$$\mathbf{y} = (y_1, y_2, \ldots, a_i, \ldots, y_n)$$

and assume that $\mathbf{x} \gtrsim \mathbf{y}$. Let f be an order-preserving value function with

$$f(\mathbf{x}) \geq f(\mathbf{y}). \tag{9.35}$$

Assuming additivity of f gives

$$f(\mathbf{x}) = \sum_{j \neq i} f_j(x_j) + f_i(a_i) \geq \sum_{j \neq i} f_j(y_j) + f_i(a_i) = f(\mathbf{y}). \tag{9.36}$$

It is obvious that this inequality should be independent of the value of $f_i(a_i)$. In other words, substituting b_i into **x** and **y** in order to produce

$$\mathbf{x}' = (x_1, x_2, \ldots, b_i, \ldots, x_n),$$
$$\mathbf{y}' = (y_1, y_2, \ldots, b_i, \ldots, y_n)$$

would still yield $\mathbf{x}' \succsim \mathbf{y}'$, and $f(\mathbf{x}') \succsim f(\mathbf{y}')$. This assumption is formalized in the following axiom:

C2: *Joint independence.* For all $x_j, y_j, a_i, b_i \in X_i, i = 1, \ldots, n$,

$$(x_1, x_2, \ldots, a_i, \ldots, x_n) \succsim (y_1, y_2, \ldots, a_i, \ldots, y_n)$$

if and only if

$$(x_1, x_2, \ldots, b_i, \ldots, x_n) \succsim (y_1, y_2, \ldots, b_i, \ldots, y_n). \tag{9.37}$$

This formulation of joint independence is somewhat unusual. Typically, joint independence is expressed more generally in terms of m variable attributes and $n - m$ fixed attributes (see, e.g., Keeney and Raiffa, 1976; Krantz et al., 1971). In this formulation, for example, attributes 1 through 3 would be jointly independent of attributes 4 through n, if the following held:

$$(x_1, x_2, x_3, a_4, a_5, \ldots, a_n) \succsim (y_1, y_2, y_3, a_4, a_5, \ldots, a_n)$$

if and only if

$$(x_1, x_2, x_3, b_4, b_5, \ldots, b_n) \succsim (y_1, y_2, y_3, b_4, b_5, \ldots, b_n), \tag{9.38}$$

which clearly follows from additivity. When joint independence holds with only one variable attribute, it is called single independence or monotonicity. We used formulation C2 because the above form is implied by our more compact way of expressing joint independence.

Unfortunately, joint independence is sufficient for additivity only when there are three or more attributes. In the two-attribute case, a condition called the Thomson condition must replace joint independence. Figure 9.4 presents a graphic version of the Thomson condition. Assuming $(x_1, y_2) \succsim (y_1, y_2)$ and $(y_1, z_2) \succsim (z_1, y_2)$, the Thomson condition would require that $(x_1, z_2) \succsim (z_1, x_2)$. Formally, this should be clear from the fact that

$$f_1(x_1) + f_2(y_2) = f_1(y_1) + f_2(x_2)$$

and

$$f_1(y_1) + f_2(z_2) = f_1(z_1) + f_2(y_2)$$

imply

$$f_1(x_1) + f_2(z_2) = f_1(z_1) + f_2(x_2). \tag{9.39}$$

We obtain Equation 9.39 simply by adding the upper two equations and "canceling" the y_i's. (Because the y_i's cancel, the ordinal property related to the Thomson condition is also called cancellation.)

To understand the psychological relevance of the Thomson condition,

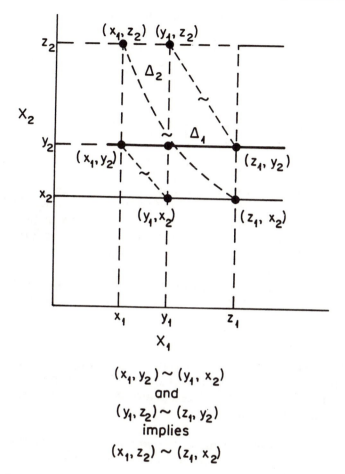

$$(x_1, y_2) \sim (y_1, x_2)$$
and
$$(y_1, z_2) \sim (z_1, y_2)$$
implies
$$(x_1, z_2) \sim (z_1, x_2)$$

Figure 9.4. Graphic illustration of the Thomson condition.

consider the increments Δ_1 and Δ_2. Adding Δ_1 to (y_1, y_2) produces a value increment equal to that produced by adding Δ_2 to it. Then, according to the Thomson condition, it does not matter where you add Δ_1 and Δ_2. They should always add equal increments in value. In particular, when Δ_1 is "added" to (y_1, x_2) and Δ_2 is "added" to (x_1, y_2), they should both "add" the same value. And since the starting points were indifferent, so should be the ending point. The Thomson condition therefore simply says that it does not matter where in the outcome space a value increment is added; it should always add the same amount of value.

Two more technical assumptions are required for the full conjoint measurement representation. These are very similar in spirit to the solvability assumption and the Archimedean assumption of difference measurement and fulfill the same purpose here: to avoid situations in which indifference equations cannot be solved (solvability) and to avoid infinitely desirable or infinitely undesirable points in **X** (Archimedean). We state these axioms here without much formal justification but briefly indicate why they are required.

C3: *(Unrestricted) solvability.* For all $i = 1, 2, \ldots, n$, a_j, $b_j \in X_j$, $x_i \in X_i$ there exists a y_i such that

$$(a_1, a_2, \ldots, x_i, \ldots, a_n) \sim (b_1, b_2, \ldots, y_i, \ldots, b_n). \qquad (9.40)$$

This condition guarantees that all standard sequences can be "solved for," in other words, that we don't run out of values in one of the attributes against which to "lay off" value increments or decrements in the others. Though probably unrealistic in practice, this assumption can be formulated as *restricted solvability* to include only subsets of each attribute, thereby avoiding "holes" in the attribute space.

The Archimedean assumption ensures that a standard sequence will not "run against" a point of infinite value or negative value in **X**. We state it here only verbally:

C4: *Archimedean.* Every strictly bounded standard sequence in each attribute is finite. In other words, a standard sequence progresses over any given point on an attribute, *or* it is finite. Obviously, if a given point is either infinitely desirable or undesirable, the standard sequence can be both infinite and never reach that point.

Given C1 through C4 we can prove the *additive conjoint measurement theorem.* If $\langle \mathbf{X}, \succsim \rangle$ satisfies C1 through C4, then there exists a real-valued function $f: \mathbf{X} \to R$ such that

$$\mathbf{x} \succsim \mathbf{y} \quad \text{if and only if} \quad f(\mathbf{x}) \geq f(\mathbf{y}), \qquad (9.41)$$

where

$$f(\mathbf{x}) = \sum_{i=1}^{n} f_i(x_i).$$

Multiattribute utility measurement[1]

We use the following somewhat simplified notation. A gamble with multiattribute outcomes is represented by a matrix $\tilde{\mathbf{x}}$,

[1] This section relies heavily on von Winterfeldt and Fischer (1975).

$$
\begin{array}{c}
\begin{array}{ccccc}
E_1 & E_2 & \dots & E_j & \dots & E_m
\end{array} \\
\begin{array}{c}
X_1 \\
X_2 \\
\vdots \\
X_i \\
\vdots \\
X_n
\end{array}
\left[
\begin{array}{ccccccc}
x_{11} & x_{12} & \dots & x_{1j} & \dots & x_{1m} \\
x_{21} & x_{22} & \dots & x_{2j} & \dots & x_{2m} \\
\vdots & \vdots & & \vdots & & \vdots \\
x_{i1} & x_{i2} & \dots & x_{ij} & \dots & x_{im} \\
\vdots & \vdots & & \vdots & & \vdots \\
x_{n1} & x_{n2} & \dots & x_{nj} & \dots & x_{nm}
\end{array}
\right]
\end{array}
$$

where the X_i's are the attributes, the E_j's are the events, and the x_{ij} is the consequence in attribute i to be received when event j occurs. The column vector $\mathbf{x}_j$ is the multiattribute outcome to be received in the event E_j, and the row vector $\mathbf{x}_i$ is the ith single-attribute gamble. We will make the idealized assumption that all options in $\mathbf{X}$ can be expressed as such matrices. This idealization greatly simplifies the presentation of the formal assumptions. The most basic assumption is, of course, that the decision maker's preferences over gambles in $\mathbf{X}$ can be modeled by a von Neumann and Morgenstern utility function. In other words, applying axioms U1-U6 to the multiattribute outcomes will provide the required representation:

$$\tilde{\mathbf{x}} \gtrsim \tilde{\mathbf{y}}$$

if and only if

$$SEU(\tilde{\mathbf{x}}) = \sum_{j=1}^{m} p(E_j)u(\mathbf{x}_j) = \sum_{j=1}^{m} p(E_j)u(\mathbf{y}_j) = SEU(\tilde{\mathbf{y}}). \quad (9.42)$$

The additive expected utility independence (AEUI) assumption in its strongest form requires that two gambles with equal marginal probability distributions be indifferent. A somewhat weaker version can be formulated as follows. Assume that all E_j's are equally likely, and construct any arbitrary option $\tilde{\mathbf{x}}$ with elements x_{ij}. Then the AEUI assumption would require that all options $\tilde{\mathbf{x}}'$ that are generated simply by permuting x_{ij}'s within attributes are indifferent to $\tilde{\mathbf{x}}$.

U7: *Additive expected utility independence.* Consider the following options $\tilde{\mathbf{x}}$ and $\tilde{\mathbf{x}}'$:

$$
\begin{array}{ccc}
\tilde{\mathbf{x}} & & \tilde{\mathbf{x}}' \\
\begin{array}{ccccc} E_1 E_2 & \dots & E_j & \dots & E_m \end{array} & & \begin{array}{ccccc} E_1 E_2 & \dots & E_j & \dots & E_m \end{array}
\end{array}
$$

$$
\begin{array}{c}
X_1 \\
\vdots \\
X_i \\
\vdots \\
X_n
\end{array}
\left[
\begin{array}{cccccc}
x_{11} x_{12} & \dots & x_{ij} & \dots & x_{1m} \\
\vdots \; \vdots & & \vdots & & \vdots \\
x_{i1} x_{i2} & \dots & x_{ij} & \dots & x_{nm} \\
\vdots \; \vdots & & \vdots & & \vdots \\
x_{n1} x_{n2} & \dots & x_{nj} & \dots & x_{nm}
\end{array}
\right]
\;\sim\;
\left[
\begin{array}{cccccc}
x'_{11} x'_{12} & \dots & x'_{1j} & \dots & x'_{1m} \\
\vdots \; \vdots & & \vdots & & \vdots \\
x'_{i1} x'_{i2} & \dots & x'_{ij} & \dots & x'_{im} \\
\vdots \; \vdots & & \vdots & & \vdots \\
x'_{n1} x'_{n2} & \dots & x'_{nj} & \dots & x'_{nm}
\end{array}
\right]
\quad (9.43)
$$

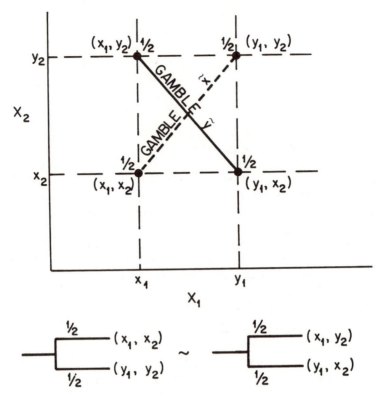

Figure 9.5. Graphic illustration of AEUI in a two-attribute example.

where all E_j's are equally likely and $\tilde{x}'$ is generated by permuting elements x_{ij} within rows. It should be true that $\tilde{x} \sim \tilde{x}'$ for all such permutations.

Figure 9.5 depicts this assumption graphically for two dimensions and equally likely events E_i, where $P(E_1) = P(E_2) = 1/2$. The necessity of AEUI can best be shown in this example. Consider the first gamble $\tilde{x}$, which can be expressed in SEU form as

$$
\begin{aligned}
SEU(\tilde{x}) &= \tfrac{1}{2}[k_1 u_1(x_1) + k_2 u_2(x_2)] + \tfrac{1}{2}[k_1 u_1(y_1) + k_2 u_2(y_2)] \\
&= \tfrac{1}{2}[k_1 u_1(x_1) + k_2 u_2(y_2)] + \tfrac{1}{2}[k_1 u_1(y_1) + k_2 u_2(x_2)] \\
&= SEU(\tilde{y}).
\end{aligned}
\tag{9.44}
$$

The multiplicative expected utility model requires the somewhat weaker assumption that preferences among options that have different uncertain consequences in some attributes are independent of common and certain attribute levels in the other attributes.

U7': *Multiplicative expected utility independence.* For all $i, j, x_{ij}, y_{ij}, a_i, b_i,$

$$
\begin{array}{c}
E_1 \ldots E_j \ldots E_n \\[4pt]
\begin{array}{c}
X_1 \\ X_2 \\ \vdots \\ X_i \\ \vdots \\ X_n
\end{array}
\left[
\begin{array}{cccc}
x_{11} & \ldots & x_{1j} & \ldots & x_{1n} \\
x_{21} & \ldots & x_{2j} & \ldots & x_{2n} \\
\vdots & & \vdots & & \vdots \\
a_i & \ldots & a_i & \ldots & a_i \\
\vdots & & \vdots & & \vdots \\
x_{n1} & \ldots & x_{nj} & \ldots & x_{nm}
\end{array}
\right]
\end{array}
\succsim
\begin{array}{c}
E_1 \ldots E_j \ldots E_m \\[4pt]
\left[
\begin{array}{cccc}
y_{11} & \ldots & y_{1j} & \ldots & y_{1n} \\
y_{21} & \ldots & y_{2j} & \ldots & y_{2n} \\
\vdots & & \vdots & & \vdots \\
a_i & \ldots & a_i & \ldots & a_i \\
\vdots & & \vdots & & \vdots \\
y_{n1} & \ldots & y_{nj} & \ldots & y_{nm}
\end{array}
\right]
\end{array}
\leftarrow \text{constant}
$$

if and only if   (9.45)

$$
\begin{array}{c}
\begin{array}{c}
X_1 \\ X_2 \\ \vdots \\ X_i \\ \vdots \\ X_n
\end{array}
\left[
\begin{array}{cccc}
x_{11} & \ldots & x_{1j} & \ldots & x_{1n} \\
x_{21} & \ldots & x_{2j} & \ldots & x_{2n} \\
\vdots & & \vdots & & \vdots \\
b_i & \ldots & b_i & \ldots & b_i \\
\vdots & & \vdots & & \vdots \\
x_{n1} & \ldots & x_{nj} & \ldots & x_{nm}
\end{array}
\right]
\end{array}
\succsim
\left[
\begin{array}{cccc}
y_{11} & \ldots & y_{1j} & \ldots & y_{1n} \\
y_{21} & \ldots & y_{2j} & \ldots & y_{2n} \\
\vdots & & \vdots & & \vdots \\
b_i & \ldots & b_i & \ldots & b_i \\
\vdots & & \vdots & & \vdots \\
y_{n1} & \ldots & y_{nj} & \ldots & y_{nm}.
\end{array}
\right]
\leftarrow \text{constant}
$$

Since outcomes in the ith attribute remain constant across events, we dropped the j index. Notice that the conditioning here is on a *single* attribute i only, in which the alternatives have the same attribute value. However, in formulation 9.45 we can include more than one conditioning attribute simply by fixing other attribute values and applying the axiom U7'. Since multiplicative expected utility independence requires conditioning that can be demonstrated in its general form only for more than two attributes, we do not provide a graphic representation. The reader is referred to Keeney and Raiffa (1976).

In the multilinear case, only one attribute is uncertain; the others are fixed, and multilinear expected utility independence requires that preferences over lotteries in *one* attribute be independent of common and certain values in other attributes. This is expressed formally in the following axiom:

U7'': *Multilinear expected utility independence.* For all $i, j, x_{ij}, y_{ij}, a_k, b_k,$

$$
\begin{array}{c}
E_1 \ldots E_j \ldots E_n \\[4pt]
\begin{array}{c}
X_1 \\ \vdots \\ X_i \\ \vdots \\ X_n
\end{array}
\left[
\begin{array}{cccc}
a_1 & \ldots & a_1 & \ldots & a_1 \\
\vdots & & \vdots & & \vdots \\
x_{i1} & \ldots & x_{ij} & \ldots & x_{1n} \\
\vdots & & \vdots & & \vdots \\
a_n & \ldots & a_n & \ldots & a_n
\end{array}
\right]
\end{array}
\succsim
\begin{array}{c}
E_1 \ldots E_j \ldots E_m \\[4pt]
\left[
\begin{array}{cccc}
a_1 & \ldots & a_1 & \ldots & a_1 \\
\vdots & & \vdots & & \vdots \\
y_{i1} & \ldots & y_{ij} & \ldots & y_{in} \\
\vdots & & \vdots & & \vdots \\
a_n & \ldots & a_n & \ldots & a_n
\end{array}
\right]
\end{array}
\leftarrow \text{variable}
$$

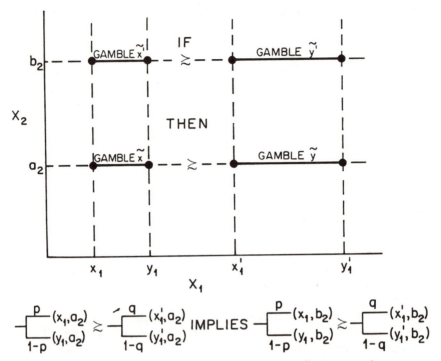

Figure 9.6. Graphic illustration of MEUI in a two-attribute example.

$$\text{if and only if} \tag{9.46}$$

$$
\begin{array}{c}
X_1 \\ \vdots \\ X_i \\ \vdots \\ X_n
\end{array}
\begin{bmatrix}
b_1 & \cdots & b_1 & \cdots & b_1 \\
\vdots & & \vdots & & \vdots \\
x_{i1} & \cdots & x_{ij} & \cdots & x_{in} \\
\vdots & & \vdots & & \vdots \\
b_n & \cdots & b_n & \cdots & b_n
\end{bmatrix}
\gtrsim
\begin{bmatrix}
b_1 & \cdots & b_1 & \cdots & b_1 \\
\vdots & & \vdots & & \vdots \\
y_{i1} & \cdots & y_{ij} & \cdots & y_{in} \\
\vdots & & \vdots & & \vdots \\
b_n & \cdots & b_n & \cdots & b_n
\end{bmatrix}
\leftarrow \text{variable}
$$

A graphic representation of multilinear utility independence is provided in Figure 9.6 for two dimensions and two outcome gambles. One interpretation of multilinear utility independence is, or course, that indifferences between lotteries in a single attribute should not change when other attribute levels are changed, and, in particular, certainty equivalents should remain constant.

Formal relationships between models and axioms

Examining the "primitives" of the three theories, we note that conjoint measurement theory is the simplest in terms of the set over which relations are defined and in terms of the relation. The difference system $\langle X \times X, \gtrsim \rangle$ and

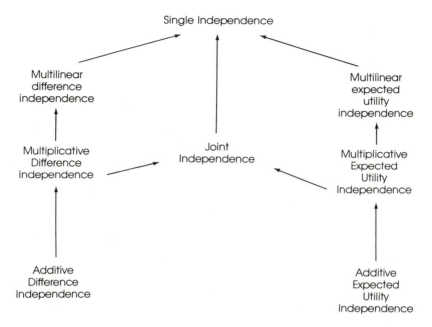

Figure 9.7. Relation among independence assumptions.

the conjoint measurement system $\langle X, \gtrsim \rangle$ can be related by defining

$$X \times a = X' \quad \text{and} \quad (x, a) \overset{\circ}{\gtrsim} (y, a) \quad \text{if} \quad x \gtrsim y. \tag{9.47}$$

And by restricting one's attention to degenerate gambles only, an SEU system can be reduced to a conjoint system. (No such match can be created between a difference system, on one hand, and an SEU system, on the other.)

Figure 9.7 shows some relationships between the models and assumptions, which we state without proof (for more details, see Dyer and Sarin, 1979; Keeney and Raiffa, 1976; von Winterfeldt, 1975). One relationship requires a comment, however. The multiplicative *and* the additive difference models imply that there exists an additive conjoint measurement representation. How can that be true?

In conjoint measurement theory, two representations f and f' are equivalent if they both preserve the order of preferences over X and can be additively decomposed into f_i's. Therefore, a positive multiplicative model of the form

$$f(\mathbf{x}) = \prod_{i=1}^{n} f_i(x_i), \qquad f_i > 0 \tag{9.48}$$

can be transformed into an additive conjoint measurement model by taking logarithms:

$$f'(\mathbf{x}) = \ln f(x) = \sum_{i=1}^{n} f'_i(x_i). \tag{9.49}$$

Therefore, a multiplicative difference model (which by definition of multiplicative difference independence is positive) can be transformed into a conjoint model by a logarithmic transformation. Note, however, that by that transformation the value functions that preserved strength of preferences are destroyed. Since strength of preferences has no meaning in conjoint measurement anyway, that destruction is admissible in a conjoint representation.

The relation between u and v has been explored by a number of authors.[2] It is relatively trivial to establish that u and v are related by a strictly increasing transformation $u = h(v)$, since both are order-preserving functions (see, e.g., Keeney and Raiffa, 1976; Krantz et al., 1971; Raiffa, 1969). But neither SEU theory nor difference measurement provides by itself a rationale for any specific closed-form relations between u and v. In principle, the shape and aggregation form of u and v can be quite different. For example, v may be additive, while u may be multiplicative or not decomposable at all. All v_i's may be linear in attribute scales, while all u_i's could be nonlinear, and vice versa.

Establishing closed-form functional relations is possible, however, when special decomposition forms are assumed. Scattered throughout the measurement-theoretic literature are results that relate utility functions and (conjoint or difference) value functions by some specific class of transformations – for example, exponential or logarithmic (see Bell, 1982; Dyer and Sarin, 1979; Keeney and Raiffa, 1976; Krantz et al., 1971; Pollak, 1967; Sarin, 1982; von Winterfeldt, 1979). A common way to relate u and v is to apply the uniqueness theorems of their respective measurement-theoretic representations. For example, an additive order-preserving function v on X is unique up to a positive linear transformation. Consequently, any other additive order-preserving function v' on X must be related to v by

$$v' = av + b, \quad a > 0. \tag{9.50}$$

In particular, if both u and v are additive and order preserving, then there exist constants $a > 0$, b such that

$$u = av + b. \tag{9.51}$$

Dyer and Sarin (1979) used the uniqueness property to derive closed-form functional relations between u and v for the cases where u or v is addi-

---

[2] The following section relies on von Winterfeldt, Barron, and Fischer (1980).

Table 9.1. *Functional relation between u and v*

	v is	
u is	Additive	Multiplicative
Additive	$u = v$	$u = \dfrac{\ln(1 + wv)}{\ln(1 + w)}$
Multiplicative	$1 + ku = (1 + k)^v$	$1 + ku = (1 + wv)^{\ln(1+k)/\ln(1+w)}$

Source: Barron, von Winterfeldt, & Fischer (1984).

tive or multiplicative. Keeney and Raiffa (1976, pp. 330–2) showed that an additive value function in combination with a multiplicative utility function implies that the utility function is constantly risk averse or risk prone in value. Therefore, value and utility functions must be related by a linear, logarithmic, or exponential transformation if both are either additive or multiplicative. Barron, von Winterfeldt, and Fischer (1984; see also von Winterfeldt, Barron, and Fischer, 1980) used a very simple proof method in which the fundamental equation

$$F(u_1, u_2, \ldots, u_n) = h[G(v_1, v_2, \ldots, v_n)] \qquad (9.52)$$

is reduced to a fundamental Cauchy-type equation. The results of that exercise are shown in Table 9.1.

9.4. Qualitative model tests and consistency checks

In this section we translate the formally stated assumptions into tools for selecting possible models. In addition to providing some ideas about how the practicing analyst can test the axioms, we describe consistency checks that can be performed during the assessment to amplify possible errors in modeling. Obviously, the model assumptions are very strong and will almost certainly fail in practical tests – partly because of systematic and intended violations and partly because of unsystematic error. The reason for using axiomatic model tests is not, therefore, to find a correct model. Rather they are meant to rule out obviously unsatisfactory models that the decision maker violates systematically and intentionally. In addition the tests and consistency checks are meant to sharpen the analyst's eye for places where things can go wrong with a model so that he or she can avoid pitfalls.

Riskless or risky models?

We argued earlier that the distinction between riskless and risky models is blurred, in theory and in practice. We consider practical issues related to

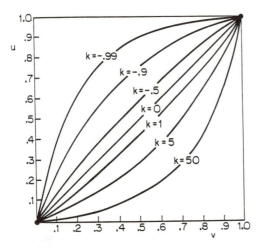

Figure 9.8. Theoretic relation between utility and value for various values of k, assuming an additive value function and a multiplicative utility function. (*Source:* von Winterfeldt, Barron, & Fischer, 1980.)

that distinction in a later section. In the following we examine its conceptual and theoretical foundations and the implications for multiattribute analysis, particularly for elicitation methods.

The first bridge between risky utility and riskless value models is provided by the functional equations in Table 9.1. Figure 9.8 shows the functional relation for two of the cells, where v is additive and u is either additive or multiplicative. We argue later that these two cells are by far the most plausible based on practical and empirical evidence.

Figure 9.8 has some remarkable features. For a wide range of k values the relation between u and v is virtually linear (i.e., for $-.5 < k < 5$). If, therefore, the multiplicative u/additive v case is valid, there are good reasons to assume that the two functions will not differ to any practical extent in many situations. One interpretation of Figure 9.8 is that the decision maker is exhibiting risk aversion in value (if $k < 0$) or risk proneness in value (if $k > 0$). In other words, he or she acts as if looking at lotteries with value indices as outcomes and then taking risk attitude into account. The parameter k therefore expresses the degree to which such risk aversion or proneness changes utility from value. Of course, that interpretation is valid only if v is actually additive.

Does it make sense to be additive in v and nonadditive in u? In other words, is this rational behavior that a decision maker might want to follow? In principle, the answer is: why not? However, this type of risk attitude superimposed in value can lead to behavioral peculiarities that a rational decison maker might want to avoid – and that a decision analyst might want to discourage by proper structuring of the decision problem.

Consider the "richest" measurement structure that combines difference and SEU measurement by defining a strength-of-preference relation over lotteries. In other words, its primitive would be $\langle \tilde{X} \times \tilde{X}, \overset{\circ}{\succsim} \rangle$. We can deduce SEU from this structure by defining the substructure $\langle \tilde{X} \times a, \succsim \rangle$ where $\tilde{x} \succsim \tilde{y}$, if $(\tilde{x}, a) \overset{\circ}{\succsim} (\tilde{y}, a)$. We can deduce difference measurement by defining the substructure of degenerate gambles, $\langle X \times X, \overset{\circ}{\succsim} \rangle$.

There is nothing wrong with such a structure. In fact, we argued earlier that most "outcomes" are indeed only gambles, and one might conclude that a "riskless" difference structure is nothing but such a complex difference structure over gambles. But the consequences are quite strong: if strengths of preferences between gambles are independent of events in which they have identical outcomes, then $u = v$. This assumption is a strong version of the sure-thing principle (see Section 9.2) and was first suggested by Sarin (1982). The equality $u = v$ simply follows from the fact that v has an additive decomposition over events, if this version of the sure-thing principle holds.

We therefore have two lines of argument which indicate that riskless and risky modeling might not differ after all. The first relies on the assumption that we can usually construct an additive v and an additive or multiplicative u in a multiattribute evaluation problem. We are rather certain of this assumption and have yet to see an example in which we could not perform the appropriate restructuring of attributes to achieve just that. This argument allows $u \neq v$ only if the decision maker is constantly risk averse or prone in value. The strengthened sure-thing principle disallows even that.

Our conclusion, if we accept that $u = v$, is that *other criteria* for selecting a risky versus a riskless approach to elicitation should be used. For example, one might ask whether the decision maker is familiar with lottery-type questions or comfortable with strength-of-preference judgments. Or one might ask if he or she can learn something by looking at lotteries, preferences, or differences.

Tests for difference measurement

The axioms in Section 9.3 include independence assumptions, which are the cornerstones of any multiattribute modeling. In this subsection we discuss implications of these axioms and try to lay out some rules for using them in practice. In general, these independence assumptions state which variations of the alternatives leave preference or difference judgments unaffected. An extremely weak independence assumption is, for example, *independence of irrelevant alternatives,* which is implicit in all multiattribute utility models. In short, independence of irrelevant alternatives requires that the addition (or deletion) of alternatives to a given set does not change the preference or difference judgment about the alternatives in the original set. For example, a car buyer's preference for a Mercedes over a Porsche should not change after some friend suggests a Maserati as a third alternative.

It is important to stress that the independence assumptions discussed above refer to judgments and preferences, not to physical relations between variables in the market or decision environment. Therefore, we sometimes call these assumptions by the generic term *judgmental independence assumptions.* In contrast, *environmental independence assumptions* are stated in terms of probabilistic dependencies or independencies of variables. To illustrate the difference, consider two attributes of a car: cost and quality. Judgments about quality are probably independent of the costs. For example, relative preferences for riding comfort and acceleration might be the same for an expensive and an inexpensive car. The quality attribute would therefore be judgmentally independent of the cost attribute. However, cost and quality are environmentally correlated because cars of higher quality cost more.

The reverse case of judgmental dependence and environmental independence can be illustrated by the attributes distance from the office and transportation facilities in an apartment evaluation problem. Aside from the vagaries of a special market, distance and transportation facilities should be uncorrelated. Therefore, these attributes will most likely be environmentally independent. However, they certainly will be judgmentally dependent. For example, when the distance from the office is large, transportation facilities will matter more (the weight should increase) than they do when the distance is small.

In value modeling we are concerned mainly with judgmental independence, and in most of this section we describe checks for such dependencies. Judgmental independence is important because it allows the construction of simple models. Judgmental dependencies can cause several things to go wrong: first, the decision maker may find it impossible to think of one attribute at a time, because the judgments obviously depend on other attributes; second, the model may not make sense (i.e., it may have little face validity because of the dependencies); and third, the model may make grossly incorrect value assignments. The first area in which to avoid such judgmental dependencies is the structuring of the attributes. In general, if the decision maker is uncomfortable answering questions about a single attribute without thinking about other attributes, the attribute in question or the whole set should be reformulated. *Thought experiments* can help the analyst uncover such dependencies.

Two common examples of dependencies are as follows. Judgments about the performance of a product tend to depend on its reliability (who cares about performance when the product doesn't work?) and judgments about the length of an activity depend on the pleasure received from that activity (longer is better if it's fun; shorter is better if it's painful), and so on.

If thought experiments do not uncover any gross dependencies, the analyst can perform some simple *independence tests*. Additive difference independence, multiplicative difference independence, multilinear difference independence, and single and joint preference independence can all be tested systematically. Practically, the analyst will pick some potentially dependent attributes and swing the constant values in the tests through their range to detect possible effects. To test additive difference independence, for example, the analyst first finds the worst and the best levels in each attribute, say x_{i*} and x_i^*, and then checks systematically, for each i, whether the judged value difference between the extremes in that attribute remains the same when the other attributes are swung from their worst to their best level. Formally, this test is a check for each attribute i if

$$[(x_i^*, \bar{\mathbf{x}}_{i*}); (x_{i*}, \bar{\mathbf{x}}_{i*})] \succsim [x_i^*, \bar{\mathbf{x}}_i^*); (x_{i*}, \bar{\mathbf{x}}_i^*)], \qquad (9.53)$$

where $\bar{\mathbf{x}}_{i*}$ and $\bar{\mathbf{x}}_i^*$ are the vectors of worst or best attribute levels in the other $n - 1$ attributes.

Similarly, the analyst can test multiplicative and multilinear difference independence. First, an indifference is constructed between two pairs of objects that vary in only one attribute while the other attributes are held at their worst level. Then the other attributes are swung to their best level, and the indifference is rechecked. Formally, this test is a check for attribute i if the following holds:

$$[(x_i, \bar{\mathbf{x}}_{i*}); (y_i, \bar{\mathbf{x}}_{i*})] \succsim [(x_i', \bar{\mathbf{x}}_{i*}); (y_i', \bar{\mathbf{x}}_{i*})]$$

and

$$[(x_i, \bar{\mathbf{x}}_i^*); (y_i, \bar{\mathbf{x}}_i^*)] \succsim [(x_i', \bar{\mathbf{x}}_i^*); (y_i', \bar{\mathbf{x}}_i^*)]. \qquad (9.54)$$

As a final qualitative check, the analyst can test independencies in the actual *construction of the value functions*. First, he or she can ascertain whether the shape of single-attribute value functions changes at different levels of other attributes and, next, whether weights change as a result of changing attribute values. If neither weights nor single-attribute value functions change, the additive model is valid. If only weights change but the single-attribute value functions remain constant, a multiplicative model or a multilinear model may be applicable. The analyst can perform another constructive check of the additive model by determining whether the single-attribute weights w_i add to 1. If they do not, the additive model may have to be rejected and replaced by a multilinear or multiplicative one.

Subadditivity ($\Sigma w_i < 1$) and superadditivity ($\Sigma w_i > 1$) of the scaling factors w_i have some interesting qualitative analogues, which in economic theory are related to the complementarity and substitutability of goods. If the weights w_i systematically add to less than 1, then $w < 0$, and consequently, some interactive terms "subtract" from the overall value of an option. This is the economic equivalent of substitution. In contrast, when $w > 0$, the multiplicative terms "add" to the additive terms and to the overall value of the options. A qualitative check of the sign w would therefore determine the nature of the interaction between two or more dimensions.

An interesting example of complementarity is the case in which the two attributes are incomes of two people. When two married people are looking for jobs, they may want to avoid a situation in which one person earns very much, the other very little. Therefore, given identical sums, they may attach a premium to similar amounts, suggesting a multiplicative model of the form

$$v(x_1, x_2) = w_1 v_1(x_1) + w_1 v_2(x_2) + w w_1 w_2 v_1(x_1) v_2(x_2), \tag{9.55}$$

where x_1 and x_2 are the respective incomes and $w > 0$. The case of equality reduces this further to

$$v(x_1, x_2) = v(x_1) + v(x_2) + w v(x_1) v(x_2). \tag{9.56}$$

Such interactions often occur because the analyst has left out an attribute. In this case the attribute "equivalence of incomes" was left out. There are many instances in which a careful examination of the source of an interaction leads to the addition of an appropriate attribute that captures the interaction and thus reestablishes the simple additive model (see also Keeney, 1981).

Test for utility measurement

As in the test of riskless independence assumptions, the analyst has several options: thought experiments, direct independence tests, and consistency checks. A first test of additivity is a thought experiment to check whether the decision maker can *think* independently about lotteries in single attributes. Can he or she assess certainty equivalents over gambles in one attribute without thinking about uncertainties in other attributes?

A second check of the additivity assumption can usually be made by the examination of some very simple two-attribute forms of additive expected utility independence, as demonstrated in Section 9.2. The analyst should select extreme points on each attributes (i.e., x_{i*}, x_i^*, x_{j*}, x_j^*) and construct the following even-chance gambles:

	$\tilde{a}$		$\tilde{b}$	
	Heads	Tails	Heads	Tails
X_i	x_i^*	x_{i*}	x_i^*	x_{i*}
X_j	x_j^*	x_{j*}	x_{j*}	x_j^*

Additive independence would, of course, require the decision maker to be indifferent. Often the decision maker will point out that he or she prefers the right-hand side, because it has "more balanced" outcomes. At this point the analysts should carefully interrogate the decision maker about the reasons for such a preference and point out why one might be indifferent: because, attribute by attribute, the gambles are indistinguishable. Furthermore, the analyst may wish to vary the entries in the gambles to examine whether the strength of preference for either side changes in accordance with the predictions of the "balance" hypothesis. An experiment by von Winterfeldt (1980a) found that the preference for the less extreme gamble increases with the difference in the value of the extreme outcomes. Because this preference is similar to the usual (single-attribute) risk aversion, von Winterfeldt called it *multiattribute risk aversion*.

Determining the reasons for possible multiattribute risk aversion is important. For example, the reasons for the decision maker's preference for the more balanced gamble may be essentially the same as those for the decision maker's single-attribute risk aversion. Assume that two attributes in the above gamble are two outcomes of an investment: immediate cash return and amount of equity built up in a year. Assume further that there are no direct means of transforming these two numbers into one, because the second amount is nonliquid. Two investments might look like this:

$$
\begin{array}{cc}
.5 \qquad .5 & \qquad .5 \qquad .5 \\
\begin{array}{l} \text{Cash} \\ \text{Equity} \end{array}
\begin{bmatrix} 10{,}000 & 0 \\ 50{,}000 & 0 \end{bmatrix}
&
\begin{bmatrix} 10{,}000 & 0 \\ 0 & 50{,}000 \end{bmatrix}
\end{array}
$$

Although equity and cash cannot be directly transformed, the decision maker might argue that a reasonable index of overall value (in the riskless sense) of a package of cash and equity would be a weighted sum of both, expressed as "net financial gain." The decision maker might also argue that his or her utility function over net financial gain is risk averse in the single-attribute sense discussed earlier. In that case, of course, the decision maker should prefer the right-hand gamble over the left-hand gamble. The reasons for multiattribute risk aversion are then exactly the same as those for single-attribute risk aversion. Note that, by multiattribute risk aversion, the decision maker violates the additive expected utility model even though he or she employs a riskless additive model.

Assume that a decision maker follows the additive difference model and that his or her strength-of-preference judgments among riskless outcomes X can be represented by an additive value function:

$$
v(\mathbf{x}) = \sum_{i=1}^{n} w_i v_i(x_i). \tag{9.57}
$$

Further assume that the decision maker wants to evaluate each outcome by first assessing its overall value v. One compares lotteries in essence by looking at "single-attribute" lotteries where v takes the place of the original multiattribute outcomes. This could lead to a von Neumann and Morgenstern utility function over "outcomes" v, which would be of the following form:

$$u(\mathbf{x}) = h \left\{ \sum_{i=1}^{n} w_i v_i(x_i) \right\}. \tag{9.58}$$

If h is nonlinear, the additive expected utility model will be violated. If h is concave, the decision maker will exhibit multiattribute risk aversion. If h is convex, the decision maker will exhibit multiattribute risk proneness, which in this case is nothing but single-attribute risk proneness over the attribute v. If the decision maker exhibits such nonlinearities, they should be further probed. We argued earlier that value v should in many instances be equal to utility u. The reasons for that argument should be made clear to the decision maker, and various consistency checks and tests should be made to determine whether a nonlinear utility–value relationship should be maintained.

It is, in principle, possible that the decision maker is risk neutral in all attributes, but multiattribute risk averse or prone. To illustrate that point, we present a multiplicative model for the above investment example. The investor might argue that more equity increases the value of the cash in hand. Assume that in all cash gambles and in all equity gambles the decision maker indicates risk neutrality. The multiplicative model could then have the following form:

$$u(c, e) = k_1 c + k_2 e + k k_1 k_2 c e, \tag{9.59}$$

where c and e represent certain amounts of cash equity, respectively. For $k > 0$, this model would still lead to multiattribute risk proneness; for $k < 0$, it would lead to multiattribute risk aversion. In this case we have created multiattribute risk proneness simply by arguing for *riskless* interaction phenomena that add surplus value for cash given equity. The term *multiattribute risk proneness* in such a case is actually misleading because the preference for the more balanced gamble has nothing at all to do with risk attitude.

In summary, there are at least two important instances of multiattribute risk attitude. The first occurs when the riskless preferences are actually additive, but the decision maker exhibits risk aversion or proneness in value. The second occurs when the decision maker sees positive or negative interactions between attributes in a riskless sense but is actually risk neutral in value. There may, of course, be other peculiar preferences in the riskless and risky sense that lead to multiattribute risk aversion, proneness, or neutrality. (For example, von Winterfeldt [1979] argued that it is in principle possible to follow a riskless multiplicative model with marginally decreasing single-attribute value functions, exhibit risk proneness in value, and thereby *not* show multiattribute risk attitude.) But the two cases discussed above seem to us the most typical.

If an analyst wants to maintain an additive SEU model in the face of strong multiattribute risk attitude, there are two options. If multiattribute risk attitude is due to single-attribute risk attitude over value, the option is to explore the rationality of that transform with the decision maker. This could involve, for example, testing the strength of the decision maker's risk aversion, exploring with the decision maker the usefulness of *not* being risk averse, and so on. If multiattribute risk aversion is due to riskless interaction phenomena like substitution or complementarity, the option is to use a multiplicative or multilinear riskless model or to restructure attributes to remove the interactions. We prefer the latter, because it simplifies modeling and assessment.

Finally, of course, the analyst always has the option of accepting multiattribute risk attitude, rejecting the additive model, and exploring the multiplicative model instead. In that case, a careful examination of the multiplicative expected utility independence assumptions should be made. We mentioned earlier that one critical way of checking these assumptions is to see whether certainty equivalents for gambles in subsets of attributes vary as a function of a bonus or penalty in other attributes. If thought experiments indicate that this may be the case, some simple independence tests should be carried out.

These independence tests should be designed to encourage violations. One way to do this is to consider an extreme lottery in one attribute and assess a certainty equivalent. For example, the decision maker is asked to set x_1 such that

$$\begin{array}{ccc} \text{Sure} & \text{Heads} & \text{Tails} \\ x_1 & \sim & [x_1^* & x_{1*}] \end{array}$$

The decision maker is specifically asked *not* to think about other attributes when making this assessment. Next, the analyst "adds" a bonus or a penalty in another attribute to the above gamble and sure thing:

$$\begin{array}{cccc} & \text{Sure} & \text{Heads} & \text{Tails} \\ X_1 & x_1 & \begin{bmatrix} x_{1*} & x_1^* \\ x_{2*} & x_{2*} \end{bmatrix} \\ X_2 & x_{2*} & \sim & \end{array}$$

and

$$\begin{array}{cccc} & \text{Sure} & \text{Heads} & \text{Tails} \\ X_2 & x_1 & \begin{bmatrix} x_1^* & x_1^* \\ x_2^* & x_2^* \end{bmatrix} \\ X_2 & x_2^* & \sim & \end{array}$$

If the decision maker now shifts his or her certainty equivalent in a systematic and intentional manner, violations of the multiplicative and the multilinear model are indicated. Such violations should then be explored in consistency checks.

9.5. Implications for decision-analytic practice

Let us assume that you have just completed your structuring activity for a multiattribute evaluation problem. You have defined the options and generated the value-relevant attributes on which to evaluate the options; you think that the attributes are probably independent. You therefore decide to use a simple additive value function.

Having just read the previous theoretic exposition, you dutifully carry out various tests, such as additive difference independence (ADI), and, for good measure, you even test the transitivity of some simple strength-of-preference judgments. ADI fails, but you have an impression that it is a minor violation; additive expected utility independence (AEUI) is grossly violated, and the decision maker seems to insist on the preference for the more balanced lottery. Transitivity of strength of preferences, the fundamental assumption of difference measurement, fails, but you are not sure whether by random error or intention. You probably wish you had never tested the assumptions (or read this chapter for that matter). What should you do?

First, you should decide which violations are systematic, intended, and strong and which are unsystematic, unintended, and minor. Ignore the latter; the flat-maximum property is likely to protect you (see Chapter 11). Second, ask yourself and the decision maker why the remaining violations occur. Are they reasonable? Should they occur? Are the implications of these violations acceptable to the decision maker? For example, the fact that ADI is acceptable, but AEUI is not, means that the decision maker should be risk averse or risk prone in value. Is that desirable? Third, if peculiar violations occur, restructure the problem. For example, if additive, multiplicative, and multilinear difference independence fail, you are probably working with an inappropriate attribute set. If ADI is (approximately) valid but AEUI fails, you may have neglected to include a regret or quasi-ruin attribute. Fourth, if the violations persist, ignore them. Carry out the analysis with the additive model and add a sensitivity analysis with a multiplicative or multilinear model to see whether the violations make a difference. If they do, you may want to build more complex models.

10   Experiments on value and utility measurement

10.1. Introduction: experiments are relevant

In this chapter we attempt to bring the rather abstract ideas of utility measurement and utility or SEU maximization into contact with two sets of realities: those of introspection and those of experimentation.

We begin by examining the obvious experiential fact that we do not normally find utilities, numbers representing the subjective values of objects or situations, lying around in our heads waiting to be elicited. This requires linking utility measurement to the more general topic of psychophysical measurement, of which it is simply an instance.

We turn next to arguments, based partly on introspection and partly on experimental data, that values are labile, evanescent, inconsistent, and, by implication, either hard to measure or not worth measuring or both. In part our view is that this is indeed so and constitutes a problem for which decision analysts have only partial solutions. In part our view is that the experimental data by no means fully support these arguments.

Then we examine the experimental evidence for the validity of multiattribute utility elicitation procedures, which is generally encouraging.

Next we turn to broad questions about the SEU model, both descriptively and normatively interpreted. We present an alternative, developed on the basis of experiments about choices among hypothetical bets: prospect theory. We then offer introspections about our own behavior with respect to money, coming to conclusions that resemble rather closely some of the ideas of prospect theory. Using the ideas and vocabulary thus made available, we examine a smattering of experiments of the kind on which prospect theory is based. We also explore what the theory means for the practice of decision analysis.

10.2. Numbers in the head?

Lessons from psychophysics

The traditional discipline that involves the study of numbers in the head is psychophysics. We argued earlier that decision analysis resembles psychophysics. Unlike psychophysicists, however, many decision analysts believe that values and utilities are numbers in the head waiting to be elicited. Psychophysicists do not hold this belief because they know that irrelevant details about the stimulus, nature of the response mode, and context effects can all influence judgments. Poulton (1979) reviewed the psychophysical literature and summarized five stimulus and response mode biases that affect judged sensory magnitudes:

1   Centering bias
2   Stimulus and response equalizing bias
3   Contraction bias
4   Stimulus spacing bias
5   Log bias

The *centering bias,* closely related to Helson's (1964) adaptation-level theory, refers to the fact that the set of available responses is well spread out over the set of stimuli presented. If the set of stimuli changes, the respondent will only gradually change the definition of the responses. *Stimulus and response equalizing biases* are close relatives of the centering bias. Responses are well distributed over the available response scale, independent of or spuriously affected by the range of stimuli. The *contraction bias,* also called the regression effect, is simply that large stimuli are underjudged and small stimuli are overjudged. Responses are too close to the middle of the range. The *stimulus spacing bias* equalizes uneven differences among stimuli and maps them into equal response scale differences. Finally, the *logarithmic bias* refers to the fact that, at least for some subjective magnitudes, 1,000 is twice, not 10 times, as large as 100. The universality of Weber's law suggests that this is indeed true for many continua. Stevens (1951) suggested that something of the sort occurs for continua created by increasing the magnitude of a sensory experience but does not occur for changes in sensory experience (e.g., pitch of a pure tone) that are not experienced as magnitudes.

These biases, identified for simple sensory magnitudes by a psychophysicist, certainly seem to imply that numbers representing those magnitudes are not simply awaiting elicitation. But it is not Poulton's purpose to argue that reports of sensory magnitudes are useless. He wants us to pay careful attention to the nature of stimulus and response scales and the relation between them and to design explicitly and with awareness the procedures that specify anchors and end points. In short, Poulton considers useful psychophysical procedures to be the result of careful and knowledgeable design.

Decision analysts would certainly agree. However, they also face a non-psychophysical fact: a set of formal models specifies the relations among responses. This fact is both a blessing and a nuisance. It is helpful because it enables the decision analyst who is knowledgeable about those logical relations to exploit them in testing the subjective numbers the respondent has produced. This gives the decision analyst an advantage over sensory psychophysicists, who must design elicitation procedures as best they can and then abide by the results. It is a nuisance because it injects the process of interaction between analyst and client into the number elicitation task. This takes time and raises some intellectual and even ethical questions.

The position we take is that no one has (cardinal) numbers in his or her head waiting to be elicited. This is true of decision-analytic quantities and also of at least some other psychophysical quantities. Nevertheless, in both cases, very useful numbers can be elicited from respondents. Here are our very speculative guesses about numbers in the head:

1   With respect to any genuine subjective continuum, ordinal judgments reside in the head and can easily be elicited. This statement requires explication. First, it applies only to genuine subjective continua. Human beings are embarrassingly willing to do whatever task is asked of them. Stevens once persuaded respondents to judge the "orthosonority" of pure tones; the respondents did so, but the judgments did not behave in an orderly way. How can we recognize a genuine subjective continuum? Fortunately, a fairly straightforward answer suggests itself: if people can, in fact, make coherent and orderly judgments about a proposed subjective continuum, it is genuine. The circularity of this definition is more apparent than real; one can easily recognize intellectual difficulties in making judgments, both by watching the process and by looking at the products. Second, ordinal relations reside in the head. Cardinal ones are constructed out of them.

2   Ordinal judgments of differences on genuine subjective continua can also be constructed by a little introspection. This, we think, is the fundamental thought process by which ordinal intuitions are converted to cardinal magnitudes.

3   The task of eliciting a cardinal number, unaided by analytical intervention, consists of four steps. (a) Identify the subjective continuum to which the task refers. (b) Recover the ordinal information. (c) Perform whatever processing steps are required to convert it to a cardinal intuition. (d) Shoehorn it into the response mode that happens to be available, using your best understanding of what each response means.

We believe that most of the biases Poulton discussed occur at steps (c) and (d). Since response modes of virtually limitless diversity are easy to design, the task of designing one that creates a one-to-one correspondence between the output of step (c) and the output of step (d) is primarily an exercise in technical psychophysical skill.

The decision-analytic task adds a fifth step: with the aid of the decision analyst, fit the numbers elicited with previous ones. If the fit is good, go on to the next task. If the fit is not good, reexamine numbers (typically with the help of the analyst to consider which ones to reconsider) until the formal rules of logical coherence are satisfied. If this proves too difficult, go back to the original structure that generated the rules of logical coherence and revise it, and then start the judgmental process again, paying special attention to the ease with which the respondent thinks about continua on which judgments are required.

We ignore as too complex for careful examination here the strong psychological assumptions made above and turn instead to the equally strong statement made in the preceding paragraph about the role of the decision analyst.

Role of the analyst

The traditional view is that the function of the analyst is to help the client implement preferences. By now it should be clear that we believe no such thing. Our lack of belief is based primarily on experience. Too seldom do we encounter a client who knows the available options, much less has preferences among them. If the client knew both (and was of one mind), the only function an analyst could serve would be that of providing formal justification for a choice already made. We know of such instances, but they are rare.

In our discussion of structuring, we stated that most clients we encounter are scratching their heads, faced with a dilemma and wondering what to do. The first analytic task is to turn the dilemma into a decision problem by constructing options relevant to it. The values the client brings to the problem are often far better structured than the options initially are. Options often grow from values.

But options also shape values. You might not have regarded quality of the view from the living room window as a value relevant to a choice among houses, until you encountered one that sat high on a hill. We have had experiences in which options were given and values evolved, and ones in which values were given and options evolved, but the most common experience has been one of reciprocal growth of both at the same time.

The analyst plays a major role in this. Even the most diligent analyst cannot help but have values too. Most analysts try their best to avoid shaping their clients' values – to the point where clients may become irritated at analytic blandness and amorality – but of course we doubt that they fully succeed. Decision analysis is a clinical endeavor, and any clinician who denies the relevance of personal views to outcomes is kidding. At least in decision analysis we have a final defense: according to a strongly built in code, the client has the final word. If the client is dissatisfied, either the analysis will be revised or it won't be used. But the client who uses the analysis is not the same individual or group as the client who sought help. A great deal of learning, and therefore change, has taken place.

Fortunately, the most strongly held professional value for most analysts is coherence among beliefs, values, and actions. Much analytic effort is spent transmitting that value to clients and teaching them how it can and should be implemented. Although that is a strong value, it is typically neutral among action options. Most analysts have, and communicate to clients, much stronger biases about methods of thought than about goals that thought or action should serve. We can easily think of one or two instances in which analysts of our acquaintance were deceived about what values were crucial to a client. We can recall no instance in which we felt, on reading an analysis, that it reflected the analyst's substantive, as distinct from methodological, values.

Only a few experimental studies have explored the impact of the analyst, or of the analyst's arguments, on subjects, judgments, and preferences. John (1984) confronted subjects with obvious ordinal discrepancies between the results of a multiattribute model and their intuitive rankings of the options. He gave subjects six choices for resolving the discrepancy:

1   Reject the MAUT model as being too simplistic
2   Add objectives or attributes
3   Change the operationalization of some attributes
4   Change weights
5   Change single-attribute utilities
6   Change intuitive (holistic) rankings

All subjects expressed a desire to achieve consistency and rejected options 1 to 3. The most prevalent response was that of changing weights, followed by changing ratings and/or holistic judgments. Unfortunately, the number of subjects involved in this study was relatively small, and the demand situation of the experiment may have been different from the climate one usually encounters in decision analysis. However, it is worth noting that the subjects were uncomfortable with the inconsistencies, wanted to make changes, and chose, at least in some cases, to adjust their intuitive rankings as well as parameters of the MAUT model.

Several studies examined how people react when confronted with their own violations of the SEU axioms (MacCrimmon, 1968; MacCrimmon and Larsson, 1979; Moskowitz, 1974; Slovic and Tversky, 1974). Efforts to convince subjects to change their responses in order to bring them into agreement with the SEU axioms had only moderate success. From our point of view the crucial fact about these experiments is that subjects were not persuaded by the arguments for the SEU axioms. An interesting question, not addressed in these experiments, is: how do you make such arguments persuasive?

10.3. Consistency and reliability of value and utility judgments

Labile values?

Three articles by experimental psychologists question the assertion that value judgments are orderly and consistent. Fischhoff, Slovic, and Lichtenstein (1980, p. 118) argue that values are often labile:

The recurrent theme of this paper is that subtle aspects of how problems are posed, questions are phrased, and responses are elicited have substantial impact on judgments that supposedly express people's true values. Furthermore, such lability in expressed preferences is unavoidable; questions must be posed in some manner and that manner may have a large effect on the responses elicited.

Fischhoff et al. contend that values are labile most often when people do not know what they want. The authors argue that in such cases the experimenter (or analyst) can influence the respondent by controlling problem formulation, the respondent's confidence in his or her judgments, existing perspectives, and so on.

Fischhoff, Goitein, and Shapira (1982) pursue this line of argument a bit farther, stating that, with the types of value judgments usually required in social judgment tasks, test–retest reliability is often low (e.g., .5 to .6). However, they also argue that "people are most likely to have clear preferences regarding issues that are familiar, simple, and directly experienced" (p. 26). Of course, an analyst would want to establish exactly those conditions for any elicitation.

Fischer (1979) supports this statement by arguing that, when the consequences of decisions are novel or too complex, the decision maker may be confused and uncertain about his or her preferences. The result could be random error or systematic biases in value and utility assessment. Fischer suggests that this can often be an asset rather than a liability. He argues that, in cases of uncertain or labile judgments, the utility and value measurement process should be viewed as a constructive process rather than as an elicitation process; this means, among other things, that the analyst becomes an active partner in utility and value construction rather than a passive psychologist or clinician. We agree.

Perhaps we should express our interpretation of Fischer's point more bluntly. Preference is often taken to be a primitive of decision theory without attention to the nature of the objects or acts among which preferences are expressed. If that were the case, we would wonder why anyone would bother with a multiattribute utility – or any other form of decision-analytic decomposition. The crux of the matter is that order of preference, like any other order relationship, is intuitively available only for genuine subjective continua. Such tools as multiattribute utility exist exactly for contexts in which the objects among which preference must be constructed array themselves naturally, not on one such continuum, but on many, and some means of aggregating over these continua must be supplied and used by the decision maker in order to make a meaningful choice.

All three of the papers we have cited argue that values may be labile, but they cite few data from experiments explicitly designed to measure utilities or values in a decision-analytic situation. In fact, surprisingly little evidence about the (un)reliability of value and utility judgments exists. The few relevant data that we know of tell a slightly more optimistic story.

Gardiner (1974) asked expert subjects (mostly members of the Coastal Commission of Los Angeles) to rate the overall quality of 15 plans for coastline developments. Test–retest reliabilities in a 36-day interval fell between .40 and .97 with a mean of .75. Considering the complexity of the stimuli (eight attributes had to be considered simultaneously) and the time interval between ratings, these results are encouraging. In another experiment von Winterfeldt and Edwards (1973a) asked subjects to rate and rank-order the overall values of 20 apartments described on 14 attributes. Though initial reliabilities were low (mean .56), after some training reliabilities increased substantially (mean .89). In a related study von Winterfeldt (1980a) asked subjects to judge even-chance gambles for commodity bundles. Certainty equivalents and strength-of-preference judgments for pairs of gambles were assessed. These certainty equivalents had a median reliability of .79 (.84 for the strength-of-preference judgments).

Our conclusion is this. Yes, failures of reliability in utility and value judgments occur. They can be substantial but seldom cover more than 5 to 10% of the range of the scale. In many situations subjects are also surprisingly consistent, even if the number of attributes makes comparisons among options relatively complex. There is a slight tendency for reliability to decrease with the complexity of stimuli (see also Gardiner, 1974; Slovic and Lichtenstein, 1971).

Effects of stimuli and response modes

A key argument in the labile-value hypothesis is that variations in contexts, procedures, and perspectives lead to lability. Let us examine the experimental evidence by analyzing the convergent validity of different types of response modes. Perhaps the most striking result is Fischer's (1976). His subjects assigned values and utilities to jobs described on three attributes (types of job, location, salary). Subjects first rated values for 27 jobs, then assigned utilities for the same jobs using the variable probability method. Root mean square errors resulting from predicting u from v directly fall between .015 and .203 with a median of .06, which represents 6% of the total range of values and utilities. Figure 10.1 shows u–v plots for the two extreme subjects (6 and 9) as well as two plots for the two subjects with median differences between u and v.

In a related experiment, Fischer (1976) asked subjects to assess the quality of hypothetical compact cars that varied on either three or nine attributes. Subjects rated the cars by means of the variable probability method and assigned a dollar value to them. The product–moment correlations taken over the cars, within subjects, were extremely high between procedures; medians fell between .84 and .95. In the above-mentioned experiment by von Winterfeldt (1980a) strength-of-preference judgments for pairs of lotteries and differences between dollar amounts assigned to the alternatives correlated reasonably well (median .74), supporting the conclusion that the convergent validity was good.

An especially interesting question concerns the empirical relationship between value measurement and utility measurement. A series of theoretic investigations (Bell and Raiffa, 1979; Dyer and Sarin, 1979; von Winter-

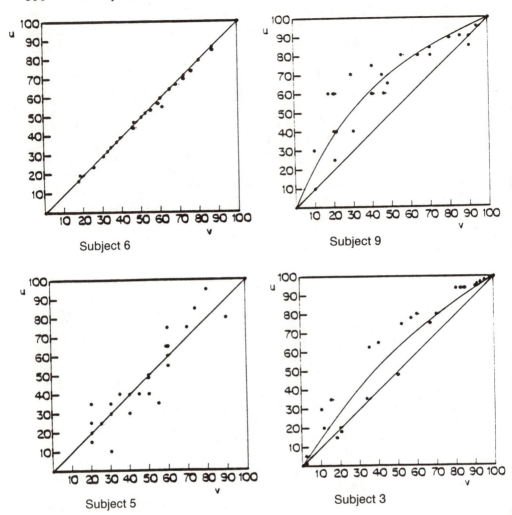

Figure 10.1. Relationship between elicited utilities *u* and values *v* for four subjects. Curves are exponential fits. (*Source:* von Winterfeldt, Barron, & Fischer, 1980.)

feldt, 1979) showed that utilities and values are, under most reasonable conditions, either linearly or exponentially related. In an experimental investigation, Barron, von Winterfeldt, and Fischer (1984) found that in most cases a linear relation between utility and value provided a good fit and that an exponential transformation, derived from theoretic considerations, improved very little on the linear relation. Especially considering the random error inherent in the data, such curvilinearities are negligible.

Slovic and Lichtenstein (1968) found that subjects' bidding responses to gambles were markedly different from their ratings of the attractiveness of the same gambles. The former response was related to the *amount* that could be lost or won, the latter to the probability of losing or winning. In two experiments Lichtenstein and Slovic (1971, 1973) demonstrated an even more striking response mode effect. They constructed gambles in which a subject could win either a medium amount of money with a high probability (A) or a large amount with a low probability (B). Both student subjects playing for small amounts and gamblers in a casino playing for high stakes showed a reversal of judgments: when asked to make a choice or rate the attractiveness of the two gambles, they tended to prefer A; when asked to place a bid, they bid higher amounts for B.

Slovic and Lichtenstein (1983) review several studies that replicated this response-mode-induced reversal in spite of efforts to provide explanations and incentives for subjects to be consistent (e.g., Grether and Plott, 1979; Pommerehne, Schneider, and Zweifel, 1982; Reilly, 1982). Slovic and Lichtenstein interpret these findings as reflecting different information-processing strategies induced by the different response modes. In choice questions and in ratings of the attractiveness of gambles, subjects seem to focus on probabilities; in bidding questions, subjects seem to focus on dollar amounts.

These response mode effects combine with several studies showing the influence of stimulus contexts and instructions on patterns of preference. Fryback, Goodman, and Edwards (1973) asked subjects to choose among equal EV gambles with often high stakes. (The experiment was carried out in a casino setting.) They observed patterns of choices at odds with most expectation models, since the desirability of a gamble depended not only on the characteristics of the gamble, but also on the context gambles (i.e., the list from which the gamble was chosen). In particular, subjects who first chose among relatively high variance gambles later preferred high-variance gambles embedded in lists of low-variance gambles and vice versa.

A peculiar instruction effect was found in Schoemaker's (1980) investigation of insurance-buying behavior. When a choice between a sure loss and a gamble with a zero outcome and a negative outcome was presented as an opportunity to buy insurance, subjects tended to be more risk averse than when the same options were presented as simply monetary gambles.

The message of these experiments on the effects of lability, stimulus, and response mode effects is mixed. Studies performed in applied settings with the usual decision-analytic elicitation procedures have shown a reasonable degree of consistency and only moderate response mode effects. However, numerous studies of response mode framing and reversal effects have shown them to be strong and stable in many contexts. One possible explanation of this discrepancy is the difference in the homogeneity of the stimuli and response modes used. Decision-analytic studies typically examined a broad spectrum of stimuli that covered a wide range of utilities or SEUs. In addition, the usual decision-analytic response modes are relatively similar to one another. Preference reversal experiments, in contrast, focused on specific stimuli (usually with similar or equal expected value) that would magnify the chances for reversals and inconsistencies. In addition, response modes were made to be rather dissimilar to one another.

Another explanation is the difference in the experimental design. Decision-analytic studies usually examine within-subject consistency across many stimuli, which offers a subject opportunities for both consistency and inconsistency. Preference reversal experiments more often study responses across many subjects for a few sensitive stimulus and response mode combinations.

Biases in gamble-based utility elicitation

Consider a bet in which you win an amount $W+$ with probability p or lose an amount $W-$ with probability $1 - p$. By changing S, a sure amount, the probability of winning p, the larger amount $W+$, or the smaller amount $W-$, the intent is to find values of S such that the respondent regards the utility of the sure thing as equal to the utility of the gamble. But how should that thought be operationalized? One possibility is to offer the bet for sale (see Goodman, Saltzman, Edwards, and Krantz, 1979), encouraging the respondent to bid as much as it seems to be worth. But this complicates the definition of the status quo. If the transaction takes place, the individual is poorer by S and richer by the bet. How to interpret the effect of paying S and receiving the bet on total fortune is far from obvious, though the assumption is that it leaves total utility unchanged.

An alternative is to give the gamble to the respondent and to consider S the minimum price for which the recipient would sell it. This simplifies the transaction, but if the bet has nonzero EV, then giving it to the respondent affects total fortune; it is an asset but of undetermined magnitude in utility. This procedure is regarded as intellectually preferable by most serious researchers on choices among bets, though it is often more difficult to execute in practice, especially if it implies giving the respondent a negative EV bet.

Utility elicitations typically solve such problems by leaving the actual set of transactions undefined and by never actually playing any bets or otherwise allowing money to change hands. The lack of realism of such procedures is obvious.

Hershey, Kunreuther, and Schoemaker (1982) discuss various biases in gamble-based utility elicitation. They note that one can establish the certainty equivalent of the bet by varying any of the four numbers entering into it; by far the most common procedures are those of varying S or varying p. They consider various procedural issues, such as the selection of $W+$ and $W-$. In particular, both could be gains, both could be losses, or one could be a gain and one a loss. Such procedural changes produce changes in behavior. These writers also note that the same lottery can be expressed in various ways, leading to nonequivalent behaviors (for numerous examples, see Tversky and Kahneman, 1981). They cite work reviewed by Fishburn and Kochenburger (1979) that seems to show that varying S produces risk aversion above the status quo and risk seeking below it, while varying p produces the opposite. They present experimental data of their own, collected from Wharton undergraduates by questionnaire methods, showing the same sorts of effects. However, they found risk seeking for low probabilities of large gains. Their conclusion, well justified by their data, is that the procedures they used should not be used to elicit utilities. We agree. However, we know of no decision analyst who would use such procedures. The kinds of phenomena this paper reports are exactly what a decision analyst would focus on to encourage respondent(s) to think more deeply about the meaning and implications of the responses.

Hershey and Schoemaker (1980) followed similar procedures and reported some closely related findings. They essentially looked for what might be called hysteresis effects. That is, suppose a utility is elicited by finding the certainty equivalent of a gamble. Then the amounts of money involved, including the certainty equivalent, can be used in a variable probability elicitation designed to reveal the same information. They found just such effects, but in a curious pattern that depends on whether the bets involve only gains or only losses, on whether, within the domain under study, the respondents could be classified as risk seeking or risk averse, and on the order in which the procedures were used.

From experience with gamble-based methods, we have a few notes to add. First, methods that vary probability, especially if they uniformly use a fixed upper and lower payoff, look very much like rating scale methods to respondents and seem to be understood as such. Methods that vary certainty equivalents assume the existence of an underlying continuous or densely spaced variable and are most commonly used with money as that variable. If, as is often done, the probabilities of a two-outcome bet are set at .5–.5, then these methods seem very much like direct rating methods for the gambles and indeed invite a procedure in which the EV of the gamble is first calculated and then the respondent adjusts the response. This is, of course, a procedure well designed to produce the anchoring and insufficient adjustment kind of judgmental phenomenon of which Tversky and Kahneman (1974) have written.

We tend to prefer non-gamble-based methods but like to check the results by asking for a few judgments about gambles. Numerical inconsistencies are highly valued by most decision analysts because they offer such fine occasions for harder thought.

10.4. Experimental validation of multiattribute utility structures

Validating MAUT: issues and approaches

In Chapter 8 we described a large number of MAUT models and techniques and their formal assumptions. In this section we summarize empirical research on the validity of these models, assumptions, and techniques.

The question of the validity of MAUT has given rise to a fairly large number of experimental studies comparing the results of different techniques of testing models and independence assumptions. The key problem in these validation studies is the difficulty of finding a validation criterion. Unlike probability studies, in which statistical data and models are the criteria, MAUT has few external criteria because all inputs and models of MAUT are inherently subjective. In the absence of objective criteria MAUT researchers have invented several second-best validation strategies: convergent validation, predictive validation, and axiomatic validation.

The first, and oldest, approach was to compare the model results with "holistic" judgments of the decision maker or experimental subject. For example, a MAUT model would be constructed for evaluating apartments described on several dimensions. One would then evaluate the options both by determining the model's utility and by asking the respondent to assign a utility directly to them. This procedure is a variation of *convergent validation procedures,* which are based on the assumption that different modes of measuring the same quantity (utility or value) should covary. Several authors have noted that convergent validation is a rather weak test and sometimes can even be misleading (e.g., Slovic, Fischhoff, and Lichtenstein, 1977). We have already commented on the fact that, especially with complex options, the respondent may not have a real preference. Since most respondents kindly do what they are told, when asked for a nonexistent or confused preference they are likely to invent simplifying strategies. In such cases, we would expect a low correlation between holistic judgment and MAUT model. However, we believe that, with relatively simple options, such studies have some value.

The second MAUT validation paradigm grew out of the recognition that value or utility is often simply shorthand for future pleasures or pains. In other words, value or utility indices should be predictive of future outcomes. This idea of *predictive* validity has been expressed by various authors (e.g., John, Edwards, and Collins, in press; Pearl, 1977; Schmitt, 1978). Examples of predictive value are the evaluation of applications for admission to graduate study, which should be predictive of future success in graduate school, and evaluation of bank credit applications, which should be predictive of default probability of the applicant. On a larger scale, the evaluation of a site for industrial facilities should be predictive of the eventual success of the company if it locates on that site, and so on. In the predictive validation paradigm MAUT results would be correlated with appropriate probabilistic indices of the eventual success or failure of an action taken on the basis of the evaluation.

The most desirable predictive validation would use an actuarial data base for such successes or failures. However, such data bases are rare and have therefore been used in only a very few studies. A variation is to *create* experimentally a predictive relationship between utility assignments and outcomes. For example, the experimenter could create a utility function with some functional form and given parameters, teach that utility function to subjects by means of a payoff scheme encouraging precise assessment, and then examine whether MAUT procedures could actually recover that utility function.

The third approach, *axiomatic validation,* is structured around the model assumptions described earlier. In that approach the axiomatic tests are applied experimentally to see where models are most likely to fail. For example, one could test additive expected utility independence with several stimuli to determine whether this assumption is typically violated by subjects. The problem with axiomatic tests is that they are very strong and almost inevitably prove the model wrong. Consequently, the analyst has to ask how seriously one should take such violations. If, for example, axiomatic violations are not intentional and if the decision maker instead wants to follow the assumptions, violations should probably be disregarded – unless, of course, the violations influence and distort the judgments required to build the model itself.

Early MAUT validation attempts relied almost exclusively on the convergent validation approach (see Fischer, 1972, 1976, 1977). The predictive validation paradigm had been used extensively before the development of MAUT (see, e.g., Slovic and Lichtenstein, 1971) to study the validity of statistically derived models of judgment (e.g., regression models), but the application of this paradigm to MAUT is relatively recent. In particular, the use of the multiple cue probability learning paradigm (see Hammond, Stewart, Brehmer, and Steinmann, 1975; see also Hammond, McClelland, and Mumpower, 1980) to teach and recover utility functions has been explored only since 1978. Axiomatic studies have been relatively rare. A summary of the few experiments can be found in von Winterfeldt (1980a). Recently, the focus of MAUT research has shifted in two ways. First, there has been a revival of interest in the search for external validation criteria; and second, several studies have begun to investigate relatively specific questions about response mode and context effects in MAUT.

Table 10.1. *Comparisons of MAUT and holistic judgments*

Study	Evaluation objects	Number of attributes	Median or mean correlations
Pollack (1964)	Jobs	8	.7
Hoepfl and Huber (1970)	Teachers	1–6	.89–.98
Huber, Daneshgar, and Ford (1971)	Jobs	?	.62–.67
Pai, Gustafson, and Kiner (1971)	Universities	4	.77–.81
von Winterfeldt and Edwards (1973a)	Apartments	14	.68–.73
Gardiner (1974)	Coastal development plans	8	.62–.73
Fischer (1977)	Cars	3–9	.93–.95
Fischer (1977)	Jobs	3	.97
Beckwith and Lehmann (1973)	Television shows	?	.75
Cook and Stuart (1975)	Financial aid applications; graduate applicants	3–6	53–75% variance accounted for
Schoemaker and Waid (1982)	College applicants	4	.69–.75

MAUT validation experiments

Since Fischer (1975) provides a summary of validation studies up to about 1973, we only summarize these studies here, and then review more comprehensively a few studies conducted between 1973 and 1985.

The convergent validation approach has been implemented in a variety of contexts. Examples include the evaluation of jobs (Fischer, 1977; Hoepfl and Huber, 1970; Pollack, 1964) of airplane landing situations (Yntema and Klem, 1965), of professors and teachers (Hoepfl and Huber, 1970), of universities (Pai, Gustafson, and Kiner, 1971), of apartments (von Winterfeldt and Edwards, 1973a), of cars (Fischer, 1972, 1976), and of coastal development permits (Gardiner, 1974). The typical MAUT model was the riskless additive type with directly assessed importance weights. The correlations between this model and the intuitive rankings of ratings of a set of alternatives (cars, students, etc.) was typically in the .7 to .9 range, which was interpreted as supporting the convergent validity of MAUT. Table 10.1 summarizes some of the results of these studies. One important finding is that the validities tend to decrease as the number of attributes increases (an exception is Fischer's .93 correlation for nine dimensions). This is, of course, to be expected since the *reliability* of holistic judgments decreases as the number of attributes increases (see also Gardiner, 1974). One should not expect a procedure to show a higher correlation with some other procedure than with a replicate of itself.

Such studies clearly support the notion that MAUT and the direct intuitive assessment of value capture the same sort of thing. They highlight an interesting dilemma. Since the direct assessment of value is always easier than any MAUT procedure, why bother with MAUT? The answer seems to us to lie in two arguments. One is that the correlations, though high enough to be encouraging, are by no means 1.0. We believe that the MAUT procedures, by demanding more thought and time, provide a better representation of underlying values than do the holistic judgments. The other argument is that the MAUT information serves many purposes other than simply entering into an aggregate value measure. We illustrate in Chapter 11, for example, how a multiattribute decomposition can be used as a tool for option design; holistic procedures would not serve this purpose. This point is especially important in the applications of MAUT as a technique for conflict diagnosis and mediation hinted at below.

While the above studies compared the model with holistic judgments, another group of studies examined the convergence of weights between different elicitation techniques. The first finding of these studies was that the composites (MAUT indices) calculated with different weight sets converged quite well (see, e.g., Fischer and Peterson, 1973; O'Connor, 1972; von Winterfeldt and Edwards, 1973a). However, this convergence was found even in instances in which the weight vectors themselves showed marked differences, indicating the robustness of the additive model rather than convergence of weights.

When weights were directly compared (e.g., by correlating weight vectors), several discrepancies were found. For example, von Winterfeldt and Edwards (1973a) found that weight vectors from three different weighting procedures correlated only modestly, and Aschenbrenner and Kasubek (1978) found a rather low degree of convergence between a direct assessment of weights and an indirect weight assessment based on indifference judgments. In addition, a number of systematic effects were discovered: weights elicited from hierarchical MAUT structures are steeper (have a higher variance) than weights elicited on the attribute level (see, e.g., John, Edwards, and Collins, in press; Fischer and Peterson, 1973). And, finally, weights derived from statistical models are steeper than directly assessed weights (see John and Edwards, 1978; John, Edwards, and Collins, 1980, in press).

Schoemaker and Waid (1982) tried five different approaches to weight assessment, including multiple regression, swing weights, Saaty's (1980) analytic hierarchy approach, and equal weights. They found the usual robustness of linear models, except that equal weights were clearly inferior to any other procedure tested. Although the weights produced were indeed different, the resulting aggregated scores correlated highly. The authors could find no basis for preferring any weight elicitation technique to any other.

Yet another version of the convergent validation strategy is to compare MAUTs of different people or of different groups. To the extent that these people or groups should represent the same judgments, the corresponding MAUTs should agree. For example, when different doctors evaluate a drug using MAUT, one would expect high interjudge agreement. (Of course, the more idiosyncratic and personal the evaluation problems, the less agreement one would expect.) Indeed, Aschenbrenner and Kasubek (1978) found a very high agreement between weights and composites of doctors who evaluated cortisone drugs. The direct procedures produced more agreement than the indirect ones. Holistic procedures produced more disagreement among judges than decomposed ones. Similarly, Eckenrode (1965) found high interjudge convergence of importance weight procedures. On the other hand, the intrajudge intermethod convergence was relatively low.

Early studies on the *predictive validation paradigm* were, as mentioned earlier, concerned mainly with the validity of statistical models of holistic judgments. In other words, they addressed the question: how well does a statistical model of a judge capture his or her judgments, or how well does that model perform against a real statistical criterion? But already in the late 1960s and early 1970s many studies had elicited explicitly judged numerical weights together with the regression weights of the statistical models. The typical question of these studies was: can respondents explicate their implicit weighting policy in direct numerical judgments of importance?

Early studies of this kind indicated that statistical weights are typically steeper than directly expressed weights (e.g., Hoffman, 1960; Pollack, 1964; Slovic, 1969; Summer, Taliaferro, and Fletcher, 1970). For example, subjects in the study by Pollack tended to put most of their weight on the three most important dimensions when making intuitive judgments.

Several studies have examined the question of whether experience influences the ability of judges to report their implicit weighting schemes. The evidence is mixed. In a study by Wright (1977), first- and second-year MBA students had to evaluate stocks using both statistical and self-expressed weighting procedures. The second-year students had a higher correlation between statistical weights and self-expressed weights. Studies by Huber, Daneshgar, and Ford (1971) and Slovic (1969) showed the reverse trend: inexperienced subjects tended to have a better correlation between self-expressed weights and statistical weights than did more experienced ones.

Three studies have examined self-expressed weighting schemes in the *MCPL paradigm* (Hammond et al., 1975). In this paradigm the experimenter arbitrarily defines a value function and determines the statistical properties of the stimuli. Subjects then have to estimate the value of the stimuli and receive feedback. After extensive training, MAUT procedures are used to recover the learned value function.

Yntema and Torgerson (1961) taught subjects the relation between various cues and an arbitrary (nonadditive) "worth" function (see also Yntema and Klem, 1965). After extensive training subjects' holistic judgments and the worth function correlated about .8 and higher. A decomposed model based on MAUT and the "true" worth function had an even higher correlation, indicating that MAUT can, indeed, recover a taught value function. Schmitt (1978) found no differences between regression weights and directly assessed weights in predicting the criterion of an MCPL study. John, Edwards, and Collins (in press) also found little difference in the predictive capacity of various weighting schemes in an MCPL study in which subjects had learned to evaluate diamonds described on four dimensions. Although directly assessed weights tended to be flatter than weights derived from regression analysis, resulting composites did equally well in the prediction of "true" composites. In fact, the overall correlation between the derived models and the "true" model was remarkably high, in the .90s.

A few studies have employed an external validation criterion. Lathrop and Peters (1969) studied a course and teacher evaluation problem in which they treated average students' evaluations as an "objective" measure of course quality. Subjects then were asked to predict this measure using both holistic and MAUT-type judgments. The decomposed models outperformed the holistic models in predicting the average criterion score.

Eils and John (1980) studied students' evaluation of 10 hypothetical credit applicants. The criterion was a model, developed by a bank, that was based on statistical data about the successes and failures of credit applications. The study revealed that a simple additive rating scale procedure improved the ability of groups to predict the bank model criterion.

Stillwell, Barron, and Edwards (1980, 1983) used a similar paradigm, but the subjects were experts. Several MAUT models were constructed from judgments of 22 credit officers of a major California bank. The judgments were compared against the lending institution's own credit-scoring model, which was based on discriminant analysis for separating defaults and non-defaults on several dimensions. The results demonstrated that subjective importance judgments showed a high degree of convergence with the criterion model. Correlations were generally above .9, and a very high percentage of "total utility" was captured by the models. Only the models based on holistic judgments did somewhat worse.

Axiomatic validation studies have typically tested specific independence assumptions like joint independence or additive expected utility independence. Joint independence versions were tested by Tversky (1967) for a two-dimension problem involving combinations of cigarettes and candy and by Fischer (1977) in a three-dimensional car evaluation problem. Both these studies essentially supported the joint independence assumption.

Additive expected utility independence (AEUI) does not fare as well. Two studies have analyzed this assumption so far. First, Delbeke and Fauville (1974) examined a number of stimuli ranging from vacation trips that varied on the attributes location and mode of transportation to combinations of job types and salaries. Although the small number of subjects did not allow a firm conclusion to be drawn, Delbeke and Fauville indentified systematic patterns of violations of AEUI that point in the direction of multiattribute risk aversion. Second, von Winterfeldt (1980a) studied subjects' preferences for even-chance gambles with two outcomes: gasoline and ground beef. Subjects exhibited clear patterns of multiattribute risk aversion and violated AEUI. These two studies, together with other tests of the additive expected utility model, cast doubts on risky additivity as a good descriptive model of human preferences. Another question is, of course, whether or not people *should* be additive expected utility independent and multiattribute risk neutral.

Fischer (1977) and Barron, von Winterfeldt, and Fischer (1984) examined the functional relationships between risky and riskless multiattribute utility functions and found high convergence. They also determined that most riskless functions were additive, while many risky functions were nonadditive. However, the pattern of violations of risky additivity was such that a simple exponential relationship between risky and riskless functions predicted the actual relationship quite well.

All of the studies mentioned above were in one way or another concerned with validation of the MAUT approach, a particular model, or a special response mode. In the following we describe some studies that looked at some special phenomena arising in MAUT. One such phenomenon is the so-called range effect. From the MAUT models and the definitions of ranges, single-attribute utilities, and weights, it should be clear that, as the ranges of single attributes change, the weights should change, too. If the ranges increase, the weights should increase, and if the ranges decrease, the weights should decrease. This range sensitivity property of weights is automatically built into all procedures that are based on indifferences or strength of preferences. But in direct importance assessment nothing guarantees range sensitivity.

Gabrielli and von Winterfeldt (1978) investigated this problem. Using two stimuli (an industrial facility-siting problem and a contrived car evaluation problem), they found that importance weights were range insensitive. Although problems with the experimental procedure allowed no firm conclusion to be drawn, the experiment raises some intriguing questions about the relation between ranges and weights.

The range effects studies and statistical studies comparing regression weights with self-expressed weights have taken the first steps in the direction of defining the psychological concept of importance. Although that concept is obviously measurable and it makes sense for people to make importance judgments, its psychological content is still somewhat unclear. Is it, for example, related more to the variance of the values or utilities in single attributes (high variance would indicate a higher importance) or to the ranges of values (high range would indicate higher importance)? Some usages of the term suggest that it may be unrelated to either. For example, the sentences "Health and safety are always the most important consideration in technological decisions" and "Money is always the most important consideration in job choices" are frequently heard, although importance obviously should depend on the available alternatives and their associated ranges.

MAUT has found some interesting experimental applications in the analysis of conflicts between groups who approached the evaluation problem from different perspectives. Gardiner (1974) was the first to study conflict with MAUT. In his study 12 subjects evaluated coastal development plans both holistically and with MAUT. Gardiner classified his subjects into two groups: those favoring development and those favoring conservation. These groups differed substantially in their holistic evaluations of a set of hypothetical development plans (see Figure 10.2). However, the corresponding averages on the MAUT models showed much greater agreement. A similar result of convergence through decomposition was reported by Aschenbrenner and Kasubeke (1978). In their study decomposed models for drug evaluations were more similar across experts than were their holistic evaluations. One interpretation is that this convergence is produced by more reliable and balanced judgments in decomposed models.

An important question is whether disagreement in evaluations is due more to perceptions of how the options perform in single attributes, to single-attribute evaluations, or to trade-offs and importance weights. Evidence obtained by Stillwell, von Winterfeldt, and John (1981) indicates that the "action" may be more in the single-attribute ratings than in the weights. In contrast, Marks and von Winterfeldt (1984) and John (1984) identified weights as the main source of disagreements among subject groups with different perspectives about technologies.

10.5. Bets, money, and the fate of static models in a changing world

The issues examined in this chapter so far have been essentially technical. They have had to do with elicitation methods, variability, reliability, and even the validity of value and utility measurement. In the remainder of the chapter we focus on a deeper topic: the appropriateness of the SEU model. Does SEU make sense?

Make sense for what? We offer three interpretations.

1   SEU might be a useful model of how risky decisions are made. In that descriptive sense, is it valid?

2   SEU might be useful for prescribing how risky decisions ought to be made. Is it? If so, how should it be used?

3   SEU is assumed to be descriptively valid by users of elicitation methods that depend on choices among bets. Is that assumption safe, and are the numbers so elicited trustworthy?

Question 1 can be given a summary answer: no. An inordinately long history of discrepancies between the predictions of the model and experiments on choices among bets makes it clear that it does not predict the details of those choices well. We need not elaborate on that assertion here.

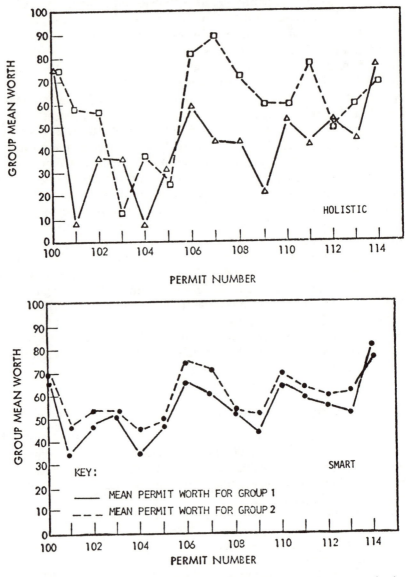

Figure 10.2. SMART produces agreement between developers and conservationists. (*Source:* Gardiner, 1974.)

For reviews of the literature see Edwards (1954d, 1961), Becker and MacClintock (1967), Rapoport and Wallsten (1972), Slovic et al. (1977), Einhorn and Hogarth (1981), and Pitz and Sachs (1984).

Our answer to question 2 is yes, and that to question 3 is sort of. But these answers need much elaboration, and we must prepare the ground.

Static models and a dynamic world

SEU is a static model. Its inputs are personal probabilities and utilities, based on an analysis of a decision problem. Its output is a decision and an explanation of why the recommended option is best. Except in decision problems structured as decision trees, that decision is made once – and then the world ends. Even in decision trees, one reaches the right-hand side of the decision tree and finally ends up at a consequence node, at which point the world ends. No version of the SEU model recognizes the continuity of life. No version includes any conception of the process of learning from experience except Bayes's theorem – a very important learning model but hardly adequate to cover all the kinds of learning decision makers do. Why should we expect so impoverished a conception of reality to be useful in either predicting or making real decisions?

A part of the answer is that the distinction between *static* and *dynamic* is far more subtle than it appears. The world is always changing, and *all* models are, by one definition, static. The function of a model is to capture the nature of some set of changes in the world, such as a decision and its consequences. The description of such changes contained in the model is itself unchanging – that is, static. One way of putting it is that the function of any model is to take a changing environment and make it static by modeling the nature of the change. This very general statement fits all kinds of models, decision analytic and other.

Another part of the answer is that no model of human behavior should mimic that behavior. Behavior is enormously complex. The function of a model of behavior is to simplify it to the point at which it can be understood. We believe that a model should be like a map: a representation of reality that resembles the real thing enough to serve some useful purpose but that is otherwise far simpler and easier to work with.

These generalizations apply to normative as well as descriptive models. Above all, a normative model must be tractable, which means it must be simpler than the problem it represents. Since it is a model, it is an unchanging representation of everchanging reality.

The test of the merit of a model, like that of other artifacts, is usefulness. Usefulness at description is tested by prediction. Usefulness at prescription is tested by effective use – a weak test, since in prescriptive contexts control groups are hard to find.

An alternative to SEU

Our major task in this section is to think about choices among bets with monetary payoffs. The restriction to monetary payoffs may seem harsh, because most decision situations are far more complex. We justify it on two grounds. (1) Money is very important. For some, it is by far the most important measure of value. For all, it is at least a useful surrogate for many non-financial values. Money was invented to facilitate transactions by permitting value comparisons to be made. As a mechanism for evaluation it is notoriously imperfect – but it is by far the most operationally useful measure of value we have. (2) The topic of utility was originally defined as being concerned with a function of current monetary value of the decision maker's total assets that would explain certain risk-relevant decisions, such as buying insurance (Bernoulli, 1738). For some economists, the argument of the utility function continues to be the current financial value of the decision maker's total assets. Most experiments involving gambles have used imaginary or, occasionally, real monetary payoffs.

The position we take is somewhat different. We believe that decision theory is simply silent about what the appropriate argument or arguments for utility function(s) should be. But since money is important, choices involving it are important too. We need a vocabulary and set of ideas with which to talk about experiments. One way to get at them is to present SEU's most illustrious contemporary competitor as a descriptive theory of choice.

Prospect theory (Kahneman and Tversky, 1979b) is based on a series of experimental observations, some of which we review below. The theory includes two main sets of ideas. One has to do with editing operations on gambles. Decision analysts would call this process *structuring*. Here, as elsewhere in this book, we attach more importance to structuring than to computation. Consequently we focus on this aspect of prospect theory to the virtual exclusion of some of its other features.

Kahneman and Tversky's experiments led them to propose four effects observable in the process of choosing among bets.

1   *Certainty effect.* "People overweight outcomes that are considered certain, relative to outcomes which are merely probable" (Kahneman and Tversky, 1979b, p. 265).

2   *Reflection effect.* "The reflection of prospects around 0 reverses the preference order" (p. 268).

3   *Aversion to probabilistic insurance.* Probabilistic insurance pays off with probability less than 1 but diminishes premiums. Respondents don't like the idea.

4   *Isolation effect.* "In order to simplify the choice between alternatives, people often disregard components that the alternatives share, and focus on the components that distinguish them" (p. 271).

The idea of editing operations is central to the way in which prospect theory accounts for these observations. Six major editing operations are proposed:

1   *Coding.* Outcomes are recoded as gains or losses with respect to some reference point, which usually corresponds to the current asset position.
2   *Combination.* Prospects are sometimes simplified by combining the probabilities associated with identical outcomes.
3   *Segregation.* "Some prospects contain a riskless component that is segregated from the risky component in the editing phase" (p. 274).
4   *Cancellation.* Common constituents of options, such as common outcome-probability combinations, can be discarded before bets are compared.

The other two editing operations, simplification (rounding) and detection of dominance, play a lesser role in prospect theory; we ignore them here.

The concept of framing options (Tversky and Kahneman, 1981) builds on the ideas of prospect theory but adds one more key idea. The frame of a decision is simply the decision maker's concept of the decision problem – its structure, as a decision analyst would say. The additional key idea of the framing paper is that people maintain psychological accounts. "To describe the framing and evaluation of compound outcomes, we use the notion of a psychological account, defined as an outcome frame which specifies (i) the set of elementary outcomes that are evaluated jointly and the manner in which they are combined, and (ii) a reference outcome that is considered neutral or normal" (Tversky and Kahneman, 1981, p. 456). The discussion makes clear that psychological accounts may vary in scope, from minimal accounts that are, so to speak, heavily reduced by the editing operations to more elaborate ones that include more of the context in which the decision is being made.

Although there is much more both to prospect theory and to the concept of framing than this brief discussion presents, these are the key structuring ideas – and our focus is on structures.

Introspections

Rather independently of the preceding ideas (though of course with prior knowledge of them), we set ourselves two closely related introspective and argumentative tasks. One was to understand how we ourselves face and decide about risky prospects. The other was to examine what advice we, as decision analysts, would give to individuals (not organizations) facing similar prospects. The result was fruitful enough for us to report.

The first idea, completely consistent with prospect theory, is that we evaluate decisions of all kinds, particularly decisions about gambles, not on the basis of final asset positions to which they might lead, but rather with respect to reference points.

This thought has a long history in the psychology of risky decision making. Originally it was seen as a methodological problem. Mosteller and Nogee (1951), Edwards (1954a,b,c), and others in the late 1940s and 1950s recognized that playing gambles during the course of an experiment changed asset position, over which the utility of money had been traditionally defined, but nevertheless chose to plot the utility of winning $10 at a point $10 away from the origin of the utility function, regardless of intervening transactions. Davidson, Suppes, and Siegel (1957), recognizing the problem, postponed all plays until all choices had been made, exactly to avoid it; this strategy was later used by many researchers (see, e.g., Coombs, Bezembinder, and Goode, 1967; Coombs and Huang, 1976). Curiously, it took a while for those who understood the methodological issue to understand the substantive one. Markowitz (1959) proposed that investments should be evaluated relative to one's customary financial position. Edwards (1962b) proposed that zero utility for money was always at the status quo, almost no matter how the status quo changed.

If bets and other prospects are evaluated with respect to a reference point, where is it? Edwards (1962b) put it at the status quo, and prospect theory puts it there sometimes. But the harder we thought about the status quo, the more elusive the idea became.

We came to realize that the status quo is, at least for us, a set of streams of transactions in which we are embedded. Though none could occur without our willingness, many are automatic, and many more are so necessary that they might as well be.

Since it seemed both normatively and descriptively relevant, we tried to sort out the transaction flows that affect our lives. The following list describes those that involve both of us; if your life is different from ours, you probably will have a different list. Ideas relevant to business or organizational contexts would be very different.

1   *Quick cash stream.* This includes what we carry in our wallets. It also includes credit card transactions (we do not allow significant debt to accumulate on them). It also includes some of our normal check writing, particularly the checks we write to replenish our wallets. Since most gambling experiments are concerned with hypothetical or real quick cash transactions, we assume that this stream is most relevant to them. But since it is composed primarily of outflows fed from other streams, the concept of the status quo is particularly hard to define with respect to it. Nor is it usually necessary. A much simpler idea, namely, that no change occurs in the quick cash stream as a consequence of a particular decision, defines a more meaningful reference point.

2   *Capital assets stream.* This stream includes house, car, investments, inheritance prospects, and retirement accumulations. It requires attention and decision making fairly infrequently.

3   *Income and fixed expenditures stream.* This includes our salaries (which we see only as deposit slips from our banks), taxes, house payments, utilities,

insurance, and so on). The checks that fill stream 1 are treated as fixed expenditures in stream 3.

4   *Play money stream.* This stream includes money reserved for risky invest-ments, for expensive vacations, and for household extravagances. For some, a car would fall into this stream rather than the capital assets stream.

There may be more streams than that, and your case will certainly differ from ours. But the idea should be clear.

This formulation leads us to a host of questions. How and when does a change of status become assimilated into a stream and lose its individual identity as a transaction? The process of paying bills is so mechanical that a first answer in that case would be "immediately and without thought." But a bad evening at the poker table can leave the poker addict morose for a day. Can a change be assimilated into a stream before it happens? Clearly, yes; that is exactly how we think about salaries. Equally clearly, such changes are not always assimilated so easily or quickly. Many of the exper-iments that involve compounding bets raise exactly this issue.

Cross-stream transactions are frequent. Current income feeds all other streams. Insurance on capital assets is a device for moving a potential gam-ble out of the capital assets stream and making it a part of the income and fixed expenditures stream. (That, we speculate, is why probabilistic insur-ance is unappealing; it fails to accomplish that move.) Life insurance does not fit that description well.

The concept of transaction streams is similar to, but broader than the concept of psychological accounts. The concept of psychological accounts has separate intuitive appeal. When Edwards played poker once a month, he kept a running record of how he did, as many other poker players do. This was clearly a psychological account written down. However, it played no role in decisions made away from the poker table; its main virtue was that it served as an element in a strategy for self-education. The amounts won or lost each month entered into the quick cash stream and were imme-diately assimilated, but the psychological account remained distinct.

Risk attitudes differ within each stream. Within the quick cash stream, both of us are risk neutral. Within the capital assets and income and fixed expenditure streams, we tend to avoid risks. Within the play money stream, we seek risks. One reason we keep these streams distinct to some degree is so that we can behave differently with regard to risk within different kinds of expenditures.

Our introspections raise questions in our minds about the interpretation of risk attitude in terms of shapes of utility functions. Risk aversion in the capital assets stream is clearly related to the concept of quasi ruin discussed in Section 1.3. For that reason it is not an effect to be interpreted by means of a nonlinear utility function at all. Risk aversion below the reference point in the income and fixed expenditure stream is based, at least for us, on the desirability of managing that stream in as smooth and effortless a way as its importance permits. Major losses in that stream simply produce complications, which are unpleasant. Above the reference point, in that stream, we are risk neutral. When the amount withheld from income changes in mid-year because the annual contribution to Social Security has been paid, our take-home pay goes up, but no aspect of our behavior with respect to this stream changes. Now and then we inspect our bank balances and transfer any excessive amount to either the investment or the play money stream. The only reason we have play money streams is so that we can do things that might be financially hard to justify – such as taking an expensive vacation or making a speculative investment. Both are fun. The message of this paragraph, then, is that most of the instances of risk aversion or risk seeking in our own behavior are related to nonfinancial dimensions of a multiattribute utility function rather than to curvature of a function describing utility of money. This view, if taken seriously, is very discouraging to those who are interested in a general theory of consumer behavior, because it implies that the money-related motives of different consumers will be different. But both introspectively and experimentally, we believe that to be clearly the case.

As it happens, we have both had extensive decision-analytic training, and consequently we can, especially within the quick cash stream, adjust our risk-taking behavior so that it is essentially unaffected by the reference point. But we believe ourselves to be atypical in this respect. Though the perfect symmetry implied by the term *reflection effect* does not fit well, there can be little doubt that most subjects in gambling experiments prefer not to lose and will take risky options in which not losing is a possible outcome in preference to sure losses. Edwards (1953, 1954a) found that, faced with various options involving various probabilities and amounts of loss, with not losing as the other possible outcome, subjects almost routinely picked the option with the higher probability of not losing. If given a choice between a 50:50 chance of winning $1,000 or nothing or a sure $500, subjects may or may not take the sure thing; more often than not, they will. When given a choice between a 50:50 chance between losing $1,000 or nothing and a sure $500 loss, subjects will very often take the gamble. Such effects are reported in Kahneman and Tversky (1979b), Tversky and Kahneman (1981), and Schoemaker (1980). Tversky and Kahneman (1981) report similar effects in problems about lifesaving policies; people are risk averse with respect to decisions stated in terms of lives saved and risk seeking with respect to decisions stated in terms of lives lost, though the options are identical for both phrasings. Other data suggest that, above the reference point, people are often risk neutral. Perhaps one reason for the universality of the assumption of risk aversion in the decision-analytic literature and its absence from many experimental findings is that most decision analytic thinking concerns major decisions, which tend to fall into individual capital assets streams or corporate equivalents thereof. These comments raise questions about the symmetry of the reflection effect.

Option packaging effects

The implication both of prospect theory and of our introspections is that the packaging of options can make a great deal of difference in the way they look. Of special importance is the question of how quickly assimilation of a gain or loss into a stream occurs, prospectively or retrospectively. We should expect options that can be treated in multiple stages, so that one can assimilate the first stage before the second comes along, to be quite different from single-stage options. This is another way of describing the operation in prospect theory called segregation.

Our intuitions about how much assimilation occurs conflict. Consider a 50:50 bet with $100 and $200 as the payoffs. Edwards, if he were given such a bet by some intrigued philanthropist, would assimilate $100 into his quick cash stream and think of the payoffs as $0 and $100; von Winterfeldt would assimilate about $150 and would think of the bet as a plus-or-minus $50 gamble.

The effect of assimilation of sure gains into an income stream is dramatically illustrated every month as millions of people write checks to pay their bills, knowing (1) that as the checks are written their account cannot cover them and (2) that by the time they are cashed and clear, next month's salary will have been deposited.

What are the normative decision-analytic implications of these ideas about income streams?

1   Except for potential ruin problems or other decisions that require it, such as large bank loans, forget about final asset position. You cannot know it, and it is rarely relevant.

2   Define your financial streams clearly, and account for each well. The liberty to adopt different risk-taking behaviors with respect to different streams is useful. We consider EV maximization within the quick cash stream to be highly desirable, and risk avoidance within the capital assets stream to be almost essential. The sizes of loss in that stream can be large enough to produce quasi ruin.

3   Whenever you are considering a cross-stream transaction, aggregate the streams involved. Normally, such aggregation is a tedious task; most of us perform it once per year, at income tax time, and then only partially. We may track our capital assets stream much more infrequently than that. The cost of broad pictures is not inconsequential; for a given decision, you may not need one.

4   Treat psychological accounts as learning tools, not rules of behavior. Investors and poker players alike must learn to write off sunk costs.

Experiments

Now that we have a language with which to talk about these ideas, we shall describe a few of the experiments that led to them.

The Allais paradox

Allais (1953; see also Allais and Hagen, 1979) was one of the earliest critics of SEU theory. His famous utility paradox consists of a clever pair of choices among imaginary lotteries in which the predominant pattern of preferences suggests a systematic violation of SEU. Since he stated the sums involved in millions, we present a version of it taken from Kahneman and Tversky (1979b).

Problem 1: Choose between
A: $2,500 with probability .33   B: $2,400 with certainty
   $2,400 with probability .66
   $0 with probability .01

Problem 2: Choose between
C: $2,500 with probability .33   D: $2,400 with probability .34
   $0 with probability .67 $0 with probability .66

Among their subjects, 82% preferred B over A, and 83% preferred C over D. A preference for B in problem 1 and for C in problem 2 violates any form of SEU maximization. The first preference means that

$$u(\$2,400) > .33u(\$2,500) + .66u(\$2,400) + .01u(\$0), \qquad (10.1)$$

or

$$.34u(\$2,400) > .33u(\$2,500) + .01u(\$0). \qquad (10.2)$$

The second preference implies the opposite:

$$.33u(\$2,500) + .67u(\$0) < .34u(\$2,400) + .66u(\$0) \qquad (10.3)$$

simplifies to

$$.34u(\$2,400) < .33u(\$2,500) + .01u(\$0). \qquad (10.4)$$

(An EV maximizer would choose A and C.)

Kahneman and Tversky (1979b) call the Allais paradox an instance of the certainty effect. It is perhaps no more than a rephrasing of that thought to suggest that problem A presents the decision maker with a reference point difficulty. If the sure thing is chosen, the reference point changes by $2,400. Even if the gamble is chosen, you are virtually certain to win. But the gamble offers, relative to a new reference point defined by the sure thing, a .33 probability of winning $100 and a .01 probability of losing $2,400. Risk aversion to losses in the quick cash stream could make that gamble undesirable. In contrast, the implications of problem 2 about the reference point are much less dramatic.

Like Allais, Kahneman and Tversky chose rather large payoffs for their version of the Allais paradox. If all payoffs were divided by 100, we think the choices in problem 1 might well be reversed. As it is, only 61% of their respondents showed the paradox. Versions with higher payoffs might produce more unanimity.

Slovic and Tversky (1974) presented a version of the Allais paradox to subjects with a hypothetical $1 million payoff. Of 29 respondents, 17 showed the paradoxical pattern. Each respondent was then given a written version of an argument in conflict with the choices made. Retest showed that very few respondents changed responses. The arguments were succinct and abstract. A second experiment was like the first, except that the arguments were expanded and more carefully presented. This procedure seemed to produce slightly better results. MacCrimmon and Wehrung (1977) also found giving explanations to subjects not very helpful.

Providing concreteness helps – a little. Keller (1985) showed that the form in which gambles are presented (written statements, graphs, urns, matrices, etc.) has a significant effect on the degree to which the axioms are violated. Matrix representations seem to be the best.

Multistage option packaging problems

So far we have been discussing single-stage choices in which a reference point problem was induced by the presence of a sure thing. An even more dramatic means of producing option packaging difficulties exists: present the respondent with a sequence of transactions or choices but require that all be made before any are acted on. This implies presenting at least some of the options in unpackaged form, with instructions to the respondent to treat them as a package. Quite powerful violations of SEU maximization can be produced in this way.

There are two general classes of such effects. One is produced when the first stage is a random event or a bet; typically the second event involves a sure thing, and the result is interpreted as a version of the certainty effect. The other class is produced when the first stage is a gift; this can have various consequences, the most dramatic of which is that the second stage changes from a winning to a losing bet. The result in interpreted as an instance of the reflection effect.

We present two dramatic examples of the first class from Tversky and Kahneman (1981), who were following up earlier studies such as those of Lichtenstein and Slovic (1971, 1973) and Kahneman and Tversky (1979b). The number in parentheses following the description of an option represents the percentage of subjects choosing that option:

Problem 3 (*N* = 150). Imagine that you face the following pair of concurrent decisions. First examine both decisions, then indicate the options you prefer.

Decision i. Choose between (A) a sure gain of $240 (84%) and (B) a 25% chance to gain $1,000, with a 75% chance to gain nothing (16%).

Decision ii. Choose between (C) a sure loss of $750 (13%) and (D) a 75% chance to lose $1,000, with a 25% chance to lose nothing (87%).

The following results are reported:

The majority choice in decision i is risk-averse. A riskless prospect is preferred to a risky prospect of equal or greater expected value. In contrast, the majority choice in decision ii is risk taking: A risky prospect is preferred to a riskless prospect of equal expected value ... because decisions i and ii were presented together, the respondents had in effect to choose one prospect from the set: A and C, B and C, A and D, B and D. The most common pattern (A and D) was chosen by 73% of respondents while the least popular pattern (B and C) was chosen by only 3% of respondents. However, the combination of B and C is definitely superior to the combination A and D, as is readily seen in problem 4:

Problem 4 (N = 86). Choose between (A and D) a 25% chance to win $240 and a 75% chance to lose $760 (0%) and (B and C) a 25% chance to win $250 and 75% chance to lose $750 (100%).

When the prospects were combined and the dominance of the second option became obvious, all respondents chose the superior option. The popularity of the inferior option in problem 3 implies that this problem was framed as a pair of separate packages. The violations of dominance observed in problem 3 do not disappear in the presence of monetary incentives. A different group of respondents who answered a modified version of problem 3, with real payoffs, produced a similar pattern of choices [Tversky and Kahneman, 1981, pp. 8–9].

Here failure to package a win-or-break-even gamble together with a lose-or-break-even gamble, though the rules required it, led to violation of dominance, one of the two most compelling principles of rationality. Incidentally, Grether and Plott (1979) and Grether (1979) found similarly that financial incentives (within the range usable in such experiments) do not have much rationality-enhancing effect.

Next we turn to the second, somewhat similar example. The parenthetical percentages are percentages of subjects choosing that option.

Problem 5 (N = 77). Which of the following options do you prefer: (A) a sure win of $30 (78%) or (B) an 80 percent chance to win $45 (22%).

Problem 6 (N = 85). Consider the following two-stage game. In the first stage there is a 75% chance to end the game without winning anything and a 25% chance to move into the second stage. If you reach the second stage, you have a choice between (C) a sure win of $30 (74%) and (D) an 80% chance to win $45 (26%).

Your choice must be made before the game starts; that is, before the outcome of the first stage is known. Please indicate the option you prefer.

Problem 7 (N = 81). Which of the following options do you prefer: (E) a 25% chance to win $30 (42%) or (F) a 20% chance to win $45 (58%)?

Again, the authors add for readers:

Let us examine the structure of these problems. First, note that problems 6 and 7 are identical in terms of probabilities and outcomes, because prospects C and E offer a .25 chance to win $30 and prospect D offers a probability of .25 × .80 = .20 to win $45 as does prospect F. Consistency therefore requires that the same choice be made in problems 6 and 7. Second, note that problem 6 differs from problem 5 only by the introduction of a preliminary stage. If the second stage of the game is reached, then problem 6 reduces to problem 5; if the game ends at the first stage, the decision does not affect the outcome. Hence, there seems to be no reason to make a different choice in problems 5 and 6. By this logical analysis problem 6 is equivalent to problem 7 on the one hand and problem 5 on the other. The participants, however, responded similarly to problems 5 and 6 but differently to problem 7 [Tversky and Kahneman, 1981, p. 10].

Problem 6 can be thought of as a two-stage unpackaged version of problem 7. The key point of the example is that the respondents think of problem 6 in unpackaged form even though explicitly instructed that they must make both choices before the game starts – that is, should treat them as a single package.

Another example, from Kahneman and Tversky (1979b), is yet another version of the certainty effect. Consider the following two problems:

Problem 1
A: .20 chance of winning $4,000
    .80 chance of winning nothing
B: .25 chance of winning $3,000
    .75 chance of winning nothing

Problem 2
This is a two-stage problem. In the first stage there is a .75 chance that the game will stop without your having gained or lost anything. In the second stage you have the choice between (b) $3,000 for sure and (a) a gamble which gives you $4,000 with a probability of .80, nothing with a probability of .20. You have to decide on the second choice before entering the first stage.

Note that these are identical problems, yet subjects may prefer A in the first problem and b in the second.

Such packaging difficulties can be combined in a mix-and-match fashion with other phenomena of risky choice. Tversky (1969) combined them with risk aversion for losses:

Problem 1
First, you receive a gift of $1,000, then you have the choice of one of the following two options:
A: .50 probability of winning $1,000
    .50 probability of winning nothing
B: $500 for sure

Problem 2
First, you receive $2,000 as a gift, then you have the choice of one of the following two options:
a: .50 probability of losing $1,000
    .50 probability of winning nothing
b: losing $500 for sure

Subjects tend to ignore the gift and choose b and a.

The phenomenon of avoiding sure losses and seeking sure wins has been described in the literature for a long time, though not in this kind of combination with packaging problems. Kahneman and Tversky (1979b) call it the reflection effect. Schoemaker (1980) has also studied it. McNeil, Pauker, Sox, and Tversky (1982) and Tversky and Kahneman (1981) reported such effects in a variety of problems, including realistic questions about lifesaving policies.

Field observations suggest that the idea of assimilating events in a stream as preferable to dealing with them in discontinuous clumps has a great deal of applicability to problems other than gambles for money. Society takes stronger action to avoid multideath disasters (e.g., a core meltdown in a nuclear power plant) than to avoid repetitive small accidents that accumulate to similar or larger numbers (e.g., car accidents). Even the well-known distinction between an identified and an anonymous life fits the paradigm. Loss of an identified life is a clear disruption of a normal pattern of events; loss of an anonymous life is simply a part of a flow of births and deaths that goes on all the time.

Oddball violations of SEU

We have discussed the systematic and classifiable violations of SEU as a descriptive model that we know of. A few other violations resist our intuitive notion of the problem.

Perhaps the most notable among them is the Ellsberg paradox, first discussed by Daniel Ellsberg (yes, he went on to other interests and claims to fame) in 1961. You have in front of you two urns, labeled urn I and urn II. Urn I has 100 red and black balls, but you do not know in what proportion. Urn II contains exactly 50 red and 50 black balls. Most people are indifferent between betting $100 on red or black in both urns. After all (their reasoning would be) they have equal chances of winning in either case. However, most respondents also prefer betting on red in urn II over betting on red in urn I, and also prefer betting on black in urn II over betting on black in urn I, presumably because they know the precise proportion of red and black balls in urn II. It turns out that this pattern of preference is inconsistent with the SEU model, since it implies that both $P(\text{red in urn I}) > 1/2$ and $P(\text{black in urn I}) > 1/2$, which is impossible.

Like the Allais paradox, the Ellsberg paradox has been found with naive subjects and experts as respondents and even with theoreticians and some practitioners of decision analysis. Furthermore, such violations of SEU theory have been remarkably resistant to reversal even after the nature of the paradoxes and reasons for the validity of the axioms have been pointed out.

Recent attempts have been made to invent alternative theories that could accommodate the seemingly paradoxical behavior. Of the many theoretic proposals, the one of Bell and Raiffa (1979; see also Bell, 1981, 1982) is perhaps the most interesting. According to Bell and Raiffa the problem lies in the fact that utility is defined over final assets only; people usually have an additional concern with the possibility of regret – an after-the-fact feeling.

By incorporating regret as a second attribute of the decision problem and by defining a two-attribute utility function over final outcomes and regret, Bell and Raiffa showed that both the Allais and the Ellsberg paradox are predicted by the SEU model.

One other basic truth of SEU theory is that one can never do better by choosing a probability mixture of options than by choosing the best of the options that enters the mix. This seems to be a trivial assumption, both normatively and descriptively, yet it has been shown to be violated in some experimental settings.

Becker, DeGroot, and Marschak (1963) presented subjects with two 50:50 lotteries and one lottery that included each of the four outcomes of the other two with a probability of .25. Thus, the last lottery was simply a 50:50 mixture of the first two. A sizable number of subjects chose the mixture over both of the other two lotteries. Similar results are reported by Coombs and Huang (1976). In this experiment, about half the subjects preferred the mixture over both extremes. To explain this phenomenon Coombs proposed a theory of ideal risk in which subjects trade off EV against risk.

Clearly, preferring gambles over all elements entering the mix contradicts rational behavior in general, not only SEU. It would therefore be instructive to see whether subjects who are instructed in the simple principles that a gamble can never be better than all of its outcomes would still prefer the gamble.

Another oddball violation of SEU consists of a failure to appreciate the implications of very small probabilities. Kahneman and Tversky (1979b) presented the following example:

Problem 7
Option A: Win $6,000 with probability .45
Option B: Win $3,000 with probability .90

Problem 8
Option A: Win $6,000 with probability .001
Option B: Win $3,000 with probability .002

Of 100 subjects, 96 chose option A in problem 7, and only 27 chose option A in problem 8. Kahneman and Tversky interpreted this as a tendency to overweight very small probabilities. Our thought, not very different, is that given a good reason, such as a big payoff difference, subjects simply don't pay attention to very small differences in probability. (It would be interesting to teach subjects about odds and then do the experiment with the uncertainties presented in odds form.)

10.6. Implications for decision-analytic practice

Since this discussion started with the assertion that a very long history of literature shows that the SEU model is not a good description of the way choices are actually made, it is no surprise that effects of the sort we have been reviewing exist. But it does raise two questions. One is whether the decision-analytic model, which is initially always some version of maximization of SEU, deserves credence as a normative principle. The other is whether decision-analytic elicitation methods that depend on the SEU model for their interpretation can be expected to work.

The first issue is obviously of great import to us, but we have found little in the literature that bears on it. Experiments showing that people violated normative principles and were somewhat reluctant to be persuaded that these violations were mistakes do not imply nearly as much about the principles as about the methods of persuasion. Moreover, researchers in the field hold views of what the normative rules refer to that we do not share. Kahneman and Tversky (1979b, p. 287) stated, "Another important case of a shift of reference point arises when a person formulates his decision problem in terms of final assets, as advocated in decision analysis, rather than in terms of gains and losses, as people usually do." We agree that people usually formulate decision problems in gains and losses. As we argued earlier in this chapter, they should. Indeed, they should define those problems according to the transaction stream they are in. The normative rules are simply silent about the argument of the utility function; they only help one to use that function in a consistent way. That is why some of the effects we have labeled oddball seem especially disturbing. Intentional intransitivity would disturb us. Deliberate violations of SEU of the Ellsberg paradox type do disturb us. (We must be brainwashed. Neither one of us feels the tug of the Ellsberg paradox at all. To us, the paradoxical set of judgments simply looks like a mistake.)

The world analysts live in is different from that portrayed in many experiments. Like experimental psychologists, analysts encounter inconsistencies and violations of SEU, and many also see the power of stimuli and response modes in forming judgments. But what experimenters usually consider as the final product of their research is only the beginning for analysts. Observing incoherence, analysts attempt to find reasons for it and seek to resolve it.

The reasons for incoherence typically vary from random error to disregard of some obvious rules of rationality to willful and systematic arguments against the logic implicit in the EV or SEU model.

Random errors usually take the least effort – simply establish the fact that they are indeed random and align the responses to reestablish coherence. A typical instance of random error occurs when the points inferred from the responses in a utility function elicitation do not fit on a smooth curve. Unless the deviations from a smooth curve are peculiar and systematic, the analyst probably would not even invite the respondent to adjust his or her judgments and instead would simply use statistical procedures for curve fitting. Most analysts would inform the respondent that from now on the fitted curve would be used as an idealized representation of the response. Respondents who considered this inappropriate would have an opportunity to object at this point, but usually such curve-fitting procedures would be accepted without much discussion.

Sometimes unintended incoherence occurs that is not quite random and still not quite counter to any principle of rationality. Two examples are partial concavity or convexity in utility functions elicited with gambles and disagreements between holistic judgments and the outputs of a MAUT model. Such incoherences usually promote creative discussions between the analyst and the client. Even without appealing to any principles of rationality, the analyst can usually convince the respondent that common sense requires consistency. Subsequently, the analyst probes: "Why are you inconsistent, and which numbers would you like to change?" John's (1984) experiment addressed these questions in the MAUT context. All subjects attributed the incoherence to faulty judgment (either in their intuition or in the model parameters) and were very explicit about what they wanted to change.

The finding that an elicited utility function is reflected around the origin is another example of a response leading to creative analyst–client interactions. It may turn out, as is often the case, that an important attribute (e.g., regret) has been left out, which is the "cause" of the reflection.

Error, inconsistency, and "lability" viewed in this context are an asset rather than a liability. They force both the analyst and the client to think hard and provide them with an opportunity to gain insights into the decision problems. Although both analyst and client may use this insight to produce a coherent reformulation of the problem, often the "creative stress" between the demands of the models and intuition is itself a useful product of decision analysis.

A more difficult problem arises with obviously nonrational responses. It does not make sense to be risk averse when considering the lives saved as a result of a social program and risk seeking when considering the loss of lives resulting from the same program. This instance of a preference reversal as a function of framing the same question must be as disconcerting to most respondents as it is to many analysts, and the answers may produce stronger feelings than "creative stress." We suspect that in many such instances of obvious violations of rationality a respondent would choose one of two solutions: accept one of the two initial responses as valid or restructure the problem, in particular reformulate the status quo and the attribute over which losses and gains are defined. For example, in the lives saved versus lives lost case it seems more natural to accept the risk-averse lives-saved response and question the reasons for reacting differently in the lives-lost case. On introspection it seems that perhaps the problem of accountability and liability artificially entered the lives-lost version, causing risk-seeking behavior. At the risk of sounding clinical, we must confess that in many decision analyses, particularly with individual clients (organizations pose problems quite different from the ones discussed here), we structure and restructure and identify and resolve inconsistencies until the model and the client are at peace and previous responses that are at odds with the model have been explained away.

If it is correct, as Daniel Ellsberg asserts, that some decision theorists violated his paradox cheerfully and "with gusto" and chose not to realign theory and intuition, his respondents would pose a much more difficult dilemma for a decision analyst. Allais's and Ellsberg's paradoxes as well as the certainty and isolation effects describe a much more fundamental form of incoherence than the other examples discussed in this chapter. Restructuring is helpful – but apparently that structure (or "frame," as Tversky and Kahneman call it) produces a different solution. So which solution should the analyst and the client accept? This is a more profound version of the violation of principles of rationality than the previous case, because now the principles are neither obvious nor completely acceptable. The sure-thing principle certainly looks acceptable, but why should you trust it more than your intuition in Allais's paradox? The substitution principle is not even obvious – unless you have had sufficient exposure to expected utility calculations.

Ultimately the client has to take sides. We have no problem accepting the sure-thing and the substitution principles and, when in doubt, would trust those principles more than our intuition. Our task as analysts is to make the process by which we arrived at this acceptance of principle over intuition as meaningful as possible to our clients.

11   Sensitivity analysis and flat maxima

11.1. Introduction: now that you have the numbers ...

The fundamental topic of this chapter is sensitivity analysis. It begins, once you, the analyst, think you have a grasp of the problem and at least some notion of the model and numbers relevant to it. You embody the problem in a mathematical structure (e.g., a MAUT model or a Bayesian inference model), plug some (usually) rough numbers in, and calculate. You repeat this process numerous times, varying structures and numbers.

The goals are (1) to gain insights into the nature of the problem, its relation to the formalizations that have occurred to you, and the possible solutions suggested by you, the decision maker, and the model; (2) to find a simple and elegant structure that does justice to the problem; (3) to check both the correctness of the numbers and the need for precision in refining them.

This characterization of sensitivity analysis is not special to decision analysis. Many operations researchers and management scientists describe sensitivity analysis in similar terms. But decision-analytic sensitivity analysis is different from that typical of operations research and management science in at least two ways. One is that only the decision is important, and its values, utilities, or SEUs are seldom greatly affected by the precision of the model form or of the input numbers. This strong statement needs much justification, which we will provide. The second difference is that decision analysis is a joint activity of client and analyst. There are many brands of clients and many brands of analysts, but we shall treat as typical the case in which the analyst has available all the formal tools anyone might wish to use, but the client does not understand them. This implies, and we shall assert, that there are two kinds of sensitivity analysis for decision-analytic purposes: sensitivity analysis for the analyst and sensitivity analysis for the client. These occur in sequence. Once the analyst, using a battery of formal tools, has an insight about the problem that the client will find illuminating, the analyst must find a minimally demanding way of passing that insight on to the client.

This picture of decision-analytic sensitivity analysis structures this chap-

387

ter. We start with a discussion of dominance, because the existence of dominance makes sensitivity analysis almost unnecessary and because sensitivity analysis should be carried out only on undominated options. Then we present technical tools suitable to the analyst for sensitivity analysis and make suggestions about how the insights to which they lead can be communicated to clients. Then in a highly technical section we discuss flat maxima in order to provide formal justification for our assertion that the precision of model forms and numbers is seldom crucial.

11.2. Dominance

Ordinal and cardinal dominance among gambles

The concept of dominance is important both theoretically and practically. When a dominant option exists, it is unambiguously the best option available, and no further analysis is required. To put it another way, dominance is completely insensitive. As a practical matter, then, one would like to find a dominant option, because then one will have no trouble deciding or convincing others that it is best. As a theoretic matter, since dominance makes sensitivity analysis unnecessary, such analyses should be conducted only on undominated options.

The concept of dominance is easy to understand. Suppose you are considering bets A and B, both dependent on the flip of a coin. In bet A, you win $1 if the coin comes up heads and lose $1 if it comes up tails. In bet B, you win $2 for heads and lose $1 for tails. Then, B dominates A, and A should be eliminated from consideration. The concept works in an exactly analogous way in multiattribute utility contexts. Suppose you are buying a new car, and you care about acceleration, comfort, and price. Car A and car B are equivalent in acceleration and in comfort, but B is cheaper than A. Then B dominates A, and you should eliminate A from the list of cars to be considered. In both examples, A is called *ordinally dominated*. Options that are not ordinally dominated are called *ordinally admissible*.

Most of the following discussion is concerned with gambles. As the preceding paragraph shows, the notion of dominance is the same in structure whether it appears in gambles or in multiattribute utilities. We start by presenting the idea of conditional values. You may remember that the notion of utility was presented in Chapters 1 and 7 as a representation of the fact that every branch of a decision tree must be cut somewhere. The point at which it is cut is called the outcome associated with that branch and has a measure associated with it called its utility. That utility is a numerical surrogate for the fact that the tree is cut at that point. In this chapter we work with the same thought, but we call such numbers conditional values. (This chapter is not concerned with the value–utility distinction.)

Using the EV maximization model and considering only simple gambles

Table 11.1. *Gambles and their conditional values: an illustration of dominance*

	Event	
Gamble	E_1	E_2
g_1	2	3
g_2	2	6
g_3	3	5
g_4	6	4
g_5	7	3
g_6	1	1

Note: The outcomes in the payoff matrix are the conditional values of the respective gambles, e.g., $CV_2(g_3) = \$5$.

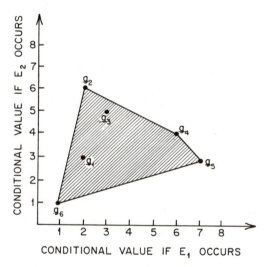

Figure 11.1 Conditional values of six gambles.

with a finite number of events and real-valued outcomes of each, we write

$$EV(\mathbf{g}) = \sum_{i=1}^{n} p_i CV_i(\mathbf{g}),\tag{11.1}$$

where p_i is the probability of the ith event and CV_i the conditional value the decision maker will obtain if that event occurs. We call that the ith conditional value of gamble **g.**

Table 11.1 presents 6 two-event gambles for small dollar amounts in the form of a payoff matrix. In this case these are the conditional values. Figure 11.1 shows the plots of the 6 gambles as points in the two-dimensional space of conditional values.

Inspect Table 11.1. First, gamble 6 is hopelessly unattractive; it is ordinally dominated by all the other gambles. That is, no matter what happens, you will be better off choosing any gamble other than gamble 6. Next, compare gamble 4 with gamble 1. Clearly, gamble 4 is dominant. Similarly, gamble 1 is dominated by gambles 2, 3, and 5. Note that in the comparisons between gamble 1 and gambles 2 and 5, the conditional values are equal if one of the two events occurs and definitely better if the other occurs. This still means that gambles 2 and 5 ordinally dominate gamble 1.

Among our survivors, gambles 2, 3, 4, and 5, gamble 3 is a special case. It is not ordinally dominated, yet it cannot ever be best. Why? This is easier to understand if we look at Figure 11.1. The line that connects gamble 2 with gamble 4 can be interpreted as the locus of various gambles that could be constructed by offering gamble 2 with some probability, otherwise gamble 4. Some subset of these more complex gambles constructed out of gambles 2 and 4 ordinally dominates gamble 3. Consequently, we say that gamble 3 is cardinally dominated (by a probability mixture of gambles 2 and 4). This kind of dominance is called cardinal rather than ordinal because it depends on the measures on the x and y axes of Figure 11.1. We could construct a weird distortion of those axes that would preserve their order properties but would remove the dominance of gamble 3. However, since we regard the scales on those axes as meaningful, we consider a cardinally dominated gamble to be just as prime a candidate for omission as an ordinally dominated gamble.

The more technically oriented reader will want a bit of mathematical argument to back the words of the preceding paragraph. Let q be the probability of obtaining gamble 2, and $1 - q$ be the probability of obtaining gamble 4. Call the new gamble $\mathbf{g}_3'$. Then

$$EV(\mathbf{g}_3') = qEV(\mathbf{g}_2) + (1 - q)EV(\mathbf{g}_4). \tag{11.2}$$

If p and $1 - p$ are the probabilities of the two events, then we can rewrite Equation 11.2 as

$$EV(\mathbf{g}_3') = q[pCV_1(\mathbf{g}_2) + (1 - p)CV_2(\mathbf{g}_2)] \\ + (1 - q)[pCV_1(\mathbf{g}_4) + (1 - p)CV_2(\mathbf{g}_4)], \tag{11.3}$$

which is equal to

$$EV(\mathbf{g}_3') = p[qCV_1(\mathbf{g}_2) + (1 - q)CV_1(\mathbf{g}_4)] \\ + (1 - p)[qCV_2(\mathbf{g}_2) + (1 - q)CV_2(\mathbf{g}_4)]. \tag{11.4}$$

Inspect the terms inside the brackets of Equation 11.4. The first bracket contains a probability mixture of two conditional values if event 1 occurs and so will itself be a conditional value, conditional on the occurrence of event 1, that lies somewhere between them. The same is true for the second bracket, except that it refers to event 2. Thus, gamble $\mathbf{g}_3'$ has conditional values that ensure that it will lie somewhere on the line connecting the conditional values of gambles $\mathbf{g}_2$ and $\mathbf{g}_4$, and an appropriate choice of q will ensure that it ordinally dominates gamble $\mathbf{g}_3$.

Making generalizations to any finite number of events and of gambles is straightforward.

Definition: ordinal dominance (gambles)

A gamble $\mathbf{g}$ is called ordinally dominated by another gamble $\mathbf{f}$ if the conditional value of $\mathbf{f}$ is at least as good as that of $\mathbf{g}$ for every event and is definitely better for at least one event.

To define cardinal dominance, we must first introduce the idea of q mixtures, which we have already illustrated. A q mixture of m gambles is a gamble that has outcomes defined by the q mixture of the conditional values of the original gambles. In other words, the conditional values of a mixture $\mathbf{g}_q$ are

$$CV_i(\mathbf{g}_q) = \sum_{j=1}^{m} q_j CV_{ij}(\mathbf{g}_j). \qquad (11.5)$$

The conditional value vectors of q mixtures must lie in the area defined by the convex boundary of the original set of gambles. In Figure 11.1 the set of all possible conditional values of q mixtures is indicated by the shaded area.

Definition: cardinal dominance (gambles)

A gamble $\mathbf{g}$ is called cardinally dominated if a q mixture of gambles exists that ordinally dominates $\mathbf{g}$. This means that, in Figure 11.1 and its multidimensional equivalents, all gambles that do not lie on the northeast boundary of the figure are either ordinally or cardinally dominated.

Gambles that are not dominated either ordinally or cardinally are called admissible. A fancier name for that northeast boundary and its higher dimensional equivalents is the Pareto frontier. The Pareto frontier is always convex; this simply means that any line, plane, or hyperplane tangent to it at any point cannot cut into it at some other point. Look at Figure 11.1 and then, for the three-dimensional version of the same idea, think of a tennis ball on a plate.

Dominance among multiattributed options

The term *conditional values* applies less obviously to multiattribute utilities than to gambles, since the outcomes are not explicitly conceived of as conditional on anything. But the idea that one could always decompose a value tree into lower levels than the one at which the tree stops amounts to the same thing. Simply replace values conditional on an event by values conditional on an attribute or objective, and replace the probabilities (p_i's) by weights (w_i's).

Given that understanding, it should be apparent that the identity of formal structure between gambles and MAUT structures ensures that the arguments we made about gambles applies to multiattribute utilities also. The notions of ordinal and cardinal dominance are the same, and the argument that dominated options do not deserve consideration is also the same.

Higher level dominance

We already introduced the idea of higher level dominance without calling it that when we created a mixture of gambles to define cardinal dominance by means of ordinal dominance of a new gamble created as a probability mixture of two gambles from an original set. The idea has much more general application.

The easiest way of understanding higher level dominance is to consider how SEU or multiattribute utility leads to choice. After all values and weights or probabilities have been aggregated, the result is a set of numbers, one for each option. One of those numbers is the highest – that is, it dominates all the others (unless there happens to be a tie).

By *subaggregation* we mean aggregation to some level of a value or a decision tree that is intermediate between left and right (decision trees) or between top and bottom (value trees). It should be intuitively obvious, and is the case, that subaggregation can produce dominance among previously undominated options. Consider the choice between $10 for sure and a two-stage gamble. If you take the gamble, you flip a coin. If it comes up heads, you win $6. If it comes up tails, you flip it again. On the second flip, heads wins you $2 and tails wins you $16. The gamble is not dominated, since you can win more than $10 by taking it. But if you subaggregate by replacing the second flip with its EV, the payoffs for the first flip become $6 and $9, and the gamble is dominated by the sure thing. Exactly the same kind of dominance as a result of subaggregation can occur in MAUT problems. Note that, in both contexts, dominance resulting from subaggregation is tentative in the sense that it depends on probabilities or weights below the level to which you have subaggregated. In the example, if the probability of winning that $16 were high enough once you got to the second random event, the gamble would be better than the sure thing. To be precise, the break-even probability at which an EV maximizer would be indifferent between the sure thing and the gamble would be 1/7 for heads and 6/7 for tails on the second flip. You may recall that exactly this kind of reasoning was used in Chapter 2 for pruning von Winterfeldt's decision tree concerning whether to sue.

The most common applications of higher level dominance that we are familiar with come in pruning trees. Another important class of application is to sensitivity analysis and is explained at length in Section 11.3.

Table 11.2. *Examples of decision functions*

Decision function $\tilde{\mathbf{d}}$	
	$\begin{aligned}\tilde{\mathbf{d}}(x_1) &= \mathbf{g}_1 = \\ \tilde{\mathbf{d}}(x_2) &= \mathbf{g}_4 = \end{aligned}$ $\begin{array}{cc} E_1 & E_2 \\ \left[\begin{array}{cc} \$2 & \$3 \\ \$6 & \$4 \end{array}\right] \end{array}$
Decision function $\tilde{\mathbf{e}}$	
	$\begin{aligned}\tilde{\mathbf{e}}(x_1) &= \mathbf{g}_6 = \\ \tilde{\mathbf{e}}(x_2) &= \mathbf{g}_3 = \end{aligned}$ $\begin{array}{cc} E_1 & E_2 \\ \left[\begin{array}{cc} \$1 & \$1 \\ \$3 & \$5 \end{array}\right] \end{array}$
Decision function $\tilde{\mathbf{f}}$	
	$\begin{aligned}\tilde{\mathbf{f}}(x_1) &= \mathbf{g}_5 = \\ \tilde{\mathbf{f}}(x_2) &= \mathbf{g}_2 = \end{aligned}$ $\begin{array}{cc} E_1 & E_2 \\ \left[\begin{array}{cc} \$7 & \$3 \\ \$2 & \$6 \end{array}\right] \end{array}$

Higher level dominance has subtleties in contexts that include the possibility of purchasing information. The basic idea is that you may know the conditional distributions of the outcomes of the information purchase well but may not know the prior probabilities of the hypotheses on which these conditional distributions depend nearly so well. In such cases, it can be useful to average out the uncertainty about the information variable and subsequently to plot and look at conditional values in order to decide whether to buy the information.

We define a *decision function* as a rule that assigns an action (gamble) to each state of information. Formally, a decision function is a map from the information variables into the set of gambles whose outcomes depend on events or hypotheses that the information variable bears on. If the information variable x can take on a finite number K of possible values, then for each x_k a decision function defines a $\tilde{\mathbf{d}}(x_k) \in G$, where G is the set of gambles. If G is also finite, one can summarize a decision function simply by listing for each x_k the gamble that should be taken. Since each gamble is a vector of outcomes, conditional on the n possible events, a decision function can be expressed as a matrix of outcomes.

To illustrate these concepts, consider our introductory example of choosing one of the six gambles shown in payoff matrix form in Table 11.1. Let us assume that before choosing one of the gambles we can make an observation X that can take on two values, x_1 and x_2. We can construct decision functions by assigning for each x_k one of the six gambles. For example, one function would be "Pick $\mathbf{g}_1$ if x_1 occurs, $\mathbf{g}_2$ if x_2 occurs." Obviously, the original gambles are decision functions, since one definable function is to choose the same gamble no matter which information state obtains.

Table 11.2 gives some examples of such decision functions. Each function is represented as a 2×2 matrix with row vectors representing gambles.

Altogether we can create 6^2 decision functions. In the general case of K information states and m gambles, the total number of possible decision functions is m^K.

Some decision functions are obviously inferior to others. In particular, one would expect the constant decision function $\tilde{\mathbf{d}}(x_1) = \mathbf{g}_6$ and $\tilde{\mathbf{d}}(x_2) = \mathbf{g}_6$ to be dominated. To get a better handle on the dominance among decision strategies, we can "average out" the uncertainty about the occurrence of the information variable for each of the two events separately. Let $P(x_k | E_i)$ be the conditional probabilities of the information variable, and let d_{ij} be the outcome to be obtained when decision function $\tilde{\mathbf{d}}$ is chosen and event E_i obtains. The conditional values of the decision function $\tilde{\mathbf{d}}$ are then defined as

$$CV_i(\tilde{\mathbf{d}}) = \sum_{k=1}^{K} P(x_k | E_i) d_{ij}. \tag{11.6}$$

Of course, the EV of a decision function $\tilde{\mathbf{d}}$ would be

$$EV(\tilde{\mathbf{d}}) = \sum_{i=1}^{n} p_i CV_i(\tilde{\mathbf{d}}). \tag{11.7}$$

In order to calculate the conditional values of decision functions, one must know the conditional probabilities in Equation 11.6. In our example, we assume

$$P(x_1 | E_1) = 2/3,$$
$$P(x_1 | E_2) = 1/3,$$
$$P(x_2 | E_1) = 1/3,$$
$$P(x_2 | E_2) = 2/3.$$

Figure 11.2 shows the conditional value vectors for the 36 possible decision functions in this example problem.

It is instructive to compare Figures 11.1 and 11.2. The circled points in Figure 11.2 represent the points of the conditional values of the original gambles generated by choosing a gamble $\mathbf{g}_j$ regardless of whether x_1 or x_2 occurs. The original gambles lie within the convex mixture of the conditional value vectors of the decision functions. This should be true in general, since costless information should improve the decision maker's ability to make a wise choise. In this context, we conclude that *gambles* that ignore costless information can never dominate decision functions that do use costless information, but the converse frequently occurs. For example, the originally admissible gamble $\mathbf{g}_4$ becomes inadmissible among decision functions. In fact, only five decision functions are admissible. These are listed in Table 11.3, together with their conditional values.

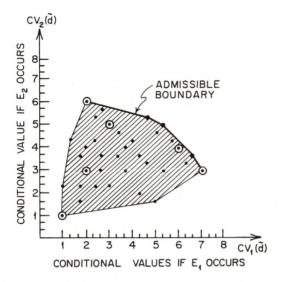

Figure 11.2. Conditional values of decision functions. (Circled points: the original gambles.)

Table 11.3. *Admissible decision functions and their conditional values in the example problem*

$$\tilde{d}_1 = \begin{bmatrix} 2 & 6 \\ 2 & 6 \end{bmatrix} \qquad CV_1(\tilde{d}_1) = 2; \qquad CV_2(\tilde{d}_1) = 6$$

$$\tilde{d}_2 = \begin{bmatrix} 2 & 6 \\ 6 & 4 \end{bmatrix} \qquad CV_1(\tilde{d}_1) = 8/3; \qquad CV_2(\tilde{d}_2) = 16/3$$

$$\tilde{d}_3 = \begin{bmatrix} 2 & 6 \\ 7 & 4 \end{bmatrix} \qquad CV_1(\tilde{d}_3) = 16/3; \qquad CV_2(\tilde{d}_3) = 5$$

$$\tilde{d}_4 = \begin{bmatrix} 6 & 4 \\ 7 & 3 \end{bmatrix} \qquad CV_1(\tilde{d}_4) = 20/3; \qquad CV_2(\tilde{d}_4) = 11/3$$

$$\tilde{d}_5 = \begin{bmatrix} 7 & 3 \\ 7 & 3 \end{bmatrix} \qquad CV_1(\tilde{d}_5) = 7; \qquad CV_2(\tilde{d}_5) = 3$$

(with E_1 E_2 column labels above the matrices)

Analysis and elimination of decision functions can now proceed as in the usual dominance analysis. Again, we should point out that this higher level dominance analysis depends on the veridicality of the inputs, in particular the conditional probabilities of the information variable.

The problem of multiple winners: the k/N paradigm

This discussion of dominance would be incomplete if there were no mention of an important case in which a simple dominance analysis fails. In all of the previous examples the task was to pick a single best option from a set of N candidates. In many contexts, that is exactly the problem, and in such contexts the above concepts of dominance apply and are useful for eliminating inferior options.

However, in some decision contexts, the task is not to pick a single option but to pick the best subset of k options out of a set of N candidates. For example, when reviewing candidates for graduate school, an admissions committee may have to pick the best five, perhaps with enough flexibility to consider only four if the overall quality of the applicants is not very good or six if the quality is exceptional. Simple dominance considerations fail in this paradigm, because after the first candidate is selected, the dominance picture can change dramatically.

The problem of the k/N paradigm, as we have called it, is to find a definition of admissibility that is equivalent to the definition in the $k = 1$ situation and thereby to generalize the concept of dominance. This turns out to be relatively tricky, both mathematically and computationally. But an idea is helpful. We can usually identify sure winners, contenders, and sure losers. Sure winners are the k/N equivalent of the dominating option, if it exists. Sure losers are the k/N equivalent of the dominated options. Contenders are those that might or might not be among the k selected members, depending on weights or (in the case of gambles) sets of probabilities.

We shall return to the k/N problem in our discussion of correlational analyses of flat maxima later in this chapter.

Eliminating dominance and inventing nondominated options

How to use dominance concepts should be obvious: simply check the dominance concepts and eliminate dominated options. Ordinal dominance can usually be detected by an inspection of payoff matrices or matrices of alternatives by objectives. Cardinal dominance can be visually detected only in the two-event or two-attribute case. Computer programs exist for detecting and eliminating cardinally dominated options, and both the theory and practice of such elimination procedures are rapidly progressing. Detecting and eliminating higher level dominance is a much trickier issue because it involves judgment about appropriate levels of subaggregation. In general, we suspect that the rules for subaggregating are dictated largely by the structure of the problem and the analyst's belief in the numbers entering the subaggregation process.

Dominance analysis can be used not only for eliminating options but also for generating new undominated options. One of the most creative tasks of decision analysis is to "push out" the Pareto frontier – to invent options that render previous options ordinally or cardinally dominated.

Cameron Peterson and his associates at Decisions and Designs, Inc., have developed a simple and ingenious approach to using the notion of a Pareto frontier and the additive MAUT model to refine options in certain design tasks. The procedure is very imaginatively packaged. A special conference room combines a whiteboard with rear-projection capabilities under computer control. The procedure requires two analysts (one to interact with respondents and one to operate a computer console), a group of 6 to 12 representatives of the client organization, and a computer program called DESIGN.

Suppose you and your team are considering alternative design options for a new sports car. You are at an early stage in the design process; your goal is to select a few options for detailed and costly exploration. You are, of course, concerned about costs and benefits, both of which are multiattributed. Attributes of benefit include styling, power and acceleration, handling and cornering, braking, interior space, interior comfort and luxury, and ease of access and other aspects of maintainability. Cost dimensions include design costs, assembly-line setup costs, costs of new machine tools, material costs per car, labor costs per car, purchase cost per car for parts bought from outside vendors, and warranty and dealer support costs.

The first step in the analysis consists of defining and reaching agreement on cost and benefit dimensions. We assume that this has been done and that the list in the preceding paragraph reports the result. (This usually takes about half a day.) The next step is to define the best and worst levels on each benefit dimension. For interior comfort and luxury, for example, the gold-plated best level might include leather-covered, fully adjustable power seats; a dashboard full of exotic displays, including perhaps a heads-up display of speed, voice annunciators for low gas, keys left in the ignition, and so on; an AM–FM radio with automatic cassette storage and changing, signal-seeking, and cassette-recording capabilities. The stripped-down worst level might include vinyl-covered seats with only manual front–back and back support angle adjustments, minimal dashboard displays with a maximum of idiot lights instead of gauges, and no standard-equipment radio. Between the best and worst levels, several (typically three) intermediate levels are chosen. A score of 100 is assigned to the gold-plated level and a score of 0 to the minimal level; intermediate levels are scored by reference to these anchors. A dollar cost on each dimension of cost is assigned to reach each level of each benefit dimension; these judgments are typically very crude. In this example, the assignment of dollar costs would require an assumed production volume. These steps are carried out for each benefit dimension. Finally, the benefit dimensions are weighted, using an additive model and a SMART procedure like ratio weighting or swing weighting.

This example has seven benefit dimensions. Assume each has five levels.

Then one might consider $5^7 = 78,125$ different designs. Of these, perhaps 10 will lie on the cost–benefit Pareto frontier; the others will be dominated. Once the benefit–cost structure has been entered into the computer, the DESIGN program indicates which options lie on the Pareto frontier, calculates that frontier, and displays it in a plot of aggregate benefit versus aggregate cost – all in a few minutes. The DESIGN program does not reverse the ordering of the cost dimension, as we have done in this book. Since it plots increasing benefit against increasing cost, in its display northwest is best.

The shape of the benefit versus cost plot is very important. If it is more or less linear, it tells you that you get what you pay for. But if, as is often the case, it is quite nonlinear, it tells you that some design variables contribute a great deal to benefit but not so much to cost and consequently that you can do a sophisticated designing job by gold-plating the relatively cheap design variables while economizing on the costly ones. An optimal design will be near the point of maximum curvature of the Pareto frontier, where you have gotten about as much cheap benefit as you can and further increments in benefit are becoming disproportionately costly.

Typically, the design team has thought about its problem and has some design options in mind. The next step is to elicit them, enter them into the DESIGN program, and find out where they fall in benefit–cost space. Typically they do *not* lie on the Pareto frontier. In that case, the program can usually select two dominating options to compare with a team-specified option: one that gives more benefit for the same cost and one that gives the same benefit for less cost. It then displays what they are.

This typically leads to rethinking of the benefit and cost dimensions and display of the judgments made about each level and the weights. The process iterates until the design team is satisfied with its crude benefit–cost structure. At that point, a few options on the Pareto frontier are selected for more careful study.

This whole process can typically be completed in 2 days and costs about $10,000 plus the time of the design team participants. It is very crude and makes strong assumptions. For example, it treats all 78,125 options as feasible – obviously untrue. But those issues are relevant to detailed evaluation of a very small option set rather than to initial design thinking. Decisions and Designs, Inc., has been very successful in marketing this procedure, because the insights it produces come quickly and the procedure is very cost effective.

This procedure nicely illustrates the features that, we think, characterize sensitivity analysis for the client. It is strongly decision related; the concept of a Pareto frontier is relevant only to decision making. It is transparent and simple, easy for the client to understand. It exploits the client's expertise and judgmental abilities. The functions of the analyst are to design the procedure, which requires such technical skills as knowing about dominance and

Pareto frontiers, to package the implementation, to elicit the cost and benefit dimensions and levels on each from the client, and to help the client interpret and understand the result.

11.3. Ideas for sensitivity analysis

Elimination by dominance and creation of new options by DESIGN or similar methods typically go a long way in clarifying a decision problem, perhaps even producing an obvious winner. But in many cases even a careful dominance analysis leaves a tough choice among nondominated options. This is when the analyst begins a process that some irreverently call "wiggling numbers," others call sensitivity analysis.

Ideas for the analyst

Unfortunately, sensitivity analysis is still a craft, not a science. In the course of thinking about it, we are able to uncover only three general principles.

By far the most important is that of flat maxima, which is intimately linked to the concept of dominance. In short, the flat-maximum principle says that after ordinally and cardinally dominated options are eliminated medium-sized errors in probabilities, weights, or utilities do not produce very large changes in expected or multiattribute utilities. Three intuitive arguments make sense of the rather technical material with which we will back this assertion in later sections of this chapter. The first is that elimination by dominance leaves only options that score quite well in aggregate utilities. According to the second argument decisions are often a close call, exactly because their utilities are not far apart. The third argument points to the fact that EV, SEU, and multiattribute utility are linear averages, and many take averages of averages. Averaging is a flattening operation, and averages of averages flatten aggregate utilities even more. Thus, one would not expect dramatic variability among the outputs of an expected value or MAUT model.

But even if utility, SEU, and multiattribute utility are relatively insensitive to medium changes in the model parameters, the best option produced by the analysis may not be. Small numerical changes in weights can sometimes produce quite surprising switches among preferred options. In this case the second idea of sensitivity analysis helps one to gain insights: the idea of switchover or break-even points. In a break-even analysis two or more options are equated in overall utility, and solutions are found for the parameters (weights, probabilities) for which equality holds. The point at which the parameters produce the break-even utility is called a switchover, since on one side of it the model would choose one option, on the other side another option.

Sometimes it is possible to find switchovers with more direct analytic tools, and sometimes you must tediously grind them out; in the latter case, computers are very helpful. But by either technique, what you normally look for is a change in the ordering of options.

Switchovers are important because they guide further modeling and elicitation. If the circumstances of the problem imply that both the analysis and the parameters you are using are remote from switchover points, you can be confident of your conclusions. If not, you will have to look carefully at models and numbers to see which side of the switchover you are on.

Most sensitivity analyses are one-dimensional; that is, they vary one parameter at a time. Two-dimensional sensitivity analyses are computationally complex and seldom add much more insight. We cannot recall having seen a sensitivity analysis that varied more than two dimensions, though obviously such an analysis would be computationally feasible. The reason is simply that the goal is insight, and more complex arithmetic does not often lead to insight. Computation designed to fine-tune many parameters at once in order to optimize a complex process with a well-understood mathematical structure is often done – but seldom by decision analysts.

We have already presented the third interesting idea, which is less general: subaggregation and higher level dominance. Eliminations based on higher level dominance are always conditional in the sense that the underlying structure and numbers entering the subaggregation control the ordering. Any change in the underlying structure might lead to the restoration of an option to contender status. But as long as the structure underneath the aggregation remains intact, only options that survive the higher level dominance analysis require further analysis. The same kind of upper level dominance can occur at any level of a decision or value tree and always leads to analytic simplification. Moreover, it can contribute insights into the problem. If upper level dominance eliminates an option and the elimination is strongly counterintuitive, that fact should invite the analyst to explore the possibility that the lower level structure needs to be changed. Perhaps an attribute has been left out, or a set of lower level weights is inappropriate. Or perhaps the elimination is correct, and only the reduced option set requires further sensitivity analysis. In that case, attributes that discriminated among options no longer in contention may not discriminate among the remaining ones and so can also be eliminated. We know of few instances in which these ideas have been applied but think they have considerable potential in evaluation problems.

Ideas for the client

Analysts, not clients, do sensitivity analyses; so the problem for the analyst is to communicate any insights thus acquired to the client. The most important way of doing so is to suppress the details of the analysis and focus on its decision implications. How this is done will depend on the nature of the problem itself. Many client-focused computer programs in sensitivity analysis vary parameters one at a time and use stars or similar labels to indicate the best options for each parameter value. In this way the switchover points become apparent. The client can take considerable comfort in noting that the switchover points are far from his or her best assessment of the parameter value. If not, the client can try for very careful assessments of key numbers – and the fact that this is a close call can be made more palatable by calculations showing that an error is not costly.

The preceding paragraph reveals a key point about client-focused sensitivity analyses. Clients agonize over numerical judgments, in spite of the analyst's repeated admonitions not to do so. Perhaps the most important function of client-focused sensitivity analysis is to give the client confidence in the robustness of the analysis. In our experience, didactic explanation never helps; only numerical demonstrations of robustness seem to ease the client's anxiety. Consequently, the analyst should be willing to devote considerable ingenuity and time to the task of devising such demonstrations.

If a conclusion turns out to be a close call, the client will be unhappy. But it cannot be helped. The only way to comfort the client in this case is to show that, at least prospectively, the options are essentially equivalent. Numerical demonstrations of that fact, when it is relevant, are helpful.

We now present three examples of the use of switchovers and higher level dominance. Subsequently we shall return to the more theoretical topic of flat maxima.

An investment example

Consider the problem of investing $2,000 either in a limited partnership or in the commodity market. The commodity investment promises a higher than average yield but involves moderate uncertainty. The partnership is basically a gamble, yielding a fivefold return in the case of a favorable development versus a $4,000 loss (the original $2,000 plus an equal amount that you must be willing to put up on demand in order to buy in) in the case of an unfavorable development. This decision problem can be structured in the form of a simple decision tree, as in Figure 11.3. The choice depends on the probabilities of the events and the decision maker's attitude toward taking or avoiding risks.

The structure of Figure 11.3 tells us a great deal. Obviously the key parameter of the problem is $P(+)$, the probability of success in the limited partnership option. If $P(+)$ were high enough, anyone would prefer the partnership to the option investment; if it were low enough, no one would. The fact that we are examining the problem at all suggests that $P(+)$ is somewhere in between. In intermediate range of values of $P(+)$, the limited partnership is a crap shoot; it should appeal only to someone who doesn't mind taking risks. Obviously, assessment of $P(+)$ is the crucial task. One function

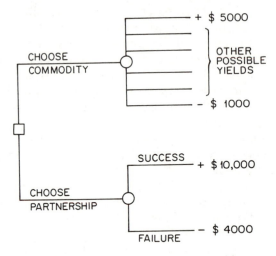

Figure 11.3. Decision tree for an investment problem.

of a sensitivity analysis will be to give numerical precision to these obvious intuitions.

Sensitivity analysis for the analyst

Consider a risk-neutral decision maker first. The EVs of the two alternatives are

$$EV(\text{partnership}) = P(+)(\$10,000) - P(-)(\$4,000) \qquad (11.8)$$

and assuming that $P(+) = 1 - P(-)$,

$$EV(\text{partnership}) = \$14,000P(+) - \$4,000. \qquad (11.9)$$

Assume that the decision makers's uncertainty about the changes in the commodity price can be approximated by a normal probability distribution with mean m and standard deviation s. The EV of the commodity investment is therefore

$$EV(\text{commodity}) = m. \qquad (11.10)$$

Without eliciting probabilities, we can conclude that the decision maker should take the partnership if and only if

$$EV(\text{stock}) > EV(\text{commodity}). \qquad (11.11)$$

The switchover or break-even point occurs when both EVs are identical – in other words, when

$$\$14,000P(+) - \$4,000 = m. \qquad (11.12)$$

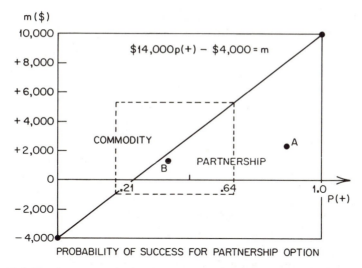

Figure 11.4. Break-even analysis of the investment decision of Figure 11.3.

Equation 11.12 defines a line that divides the $P(+)$–m parameter space into two parts. All points in the upper left part favor the commodity investment, and those in the other favor the partnership (Figure 11.4). Above the break-even line the decision maker should choose the commodity option; below it, the partnership option. For example, if $P(+) = .7$ and $m = 4,000$, the partnership option is preferable to the commodity option.

Even if we do not know $P(+)$ and m, this analysis leads to some interesting observations. First, the decision is independent of the variance of the normal distribution(s). This is, of course, true for a risk-neutral decision maker only. Second, we can restrict our attention to values of $P(+)$ between .21 and .64. These values were derived from Equation 11.12 by substitution of the minimum and maximum values of the gains or losses in the commodity option. At $P(+) = .21$, the partnership option has an EV just equal to the minimum value of the commodity option ($-\$1,000$). For that value and all values below, the decision maker should choose the commodity option. At $P(+) = .64$ the EV of the partnership option is just equal to the maximum value of the commodity option. For that value and all values above, the decision maker should select the partnership option.

Having narrowed the range of values to $.21 < P(+) < .64$ and $-\$1,000 < m < +\$5,000$, the analyst can now ask the decision maker for a *rough* estimate of $P(+)$ and m. If the answer is, for example, $P(+) = .8$ and $m = \$2,000$ (point A in Figure 11.4), no further analysis need precede a recommendation of the partnership option, since point A is outside the critical range of probabilities. However, if the rough assessment leads to $P(+) = .4$ and $m = \$1,500$ (point B in Figure 11.4), the EV is close to the break-even line, and therefore the analyst has to be careful in assessing $P(+)$ and m.

Table 11.4. *Certainty equivalent for the partnership option with P(+) = .5 and several risk-averse utility functions of the form* $u(x) = 1 - e^{-ax}$

a	*CE* ($)
0	3,000
.00002	2,512
.00005	1,799
.0001	727
.0002	−829
.0005	−2,616
.001	−3,325

Though the decision at point *B* is much tougher, the EV of both options are actually very close at *B*. At point *B*, *EV*(partnership) is only $100 higher than *EV*(commodity), while *EV*(partnership) is $5,200 higher at point *A*.

This sensitivity analysis makes the crucial assumption that the decision maker is risk neutral. We now relax that assumption and examine cases in which the decision maker has a risk-averse exponential utility function of the form $u(x) = 1 - e^{-ax}$. To get a feel for the parametric properties of this family of utility functions, we first examine the sensitivity of the partnership option to the parameter *a*. To do this, we study the certainty equivalent of the partnership option when $P(+) = .5$. The certainty equivalent *CE* of a risk-neutral decision maker would be

$$CE(\text{partnership}) = .5(\$10,000) + .5(-\$4,000) \qquad (11.13)$$
$$= \$3,000.$$

The corresponding certainty equivalent for a risk-averse decision maker with a utility function $u(x) = 1 - e^{-ax}$ would be

$$CE(\text{partnership}) = u^{-1}[.5u(\$10,000) + .5u(-\$4,000)]. \qquad (11.14)$$

Since $u^{-1} = -(1/a)\ln(1 - u)$, we have

$$CE(\text{partnership}) = \frac{1}{a}\ln[1 - .5(1 - e^{-10,000a})$$
$$- .5(1 - e^{4,000a})]. \qquad (11.15)$$

Table 11.4 lists the certainty equivalents for selected values of *a*. Tables like this are useful for exploring the implications of parameterized utility functions and for narrowing down the parameters. Using $u(x)$ but without deciding on a precise value of *a* we can perform a break-even analysis by writing out the SEU equation

$$SEU(\text{partnership}) = SEU(\text{commodity}), \qquad (11.16)$$
$$P(+)u(\$10{,}000) + [1 - P(+)]u(-\$4{,}000) = SEU[N(m, s)], \qquad (11.17)$$

where $N(m, s)$ stands for the normal distribution with mean m and standard deviation s. Fortunately, the expected value of the exponential function u with respect to a normal distribution has a simple solution:

$$SEU[N(m, s)] = 1 - e^{-am + a^2 s^2/2}. \qquad (11.18)$$

(See also Keeney and Raiffa, 1976.) We can therefore write out the break-even equation as

$$P(+)[1 - e^{-10,000a}] + [1 - P(+)][1 - e^{4,000a}] = 1 - e^{-am + a^2 s^2/2}. \qquad (11.19)$$

Earlier we analyzed the relationship between m and $P(+)$ to find the break-even points at which the decision maker would switch from the partnership to the commodity investment. We can do the same in the expected utility analysis by solving Equation 11.19 for m:

$$m = \frac{as^2}{2} - \frac{1}{a}\ln[1 - P(+)(1 - e^{-10,000a})$$
$$- [1 - P(+)](1 - e^{4,000a})]. \qquad (11.20)$$

As one would expect, m increases with the standard deviation of the probability distribution over the commodity price. But Equation 11.20 provides an even stronger result: independently of $P(+)$, m increases quadratically with the standard deviation (or linearly with the variance) of the commodity price distribution.

Another interesting result of Equation 11.20 is that, for fixed variance, m is proportional to the certainty equivalent of the partnership investment. This implication can be seen more clearly if 11.20 is written in the compact form

$$m = \frac{a}{2}s^2 + u^{-1}[SEU(\text{partnership})]. \qquad (11.21)$$

To investigate further the sensitivity of s and a, we first fix a at .00005 and examine the function $m = f(p)$ for several values of s. Figure 11.5 shows that the break-even analysis for a somewhat risk averse decision maker is not fundamentally different from that for a risk-neutral decision maker. More important, it indicates that the change in the break-even point produced by changes in the standard deviation of the commodity yield distribution is actually rather small. Therefore, s is not a very sensitive parameter of the decision problem.

Next, let us examine the sensitivity of a. Figure 11.6 shows the break-even curves for $a = 0$, $a = .00005$, and $a = .0002$ for a fixed s of 1,000.

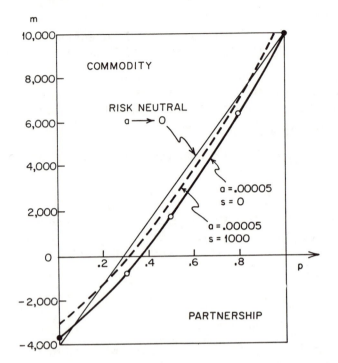

Figure 11.5. Break-even analyses for three variances of yields of the commodity option.

Break-even curves for other variances will lie parallel to these curves shifted upward if the variance is higher, downward if it is lower. It appears from Figure 11.6 that risk aversion is a sensitive parameter in determining break-even points. For example, at $P(+) = .5$ the partnership gamble seems very attractive for a risk-neutral subject. However, for a highly risk averse subject ($a = .0002$), the commodity option is still preferable at that probability. In fact, if the risk aversion gets even stronger (e.g., $a = .001$) the decision maker should *never* take the partnership option.

So far we have analyzed the influence of the variance s^2 and the risk aversion parameter a separately. However, they interact, as Equation 11.20 shows. If both the risk aversion parameter and the variance become relatively large, the break-even curve can shift substantially. For example, if $a = .001$ and $s = \$2,000$, $c = as^2/2 = 2,000$, and therefore the shift of the break-even curve can be much more noticeable than in the previous examples. However, for "reasonable" levels of risk aversion ($a < .0002$) and medium or small s ($<\$1,000$), the decision will remain insensitive to s.

Having performed a sensitivity analysis on the investment problem, we can now present some conclusions to the decision maker, even without fur-

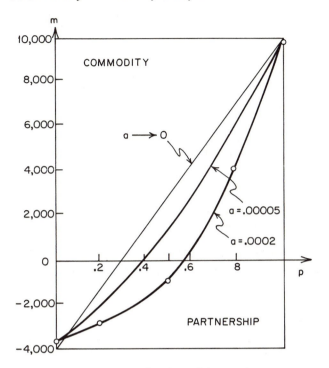

Figure 11.6. Break-even analyses for three risk aversion parameters.

ther eliciting *a*, *P*(+), *m*, or *s*:

1   For risk-neutral decision makers, the partnership option is attractive if it
        has a reasonable chance of being successful (2/3 and above) *and* the com-
        modity venture has a relatively modest expected yield ($3,000 and below).
2   Risk aversion tends to favor the commodity venture. Highly risk averse
        decision makers should enter the partnership only if the probability of suc-
        cess is very high (.8 and above) and the expected gain of the commodity
        venture is relatively modest ($3,000 and below).
3   The uncertainty about the partnership option matters more than the uncer-
        tainty about the commodity yield, unless the decision maker is very risk
        averse *and* the variance of the commodity yield distribution is very large.
        It is therefore more important to elicit precise information about *P*(+) than
        to elicit the variances precisely.

Sensitivity analysis for the client

Now the analyst, understanding the problem well, must find a convenient
way of presenting these conclusions to the client. The appropriate format
will depend on what the analyst knows about the client's risk attitudes and
ability to understand the results. The simplest display of the conclusions

Table 11.5. *Recommendations from sensitivity analysis for selected parameters and risk aversion*

Probability of successful partnership venture	Decision maker's risk attitude	Return expected from commodity[a]		
		0	$2,000	$4,000
.25	Risk neutral	?	C	C
	Risk averse	C	C	C
	Very risk averse	C	C	C
.50	Risk neutral	P	P	P
	Risk averse	P	?	C
	Very risk averse	C	C	C
.75	Risk neutral	P	P	P
	Risk averse	P	P	?
	Very risk averse	P	?	C

[a] C, Commodity; P, partnership; ?, too close to call.

would be Table 11.5, although it would perhaps be too simple for some clients.

For a somewhat more sophisticated client or one willing to think harder about the problem, the same basic structure could be used, but the recommendations in the table could be replaced by numbers representing the SEU difference between the two options. This display would have two advantages over Table 11.5: it would help the client assess the robustness of each decision, and it would allow the client to consider how he or she feels about making a risky $2,000 investment. If the client's assessments of $P(+)$ and m are close enough to one another to make the issue important, the analyst might want to raise the issue explicitly with the client. A choice between a limited partnership and a commodity investment implies a well-off client, since both are risky relative to many alternatives. A well-off client may be risk averse about a $2,000 or $4,000 loss. But is that appropriate? Perhaps the client's risk aversion was acquired during an impoverished youth and has little to do with present financial circumstances. Such issues do not fall within the traditional purview of decision analysis. But if the analyst is to help the client make decisions he or she should assist the client in thinking about these matters.

A medical decision-making problem

Moroff and Pauker (1983) reported a sophisticated and elaborate sensitivity analysis in a medical decision-making problem.

Their basic analytic tool was the declining exponential approximation of life expectancy (DEALE). This is a technique developed by Pauker and his group (see Beck, Kassirer, and Pauker, 1982; Beck, Pauker, and Gottlieb, 1982) to approximate life expectancy information on the assumption that life expectancy follows a simple declining exponential function – an approximation that works well in many situations. The reason for DEALE's importance is that it provides a clinical decision maker with the utilities needed to make life-or-death decisions. The basic concept is that utility, in life-or-death medical contexts, should be measured by quality-adjusted life years. The adjustments are usually somewhat rudimentary; for example, in this instance they did not take dollar cost into account, but did consider pain and suffering, by subtracting time from life expectancy. Evaluating the utilities of life expectancies should be more complex than that; no one has tried to model the problem in a more general way.

In this instance, the patient was a very healthy 95-year-old man with what his primary physician believed to be cancer of the lung. The options were to perform surgery, to give radiotherapy without verification of the nature of the lesion (a medically unusual procedure), or to administer bronchoscopy and then, if the lesion were diagnosed as cancerous, to perform surgery or radiotherapy or to do nothing. Bronchoscopy was a fairly unattractive option because (1) the prior probability of stage I cancer was .90, and (2) even a negative bronchoscopic examination would have reduced that probability to only .734, mostly because this examination reveals cancer when present in only 70% of cases.

Sensitivity analysis for the analyst

The crucial fact is that a 95-year-old healthy man has a life expectancy of 2.9 years. Consequently, the mortality associated with diagnostic and therapeutic procedures is of great importance. The fundamental conclusion Moroff and Pauker reached was "that radiotherapy would provide a quality-adjusted life expectancy of our patient of 17.5 months, bronchoscopy 14.1 months, surgery 13.5 months, and no treatment 8.5 months. In a person in whom 'normal' life expectancy is just under 35 months, we regard these differences as meaningful" (pp. 326–7).

Figure 11.7 shows the sensitivity analysis for perioperative mortality (i.e., mortality caused by surgery), the baseline figure of which for this patient was .35. Clearly, given the other numbers in the calculation, the decision was not at all a close call between surgery and any other procedure, except bronchoscopy. Bronchoscopy was a close call and did make a difference, since a negative result would have meant the patient would receive no treatment, given baseline numbers.

A particularly dramatic two-way sensitivity analysis is presented in Figure 11.8. It shows the trade-off between surgery and radiotherapy for various annual mortality rates assumed to go with each. It includes two lines, cor-

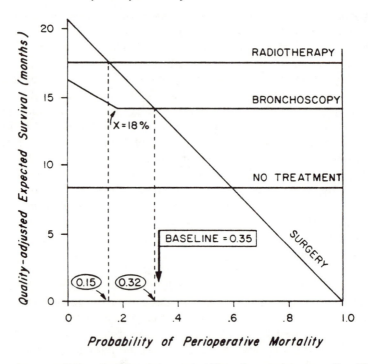

Figure 11.7. Sensitivity analysis of the probability of operative mortality. The dashed vertical lines denote threshold values of 13 and 32%; *X* marks the point above which bronchoscopy, if positive, leads to radiotherapy and below which it leads to surgery. (*Source:* Moroff & Pauker, 1983.)

responding to two different perioperative mortality rates for surgery. The figure shows that the conclusion in favor of radiotherapy over surgery in this case is insensitive to the specific numbers inferred from the review of the medical literature on which Moroff and Pauker based their baseline figures for mortality rates for the two procedures.

These two displays should whet your appetite for the article itself. The general conclusion to which it leads is that a quite unconventional piece of advice (give radiotherapy without prior bronchoscopy; if the radiotherapist refuses, do the bronchoscopy and give radiotherapy if it comes out positive) is clearly appropriate to this admittedly remarkable case. The numerous other sensitivity analyses contained in the article are textbook examples of the way sensitivity analyses for decision trees should be done and presented.

It is worth noting that none of the analyses presented in the article took the patient's attitude toward risk into account. If they had done so, the fact that surgery carries a risk of immediate iatrogenic death while radiotherapy does not could only have reinforced the conclusions already reached.

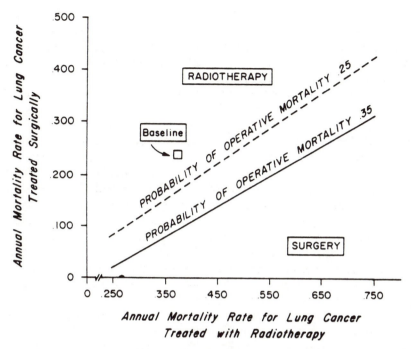

Figure 11.8. Sensitivity analysis of the effect of lung cancer treatment-specific mortality on the decision between surgery and radiotherapy. The solid diagonal line represents the baseline assumption of 35% probability of operative mortality; the dashed line, representing 25% operative mortality, expands the zone for surgery and shrinks that for radiotherapy. (*Source:* Moroff & Pauker, 1983.)

Sensitivity analysis for the patient

Although the computations involved in the DEALE require at least a programmable handheld calculator and a fair understanding of the models, the calculations involved in the decision process itself are extremely simple, depending as they do on five probabilities and five utilities. Indeed, for most purposes two of those probabilities and one of the utilities can be ignored, since the option of bronchoscopic examination is never best, and one of the utilities and two of the probabilities are associated with it.

Consequently, a simple display of the two figures should be adequate as sensitivity analysis for the patient. The conclusion is extremely insensitive to the numbers included in the analysis. Inspection of Figure 11.7 shows that radiotherapy without bronchoscopy is preferable to any option in which bronchoscopy comes first, for the baseline numbers. That conclusion obviously depends strongly both on the prior probability of cancer and on the two probabilities that describe the bronchoscopic test.

A very interesting sensitivity analysis holds the bronchoscopic probabilities constant but varies the age of the patient. This shows that, for the given input probabilities (adjusted where appropriate for age change) and for ages 56 and above, bronchoscopy is *never* the attractive first step, given this high a prior probability of stage I cancer.

A patient might want to understand why so common a diagnostic procedure would be inappropriate in all such cases – and dramatically so. At least we would. The following numbers would help us, and might help the patient. If cancer were present, we would expect a positive diagnosis from bronchoscopy 70% of the time; if absent, we would expect a positive diagnosis (i.e., that cancer was present) 30% of the time. Given the extreme prior probability of cancer, we would expect with probability $.9(.7) + .1(.3) = .66$ to get a positive result from bronchoscopy followed by radiotherapy. The probability of a negative bronchoscopic examination, and therefore of no treatment, is, of course, .34. But given a negative bronchoscopic examination, the probability of cancer is still .734. So the net result of bronchoscopy would be radiotherapy (needed or not) with probability .66, no radiotherapy but cancer with probability $.34(.734) = .25$, and no radiotherapy and no cancer with probability .09. This set of outcomes compares to the strategy of giving radiotherapy with probability 1, in which case it is appropriate with probability .9 and inappropriate with probability .1. So the decision about bronchoscopy is between a probability of .1 of unnecessary radiotherapy and a probability of .25 of failing to give radiotherapy to a patient with cancer but saving the patient from unnecessary radiotherapy with probability .09. The choice does not seem hard to make.

This is a dramatic instance of the effect of extreme priors and dichotomous tests of fairly weak diagnostic power (see Meehl and Rosen, 1955). We should emphasize that such effects cannot occur if the initial output of the test can be thought of as a continuum of scores, dichotomized by a cut point the location of which reflects prior probabilities, as in signal detectability theory examples. As far as we are aware, bronchoscopy does not fit this description.

A multiattribute example

We return to the Drug-Free Center example of Chapter 8. You may recall that the director of the center had evaluated six sites to which the center might move, using the value tree and weights obtained in Figure 11.9 and the numbers presented in Table 11.6. We pick up the analysis from there.

Sensitivity analysis for the analyst

The first step in the analysis is to note that, on all benefit dimensions except AD, option 6 is dominated by option 2. The director, noting that option 2 is equal to or better than option 6 on all benefit dimensions but one, and

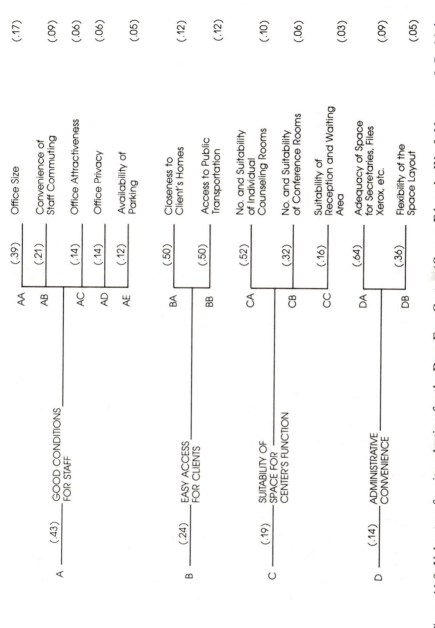

		AA	(.39)	Office Size	(.17)
A	(.43) GOOD CONDITIONS FOR STAFF	AB	(.21)	Convenience of Staff Commuting	(.09)
		AC	(.14)	Office Attractiveness	(.06)
		AD	(.14)	Office Privacy	(.06)
		AE	(.12)	Availability of Parking	(.05)
		BA	(.50)	Closeness to Client's Homes	(.12)
B	(.24) EASY ACCESS FOR CLIENTS	BB	(.50)	Access to Public Transportation	(.12)
		CA	(.52)	No. and Suitability of Individual Counseling Rooms	(.10)
C	(.19) SUITABILITY OF SPACE FOR CENTER'S FUNCTION	CB	(.32)	No. and Suitability of Conference Rooms	(.06)
		CC	(.16)	Suitability of Reception and Waiting Area	(.03)
D	(.14) ADMINISTRATIVE CONVENIENCE	DA	(.64)	Adequacy of Space for Secretaries, Files Xerox, etc.	(.09)
		DB	(.36)	Flexibility of the Space Layout	(.05)

Figure 11.9. Value tree for site selection for the Drug-Free Center. (*Source:* Edwards, W., & Newman, J. R. *Multiattribute evaluation*. Copyright © 1982, Sage Publications, Inc. Adapted by permission of Sage Publications, Inc.)

Table 11.6. *Location measures and costs for six sites*

Attribute label	Site number					
	1	2	3	4	5	6
AA	90	50	10	50	10	40
AB	50	30	100	10	5	30
AC	30	80	70	10	85	80
AD	90	30	40	10	35	50
AE	10	60	30	10	100	50
BA	30	30	0	50	90	30
BB	70	70	95	50	10	70
CA	10	80	5	50	90	50
CB	60	50	10	10	90	50
CC	50	40	50	10	95	30
DA	10	70	50	90	50	60
DB	0	40	50	95	10	40
Rental cost ($)	48,000	53,300	54,600	60,600	67,800	53,200

Source: Adapted from W. Edwards & J. R. Newman, *Multiattribute evaluation.* Copyright © 1982 by Sage Publications, Inc. Reproduced by permission of Sage Publications, Inc.

that that one has a low weight, and costs only $100 per year rental more than option 6, might well make an informal decision to eliminate option 6 at this point. (We will keep it to show that it will be dropped later because it is cardinally, though not ordinally, dominated after subaggregation). No other options are dominated on the benefit dimensions.

Table 11.6 is inconveniently complex. Moreover, it is unlikely that the weight judgments at lower levels of the value tree deserve to be included in the sensitivity analysis. Since they are at lower levels, changing them would have only minor effects on aggregate conclusions. Important sensitivities to weights arise at higher levels of the tree. A useful simplifying procedure is to aggregate to those levels. Table 11.7 shows the result.

Inspection of Table 11.7 shows that option 3 is now dominated by option 2. Option 6 is dominated by option 2 on all dimensions but cost. Option 3 should be eliminated from further consideration. Moreover, once option 3 is eliminated, dimension B becomes completely nondiscriminating. Of course, that fact was carefully contrived by appropriate selection of the original values and would never happen precisely in a real problem. But the amount of variability on a dimension could easily be so small that varying the weight of the dimension in a sensitivity analysis would be pointless.

With respect to benefits, using these weights, the options are ordered 256143. With respect to costs, they are ordered 162345. Options 3, 4, and 5 are ordinally dominated by option 2, and only the decision among options

Table 11.7. *Subaggregated utilities and costs*

Attribute label	Site number					
	1	2	3	4	5	6
A (.43)	63.6	48.4	43.9	25.6	33.8	46.1
B (.24)	50.0	50.0	47.5	50.0	50.0	50.0
C (.19)	32.4	64.0	13.8	30.8	90.8	46.8
D (.14)	6.4	59.2	50.0	91.8	35.6	52.8
Aggregate benefit (utility)	46.40	53.26	39.90	41.71	48.77	48.11
Rental cost ($)	48,000	53,300	54,600	60,600	67,800	53,200
Transformed rental cost	100	73	67	36	0	74

Source: Adapted from W. Edwards & J. R. Newman, *Multiattribute evaluation.* Copyright © 1982 by Sage Publications, Inc. Reproduced by permission of Sage Publications, Inc.

Table 11.8. *Ranges over subaggregated attributes*

Attribute label	Ranges on attributes		
	Best option	Worst option	Range
A	1(63.6)	4(25.6)	38
B	—	—	0
C	5(90.8)	4(30.8)	60
D	4(91.8)	1(6.4)	85.4
Cost	1(100)	5(0)	100

Source: Adapted from W. Edwards & J. R. Newman, *Multiattribute evaluation.* Copyright © 1982 by Sage Publications, Inc. Reproduced by permission of Sage Publications, Inc.

1, 2, and 6 need be considered. It is worth noting that option 2, not best on any of the benefit dimensions, looks like the probable winner.

The last line of Table 11.7, labeled "Transformed rental cost," is simply a linear transformation on the annual rentals, obtained by defining a rental of $48,000 as 100 and a rental of $67,800 as 0 and finding the appropriate values for intermediate rentals.

It is useful to look at best sites, worst sites, and attribute range for the top-level attributes (Table 11.8). Table 11.8 shows some interesting things. Option 1 is best on both A and transformed cost. It will be a formidable contender, cannot be dominated, and will win for high weights on A. A change in the weight on D will have the greatest effect on reordering sites in benefits, and C comes next. Both sites 4 and 5 are best on a benefit dimension; giving that dimension heavy weight will make them best in benefits. Nothing further can be done until the benefit dimensions are reexamined.

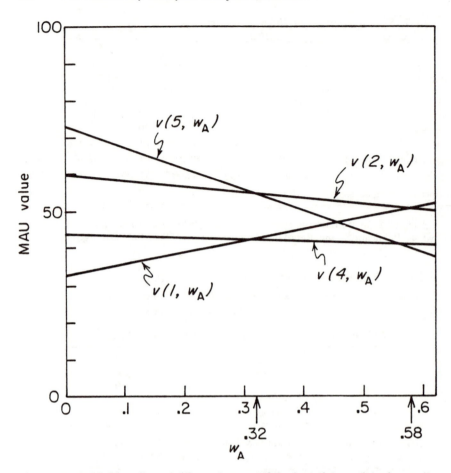

Figure 11.10. Multiattribute utility values as a function of the weight for attribute A, w_A, ignoring costs. The largest value of W_A plotted is .62 because the weights of B and D, held constant in this analysis, sum to .38. The weights .32 and .58 are switch-over points between option 2 and options 5 and 1, respectively. (*Source:* The example, though not this figure, is adapted from Edwards, W., & Newman, J. R. *Multiattribute evaluation.* Copyright © 1982, Sage Publications, Inc. Adapted by permission of Sage Publications, Inc.)

Dimension A is good working conditions for staff, and the director of the center is concerned that the staff weights for those are too high. Dimension C, suitability of the site for its intended functions, seems to her to have been weighted too low. Dimension B is irrelevant. Dimension D, administrative convenience, has been weighted .14, which the Director thinks, at least for a first cut, is high enough, even though varying the weight on D would have the greatest impact on the ordering of options in benefits. A natural sensitivity analysis would consist of varying weights for A and C, holding D con-

Table 11.9. *Aggregated benefit utilities for several weight vectors*

Weight vector	Options				
	1	2	4	5	6
(.3, .24, .32, .14)	42.34	55.29	42.39	56.18	48.20
(.43, .24, .19, .14)	46.4	53.26	41.76	48.77	48.10
(.5, .24, .12, .14)	48.58	52.17	41.35	44.78	48.06
(.6, .24, .02, .14)	51.70	50.61	40.83	39.08	47.99
Rental cost ($)	48,000	53,300	60,600	67,800	53,200

Source: Adapted from W. Edwards & J. R. Newman, *Multiattribute evaluation.* Copyright ©
1982 by Sage Publications, Inc. Reproduced by permission of Sage Publications, Inc.

stant. The effect of a variation such as this can be plotted as a series of lines
showing the multiattribute utility of each site as a function of weight of A.
Figure 11.10 shows such a plot, omitting 3 and 6. It is illuminating. If the
weight of A is below .32, option 5 is best in benefits. If it is between .32 and
.58, option 2 is best. Above .58, option 1 is best. None of these conclusions
takes cost into account. Note that the arithmetic leading to them is a trivial
form of break-even analysis.

The most important conclusion to be drawn from Figure 11.10 is that
option 4 is hopeless. Inspection of Table 11.7 shows that it could be rescued
by considerably increasing the weight on D. Would a sensitivity analysis of
this be worthwhile? Note that option 4 is also relatively high in cost. It
would take a heavy weight indeed on D to make it a winner, given that fact.
Later we explore the issue more carefully. But in a real analysis, it would be
wise at this point to forget option 4.

By now the problem is considerably simplified. Option 2 is balanced
among the values and fairly cheap. Option 5 shines on C and is most expensive. Option 1 shines, though less brilliantly, on A and is cheapest. This is
a very considerable simplification of what was initially a very confusing
problem. Along the way, for several different reasons, we have dropped
options 3, 4, and 6, though we will continue to carry all but 3 for a while,
merely to illustrate points.

Now we prepare to think about cost. Again, we decide to keep weights of
values B and D fixed at .24 and .14, respectively. We explore several values
of the weights on A and C, chosen from what we learned from Figure 11.9.
Table 11.9 shows the resulting aggregate utilities.

For all weight sets, option 4 is dominated by options 2 and 6. It should
have been eliminated long ago. Option 6, though low in benefit utility, is not
ordinally dominated in the first two weight sets but is dominated by option
1 in the last two. Option 6 varies very little in aggregated benefit utility with
these weights. Inspection of Table 11.8 shows why; it varies very little from

Table 11.10. *Increments in utilities and cost (weights: .3, .24, .32, .14)*

Site no.	Utility differences (increment)	Cost differences (increment), $	Cost/ utility, $
1	0	0	—
6	5.86	5,200	887.37
2	7.09	100	14.10
5	.89	14,500	16,292.13

Table 11.11. *Increments in utilities and costs, site 6 removed*

Site no.	Utility differences (increment)	Cost differences (increment), $	Cost/ utility, $
1	0	0	—
2	12.95	5,300	409.27
5	.89	14,500	16,292.13

Source: Adapted from W. Edwards & J. R. Newman, *Multiattribute evaluation.* Copyright © 1982 by Sage Publications, Inc. Reproduced by permission of Sage Publications, Inc.

one dimension of value to the others, and consequently weighting can have only minuscule effects.

In sum, the first set of weights yields options 1, 2, 5, and 6 as ordinally undominated contenders. The second yields 1, 2, and 6. The third yields 1 and 2. The fourth yields only 1. But these conclusions are based only on ordinal dominance. We next show how to eliminate more options by considering cardinal dominance. We illustrate it with the first weight set only. We eliminate option 4, and list the other options in order of increasing utility and cost. If ordinally dominated options are eliminated, all such two-dimensional lists will show perfect agreement in rank ordering of benefit and cost. Next we take successive differences. The result is Table 11.10.

Table 11.10 shows successive differences in utility and in rent and the ratios of these differences. The fact that the ratios of these differences (taken as dollars divided by utilities) do not increase monotonically indicates that the list includes a cardinally dominated option, option 6. Elimination of option 6 produces Table 11.11. Now all options are admissible, and the numbers in the far-right-hand column are interpretable as dollars per utility point at switchover points. That is, if one utility point is worth less than $409.27 to you, you should choose option 1 (with these weights). If it is worth more than \$409.27 but less than \$16,292.13, you should choose option 2. And if it is worth more than \$16,292.13 you should choose option 5. This is another form of break-even analysis.

How can you know the dollar value of a utility point? A way to approach the problem is to go back to the original location measures of Table 11.6. Suppose the director is particularly confident in her knowledge about twig DA: availability and suitability of space for secretaries, files, copying machine, and the like. She can ask herself, "How much rent would you be willing to pay in order to improve that twig from its minimum to its maximum – that is, swing one hundred points?" This might be a fairly clear number, say \$4,500 per year in rent. Referring to Figure 11.9, we find that the weight of twig DA is .09. Consequently, a 100-point swing on DA is a 9-point change in aggregate utility. That judgment, then, implies that utility is worth \$4,500 for 9 points, or \$500 per point. If so, then for this vector, option 2 is obviously best.

What about other weight vectors? Calculations similar to those in Table 11.11 show that for the second weight set the switchover from 1 to 2 comes at \$772.59 per utility point and that for the third weight set it comes at \$1476.32 per utility point. So the preference of option 2 to option 1 is not very robust. Careful assessment of the weights and of the dollar value of a utility point is required to choose between 1 and 2. The rest can be discarded. Fortunately, the director has already concluded that the judgment of the dollar value of a utility point is conservative. Increasing it can only strengthen the case for option 2.

The numbers in the far-right-hand column of Tables 11.10 and 11.11 are the decision-analytic version of the economic cost–benefit (more precisely, incremental cost divided by incremental benefit) ratios. In this application, we used them only to identify which options lie on the Pareto frontier by exploiting the fact that the Pareto frontier is convex.

Sensitivity analysis for the client

This example, adapted from Edwards and Newman (1982), was for the most part designed for hand computation. The authors intended that the example be sufficiently transparent that the distinction between sensitivity analysis for the analyst and sensitivity analysis for the client would disappear. However, those who read the example found it complicated and hard to understand. So we must conclude that, even though the methods are simple, what we have presented so far is a somewhat unfamiliar set of sensitivity analyses for the analyst.

From our point of view, a sensitivity analysis for the client would consist of Figure 11.10 and Tables 11.10 and 11.11, along with an examination of the appropriate trade-off between benefit utility and dollars. For a more complex case in which the cost dimension was multiattributed, we would see no alternative to using transformed costs and aggregating them with the benefits by directly judgmental means.

11.4. Flat maxima in EV models

We stated earlier in this chapter that aggregated or expected utilities are seldom much affected by the precision of the model form or of the input numbers. We have published the mathematical justification for this assertion several times, but not in publications generally available to decision analysts (see von Winterfeldt and Edwards, 1973b, 1975, 1982). Moreover, we have done additional work since then. In this section we both justify the statement and, in the process, describe some procedures an analyst might use to do sensitivity analysis for the analyst, not the client. The material is inevitably rather technical.

Reasons for flat maxima

Three very simple ideas underlie the arguments, which are no more than technical expressions of them. The first idea, central to the topic of sensitivity analysis and introduced at length in this chapter, is that of dominance. By eliminating dominated options the analyst essentially eliminates the risk of choosing a disastrous option. What remains are relatively attractive options, which for various technical mathematical reasons have aggregate or expected utilities that are severely constrained. The mathematical consequences of dominance make it virtually impossible, for example, that inadvertently misjudging a probability to be .4 instead of .5 could produce a loss larger than 10% of the range of possible losses.

The second idea has to do with the properties of decisions themselves. Take a simple example. Consider two bets, both of which depend on the flip of a coin. If you take bet A, you win $1.00 for heads and lose $1.00 for tails. If you take bet B, you win $1.05 for heads and lose $1.01 for tails. We find bet B preferable to bet A – but it is obviously a close call, and it won't make much difference which bet you take. If, however, bet A were the same and bet B paid $100 for heads and resulted in a $50 loss for tails, it wouldn't be a close call at all.

The same is true of much more complicated examples. When decisions are close calls, it makes little difference, at least prospectively, which option you choose. Regret over a "wrong" decision can be substantial, but essentially it is the kind of regret you feel when you bet on the wrong horse. We are all seduced into evaluating decisions after their outcomes are known. But, by definition, every decision made under uncertainty (and we have argued strongly elsewhere in this book that all decisions are made under uncertainty) must be made and evaluated prospectively. In the close-call decision of the preceding paragraph, if the positive payoff in bet A had been for tails, not heads, and you chose B and tails came up, you might feel some regret over your mistake. But that kind of regret is always misplaced.

Almost always, decisions that are not close calls are sufficiently obvious that detailed analysis is unnecessary. This statement, though true, is misleading; surprisingly often it takes analysis to find out that a decision is not a close call.

The third idea has to do with the process of averaging. First, note that all the techniques of decision analysis are really techniques for averaging decision-relevant numbers and then basing decisions on the averages. The EV of a bet is a weighted average of its payoffs; the weights are the probabilities. An additive MAUT structure is formally identical; location measures correspond to the payoffs, and weights correspond to probabilities. Any more complicated MAUT model is similarly an average.

Now, think about the properties of averages. An average combines several quantities and so lies somewhere among them. In that sense, averaging is a flattening operation. Many of the analytic processes inherent in decision analysis include more than one averaging step. Information purchase decisions, for example, involve two. Each successive step makes the function that relates losses to deviations from optimality flatter.

None of this implies that decision analysis cannot help one make better decisions or that choosing appropriate models and numbers is not useful. It just means that the main advantages of decision analysis lie in structuring the problem, finding new options, and sometimes collecting better information rather than in precise measurement. The general strategy of generating the most creative options and using them does much more to improve decision making than the strategy of optimizing performance within the given constraints on options and expertise.

We turn now to technical matters having to do with flat maxima. Those uncomfortable with fairly demanding mathematical reasoning would do well to go on to Section 11.5.

The fact that decision-theoretic maxima are flat has been reported repeatedly in the literature (see, e.g., Green, 1960; Murphy and Winkler, 1970; Rapoport and Burkheimer, 1971; von Winterfeldt and Edwards, 1973b, 1975, 1982), but what follows is a more general treatment.

We first present an example of flat maxima in scoring rules, a topic described in Chapter 4. As it turns out, scoring rules are more than a specific decision-making instance – they are the paradigm for flat maxima. We discuss this paradigm by examining EV changes resulting from the use of incorrect prior probabilities, incorrect decisions, and omitting information sources.

Scoring rules

In Chapter 4 we discussed the concept, form, and uses of scoring rules for probability elicitation. In this section we analyze the penalties in EV that a probability estimator encounters when misrepresenting his or her true probability in a scoring-rule situation. To recapitulate: a scoring rule is any payoff scheme $s(\mathbf{r}, E_i)$ that depends jointly on the vector of *stated* probabilities $\mathbf{r} = (r_1, r_2, \ldots, r_i, \ldots, r_n)$ and the event E_i that actually occurs; with a *proper* scoring rule, the probability estimator maximizes the expected score by stating the true probability vector **p**. In other words, a scoring rule is proper if

$$E[s(\mathbf{r}), \mathbf{p}] = \sum_{i=1}^{n} p_i s(\mathbf{r}, E_i) \leq \sum_{i=1}^{n} p_i s(\mathbf{p}, E_i) = E[s(\mathbf{p}), \mathbf{p}]. \qquad (11.22)$$

A scoring rule is strictly proper if $\leq$ in Equation 11.22 is replaced by $<$.

An ideal scoring rule should strongly reward $\mathbf{p} = \mathbf{r}$ and punish $\mathbf{p} \neq \mathbf{r}$ even for $\mathbf{r}$ in the vicinity of $\mathbf{p}$. As we shall soon find out, such sharp rewarding schemes cannot be created. Consider the simplest case of two mutually exclusive and exhaustive events E_1 and E_2, $\mathbf{r} = [r_1, (1 - r_1)]$; $\mathbf{p} = [p_1, (1 - p_1)]$, and the expected score of $\mathbf{r}$ is

$$E[s(\mathbf{r}), \mathbf{p}] = ps(r, E_1) + (1 - p)s(r, E_2). \qquad (11.23)$$

For convenience, we use the notation

$$E[s(\mathbf{r}), \mathbf{p}] = E(\mathbf{r}, \mathbf{p}) \qquad (11.24)$$

and

$$E[s(\mathbf{p}), \mathbf{p}] = E^*(\mathbf{p}). \qquad (11.25)$$

If s is proper, $E^*(\mathbf{p}) > E(\mathbf{r}, \mathbf{p})$, but by how much? The shape of the function E around its maximum at $\mathbf{r} = \mathbf{p}$ depends not only on the scoring rule s, but also on $\mathbf{p}$. As we shall see, however, E^* as a function of $\mathbf{p}$ tells the whole story about possible losses in EV in scoring-rule problems. Assume that E is bounded (which is true for the spherical and quadratic rules, but *not* for the logarithmic rule). If a scoring rule is strictly proper once E is bounded, it can be shown (von Winterfeldt and Edwards, 1973a) that E^* is convex:

$$E^*[\alpha \mathbf{p} + (1 - \alpha)\mathbf{q}] \leq \alpha E^*(\mathbf{p}) + (1 - \alpha)E^*(\mathbf{q}). \qquad (11.26)$$

The proof is rather simple, and it is presented here because it is important for our later theoretic development.

Consider a strictly proper scoring rule s and an arbitrary true probability vector **t**, which the respondent should state as his or her opinion in order to maximize $E(\mathbf{r}, \mathbf{t})$. Now consider two nonoptimal responses **p** and **q**, which are selected such that **t** can be expressed as a mixture of these two probability vectors, that is, $\mathbf{t} = \alpha \mathbf{p} + (1 - \alpha)\mathbf{q}$.

By definition of strictly proper scoring rules

$$E^*(\mathbf{t}) = \sum_{i=1}^{n} t_i s(\mathbf{t}, E_i)$$

$$= \sum_{i=1}^{n} [\alpha p_i + (1 - \alpha)q_i][s(\mathbf{t}, E_i)] \qquad (11.27)$$

$$= \alpha \sum_{i=1}^{n} p_i s(\mathbf{t}, E_i) + (1 - \alpha) \sum_{i=1}^{n} q_i s(\mathbf{t}, E_i).$$

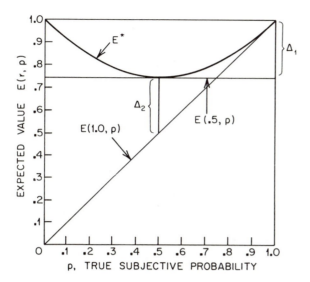

Figure 11.11. Maximum expected value E^* and possible losses in a scoring-rule example.

Again by the definition of a strictly proper scoring rule

$$\sum_{i=1}^{n} p_i s(\mathbf{t}, E_i) = E(\mathbf{t}, \mathbf{p}) < E^*(\mathbf{p}) \tag{11.28}$$

and

$$\sum_{i=1}^{n} q_i s(\mathbf{t}, E_i) = E(\mathbf{t}, \mathbf{q}) < E^*(\mathbf{q}). \tag{11.29}$$

Substituting $E^*(\mathbf{p})$ and $E^*(\mathbf{q})$ into Equation 11.27 therefore should increase the last term of that equation, and consequently

$$\begin{aligned} E^*(\mathbf{t}) &= E^*[\alpha\mathbf{p} + (1 - \alpha)\mathbf{q}] \\ &= \alpha E(\mathbf{t}, \mathbf{p}) + (1 - \alpha)E(\mathbf{t}, \mathbf{q}) \le \alpha E^*(\mathbf{p}) + (1 - \alpha)E^*(\mathbf{q}). \end{aligned} \tag{11.30}$$

[Notice that we needed boundedness to allow $E^*(\mathbf{t})$ to exist everywhere.]

Since E^* is convex in $\mathbf{p}$ and E is linear in $\mathbf{p}$, E is a hyperplane with point of support at E^* for some $\mathbf{p}$. Figure 11.11 illustrates this concept for the quadratic scoring rule $s(r, E_1) = 1 - (1 - r)^2$ and $s(r, E_2) = 1 - r^2$. The line tangent to E^* at $p = .50$ is the expected value function for the stated probability $r = .50$ as a function of p, the true probability. Δ_1 is the maximum loss in expected value that the probability estimator would incur if $p = 1.0$ or $p = 0$ were the true probability but he or she made the estimate $r = .50$. Similarly, Δ_2 is the loss he or she would incur if $r = 1.0$ and $p = .5$. These and all other losses in EV are generated by differences between E^*

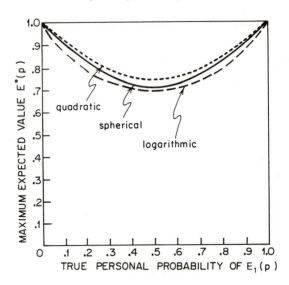

Figure 11.12. Maximum expected value functions for three scoring rules.

and its tangents (hyperplanes for $n > 2$). It is easy to see that convexity and boundedness of E^* severely limit these losses.

Figure 11.12 shows the E^* functions for the three most common scoring rules. This figure can be used directly for sensitivity analysis. To determine a particular loss, the analyst simply has to pick a true probability p and calculate the difference between $E^*(\mathbf{p})$ tangents to E^* at values in the neighborhood of p. It should be clear that neither of the three E^* functions will generate large losses; convexity and boundedness of E^* prohibit this.

Murphy and Winkler (1970) plotted $E(\mathbf{r}, \mathbf{p})$ directly as a function of $\mathbf{r}$ for various levels of $\mathbf{p}$. Figure 11.13 shows the results for the logarithmic, spherical, and quadratic two-event scoring rules. They fully confirm the results of our E^* analysis.

Similar analyses apply for $n > 2$, with E^* being a convex function in R^{n-1} and E being $(n - 1)$-dimensional hyperplanes.

The fact that proper scoring rules have flat maxima is well known by now. However, the ubiquity of proper scoring rules is not as well known. First, notice that the probability label on the response is irrelevant; proper scoring rules are not confined to situations in which the response is an explicit probability estimate. Any dense set of acts none of which is ordinally or cardinally dominated or duplicated has the same structure as a proper scoring rule: the choice of an act, in effect, signals the estimation of a probability vector, provided that the decision maker maximizes EV. Consequently, if a suboptimal act A is close to an optimal act B (in the sense that the probability vector that would make A optimal is close to the one that makes B

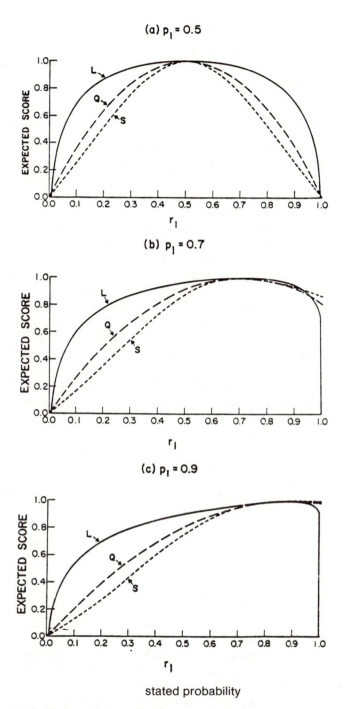

Figure 11.13. Expected scores for three scoring rules and three true probabilities. (*Source:* Murphy & Winkler, 1970.)

optimal), the decision maker will often lose little by choosing A over B. This is the essence of the flat-maximum argument that we develop more generally in the next section.

Sensitivity of prior probabilities

We denote the set of admissible gambles and decision functions by D with typical element $\mathbf{d} \in D$. For simplicity, we call elements in D decisions; $\mathbf{p}$ is the prior probability vector over states. To develop a general approach to analyzing sensitivity to prior probabilities we need three results from statistical decision theory. The first is that for each prior probability $\mathbf{p}$ there exists an admissible (not necessarily unique) decision $\mathbf{d}$ that maximizes EV. This result is, of course, trivial for finite states and bounded outcomes. [For each probability vector $\mathbf{p}$, simply calculate $E(\mathbf{d}, \mathbf{p})$, which exist by virtue of finiteness and boundedness, order the decisions according to EV, and pick the one(s) with the highest EV.] Some technical problems arise when outcomes are unbounded or when states or decisions are infinite. Ignoring such technical problems, we state the following theorem (Ferguson, 1967): if the set of states is finite and the outcomes are bounded, then for each prior probability vector $\mathbf{p} = (p_1, p_2, p_3, \ldots, p_i, \ldots, p_n)$, $p_i > 0$, a decision $\mathbf{d} \in D$ exists such that $E(\mathbf{d}, \mathbf{p}) \geq E(\mathbf{e}, \mathbf{p})$ for all $\mathbf{e} \in D$.

If $\mathbf{d}$ is optimal against $\mathbf{p}$, we label it $\mathbf{d}_p$. Obviously, several $\mathbf{d}$ can be optimal against the same $\mathbf{p}$. We label D_p the subsets of decisions that are optimal against $\mathbf{p}$.

The second result reverses the role of $\mathbf{d}$ and $\mathbf{p}$. In short, this result is that for each admissible $\mathbf{d}$ a $\mathbf{p}$ exists for which $\mathbf{d}$ is optimal. The proof of this theorem is very complicated and requires lemmas like the famous hyperplane theorem (see Ferguson, 1967). We therefore state it without proof: if the number of states is finite and the outcomes bounded, then for each admissible decision $\mathbf{d} \in D$ a prior probability $\mathbf{p}$ exists such that $E(\mathbf{d}, \mathbf{p}) \geq E(\mathbf{e}, \mathbf{p})$ for all $\mathbf{e} \in D$.

As in the preceding theorem we define the subset of prior probabilities $\mathbf{p}$ that make $\mathbf{d}$ optimal as P_d and elements in this subset we label $\mathbf{p}_d$. Furthermore, we define.

$$E(\mathbf{d}_p, \mathbf{p}) = E(\mathbf{d}, \mathbf{p}_d) = E^*(\mathbf{p}). \tag{11.31}$$

Equation 11.31 allows us to step freely from the parameter space of prior probabilities to decisions and back.

We already proved the third result in one of our previous examples. It is repeated here without proof: if the number of states is finite and the outcomes are bounded, then E^* is a convex function of $\mathbf{p}$.

We can now use the above results to analyze the losses a decision maker might encounter when using an incorrect prior probability $\mathbf{q}$ instead of the correct **p**. The use of **q** will lead him or her to choose an element of D_q, say $\mathbf{d}_q$, that will have a smaller expected value than an optimal decision $\mathbf{d}_p \in D_p$; $E(\mathbf{d}_q, \mathbf{p})$ is an $(n-1)$-dimensional hyperplane with point of support **p** at E^*. Because of this relationship between E^* and E, we can write the expected value of $\mathbf{d}_q$ purely in terms of E^*:

$$E(\mathbf{d}_q, \mathbf{p}) = E^*(\mathbf{q}) + \sum_{i=1}^{n} \delta_i (p_i - q_i), \quad (11.32)$$

where δ_i is the ith partial derivative of E^* evaluated at **q**; that is $\delta_i = \delta E^*/\delta \mathbf{q}_i$ evaluated at **q**.

Equation 11.32 is a key to any numerical sensitivity analysis of incorrect prior probabilities. It directly highlights the dependencies of the sensitivity on the slopes of E^* and on the differences $p_i - q_i$. As one would expect, flat E^* functions lead to flat maxima in expected value because $\delta_i \sim 0$. Also, losses will be small if **p** is in the neighborhood of **q**. Convexity and boundedness of E^* make large losses the exception rather than the rule.

Although Equation 11.32 is compact and can often be used effectively by fitting some convenient E^* function, it does not quite answer the question: how flat is flat? It is desirable to put expected losses into the perspective of the overall gains and losses that more or less foolish or clever decision makers could incur in the same situation. An obvious ceiling in EV is obtained by the clairvoyant, who always knows which state is true and selects the EV-maximizing decision given that state. The clairvoyant's expected value is

$$E_C^*(\mathbf{p}) = \sum_{i=1}^{n} p_i E^*(\mathbf{e}_i), \quad (11.33)$$

where $\mathbf{e}_i$ is the unit vector with zeros in all but the ith event, in which it has a 1. In geometric terms, the clairvoyant's EV is the hyperplane that connects the corner points of E^*. Figure 11.14 shows it for a two-event example.

The problem of defining bad performance meaningfully is a little trickier. We explored several such definitions, and none were fully satisfactory because they were either too foolish (e.g., always picking the decision with the worst EV) or too clever (e.g., choosing a minimax mixture). Between these is a random strategy: the decision maker eliminates dominated options and ignores priors and payoffs and chooses a decision at random. In the finite case with K decisions, the random strategy has the following expectation,

$$E_R(\mathbf{p}) = \sum_{k=1}^{K} \frac{1}{K} E(\mathbf{d}_k, \mathbf{p}), \quad (11.34)$$

which defines a hyperplane without support at E^*. In other words, the random strategy is dominated. In the two-attribute infinite case, the EV of a

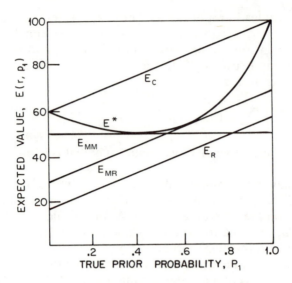

Figure 11.14. Illustration of the EV functions of three strategies.

random strategy is

$$E_R(\mathbf{p}) = 2 \int_q E^*(\mathbf{q})d_q - p_1 E^*(0) + (1 - p_1)E^*(1), \qquad (11.35)$$

which is parallel to the clairvoyant's hyperplane but completely below the E^* function without support at E^*. Figure 11.14 illustrates E_R.

Another random strategy chooses the prior probabilities $\mathbf{q}$ at random and then maximizes EV. As it turns out, this strategy gives a higher weight to decisions that have a larger region of priors that would make them optimal. This "loading the dice" strategy is identical to the original random strategy if the act space is infinite. For finite act spaces, this idea leads to as many different definitions of a lower bound on EV as there are different ways of representing $\mathbf{q}$, because the assertion that $\mathbf{q}$ is picked "at random" implies that all values of $\mathbf{q}$ are equally likely, but if that statement is true for one representation of $\mathbf{q}$, it must be false for all others.

Two more strategies are of some interest, both because they are frequently mentioned in the literature as "second-best" strategies and because they have interesting relationships with the previous strategies. They are the minimax and minimax regret strategies. For finite decisions, both can be mixed strategies, but in the infinite case they are pure strategies with some simple interpretations in terms of E^*. The minimax strategy is defined by the horizontal tangent hyperplane with point of support at the minimum of

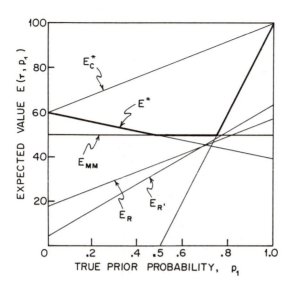

Figure 11.15. Illustration of the EVs of three decision strategies in a discrete example.

E^*. In symbols, the minimax strategy is defined by

$$E_{MM}(\mathbf{p}) = \min_{\mathbf{p}} \{E^*(\mathbf{p})\}. \qquad (11.36)$$

The minimax regret strategy minimizes the maximum difference between the highest outcome in each state and the actual outcome achieved. In terms of E^* it is the tangent hyperplane that parallels E_G^*. Formally, E_{MR} is defined by some constant c such that

$$E_{MR}(\mathbf{p}) = \sum_{i=1}^{n} p_i E^*(\mathbf{e}_i) - c. \qquad (11.37)$$

Figure 11.14 illustrates the minimax and minimax regret strategies. Figure 11.15 illustrates the same strategies in a discrete problem. It highlights the fact that randomization on $\mathbf{p}$ leads to a different E function than randomization on decisions directly. It also shows that E_R is almost minimax regret.

Using E^* as a ceiling and E_R as a floor, we can now express all expected losses in terms of the relative expected loss REL:

$$REL(\mathbf{d}_q, \mathbf{p}) = \frac{E^*(\mathbf{p}) - E(\mathbf{d}_q, \mathbf{p})}{E_G^*(\mathbf{p}) - E_R(\mathbf{p})} \, 100 \, (\%). \qquad (11.38)$$

Since $E_G^*(\mathbf{p}) - E_R(\mathbf{p}) = $ const, this usually has a convenient analytical solution.

Table 11.12. *Payoff matrix for sensitivity analysis example*

Decision	State			
	E_1	E_2	E_3	E_4
d_1	100	*0*	*0*	*0*
d_2	98	12	12	*0*
d_3	94	27	*0*	13
d_4	76	*38*	*38*	*38*
d_5	59	*59*	39	39
d_6	*0*	92	*0*	39
d_7	*0*	69	51	51
d_8	*0*	*0*	92	39
d_9	*0*	*0*	100	*0*
d_{10}	*0*	49	81	62
d_{11}	*0*	*0*	97	24
d_{12}	*0*	*0*	71	71
d_{13}	*0*	*0*	55	83
d_{14}	*0*	12	12	90
d_{15}	*0*	*0*	*0*	100
Average	22	24	43	43

Note: Boxed numerals represent maximum values in each state; italic numerals represent minimum values in each decision.

To illustrate the above theoretical development in a practical situation, consider the payoff matrix in Table 11.12. The entries in that matrix are conditional values derived either from gambles or from decision functions. Not one of the decisions in Table 11.12 is ordinally or cardinally dominated. Since all decisions are admissible, they are all potentially optimal choices.

First, we identify the corner points of E^* by determining the maximum outcome in each event E_i. They are boxed in Table 11.12. Next, we find the minimax decision. Our guess is that d_5 is a minimax decision, because it has the most evenly distributed outcomes. This guess is confirmed since the minimum payoff for d_5 is the largest of all such minima. We know, therefore, that the lowest point of E^* must be a mixture between .59 and .39. Unfortunately, we cannot define the minimum of E^* precisely, since the available decisions do not include the mixed minimax strategy that has E^* as its minimum. We make a guess that it is approximately the .25 mixture of the outcomes of the discrete minimax strategy, which turns out to have equal outcomes of 50 for all states.

So far, by simple inspection of the payoff matrix we have defined two strategies – the clairvoyant and the (approximate) minimax:

$$E^*_C = 100p_1 + 92p_2 + 100p_3 + 100p_4, \qquad (11.39)$$

$$E_{MM} = 50 \quad \text{(for all } \mathbf{p}\text{).} \qquad (11.40)$$

Next we notice that the clairvoyant's hyperplane is (almost) horizontal and that therefore the minimax regret strategy will also be (almost) horizontal. Therefore, the minimax regret strategy will be very similar to the minimax strategy. For approximation purposes we assume that they are identical, that is,

$$E_{MR} = 50 \quad \text{(for all } \mathbf{p}\text{).} \qquad (11.41)$$

Finally we derive the EV of the random strategy by averaging all outcomes conditional on the states across decisions. These averages are given in the last row of Table 11.12. The EV of the random decision strategy is

$$E_R(\mathbf{p}) = 22p_1 + 24p_2 + 43p_3 + 43p_4. \qquad (11.42)$$

Had we, instead of randomizing decisions, randomized probabilities, we would have found an EV plane parallel to the clairvoyant's plane, that is,

$$E_R(\mathbf{p}) = E^*_G(\mathbf{p}) - \text{const.} \qquad (11.43)$$

Since we had adopted E^*_C as a constant approximation, the probability randomization would have led us therefore to a constant EV. It is reasonable to assume that this line would approximately balance the skewness of the random decision strategy and therefore lie approximately at

$$E_R(\mathbf{p}) = 33. \qquad (11.44)$$

The "range" of EV in this sensitivity analysis is therefore

$$MEL = E^*_C(\mathbf{p}) - E_R(\mathbf{p}) = 67, \qquad (11.45)$$

where MEL denotes maximum expected loss. Next, we fit an E^* function. We want to make it symmetric, going through $E^*(\mathbf{e}_i) = 100$ for all corner points. That would provide a perfect fit for three E_i and only a small difference of eight outcome points for E_2. The minimum should be at $\mathbf{p} = (.25, .25, .25, .25,)$, and at that point it assumes a value of .5. We will fit a quadratic function of the form

$$E^*(\mathbf{p}) = 100 \sum_{i=1}^{n} \frac{p_i}{\sqrt{\Sigma p_i}} \qquad (11.46)$$

and ascertain that at $i \neq 2$ this function meets our corner-point and minima requirements. To check the fit of this function, we calculated E^* for several p's using the actual payoff matrix and compared the result with the E^* values. The results and differences are shown in Table 11.13. The largest dif-

Table 11.13. *Comparisons of actual maximal EV (using payoff matrix) and fitted* E* *for selected prior probabilities*

Prior	Actual maximum EV	E*	Difference (%)
1.0, .00, .00, .00	100	100	0
.90, .10, .00, .00	89	91	2
.70, .00, .00, .20	70	70	0
.00, 1.0, .00, .00	92	100	8
.25, .25, .25, .25	49	50	1
.00, .00, .50, .50	71	71	0
.00, .00, 1.0, .00	100	100	0

ference (of 8%) occurs at E_i, for $i = 2$. This difference was calculated into the fit of $E*$. The remaining differences are small and provide some justification for using $E*$ for sensitivity analysis of improper use of priors.

Substituting the specific form of $E*$ into the general EV function (Equation 11.35) we find

$$E*(\mathbf{d}_q, \mathbf{p}) = \sum_{i=1}^{n} \frac{p_i q_i}{\sqrt{\Sigma \, q_i^2}} . \tag{11.47}$$

Table 11.14 provides several examples of the losses in EVs, optimal EVs, and RELs. The REL in our specific $E*$ formula is calculated as

$$REL(\mathbf{q}, \mathbf{p}) = \frac{\Sigma \, p_i}{\sqrt{\Sigma \, p_i^2}} \frac{p_i q_i}{\sqrt{\Sigma \, q_i^2}} \frac{300}{2} , \tag{11.48}$$

since the range of losses was defined to be $E_G^* - E_R = 2/3$.

Table 11.14 shows clearly that the effect of small and moderate deviations from correct priors is not severe, and only for extreme deviations are losses substantial. Table 11.15 shows the expected values and RELs of the two limiting strategies (random and minimax). The minimax regret strategy has the same limiting behavior as the minimax strategy. It appears from this table that the decision maker can insure quite well against large losses by using the minimax strategy or the minimax regret strategy, as long as the true prior probability vector is not too steep. And even the random strategy performs reasonably well as long as the prior probabilities are evenly distributed.

By now it should be clear how the $E*$ functions can be used for sensitivity analysis. Naturally, this analysis is applicable only if the number of undominated options is large relative to the number of states. If this is the case, we recommend the following steps:

1   Calculate conditional values and put together the payoff matrix.
2   Eliminate dominated decisions.

Table 11.14. *EVs and expected losses produced by use of incorrect prior*

Correct prior **p**	Prior used **q**	$E\,(\mathbf{d}_q, \mathbf{p})$	$E^*(\mathbf{p})$	$REL(\mathbf{q}, \mathbf{p})$, %
1.0, .00, .00, .00	.80, .20, .00, .00	98	100	3
	.70, .30, .00, .00	92	100	12
	.50, .20, .20, .00	86	100	21
	.25, .25, .25, .25	50	100	75
	.00, .00, .00, 1.0	0	100	150
.75, .25, .00, .00	1.0, .00, .00, .00	75	79	6
	.90, .10, .00, .00	77	79	3
	.50, .50, .00, .00	70	79	14
	.25, .25, .25, .25	50	79	44
	.00, .00, .00, 1.0	0	79	119
.33, .33, .33, .00	.50, .20, .20, .10	52	58	9
	.25, .25, .25, .25	50	58	12
	.70, .30, .00, .00	44	58	21
	.80, .20, .00, .00	40	58	27
	.00, .00, .00, 1.0	40	58	87
.25, .25, .25, .25	.40, .40, .20, .00	42	50	12
	.50, .20, .20, .10	43	50	11
	.70, .30, .00, .00	33	50	26
	.80, .20, .00, .00	30	50	30
	1.0, .00, .00, .00	24	50	38

Table 11.15. *EVs and expected losses of limiting strategies*

Prior probability **p**	$E^*(\mathbf{p})$	E_{MM}	REL_{MM}, %	E_R	REL_R, %
1.0, .00, .00, .00	100	50	75	33	100
.90, .10, .00, .00	91	50	62	33	87
.75, .25, .00, .00	79	50	44	33	69
.60, .40, .00, .00	72	50	33	33	59
.60, .20, .20, .20	66	50	24	33	50
.50, .50, .00, .00	71	50	31	33	57
.40, .40, .20, .00	60	50	15	33	41
.33, .33, .33, .00	58	50	12	33	38
.40, .20, .20, .20	53	50	5	33	30
.25, .25, .25, .25	50	50	0	33	26

3   Find maximum values in each state [the $E^*(\mathbf{e}_i)$ values] and minimum values in each decision.

4   Determine the minimax and random decisions, and calculate their respective EVs. Identify the minimum point of the E^* function; if necessary approximate.

5   Fit a continuous E^* function through the corner points and the minimum point. Check against actual maximum EVs, if necessary iterate.

6   Use the continuous E^* approximation to calculate losses due to incorrect priors, limiting strategies, and so on.

These steps can seldom be done without computers. We hope that someone will soon write a computer package that makes use of these ideas for continuous approximation in sensitivity analysis.

Sensitivity to decisions

The results of the preceding section can be used to define a metric on decisions and decision strategies, even if they have no inherent metric characteristic. The metric is provided by the prior probabilities that would make a decision optimal. In other words, for each decision **d** we identify the set of probabilities **p** that would make it optimal; we previously labeled that set P_d. Decisions are close if their optimizing probabilities are close.

The analysis of the sensitivity of decisions can therefore build directly on the sensitivity analysis for prior probabilities. We begin by assuming that a particular d is optimal and find its associated $\mathbf{p}_d$ or set of P_d. Then we examine the expected losses produced by choosing other decisions $\mathbf{d}_q$ by calculating $E(\mathbf{q}, \mathbf{p})$ or $REL(\mathbf{q}, \mathbf{p})$.

One can perform this analysis either by using the E^* approximations to the payoff matrix or by using the payoff matrix directly. The advantage of using E^* is that it associates with each suboptimal **d** a probability and thereby provides some indication of the "distance" between the optimal and suboptimal decisions. The analysis can then concentrate on decisions that are "close" to the optimal one in terms of **p**. Since this sensitivity analysis is analogous to the analysis of prior probabilities, it need not be repeated here.

If the payoff matrix is used directly, one typically has to calculate all EVs for a given prior, a process that can be quite tedious. Table 11.16 is an example of such an extensive analysis.

Sensitivity to information

So far we have analyzed only losses generated by the choice of suboptimal but undominated decisions or by the choice of incorrect priors. Nothing guarantees that losses will be small or restricted if the scope of the analysis is extended to dominated decisions. Normally this poses no problem, since dominance is relatively easy to recognize. However, dominance can sometimes be caused by inefficient information use, and this is rather difficult to recognize.

We saw in Section 11.2 that the use of information enriches a set of gambles to decision functions by generating conditional value vectors that dominate the vectors of the original gambles. In effect, the information turns

Table 11.16. *EVs and RELs of suboptimal decisions*

Correct decision	Incorrect decision	E correct	E*	E incorrect	REL
d_1 is correct if $\mathbf{p}$ = 1.0, .00, .00, .00	d_2	100	100	98	3
	d_3	100	100	94	9
	d_4	100	100	76	36
	d_5	100	100	59	62
d_3 is correct if $\mathbf{p}$ = .75, .25, .00, .00	d_1	77	79	75	3
	d_2	77	79	76	2
	d_4	77	79	67	14
	d_5	77	79	59	27
	d_6	77	79	23	81
d_5 is correct if $\mathbf{p}$ = .33, .33, .33, .00	d_1	52	58	33	29
	d_2	52	58	41	16
	d_3	52	58	40	18
	d_4	52	58	51	2
	d_6	52	58	31	32
	d_7	52	58	40	18
	d_9	52	58	33	29
	d_{10}	52	58	43	14
d_5 is correct if $\mathbf{p}$ = .25, .25, .25, .25	d_1	49	50	25	36
	d_2	49	50	31	27
	d_3	49	50	34	23
	d_4	49	50	48	2
	d_6	49	50	33	24
	d_7	49	50	43	9
	d_8	49	50	33	24
	d_9	49	50	25	36
	d_{10}	49	50	48	2

previously undominated decisions into dominated ones. The same would presumably be true if the choice were between two producers of information (different sources, different sample sizes or strategies) one of which was better than another; that is, one would expect that the decision strategy obtained with the better information would dominate that obtained with the poorer information. As a consequence, losses encountered by using a decision strategy with poor information may actually be quite severe.

The interpretation of these concepts is simple if we use our formalizations of E^* functions. Any information variable X will generate a decision function that, after deletion of the dominated ones, will generate an E^* function. Obviously another information variable is "better" if its decision functions generate an E^* function that is higher everywhere. To denote the dependence of the E^* functions on the information variable we label them E_X^* or E_Y^*. We already defined a particular E^* function on the basis of perfect

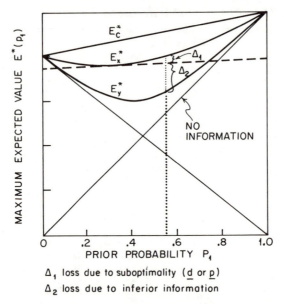

Figure 11.16. Illustration of losses caused by use of inferior information. Δ_1, loss due to suboptimality (**d** or **p**); Δ_2, loss due to inferior information.

information, namely, E_C^*. Figure 11.16 shows a hypothetical two-state example of E^* functions and indicates some losses that may be generated by suboptimality (in the sense of choosing a wrong prior or decision) or by poor information. It appears that poor information can indeed be harmful, especially when the priors are fairly uniform.

We would like to detect dominance simply by studying the probabilistic characteristics of the information variables rather than by examining E_X^* and E_Y^*. Unfortunately, it is by no means trivial to establish dominance merely on the basis of probabilistic relationships among the information variables and the states about which probabilities are to be inferred. Three relatively specific and obvious instances in which information variables could be ordered in a natural way relating to their "informativeness" or "precision" were explored in von Winterfeldt and Edwards (1975); showing that in fact this ordering led to dominance. Inadvertent use of a dominated information source would, of course, lead to relatively large losses.

11.5. Flat maxima in MAUT models

Two approaches exist for analyzing the sensitivity of parameters in MAUT models. The first builds on the formal analogy between EV models and additive MAUT models and so is very similar to the sensitivity analysis for

Table 11.17. *Attribute values of the multiattribute options in a simple two-attribute example*

Option	Attribute X_1	Attribute X_2
$\mathbf{x}_1$	20	90
$\mathbf{x}_2$	40	80
$\mathbf{x}_3$	40	40
$\mathbf{x}_4$	60	50
$\mathbf{x}_5$	80	40
$\mathbf{x}_6$	90	10

expectation models. In this analysis, utility losses or gains based on incorrect weights are assessed. The second approach, which originated in test theory, compares the "goodness of fit" of an incorrect model with that of a correct model using statistical indices like correlation coefficients.

We have already discussed the analogy between EV models and MAUT models and therefore present here only a simple example that highlights the analogy in terms of the definitions provided in the preceding section. Subsequently we shall discuss in more depth the correlational sensitivity analysis involving multiattribute utilities.

Demonstration of the analogy between EV and MAUT models

In an analysis of flat maxima in MAUT models, the weights w_i take the place of the prior probabilities p_i. For demonstration purposes we consider again the introductory two-attribute example, where options could vary on the attribute X_1 (e.g., costs) and X_2 (e.g., benefits). We consider six options characterized by their single-attribute ratings (utilities) in Table 11.17. We want to analyze the sensitivity of the decision with respect to the weight vector $\mathbf{w} = (w_1, w_2)$ assuming a simple additive model,

$$v(\mathbf{x}_k) = \sum_{i=1}^{2} w_i v_i(x_{ik}).$$

We first examine dominance by plotting the graphs

$$v(\mathbf{x}_k) = w_1 v_1(x_{1k}) + (1 - w_1)v_2(x_{2k}) \tag{11.49}$$

as a function of w_1. Figure 11.17 shows this plot for the vectors in our example. The heavy line segments on the $v(\mathbf{x}_k, w_1)$ lines connect the maximum utility that a decision maker might achieve by always selecting the best option against a given weight vector $\mathbf{w}$. In correspondence to the E^* function in expectation models, we call this function V^*. Just as E^* is only a function of $\mathbf{p}$, V^* is only a function of $\mathbf{w}$.

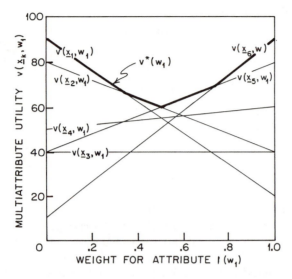

Figure 11.17. Two-attribute value functions as a function of the weight for attribute 1.

An option x_k can maximize utility only if its $v(x_k, w)$ function is tangent to the V^* function. The lines $v(x_3, w_1)$ and $v(x_7, w_1)$ do not touch the V^* function and the options x_3 and x_4 can therefore be eliminated from further consideration.

The vertices of V^* (the corner points) define the switchover (break-even) points at which the decision maker should change the decision from one option to another. They also define the points in w where two or more options have identical multiattribute utilities. Figure 11.18 shows the v and V^* function for nondominated options and indicates the switchover or break-even points. In addition, it shows some typical losses due to erroneous weight parameters. For example, Δ_1 indicates the loss that a decision maker would encounter if he or she used the weight $w_1 = .2$ when the correct weight $w_1 = .6$. The quantity Δ_2 is the loss the decision maker would encounter if he or she acted as if .6 were the correct weight when in fact .2 was true.

Just like the E^* functions in expectation models, the V^* functions are convex and bounded. In addition, the standardizations of the v_i functions imply certain boundaries in the vertices of the V^* function. In particular,

$$V^* (0) \leq 100,$$
$$V^* (1) \leq 100,$$
$$V^* (.5) \geq 50.$$

It is easy to see how convexity and the specific boundaries limit the shape of the V^* functions and, as a consequence, the losses of $v(x_{k1}w_1)$.

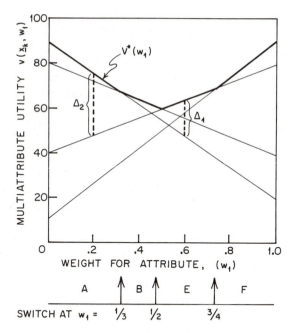

Figure 11.18. Maximum two-attribute value function V^* and illustration of possible losses.

Correlational analysis

A typical example of correlational sensitivity analysis is the selection of graduate students from a group of applicants. The faculty committee charged with the selection attempts to select students who are most likely to do well. This mixed evaluation–prediction problem has frequently been modeled by means of regression analyses (see e.g., Dawes and Corrigan, 1974; Huber, Daneshgar, and Ford, 1971). The information available to the committee includes, for example, the students' graduate record examination, undergraduate grade point average, type of school attended, and the quality of the letters of recommendation. On the basis of this information, the committee might contemplate an evaluation model of the form

$$v(\mathbf{x}) = \sum_{i=1}^{n} w_i v_i(\mathbf{x}), \tag{11.50}$$

where the v_i's are the attribute scores and the w_i's may be either directly assessed or constructed through a multiple regression model in which the w_i's are beta weights and the v_i's are standardized scores on the relevant attributes. The committee then selects those candidates having the highest v scores.

This paradigm violates our previous assumptions, since its evaluations concern both dominated and undominated applicants. Assume, for example, that an applicant with an absolutely superb record and who dominates all others is included. Obviously, this candidate would be chosen regardless of weights. But if several candidates are to be selected, students who are dominated by this outstanding applicant have to be considered too. Often, one may want to include *all* applicants in a first-cut sensitivity analysis. (Later we argue that one should look only at a subset of applicants, the so-called contenders, and omit sure losers and sure winners.)

A correlational sensitivity analysis treats such a set of applicants as a sample over which MAUT models are correlated. Models can be compared by first computing the two multiattribute utilities v and v' for each applicant. The multiattribute utilities of the models are then correlated across the sample of applicants. A correlation of $+1$ would indicate perfect agreement between the models; -1 would mean perfect disagreement. The correlation coefficient is thus an index of how well two models approximate one another for a given sample of alternatives.

This type of sensitivity analysis uses well-known results from statistical test theory. Gulliksen (1950) derived the correlation between two MAUT models differing in weights $\mathbf{w}$ and $\mathbf{w}'$ only, assuming that all attribute intercorrelations are zero and variances of the v_i's in each attribute are equal,

$$r_{vv'} = \frac{r_{ww'} \dfrac{\sigma_w}{\overline{w}} \dfrac{\sigma_{w'}}{\overline{w}'} + 1}{(1 + \sigma_w/w)^2 (1 + \sigma_{w'}/w')^2} \tag{11.51}$$

where $r_{ww'}$ is the correlation between the two weight vectors, σ_w and $\sigma_{w'}$ are the standard deviations of the weight vectors, and $\overline{w}$ and $\overline{w}'$ are the means of the two weight vectors. We can use this result to observe directly the sensitivity of the composites to changing weights. There is a strong dependence, as one would expect, on the correlation between the two weight vectors.

Assume next that one MAUT model v has differential weights; the other is a unit weighting model defined by

$$v_u(\mathbf{x}) = \sum_{i=1}^{n} (1/n)v_i(\mathbf{x}). \tag{11.52}$$

Assuming that attribute intercorrelations are equal (though not necessarily zero) v_u and v have the following correlation (see, e.g., Einhorn and Hogarth, 1975; Ghiselli, 1964),

$$r_{v_u,v}^2 = \frac{1 + (n - 1)}{1 + (n - 1) + (\sigma_w/\overline{w})(1 - \rho)}, \tag{11.53}$$

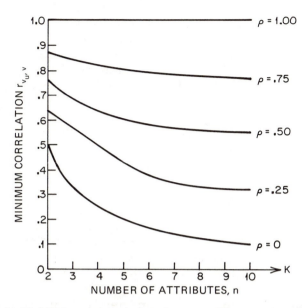

Figure 11.19. Minimum correlations between differential and unit weighting models as a function of the number of attributes and the interattribute correlation. (*Source:* Einhorn & Hogarth, 1975.)

where n is the number of attributes, σ_w and $\overline{w}$ are the standard deviation and mean of the differential weight vector respectively, and ρ is the attribute intercorrelation. Einhorn and Hogarth derive the minimum value of that correlation, which gives an indication of how poorly (or well) a unit weighting model can do under the described assumptions:

$$\min r_{v_u,v}^2 = 1 + (n - 1)(\rho/n). \tag{11.54}$$

Figure 11.19 shows plots of these minimum correlations for various levels of the attribute intercorrelation ρ. It illustrates the main results of the correlational sensitivity analysis: when attribute intercorrelations are positive and the number of attributes is small, equal weights will do a very good job of predicting the multiattribute utilities derived with a differential weighting system. Results of a similar nature and further arguments supporting the robustness of equal weights were provided by Wainer (1976). (In addition, equal weights are sometimes favorable because of the unstable nature of statistically estimated regression weights; see, e.g., Dawes and Corrigan, 1974; Einhorn and Hogarth, 1975. However, for multiattribute models such effects are of secondary importance.)

The equal-weights argument has been criticized because it ignores the potential for *negative* correlations, which are frequent in multiattribute utility analyses. McClelland (1978) considered "pick 1 out of n" situations and

Table 11.18. *Intercorrelations between MAUT models using different weighting schemes (five attributes)*

Weights compared	All (1,000) alternatives	Admissible (100) alternatives
1 × 2	.970	.959
1 × 3	.752	.514
1 × 4	.335	−.157
1 × 5	.164	−.274
2 × 3	.870	.692
2 × 4	.511	.053
2 × 5	.324	−.109
3 × 4	.869	.757
3 × 5	.743	.630
4 × 5	.968	.971

Note: Weighting schemes are as follows: 1, (81, 49, 25, 9, 1) (optimal); 2, (9, 7, 5, 3, 1); 3, (1, 1, 1, 1, 1); 4, (1, 3, 5, 7, 9); 5,(1, 9, 25, 49, 81).

demonstrated that in the two-attribute case undominated options typically have negative attribute intercorrelations. Seaver (1973), in an unpublished paper, made the same point somewhat more generally. In a simulation, he correlated several multiattribute models, differing in weights only. He first used a randomly generated set of 1,000 alternatives to compute this correlation and then repeated the analysis on a subset of 100 admissible alternatives. Table 11.18 shows that the correlations $r_{vv'}$ are generally positive for the whole set but severely depressed and occasionally negative for the subset of admissible alternatives.

Stillwell, Seaver, and Edwards (1981), building on this finding, examined how various procedures for rank weighting approach the predictive effectiveness of a "true" model. Using the rank-weighting techniques described in Chapter 8 as approximations of ratio weight assessments, they correlated both the rank-weighting models and a unit-weighting model with the "true" ratio-weighting model. In three applications of MAUT they found substantial improvements of rank weights over equal weights, because of the restriction to nondominated alternatives.

A final argument against the ubiquity of the robustness of equal weights comes from examining the k/N situation. As in graduate student selection, a decision maker is often faced with picking not one but several candidates. In such situations there often are sure winners and sure losers. It would be unfair to evaluate the weighting scheme (or any decision rule, for that matter) by including the sure winners and losers, since *any* rule would select the former and reject the latter. Including them artificially increases the agreement between models, just as the inclusion of dominated options increases the correlation between models.

John, Edwards, von Winterfeldt, and Barron (1980) carried out a simulation in which sure winners and sure losers were defined as those that any conditionally monotone model would pick or reject. Such cases were eliminated, and average attribute intercorrelations were computed for the set of contenders only. The first result of that simulation was that in many situations large proportions of sure winners and sure losers exist; that is, in many situations decisions are rather trivial. This is especially true if attributes are positively correlated over the whole set of alternatives and if the number of attributes is relatively small. Correspondingly, the number of contenders increases with decreasing attribute intercorrelations and with increases in the number of attributes.

The second result of John et al. is that average attribute intercorrelations for the contender set are much lower than those for the entire set. Indeed, in the two-attribute case average intercorrelations for the contenders become negative, even if the attribute intercorrelations of the whole set are positive. This is, of course, a generalization of McClelland's finding. The depression of the attribute correlation also appears for higher numbers of attributes, although the average correlations of attributes among contenders becomes less highly negative and in some instances is even positive (i.e., when the original correlation over the whole set is .9). These results suggest that in a k/N situation equal weights may not be as robust as initially believed.

So far we have examined only the sensitivity of weights within the additive model. Dawes and Corrigan (1974) make the more general point that additive forms can approximate nonadditive forms very well when the following conditions are met:

1   The nonadditive model is conditionally monotone in each attribute (i.e., the composite from the nonadditive model is monotone in the attribute values, no matter what the other values are).
2   Single-attribute measurements are subject to error.

In multiattribute utility measurement, both conditions are typically true.

Seaver (1973), in his unpublished note, correlated different model forms over sets of simulated alternatives. Table 11.19 shows a surprising agreement between different model forms. Correlations between models are only somewhat depressed when one looks at the admissible subset only. Fischer (1972) obtained a similar set.

In summary, simple unit weights approximate "true" weights well – when attributes are positively correlated and the number of attributes is relatively small. In other cases rank-weighting techniques provide excellent approximations. Furthermore, different model *forms* generate highly correlated composite utilities, as long as the models are conditionally monotone in attribute values.

Table 11.19. *Correlations between nonadditive*
MAUT models and an additive model

	All (1,000) alternatives	Admissible (100) alternatives
F_1	.980	.995
F_2	.690	.878
F_3	.825	.867
F_4	.660	.504

[a]Models:
$$F_1(x) = \sum_{i=1} x_i + \sum_{i \ne j} x_i x_j, \quad F_2(x) = \sum x_i + \prod x_i,$$
$$F_3(x) = (x_1 x_2 + x_3 x_4) x_5, \quad F_4(x) = (x_1 + x_2) x_3 + x_4 x_5.$$

11.6. Implications of the insensitivity of decision-analytic models

The preceding sections point to the feebleness of decision analysis – at least of the measurement aspects that are usually stressed in textbooks and journal articles. We can perhaps escape the conclusion that precise measurement does not matter by arguing that EV rather than REL is what counts – and a 1% decrease in EV in a $\$10^9$ decision is still a $\$10^7$ loss.

Another caveat against the overgeneralization of flat maxima is that sometimes the parameters of a decision problem have a peculiar functional relationship with prior probabilities. Notice that our main argument for flat maxima applies to EV and value functions defined on prior probabilities and weights only. In principle, decision parameters could be an extremely distorted function of prior probabilities or weights. Such extreme distortions may indeed produce local steepness of an EV for value functions defined over such a parameter. We personally encountered one such instance.

In a study of offshore oil operators' responses to oil discharge standards, von Winterfeldt (1982) found that the EV of an oil operator can drop sharply in the close vicinity of "cutoff" standards at which the operator should switch to improved treatment. We believe that such situations are more atypical than typical. We have seen many other instances (e.g., in signal detection analysis or in information purchasing problems) in which translations from the prior probabilities into other decision parameters did not produce more steepness.

Although there certainly will be exceptions to the rule of flat maxima, the more important point is that structuring and expertise are important as a rule. While the areas of structuring and information collection have not received nearly as much attention as they deserve, decision analysts certainly have something to offer in these areas. Option generation to *create* dominating alternatives is an obvious way to improve decisions – the gains generated by new options can be just about limitless. Conversely, failure to generate dominating options can lead to large losses.

An especially subtle form of dominance is created by an inefficient use or neglect of information and expertise. In the preceding sections we have shown how such inefficiencies can produce dominated strategies that in turn can lead to substantial losses. The obvious conclusion is that improvements in information collection and expertise are important and that decision analysts should spend a substantial amount of time aiding decision makers in these steps.

A major implication of flat maxima for behavioral studies in decision making is that experimental subjects do not suffer much from using non-optimal strategies. The suboptimality found in experimental studies may therefore be less an indication of subjects' *inability* to perform at their best than a sign of their lack of *motivation* to do so. If subjects' economic prospects in decision-theoretic experiments are essentially unaffected by the nonoptimality of their strategies, who would blame them for responding with simple strategies that do not require much thought, but pay off (on the average) nearly as much as optimal ones?

Faced with flat maxima, subjects may do various things. They may behave randomly, especially if they don't know what they are doing. Often, other facts about the experiment imply nonmonetary payoffs, and subjects are likely to pay attention to these. They may minimize effort, perhaps by as extreme a procedure as ignoring stimuli or hunting for simple strategies. Or they may look for hidden meanings and so develop self-instructions and idiosyncratic response strategies (the famous probability matching phenomenon in repetitive binary choice experiments, to the extent that it occurs at all, seems to be a result of this kind of self-instruction). Or they may just be bored.

All this makes suboptimality in decision-theoretic experiments very hard to interpret. It is perhaps encouraging to find good performance in decision making when the stakes are high and the decisions are real. Such improvement has been found in high-stakes gambling experiments in Las Vegas (see, e.g., Goodman, Saltzman, Edwards, and Krantz, 1979) and in laboratory situations (see, e.g., Swensson and Edwards, 1971). In such situations, subjects' global strategies were approximated well by a straightforward EV model.

When stakes are low, flat maxima may produce random errors, systematic errors, or both. In signal detection experiments, Green (1960) and Swets, Tanner, and Birdsall (1961) found that subjects tended to deviate from optimal cutoffs in the direction of making both responses more nearly equally often. Green concluded that "the way in which the expected value changes for various criterion levels is the crux of the problem"; that is, he had flat-maximum trouble. Others have proposed that subjects regard such tasks as being sensorily oriented or that subjects do not in fact maximize EV. Uhlela (1966) also reported nonoptimal decision criteria in an experiment requiring recognition of tilted lines. Again, the subjects tended toward an error-minimizing strategy. Similar findings have been reported in other tasks by Kubovy and Healy (1977), Healy and Kubovy (1977), A. Lieblich and I. Lieblich (1969), and I. Lieblich and A. Lieblich (1969).

Healy and Kubovy (1978) varied prior probabilities and payoffs in a memory recognition task. The subjects' likelihood ratio cutoffs β derived from a signal detection analysis were optimal ($= 1$) for symmetric payoffs and priors but suboptimal (around 1.5 instead of 3) for asymmetric payoffs and priors. Our flat-maximum analysis would suggest that subjects suffered only a small expected penalty from their conservative adjustment, especially since the actual payoffs were in fractions of a cent. Under such a condition it is not very costly for subjects to use simple heuristic strategies.

Kubovy and Healy (1980) reported results from an experiment in which subjects had to decide whether a person of a given height was male or female. This paradigm allowed the experimenter to control d' and the observations received by the subject. Again these authors found conservative cutoff locations in the case of asymmetric payoffs. However, the subjects became near optimal after they were essentially told how to achieve optimality.

Kubovy and Healy (1980) reported another experiment in which they investigated the hypothesis that subjects initially begin with a likelihood ratio of 1 and then adjust it in the direction of the optimal ratio until they no longer perceive any increase in EV. They conjectured that flat maxima would lead subjects to perceive no increase in EV even before reaching the optimal cutoff point. They tested this hypothesis by manipulating d', which influences the steepness of the EV function over k. Initial analyses favored the interpretation that subjects are less conservative for steeper EV functions.

Virtually all of these experiments combined skewed payoff matrices with quite difficult discriminations. This produces a probability distribution over p that is peaked such that p^* is well away from .5. Such procedures can be shown to lead to very flat maxima in the region of p^*.

Criterion variability is very important to the interpretation of signal detection experiments. The formal arguments summarized above suggest that it should be present in typical experiments. Hammerton (1970), using a simulated signal detection task in which subjects made inferences about parameters of normal distributions, showed that they did not adopt stable criteria. Galanter and Holman (1967) suggested a systematic criterion shift model to explain data in a probabilistic categorization task. Wherever they have been studied, the implications of flat maxima seem to have been experimentally confirmed.

Can this distressing picture be alleviated by increasing costs and payoffs? Some data reveal invariance of d' for different payoff structures and levels of motivation (see Green and Swets, 1966; Lukaszewski and Elliot, 1962; Swets and Sewall, 1963). However, Watson and Clopton (1969) and Calfee (1970) found noticeable effects of costs and payoffs on the detection rate and on d', respectively.

Aschenbrenner and Wendt (1978) studied the effects of scoring rules on probability estimates and found little effect of the steepness of the rule. The scoring rules for probability estimates are so flat that we are generally pessimistic. Although there seems to be little point in using proper scoring rules for motivation, they may be useful instructions about the meaning of probability estimates.

12 Applications and pitfalls of decision analysis

12.1. Introduction

In this chapter we summarize 11 applications of decision analysis to real-world problems. To avoid duplicating other reviews, we have concentrated on relatively recent cases, most of which were carried out in the late 1970s and early 1980s. We tried to select applications with a wide range of substantive topics and a mix of methodological approaches. The topics are diverse: environmental standard setting, the use of X rays for medical diagnosis, landslide risk assessment, capital investment decisions, bypass surgery. The applications are grouped by their methodological emphasis on probability, value, or decision making.

These applications are, of course, only a small selection of the large number of real-world decision analyses. Other applications are reviewed by Keeney and Raiffa (1976), Howard, Matheson, and Miller (1976), and Krischer (1980). Brown (1970) and Ulvila and Brown (1982) review business applications. The *Journal of Medical Decision Making* is devoted to medical applications, and *Operations Research* and *Management Science* have published special issues on decision-analytic applications. Many more applications can be found in technical reports issued by consulting firms like Decisions and Designs, Inc., Decision Science Consortium, the Maxima Corporation, Woodward–Clyde Consultants, and others.

We conclude this chapter by discussing some of the pits into which decision analysts have fallen and the lessons learned in consequence.

12.2. Applications to diagnostic and prediction problems

The American College of Radiology's efficacy study[1]

In 1971, Bell and Loop published a study of the diagnostic efficacy of radiographic examinations of the skull after a trauma. They found that if certain signs readily observable on physical examination were absent, the patient's skull was virtually never fractured. Moreover, most nondepressed skull frac-

[1] See Lusted (1977) and Lusted et al. (1980) for a detailed description of this study.

448

tures are treated in essentially the same way as other traumas to the head. They concluded that the cost of using X rays to hunt for skull fractures was more than $6,000 (in 1971 dollars) per fracture found and wondered if the hunt was worth it.

This striking finding in combination with several other considerations caused the American College of Radiology to set up a Committee on Efficacy Studies in 1971. Its first problem was to figure out what *efficacy* means. The committee members concluded that in diagnostic radiology it means three things. A diagnostic procedure is efficacious-3 if the patient is, in some long-run sense, better off as a result of having had the procedure than would otherwise be the case. Of course, efficacy-3 is the goal toward which diagnostic (and therapeutic) procedures are directed – but it is rather hard to measure. An effective measurement procedure would require that the patient's long-run well-being be known, both having had the procedure and not having had it – and so not having had any changes in therapy to which its results might have led.

The committee's conclusion that measuring efficacy-3 would be impractical led it to fall back on efficacy-2. A diagnostic procedure is efficacious-2 if the attending physician's therapeutic decisions are different, given the procedure, from what they would have been otherwise.

In case efficacy-2 might prove too hard to measure, the committee also defined efficacy-1. A procedure is efficacious-1 if it influences the attending physician's diagnostic thinking. To find that out, one need only measure the difference, if any, between a pre-X-ray prior probability distribution over possible diagnoses and a post-X-ray posterior probability distribution.

Thornbury, Fryback, and Edwards (1975), in a pretest, attempted to measure both efficacy-1 and efficacy-2. They gave up on efficacy-2, concluding (in our view incorrectly) that it would be too difficult to determine what the attending physician would have decided in the absence of radiographic information, since in fact it was available. So the large field study that the American College of Radiology conducted was a study of efficacy-1.

The operational definition of efficacy-1 comes directly from Bayes's theorem. In its log odds–log likelihood ratio form (see Chapter 5), Bayes's theorem can be rewritten

$$LLR = LFO - LIO. \tag{12.1}$$

This notation, different from that used in Chapter 5, denotes the following. Subtract the logarithm of the initial odds from the logarithm of the final odds to get the logarithm of the likelihood ratio. LLR is a natural measure of efficacy-1. For undiagnostic X rays, values of LLR cluster around zero; for diagnostic ones, they deviate from zero. Larger deviations directly indicate more diagnosticity. So the study consisted of obtaining a large number of judgments of initial odds or probabilities (before X ray) and corresponding judgments of final odds or probabilities (after the X-ray picture had been taken and the attending physician knew the result) and then calculating and doing statistics on the LLRs thus implied. A total of 381 emergency-room physicians and 52 radiologists provided approximately 14 judgments of prior and posterior quantities each; the study included 8,658 protocols. The seven X-ray procedures (skull, cervical spine, chest, abdomen, lumbar spine, extremities, and intravenous pyelogram) together account for approximately 90% of all radiographs taken in emergency rooms.

In each case the physician requesting the X-ray examination needed the information within 12 hours and typically received it much faster. (That was the main reason for choosing emergency-room settings for study.) Data for each patient consisted of a brief summary of history and physical examination, prior odds or probability assessment, posterior odds or probability assessment, and some qualitative information about the physician's reasoning. The response form asked for numerical judgments (odds or probabilities) about the most likely diagnosis (typically normal) and the most important diagnosis (typically an abnormal condition). Odds judgments were for each disease compared with its negation. Probability judgments were of the probabilities of these two hypotheses only. Since the attending physician might be considering more than one abnormal condition, they could sum to less than 1. Pilot studies had indicated that this dichotomization greatly simplified the judgmental task, without giving up important information.

The first question the investigators examined was: how well do physicians judge probabilities or odds? The data revealed a high degree of consistency in these judgments and a reasonable degree of calibration. Physicians tended to overestimate probabilities attached to abnormal diagnoses. Figure 12.1 shows the general calibration curve. Considering the respondents' lack of familiarity with the probability or odds assessment task and the limited amount of training, practice, and feedback, their calibration is quite good. Were it not for the tendency to overassess the likelihood of dangerous or undesirable events, it would be excellent.

Next the investigators examined the distributions of log likelihood ratios. Table 12.1 shows perhaps the most important result, the percentages of log likelihood ratios that were essentially zero and thus signaled inefficacious radiographs ($-.25 < \text{LLR} < +.25$). As is evident from this table, only a few radiographs truly lacked efficacy-1, regardless of the procedure. Table 12.2 also exhibits the efficacy-1 of these X-ray procedures. It shows that the percentages of "extreme" log odds increase very substantially after radiography.

A third question concerned the extent to which attending physicians order radiography for medicolegal reasons and how efficacy-1 is related to such reasons, which were reported as the primary cause of radiographic examination in 6.1% of the cases. No substantial differences turned up in the distributions of LLRs between these cases and the rest.

This application of a simple Bayesian procedure to the evaluation of the

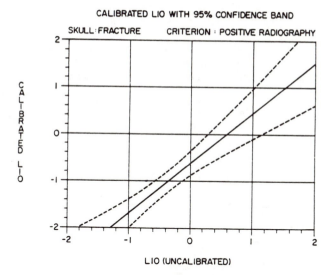

CALIBRATED LIO WITH 95% CONFIDENCE BAND

SKULL·FRACTURE   CRITERION : POSITIVE RADIOGRAPHY

Figure 12.1. Statistical calibration of emergency-room physicians' initial odds (LIO uncalibrated) for the most important diagnosis, skull fracture, compared with radiologists' interpretation of skull radiographs for fracture (calibrated LIO). (*Source:* Lusted et al., 1980.)

Table 12.1. *Percentage of near-zero initial log likelihood ratios ($-0.25 <$ LIO < 0.25)*

Skull	Cervical spine	IVP	Lumbar spine	Chest	Abdomen	Extremities	Total
2.4	0.0	2.6	12.2	2.5	12.3	1.3	4.0
(41)	(38)	(39)	(49)	(322)	(138)	(297)	(924)

Note: Number of cases in parentheses; LIO denotes logarithm of the initial odds; IVP, intravenous pyelogram.
Source: Lusted et al. (1980).

efficacy-1 of radiographs indicates that emergency-room attending physicians do a fairly good job of assessing prior and posterior probabilities or odds and shows that their diagnostic thinking usually benefits from an X-ray examination. Why, in that case, is the notion of unduly high cost and low efficacy of radiology so widespread? Critics of this study make two complaints. One is that emergency rooms are atypical of radiological practice, since they deal so extensively with the aftermath of trauma. X-ray pictures make it easy to spot or rule out broken bones. The other is that the real test of a medical procedure, diagnostic or otherwise, should be at least efficacy-2. The data from the study offer incidental support for this criticism. By far

Table 12.2. *Percentage of cases with log odds less than -1.75 or greater than $+1.25$ for the most important diagnosis*

Procedure (number of cases)	Before radiography	After radiography	Net increase
Skull (1,039)	18.0	71.2	53.2
Cervical spine (958)	23.1	78.1	55.0
IVP (285)[a]	11.3	63.2	51.9
Lumbar spine (807)	16.4	74.2	57.8
Chest (2627)	9.1	59.9	50.8
Abdomen (957)	6.5	49.1	42.6
Extremities (1,985)	10.4	79.1	68.7
All procedures (8,658 cases)	12.7	67.8	55.1

[a]IVP, intravenous pyelogram.
Source: Lusted et al. (1980).

the most common pattern in the data was this: the attending physician worried about some condition or disease consistent with known signs and symptoms and requiring treatment if present but having a medium to low initial probability, ordered X-ray pictures to check, and, reassured, assigned it very low final probability. Most of those associated with this study have concluded that future efficacy studies *must* assess efficacy-2 as well as efficacy-1.

A suicide prediction model[2]

Most people who attempt suicide complain about suicidal thoughts to friends, psychiatrists, or mental health workers first. That is, the probability $P(C|A)$ of a complaint C before an attempted suicide A is much higher than $P(C|\overline{A})$. A good model for predicting suicide attempts from complaint patterns could aid clinicians in making decisions about whether to hospitalize a client and what form of treatment to choose.

If c_i is the ith category of a suicide complaint and if complaint categories and levels within each are conditionally independent, the formal rule for determining the posterior odds of attempt versus nonattempt is

$$\frac{P(A|c_1, \ldots, c_n)}{P(\overline{A}|c_1, \ldots, c_n)} = \frac{P(c_1|A)}{P(c_1|\overline{A})} \frac{P(c_2|A)}{P(c_2|\overline{A})} \cdots \frac{P(c_n|A)}{P(c_n|\overline{A})} \frac{P(A)}{P(\overline{A})}. \qquad (12.2)$$

[2] See Gustafson, Grest, Stauss, Erdman, & Laughren (1977) for a detailed description of this application.

Table 12.3. *Suicide prediction symptoms*

Degree problems can be discussed with most trusted friend	Sex
	Marital status
Existence of suicide plan	Income
Degree of communication of suicide concern to others	Effect of patient's suicide on others
	Age
Living arrangements	Rage
Degree of self-like	Recent loss
Thought disorder	Expected future loss
Concern about achieving major goal	Drug abuse
Accident proneness	Religious attendance
Previous suicide attempt	Family history of mental disorder
Health concern	Patient's prognosis for next 24 hours
Religion	Satisfaction with life and daily activities
Frequency of suicide thought in last 24 hours	Likelihood of solving problems
	Feeling of being needed by others
Duration of current suicide thoughts	Degree of impulsivity
Chance of being dead in 1 month	U.S. citizenship adjustment problems
Alcohol abuse	

Source: Gustafson, Grest, Stauss, Erdman, & Laughren (1977).

Gustafson, Grest, Stauss, Erdman, and Laughren (1977) developed an elaborate interactive computer program to diagnose suicidal patients and to predict the probability of a suicide attempt using this straightforward Bayesian model. They first asked a group of experienced psychiatrists and residents in psychiatry to compose a list of possible symptoms of suicide attempts. The list consisted of 32 symptoms with 246 individual symptom levels (Table 12.3). Next, the researchers asked six clinicians to assess likelihoods for the symptoms and symptom levels by making judgments like the following:

Assume that 100 patients have come in your office with suicidal thoughts, and you know that all of these 100 patients will make a serious attempt within the next three months. Of these hundred patients, how many are:
1. Single _____
2. Married _____
3. Divorced _____
4. Separated _____
5. Widowed _____

Group discussions resolved inconsistent assessments. These assessments generated $P(c_i|A)$. After similarly assessing $P(c_i|\overline{A})$ the analysts were able to calculate the likelihood ratios, the crucial ingredients in the Bayesian model. For example, a future attemptor was judged to be five times more likely to have a suicide plan and to have obtained whatever was needed to carry it out (a handgun, pills, etc.) than a nonattemptor.

Table 12.4. *Sample likelihood ratios for selected symptom levels*

Symptom category	Symptom level	Likelihood ratio	Favoring attempt?
Marital status	Divorced, second time, less than 1 year	1.80	Yes
Age	13–18	1.63	No
Uses drugs	Not at all	1.08	No
Possibility of solving problems	No chance	3.31	Yes
Frequency of suicide thoughts	One to three times per year	2.34	No
	All the time	5.00	Yes
Suicide plan	Has one and has obtained the means	4.69	Yes
Self-image	Moderate	1.13	Yes
Concern about achieving a major goal	Low–moderate	2.60	No
Living arrangements	Alone, does not know neighbors	1.33	Yes

Note: The larger the ratio, the more this symptom level would support the hypothesis in the far-right-hand column.
Source: Gustafson, Grest, Stauss, Erdman, & Laughren (1977).

An interactive computer program based on the resulting model followed an efficient path in eliciting the information required to calculate the posterior odds of a suicide attempt. A typical result of such an interview is the patient profile shown in Table 12.4. All the likelihood ratios are expressed as numbers greater than 1. If they are listed as favoring an attempt, they are of the form $P(c_i|A)/P(c_i|\overline{A})$. If not, the form is $P(c_i|\overline{A})/P(c_i|A)$. Given the profile in Table 12.4 and a prior probability of a suicide attempt of 1/2, the model would assign posterior odds of 19.6 or a posterior probability of .95 to the hypothesis that this patient would attempt suicide.

The model was validated by an experiment and field studies. In the experiment, psychiatrists looked at profiles of patients similar to the one shown in Table 12.4 and made judgments about the probability of a suicide attempt for each. This assessment was compared with the output of the Bayesian model. Fifty profiles described patients who subsequently attempted to commit suicide; 50 profiles described patients who made no such attempt. Table 12.5 shows the percentages of correct predictions for the computer, residents, and experienced clinicians. The computer substantially outperformed the clinicians in predicting attempted suicides, and it was only slightly less accurate in predicting nonattempts. The result obviously reflects the fact that clinicians do not assign a prior as high as .5 to attemptors, whereas the computer worked with the appropriate prior for the experiment – but the superiority of the computer's performance is too great to be explained by that argument alone.

A second dependent measure was the probability assigned to the correct predictions. Obviously one wants the system to assign a very high proba-

Table 12.5. *Percentage of correct predictions of suicide attempts and nonattempts*

	Computer (%)	Residents (%)	Psychiatrists (%)
Attempt	70	33	38
Nonattempt	90	97	93

Source: Adapted from Gustafson, Grest, Stauss, Erdman, & Laughren (1977).

Table 12.6. *Comparison of average probability assigned to correct prediction of attempts and nonattempts by computer and clinicians*

	Computer	Psychiatrist	Resident
Attempt	0.68	0.40	0.34
Nonattempt	0.94	0.86	0.87

Source: Gustafson, Grest, Stauss, Erdman, & Laughren, (1977).

bility to the prediction that eventually turns out to be correct. Table 12.6 shows the average posterior probabilities. On this measure, too, the computer model outperformed the clinicians substantially, especially by assigning a much higher probability to the correct prediction of a serious attempt. The field studies produced similar results.

This model had a rather sad fate: in spite of its obvious success and the subsequent media attention it received, it was never implemented in an ongoing clinical practice. The reasons for this failure are complex. They include the failure of the analysts to turn the program into an aid for clinicians, the complexity and "black box" character of the model, and clinicians' lack of familiarity with computers. We shall return to this implementation failure in Section 12.5.

Assessing the risks of a landslide

A quite different application combining judged probabilities with models was carried out by Keeney and his collaborators (see Keeney, 1980; Keeney and Lamont, 1979). In this application the probability of a landslide at a proposed site had to be assessed as a major input into an overall assessment of the impacts of a proposed geothermal plant in northern California.

An earthquake was considered the main potential cause of a landslide. Figure 12.2 shows that the site was located near three faults, Maacama (MA), Healdsburg and Rodgers Creek (HR), and San Andreas (SA). The cal-

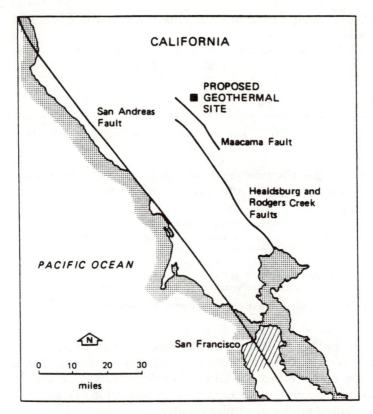

Figure 12.2. Location of the proposed geothermal power plant. (*Source:* Keeney, 1980.)

culation of the overall probability of a slide entailed a clever combination of human judgment and engineering modeling. The structure of the assessment is shown in Figure 12.3.

Let M be the magnitude of an earthquake and let $f_i(M)$, $i = $ SA, HR, MA, be the probability density that such an earthquake will occur at fault i during the 30-year lifetime of the plant. Furthermore, let $P_i(M)$ be the probability of a slide induced by an earthquake of size M. Then the overall probability of a slide induced by an earthquake from fault i during the lifetime of the plant is

$$P_i = \int f_i(M) P_i(M) \, dM. \tag{12.3}$$

Assuming that the probabilities of earthquakes at all faults are independent, the overall probability of at least one slide is

$$p = 1 - (1 - p_{\text{SA}})(1 - p_{\text{HR}})(1 - p_{\text{MA}}). \tag{12.4}$$

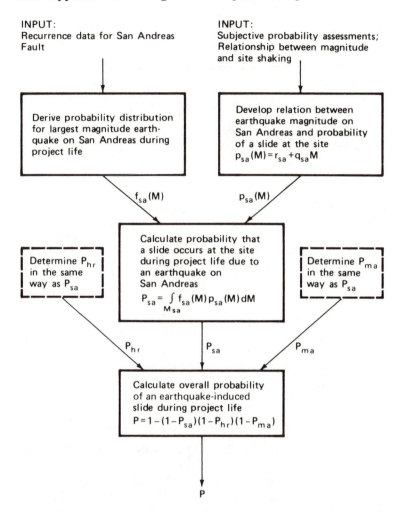

Figure 12.3. Diagrammatic representation of the steps in the landslide analysis. (*Source:* Keeney, 1980.)

The main tasks of the analysis team were to assess the parameters of the density functions f_i and to develop the functional relationships between M and p_i.

The first part of this analysis involved relatively straightforward engineering methods. The general form of the probability density that an earthquake of size M will occur in a period of less than T years is given as

$$f_i(M) = b_i T \exp[a_i - b_i M - T \exp(a_i - b_i M)]. \tag{12.5}$$

Table 12.7. *Parameters for earthquake occurrence*

Fault	a_i	b_i
San Andreas	3.93	1.22
Maacama	3.27	1.66
Healdsburg–Rodgers Creek	5.68	1.66

Source: Keeney (1980).

Table 12.8. *Earthquake acceleration and duration data*

Fault	Earthquake magnitude	Peak site acceleration (g)	Shaking duration (sec)	Probability of slide
San Andreas	7.5	0.25	≤ 40	0.0
	8.5	0.33	40	0.16
Maacama	6.0	0.40	7	0.02
	7.0	0.45	15	0.20
Healdsburg–Rodgers Creek	6.5	0.30	≤ 20	0.0
	7.0	0.35	20	0.03

Source: Keeney (1980).

The number of years T was set at 30, and Table 12.7 shows estimates of a_i and b_i based on seismological data. These values can be substituted into Equation 12.5 to obtain any desired value of $f_i(M)$.

Relating earthquake probabilities to landslide probabilities p_i requires substantial professional judgments. The methods outlined in Chapter 4 were most helpful. The first step was to relate earthquakes of various sizes to peak site acceleration and shaking duration at the site. The results, combining information from the literature with professional judgments, appear in Table 12.8.

The next question was: how are local peak acceleration and duration of an earthquake related to the probability of a landslide? Three engineers were asked to assess these probabilities for various combinations of the two variables directly. The results appear in Figure 12.4. The next step was to combine the functions in Figure 12.4 with the information about peak site acceleration and shaking duration in Table 12.8 to obtain the probability of slide column in Table 12.8. These probabilities are plotted in Figure 12.5 as a function of the earthquake magnitude M. Any desired value of $P_i(M)$ can be read from the graph. With $f_i(M)$ and $p_i(M)$ known, it was easy to calculate

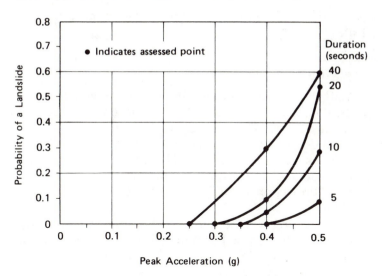

Figure 12.4. Relation between peak acceleration and shaking duration and the probability of a landslide. (*Source:* Keeney, 1980.)

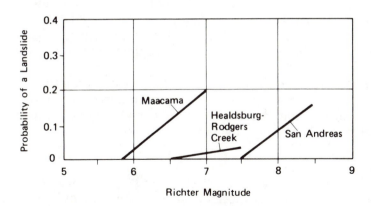

Figure 12.5. Relation between earthquake magnitude and the probability of a landslide. (*Source:* Keeney, 1980.)

the quake-induced slide probabilities for each fault over the 30-year period from Equation 12.3. They were

$$p_{SA} = .007,$$
$$p_{MA} = .003,$$
$$p_{HR} = .002.$$

From Equation 12.4, the overall probability of a landslide on the geothermal plant site over its assumed 30-year life was therefore .012. This result was a major input into the environmental impact assessment of the proposed site.

Prediction of oil spills from oil rigs

Brace yourself! We are about to describe a model that assesses the probability and the consequences of oil spills from drilling and production platforms in the sea. It uses virtually every tool of single-stage Bayesian inference and a great deal of distribution theory. This Poisson–gamma model for oil spill prediction was developed at MIT (see Council for Environmental Quality, 1974) and applied to North Sea platforms by the Central Unit on Environmental Protection (CUEP), a British environmental agency (see CUEP, 1976a,b).

Major spills at oil rigs can be caused by blowouts, structural failures, or large leakages in storage tanks. The probability density of these rare events can be approximated by a Poisson distribution of the form

$$P(n|\lambda, t) = e^{-\lambda t}(\lambda t)^n/n!, \tag{12.6}$$

where n is the number of spills, λ the average rate of occurrence of spills per unit of volume of oil handled, and t the number of units of volume handled. This model assumes that volume of oil is the appropriate "exposure variable" for the Poisson process. Since oil is incompressible, weight is linear with volume; in the remainder of the discussion volume is measured in tons.

Before observing any data, experts will be quite uncertain about the value of the parameter λ. If we assume that the prior uncertainty can be expressed by an (improper) uniform prior distribution and if we observe N spills during handling of T tons of oil, the posterior will be

$$f(\lambda|N, T) = e^{-\lambda t}(\lambda t)^{N-1}T/(N - 1)!. \tag{12.7}$$

Having thus arrived at the posterior over λ, we can calculate the predictive distribution over n, the number of possible spills, by averaging out the uncertainty over the parameter λ. A little calculation shows that this predictive distribution is a negative binomial:

$$P(n|t, N, T) = \{(n + N - 1)!t^n T^N\}\{n!(N - 1)!(t + T)^{n+N}\}. \tag{12.8}$$

Next, we are interested in assessing the *amount* of a spill. Clearly, the majority of spills are small, but there have been a few extremely large ones, like the Santa Barbara spill and the Texaco spill of 1980. Therefore, the probability density function over spill amounts will be highly skewed to the left. Such a distribution can be modeled by a gamma distribution of the form

$$f(x|\rho, w) = e^{-wx}(wx)^{\rho-1}w/(\rho - 1)!, \tag{12.9}$$

Table 12.9. *Data on oil spill rates and spill sizes in the United States*

Study	MIT	CEQ + USGS[a]
Period of observation	1964–72	1964–75
Area of observation	U.S.	U.S. (1973–5, Gulf of Mexico)
Number of accidents	9	10
Production volume (million tons)	527	718
Accident rate (λ)	$\dfrac{1}{58.6 \times 10^6}$	$\dfrac{1}{71.8 \times 10^6}$
Average size of spills (tons)	2,812	2,664
Standard deviation (tons)	3,659	3,481

[a]CEQ, Council for Environmental Quality (1974); USGS, United States Geological Survey (1976).

where x is the size of the spill and w and p are parameters of the gamma distribution. Before observing any spills, one may feel very uncertain about the parameters of the gamma distribution. Assuming an (improper) uniform prior, after a sequence of spills of sizes $x_1, x_2, \ldots, x_m$ have been observed, the appropriate posterior joint density of w and ρ is

$$f(w, \rho \mid m, s, \pi) = e^{-sw}w^{m\rho-1}/\{\Gamma(\rho)\}^m S(m, s, \pi), \qquad (12.10)$$

where $S(m, s, \pi)$ is a normalizing constant, s the sum of the x's, and π the product of the x's. Again, by averaging out the uncertainty over the parameters of the gamma distribution, we can generate a "diluted" predictive distribution over the oil spill sizes:

$$f(x \mid m, s, \pi) = \int\int f(x \mid \rho, w)f(\rho, w \mid m, s, \pi) \, d\rho \, dw. \qquad (12.11)$$

Unfortunately, this integral can be solved numerically only.

Equations 12.8 and 12.11 are all the ingredients one needs to assess the uncertainties about the number and sizes of oil spills on production platforms. In the CUEP adaptation of the methodology, the observations of T, N, and x_i were taken from U.S. Coast Guard data and some data from the North Sea (Table 12.9). Inserting these data in Equations 12.8 and 12.11, the CUEP calculated the distribution over the number of oil spills and the spill amounts (see Table 12.10 and Figure 12.6).

Several summary indices of these distributions are worth discussing in more detail. For example, the chance that there will be no platform spill of size larger then 135 tons in 1981 is 7%. The most likely number of spills is three and there appears to be a large probability (.65) of three or more spills in 1981. Figure 12.6 shows that the median size of an oil spill is about 1,600 tons. But because of the skewedness of the gamma distribution, the expected outflow per accident is relatively large: 3,451 tons for the MIT estimate. Combining the information about expected outflows and expected number

Table 12.10. *Estimated probabilities associated with the number of platform spills over 135 tonnes occurring in the North Sea, 1981*

Number of spills	Probability	Cumulative probability[a]
0	0.07	0.07
1	0.17	0.24
2	0.22	0.45
3	0.20	0.65
4	0.15	0.80
5	0.09	0.90
6	0.05	0.95
7	0.03	0.98
8	0.01	0.99
9 or more	0.01	1.00

Note: Estimated volume of oil produced = 170 million tonnes, excluding any Norwegian oil not piped to Teesside. Spill rate based on MIT data = 1 for every 57 million tonnes produced. Estimated average number of spills = 3.0.

[a]The probability that there will be no more than the corresponding number of spills. The cumulative does not always equal the sum of the probabilities because of rounding errors.

Source: Central Unit on Environmental Pollution (1976a).

of spills, one would estimate that in 1981, the first year of peak production in the North Sea, about 10,000 tons of oil will spill. Of course, there is a nonnegligible chance that no oil will be spilled and a substantial probability that, even if an accident occurs, the actual amount of spilled oil will be relatively small. The expectations are somewhat misleading, since distributions of n and of x are highly skewed. Tail probabilities are probably more useful as inputs to planning. The CUEP and the Petroleum Production Division of the UK Department of Energy used these data and the estimates derived from the Bayesian model to develop emergency plans and to assess sizes of stockpiles needed for cleanup materials.

12.3. Applications to evaluation problems

Evaluating school desegregation plans in Los Angeles[3]

In August 1963, Mary Ellen Crawford filed a suit in Superior Court claiming that the Los Angeles Board of Education was violating her constitutional

[3] This section was condensed from Edwards (1979, 1980). Multiattribute utility measurement: Evaluating desegregation plans in a highly political context, by Edwards, appeared in R. Perloff (Ed.), *Evaluator interventions: Pros and cons.* Copyright © 1979 by Sage Publications, Inc. Adapted by permission of Sage Publications, Inc.

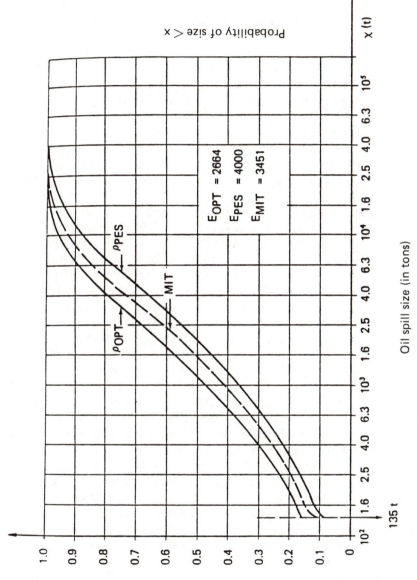

Figure 12.6. Cumulative probability distribution for oil spills of various sizes.

rights in that her school was segregated. This lawsuit initiated a 20-year-long legal battle, which included, at its peak, a multiattribute evaluation of school desegregation plans.

First, some historical background. In 1970, the Superior Court found that the Los Angeles Unified School District (LAUSD) was indeed violating Mary Ellen Crawford's rights and ordered it to desegregate. In 1975, that decision was reversed by the Court of Appeals, and the Court of Appeals was in turn reversed by the California Supreme Court in June 1976. The California Supreme Court found that Mary Ellen Crawford's rights under the Constitution of the State of California, not the U.S. Constitution, had been violated, so their decision was treated as final. On June 28, 1976, the California Supreme Court ordered the district to desegregate. The nature of the order was inevitably relatively general. In a key passage the board was ordered to "immediately prepare and implement a reasonably feasible desegregation plan."

The California Supreme Court decision directed that a Superior Court judge be appointed to monitor and supervise both the planning and execution of the process of desegregating LAUSD. Judge Paul Egly was appointed. Subject to various potential appeals, this made Judge Egly the ultimate arbiter responsible for the evaluation of both the planning and execution of this enormous task. Ultimately (subject to appeal), he would decide what "reasonable and feasible" meant and whether the proposed plans and their execution did or did not meet this vaguely worded mandate.

It is worth pointing out the awesome difficulties of desegregating the LAUSD. The district is huge; in 1976 it included 559 schools and about 600,000 pupils. It sprawls. The maximum linear distance from one end to the other is 58 miles. Freeway distances are longer. Unlike most school districts that are ordered to desegregate, it is for most purposes quadriracial. Its pupils are classified as black, Hispanic-Americans, Asian-Americans and other minorities, and other whites. At the time of the case LAUSD predicted that in the early 1980s Hispanic-Americans would constitute more than 50% of the LAUSD pupil population. Blacks and other whites, both decreasing in number and percentage, would constitute about 20% each. The remaining 10% would be Asian-Americans and other minorities. (These demographic projections did not take into account any changes that might be produced by a desegregation plan.) These predictions have proved correct. A considerable amount of instruction was given then and is given now in Los Angeles schools in languages other than English.

The district, though it extends from the San Fernando Valley to San Pedro, does not include many areas that most would think are part of Los Angeles. Among these areas are Santa Monica, Beverly Hills, Culver City, Burbank, Glendale, Inglewood, Pasadena, Palos Verdes, Torrance, and Compton. Some of them are overwhelmingly white. It would make geographic sense for all of them, except perhaps Pasadena, to be part of the district. Their noninclusion is the result of long-standing political boundaries and was never an overt issue in the case.

No planner in the district seriously considered a metropolitan plan, that is, a plan that would include nondistrict pupils. Only one external plan was of that type (and the evaluation scheme described here was not applied to it). Those in a position to know told Edwards that any metropolitan plan would delay desegregation, because of legal battles, for at least 10 more years.

In the face of these difficulties, several compromise plans were drafted by various interest groups. The Citizens' Advisory Committee on Student Integration (CACSI), originally created by the District to help it formulate a plan, developed a plan that was subsequently rejected by the school board. A modified, less sweeping version of the CACSI plan was submitted to Judge Paul Egly by the school board in June 1977. On July 5, 1977, Egly issued a minute order finding that the board plan was insufficient. It also directed the board to present within 90 days a plan or plans that would realistically commence the desegregation of the district no later than February 1978, to consider all reasonable alternative plans, and to accompany and support its plan or plans and the alternatives by detailed findings and conclusions.

At this point the school board staff decided to devise a method for assembling plans, assessing their impacts, and providing an evaluation system. Edwards was asked to aid in the evaluation of the alternative plans. The procedure used was a simple version of multiattribute utility analysis, SMART (see Chapter 8), which in this application was renamed VAS (value analysis system).

The first step was to identify the decision maker(s). In this case the board made the decisions subject to court review. The second step was to define what dimensions of value were important enough to consider. In a complex topic like school desegregation, such dimensions of value are hierarchically arranged. The first requirement of VAS was to identify the elements of this hierarchy and to determine its structure. The result was a value tree.

Staff members of the school board, together with the analyst, prepared the value tree. It was, inevitably, excessively complex. Comments on early versions by members of the Board of Education and by representatives of the plaintiffs and intervenors led to the addition of many more value dimensions, but not to a restructuring of the tree and certainly not to any simplification. In fact, it was an effort to resist suggestions that would have made it even more complex. The final version of the tree, discussed here, was the eighth.

Figure 12.7 shows the structure of that tree only. The letters in the figure refer to the values included in the tree and are described (in less than full

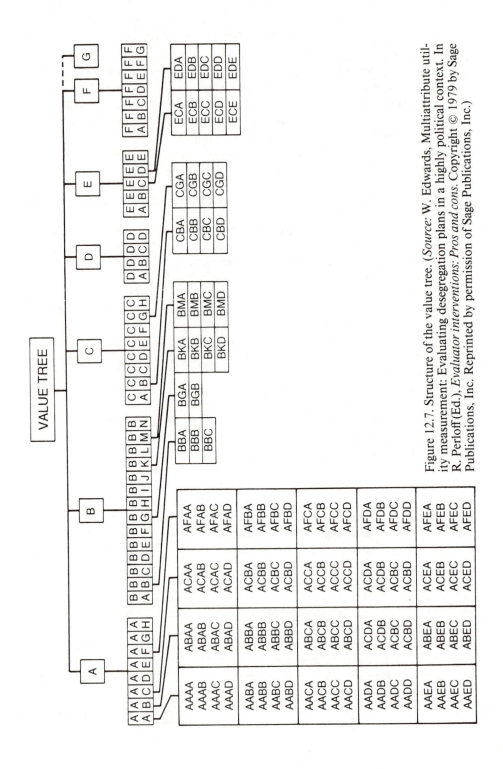

Figure 12.7. Structure of the value tree. (*Source:* W. Edwards, Multiattribute utility measurement: Evaluating desegregation plans in a highly political context. In R. Perloff (Ed.), *Evaluator interventions: Pros and cons.* Copyright © 1979 by Sage Publications, Inc. Reprinted by permission of Sage Publications, Inc.)

detail) in the following:

The value tree, model 8

A   Effect of a desegregation plan on racial–ethnic composition.
B   Effect of a desegregation plan on educational quality.
C   Community acceptance of a desegregation plan.
D   Implications of a desegregation plan for district personnel.
E   Destabilizing effects of a desegregation plan.
F   Provisions within a desegregation plan for monitoring and evaluation.

AA   Racial–ethnic proportions of pupils moved from local schools.
AB   Racial–ethnic proportions in resulting schools.
AC   Racial–ethnic proportions of pupils bused. (*Note:* originally LAUSD expected some nonbusing plans. None were submitted, so this branch was treated like AA.)
AD   Number of grades affected by reassignments.
AE   Duration in weeks of integrated educational experience.
AF   Numbers of students remaining in isolated schools.
AG   Provisions for reduction of racial–ethnic isolation in still segregated schools.
AH   Provisions for effectively preventing the resegregation of integrated schools.

>   AAA, AAB, AAC, AAD, AAE. These are proportions of pupils moved from local schools broken up by grade levels. AAA refers to kindergarten; AAB refers to grades 1–3; AAC refers to grades 4–6; AAD refers to 7–9; AAE refers to 10–12. These were all further partitioned in the full value tree.
>
>   AAAA, AAAB, AAAC, AAAD. These refer to proportions of kindergarten pupils moved from local school who are black, Hispanic-American, other white, and Asian-American and other minority, respectively.
>
>   AABA–AAED. These are like AAAA–AAAD in all respects except that different grade levels are referred to.
>
>   ABA, ABB, ABC, ABD, ABE. These are racial–ethnic proportions of pupils in resulting schools broken up by grade levels, in the same manner as for AAA–AAE. They were all further partitioned in the original value tree.
>
>   AABA–ABED. These are like AAAA–AAED except that they refer to racial–ethnic proportions in resulting schools instead of among those moved.
>
>   ACA, ACB, ACC, ACD, ACE. These are racial–ethnic proportions of pupils bused broken up by grade levels, in the same manner as for AAA–AAE. They were all further partitioned in the original value tree.
>
>   ACAA–ACED. These are like AAAA–AAED, except that they refer to racial–ethnic proportions within grade levels among pupils bused instead of those moved.
>
>   AFA, AFB, AFC, AFD, AFE. These are numbers of students remaining in racially or ethnically isolated schools broken up by grade levels, in the same manner as for AAA–AAE. They were all further partitioned in the original value tree.
>
>   AFAA–AFED. These are numbers of students remaining in racially or ethnically isolated schools broken up by grade levels and by racial–ethnic category.

BA	Impact of a plan on student–teacher ratios.
BB	Impact of a plan on classroom heterogeneity.
BC	Impact of a plan on staff attitudes.
BD	Impact of a plan on student attitudes.
BE	Impact of a plan on learning of basics.
BF	Impact of a plan on participation of volunteers.
BG	Impact of a plan on availability of pupil options.
BH	Impact of a plan on average teacher–student contact hours per day.
BI	Impact of a plan on availability of multicultural education.
BJ	Impact of a plan on teacher quality.
BK	Impact of a plan on adequacy and use of facilities.
BL	Impact of a plan on identification of pupils with their home schools. (A home school is not necessarily a neighborhood school. It is the school to which the pupil is regularly assigned.)
BM	Availability of special programs for pupils with special needs.
BN	Impact of a plan on learning of interracial and interethnic acceptance.
BBA	Impact of a plan on socioeconomic heterogeneity.
BBB	Impact of a plan on heterogeneity of past educational achievement.
BBC	Impact of a plan on heterogeneity of lingual skills.
BGA	Impact of a plan on pupil curricular options.
BGB	Impact of a plan on pupil extracurricular options.
BKA	Impact of a plan on needs for double and short sessions.
BKB	Impact of a plan on reduction of concentration of pupils at high-density schools.
BKC	Provision within a plan for reduction of maintenance backlog.
BKD	Extent to which space is available for new facilities required by a plan.
BMA	Availability of a special program for beginning learners.
BMB	Availability of special programs for educationally disadvantaged pupils (Title 1, SB 90).
BMC	Availability of special programs for gifted pupils.
BMD	Availability of special programs for bilingual and bicultural pupils.
CA	Effect of a plan on parent, community member, teacher, and pupil participation in local school decision making.
CB	Effect of a plan on parental attitudes.
CC	Effect of a plan on the attitudes of opinion leaders.
CD	Effect of a plan on pressure group attitudes.
CE	Effect of a plan on the attitudes of political leaders.
CF	Effect of a plan on media.
CG	Effect of a plan on producing or avoiding family flight.
CH	Existence within a plan of explicit provisions and plans for enhancing community acceptance.
CBA	Effect of a plan on attitudes of black parents.
CBB	Effect of a plan on attitudes of Hispanic-American parents.
CBC	Effect of a plan on attitudes of other white parents.
CBD	Effect of a plan on attitudes of Asian-American or other minority parents.
CGA	Impact of a plan on producing or avoiding flight of black families from LAUSD.
CGB	Impact of a plan on producing or avoiding flight of Hispanic-American families from LAUSD.
CGC	Impact of a plan on producing or avoiding flight of other white families.

CGD	Impact of a plan on producing or avoiding flight of Asian-American or other minority families.
DA	Implications of a desegregation plan for new hires of district personnel.
DB	Implications of a plan for transfers or relocation of district personnel.
DC	Implications of a plan for teacher and other staff development.
DD	Impact of a plan on maintenance of harmonious employee–employer relations within the district.
EA	Number of additional classrooms required.
EB	Planning for phase-in of plan.
EC	Number of students bused.
ED	Average amount of time per bused pupil per day spent riding buses.
EE	Effect of a desegregation plan on the safety of the pupils, teachers, and facilities and equipment.
ECA	Number of kindergarten students bused.
ECB–ECE	Like ECA except that they refer to grades 1–3, 4–6, 7–9, and 10–12, respectively.
EDA–EDE	Average amount of time per bused pupil per day spent riding buses, broken down by the five grade categories.
FA	Provisions within a plan for monitoring and evaluating racial–ethnic compositions.
FB	Provisions within a plan for monitoring and evaluating educational quality.
FC	Provisions within a plan for monitoring and evaluating community acceptance.
FD	Provisions within a plan for monitoring and evaluating implications for district personnel.
FE	Provisions within a plan for monitoring and evaluating destabilizing effects.
FF	Provisions within a plan for monitoring and evaluating the monitoring and evaluation system itself.
FG	Provisions within a plan for monitoring and evaluating its financial implications.

One obvious omission in the value tree is cost. Monetary costs were calculated separately, at least at first approximation, by a relatively simple procedure previously devised by the school board staff. For the most part, district budget experts made cost calculations on the basis of information provided by those preparing plans. The value tree included, of course, non-monetary costs, like travel time and destabilizing effects. In spite of the pitfalls of such numbers, benefit-to-cost ratios seemed useful for the overall evaluation of alternative plans. Such ratios require that both benefits and costs have an origin. Zero benefit was defined as the benefit obtained, using the value tree and weights, from operating LAUSD in 1976–7. Similarly, zero costs were defined as the dollar cost of that year's operation.

Given the value tree in final form, the next step was to elicit importance weights. These were elicited from five of the seven board members, and average weights were computed. Individual weights were and are confidential; it seemed necessary to make them confidential in order to persuade

Table 12.11. *Average board weights for single-letter values*

Top-level attribute	Weight (%)
A: Racial–ethnic compositions	16
B: Educational quality	40
C: Community acceptance	23
D: Implications for district personnel	8
E: Destabilizing aspects	11
F: Monitoring and evaluation	3

Source: W. Edwards, Multiattribute utility measurement: Evaluating desegregation plans in a highly political context. In R. Perloff (Ed.), *Evaluator interventions: Pros and cons.* Copyright © 1979 by Sage Publications, Inc. Reprinted by permission of Sage Publications, Inc.

these elected officials to specify weights at all. Information about the relative importance of racial–ethnic composition and educational quality to board members still active in politics would even today make a lively newspaper story. Representatives of each of the plaintiffs and intervenors in the Crawford case were requested to contribute weights. The plaintiffs, CACSI, and the Integration Project (a probusing organization) chose not to do so. Two antibusing groups (BUSTOP and BEST) prepared weights, but only BEST weights could be considered, because BUSTOP submitted its weights too late. Finally, three highly qualified experts in integration and educational problems contributed weights.

Because of the difficulty of eliciting 144 twig weights, weights were elicited in the hierarchical form described in Chapter 8. The SMART triangular ratio procedure described in Section 8.2 was used. All respondents received extensive instructions and had the opportunity to ask the analyst for help during assessments. Both instructions and individual help emphasized the concept of trade-offs and the dependence of weights on the attribute ranges. Table 12.11 shows the average school board weights for the five top-level attributes.

Educational quality is overwhelmingly the most important issue. Community acceptance is next. Then comes racial–ethnic compositions. Destabilization effects are weighted only 14%; the other values still lower. At this level of generality, the message is clear but not surprising: design an integration program meeting Crawford's requirements that is of high educational quality and engenders community acceptance; those issues are more important than the details of racial–ethnic balance and the problem of destabilization.

Once the value tree and weights were obtained, the next task was to construct single-attribute utility functions for each twig attribute. The assumption that single-attribute utility functions were either linear or triangular (single-peaked and piecewise linear) greatly simplified the assessment. About 70 experts of LAUSD, working in small committees, identified the appropriate type of function and the two (or, for triangular functions, three) extreme points required to specify it.

The following plans were assessed:

1   A plan submitted by an organization called Better Education for Students Today (BEST) emphasizing voluntarism and centers for excellence
2   The plan submitted by the CACSI and rejected by the board, as updated by the CACSI; not voluntary
3   A plan submitted by the Council of Black Administrators (COBA), an advisory group composed primarily of principals of LAUSD schools; also not voluntary
4   A fairly thorough plan developed by a UCLA professor emeritus of history and his students (CAUGHEY)
5   A plan developed by the Integration Project, a probusing group, that called for sweeping busing measures (Integration Project)

Also included in the evaluation were plan A, the school board plan originally rejected by Judge Egly, and plan 0, the no-plan alternative that described the state of the district in 1976–7.

Given weights, utility functions, and expert assessments of the performance of the plans on the twig attributes, the calculation of overall utilities was now merely a matter of computation. Added to this computation of benefits were the calculation of costs and the final derivation of incremental benefit-to-cost ratios. The results are shown in Table 12.12. Plan A, the original plan submitted by the board and rejected by Judge Egly, was the clear winner for all weight sets. Table 12.13 presents scores subaggregated to the six major values of the tree, based on board weights only. Though the plans vary substantially from one dimension to another, their major features are highly visible. For example, the CACSI and Integration Project plans do well on racial–ethnic composition, the CACSI plan does well on destabilizing effects, and plan A does well on educational quality. It surprised many that the two voluntary plans did not do better than they did on educational quality.

Meanwhile, the board was developing yet another plan for submission to Judge Egly. The development of that plan may have been aided by VAS because it could be fine-tuned to score highly on attributes that were considered important. Because of time pressure, the final board plan was not evaluated with the MAUT system. The board adopted the plan and submitted it along with the other plans and their evaluation to Judge Egly. He ordered the second board plan to be implemented to meet the requirements of the Crawford decision.

The case had one more twist. In 1980 a referendum was placed on the California ballot opposing forced busing as a means of achieving desegre-

Table 12.12. *Summary of benefits and costs*

	BEST	BUSTOP[a]	CACSI	CAUGHEY	COBA	Integration project	Plan A	Plan O
Year: 1978–9								
Benefit/cost ratio								
5 board members	.071	—	.027	—	.005	.005	.222	—
Overall benefit								
5 board members	57	50	66	49	54	56	68	53
BEST	55	55	63	50	51	58	70	52
Dr. Havighurst	52	48	64	53	52	58	63	51
Dr. Miller	56	52	63	43	62	51	70	52
Dr. Sullivan	50	46	56	43	47	50	64	52
Annual incremental operating costs (noncumulative)	37.2	NA	69.4	50.9	41.1	122.1	52.7	—
+ Incremental capital costs (cumulative)	18.8	NA	412.5	327.1	168.5	496.3	14.8	—
= Cumulative incremental cost	56.0	NA	481.9	378.0	204.6	618.4	67.5	—
Year: 1981								
Benefit/cost ratio								
5 Board members	.039	—	.026	—	.014	.007	.177	—
Overall Benefit								
5 Board members	60	51	69	52	62	58	71	53
BEST	63	54	68	50	56	59	74	52
Dr. Havighurst	58	48	69	57	60	59	67	51
Dr. Miller	62	53	68	45	66	51	74	52
Dr. Sullivan	50	49	60	46	55	50	69	52
Annual Incremental operating cost (noncumulative)	95.1	NA	94.9	92.0	143.7	151.6	73.0	—
+ Incremental capital costs (cumulative)	83.3	NA	516.4	520.2	517.0	549.2	28.9	—
= Cumulative incremental costs	180.4	NA	611.3	612.2	660.7	700.8	101.9	—

[a]NA denotes not applicable

Source: W. Edwards, Multiattribute utility measurement: Evaluating desegregation plans in a highly political context. In R. Perloff (Ed.), *Evaluator interventions: Pros and cons.* Copyright © 1979 by Sage Publications, Inc. Reprinted by permission of Sage Publications, Inc.)

Table 12.13. *Value profile for each plan using board weights*

5 Board members	BEST	BUSTOP	CACSI	CAUGHEY	COBA	Integration project	Plan A	Plan 0
Year: 1978–9								
A. Racial–ethnic composition	46	43	73	71	51	83	50	28
B. Educational quality	57	57	72	47	54	53	77	54
C. Community acceptance	66	43	57	34	56	52	69	55
D. Effects on district personnel	34	42	36	35	29	28	48	66
E. Destabilizing effects	69	55	80	63	66	58	73	72
F. Monitoring and evaluation	50	50	50	50	66	45	71	50
Year: 1981–2								
A. Racial–ethnic composition	60	43	70	77	79	84	51	28
B. Educational quality	62	57	80	48	59	54	81	54
C. Community acceptance	68	43	54	35	57	55	70	55
D. Effects on district personnel	24	51	50	46	39	36	57	66
E. Destabilizing effects	68	55	82	70	74	57	82	72
F. Monitoring and evaluation	50	50	50	50	66	41	61	50

Source: W. Edwards, Multiattribute utility measurement: Evaluating desegregation plans in a highly political context. In R. Perloff (Ed.), *Evaluator interventions: Pros and cons.* Copyright © 1979 by Sage Publications, Inc. Reprinted by permission of Sage Publications, Inc.

gation. The referendum passed, and the California Supreme Court held it to be constitutional. With that decision, forced busing ended in Los Angeles.

Prioritizing research projects for the Construction Engineering Research Laboratory[4]

The Construction Engineering Research Laboratory (CERL) is a major research laboratory of the U.S. Army Corps of Engineers. Its research produces products and systems in response to construction-related army needs and requirements. Environmental problems, energy systems, and information technologies have received the most attention in the past few years. Examples of CERL product/systems (as they call their projects) include systems for energy conservation in army installations, techniques for noise reduction at training facilities, and computer-aided engineering and architectural design systems. Almost all work is done in-house, not on contract.

As in any other research laboratory, the total amount of money requested to implement the ideas proposed each year typically exceeds the funds available. Of approximately 200 proposals made each year, only about 100 are funded. Consequently, the management of CERL has the yearly task of selecting attractive new research projects, deciding on the desirability of continuing old ones, selecting funding levels for all projects to be funded, and rejecting other projects. This problem is complicated by the diversity of CERL's product/systems and by the fact that several divisions within CERL in effect compete for research funds.

The management of CERL sought to develop more rational procedures for selecting funding levels for product/systems. They wanted a formal prioritization system for research proposals and projects. After several unsuccessful attempts at developing such a system (which included cost–benefit approaches and attempts to assess return on investment for selected product/systems) management decided to try multiattribute utility measurement for evaluating and prioritizing projects. What follows is a description of the procedures we used to apply SMART (see Chapter 8) to the task. This time the output was called a multiattribute aid for prioritization (MAP). It seems to be the fate of SMART to be relabeled each time it is used; perhaps Edwards's original choice of that acronym wasn't smart at all.

The first and most important task was to develop a value tree capturing the values of CERL scientists, managers, and others involved in setting product/system priorities. We spent 4 days at CERL interviewing the key

---

[4] This section was condensed from Edwards, von Winterfeldt, and Moody, Simplicity in decision analysis: An example and a discussion. Copyright © by the President and Fellows of Harvard College. Condensed by permission of the Harvard Business School. To appear in D. Bell (Ed.), *Decision making: Descriptive, normative, and prescriptive interactions.* Cambridge, Mass.: Harvard Business School, in press.

CERL scientists and managers in depth. Of particular interest was the issue of divisional specificity of the value dimensions. CERL has four main divisions: Facility Planning and Design, Construction Management and Technology, Energy and Energy Conservation, and Environmental Quality. The Energy and Environment divisions are budgeted separately, but Facility Planning and Design and Construction Management and Technology essentially compete for the same budget. These four divisions shared a total budget of more than $7 million in fiscal year 1981. In addition, several smaller sets of activities do not fit the divisional boundaries. These include basic research, combat engineering, and mobilization. An early decision was to apply the prioritization system only to the major divisions.

Management wanted to develop a prioritization system that cut across budgetary boundaries. This offered an interesting challenge. Would it be possible to abstract from divisional values and find value dimensions that would apply to all programmatic activities? As we mentioned earlier, the product/systems CERL develops are extremely diverse. If proposals in the environmental division were evaluated using contribution to environmental quality as a criterion, that criterion might be quite inapplicable to new information technologies. Fortunately, we realized very early in our interviews that divisional objectives were in fact quite similar. They had to do with user requirements, the extent of army need for the product/system and of army perception of that need, and the ability to transfer CERL's output to its intended users. We suspect that such abstract values necessarily develop in a laboratory that produces a very broad spectrum of products and services.

Our interviews were relatively informal but focused on eliciting value structures. We asked questions like what is a high-priority product/system? We probed intradivisional values, the need for staff continuity, for example. And we suggested some values of our own, such as the value of enhancing professional stature. The result was the value tree, model 1, shown in Figure 12.8. A copy of this value tree was circulated to all division heads and to top-level management for comment. Subsequently one of us (Edwards) visited CERL again to explore in detail their responses to the proposed tree. The numerous changes that had been made were supposed to have resulted in a final tree; however another visit was necessary to make additional modifications and to establish consensus. The final tree is shown in Figure 12.9. It differs from the initial tree not only in wording, but also in general structure. The final tree is simple – it only has two levels and it is more precise than the first tree about the mission-oriented values.

The next task was to obtain weights. Division chiefs, clear that weights were expressions of priorities among values, were quite content to have the two top managers of CERL provide them. Edwards arranged to spend an uninterrupted afternoon with the managers, away from phones and other distractions. Weight elicitation began with a rather careful explanation of

A. CERL-wide issues
  - AA. Relevance to CERL mission
  - AB. Conformity to guidance from STOG, QCR, MAD, and similar sources
  - AC. Contribution to strategy
    - ACA. Conformity to a well-developed and accepted strategy
    - ACB. Contribution to or initiation of a developing or new strategy
  - AD. Degree of uniqueness
  - AE. Contribution to CERL program diversification

B. Division-specific issues
  - BA. Prior effort in this product/system should be carried to completion
  - BB. Appropriate use of available people and/or equipment resources

C. Proponents, users, champions
  - CA. Type of external support
    - CAA. Rank
    - CAB. Organizational location
  - CB. "Loudness" of external support
  - CC. Importance of the problem addressed by the product/system

D. Anticipated degree of success
  - DA. Anticipated degree of technical success
  - DB. Timeliness
    - DBA. Likelihood of completion on schedule
    - DBB. Duration of anticipated need for product/system after completion
  - DC. Ease of technology transfer
    - DCA. Anticipated life-cycle cost of product/system to user(s)
    - DCB. Availability of user resources needed for successful transfer

E. Direct cost to CERL

F. Anticipated cost savings to user(s)

Figure 12.8. Value Tree for CERL, model 1. (*Source:* W. Edwards, D. von Winter-feldt, & D. L. Moody, Simplicity in decision analysis: An example and a discussion. Paper delivered at the Harvard Business School 75th Anniversary Colloquium on Decision-Making: descriptive, normative, and prescriptive interactions, June 1983. Copyright © 1983 by the President and Fellows of Harvard College. Reprinted by permission of the Harvard Business School, in press.)

weights, with emphasis on the notion of trade-offs, the fact that ranges are weights, and the counterintuitive nature of range effects. Then each manager, working independently, judged weights using the SMART procedure with triangular consistency checks. Finally, the managers compared normalized weights and revised them until they had an agreed-on and consistent additive weight structure with agreed-on and consistent triangular consistency checks. The whole process took about $3\frac{1}{2}$ hours. Table 12.14 shows the result. Values related to need (mission-oriented values) and use (anticipated benefits) received the highest weights. The weight for direct cost was relatively low. CERL is a very stable and secure organization; neither its own funding nor that of elements within it is subject to much year-to-year fluctuation.

A. Mission-oriented issues
    AA. Relevance to army mission areas
    AB. Conformity to validated requirements
    AC. Well-defined problem and solution fits into (mission-related) activities
    AD. Opportunity for technological breakthrough

B. Resources and effort issues
    BA. Future effort required for completion of product/system
    BB. Appropriate use of resources

C. Characteristics of champion and/or champions
    CA. Position of champion
    CB. Emphasis of external support

D. Anticipated degree of success
    DA. Anticipated degree of technical success
    DB. Timeliness
    DC. Duration of anticipated usage for product/system after completion
    DD. Ease of technology transfer

E. Direct remaining research and development cost to CERL

F. Anticipated benefits to users
    FA. Tangible benefits
    FB. Other benefits

Figure 12.9. Value tree for CERL, model 4. (*Source:* W. Edwards, D. von Winter-feldt, & D. L. Moody, Simplicity in decision analysis: An example and a discussion. Paper delivered at the Harvard Business School 75th Anniversary Colloquium on Decision-Making: Descriptive, Normative, and Prescriptive Interactions, June 1983. Copyright © in 1983 by the President and Fellows of Harvard College. Reproduced by permission of the Harvard Business School, in press.)

Once the value structure and weights were firmly established, each division chief established a small committee on which he sat to rate that division's product/systems on each branch of the tree. Working with the program office managers, we had prepared detailed worksheets for scoring the product/systems on each twig; each worksheet included a careful definition of the scores. Table 12.15 presents two examples. These definitions had an interesting history. Initially, the program office managers wanted much more objective definitions, preferably using either more objectively measurable values or proxy variables for the subjective values or both. Attempts to develop such objective definitions were vigorously rejected by the top managers and division leaders alike; they wanted values that expressed what they really cared about, subjective or not, but they also wanted guidelines for judgment. In our experience, those two preferences are common in secure organizations. Most managers acknowledge that evaluations are and should be subjective; they want guidance about how to make a complex subjective task simpler and more orderly, not less subjective. In the applications we have conducted, insecurity, need for organizational self-justification, and a knee-jerk belief that "subjective" implies "inferior" characterize

Table 12.14. *CERL weights for the value tree, 1982*

Node code	Normalized weight	Twig weight
A. Mission-oriented values	.39	
AA	.50	.1950
AB	.13	.0507
AC	.06	.0234
AD	.31	.1209
B. Resources and effort issues	.05	
BA	.50	.0250
BB	.50	.0250
C. Characteristics of champion(s)	.18	
CA	.67	.1206
CB	.33	.0594
D. Anticipated degree of technical success	.12	
DA	.15	.0180
DB	.46	.0552
DC	.08	.0096
DD	.31	.0372
E. Direct remaining cost to CERL	.02	.0200
F. Anticipated benefits to user(s)	.24	
FA	.67	.1608
FB	.33	.0792

Source: W. Edwards, D. von Winterfeldt, & D. L. Moody, Simplicity in decision analysis: An example and a discussion. Copyright © 1983 by the President and Fellows of Harvard College. Reproduced by permission of the Harvard Business School. To appear in D. Bell (Ed.), *Decision making: Descriptive, normative, and prescriptive interactions.* Cambridge, Mass.: Harvard Business School, in press.

organizations for which the use of inherently subjective dimensions has presented problems.

Independently of these ratings by the division chiefs, two office program managers rated the 97 product/systems that were evaluated on all attributes. We made arrangements for disagreements to be resolved by top management; they were unnecessary. Disagreements were easily resolved in the discussions between division chiefs and the program office managers.

The overall value of each product/system could now simply be computed using the additive model and the weights provided by top management. Top management and each division leader discussed the results and made decisions about support and funding level or exclusion of that division's existing and proposed product/systems. There was surprisingly little disagreement; all participants felt that MAP substantially facilitated these tough decisions.

This application of multiattribute utility measurement was unique (as far

Table 12.15. *Examples of scoring instruction for rating product/system (P/S)*

AA. Relevance to army mission areas
    100: P/S directly supports five sub-mission areas
     90: P/S directly supports four sub-mission areas
     75: P/S directly supports three sub-mission areas
     60: P/S directly supports two sub-mission areas
     50: P/S directly supports one sub-mission area
      0: P/S supports *no* sub-mission area

    Sub-mission Areas: Base/facility development
                           Installation support activities
                           Energy conservation and alternate sources
                           Environmental quality
                           Military engineering

FA. Tangible benefits to users
    100: P/S provides for reduction in work efforts and/or improvement in productivity plus reduction in equipment, training, materials, and operating costs
     80: P/S provides reduction in work efforts and/or improvement in productivity plus reduction in equipment and materials
     60: P/S provides reduction in work effort and/or improvement in productivity
     40: P/S provides reduction in work effort and/or improvement in productivity *but* higher costs for materials and equipment
      0: P/S provides no tangible benefits

Source: W. Edwards, D. von Winterfeldt, & D. L. Moody, Simplicity in decision analysis: An example and a discussion. Copyright © 1983 by the President and Fellows of Harvard College. Reproduced by permission of the Harvard Business School. To appear in D. Bell (Ed.), *Decision making: Descriptive, normative, and prescriptive interactions.* Cambridge, Mass.: Harvard Business School, in press.

as we know) in that it involved a large number of objects of evaluation. Some of the statistics that describe the judged twig ratings for the 97 product/systems are instructive. Table 12.16 shows the means, standard deviations, and ranges of these ratings, together with the twig weights. The most obvious finding is that all mean ratings are greater than 50 except on twig BA. Ratings on the attributes related to the anticipated degree of success are particularly high. This is to be expected; informal processes eliminate obviously unattractive product/systems before they reach formal evaluation. The next finding is that the attribute intercorrelations are generally low (see Table 12.17). There are no dramatic halo effects. The five high attribute intercorrelations have obvious explanations. For example, a highly placed champion (CA) is in a position to create validated requirements (AB).

The third finding is that the entire range was used for most attributes. The serious exceptions are AA, BB, and DB. Exceptions such as these raise several questions. Were the ranges and end-point definitions initially plausible? At least in the case of DB, we believe the definition of the zero point

Table 12.16. *CERL twig weights and descriptors*

Twig	Weight	Mean	Standard deviation	Range Min	Max
AA	.1950	61	11.0	50	90
AB	.0507	69	26.5	0	100
AC	.0234	71	20.1	0	100
AD	.1209	71	20.7	0	100
BA	.0250	45	27.0	0	100
BB	.0250	89	11.1	50	100
CA	.1206	59	29.1	0	100
CB	.0594	53	27.6	0	100
DA	.0180	80	15.7	25	100
DB	.0552	94	6.5	70	100
DC	.0096	87	16.7	20	100
DD	.0372	73	22.4	0	100
E	.0200	63	21.0	25	100
FA	.1608	68	15.2	20	100
FB	.0792	64	20.0	0	100

Source: W. Edwards, D. von Winterfeldt, & D. L. Moody, Simplicity in decision analysis: An example and a discussion. Copyright © 1983 by the President and Fellows of Harvard College. Reproduced by permission of the Harvard Business School. To appear in D. Bell (Ed.), *Decision making: Descriptive, normative, and prescriptive interactions.* Cambridge, Mass.: Harvard Business School, in press.

was not. Do the weight judgments reflect the ranges actually stated, even though they were not realized? We think so – on the basis of some informal ex post facto trade-off judgments we asked the decision makers to perform. Should we have expected all of the plausible range to be used for each twig? Clearly not. In instances like this in which the entire evaluation scheme, including weights, must be in place before evaluations are made, even 97 product/systems may not be enough to span the full range of 15 variables, especially since they are subject to informal preselection. A far smaller number of options characterizes most applications; one would expect few if any ranges to be fully covered. As long as the weights are appropriately related to the ranges, that fact makes no difference to the order or spacing of the output values. We like procedures based on plausible ranges even in contexts in which the single-dimension values for all options are known before the weights are assessed. If procedures based on trade-offs or gambles are to be used for weight elicitation, they can equally well be based on the option locations on scales defined by plausible rather than actual ranges. If you find such procedures harder to use with end points other than 0 and 100, that finding should raise questions about the meaning of intermediate numbers obtained from questions in which the end points are 0 and 100. If the trade-

Table 12.17. *Interattribute correlation matrix*

	AA	AB	AC	AD	BA	BB	CA	CB	DA	DB	DC	DD	E	FA	FB
AA	1.00														
AB	0.03	1.00													
AC	−0.05	0.25	1.00												
AD	−0.13	0.15	0.28	1.00											
BA	−0.16	−0.16	0.05	−0.09	1.00										
BB	−0.10	0.07	0.05	0.02	0.26	1.00									
CA	0.07	0.69	0.32	0.06	−0.11	0.04	1.00								
CB	−0.01	0.54	0.31	0.08	−0.11	−0.06	0.69	1.00							
DA	−0.04	0.01	−0.28	−0.23	0.23	0.29	0.02	−0.06	1.00						
DB	0.00	−0.36	0.03	−0.11	0.24	−0.10	−0.34	−0.32	0.21	1.00					
DC	−0.09	0.26	0.22	−0.14	−0.11	−0.02	0.28	0.22	0.18	−0.25	1.00				
DD	−0.22	0.32	0.55	0.21	0.06	0.09	0.14	0.28	0.30	−0.05	0.29	1.00			
E	−0.24	−0.29	−0.01	−0.16	0.79	0.27	−0.29	−0.27	0.12	0.28	−0.19	0.00	1.00		
FA	−0.04	−0.15	0.20	0.30	0.20	0.02	0.00	−0.07	0.03	0.08	0.05	−0.02	0.14	1.00	
FB	0.20	0.28	0.14	0.37	−0.14	0.03	0.27	0.13	−0.08	−0.09	0.23	−0.03	−0.23	0.10	1.00

Source: W. Edwards, D. von Winterfeldt, & D. L. Moody, Simplicity in decision analysis: An example and a discussion. Copyright © 1983 by the President and Fellows of Harvard College. Reproduced by permission of the Harvard Business School. To appear in D. Bell (Ed.), *Decision making: Descriptive, normative, and prescriptive interactions.* Cambridge, Mass.: Harvard Business School, in press.

off judgments or gambles are expressed in physical units, the issue should not arise, since only by accident (or approximation) will the arbitrary definitions of 0 and 100 coincide with convenient round values of the physical variables.

Both top managers and division chiefs in CERL were highly satisfied with MAP and have continued to use it. They have come to realize that MAP, like any useful evaluation procedure, is also a program design tool and a monitoring guide. New internal proposals in CERL have taken the MAP format to some extent and routinely deal with the issues specified by it. In ongoing monitoring of programs in progress, managers make sure that they track the MAP dimensions. If you have an evaluation tool in which you believe, it is entirely appropriate to do whatever you can to optimize the aspects of performance it measures.

A final note: MAP contributed to decision making about allocations of roughly $10,000,000 in 1982 and even more in 1983. It cost less than $30,000 as well as a great deal of CERL staff time, to develop and use once. We deliberately gave CERL a bargain, for various reasons not relevant here, but a normal price for this job should not be greater than $75,000, in 1982 currency. CERL actually spent an identifiable .3% of the amount to be allocated in order to buy a tool to help perform the allocation. Either that figure or the .75% that we suggest would be a normal price is extremely low. A common rule of thumb is that, for any given expenditure, one should add 10% for thinking about how to spend the original amount properly. Our experience suggests that sophisticated assistance in such thought processes seldom costs anything like 10% – and typically saves much more than that.

Evaluation of pumped storage sites[5]

So far we have described two applications of Edwards's SMART procedure. In this section we report Ralph Keeney's (1979, 1980) evaluation of alternative sites for a pumped storage electricity generation facility, in which lotteries were used to assess utility functions. An electrical utility that foresees future inability to meet demand can increase its capacity in two ways. It can enhance its ability to supply base load by building a large generating facility with oil, coal, or nuclear power. Such facilities are cornerstones of any electrical system. Peak load supply facilities provide additional supplies for short periods of time when demand peaks and threatens to create shortages. A favored method for supplying peak load electricity is to pump water up a hill to a reservoir using the surplus electricity available during off-peak hours. During peak hours, the water moves to a downhill reservoir through turbines that drive generators and produce additional electricity.

---

[5] This section was adapted from Keeney (1980).

Table 12.18. *Preliminary list of general concerns and considerations*

General concerns	Considerations
Health and safety	Consequences of dam breach
	Impact on water quality due to reservoir development
Environmental effects	Terrestrial ecological impact
	Aquatic ecological impact
	Equalization of species composition between reservoirs
	Ecological impact from disposing of blowdown waters
	Transmission line impacts
Socioeconomic effects	Recreation potential
	Preemption of resources
	Archaeological features
	Land acquisition
	Sociopolitical system effects
Economics	Cost for adequate safety and operability
	System reliability
	Reserve capacity
Public attitudes	Public acceptance

Source: Keeney (1980).

Although the technology for pumped storage facilities is relatively straightforward, finding appropriate sites for such facilities is not. A facility has to be reasonably close to the areas it will supply. The site must have a steep gradient to produce a substantial height differential between the uphill and downhill reservoir. The site should be fairly small, and the land cheap and accessible. Building and using the facility should not damage the environment. These objectives normally conflict.

A Southwest utility company asked Keeney and his colleagues from Woodward–Clyde Consultants to screen potential pumped storage sites and aid in selecting an appropriate one. They used a multiattribute utility approach adapted to the sequential nature of the screening, evaluation, and selection process that typifies siting decisions (see also Keeney, 1980).

The first step was to evaluate the vast area in which pumped storage facilities could be located. Regions with scenic, cultural, aesthetic, or archeological significance were eliminated, as were highly populated areas. Other areas were eliminated on the basis of more technical criteria. For example, the height differential between reservoirs had to be at least 500 feet, with a relatively steep gradient and large potential reservoirs. This process left about 70 candidate *areas*. Aerial reconnaissance eliminated 50 areas, and on-site inspection reduced the candidate set to 10 sites.

A detailed multiattribute utility analysis was then undertaken. The analysts, working with utility representatives, first generated a list of general concerns and values (Table 12.18). Not all values in Table 12.18 differen-

Table 12.19. *Final objectives and attributes*

Objective	Attribute
Minimum cost	Capital and operations cost
Minimum transmission line impacts	Aesthetic and environmental damage
Minimum ecological and environmental impacts	Pinyon–juniper forest destruction; riparian community

Source: Adapted from Keeney (1980).

tiated among the sites; not all seemed important. For example, archeological impact seemed irrelevant for all sites and was therefore left out. Table 12.19 shows the very simple final set of attributes.

The analysts carefully operationalized each of the four main attributes. Costs were defined as first-year capital plus operational costs. Ecological and aesthetic impacts of transmission lines were measured judgmentally on a scale labeled "mile equivalents." One mile equivalent was defined as a mile of transmission lines having minimal environmental impact: not visible from highways, passing through only unpopulated rangeland, not having any harmful effect on endangered species, and not passing through pristine areas. Ten mile equivalents were defined as one mile of transmission lines having maximum environmental impact: traversing state or national parks, wildlife refuges, historic monument sites, or habitats that contained unusual or unique animal communities or supported endangered species. The aesthetic and environmental damage produced by transmission lines was assessed by measuring mileage in each area and then multiplying that measurement by the mile equivalent figure judged appropriate to the characteristics of that area. The sum of such products was then treated as a one-dimensional value scale. Note that two points were defined, conforming to the tradition that utilities are defined up to a linear transformation and thus have two free parameters. If one makes the quite reasonable assumption, implicit in the method of using mile equivalents, that the (negative) utility of having no transmission line is 0, then these definitions amount to the strong assumption that no single mile of transmission line through areas relevant to these sites could be worse than 10 times as bad as the best possible mile, considering only aesthetic and environmental effects. Of course, if the assessors had regarded that assumption as dubious, they would have chosen a larger ratio.

Ecological and environmental impacts at the site were operationalized as acres of pinyon–juniper forest lost and yards of riparian community lost as a result of building the facility. Table 12.20 lists the attributes and the plausible ranges chosen for them. The measurements and judgments of the site impacts were performed by financial experts of the utility company for the

Table 12.20. *Final attributes for pumped storage ranking*

Attribute	Measure	Range	
		Best	Worst
x_1 = first-year cost	Millions of 1976 dollars	50	75
x_2 = transmission line distance	Mile equivalents	0	800
x_3 = pinyon–juniper forest	Acres	0	800
x_4 = riparian community	Yards	0	2000

Source: Keeney (1980).

Table 12.21. *Data for evaluating pumped storage candidate sites*

Candidate site	First-year cost (millions $)	Transmission line (mile equivalents)	Pinyon–juniper (acres)	Riparian community (yards)
		Base data		
S1	56.01	97.8	230	0
S2	59.18	140.0	150	0
S3	61.48	163.0	0	0
S4	59.68	342.3	0	0
S5	64.47	91.0	270	0
S6	61.36	152.7	721[a]	2,000
S7	58.23	681.0	0	0
S8	59.92	704.0	240	0
S9	49.71	84.2	260	1,900[b]
S10	75.42	392.7	419[c]	1,600
		Alternative data		
S9*	49.71	84.2	260	1,900[d]
S6*	51.64[e]	152.7	721[a]	2,000
S8*	52.98[e]	704.0	240	0
S7*	65.19[f]	681.0	0	0

[a]Includes addition of 350 acres for damage to arroyo seeps.
[b]Assumes this 1,900 yards is a unique riparian community.
[c]Includes addition of 200 acres for impact on raptors.
[d]Assumes this 1,900 yards is a "normal" riparian community.
[e]Assumes upper reservoir is not completely lined.
[f]Assumes upper reservoir is completely lined.
(*Source:* Keeney, 1980.)

first attribute and by Woodward–Clyde Consultants for the other three. The results for the 10 sites are shown in Table 12.21.

The next step was to construct a utility model based on judgments by representatives of the utility company. In tests of the three key assumptions of the additive and multiplicative expected utility models, joint indepen-

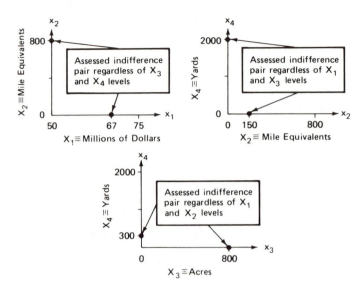

Figure 12.10. Invariant value trade-offs, indicating preferential independence. (*Source:* Keeney, 1980.)

dence and multiplicative utility independence were approximately satisfied, and additive utility independence was not. Figures 12.10 and 12.11 show some of the tests that led to these conclusions. The following model was selected to represent the structure of the utility company's preferences:

$$1 + ku(x_1, x_2, x_3, x_4) = \prod_{i=1}^{4}[1 + kk_iu_i(x_i)]. \qquad (12.12)$$

The lottery procedures outlined in Chapters 7 and 8 were used to construct single-attribute utility functions. Figure 12.12 shows the results. Note that the scale for utility used in the figure is 0 to 1, not 0 to 100. Additional indifference judgments were needed to obtain the scaling factors k_i and k. The analysts used a version of the BRLT procedure described in Chapter 8. First they fixed x_3 and x_4 at their worst levels. This means that $u_3(x_3^*) = u_4(x_4^*) = 0$. This causes all terms of Equation 12.12 that involve u_3 or u_4 or both to drop out. For any such option, Equation 12.12 can therefore be rewritten as

$$u(x_1, x_2, x_3^*, x_4^*) = k_1u_1(x_1) + k_2u_2(x_2) + kk_1k_2u_1(x_1)u_2(x_2). \quad (12.13)$$

Bear in mind that a BRLT is a lottery between the best and worst options. In this case, since x_3 and x_4 are fixed at their worst levels, the two possible outcomes of the BRLT are $(x_1^*, x_2^*, x_3^*, x_4^*)$. and $(x_1^*, x_2^*, x_3^*, x_4^*)$. By defini-

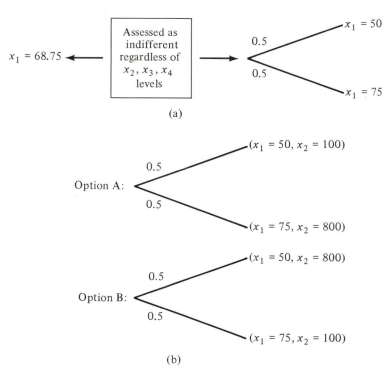

Figure 12.11. Examining potential independence conditions. (a) Invariant difference indicates x_1 multiplicative expected utility independent of (x_2, x_3, x_4). (b) Preference for option B violates additive expected utility independence.

tion $u_1(x_1^*) = u_2(x_2^*) = 0$. Consequently,

$$u(x_1^*, x_2^*, x_3^*, x_4^*) = k_1 + k_2 + kk_1k_2 \qquad (12.14)$$

and

$$u(x_1^*, x_2^*, x_3^*, x_4^*) = 0. \qquad (12.15)$$

Thus, a BRLT having probability p of winning $(x_1^*, x_2^*, x_3^*, x_4^*)$ and probability of $1 - p$ of winning $(x_1^*, x_2^*, x_3^*, x_4^*)$ has expected utility $EU(p) = p(k_1 + k_2 + kk_1k_2)$. Next, consider an option in which all dimensions except x_1 are set at their worst levels, and x_1 is set at its best level. Inspection of Equation 12.12, given that all u_i's except that for x_1 are zero and that $u_1(x_1)$ is 1, shows that the value of such an option is k_1. This result is general; if the ith attribute is set at its best level and all other attributes are set at their worst levels, the utility of the option thus defined is k_i. So k_2 is the utility of $(x_1^*, x_2^*, x_3^*, x_4^*)$. If p_1 is the BRLT judgment made when x_1 is set at its best

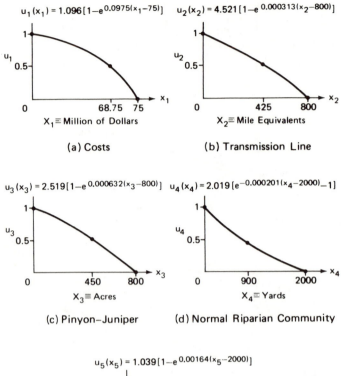

$u_1(x_1) = 1.096[1-e^{0.0975(x_1-75)}]$ $u_2(x_2) = 4.521[1-e^{0.000313(x_2-800)}]$

(a) Costs

(b) Transmission Line

$u_3(x_3) = 2.519[1-e^{0.000632(x_3-800)}]$ $u_4(x_4) = 2.019[e^{-0.000201(x_4-2000)}-1]$

(c) Pinyon–Juniper

(d) Normal Riparian Community

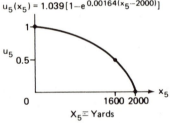

$u_5(x_5) = 1.039[1-e^{0.00164(x_5-2000)}]$

(e) Distinct Riparian Community

Figure 12.12. Assessed utility functions. (a) Costs; (b) transmission line; (c) pinyon–juniper; (d) normal riparian community. *x_4 had a different shape for site 9, which involved destruction of a rare riparian community. (*Source:* Keeney, 1980.)

level and p_2 is that judgment made when x_2 is set at its best level, then

$$k_1 = p_1(k_1 + k_2 + kk_1k_2) \tag{12.16}$$

and

$$k_2 = p_2(k_1 + k_2 + kk_1k_2). \tag{12.17}$$

Keeney found that p_1 and p_2 were .75 and .40, respectively.

We are dealing with a problem having five unknowns, the four k_i's and k. We have two equations; we need three more.

Keeney got two more equations from the judgments reported in Figure 12.10. The second panel of the figure shows that, regardless of x_1 and x_3 levels, the worst value of x_4, 2000 yards, was judged equivalent to 150 mile equivalents. More precisely, the judgment was

$$u(x_1^*, x_2^*, x_3^*, x_4^*) = u(x_1^*, x_2 = 150, x_3^*, x_4^*). \tag{12.18}$$

In other words, the respondent could just be compensated for a change in x_2 from its best value, 0 miles, to 150 miles by changing x_4 from its worst value, 2000 yards, to its best value, 0 yards. Moreover, this was true for any fixed values of x_1 and x_3. Therefore,

$$k_2 = k_4 + k_2 u_2(150) + kk_4 k_2 u_2(150). \tag{12.19}$$

Exactly the same procedure can be applied to the judgment reported in the third panel of Figure 12.10. The result is

$$k_4 = k_3 + k_4 u_4(300) + kk_3 k_4 u_4(300). \tag{12.20}$$

Now we have four equations. But since there are five unknowns, we need a fifth equation to solve for them. We can easily obtain one simply by considering the utility of $(x_1^*, x_2^*, x_3^*, x_4^*)$, the option composed of the best levels on all four attributes. Of course, all u_i values for that option are 1. If we substitute those 1's into Equation 12.12, we obtain

$$1 + k = \prod_{i=1}^{4}(1 + kk_i). \tag{12.21}$$

Now at last we have five equations; solving them for our five unknowns is simply a matter of fairly complex number-crunching. To do that, of course, we must know the values of $u_2(150)$ and $u_4(300)$. These come from the equations in panels b and d of Figure 12.12.

The final output of this work is

$$k_1 = .716,$$
$$k_2 = .382,$$
$$k_3 = .014,$$
$$k_4 = .077,$$
$$k = -.0534.$$

The negative value of k means that the decision maker is multiattribute risk averse. Table 12.22 shows the resulting utilities for the possible sites. To make the interpretation of the utilities easier, the last column indicates equivalent first-year costs. That is, each such number is a dollar amount x_1' such that, according to the model, the decision maker would be indifferent between the vector (x_1, x_2, x_3, x_4) that actually characterized the site and the

Table 12.22. *Evaluation of pumped storage candidate sites*

Alternative	Rank	Utility	Equivalent first-year cost (millions $)
		Base data	
S1	1	0.931	58.7
S2	2	0.885	62.0
S3	3	0.846	64.1
S4	4	0.820	65.3
S5	5	0.809	65.8
S6	6	0.799	66.2
S7	7	0.732	68.6
S8	8	0.697	69.7
S9	9	0.694	69.8
S10	10	0.196	78.7
		Alternative data	
S9*		0.941	57.8
S6*		0.905	60.7
S8*		0.780	66.9
S7*		0.596	72.2

Source: Keeney (1980).

vector $(x'_1, x^*_2, x^*_3, x^*_4)$. This procedure can be used to make the results of any (risky or riskless) multiattribute utility procedure that uses money as an attribute easier to interpret; it is often called *pricing out*.

The outcome of this analysis shows the importance of sensitivity analysis and critical thought about models. The final recommendation was that sites S1, S6, and S9 be studied in depth, and the final decision was to accept S9. Why? Site S9 scored poorly primarily because its impact on the riparian community was severe, and that dimension had been given a heavy weight that was different from the weight used for other sites. In the alternative analysis of the site (S9*), its riparian effects were not given such heavy weight. Similarly, S6 was relatively expensive because its cost data assumed a high construction cost about which the decision makers had doubts. The final choice of S9* represented a decision to give its riparian community effects no greater weight than had been given to riparian community effects at the other contending sites.

Evaluation of alternative radiocommunication systems for the U.S. Army

A version of multiattribute utility measurement that falls between Edwards's SMART procedure and Keeney's methods helped the U.S. Army to evaluate alternative radiocommunication systems. The project, conducted by Decisions and Designs, Inc. (DDI), had two parts: a multiattribute evaluation of the benefits of alternative systems and a probabilistic analysis of their costs. In this section we describe only the multiattribute analysis of benefits. Our description is based largely on the report by Chinnis, Kelly, Minckler, and O'Connor (1975).

In 1974 an army special task force was established to study possible improvements on the current army combat net radio system. The task force was called the Single Channel Ground and Airborne Radio System (SINGCARS) Special Task Force. DDI subsequently assessed and evaluated several alternative radio systems. The first step was to identify the technical alternatives for SINGCARS.

Alternative 1: current combat net radios (CNRs)

The then current system consisted of three fairly independent radios: one for vehicles, one carried by personnel ("manpack"), and one for use in airborne operations. Although these radios operated on the same channel, their independent development and characteristics prevented any interchange of parts. Each system could be technically improved, but such separate improvements would diversify the total system rather than integrate it. This alternative was to leave the total system unchanged.

Alternative 2: product improvement of the current system

This alternative consisted simply of improving the separate radios then in use, increasing the number of channels used, and spreading the channels farther apart in frequency.

Alternative 3: development of a new integrated system called AN/URC-78

This integrated system would have identical receiver–transmitter VHF-FM modules for all three uses (airborne, manpack, and vehicular). Specific requirements could be met by changing power amplifiers, antennas, and vehicular mounts. It would have several unique features that substantially modernized the old system but would lack electronic means for avoiding enemy surveillance.

Alternative 4: development of a new conceptual design based on latest technology

This would be technologically the most advanced (and also probably the most expensive) alternative; it would include electronic avoidance of enemy surveillance of radio communications.

The next step was to develop an appropriate value tree. Figure 12.13 displays the general structure of that tree. It has a number of unique features. First, the major value dimensions (operational acceptability, technical system utility, cost) and the system parameters (attributes) are linked through

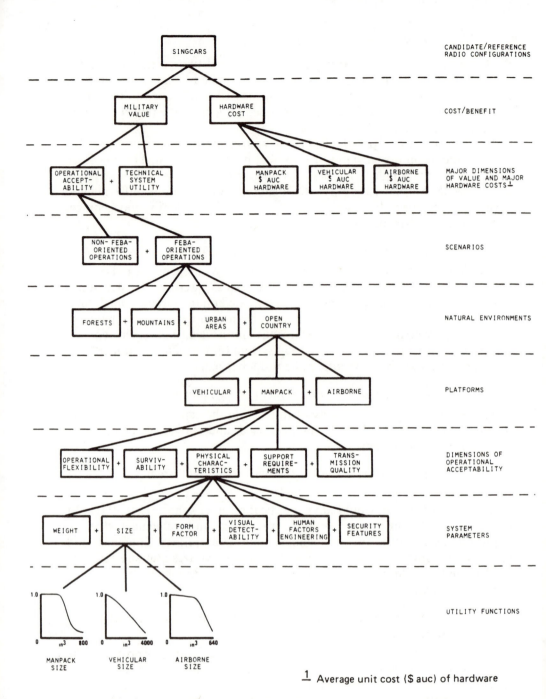

Figure 12.13. General structure of the SINGCARS evaluation model highlighting technical system utility. $AUC denotes average unit cost; EMC, electromagnetic compatibility. (*Source:* Reprinted by permission of Decisions and Designs, Inc., from Chinnis, Kelly, Minckler, & O'Connor, 1975.)

a series of conditioning variables:

1   *Scenarios of use.* FEBA- versus non-FEBA-oriented operations (FEBA denotes forward edge of the battle area)
2   *Natural environments* in which the radios would be used (forests, mountains, urban, open country)
3   *Types of platforms* on which the radios would be used (manpack, vehicular, airborne)

These are not value dimensions; they are essentially scenarios. They were introduced into the evaluation structure because both single-dimensional values and weights of specific dimensions can vary with the context in which the radios are used. Thus, vehicular use is more important in open country than in forests; dependability is more important near the FEBA than in the rear, where maintenance is easier to obtain. Assessments were, where appropriate, made on the basis of these scenario variables. In order to aggregate them into overall assessments, the scenarios were weighted. Such weights can be thought of as an unspecified blend of probability and importance. Thus, FEBA-oriented operations received heavier weights than non-FEBA-oriented operations, even though they might have been less frequent. Figure 12.14 lists the attributes of technical performance not listed in Figure 12.13. Figures 12.15 to 12.18 show the remaining structure of the value tree for SINGCARS.

The analysis team next elicited the 94 value functions implied by the SINGCARS structure from experts on the task force staff. Most of these directly related performance characteristics to values. Figures 12.19 and 12.20 are examples; the latter is conditional on FEBA operations. The elicitation method most nearly resembled the curve-drawing method described in Section 7.3.

The aggregation rule for this rather complex model combines most weighted values by addition, but a few by multiplication. A system that performs very well but is utterly unreliable is as worthless as a system that is perfectly reliable but scarcely performs. Multiplicative aggregation of these dimensions ensures that either will get a score of zero on technical system utility.

Weight judgments by the task force staff were based on the contribution of each attribute to the overall utility of the system; the elicitation procedure was essentially that for swing weights (see Chapter 8). The weights were assessed at each level of the hierarchy and combined by multiplying through the tree.

Tables 12.23 and 12.24 show some of the major results concerning benefits. Surprisingly, system 4, though based on the latest technology, has lower technical system utility than system 3, a developmental system. The reasons become clear from an inspection of Table 12.24. System 3 is slightly more dependable, has slightly higher technical performance, and is substantially more interchangeable than the brand new conceptual system.

The benefits are, of course, only half the story. Table 12.25 summarizes

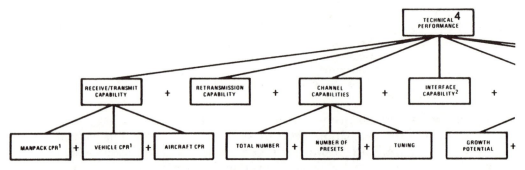

Figure 12.14. Technical performance. 1, Communications planning range; 2, with tactical data and automatic switching systems; 3, manpack to vehicle; 4, the subdimensions in this figure appear in a somewhat different order than in Figure 12.13 for convenience of presentation. (*Source:* Reprinted by permission of Decisions and Designs, Inc., from Chinnis, Kelly, Minckler, & O'Connor, 1975.)

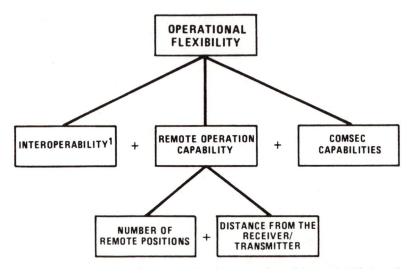

Figure 12.15. Operational flexibility. 1, With other service, older and Allied radios. (*Source:* Reprinted by permission of Decisions and Designs, Inc., from Chinnis, Kelly, Minckler, & O'Connor, 1975.)

the output of an elaborate probabilistic cost analysis for the four alternative systems. Alternative 4 turns out to be somewhat cheaper overall than alternative 3, thus offsetting its utility disadvantage in technical performance. The analysts concluded that

inasmuch as alternative 2 was far more expensive than either alternative 3 or alternative 4, the latter two alternatives are better options from a combined cost/benefit point of view. Because alternative 4 has lower hardware cost than alternative 3, and

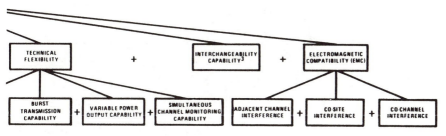

Figure 12.14. (*cont.*)

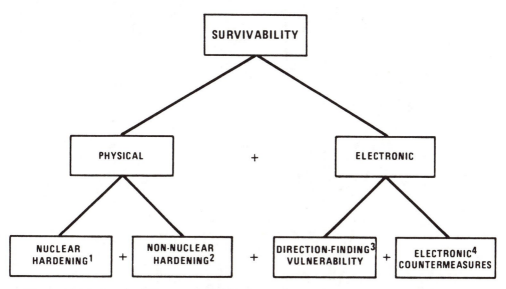

Figure 12.16. Survivability. 1, Reflecting hardening against radiation, thermal, and blast effects; 2, reflecting receiver–transmitter case penetration protection against projectiles (small arms, shrapnel, etc.); 3, in terms of the effective radiated power of the transmitter; 4, electronic countermeasures, in terms of antijamming protection. (*Source:* Reprinted by permission of Decisions and Designs, Inc., from Chinnis, Kelly, Minckler, & O'Connor, 1975.)

military value of alternatives 3 and 4 are approximately equal, alternative 4 is considered the most cost/beneficial option [Chinnis et al. (1975), pp. 33–4].

A number of sensitivity analyses showed how the other alternatives could be improved to become winners. For example, a reduction of the number of receiver–transmitters in alternative 3 to only one lowered hardware costs by about $500, making alternative 3 a stiff competitor of alternative 4 from a cost–benefit perspective.

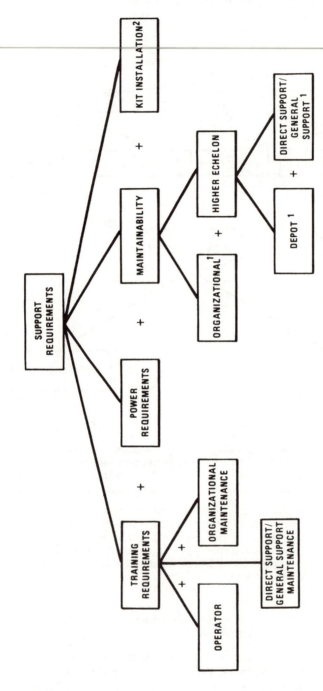

Figure 12.17. Support requirements. 1, Reflecting mean time to repair; 2, reflecting time required to mount radio with vehicle or aircraft. (*Source:* Reprinted by permission of Decisions and Designs, Inc., from Chinnis, Kelly, Minckler, & O'Connor, 1975.)

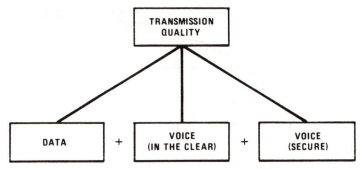

Figure 12.18. Transmission quality. (*Source:* Reprinted by permission of Decisions and Designs, Inc., from Chinnis, Kelly, Minckler, & O'Connor, 1975.)

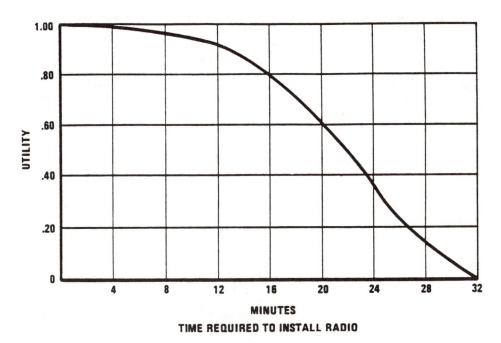

Figure 12.19. Basic utility function for kit installation. Abscissa represents time required to install radio in aircraft console. (*Source:* Reprinted by permission of Decisions and Designs, Inc., from Chinnis, Kelly, Minckler, & O'Connor, 1975.)

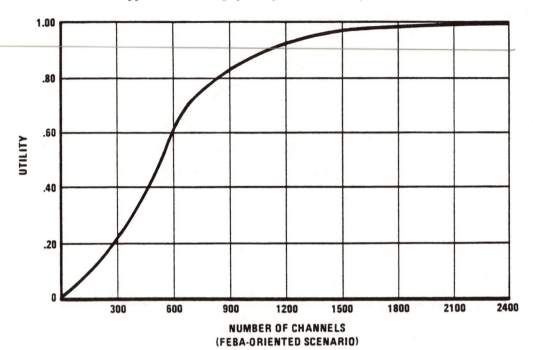

Figure 12.20. Basic utility function for the total number of channels. (*Source:* Reprinted by permission of Decisions and Designs, Inc., from Chinnis, Kelly, Minckler, & O'Connor, 1975.)

Table 12.23. *Summary of the military values of alternative radio system configurations*

	Alternative radio system configurations			
Major dimensions of value	Current system (alternative 1)	Product-improved system (alternative 2)	Developmental system (alternative 3)	Conceptual system (alternative 4)
Operational acceptability	.69	.73	.74	.80
Technical system utility	.34	.39	.67	.65
Overall military value	.51	.56	.71	.72

Note: It is assumed that operational acceptability and technical system utility are weighted equally in determining overall military value.
Source: Chinnis, Kelly, Minckler, & O'Connor (1975).

Table 12.24. *Technical system utility and operational acceptability by dimensions/subdimensions for alternatives 1–4*

	Alternative 1	Alternative 2	Alternative 3	Alternative 4
Technical system utility	.34	.39	.67	.65
Dependability	.49	.53	.79	.78
Technical performance	.70	.73	.84	.83
Receiver–transmitter capability	.80	.79	.88	.86
Retransmission capability	.90	.90	.90	.90
Channel capabilities	.76	.88	.92	.97
Interface capabilities	1.00	1.00	1.00	1.00
Technical flexibility	.37	.37	.43	.51
Interchangeability	.00	.00	1.00	.80
Electromagnetic capability	.70	.74	.52	.51
Operational acceptability	.69	.73	.74	.80
Operational flexibility	.87	.87	.87	.99
Survivability	.41	.61	.62	.58
Physical characteristics	.69	.69	.75	.86
Support requirements	.87	.87	.88	.89
Transmission quality	.62	.62	.62	.62

Source: Chinnis, Kelly, Minckler, & O'Connor (1975).

Table 12.25. *Average unit cost*

	Most likely average unit cost of alternative systems ($)		
Platform	2	3	4
Manpack	1,090	1,590	1,550
Vehicular	3,190	2,980	2,570
Airborne	3,980	1,990	1,970

Source: Chinnis, Kelly, Minckler, & O'Connor (1975).

12.4. Applications to decisions under uncertainty

Setting standards for oil production platforms in the North Sea[6]

Offshore oil production brings economic benefits to oil-producing and oil-using countries but also pollutes the seas. One major source of oil pollution

[6] This section was adapted from von Winterfeldt (1982).

is production platforms. They discharge oil into the sea in two ways: occasional blowouts and chronic oily water discharges. Although accidental spills like the Santa Barbara blowout in the Pacific (see Straughan, 1971) and the Ekofisk blowout in the North Sea (see Fischer, 1978) are more dramatic and have a more visible impact on birds and beaches, chronic discharges may be at least as dangerous. If discharges continue throughout the life of a platform, they may poison marine organisms, change the spawning behavior of fish, and upset the ecological balance.

Oil emission standards set on the concentration of oil (measured in parts per million, ppm) in the discharge water are the most common regulatory tool for reducing oil pollution from production platforms in the North Sea. In 1978 government officials in the United Kingdom and Norway explored appropriate standards for their new North Sea oil production platforms. One of us (von Winterfeldt) participated in this process, both to observe an ongoing standard-setting task and to develop a decision-analytic model for improved standard setting.

The first step in the analysis was to understand the standard-setting problem the UK government faced. There was no single decision maker. The Petroleum Production Division (PDD) of the UK Department of Energy set the standard with advice from the CUEP. The multinational oil firms affected by the standards engaged in discussions and negotiations with the PPD throughout the process. The major possible beneficiaries of the standard were the fishermen, whose voices were heard through governmental marine institutes. Each decision-making organization saw the problem from a somewhat different perspective. Each controlled different types of alternatives, each had different objectives and perceived different uncertainties as important. Table 12.26 summarizes these differing perspectives.

Decision analysis seemed to provide an appropriate starting point for modeling the standard-setting task, but the traditional form of analysis had to be adapted to take multiple decision makers into account. Three separate analyses interlinked through the respective actions of the decision makers seemed preferable to modeling the whole process from the perspective of the PPD alone. Figure 12.21 shows a decision tree structure interlinking the three analyses.

The regulator model consisted of a simple multiattribute evaluation of possible standards against the highly political and "soft" objectives of the regulator. After this initial evaluation, an SEU maximization model determined the operator's optimal treatment response to a standard. Considered in the evaluation of treatment alternatives were uncertainties about equipment performance, uncertainties about possible violations of standards and subsequent detections, and uncertainties about the costs of treatment and detection. Given the treatment decision and possible improvements, the impact model evaluated the possible environmental effects. The uncertain emission levels were used as a proxy for environmental impacts; this

Table 12.26. *Alternatives, objectives, and uncertainties for three decision makers*

Decision maker	Alternatives	Objectives	Main uncertainties
Petroleum Production Division, UK	1. Standard Level 2. Sanctions 3. Sample size, exemptions, inspection procedure	1. Agree with standards of other nations 2. Satisfy international demands for a clean North Sea 3. Agree with national energy policy 4. Agree with national environment policy	None considered
Offshore oil operators	1. No treatment 2. Simple gravity tank 3. Corrugated plate interceptor (CPI) 4. CPI and gas flotation (GF) 5. CPI, GF, and filters (F) 6. CPI, GF, F, and biological treatment 7. Reinjection of oily water into empty reservoir	1. Minimize investment cost for treatment 2. Minimize operation cost for treatment 3. Minimize penalties due to regulation violation	Equipment performance and detection of violations of standards
Fishermen	No actions considered; viewed as "sufferers"	1. Minimize mortality of commercial marine organisms 2. Minimize tainting and chronic toxicity of fish and other marine organisms 3. Minimize ecological disturbances	Environmental effects

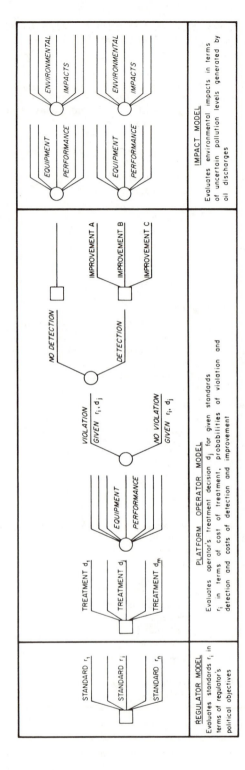

Figure 12.21. Decision tree for regulating offshore oil pollution. (*Source:* von Winterfeldt, 1982. Reprinted with permission from *Operations Research, 14,* 247–56, Operations Research Society of America. No further reproduction permitted without the consent of the copyright owner.)

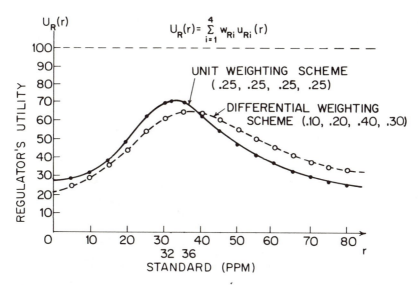

Figure 12.22. Regulator's utility as a function of standard *r*. (*Source:* von Winterfeldt, 1982. Reproduced with permission from *Operations Research, 14,* 247–56, Operations Research Society of America. No further reproduction permitted without the consent of the copyright owner.)

amounted to assuming that those effects were linear with the amount of oil entering the sea. An exploration of more sophisticated effects models was discouraging; too many model parameters were too uncertain.

The regulator model was based on interviews with the key decision makers in the PPD and the CUEP. These discussions elicited the objectives listed in Figure 12.21. All of the objectives were soft and political, and no direct operationalization was available. Value functions were constructed directly over the standard level so that each value function expressed the perceived degree to which the standard would meet each of the four objectives. Two alternative weighting schemes were used: a unit weighting scheme and one that appeared to correspond more closely to the weights of the PPD. Figure 12.22 shows the resulting overall value functions.

The utility function for the environmental effects was defined directly on random emission levels. If the operator's treatment decision d_j produced a level of emissions l_j, then

$$u_A(d_j) = -l_j.$$

The term $u_A(d_j)$ was standardized so that the utility of no discharge was 100 and the utility of 1,000 ppm was 0.

The platform operator model, which determined optimal treatment responses given a standard, was the heart of this effort. The operator's alternatives d_j are listed in Table 12.27 together with approximate investment

Table 12.27. *Illustrative cost estimates for treatment alternatives*

Alternative	Installation	Operation/yr	$c(d_j)$ Total (no discount)
d_1: No treatment	0	0	0
d_2: Gravity tank	0	3	45
d_3: Corrugated plate interceptor (CPI)	70	5	145
d_4: CPI + gas flotation (GF)	140	10	290
d_5: CPI + GF + filter (F)	200	15	425
d_6: CPI + GF + F + biotreatment	500	50	1,250
d_7: Reinjection	2,100	115	3,825

Note: Entries in £1000. Data for a platform with a production volume of 100,000 tons; sources of data: CUEP (1976b), National Research Council (1977), manufacturers' data; all estimates are very rough.

Source: D. von Winterfeldt, Setting standards for offshore oil discharges: A regulatory decision analysis. Reprinted with permission from *Operations Research, 30,* 5, copyright © 1982, Operations Research Society of America. No further reproduction permitted without the consent of the copyright owner.

and operation costs for a single platform. Total costs $c(d_j)$ were based on a 15-year lifetime. On the assumption that cost escalation during the 15 years would be approximately equal to the discount rate, it seemed reasonable not to discount operational costs. The alternatives d_j are ranked in increasing order of undiscounted cost and effectiveness. The operator's decision depends crucially on whether a treatment decision may lead to a violation of a standard (Q_1) or not (Q_0). Table 12.28 presents the decision problem in the form of a payoff matrix. When no violation occurs, the operator pays just the cost of treatment. If a violation occurs and is detected, the operator pays the cost of treatment, plus a penalty K_0, plus an incremental cost $K(d_j)$ to improve treatment from d_j to d_{j+1}. Since equipment units are combined to improve treatment, the model assumes that $K(d_j) = c(d_{j+1}) - c(d_j)$. Therefore, the operator has to pay $c(d_{j+1}) + K_0$ in the case of a detected violation.

The probability of a detected violation depends on the choice of treatment d_j, the standard r, and the definition of the inspection and monitoring procedure. In general, oil pollution standards were defined as follows. The average $\hat{l}$ of n measurements taken during time period t should not exceed the standard r more than m times during time period T ($t \ll T$). For example, the 1978 U.S. oil discharge standard (Environmental Protection Agency, 1975) of 48 ppm is not to be exceeded by the average of four samples ($n = 4$) taken daily ($t = 1$) more than twice ($m = 2$) in any 1 month ($T = 30$ days). The sampling and monitoring procedures are thus defined by (t, n, T, m). The model explored the following specific values, which roughly correspond to U.S., UK, and Norwegian definitions of maximum

Table 12.28. *Payoff matrix representation of the operator's decision problem*

	Violation state	
Alternative	No violation (Q_0)	Violation (Q_1)
d_1	0	45 + 100
d_2	45	145 + 100
d_3	145	290 + 100
d_4	290	425 + 100
d_5	425	1,250 + 100
d_6	1,250	3,825 + 100
d_7	3,825	—[a]

Note: K_0 = £100,000; all entries in £1,000.
[a]No violation is possible for d_7.
Source: D. von Winterfeldt, Setting standards for offshore oil discharges: A regulatory decision analysis. Reprinted with permission from *Operations Research, 30,* 5, copyright © 1982, Operations Research Society of America. No further reproduction permitted without the consent of the copyright owner.)

and average standards:

1   UK definition of a maximum standard (UK-MAX): Two samples are taken per day. During any one month not more than two single samples (no averaging) may exceed the standard r ($t = \frac{1}{2}$, $n = 1$, $T = 30$, $m = 2$).
2   EPA definition of an average standard (EPA-AV): The daily average of four samples may not exceed the standard r more than twice during any 1 month ($t = 1$, $n = 4$, $T = 30$, $m = 2$).
3   Norwegian definition of an average standard (NWY-AV): The daily average of continuous sampling may not exceed the standard r more than once during any 1 month ($t = 1$, $n \to \infty$, $T = 30$, $m = 1$).
4   UK definitions of an average standard (UK-AV-0, UK-AV-1): The monthly average of two daily samples may not exceed the standard r (or may not exceed it more than once) during the lifetime of the plant ($t = 30$, $n = 60$, $T = 5,400$, $m = 0, 1$).

In these definitions a month is approximated by 30 days. The lifetime of a plant is assumed to be 15 years. A violation of a standard occurs if the regulator detects more than m times that the sample mean $\hat{l}$ was above the standard r during the time period T. The expected utility of the operator is then

$$u_D(d_j, r) = P_D(Q_0 | d_j, r)u_D\{c(d_j)\} + P_D(Q_1 | d_j, r)u_D\{c(d_{j+1}) + K_0\}, \qquad (12.22)$$

where $P_D(Q_1 | \cdot)$ and $P_D(Q_0 | \cdot)$ are the probabilities of violation and non-violation, respectively. The objective of the operator is to maximize U_D (d, r) with respect to $j = 1, 2, \ldots, 7$, given r. For the purpose of sensitivity analysis, the utility function $u_D(c)$ was assumed to take one of the following forms:

$$u_D(c) = -2 \times 10^{-6}c,$$
$$u_D(c) = \exp(-2 \times 10^{-6}c), \qquad (12.23)$$
$$u_D(c) = -\exp(2 \times 10^{-6}c).$$

These utility functions represent a risk-neutral, a highly risk prone, and a highly risk averse decision maker, respectively. To determine violation probabilities, the following assumptions were made:

1   Each piece of equipment performs at a random oil concentration level l, which is normally distributed with unknown mean $\bar{l}_j$ and known standard deviation s_j.
2   The uncertainty about the mean performance can be expressed by a normal prior probability distribution with mean $\bar{l}_j$ and standard deviation $\bar{s}_j$.

Let $\hat{l}$ be the average of n measurements. The marginal distribution of $\hat{l}$ given the above assumption is then normal with mean $\bar{l}_j$ and standard deviation

$$\hat{s}_j = \sqrt{(s_j^2 + s_j^2/n)}. \qquad (12.24)$$

With these inputs the probability that $\hat{l}$ will not exceed the standard is

$$p_0 = Pr(\hat{l} < r \mid d_j) = \int_{-\infty}^{r} N(\hat{l}_j, \hat{s}_j) \, dl, \qquad (12.25)$$

where N stands for the normal distribution.

A violation is defined as m or more cases in which $\hat{l} > r$ during any one inspection interval T. If there are $M = T/t$ chances of violations in an inspection interval, the probability of no violation in that interval is

$$p_m = \sum_{i=0}^{m} \binom{m}{i} (1 - p_0)^i p_0^{m-i}. \qquad (12.26)$$

Finally, from single sample violations, the probability of not detecting a violation during the lifetime of the platform can be computed as

$$P_D(Q_0 \mid s_j, r) = p_m^N, \qquad (12.27)$$

where N is the number of inspection intervals.

Table 12.29 lists estimates of l_j, $\bar{s}_j$, and s_j, which were used to calculate violation probabilities. In addition, it lists ranges of literature estimates of average treatment performances. On the basis of the probabilities and the utilities for costs of investment, operation, and violations, SEUs could be calculated to evaluate and optimize the platform operator's treatment decision.

Figure 12.23 shows the optimal decisions and the associated SEU for a linear (risk-neutral) utility function, for $K_0 = 100,000$ and for the EPA-AV definition. Read the figure from right to left. For lax standards, say about

Table 12.29. *Parameter estimates of distributions characterizing equipment performance uncertainty*

Treatment[a]	Range of average performance(ppm)[b] $l_{j,min} - l_{j,max}$	Normal distribution over l_j $\bar{l}_j$	$\bar{s}_j$	Performance standard deviation s_j
d_1 (none)	300–3,000	500	100	100
d_2 (gravity)	50–150	100	20	20
d_3 (CPI)	~50	50	5	10
d_4 (CPI + GF)	15–35	20	5	5
d_5 (CPI, GF, F)	3–10	5	2	3
d_6 (CPI, GF, F, B)	—	1	.2	.4
d_7 (reinject)	—	0	0	0

[a]CPI, Corrugated plate interceptor; GF, gas flotation; F, filter; B, biotreatment.
[b]Data from CUEP (1976b) and equipment manufacturers.
Source: D. von Winterfeldt, Setting standards for offshore oil discharges: A regulatory decision analysis. Reprinted with permission from *Operations Reserach, 30,* 5, copyright © 1982, Operations Research Society of America. No further reproduction permitted without the consent of the copyright owner.

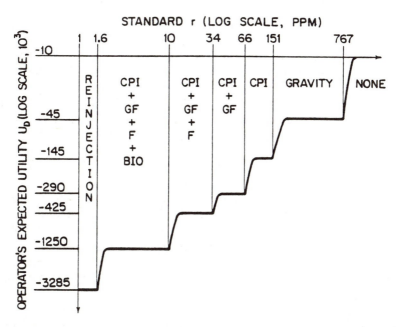

Figure 12.23. Operator's maximal SEU as a function of the regulator's standard r. CPI, Corrugated plate interceptor; GF, gas flotation; F, filter; B, biotreatment. (*Source:* von Winterfeldt, 1982. Reproduced with permission from *Operations Research, 14,* 247–56, Operations Research Society of America. No further reproduction permitted without the consent of the copyright owner.)

900 ppm, the operator model chooses no treatment as its optimal decision, and the cost of that decision is small, since the probability of violation of such a lax standard is very low (e.g., $p_D(Q_1 | d_1, 900) = .0000043$). If the standard is tightened, the probability of a violation will increase until the expected utility $u(d_1)$ is just equal to the utility of the cost of the next best treatment decision d_2. As can be seen, if the standard is further tightened, the utility $u(d_2)$ remains constant, since the probability of detection remains small. At stricter levels (e.g., around 160 ppm) this probability increases rapidly and adds to the cost of d_2 the expected penalty cost, further decreasing the utility $u(d_2)$ until the next cutoff point is reached.

The corresponding figure for other definitions of the monitoring and inspection procedure is similar, although the cutoff values are shifted, and the slope of $u(d_i)$ functions in the area of the cutoff value changes.

Several sensitivity analyses revealed the following results:

1   The operator's decision cutoffs are sensitive to the amount of information and to the monitoring and inspection procedures.
2   The operator's decision cutoffs are relatively insensitive to the amount of the penalty imposed by the regulator.
3   The operator's decision cutoffs are relatively insensitive to the shape of the utility function for money.

The next steps are to investigate the regulator's utility $u_R(r)$, the operator's utility $u_D[d_j(r)]$, and the environmental impact utilities $u_A[d_j(r)]$ directly as a function of the standard r. This allows further sensitivity and dominance analyses to be made in order to identify possible candidates for standards.

Table 12.30 shows that there are, in fact, many dominated standards, that is, standards that are not better than others for any decision maker and worse for at least one. For example, the 50-ppm standard leads to utilities of 48 for the regulator, 28 for the operator, and 80 for the environmental impacts. However, the 40-ppm standard results in the same decision by the operator, and thus the same utilities for the operator and environmental impacts, while the regulator's utility increases to 62. So the 50-ppm standard, dominated by the 40-ppm one, should not be considered.

Which standards survive the dominance test? In strict mathematical terms no standard is dominated, since the operator's utility function changes slightly for standards just below each cutoff point. However, for most practical purposes, the standards 36, 70, and 160 ppm dominate the remaining standards.

Regulators and other interested parties were briefed about the model structure, the model runs, and the sensitivity and dominance analyses. Although the lack of precise quantification and the relatively arbitrary use of the utility functions did not make the final numerical recommendations of the model acceptable without further analysis, the sensitivity analyses produced many insights for the regulators. In particular, the importance of

Table 12.30. Regulator's, operator's, and impact utilities as a function of the regulators' standard r

r	$d_j(r)$	$u_R(r)$	$u_D[d_j(r)]$	$u_A(d_j)$
0	d_7	26	-856	100
1	d_7	26.5	-856	100
2	d_6	27	-213	99
5	d_6	29	-213	99
10	d_6	30	-213	99
15	d_5	38	-6	95
20	d_5	48	-6	95
35	d_4	65	28	80
40	d_4	62	28	80
50	d_4	48	28	80
100	d_3	28	64	50
150	d_3	26	64	50
500	d_2	25	89	0
1,000	d_1	25	100	-400

(*Source:* D. von Winterfeldt, Setting standards for offshore oil discharges: A regulatory decision analysis. Reprinted with permission from *Operations Research, 30,* 5, copyright © 1982, Operations Research Society of America. No further reproduction permitted without the consent of the copyright owner.)

the monitoring and inspection procedures led the regulators to revise some of their analyses and to adjust some of their thinking. Some time after the analysis the United Kingdom adopted a standard of 40 ppm with the UK-AV definition and Norway adopted a 30-ppm standard with continuous monitoring. As the model results indicated, both are quite comparable in their impact on the operator's decision and thus in their environmental benefits. The numerically smaller Norwegian standard may, however, serve Norway's political objectives better.

Bypass surgery decision

The following decision analysis by Stephen Pauker (1976) is representative of the growing field of medical decision analysis, which tailors physicians' diagnostic thinking and decision making to each patient's signs and symptoms and to the patient's evaluations of the outcomes of medical decisions. Pauker's analysis did not involve direct assessments of probabilities and utilities. Instead he developed prototypical utility functions and estimated the probabilities of medical outcomes from the medical literature.

The decision problem is whether to perform bypass surgery on patients with a history of coronary heart disease. Such patients can have a variety of

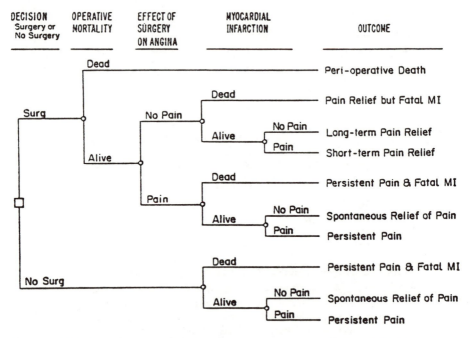

Figure 12.24. Decision tree for chronic coronary artery disease. MI, Myocardial infarction. (*Source:* Pauker, 1976.)

symptoms, depending on the location and type of coronary artery lesions and on the patients' ventricular functioning. These signs and symptoms, coupled with other patient information (age, sex) and the past success of the surgical team, determine the probabilities of a successful operation and of operative and postoperative complications. The ultimate outcomes of the surgery–no surgery decision include long life in pain, short life without pain, instant death, and others. Not only the probabilities of these various outcomes, but also the patient's evaluation of them should influence the physician's decision making.

Figure 12.24 shows a simplified structure of this decision problem. It assumes a 2-year postoperative time horizon and the possibility of one myocardial infarction (heart attack) at the end of the first year. The tree is self-explanatory; note that, except for the initial decision, it is an event tree rather than a decision tree. The outcomes at the tips of the tree indicate whether or not the patient survives the first and the second year and whether he or she suffers from pain during that time. For example, successful surgery can lead to initial pain relief but death from a myocardial infarction (MI) after 1 year, or it can lead to life for at least 2 years but with persistent pain. Pauker's detailed analysis included many more branches than this tree has.

He treated his 5-year time horizon as five separate occasions in which an MI might occur. Sensitivity analyses, however, indicated that the simplified tree of Figure 12.24 is an excellent first approximation of the more complicated tree in determining the optimal decision.

The transition probabilities in the tree depend on two variables: the patient's signs and symptoms and the experience and success record of the surgery team. Pauker created three classes of patient coronary anatomy: good, fair, and special lesion (LAD). In addition, he classified patient ventricular functions as either good or fair. Excluding the two worst patient types (LAD–fair and fair–fair), this classification generated four basic patient profiles. For each of these profiles, Pauker considered three surgery success rates: excellent, good, and average. This created 12 distinct decision situations. With this classification, a physician, examining a patient, could conclude, for example, that a patient who had a fair coronary artery condition and good ventricular functions would be well qualified for surgery if performed by an experienced, successful team.

These conditions influence not only the probability of a successful operation, but also the probabilities of postoperative complications (graft closure and death with graft closure). Table 12.31 shows these probabilities, conditional on the type of patient and on surgical experience. Pauker made these estimates on the basis of the medical literature.

Next, Pauker considered patients' preferences for the outcomes of the surgery–no surgery decision. He assumed that patients would be interested in two attributes of the decision outcomes: years free of pain and years alive. He further assumed that patients were of two types. Type "pain" patients, primarily concerned with years free of pain, were assumed to put all their weight on that attribute and to display only slight risk aversion. Type "life" patients were assumed to put all their weight on years alive, independent of pain, and to be more risk averse. Pauker did not assess any of these utility functions but assumed that the two forms shown in Figure 12.25 characterized two basic patterns of patient preferences.

In addition to these two types, Pauker assumed two mixed utility functions, which were essentially additive or multiplicative combinations of the type "pain" and the type "life" utility functions. The additive combination was an arithmetic average of the two functions in Figure 12.25 that characterized a patient ("either") concerned about years without pain and years of life and willing to trade one against the other. The multiplicative combination was a geometric average of the two functions and characterized a patient ("both") concerned with both but especially eager for years of life if they would also be painless.

For each possible outcome, the analyst can now determine the patient type, estimate the length of life and the amount of pain associated with that outcome, and then estimate the patient's utility for that outcome. Combining utilities of the outcomes with the probabilities of the branches leading

Table 12.31. *Probabilities of chance events*

Coronary anatomy: Ventricular function: Past surgical results:	Disabling angina									Asymptomatic[a]		
	Good Good Exc	Good Good Good	Good Good Avg	Fair Good Exc	Fair Good Good	Fair Good Avg	Good Fair Exc	Good Fair Good	Good Fair Avg	LAD Good Exc	LAD Good Good	LAD Good Avg
Outcome												
Surgery												
Operative mortality	0.01	0.03	0.06	0.02	0.06	0.12	0.04	0.12	0.24	0.02	0.04	0.08
Operative success with pain cure	0.90	0.85	0.80	0.80	0.70	0.60	0.88	0.80	0.70	0.95	0.90	0.85
Graft closure/year	0.05	0.10	0.15	0.10	0.20	0.30	0.07	0.15	0.25	0.05	0.10	0.15
Annual mortality with patent graft	0.04	0.04	0.04	0.07	0.07	0.07	0.12	0.12	0.12	0.05	0.05	0.05
Annual mortality with closed graft	0.07	0.07	0.07	0.12	0.12	0.12	0.18	0.18	0.18	0.12	0.12	0.12
Spontaneous pain cure/year	0.03	0.03	0.03	0.02	0.02	0.02	0.03	0.03	0.03	0.03	0.03	0.03
Spontaneous pain recurrence/year	0.04	0.04	0.04	0.04	0.04	0.04	0.04	0.04	0.04	0.04	0.04	0.04
Natural history												
Annual mortality	0.05	0.05	0.05	0.10	0.10	0.10	0.15	0.15	0.15	0.10	0.10	0.10
Spontaneous pain cure/year	0.03	0.03	0.03	0.02	0.02	0.02	0.03	0.03	0.03	0.03	0.03	0.03
Spontaneous pain occurrence/year	0.04	0.04	0.04	0.04	0.04	0.04	0.04	0.04	0.04	0.04	0.04	0.04

[a]LAD, Proximal obstruction of the left anterior descending coronary artery.
Source: Pauker (1976).

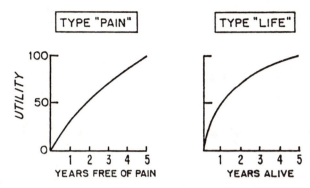

Figure 12.25. Prototypical utility functions for type "pain" and type "life" patients. (*Source:* Pauker, 1976.)

to them, the analyst can then calculate the expected utilities for the decisions surgery and no surgery. Table 12.32 summarizes the results and indicates which procedure is preferable in an expected utility sense depending on patient type, patient symptoms, and surgery success.

The preferred therapy for the type "pain" patients, except for the asymptomatic type LAD patients, was surgery. For type "life" patients the better decision was medication, except in one case: when the LAD symptoms occurred and the surgical team had an excellent record. For patients of type "either" or "both," surgery was generally preferred, except when the LAD symptoms were present. A series of sensitivity analyses supported these general trends of the analysis.

A capital investment decision

Hax and Wiig (1977) described an application of decision analysis to a complex capital investment problem faced by a major U.S. mining company. This interesting application dealt mainly with the uncertainty side of the investment problem, had a relatively straightforward objective function (net present cash value and product volume), and involved the highest levels of corporate decision making.

The problem the mining company faced was actually an opportunity: the U.S. government had invited bids for two parcels of land (labeled A and B in the subsequent analysis) that had extensive and valuable ore deposits. The company had to decide whether to bid, how much to bid, whether to bid alone or with a partner, and how to undertake exploration and production if the bid were won. A critical uncertainty was a competing venture the company was considering. That venture would substantially change the company's overall financial situation, forcing it to carry out exploration and

Table 12.32. *Benefits of surgery and expected values*

	Disabling angina								Asymptomatic		
Anat:	Good	Good	Fair	Fair	Fair	Good	Good	Good	LAD Good	LAD Good	LAD Good
Funct:	Good	Good	Good	Good	Good	Fair	Fair	Fair	Good	Good	Good
Surg:	Exc	Avg	Exc	Good	Avg	Exc	Good	Avg	Exc	Good	Avg
Patient type[a]											
Pain	58.2[b]	37.9	43.8	28.5	17.1	44.2	30.0	16.7	−15.7	−26.5	−36.6
	64.0[c]	43.7	47.2	31.9	20.5	48.5	34.3	21.0	80.8	80.8	80.8
Life	−0.4[b]	−5.6	−0.3	−4.6	−10.5	−1.9	−9.4	−20.5	1.9	−0.4	−4.6
	95.4[c]	95.4	91.1	91.1	91.1	87.0	87.0	87.0	93.0	91.1	91.1
Either	28.9[b]	16.1	21.8	12.0	3.3	21.1	10.3	−1.9	−6.9	−13.4	−20.6
	79.5[c]	66.7	69.0	59.2	50.5	66.8	55.9	45.7	85.9	85.9	85.9
Both	63.9[b]	43.9	50.2	34.5	22.0	50.6	35.7	21.0	−12.3	−22.8	−33.2
	71.4[c]	51.4	54.6	38.9	26.4	56.2	41.3	26.6	85.2	85.2	85.2

Note: The time horizon is 5 years and the cost of surgery is equivalent to 1 year of disabling angina. Anat, Coronary anatomy; Funct, ventricular function; Surg, past surgical results; LAD, proximal obstruction of the left anterior descending coronary artery.

[a] Patient type denotes type of patient preferences (utilities); type "pain" is concerned with freedom from pain; type "life" is concerned with life expectancy; types "either" and "both" are concerned with both. For details, *see* text.

[b] The first number is the benefit of surgery ($EV_{Surg} - EV_{No\ surg}$), where EV_{Surg} is the expected value of surgery and $EV_{No\ surg}$ is the expected value of medical therapy; a positive benefit implies that surgery is preferable, whereas a negative benefit implies that medical therapy is preferable.

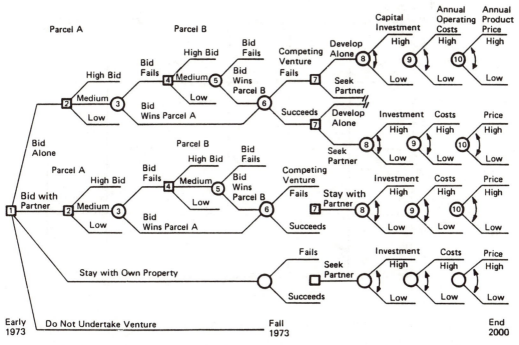

Figure 12.26. Decision tree for capital investment project. Like nodes and branches are suppressed. (*Source:* Hax & Wiig, 1977.)

production with a partner whether or not it had bid alone. The project required approximately 3 years of planning, 5 years of construction, and 20 years of plant operation. The total capital commitments were $500 million.

The structure of this problem is represented in the decision tree form of Figure 12.26. The tree is self-explanatory. The key probabilities were the following:

1   Probability of winning the bid
2   Probability of success of the competing venture
3   Probability distribution over amounts of capital investment
4   Probability distribution over product market prices
5   Probability distribution over operation costs

The probability of winning the bid is obviously a function of the amount bid. To construct this relationship, the decision maker assessed fractiles of the cumulative probability distribution of winning (Figure 12.27). The tree analyzed only three discrete bids: low, medium, and high, with their associated probabilities of winning and losing. The probability of a successful competing venture was assessed as .10. The other three uncertainties were taken into account by using relatively crude ranges of the respective vari-

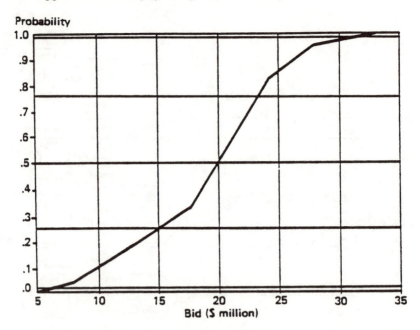

Figure 12.27. Probability of winning bids, encoded by decision maker at 1, 25, 50, 75, and 99%. (*Source:* Hax & Wiig, 1977.)

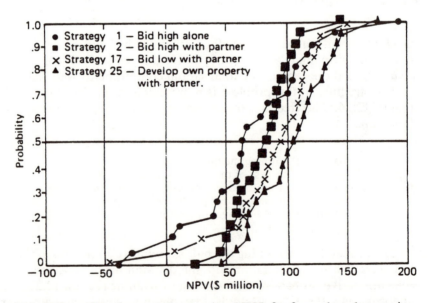

Figure 12.28. Risk profiles (in net present value, NPV) for four selected strategies. Mean NPV for strategy 1 was $71 million; for strategy 2, $81 million; for strategy 17, $87 million; and for strategy 25, $101 million. (*Source:* Hax & Wiig, 1977.)

ables and incorporating them in the form of a probabilistic sensitivity analysis.

Every path through the tree in Figure 12.26 defines an outcome state. From the point of view of the decision maker two variables were important for defining preferences among these states: net present cash value (NPV) and product output (PO). Both were, of course, uncertain.

The analysis considered 26 strategies, a small subset of the total number of paths through the tree specified by acts under the decision maker's control. A probability distribution was constructed for each of the objectives, NPV and PO, for each of the 25 strategies. Figure 12.28 shows such distributions for NPV for some of the strategies. Strategy 25 is stochastically dominant over the other strategies. That is, virtually regardless of the value of p, its cumulative distribution function lies to the right of all others and so should produce a higher NPV.

Next, the analysts assessed utility functions over NPV and PO. They assumed a multiplicative utility function of the familiar form

$$u(\text{NPV}, \text{PO}) = k_1 u_1(\text{NPV}) + k_2 u_2(\text{PO}) + k k_1 k_2 u_1(\text{NPV}) u_2(\text{PO}). \quad (12.28)$$

Using procedures described in Chapter 8, the analysts assessed this utility function as

$$
\begin{aligned}
u(\text{NPV}, \text{PO}) = \ & .988\{1 - \exp[-.005(\text{NPV} + 100)]\} \\
& + .197[1 - \exp(-.03\text{PO})] \\
& + .067\{1 - \exp[-.005(\text{NPV} + 100)]\}[1 - \exp(-.03\text{PO})].
\end{aligned}
$$
$$(12.29)$$

Figure 12.29 is a two-dimensional representation of this two-attribute utility function. Table 12.33 shows the expected utilities that will result from the probability distributions over NPV and PO and the two-attribute utility function. The stochastic dominance of strategy 25 disappears in the two-attribute analysis. Instead strategies 1 and 2 seem rather attractive.

The authors summarized the results and impact of the study as follows:

The decision maker chose strategy 2 as a result of the analysis outlined in this paper. He had been frustrated by his inability to handle the two objectives and resolve tradeoffs (or conflicts, as he expressed it). With the multiattribute utility analysis he was satisfied that his views and values were properly represented and, hence, he had no hesitation in accepting the optimal strategy [Hax and Wiig, 1977, p. 294].

12.5. Pitfalls of decision analysis: examples and lessons[7]

All of the applications described in the preceding sections were basically successful. But their success depended on the analysts' ability to avoid numer-

---

[7] We would like to thank R. V. Brown, D. Seaver, J. L. Dyer, D. Gustafson, P. Humphreys, and L. D. Phillips for their frankness and for letting us use their cases and materials for this section, which is adapted from von Winterfeldt (1983).

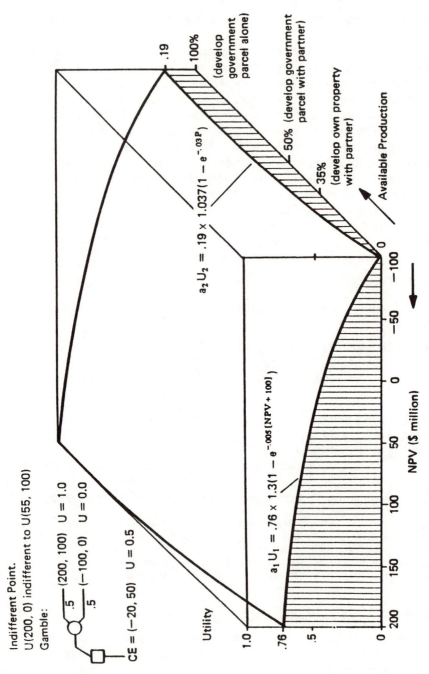

Figure 12.29. Multiattribute utility functions for NPV and production. (*Source:* Hax & Wiig, 1977.)

Table 12.33. *Expected utilities and equivalent net present cash values of main strategies*

	1 Bid high alone	2 Bid high with partner	17 Bid low with partner	25 Develop own property with partner	26 Do nothing
Expected two-objective utility	.719	.722	.706	.710	.386
Certainty equivalent ($ million NPV) (assessed at $P = 50$)	51	52	45	47	—

Source: Adapted from Hax & Wiig (1977).

ous pitfalls. Some failed to do so. In this section we survey some of these potential pitfalls and describe some of the ways in which an analyst can be more effective. We organize them by their relation to the stages of decision analysis:

1   Developing an analyst–client relationship
2   Defining the problem
3   Organizing the analysis
4   Structuring and modeling
5   Eliciting probabilities and utilities
6   Using and implementing the model

We describe the general nature of the pitfalls at each stage, give several examples, and briefly discuss the lessons to be learned.

Developing an analyst–client relationship: users and hidden agendas

Decision analysis is still an emerging discipline and therefore largely sold by suppliers rather than sought by customers. Often the analyst identifies a problem area for which decision analysis is useful and then approaches the potential client. Though this picture is rapidly changing, the analyst must often convince government agencies, businesses, or individual clients that decision analysis is useful. This need to sell, as well as the eagerness of the analyst to practice his or her profession, produces errors. These include misidentification of the client, misunderstanding of the client's motives, and confusion about who is to be served by the analysis and why. The problem is worse if the sponsors themselves are not sure about the ultimate user or uses of the analysis, as is normally the case.

An example of a decision problem involving multiple clients was a decision-analytic evaluation of community anticrime (CAC) programs (see Snapper and Seaver, 1978). The sponsor of this evaluation was the Law Enforcement Administration Agency (LEAA), which also funded the programs that were to be evaluated. One of the purposes of the evaluation was therefore easily identified: to aid LEAA in its planning and funding decisions. However, other users of the proposed evaluation soon emerged: the CAC project managers, who wanted to learn how their projects could be improved, and Congress, which had to set policy about CAC programs and about LEAA.

A natural pitfall of decision analysis in this situation would be to focus the evaluation solely on the needs and concerns of LEAA, in essence becoming a watchdog over the subordinate project managers and using the evaluation to sell the program as a whole to Congress. The analysts avoided this pitfall with an elegant solution: they constructed a three-level value tree. The upper level represented the values of Congress; one second-level branch included LEAA's overall program objectives; one branch of LEAA's objectives coincided with the local CAC program objectives. This approach may have idealized somewhat the degree of harmony of the objectives of these major stakeholders, but it helped everyone maintain an open mind about the use and users of the analysis. As it turned out, one of the most interesting implementations of the evaluation system was project management (see Snapper and Seaver, 1980b) rather than planning.

Another pitfall in the client–analyst relationship is hidden agendas: a client wants a favorable evaluation of an activity; a decision, already made, needs justification; or the analyst's technical skills and professional stature are expected to enhance the image of a project. None of these are *necessarily* detrimental to the analysis, but they are better handled when made explicit early.

Clients may hide parts of their agendas because they consider them confidential or not socially acceptable or because they do not understand them well enough. But most decision analysts are neither blabbermouths nor moralists, at least in their professional roles. And much of what analysts do consists exactly of uncovering values and reducing them to an orderly structure. They may be insightful enough to identify hidden agendas and incorporate them into the analysis; almost every value we have seen in an analysis could be understood and expressed in a socially acceptable way. But frankness, insight, and the willingness to be honest with the analyst are very helpful.

Hidden agendas sometimes occur in risk analysis applications of decision analysis. The client's intention may be to use the analysis to prove that a given product or technology is safe (or unsafe) rather than to solve a decision problem related to the safety of the product. In many such instances the analysis is being undertaken in response to public or governmental concern about safety, and the client (normally an organization) expects results that favor its position and will therefore help resolve the controversy in its favor. Ironically, risk analyses frequently stir up controversy rather than quell it (Mazur, 1980), partially because the public suspects such hidden agendas.

A third pitfall is a direct consequence of the fact that analysts like to please their clients: they sometimes promise too much. An example is the American College of Radiology study of the efficacy of radiology described above (see Lusted et al., 1977, 1979). The sponsor of the research originally thought that many radiographs were a waste of money and expected the study to show exactly that. The analyst did too little to temper this expectation. But the large-scale study showed that radiographs were indeed efficacious-1. They did change the diagnostic judgments of the physicians. Some of the researchers, convinced that a larger number of radiographs would not meet the efficacy-2 criterion (change physician's treatments), proposed a study of efficacy-2. That study was never funded, partly because the sponsor's expectations of the first study were not fulfilled.

What can be learned from these examples? First, understand your client, probe his or her motives, and carefully define the purposes of the analysis. This is usually simple when the client comes with a problem, so be more alert when you approach a client. Second, search actively for organizations or individuals with stakes in the decision in order to identify the conflicting interests and motives. Third, establish an atmosphere of trust, encourage the client to reveal hidden agendas, stress that such agendas can become a legitimate part of the analysis. And finally, don't promise too much or draw conclusions too early.

Defining the problem: apparent and convenient problems

Perhaps the first step in every decision analysis is to define the problem. A common pitfall is to take the client's definition at face value. Another trap is to accept the client's restrictions on the parts of the problem for which he or she wants answers. Analysts like to reformulate problems to make them accessible to decision-analytic modeling, thereby fitting the problem to the model. That, too, can be a trap. Common to many of these problems are the difficulties of defining the level of abstraction of alternatives (e.g., strategic vs. tactical) and objectives (e.g., overall organizational vs. costs–benefits) in response to an initially vague problem formulation.

The first pitfall is illustrated by the study of chronic oil pollution from North Sea oil production platforms (CUEP, 1976a; von Winterfeldt, 1982) that we described earlier in this chapter. The decision maker, the UK Department of Energy, had to set standards on oily water discharges from offshore oil production platforms. These standards were intended to prevent damage to the environment while avoiding costly restrictions on offshore oil development. This appears to be a straightforward choice-among-standards problem, and it was indeed handled that way informally by the

CUEP and formally, though experimentally, by von Winterfeldt (1982). During the course of interaction with the UK government agencies, the analyst began to suspect, however, that setting oil pollution standards was not really the problem. Apparently, several countries of the European Community had been pushing very hard for a clean North Sea, enforced by uniform European standards. In the past, the UK government had avoided setting numerical standards and instead had stressed the flexible nature of the pollution sources and of the local environmental carrying capacity. Setting numerical standards therefore required a change in policy. Perhaps a better problem formulation would have been: how can the United Kingdom best counter the European Community's push for uniform standards? Obviously, the options would have been very different from the oil concentration standards that both the CUEP and von Winterfeldt analyzed.

Inadequate problem formulations frequently occur in analyses of personal decisions. In an experimental study of such decisions (see John, von Winterfeldt, and Edwards, 1983), a woman initially believed that she had an apartment selection problem. The real problem turned out to be much more complex and involved financial questions and family interactions. The problem could have been formulated, for example, as a problem about the woman's management of her relationship with her parents. Another problem formulation would have focused on the ways the woman managed her financial situation. After these deeper aspects of the "apartment selection" problem were identified, they were incorporated into objectives, and apartments were maintained as the alternatives. It was clear, however, that each apartment represented a complex alternative for managing the subject's life style.

Vari and Vecsenyi (1983) described another example of addressing only part of the real problem. The decision maker, a Hungarian governmental agency, had to choose one among several mixes of research and development projects in a typical resource allocation problem. The analysts intended to consider the complementarities and redundancies among projects in an explicit model of conditional utilities and probabilities. However, the decision makers preferred to obtain the utilities of the single projects separately and to use their own heuristics in combining the single project utilities into an overall evaluation. One reason for this preference was, presumably, that the decision makers wanted to engage some of their own values about projects and project interdependencies without making them an explicit part of the analysis. The same preference, for the same reasons, is common in resource allocation problems and was illustrated in the CERL resource allocation problem for research and development projects earlier in this chapter.

Ulvila and Brown (1981) provide an example of concentrating on those parts of a decision problem that lend themselves easily to decision-analytic tools. They developed a decision-analytic model to aid the International

Atomic Energy Agency in allocating inspection resources. On later reflection, it seemed that it might have been more useful to have developed and evaluated alternative strategies for motivating inspectors within a given resource allocation context.

One implication of these examples is that a decision analyst should keep an open mind about problem formulations, including those to which decision analysis does not seem especially well suited. Another conclusion is that one should often examine several different organizational levels, and consequently several different levels of problem formulation, in the early stages of analysis. Problems usually come in hierarchies. In the oil pollution example the most general problem formulation would have involved alternative policies for dealing with international pressure on the UK government to clean up the North Sea. Once regulation strategies were accepted, the United Kingdom would have faced alternatives for regulating oil pollution: case-by-case regulation, emission taxes, standards, among others. Once standards were decided on, additional decisions concerning the levels of these standards, the monitoring and inspection procedures, and so on, would have had to be made. Each of these decisions would have involved different elements of the UK government.

Decision makers sometimes like to narrow the problem definition because doing so makes the analysis more technical, requires fewer sensitive political judgments, and keeps the alternatives within their own decision-making discretion. This tendency to suboptimize is not necessarily bad. A wider problem formulation does not always lead to substantially greater attainment of the overall organizational objectives and usually leads to a more expensive analysis. Yet the analyst should be aware of higher order problem formulations and the trade-offs involved.

A chronic hindrance to good problem formulation is the analyst's ego. To be effective, an analyst must talk with clients about ideas in a language that makes sense to the client – preferably from day 1. The pressure on the analyst to become an instant expert is enormous, and the difficulty of recognizing one's own ignorance may be severe. In an analysis in which we are still involved as we write, our initial formulation identified what we thought was a crucial decision point in a development versus environment controversy. Our attempt to structure the problem too much too soon led us to misidentify the relevant decision and so to appear uninformed in early interactions with stakeholders. We later learned that what we had thought to be the key decision was (1) made by an automatic rule and (2) so unimportant that a later revision of procedures completely abolished it. Still later, the rules changed again, and at this moment the original formulation again looks good. But the formal and informal rules are in flux. They will, for example, change radically if the party in power changes with the next election. Whether our problem formulation will ultimately make sense depends on political events beyond our prediction or control.

Organizing the analysis: institutional obstacles and obstinate individuals

Setting up an analysis in an institutional environment often requires substantial managerial skill and political savvy. Decision makers have to be convinced that the analysis is useful and does not interfere with their activities or threaten their jobs. Experts have to spend valuable time performing assessments they may consider tedious and boring. In politically controversial decisions, opposing stakeholder groups are involved in the analysis. Sometimes the institutional constraints prevent the analysis from being done or from being effectively implemented. Sometimes individuals or organizations simply refuse to cooperate. A particularly interesting set of institutional constraints was discovered in a descriptive case study of the power plant siting process of the Tennessee Valley Authority (TVA) (see Knop, 1979). One purpose of the descriptive study was to examine how a decision analysis process could improve the siting procedure then in use by TVA. In the first stage of that procedure candidate areas were selected on the basis of power system requirements. In the second stage numerous candidate sites were screened, mainly on the basis of engineering, construction, and land use issues. More detailed comparative evaluations of cost, engineering, and environmental factors were done on the three to five sites that survived the screening. Finally, the preferred site was studied in great detail, mainly to meet federal and state regulations on environmental impact.

An interesting feature of this process was the organizational arrangement. In the first two stages the process was coordinated and, in effect, controlled by the Division of Power Resource Planning; in the last two stages, by the Division of Engineering Design and Construction. The Environmental Division, while technically reporting to the board of directors, was in effect a subcontractor to the lead division for surveys and research. It became involved only in the later stages of the siting process. This institutional arrangement seemed to contradict TVA's policy of putting environmental considerations on an equal footing with cost, engineering, and power system considerations. Decision making was really a sequential elimination process with shifting priorities: power systems (first stage), engineering (second stage), cost (third stage), and environmental (fourth stage).

Because of its emphasis on trade-offs, decision analysis could have been implemented only with some organizational rearrangements. Such reorganization was a focal point of discussion at TVA at the time of the case study; most divisions, especially the Environmental Division, pushed strongly for more lead time and an earlier involvement in the siting process as an institutional way of redressing the balance among TVA's multiple objectives.

A more straightforward pitfall of decision analysis is the refusal of important experts or stakeholders to cooperate. An example is Edwards's school board study (Edwards, 1979, 1980) described in Section 12.3. Although the general level of cooperation of stakeholders was remarkable, there were notable exceptions: two probusing groups and two members of the school board refused to provide inputs to the analysis. This did not cause the analysis to fail, but it highlighted a potentially severe problem with decision analysis in politically controversial situations.

Institutional constraints on any form of analysis abound. Some can be very serious; many courts do not allow probabilistic testimony. Others are more amusing; some experts refuse to express opinions probabilistically, because of a lack of "hard" knowledge. What can be done about it? Awareness of the institution involved, the political arrangements, and individual psyches is important. Don't try to force an analysis that does not respect institutional and personal barriers – it is likely to fail. Meshing analysis, institutions, and individuals requires that everyone make compromises, especially the analyst.

Structuring and modeling: bushy messes and analytic myopia

A frequent structuring pitfall is the acceptance of a traditional decision-analytic paradigm that does not quite fit the problem. A problem is quickly labeled a typical riskless multiattribute problem or a typical signal detection problem. Dynamic aspects and feedback loops in decision problems are often overlooked, because they are not handled well by the traditional static structures of decision analysis. A related pitfall is structuring a problem too quickly in too much detail. Bushy messes (i.e., overly detailed and often redundant decision, value, and inference trees) are a frequent problem for beginning decision analysts. The development of an appropriate inference, evaluation, or decision model presents additional pitfalls: dependencies in inference models, redundancies in evaluation models, and dynamic features in decision models, to name only a few.

The previously mentioned school board study illustrates a structuring pitfall. Edwards's value tree had 144 twigs, far too many according to his own rules (Edwards, 1979, 1980). Edwards began the value tree building process by constructing a relatively modest "strawman" tree. The tree was then shown to members of various stakeholder groups, and each group typically added values. These additions not only increased the size of the tree but also created interdependencies and redundancies. The analyst accepted both the dependencies and the redundancies as a fact of life and the only reasonable way to deal with the political nature of the task he had set out to do.

A fascinating case of misstructuring and mismodeling lies behind Ford's decision about whether to place the Pinto gas tank in front of or behind the rear axle. The decision was based on a probabilistic cost–benefit analysis in which the chances of fire in rear-end collisions were traded off against the costs of lives lost in these fires. As it turned out, the expected dollar value of lives saved by placing the tank in front of the rear axle was smaller than the cost of the tank relocation. Ford therefore chose not to relocate it.

The problem with this structure is its myopia, both in foreseeing possible consequences and in identifying relevant dimensions of value. It neglected the possible negative publicity that would result from frequent fires caused by rear-end collisions and it did not consider the possibility of punitive damages in liability suits. The analysis derived the value of lives from insurance premiums and past court awards – a standard myopic approach to a MAUT problem. At the time of the analysis the value was estimated to be between $300,000 and $400,000 (in 1970 dollars). From the company's point of view, this number represented the average loss it would face if sued for liability. Punitive damages could, of course, be in the millions.

The case had an ironic twist. Ford was sued several times because of fatalities and injuries caused by rear-end collisions that led to fires. In one suit the analysis was made public; that publication was partly responsible for an assessment of millions of dollars in punitive damages. The irony is that, had Ford considered the possibility of such punitive damages, it might very well have concluded that the expected costs of not relocating the tank were larger than the costs of relocating it.

Perhaps the best way to avoid the pitfalls described in this section is to develop several alternative structures and models early in the decision analysis and to run several sensitivity analyses to see what matters and what does not. Furthermore, the analyst should encourage creativity in structuring and in inventing events and anticipating obscure secondary and tertiary impacts of the decision. One way to improve this process is to involve groups of decision makers and experts covering a wide range of experiences, opinions, and values.

Eliciting probabilities and utilities: gamed numbers and numbers games

The elicitation of utilities and probabilities is technically the most highly developed part of decision analysis. The main problems an analyst encounters in this phase are inadvertent biases, misrepresentations, and even lies. A frequent bias is optimism or pessimism in the assessment of probabilities of events in which the assessor has a stake. Misrepresentations also occur in utility assessment. Respondents may bias the trade-offs in order to make one alternative come out better than the others. And finally, respondents may simply game the numerical inputs to the analysis.

Perhaps the most intriguing example of this sort occurred in Dyer and Miles's (1976) evaluation of alternative trajectories for NASA's Jupiter–Saturn mission. In this study, several science teams assigned utilities to alternative trajectories by considering the value of the research contribution made by each trajectory. Since different science teams had different research tasks and interests, these utilities varied widely. With the single-team evaluations as inputs, several formal rules for collective decision making were applied to find an acceptable trajectory.

The science teams involved in the assessment knew, of course, that the purpose of the study was to develop a compromise evaluation, and they were knowledgeable enough about collective decision rules to be able to game them if they wished to do so. In fact, two types of gaming occurred. The first was simply to give the trajectories that were considered good an extremely high evaluation and to give all the others an extremely low rating. This type of gaming gave the trajectories that a group preferred a better chance of surviving. Another type of gaming was coalition formation. Dyer and Miles reported that some groups met during the evaluation process, and it is conceivable that they coordinated their assessments. The analysts were, of course, aware that such gaming could occur, and they used several strategies to ensure that gamed numbers would not distort the analysis too much. Nevertheless, some groups, after the evaluation was completed, actually celebrated their victory over the evaluation system.

Humphreys and McFadden (1980) observed numbers games that people played with the interactive computer program MAUD. In a group decision-making task, individual members typically argued for increased weights for those attributes on which their favored alternative scored most highly. If an individual was sufficiently persuasive, the group's evaluation would be biased in favor of the alternative that the game player originally preferred. It turned out that such gaming was much more difficult in interaction with MAUD than in interactions with group members.

Though utilities are easier to game than probabilities, unintentional biases in probability judgments can occur quite easily. Much of the decision-theoretic research literature in psychology focuses on cognitive biases in probability judgments, but the more obvious biases are probably motivational. For example, researchers are notoriously optimistic in their point estimates of the amount of time it takes to finish papers. The original schedule for this book has slipped more than 3 years.

To counteract gaming strategies, the analyst first has to know the motives of the decision makers and experts. This requires a good client–analyst relationship and mutual trust. Utility assessment is facilitated by the use of careful anchors for scales and relative judgments rather than absolute ones. The analyst can often counteract unintentionally optimistic or pessimistic probability assessments by phrasing the questions in terms of low-stake lotteries. Other debiasing procedures that address specific cognitive illusions have been discussed in the literature. We review the topic in Chapter 13.

Being better is not good enough

This section is about the unfortunate analyst who successfully avoids all the pitfalls we've described only to fall into the last one: failure of the analysis to be implemented or used. Decision makers can ignore an analysis in many ways. One-shot decision analyses may simply gather dust on office and library shelves. Parts of the analysis may be used to justify a decision already made. Perhaps the most severe form of the implementation pitfall occurs when a decision analysis system that is built for repeated use is never implemented.

A particularly sad case of this nature is the system of Gustafson, Grest, Stauss, Erdman, and Laughren (1977) for predicting suicide attempts, described in Section 12.2. The capacity of the computer to detect individuals who were relatively likely to attempt suicide was much better than that of expert clinicians. But even though this research has been published in several academic journals, even though the results were described in *Time* magazine, and even though the system was set up for full-scale implementation, nobody is using it. The many expressions of interest have led nowhere.

Why? The system's developers could not overcome the organizational and psychological effects that can hinder the implementation of any formal decision-analytic system. Though patients like to interact with computers, clinicians resist it. One reason is that clinicians and other users in mental health counseling and guidance are not familiar with computers and thus are skeptical about their use. Another reason is that computers challenge the authority of the clinician, because they can replace clinical psychologists and psychiatrists in some critical professional tasks. Furthermore, although research scientists are very fond of the Bayesian processing model, it is hard to explain and somewhat obscure to clinicians – another reason for their lack of trust.

Edwards's probabilistic information-processing (PIP) system (Edwards, Phillips, Hays, & Goodman, 1968) is another inference system that has never had significant real-world applications. PIP was developed mainly to facilitate the task of processing intelligence-system information that bears on hypotheses relevant to foreign policy. PIP is built on a simple Bayesian inference structure. It uses likelihood ratios to quantify the diagnostic impact of information and prior odds to quantify a priori knowledge. It then computes the posterior probability or odds of the relevant hypotheses. In a simulation study (Edwards et al., 1968), PIP was found to be superior to other on-line systems that were evaluated. Yet PIP has never been used. (Or has it? PIP is no more than an implementation of Bayesian ideas, which have certainly been used; the distinction is hard to make.)

The inference structure in PIP was too simplistic. Schum's recent research and thought, summarized in Chapter 6, has generated generic inference structures that are much more realistic than the one-stage Bayesian structure used in PIP. Moreover, PIP was an information-processing system with no direct links to decision making.

Less dramatic examples of the implementation pitfall also exist. The previously mentioned study of oil pollution standards was never used. Though the analysis sharpened the decision maker's eye for the sensitive places in the process (monitoring procedures, sampling methods), it did not have precise numerical inputs, nor were the environmental impacts modeled sufficiently thoroughly. Consequently, the numerical analysis was not taken seriously.

Edwards's school board study had a unique fate. The study was successful in that it produced an evaluation system and the desegregation plans were actually evaluated. However, after the initial evaluation was completed, the school board developed its own plan, which was never evaluated by the multiattribute system. The reasons for this seem fairly clear. The judicial mandate for a cost–benefit analysis of submitted plans did not require such an analysis for the board's own plan. And it would have been extraordinarily embarrassing for the board to have had to report that its new plan scored worse on its own evaluation system than did its original plan, which the judge had already rejected – a very likely outcome.

What can be done to avoid the nonimplementation pitfall? First, avoid all the others that precede it. Second, during the process of the analysis keep in mind that the decision maker, not the analyst, has to use the analysis: avoid excessively complex modeling, the extensive use of incomprehensible or inaccessible machinery, and ideas or devices that may threaten the client. Third, present the analysis or model as an aid, not a substitute for decision making; the interaction between model and client should be "user-friendly."

13   Cognitive illusions

13.1. Messages of despair, confidence, and help

Decision analysis assumes that people can make disaggregated judgments about probabilities and about the elements of multiattribute utilities and that the aggregation rules make sense. To justify those assumptions, we must reflect on a large literature concerned with errors of human judgment. Our treatment is not exhaustive; a thorough review would require a book. Indeed, such a book was prepared in 1982: *Judgment under Uncertainty: Heuristics and Biases,* edited by Daniel Kahneman, Paul Slovic, and Amos Tversky. Hogarth (1980) defined at least 27 sources of bias or error in judgment and decision making. In this chapter, we can only hope to summarize a few of the key studies, to present some cognitive illusions that fall outside the scope of the work cited above, and reflect on what cognitive illusions mean for decision analysis.

Cognitive illusions is our own term for certain kinds of systematic human errors of judgment. Some researchers in the field consider it pejorative; others have used it to describe their work. The intent of the phrase is to draw an analogy between systematic judgmental errors and the kind of systematic perceptual errors to which the Gestalt psychologists called attention in the 1930s and 1940s.

Kahneman and Tversky say that "there are three related reasons for the focus on systematic errors and inferential biases in the study of reasoning. First, they expose some of our intellectual limitations and suggest ways to improve the quality of our thinking. Second, errors and biases often reveal the psychological processes that govern judgment and inference. Third, mistakes and fallacies help the mapping of human intuitions by indicating which principles of statistics or logic are non-intuitive or counterintuitive" (Kahneman and Tversky, 1982, p. 494). This research strategy has led to many insights into human information-processing abilities and limits. One aspect of it is of concern to us, however. A research focus on systematic errors and inferential biases can lead those who read the research with an uncritical eye to the notion that such errors and biases characterize all human thinking. This notion, carried to an unwarranted extreme, could lead

530

readers to believe that people cannot perform the tasks required by decision analysis, such as assessing prior probabilities, likelihood ratios, or utilities. The writers of this literature have seen clearly and said repeatedly that the problem is not whether people can perform such tasks but how they can be helped to do them better. A literature on debiasing (e.g., Fischhoff, 1982; Kahneman and Tversky, 1979a) examines methods by which systematic errors and inferential biases can be averted or ameliorated. But a sense of the inevitability of specific kinds of intellectual errors has been more widely disseminated than, we believe, the literature proposes or justifies. One author wrote to one of us, "Many serious decision makers are concerned about cognitive illusions and refuse to use decision analysis. I do not wish to justify this attitude but it is very common." So we are not the only ones who feel this way. One of our purposes in this chapter is to communicate a message of confidence and help to counteract what we and others consider to be a message of despair.

Research paradigm for finding cognitive illusions

Webster's Dictionary defines *illusion* as, among other things, "the state or fact of being intellectually deceived or misled." In the case of perceptual illusions, the definition is slightly misleading. The bent-stick illusion, for example, refers to the fact that a straight stick put into water at an angle and viewed from one side seems to be bent at the point at which it passes through the surface. No adult believes the stick is really bent. (What do children believe?) The error is perceptual, not intellectual. But cognitive illusions fit the definition exactly.

The elements of every cognitive illusion are the same:

1   A formal rule that specifies how to determine a correct (usually, *the* correct) answer to an intellectual question. The question normally includes all information required as input to the formal rule.
2   A judgment, made without the aid of physical tools, that answers the question.
3   A systematic discrepancy between the correct answer and the judged answer. (Random errors don't count.)

Sometimes it takes two or three questions to demonstrate the presence of a cognitive illusion; the principle is the same.

We know of four research topics within which cognitive illusions have been experimentally studied: probabilistic reasoning and inference; violations of the SEU model in decision making; logic and arithmetic; and intuitive physics. Although this list exhausts the literature we know about, it obviously does not exhaust the topics to which the paradigm as we have defined it could be applied. To take an extreme example, linear programming is a formal procedure that specifies answers to interesting questions. Such questions can also be, and often are, answered intuitively. If the intuitive answers were compared with the formal one, there would surely be systematic discrepancies.

Why are the four classes of formal rules that we listed above of special interest to psychological experimenters? We can see two possible answers; both seem to apply. One is that real-world analogues of these laboratory tasks seem particularly common, and consequently the research seems to be especially relevant. The other reason, probably more important, applies to two of them. Probabilities and utilities are, according to decision theory and decision analysis, a central topic of decision making. Many cognitive psychologists and others regard decisions as a central output of human intellectual activity. So systematic errors in assessing probabilities or failures to maximize SEU would, and perhaps do, lead to systematic errors in decision making, and such errors are obviously important.

In the following sections we describe four classes of cognitive illusions. This description is not intended to be a thorough review of all the evidence for the existence of these illusions, nor a discussion of the theoretical constructs and psychological processes that may underlie these illusions. Much literature in cognitive psychology deals with such constructs, and a major purpose of descriptive research on cognitive illusions has been to identify psychological processes that explain their existence.

Our purpose in discussing cognitive illusions is threefold: to warn decision analysts, researchers, and real-world decision makers about some traps of intuitive thought; to examine, briefly, how decision analysis may help overcome these traps; and, perhaps most important, to put the cognitive illusion literature in a larger context of people's cognitive abilities and limits.

To achieve the first two purposes, we present the illusions with relatively simple examples and demonstrations, usually taken verbatim from the early experiments that identified them. Then, using the applied and experimental literature as our basis, we speculate about possible remedies, so-called debiasing techniques (see, e.g., Fischhoff, 1982; Kahneman and Tversky, 1979a). The evidence about the possibilities for debiasing and about the generalizability and robustness of cognitive illusions is mixed, but this is not the issue of this chapter. Instead we take a "what if" attitude toward debiasing and leave it to the reader (and aspiring decision analyst) to decide whether a particular illusion is likely to arise in his or her work.

We have struggled for a long time to achieve the third purpose of this chapter: to put the cognitive illusions literature into a perspective of people's cognitive abilities and limitations. Our investigation of the cognitive illusions in physics and arithmetic has given us a glimpse of what may lie at the heart of our struggle with cognitive illusions: the ill-understood concepts of intuition, mental effort, and intellectual tools. We conclude this chapter with speculations about how these concepts are related to cognitive illusions and to people's abilities to overcome them.

13.2. Cognitive illusions in probability and inference: conservatism

In the late 1950s, mostly as a result of Savage's (1954) work, psychologists became aware that probabilities describe opinions and that Bayes's theorem is a normative rule specifying how opinions should be revised in the light of new evidence – an important cognitive task.

Phillips, Hayes, and Edwards (1966) did the first study. In an unnecessarily complex task, chosen by the authors because they wrongly supposed that simple tasks would lead to uninteresting right answers, they found that no subject revised opinions nearly as much as the optimal Bayesian rule required. This inability has come to be called conservatism in probabilistic inference. Phillips and Edwards (1966) thereupon developed the simplest task they could invent that still embodied the basic Bayesian idea, the book-bag and poker chips task. (Rouanet, 1961, had anticipated them, but they were unaware of that fact.) In this task a subject is presented with two book-bags. One contains, for example, 70% red chips and 30% blue chips; the other has the opposite composition. One bag is chosen at random, so that the prior probability of the predominantly red bag is .5. Then a sample is taken with replacement, generating, for example, six red chips and four blue chips. The subjects are asked to provide posterior probabilities or odds in favor of the bag favored by the data. Typical responses in this example are .6 to .7, quite different from the normatively correct .84. The major finding in experiments like these has been that human inference is routinely conservative.

Early explanations of this phenomenon included response bias (people do not like to respond with extreme numbers), misperception (people underestimate the diagnostic impact of the data), and misaggregation (people perceive the impact of a single datum correctly but fail to aggregate properly the joint impact of several data) (see Edwards, 1968; Wheeler and Edwards, 1975). These explanations, together with the orderly nature of the conservatism phenomenon, led to the relatively straightforward design of tasks and procedures to avoid conservatism in decision-analytic assessment. A particular form of redesigning the tasks was the early PIP system (Edwards, Phillips, Hays, and Goodman, 1968), in which respondents are asked for prior odds and likelihood ratio judgments for single data, which are then aggregated mechanically. Another procedure for reducing conservatism is the use of response modes that call for responses in the midst of, rather than far away from, the numerical representations of the information to be aggregated (Eils, Seaver, and Edwards, 1977). Both procedures help circumvent conservatism.

In the 1970s, the conservatism literature encountered a host of criticisms that challenged both the previous explanations and the corrective mechanisms that they suggested (see, e.g., Beach, Wise, and Barclay, 1970; Kahneman and Tversky, 1972b; Marks and Clarkson, 1972; Slovic and Lichtenstein, 1971; Vlek and Wagenaar, 1979). The crux of many of these criticisms was that the Bayesian inference task is too complex for unaided human performance and consequently that subjects asked to perform Bayesian tasks seek and find simplifying strategies. Perhaps the most commonly proposed simplifying strategy, called the r/N hypothesis, is that in which subjects report a posterior estimate approximately equal to the proportion of red balls in the observed sample.

The r/N hypothesis seemed to fit the data from tasks in which samples were presented simultaneously but did not do nearly as well at explaining the data obtained from sequentially presented samples (see, e.g., Grether, 1979; Leon and Anderson, 1974; Shanteau, 1970; Ward, 1975). People seem to be in reasonable agreement with the Bayesian model when judging posterior probabilities based on a single datum (Wheeler and Edwards, 1975) or the probability of a sample given a hypothesis, and violate Bayesian principles mainly when judging the probability of a hypothesis given an aggregate sample (Bar-Hillel, 1980).

A more general criticism, not only of conservatism experiments but of other experiments on probability assessment, arose in the 1970s. Its essence was that laboratory experiments used contrived inference problems of types that rarely occur outside the laboratory and were misleading in their structure (Navon, 1978; Winkler and Murphy, 1973). In particular, real-world inference problems usually involved unreliable source data and conditional dependencies among data and among intermediate hypotheses.

We now believe that simple cures for conservatism like PIP are probably less useful than detailed structuring of actual inference problems to reflect such facts of life as the unreliability of many data and the existence of complex, conditionally dependent inference structures. Such structures call for disaggregated judgments of probabilities, but the appropriate combination rule for these probabilities is much more demanding than the simple single-stage formulation of Bayes's theorem.

Ignoring base rates

Bayes's theorem specifies that proper inference from fallible evidence should combine that evidence with prior probabilities, that is, the opinions the inference maker held before the new evidence became available (see Edwards, Lindman, and Savage, 1963). In more recent years, a number of experiments have called into question whether people actually use base rates in making probability judgments as required by the normative model.

The seminal study of neglect of base rate was done by Kahneman and Tversky (1973). One group of subjects was given the following cover story:

A panel of psychologists have interviewed and administered personality tests to 30 engineers and 70 lawyers, all successful in their respective fields. On the basis of this information, thumbnail descriptions of the 30 engineers and 70 lawyers have been written. You will find on your form five descriptions, chosen at random from the 100 available descriptions. For each description, please indicate your probability that each person described is an engineer, on a scale from 0 to 100 [p. 241].

Subjects in another large group were given the same story, except that it referred to 30 lawyers and 70 engineers. Both groups were then presented with five descriptions. For example:

Jack is a 45-year-old man. He is married and has four children. He is generally conservative, careful, and ambitious. He shows no interest in political and social issues and spends most of his free time on his many hobbies, which include home carpentry, sailing, and mathematical puzzles [p. 241].

On the basis of this description, the subjects were expected to judge the probability that Jack is a lawyer (or, for some subjects, an engineer). The experiment was so designed that it was unnecessary to recover likelihood ratios in order to discover whether the between-group manipulation of base rates (30–70 vs. 70–30) made any difference to the judged probabilities. The data indicated that base rates did not make much difference, although when the same subjects were asked what their judgment would be in the absence of the personality description, they indicated that they would use the base rates. Kahneman and Tversky concluded that, in the presence of specific individuating evidence, prior probabilities, by which they mean base rates, are ignored.

This neglect of base rates has been replicated in a number of studies using various stimuli, including some in which the numerical diagnosticity could be inferred, thus providing the ingredients for a straightforward Bayesian calculation (see, e.g., Bar-Hillel, 1980; Carroll and Siegler, 1977; Hammerton, 1973; Lyon and Slovic, 1976). Although these studies generally supported the existence of a base rate fallacy, they also showed that base rates are sometimes taken into account: when the link between base rate and target event is causal, when base rates appear relevant, when the base rates are related to individuating information, and when both diagnostic and base rate information are essentially statistical.

This body of experimental evidence, in combination with a number of real-world observations, generates a picture of a robust phenomenon. The seminal paper about the real-world consequences of that neglect was written by Meehl and Rosen (1955). Dershowitz (1971) and McGargee (1976) called attention to the consequencs of failure to consider base rates in judicial contexts. Lykken (1975) noted the contribution of that failure to misinterpretations of lie detector tests. Oskamp (1965) complained of it in connection with interpreting case studies. Eddy (1982), in a very stimulating article, showed how not only medical doctors but also their teachers and textbooks fall into the base rate trap.

Bar-Hillel (1980) put all this evidence and thought together in a most orderly and persuasive way. She summed it up as follows:

People integrate two items of information only if both seem to them equally relevant. Otherwise, high relevance information renders low relevance information irrelevant. One item of information is more relevant . . . than another if it somehow pertains to it more specifically [p. 230].

She suggested that this could happen in two ways:

(1) the dominating information may refer to a set smaller than the overall population to which the dominated items refer . . . (2) the dominating information may be causally linked to the judged outcome, in the absence of such a link on behalf of the dominated information. This enhances relevance because it is an indirect way of making general information relate more specifically to individual cases [p. 230].

Thus, Bar-Hillel considers the Tversky–Kahneman findings about causality to be a special case of her more general principle of relevance.

In real-world applications of Bayesian inference models, one constructs a problem structure that appropriately reflects the statistical properties of the environment and meets the analytic requirements of the Bayesian model. We believe that appropriate structures go a long way toward helping people avoid the base rate bias. In almost every experimental situation that we reviewed, a little help from an analyst would have improved the subjects' performance enormously (or shown that the subjects had, indeed, a different problem structure in mind). One part of problem structuring is to identify classes of hypotheses and events that are useful for decision making and that enable one to discriminate among data. Often these classes are constructed such that the prior distribution is relatively flat. (If it is very steep, one often tries to find subdivisions of the high-probability hypothesis.) Flat or gently sloping priors can be ignored. The structuring process also decomposes the problem in a way that highlights the separate relevance of priors, diagnostic information, reliability information, and their dependencies. This decomposition alone should enhance the decision maker's awareness of base rates, priors, diagnosticities, and their interlinkages.

Once the problem is appropriately structured, the simplest way to avoid the base rate fallacy is to model priors explicitly, assess likelihoods or likelihood ratios, and make use of Bayes's theorem to aggregate. Subjects thus would never be asked to aggregate base rates and diagnostic information intuitively. But sometimes intuitive aggregation cannot be avoided, and if Bar-Hillel's (1980, p. 230) explanation is correct, aggregation of two nonequally relevant items of information can lead to distortions when the aggregation is done in the head. In such a case, the literature suggests the following strategies:

First, if both diagnostic data and base rate information are essentially statistical, their statistical nature and interlinkages should be stressed. Second, if both can be related causally to the target event, the causal chains should be pointed out for both. Third, one could provide individuating information about base rates (as is usually implicit in diagnostic information). Fourth, Nisbett and Borgida (1975) suggested and Nisbett, Borgida, Crandall, and Reed (1976) demonstrated that one can make the base rate information more dramatic and less abstract by using a few concrete examples instead of a set of descriptive statistics. Essentially, all of these strategies are attempts to put base rate information and diagnostic data on an equal footing. Of course, the same strategies apply if two pieces of the same kind of information (e.g., two pieces of base rate information; two pieces of diagnostic information) have different degrees of relevance.

Ignoring sample size

A series of experiments by Tversky and Kahneman (1971, 1973) showed that subjects tend to ignore sample size when constructing subjective sampling distributions and that even experienced and statistically trained psychologists fail to appreciate the power (or lack of power) of a small sample test. The result is what they call a human belief in the "law of small numbers." Tversky and Kahneman argue that this effect is due to the representativeness heuristic, according to which a sample that is similar to the population is considered to be far more likely to be obtained than one that is dissimilar. Similarity thus can override other considerations like sample size.

In a particularly striking demonstration, Kahneman and Tversky (1972b) asked subjects to construct sampling distributions for the mean height of 10, 100, and 1,000 men drawn randomly from a population with a mean height of 170 cm (the variance was not specified). Subjects gave individual probability estimates for five equal 5-cm intervals between 160 and 185 cm, plus estimates of the probabilities that the respective means would fall below 160 cm or above 185 cm. Sampling theory would, of course, prescribe that the variance of the subjective sampling distributions decrease with N. However, in Kahneman and Tversky's experiment, the median sampling distributions were constant across N. Thus, subjects appeared to be insensitive to sample size. Kahneman and Tversky (1972b) reported similar results for binomial sampling distributions, as well as for simpler questions about the probability that the proportion of elements in a sample would exceed a specified amount. For example, when subjects were asked to judge the probability that a random sample of newborn babies would contain at least 60% males, 56% of them gave the same answer independently of whether the sample was generated in a large hospital (large daily N) or a small hospital (small daily N) and the rest split evenly between the two hospitals.

These findings apply to sophisticated as well as naive subjects. Mathematical psychologists trained in statistics were found to be too confident in the replicability of statistically significant results. For example, they thought that a sample of 10 subjects would very likely reproduce a result that had previously been found to be significant with 20 subjects at the .05 level (Tversky and Kahneman, 1971).

When the "law of small numbers" occurs, several precautions can be taken against it. One, as usual, is an appropriate problem structure, decomposing samples, data, and hypotheses to avoid judgments prone to the bias. This is especially true for the confidence judgments about samples, which can be structured and modeled in various ways (see, e.g., the two structures that Tversky and Kahneman (1981) proposed to construct a normative model for the significance test replication; there are many more of this sort). The findings of Bar-Hillel indicate that it is important to discuss with the experts and decision makers the nature of the sampling process, particularly considering replacement versus nonreplacement, proportions of samples to populations, and the effect of sample sizes on sample statistics. Especially important, in our opinion, is a search for reasonable hypotheses about parent populations, given particular samples. One of the first things experts and decision makers may do when faced with questions of the likelihood of a sample, is to generate hypotheses that make the data likely. If the sample makes the hypotheses about the population proposed by experiment or scenario seem absurd, it is entirely predictable that subjects will consider others. Every model of a data-generating process should be judged on its merits; none ever deserves unlimited credence. For a detailed discussion of such issues, see Edwards, Lindman, and Savage (1963).

Nonregressive prediction

When experts or statistically unskilled human subjects have to predict a variable y from knowledge of another variable x and the correlation between x and y is less than perfect, traditional statistical models require that the estimate be regressive. In the extreme, if there is a zero correlation between the variables, the conditional estimate of y given x should coincide with the unconditional mean of y. The higher the correlation, the closer the estimate should fall to the 45° line (assuming standardized variables), in the graph of y as a function of x. Normative regressiveness of prediction makes several assumptions about the nature of the prediction task, but these are general enough that, in most situations, predictions of imperfectly correlated variables should be regressive.

Several studies have shown that subjects instead tend to predict by matching the dependent to the independent variable and do not sufficiently account for the lack of perfect correlation. Kahneman and Tversky (1973) found this effect when asking subjects to predict a student's grade point average. In this task, as in others, the subjects showed a marked lack of regressiveness. As with the base rate and the sample size biases, Kahneman and Tversky (1973, p. 249) attribute nonregressiveness to the representativeness heuristic in that "the degree of confidence one has in a prediction reflects the degree to which the selected outcome is more representative of the input than are other outcomes."

Several other studies revealed nonregressive prediction in a variety of settings (see, e.g., Jennings, Amabile, and Ross, 1982; Nisbett and Ross, 1980). These studies also showed that subjects typically overestimate the amount of covariation between two variables; in other words, they have "illusions of reliability and validity" (see, e.g., Chapman and Chapman, 1967, 1969). This illusion is stronger when covariation is estimated on theoretic grounds and prior expectations, smaller when based on data (Jennings et al., 1982).

Real-world evidence also suggests nonregressiveness. Teachers of statistics often find the notion of regressive estimates difficult to teach. Statistically experienced psychologists often cling to arguments about test validities in spite of contrary statistical evidence. Less sophisticated social scientists interpret regressive data as meaningful effects.

Should predictions be regressive? Often, but not always. A very simple case for regressiveness arises from the fact that, in a typical simple or multiple regression case, the prediction of y dependent on a single x or a vector of x's is a conditional mean; that is, it is the mean that y would have if the population under consideration were confined to those elements having exactly the specified value of x or of the vector $\mathbf{x}$. Since the mean is a best guess about the value of a random variable under a wide variety of conditions, it seems reasonable to think of it as a best guess in this case too. And conditional means are always regressive for less than perfect correlations.

Kahneman and Tversky (1979a) propose a heuristic procedure to correct nonregressive predictions. It consists of five steps. The first is to identify the reference class (the relevant population). The second is to assess the distribution of y in that class. (Some of the language of the paper suggests, appropriately, that that distribution should be assessed separately conditional on several different values of x or of the vector $\mathbf{x}$.) The third is to obtain an estimate of the correlation between x and y, preferably by statistical means. The fourth is to correct the intuitive estimate of y by means of a computation based on that correlation. Kahneman and Tversky (1979a) do not expect that suggestion to lead to immediate acceptance of the revised estimate; instead, they hope it can be used as a basis for persuasion.

Overconfidence

A number of papers have proposed that overconfidence is another cognitive error. We reviewed the rather confusing evidence about it in our discussion of calibration and scoring rules in Chapter 4. The conclusions we reached there were that (1) overconfidence is a reliable, reproducible finding; (2) in work with continuous distributions a change in reponse modes can do a great deal to correct it; (3) in work with discrete distributions the picture concerning correction by reponse modes is very confusing; and (4) the experts, especially those expert both about the appropriate form of substantive knowledge and about how to estimate probabilities, can do a very good job indeed and are not at all overconfident.

Hindsight

Two cognitive illusions have been cleverly studied by Fischhoff (1975, 1976; Fischhoff and Beyth, 1975); they are called the hindsight illusions. Fischhoff (1982) summarizes them as follows:

In hindsight, people consistently exaggerate what could have been anticipated in foresight. They not only tend to view what has happened as being inevitable, but also to view it as having appeared "relatively inevitable" before it happened. People believe that others should have been able to anticipate events much better than was actually the case. They even misremember their own predictions so as to exaggerate in hindsight what they knew in foresight [p. 428].

These phenomena seem to be a probabilistic version of "I told you so." Fischhoff's studies leave no doubt about their reality.

Fischhoff himself (1982) reviewed all the published hindsight studies to examine whether it is possible to eradicate hindsight illusions. He concluded that "few [experiments] have successfully eradicated the hindsight bias; none has eliminated it" (p. 428). Attempts included simplifying the task, reducing the self-flattery inherent in a high post hoc estimate, instructing subjects and warning them against the bias, asking subjects to think and work harder, and varying expertise. The only strategy that fared well was that of instructing subjects to ask themselves why the event that actually occurred might not have occurred (Slovic and Fischhoff, 1977).

Of all cognitive illusions, the hindsight illusions would seem to be the easiest to correct: one simply writes down the probability estimate before the event occurs, or before the estimator learns the answer. But Fischhoff was motivated by the plight of historians, condemned to look back at events that have already occurred and to wonder what chance, if any, they had of occurring differently. (See Fischhoff, 1980, for a detailed discussion of these problems.) Writing history is an exercise in hindsight. Are the hindsight illusions inevitable occupational diseases of historians?

Perhaps. Still, the ideas of this book may help to reduce this concern a bit. A formulation like "Twenty-four hours before the battle started, how probable was it that Napoleon would lose at Waterloo?" is at worst nonsense and at best incomplete, since it specifies neither whose the probability is nor the information on which it is based. The question "Twenty-four hours before the battle started, how probable did Napoleon consider it to be that he would lose at Waterloo?" is at least well framed; historians might try to answer it. To do so, they would have to find out what Napoleon believed about his record of successes and failures and about the state of his enemies' forces and what battle scenarios he was considering. This would strip the problem to at least potentially manageable size. The sunken wall, for example, is irrelevant; Napoleon didn't know it was there. Thus formulated, the apparent inevitabilities of history seem less inevitable.

Proper formulation of the probability question is not necessarily a cure. Fischhoff's studies imply that the historian's post hoc point of view fairly well ensures the first bias. They are silent about what would happen if the historian were to try to see the world the way Napoleon saw it – admittedly an extraordinarily difficult exercise of imagination.

Anchoring

When people are asked to make an estimate, they frequently anchor on an obvious or convenient number (e.g., the mean, the mode) and then adjust upward or downward if they feel it necessary to do so. In many situations that strategy works well, particularly when anchors are finely graded over the scale of estimates. Diamond evaluation is an example. The four standard dimensions of such evaluations are cut, color, clarity, and carats. Carats are, of course, easily measured on a balance. Diamond experts disagree about whether cut should be evaluated by a complex formula based on physical measurements or by intuitive judgments. But all agree that color and clarity must be assessed judgmentally. The training process involves many exemplars; the judgment reduces to assessing the similarity of the new diamond to remembered or currently available exemplars.

In other situations, anchoring and adjustment can lead to misjudgments. Slovic, Fischhoff, and Lichtenstein (1977) reviewed a number of studies showing the effect. Tversky and Kahneman (1974) argued that in probability judgments people frequently underadjust and thereby produce predictable biases in their numerical estimates.

Bar-Hillel (1973) and Cohen (1972) showed that the probability of compound events is typically overestimated, and this seems to be an anchoring effect. People anchor on one event and fail to appreciate that multiplying two probabilities less than 1 by one another will produce a number less than either of them.

The previously discussed overconfidence bias has also been interpreted as an anchoring and adjustment bias (see, e.g., Slovic and Lichtenstein, 1971). By centering judgments around some median or modal value, subjects may attempt to find fractiles that are not sufficiently far removed from the anchor values.

In decision-analytic practice, the keys to reducing anchoring and adjustment biases are the use of multiple anchors and convergent validation techniques. When assessing continuous probability distributions, for example, one can begin by identifying the mean, mode, and plausible range of the random variable. In addition, the analyst can use the two variations of assessment techniques discussed in Chapter 4: fractiles and direct probability estimation. The inevitable inconsistencies should lead to insights, discussions, and resolution. Sometimes an analyst may have a suspicion that respondents will anchor on some value like the most likely value or on a very low or very high value. In that case it is good practice to provide respondents with "counteranchors" to "break" their intuitive anchors. In other cases, it is useful to construct probabilities over different random variables that can be formally related but invite anchors that produce divergent assessments.

Retrieval and scenario-based availability

Tversky and Kahneman (1973) presented a number of studies concerned with the effect of availability of instances or answers on judgments. Since we are trying to categorize instances by the nature of the normative principle that leads to the right answer rather than by the underlying psychological mechanism, we shall discuss only some of those studies here, along with others conducted since.

The form of availability we discuss here has been called a bias, but the name may be inappropriate. Subjects tend to estimate a higher probability for those events for which they can easily generate or recall instances. In the most familiar real-world examples, extensive publicity about some atrocious crime or unusual disaster enhances lay assessment of the probability of the event. Every light-plane pilot knows that the true statement "The most dangerous part of the flight is the drive to and from the airport" is shocking and objectionable to most nonpilots, since plane crashes are normally publicized, while automobile crashes, except unusual ones, are not.

Tversky and Kahneman (1973) asked subjects to state whether words that begin with R are more or less common in the English language than those in which R is the third letter. Most subjects said that words beginning with an R were more common. The statistical fact is the reverse. Words that begin with R are easier to recall or to list than words in which the third letter is an R. One interpretation of availability is that people overassess the probability of easily retrieved events and fail to recognize that that is an error.

Even more complex problems arise when judgments of probability must be based on scenarios about the future. This form of probability assessment has been formalized by the technical device known as a "fault tree," with which one attempts to assess the probability of a low-probability event by drawing a schematic of all the ways in which that event may occur and assessing the likelihood of each. For a full technical presentation see Green and Bourne (1972). For the most famous application see U.S. Nuclear Regulatory Commission (1975). The method is used extensively. Anxiety about its validity among the engineers who developed it seems to focus primarily on whether its assumptions are satisfied. Much more dramatic problems are implied by a study by Fischhoff, Slovic, and Lichtenstein (1978), which showed that experienced automobile mechanics, asked to deal with various representations of the possible reasons for the failure of a car to start, did not recognize the omission of major branches of the fault tree. Kahneman and Tversky (1982) discussed other problems with simulations as bases for probability assessment.

Evidence for successful statistical intuitions in inductive reasoning

Rather recently, a countercurrent to the line of research summarized so far has appeared. By far the best summary of its content and the thinking involved is contained in an important paper by Nisbett, Krantz, Jepson, and Kunda (1983). The authors, starting from the premise that some intuitive judgments that should depend on statistical principles do and some do not, attempt to explore what problem and respondent characteristics favor the use of statistical principles. They note the important work of Piaget and Inhelder (1951/1975), which shows that children develop statistical intuitions as they grow older and that understanding of the behavior of physical objects that obviously behave randomly emerges as a function of age. They suggest that, here as elsewhere in development, the development of the individual to some extent resembles the development of human understanding in general. They identify three task variables that can influence the ease with which adults think statistically: the degree to which the random nature of the data-generating device or process is visible and obvious, familiarity with the randomness of a sequence of events resulting from experience with it or comparable sequences, and cultural prescriptions to reason statistically (e.g., the incessant baseball-season bombardment with statistical information, implying random variability, about aspects of individual and team performance).

Nisbett et al. conducted some very stimulating experiments. In one, subjects were far more willing to generalize from a very small number of consistent instances about what seemed to be a nonrandom process (electrical conductivity of a metal) than about an obviously more variable one (obesity of a Pacific island dweller). Another was built on a previous study by Quattrone and Jones (1980), which showed that subjects were more likely to suppose that a population would behave in the same way as a few individuals in it if they were unfamiliar with the population than if they were familiar with the population. They repeated the study, adding a manipulation intended to call to the respondents' attention the fact that the populations were about equally heterogeneous. This manipulation destroyed the ingroup versus outgroup effect Quattrone and Jones had found. A third showed that the enumeration of a sample space and recognition that a subset of observations from it was, in fact, a sample made that sample less important and thus enhanced the importance of other conflicting information. A fourth showed that experienced athletes and actors were more likely than inexperienced ones to recognize that a poor performance could be random. Nisbett et al. (1983) concluded from these and other arguments and data that

... some of our subjects showed ... an appreciation of the statistical principles that in previous work other subjects failed to appreciate. It seems more reasonable to explain [this success] by saying that they are more skilled at statistical reasoning than the other subjects than by saying that they saw through the experimenters' tricks. . . . We see a powerful argument in the work we have reviewed for the role of cultural evolution. It does not require unusual optimism to speculate that we are on the threshold of a profound change in the way that people reason inductively. . . . Most people today appreciate entirely statistical accounts of sports events, accident rates, and the weather. . . . Will our own descendants differ as much from us as we do from Bernoulli's contemporaries [pp. 360–2]?

These conclusions convey perhaps a more dramatic message of hope even than the one we are offering. Our emphasis on understanding and expertise is like that of Nisbett et al., as is our recognition of gradual emergence of inductive skills during maturation and education. We think of decision analysis as a technique for honing those skills when they are needed. If we take the argument about cultural evolution seriously, we might look for the disappearance of decision analysts. There is a precedent. At one time, professional scribes wrote for those who could not. Later, professional arithmeticians served the needs of merchants deficient in arithmetical skills. Both professions have disappeared.

13.3. Other classes of cognitive illusions

Violations of SEU

In Chapter 10 we reviewed at length a substantial experimental literature showing that people do not, unaided, always make choices that maximize SEU. Such mistakes fit the paradigm of cognitive illusions. The formal combination rule is considerably simpler than Bayes's theorem. Some of the violations are dramatic: for example, cleverly designed option unpackaging techniques can cause subjects to choose dominated options.

The literature reviewed in Chapter 10 differs from the probability and inference literature in two important respects. One is that a formal model, prospect theory, has been proposed to account for the violations of SEU, while no corresponding model exists for cognitive illusions about probability and inference. Another is that a few of the studies reported in Chapter 10 include unsuccessful attempts to convince subjects, some of them sophisticated about decision theory, that they were making errors. The cognitive

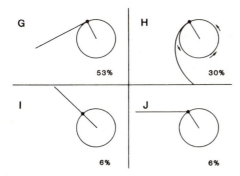

Figure 13.1. Illustration of a physical illusion. After the string breaks, the ball moves in the direction indicated by G. Only 53% of subjects chose G as the correct answer. (*Source:* McCloskey, Caramazza, & Green, 1980. Copyright © 1980 by the American Association for the Advancement of Science.)

illusions about probability can be found with sophisticated respondents, but we know of no comparable work showing any difficulty in arguing them out of these errors. The information presented in Chapter 10 suggests that the wrong kinds of arguments were used: defense of axiom systems rather than examples of the cost of error. But that suggestion is very speculative.

Cognitive illusions in physics

Probably the most famous errors in intuitive physics were originally reported by Piaget and Inhelder (1951/1975) and are known as conservation errors. Suppose a beaker of a colored liquid is shown to a young child and then poured into another glass container of a different shape. Will the child recognize that the amount of liquid has not changed? Piaget and Inhelder found that the answer is no, not if the child is under 7.

For many years Piaget and his colleagues studied a wide variety of physical conservation tasks: conservation of quantity, length, number, and so on. None of these conservation rules taken so for granted in adult thinking are demonstrable in young children. We seem to learn such simple physical principles.

Adults also show a lack of appreciation of physical rules that they might reasonably be expected to have learned in the course of a lifetime of observation, combined with some classroom teaching. McCloskey, Caramazza, and Green (1980) conducted some ingenious experiments on intuitive assessments by college student subjects of motions and trajectories. Consider a stimulus like that in Figure 13.1. It represents a view from above of a ball attached to the end of a string. The string is attached to something (with a swivel; it does not roll up around a pole), and the ball maintains a circular trajectory. Now, imagine that the string breaks. Draw a line representing the direction in which you think the ball will move.

The physical principle involved is that an object will continue in a straight line unless affected by an external force. Once the string is broken, the only external force acting on the ball is gravity, which does not show its effect in a view from above. Consequently, the correct answer is that the ball will continue in a straight line tangent to the circular path it was following before the string broke. The authors reported that more than 30% of their student subjects failed to recognize this fact. Caramazza, McCloskey, and Green (1981) studied a more sophisticated prediction-of-motion problem and found that only about 25% of their college student subjects produced the right answers. We ourselves have tried the task presented in Figure 13.1 informally on respondents in the Social Science Research Institute and found that even graduate students with considerable training in physics get it wrong. We also tried a manipulation not reported in the other studies: we explained the reasoning that would lead to the correct answer. In every instance, an adequate explanation caused the respondent to give the right answer.

Although this class of cognitive illusions seems particularly fragile, in the sense that some versions appear only if the respondents are children and others are easy to correct by explanation, the reason may well be that the physical principles explored so far are matters of daily experience. More complex principles of physics are surely less intuitive. Those of relativistic physics, if intuitive to anyone, have become so only during the twentieth century. The existence of billiard and pool sharks and of skilled ship handlers shows that originally nonintuitive principles of physics can become intuitive by extensive experience; the existence of professors of physics shows that they can become intuitive by precept. Intuitive physics seems to share with intuitive arithmetic the property of presenting a much wider range of intellectual difficulty than intuitive Bayesian inference, for example. The thrust of this comment is not that intellectual tasks like Bayesian inference cannot become intuitive. We offer ourselves and many others we know well as counterexamples. The point is simply that the extent to which a normative rule becomes "intuitively obvious" depends, among other things, on the inherent difficulty of the rule.

Cognitive illusions in logic and arithmetic

We group these topics, studied for different purposes and at different times, because they represent the application of particularly explicit formal rules, the violation of which seems especially shocking.

The conjunction fallacy

Perhaps the most shocking example is presented in the work of Tversky and Kahneman (1983) on what they call the conjunction fallacy. They presented 260 students at the University of British Columbia and Stanford with the following problem:

Consider a regular six-sided die with four green faces and two red faces. The die will be rolled 20 times and the sequence of greens (G) and red (R) will be recorded. You are asked to select one sequence, from a set of three, and you will win $25 if the sequence you chose will appear on successive rolls of the die. Please check the sequence of greens and reds on which you prefer to bet.
1. RGRRR
2. GRGRRR
3. GRRRRR

Then they gave the following explanation:

Note that Sequence 1 can be obtained from Sequence 2 by deleting the first G. By the conjunction rule, therefore, Sequence 1 must be more probable than Sequence 2. Note also that all three sequences are rather unrepresentative of the die, since they contain more R's than G's. However, Sequence 2 appears to be an improvement over Sequence 1, because it contains a higher proportion of the more likely color [Tversky and Kahneman, 1983, p. 303].

About half of the 260 subjects actually played the bet chosen, for real payoffs. The percentages of subjects who chose the dominated sequence 2 was 65% with real payoffs and 62% in the hypothetical format. Only 2% in both groups chose Sequence 3.

This dramatic finding of a violation of dominance produced by an inclusion relation was reproduced in various forms in the same paper. It is only minor consolation that when the logic of the situation was presented 76% of subjects (Stanford students in this study) found it persuasive. One wonders about the other 24%. The arguments were presented in written form, and students were asked which they found correct. We suspect that their lack of agreement represented a lack of understanding rather than obstinate adherence to a logically untenable judgment. But the argument that such errors are attributable to sheer naivete is wrong. Appropriate versions of the same logical structure were presented to trained physicians and to professionals involved in forecasting and planning. A variable but substantial percentage of them showed the same kind of error. We can only hope that an attempt to reproduce these results with professional logicians would fail.

A weaker form of the same kind of phenomenon was studied by Bar-Hillel (1973), Beyth-Marom (1981), Cohen and Hansel (1957), Goldsmith (1978), and Wyer (1970).

Illusions in syllogistic reasoning

A much earlier literature documents studies of systematic errors in syllogistic reasoning. For example, Wilkins (1928) compared syllogisms stated in the form traditional in textbooks of logic, in which a premise is stated as "All *X* are *M*," with versions in which the premise is stated as "All good ballet dancers have many years of training." She found, as seems reasonable, that the more specific phrasing was very helpful for recognizing the right conclusion to be drawn from the premises. The differences, however, were surprisingly small.

Woodworth and Sells (1935), Morgan and Morton (1944), and others studied the atmosphere effect in syllogistic reasoning. The history of such studies goes back to before 1900; for a review, see Woodworth (1938). The hypothesis was that an affirmative atmosphere in the premises makes it easy to accept an affirmative conclusion, and vice versa. The data confirmed the hypothesis. Morgan and Morton's study combined the atmosphere effect with the specificity effect and found that both helped subjects arrive at correct conclusions.

We are unaware of research on syllogistic reasoning since World War II, and no other review of cognitive illusions has discussed these errors. A hypothesis is that the interest in cognitive illusions grew out of concern with decision making. Deterministic reasoning is obviously relevant to decision making but has been studied relatively little. Yet we cannot see why failure to get the right answer to problems concerned with multiplication or combinatorics or Bayesian inference, in all of which firm conclusions follow from input information and human beings produce answers at variance with those conclusions, should be considered to fit the cognitive illusions paradigm but errors in syllogistic reasoning should not.

We are also confident that with careful thought, perhaps combined with some guidance, one can overcome almost any error of syllogistic reasoning, though we have no data to offer.

Errors in arithmetic

The literature on errors in arithmetic is enormous; we cannot hope to summarize it here. Arithmetic is a major element of early education. Apparently every isolable skill that goes into it, beginning with counting, is a product of early learning. Consequently, virtually any arithmetical error that one can think of can be found at some age or another, in some task or another. Many such errors are systematic, but their nature depends on experimental arrangements. A review of the literature on numerical skills and concepts in children appears in Flavell (1977, pp. 86–97).

Adults make errors in arithmetic too. Tversky and Kahneman (1973) asked college students to multiply, within 5 seconds, either the numbers from 1 through 8 or the numbers 8 through 1. The product is 40,320. All the subjects grossly underestimated it, but those who worked with the descending sequence erred to a far lesser extent than those who worked with the ascending sequence. The requirement that the subjects respond within 5 seconds, of course, prevented them from actually doing the multiplications, either on paper or in their heads. (The latter is perfectly possible. Try it. One of us arrived at the solution in about 90 seconds.)

In the same study Tversky and Kahneman asked respondents to perform much more difficult mathematical tasks. The subjects made systematic errors in assessing permutations, combinations, and binomial distributions. Kahneman and Tversky explain that all of these errors illustrate the effects of the availability heuristic. For example, subjects routinely judge that the number of different two-person committees that can be formed from a total of 10 people is larger than the number of eight-person committees that can be so formed. The two numbers must obviously be identical, since a two-member in-group automatically defines an eight-member out-group. In this problem, the dramatic result was not the difference between small and large committees, but rather the very large discrepancy between judged and correct number of committees for all sizes of membership greater than two. Tversky and Kahneman (1973) argue that "people estimate combinatorial values by extrapolating from an initial impression. What a person sees at a glance or in a few steps of computation gives him an inadequate idea of the explosive rate of growth of many combinatorial expressions. In such situations, extrapolating from an initial impression leads to pronounced underestimation" (p. 215).

A closely related group of studies compared intuitive with calculated extrapolations of exponential growth. Wagenaar and Sagaria (1975) asked subjects to extrapolate from the early terms (usually five) of an exponential growth process and found that the resulting extrapolations were dramatically too small. Nor were either prior instruction or experience with exponential growth processes very helpful. Wagenaar and Timmers (1978) point out that such inability to recognize the consequences of exponential growth is a matter of great social concern, since exponential growth processes are so common in the environment.

Arithmetic and mathematics are clearly the best topics to use in introducing the idea of intellectual tools and their embodiment in physical tools. The acquisition of virtually every new idea in the course of learning arithmetic and mathematics depends on tools. In the early stages of learning to count, children use pebbles or other physical objects that they can manipulate (Inhelder and Piaget, 1958). Later, counting is easy, but a convenient representational system, the decimal system, is needed to facilitate the tasks of arithmetic. Few casual users of calculus can get along without tables of integrals. The tools required to perform arithmetic and other forms of mathematics are numerous, diverse, and effective. We do not believe that those facts make them any different in kind from the tools used to perform other intellectual tasks. It simply makes them more familiar and easier to use and understand.

13.4. Reflections on cognitive illusions

Making sense of cognitive illusions

We have found it extraordinarily difficult to make sense of cognitive illusions – this chapter has been preceded by many unsuccessful, unpublished attempts to write about the topic. Several thoughts have helped us:

1. The paradigm of cognitive illusions has been difficult to bring into sharp focus, perhaps in part because the work with which we have been most familiar has concentrated on intellectual tasks that lie at or beyond the limits of ability of most adults. It has been very helpful to think about intuitive arithmetic and intuitive physics – both easier tasks, at least in the forms in which we have thought about them. Obviously, both arithmetical and physical tasks can be devised that are well beyond the reach of adult human intuition. The point is that intuitively easy tasks of these kinds can also be devised. We know of no intuitively easy version of Bayesian inference. It has been helpful for us to be able to consider a full range of task difficulty.

2. We started out believing we knew the meaning of the word *intuition*. We also started out believing that a *cognitive process* is a fixed method of doing intellectual business. Both ideas now seem absurd. We could find no agreed-on definition of intuition in the literature, and we found that we ourselves disagreed about its meaning. Cognitive researchers better acquainted than we with the literature of developmental psychology helped us to understand that cognitive processes are not givens. They develop and change over time as a function of maturation, experience, and training.

Research on cognitive processes as it is normally done with adult subjects gives the appearance of reporting static processes for two reasons: because we like to describe those processes by means of static models and because the time periods of such studies are normally short relative to the periods over which development and learning take place. Consequently, such experiments study "snapshots" – pictures of how a given cognitive process works at a certain level of development and training.

These two lines of thought have helped us. Many cognitive psychologists interested in cognitive illusions among adults say that they study them in order to learn more about intuitive cognitive processes; we quoted Kahneman and Tversky to that effect earlier in this chapter. It is very helpful to recognize that, as Hammond and his colleagues put it, "intuition is what analysis is not" (Hammond, Hamm, Grassia, and Pearson, 1983, p. 2) and that cognitive processes are responsive to maturation, experience, and education, even if we do try to capture them by means of static models that imply the contrary.

3. Another crucial recognition has been that the notion of intellectual effort is central to understanding thought. Since "intellectual effort" is a thoroughly subjective concept, experimentalists have tended to use objectively measurable stand-ins for it; the most common of these is incentives.

4. The notion of intellectual tools is important. Decision analysis is a collection of intellectual tools. Only recently have we come to think about the relation of intellectual tools to the physical tools that implement them. Intellectual tools, we believe, are used if the user knows they exist, knows how to use them, and considers it worthwhile to make the intellectual effort. If they are useful they become embodied in physical tools. Then the former user of an intellectual tool often delegates the task performed by it to the physical tool and may even forget how to use the intellectual tool.

The topic of intellectual tools is related to expertise. Experts become expert in the use of intellectual tools as well as acquiring factual knowledge. They may use physical tools to implement the intellectual ones; experts on Bayesian statistics, though they have no difficulty recognizing a Bayesian problem, may need a hand calculator or even a computer to get the right answer. If an experiment requires its subjects to perform a task that even an expert would need physical tools to perform but forbids the subjects from using tools, the implication is that getting the answer right is not important enough to require a major intellectual effort.

Task difficulty, mental effort, and intellectual tools

The crucial question, it seems to us, presented by any cognitive illusions study is this: what is the difference between the experimenter and the subject, other than that the former gets the answers right and the latter gets them wrong? We see two ways of thinking about this question. One is to focus on the processes that produce wrong answers. The literature reviewed in this chapter has for the most part addressed this question and has proposed a number of processes of this kind.

Our question is different. What are the processes that enable a respondent (e.g., an experimenter) to find the correct answer to a problem? As long as the tasks we considered were so difficult that most adults without physical tools produced wrong answers, the only answer we could come up with was that physical tools are important – hardly an astonishing discovery. But by considering a sequence of tasks that ranged from trivially easy to impossible we came to a better understanding of our question.

Our insights began to develop when we considered mental arithmetic. We would like to take you through a series of problems in mental arithmetic with the hope that it will lead you to the same lines of thought to which it led us. In so doing, we will exploit the fact that the examples can be presented on the page. This idea dates back at least to the Gestalt psychologists, who used examples on the page to study visual illusions. The experimental cognitive psychologists of the present day collect data, but they also present the examples on which they base their arguments as part of the text of each article. We assume that they expect the examples on the page to support, or perhaps to be even more compelling than, the experimental evidence. We use our examples for the same reason. Please, therefore, do not just read each problem as we present it. Make a genuine mental effort to solve it, and do not read on until you have succeeded. If you must, you can use paper and pencil – but it should not be necessary for examples 1 through 8 and if you do so some of the vividness of the example will be destroyed.

In order to discuss our examples, we must first examine the meaning of the word *intuition.* We propose four definitions bearing a family resemblance to but not exactly the same as the three proposed by Kahneman and Tversky (1982).

Intuition-I is the dictionary definition of *intuition.* Different dictionaries phrase it differently, but the key idea is that of immediate, effortless understanding. It is often contrasted with reason or deliberate inference. *Webster's New Collegiate Dictionary,* for example, gives two relevant definitions: "Immediate apprehension or cognition"; "The power of attaining to direct knowledge or cognition without evident rational thought or inference."

Intuition-R is a judgment that is a rough cut, an approximation. Though this does not correspond to the dictionary meaning, it closely corresponds to what experimenters on cognitive illusions study. Such experimenters often encourage mental effort but do not permit the use of physical tools. As later examples will suggest, such conditions often produce partial answers or approximations.

Intuition-M is our name for a situation in which the method of attack on the problem is obvious and intuitive even though the answer requires the use of physical tools. Long division is a good example for problems of reasonable difficulty.

Intuition-V is the kind of judgment you make when, looking at the sum of a long column of figures, you say that you do not plan to do the arithmetic but that the answer looks reasonable. This is an intuitive verification of an answer arrived at by other means. Perhaps the most extreme, fully subjective version of it is the tip-of-the-tongue phenomenon in which you know what someone's name is but cannot remember it. You usually can reject wrong answers that you or anyone else proposes without trouble and feel embarrassed at your stupidity when you finally have to ask for the right name.

Some arithmetic problems

The following text presents 13 arithmetic problems graded in difficulty. After each is presented, stop reading and try to solve it in your head. Note both what you do and how well you do. Try to compare your intuitions with ours.

1. $2 + 2 =$
2. $8 \div 4 =$
3. $\sqrt{9} =$

All three of these problems seem completely intuitive-I. They require no effort, the answer is transparent, and any adult with reasonable education will get them right. It is helpful to remember that the same comment does not apply to children. It might be as long as 2 or 3 years before a child who found problems 1 and 2 intuitive-I could even understand what problem 3 means. For most of you the answer to all three of these problems comes not from knowing how to do arithmetic but from memory.

Next, consider these problems:

4. $37 + 18 =$
5. $78 \div 13 =$
6. $\sqrt{441} =$

None of these problems is intuitive-I, at least for us. We can get all three right, but it takes mental effort. A cognitive process, which might as well be called mental arithmetic, is clearly required. Problem 6 is interesting both because it requires more mental effort than 4 or 5 and because the effort is of a different kind. We do not know how to extract square roots in our heads – or on paper, for that matter. To solve 6, it helps to combine search with mental multiplication. First, note that $20 \times 20 = 400$. Search the integers upward from there. The first trial after that gives the right answer, so your search stops. Had the problem been $\sqrt{529}$, you might have used the same starting point but skipped a number or two in the search, recognizing that the difference between 400 and 529 is large enough that trying 21 is unnecessary. With harder thought you might also have recognized that the last digit of $\sqrt{529}$ must be odd and can only be 3 or 7, and consequently trying 22 would be unnecessary. If you find that comment nontransparent, as many will, read no farther until you see why it must be so. This will give you a direct experience of what mental effort is. It took one of us hours, after recognizing the specific point, to discover the underlying principle and to see why no square can end in 2, 3, 7, or 8. We needed paper and pencil to understand that. Do you?

These problems require effort. For some, problem 6 may be intuitive-R; why bother with more than an approximation? For all, they are intuitive-M and intuitive-V. Many of those tempted by the fact that problem 6 is very intuitive-R might settle for the thought that the answer is more than 20, but not much more – unless some good reason for getting the answer right provided an incentive for harder thought.

The next three problems are

7. $48{,}512 + 659{,}871 =$
8. $2{,}365 \div 43 =$
9. $\sqrt{20{,}449} =$

Problems 8 and 9 push us almost beyond our ability to do mental arithmetic. We can do problem 7 in our heads but need more mental effort than we would normally be willing to use in order to remember the digits or the answer in the right order, since we arrive at them from right to left. But little mental effort is involved in 7 or 8 if pencil and paper are allowed.

Problems 7 and 8 are naturals for intuition-R. Problem 7 is obviously roughly 700,000. Problem 8 is a little less obvious. A first approximation is $2,000 \div 40 = 50$. For a more thoughtful approximation, note that $50 \times 43 = 2150$. So 50 is too small. Really hard thought can produce an answer without any physical tool. Still more thought is needed to approximate the answer to problem 9. A first thought is that $150 \times 150 = 22,500$, so the answer must be near but smaller than 150. Try 140 next; its square is 19,600. Now we have the answer trapped. Using the principle that you figured out in connection with problem 6, you can see that the answer must be either 143 or 147, and obviously 147 is too large. But this is harder intellectual work than almost anyone routinely does without physical tools. As usual, these problems are intuitive-M and intuitive-V.

Problem 9 brings up another issue about tools. A few of you may know how to take square roots using only paper and pencil. We do not, though Edwards was taught how in high school. We doubt that any schoolchildren learn how to do it in this era of the hand calculator. For such problems paper and pencil have become technologically obsolete.

The first six problems focused attention on the meanings of intuition. This set focuses on the meaning of the notion of cognitive process. Is an intellectual process that *requires* external physical tools for its correct execution a cognitive process? We say yes. We think a cognitive process is a learned intellectual or judgmental skill executed with whatever tools seem necessary.

The implications of this definition are dramatic. Children learn to do arithmetic. These problems would probably do a fairly good job of sorting children by age and grade level. Only the simplest are intuitive-I to us, though problems 4, 5, and 6 would probably be intuitive-I to someone who does arithmetic all day for a living. For young children, none are intuitive in any of the four senses. For those without access to (or knowledge about) calculators, 9 may not be intuitive-M. For most educated adults, all are intuitive-V and intuitive-R.

Consider another set of problems:

10. $e + \pi =$
11. $\pi \div e =$
12. $\sqrt{\pi e} =$

Most of you could answer these three problems but would have to look up the values of π and e first. Now the source of that information becomes an intellectual tool. How well can one do without the information? If you have no idea what the value of either π or e is, it is hopeless. If you remember, as we do, that $\pi = 3.14159\ldots$ and $e = 2.7\ldots,$[1] an approximate answer to problem 10 is 5.84. (To three significant figures, the right answer is 5.86; the fact that we couldn't remember the third significant digit of e was misleading.) Problem 11 is just about out of reach, except that the first significant digit obviously is 1. Problem 12 again is easy to the first significant digit, which must be 2. The next must be greater than .5, but not even hard intellectual work tells how much greater.

Is looking up something in a book an acceptable element of a cognitive process? Though we feel lonely and exposed doing so, we feel that we have no choice but to say yes.

Now we should test the limits of the definition of cognitive process that admits physical tools. Doing problem 12, even if the values of π and e are available, is tedious if, say, eight significant digits are desired. But a sophisticated hand calculator can do the task, including the looking up, in seven keystrokes. This clearly exploits intuition-M where intuition-I is absent and intuition-R is very weak.

Is this still a cognitive process? A great deal of responsibility for the thinking has now been delegated. Each of the symbols in problem 12 specifies a task. The only thinking required is the exploitation of intuition-M: the ability to recognize what each task is and to identify the sequence of keystrokes that accompanies it. These identification and sequencing tasks are clearly cognitive processes, but they are not mental arithmetic.

There is a further complication. The calculator is programmable. The seven button pushes can be reduced to one. This separates the task of recognizing the visual input of problem 12 from the task of knowing the appropriate sequence of keystrokes required. The mind that recognizes the task now delegates intellectual effort not only to the calculator, but also to the mind, which may reside in a different head, that entered the program into the calculator.

Computers can perform extraordinarily complex cognitive tasks at the (figurative) push of a button. The system composed of person and computer is clearly thinking. But is the person? Which person – the button pusher, the programmer, the task analyst, the user of output? This definition of cognitive processes is misty at the upper end. Once any object external to one person's skin is allowed into it, no clear lines can be drawn. Those who write about or experiment on cognitive processes ordinarily forbid the use of physical tools. The reason for this has now emerged. Once you allow any physical tool at all, even a book, to be used, where do you stop?

---

[1] D. von Winterfeldt did not remember any more digits of e but recalled that

$$e = \lim_{n \to \infty} \left(1 + \frac{1}{n}\right)^n.$$

It would be misleading to focus too much attention on physical tools. Consider problem 13:

13. LXIV ÷ IV =

In working on it, remember that you are a Roman, familiar with the symbols ÷ and = but not with the decimal system. A bit of casual historical reading led us to believe that Roman mathematicians could do some but not all division problems and that Roman merchants found such problems hard. The secret seems to have been finding tricks to make the problem convenient. This example offers one: LXIV = XX + XX + XX + IV. XX ÷ IV = V, and of course IV ÷ IV = I. So the answer must be V + V + V + I = XVI.

To a Roman mathematician, this problem would have been intuitive-V, but probably not intuitive in any other way. (Multiplication by successive addition was well known.) To many of us, 64 ÷ 4 = 16 is intuitive-I. The difference is a convenient notational system – an intellectual tool so deeply ingrained that we forget it is there. Good intellectual tools are crucial to good intellectual performance. Their embodiment in physical tools is a by-product of that importance.

For us, at least, the preceding discussion of mental arithmetic has clarified the issue of cognitive illusions. A fairly seamless sequence of intellectual tasks, and of methods for their performance, exists. At one end, the task is simple, easy, and intuitive. At the other, it is massive, and difficult and may involve many people and complex physical machinery. No obvious boundary exists on the intellectual continuum defined by the idea of a tool. Simple arithmetic can easily be done in the head. If the problem is simple enough, it normally is. More complex arithmetic may or may not be done in the head, depending on training, ability, need, willingness to make an effort, and the availability of physical tools. Really complex arithmetic absolutely requires physical tools. Where is the boundary between cognitive processes and the use of tools? Tradition answers: at the skin. But the idea of intellectual tools challenges the tradition. Intellectual tools have no clear residence. Do they reside inside the head? If so, they are presumably cognitive processes. But tools resident inside the head at one time may later move out, as the examples illustrate. The notion of an intellectual tool makes the boundary of the skin, of such great philosophical and psychological importance, less and less meaningful. This seems to be an intellectual trap.

Let us be radical for a moment and ask why the skin is such an important boundary. Senses exist to make it easy for information to be passed from one side of the skin to the other. The issue is where that information and its processing reside.

The sharp delineation of the boundary at the skin is unsatisfactory because the process of education moves both information and information processing from one side of the skin to the other. As examples 9 and 12 illustrate, technological innovation moves both back outside. It would be easier to think about the problem if we ignored the boundary.

That, of course, is exactly what many serious thinkers do. Few laypeople care what information is processed inside the head and what outside. What seems critical is that the processing be done, and done well. The tool-using human species has no hesitation about inventing and using tools, including intellectual tools that make possible information processing that otherwise no head could possibly perform. This point of view seems to us to be task analytic with respect to intellectual tasks. Yet the distinction between what the mind does and what the computer does matters enormously to us all. Most of us stridently insist that computers cannot think but never say what thinking is.

In these few pages we have gone from trivial arithmetical problems to philosophical dilemmas. We have made at least one important point. It is often argued (e.g., by Edwards et al., 1968) that one should deal with human cognitive limitations by designing intellectual tools and consequently that the research on, for example, cognitive illusions strengthens the case for the use of intellectual tools like decision analysis. From our point of view, the case for intellectual tools, like that for physical tools, rests on the fact that tool building and tool using are as natural to human beings as is the desire to be right rather than wrong. Tools may transcend intellectual limitations; calculators can do things that are beyond the reach of mental arithmetic. Tools may transcend other tools; computers transcend calculators. Computers were not designed because mental arithmetic is difficult. Linear programming was not designed because intuitive allocation is difficult. Human beings build tools because the reach of their minds exceeds their present grasp – because they want to do better than they now can. Awareness of what is possible, not dissatisfaction with what exists, stimulates tool building, intellectual or physical. And in our experience resistance to the use of any tool, physical or intellectual, is produced almost entirely by reluctance to make the effort necessary to learn how. Skilled tool users are proud of the tools they use and of the results of that use.

Returning to the topic of this chapter, perhaps it is appropriate to accept the psychological tradition that establishes the skin as an important boundary. But the function of education is to move information and processing skills from outside the boundary to inside. We still can find no intelligible meaning for the notion of a cognitive process other than that of a learned intellectual skill.

Does the literature offer any substantiation? Yes. The most important substantiation is simply that the literature exists. If the authors of the papers on cognitive illusions did not know how to find the right answers to the questions they asked, the literature would not exist. If the respondents answered correctly, it might exist, but it would be much smaller and less interesting.

It would be unfair to say that such researchers exploit the differences in expertise between themselves and their respondents, for two reasons. (1) Their key point is that errors are systematic, not that they occur. (2) Experts as well as naive respondents make these errors.

What is the difference between the researchers and their respondents? One is that the researchers have to, and do, make the mental effort required to get the right answers. The other is that, in doing so, the researchers have access to, and use, whatever intellectual tools they need, including books, calculators, computers, and whatever else the intellectual task requires.

Checking operations

In mental arithmetic and in most cognitive tasks, checking operations are available. The label *checking operation* implies two kinds of tools. The first is a set of heuristics with which to ensure that an answer is reasonable. One uses checking operations in this sense to make sure that an answer is intuitive-V. An obvious example is illustrated by the following problem:

$$45,876 \times 217,978 =$$

Few are likely to get the right answer without physical tools. But if we were to write that the right answer is 92,200,208, you would be sure we were wrong. The product of a five-digit number and a six-digit number cannot have only eight digits.

This example illustrates the approximate nature of some checking operations. How many digits should the answer have? As it happens, it has 10. But if either number were increased by 1, it would have 11. Counting digits is a useful heuristic. Many others, of various degrees of precision and usefulness, apply to mental arithmetic.

Checking operations of another kind also exist. It is a considerable mental comfort, when one is doing an intellectual task without tools, to know that the tools required are available. One can add a column of numbers in the head if a calculator is available to check the result almost twice as fast as one can do so without this means of checking the answer. This form of checking operation is psychologically similar to the fondness that many scientists feel for objectivity. It is simply reassuring to know both that there is a right answer and that some effort and some tools, appropriately used, will yield it. At least for the kinds of arithmetical tasks we have used as examples, a trade-off exists between mental effort and the availability of checking operations.

One interpretation of the difficulty laypeople have in working with decision-analytic ideas is simply that their inherent subjectivity precludes the use of checking operations of this kind. You can never be sure that a subjective probability estimate or a multiattribute utility is *right* – well elicited and plausible, perhaps, but not right.

Implications of the argument

In the preceding pages we have erected a great deal of philosophical scaffolding on the rather shaky foundations of intuitive arithmetic. What lessons, if any, have emerged?

1   The seamless nature of the intuitive arithmetic task, by presenting a spectrum of task difficulty ranging from trivial to impossible, has made it possible to disentangle ideas that we normally mix up. For example, it disentangles expertise from mental effort, it distinguishes between checking operations that are heuristics and checking operations that are exact, and it enables us to understand that there are at least four brands of intuition.

2   The obvious fact that we learn a wide variety of mental operations in order to perform intuitive arithmetic and that we must be able to perform all of these operations well in order to get correct answers invites attention to learning. The facts that mental arithmetic can be learned and that skills at doing it are gained both by formal precept and by experience invite the speculation that the same thing applies to other cognitive operations. Just as ability to perform mental arithmetic is labile, so other cognitive skills are probably labile. And just as the amount of time required to learn how to do mental arithmetic is measured in years, so the amount of time required to acquire other cognitive skills is probably measured in years.

3   Thought about mental arithmetic has helped us to differentiate expertise from mental effort. Obviously no amount of mental effort can create expertise where it does not exist. But an expert who is not making a mental effort is likely to come up with poorer answers than one who is making a mental effort.

4   Mental effort almost always requires the use of tools. Tools must, then, characterize almost every serious task in our mental life. Most cognitive tasks require numerous tools, and usually numerous heads, for effective execution.

14   Some idiosyncratic history and guesses about things to come

14.1. Introduction

This chapter serves two purposes. It gives a smattering of the post–World War II history of decison analysis, tracing, especially, its linkages to behavioral decision theory. And it specifies some of the elements of a research agenda for decision analysts.

It would take a book to do justice to the history of decision analysis and a long chapter even to summarize it. We will sketch briefly a few major events, ideas, and personalities, attending almost entirely to the period since 1944. To help structure our exposition, we have chosen some arbitrary dates and some key fields and people, leaving out many other major events and people to save space.

If you want to read more about the history of decision analysis than we offer here, we can do surprisingly little to help you. Edwards (mostly in 1954d; to a lesser extent in 1961) gives a historically oriented presentation of the origins of behavioral decision theory in economics and psychology. Adams (1954, 1960) surveyed Bernoullian utility theory. Its history since then in psychology is well reported in the series of *Annual Review of Psychology* chapters covering the topic (see Becker and McClintock, 1967; Einhorn and Hogarth, 1981; Pitz and Sachs, 1984; Rapoport and Wallsten, 1972; Slovic, Fischhoff, and Lichtenstein, 1977). For other psychology-oriented reviews and compendia, see Hogarth (1980), Kahneman, Slovic, and Tversky (1982), Nisbett and Ross (1980), Peterson and Beach (1967), and Slovic and Lichtenstein (1971). Luce and Suppes (1965) review past work and present their own ideas about probability of choice. More recent work is covered in detail in other chapters of this book. For an economist's point of view on the history of riskless utility, see Stigler (1950); for a similarly economically oriented review of utility in risky situations, see Arrow (1951). We cannot offer as many bibliographic details on the relevant parts of operations research, human engineering, or psychometrics. Savage's (1954) book is not a history, but Savage cared about intellectual origins and presented those of his approach to statistics well. Some of the relevant early work is reprinted in Kyburg and Smokler (1964), who focus on statistics, and Edwards and Tversky (1967), who focus on psychology.

14.2. Background: pre–World War II

The ideas of utility and probability, their combination via the notion of EV and SEU, and the view that it is rational, and perhaps common, to make choices by selecting from the options available the one with the most utility or SEU have a history reaching back 400 years or more; we ignore it here. A few key events of the 1920s and 1930s deserve mention. Most important was the behaviorist revolution in economics. Edgeworth (1881) had provided the key tool by showing that orderly preferences among commodity bundles can be represented by indifference curves or surfaces rather than by inherently subjective utility functions. Indifference, unlike (cardinal) utility, is in principle observable or inferable from choice behavior in riskless situations. In 1906 Pareto noted that indifference curves can be derived from ordinal rather than cardinal utility. Economic theory of consumer choice came to depend more and more on indifference curves. Finally, in 1934, Hicks and Allen set out to purge the theory of consumer choice of its last introspective elements by deriving it from indifference and preference observations only, with no reference to utility. We know of little evidence that this behaviorist revolution in economics drew on the earlier behaviorist revolution in psychology, but it would be strange if it did not.

Three other pre-war events deserve mention. One was Emile Borel's (1924a,b) formulation of the basic ideas that provide the framework for the theory of games, including the minimax theorem. Borel speculated that the minimax theorem was not true in general. John von Neumann (1928) proved that, if mixed strategies are allowed, every two-person zero-sum game has a minimax solution – the fundamental theorem of game theory.

The other two events were isolated emergences of the notion that probabilities are in some sense subjective, one published in articles by Ramsey (compiled into Ramsey, 1931, after his untimely death) and the other in a lonely article by Bruno de Finetti, a statistician, in 1937. Both lines of thought were essentially ignored at the time but became important stimuli to later thinkers.

14.3. 1944–1954

Economics: von Neumann and Morgenstern

The one pair of ancestors that would be included in every decision analyst's intellectual family tree is von Neumann and Morgenstern. The modern history of decision analysis clearly starts with them.

John von Neumann was a mathematician; Oskar Morgenstern was an economist. They performed a crucial function for decision analysis: they made subjectivity respectable again in economics and thus undid the harm that Hicks and Allen had done.

Curiously, they did it by accident, more or less. When von Neumann published the minimax theorem in 1928, it had no massive effects. But in 1944 and again in 1947 von Neumann and Morgenstern published *Theory of Games and Economic Behavior* – and in less than a year (after the 1947 publication, which is the standard one) it had become virtually required reading for every mathematical economist and statistician. Its crucial ideas were the minimax property, the minimax theorem, and the extensions of those ideas to various classes of games. Indeed, the prestige of the work was such that those ideas became a major focus of mathematical and economic study – but with remarkably little applied result. Central to the development of decision analysis was the rehabilitation of cardinal or interval-scale utility, done mostly in an appendix in the 1947 volume, very much a by-product. The theory of games was the topic of much mathematical and some experimental study, well summarized in Luce and Raiffa (1957). It still turns up in the thinking of researchers on conflict and its resolution, but it has clearly not had the long-range and profound impact that the rehabilitation of cardinal utility has had.

The argument that rehabilitated cardinal utility was not fully subjective and would not have worked if it had been. It was simply an axiom system that produced as a theorem the conclusion that people will, if they obey the axioms, choose among bets in such a way as to maximize expected interval-scale utility. The difference between this conclusion and Hicks and Allen's is based on the fact that von Neumann and Morgenstern focused on bets as objects of choice, while Hicks and Allen were concerned with riskless preferences. Ordinal utilities are adequate in a riskless environment; cardinal utilities are needed to produce orderly behavior in an uncertain environment (for von Neumann and Morgenstern, in a game), and their theorem showed how cardinal utilities could be constructed out of preferences among bets. Perhaps "showed how" is too strong; it took two interpretive articles by Friedman and Savage (1948, 1952) to prepare the way for operational use of the ideas. But those articles added little to the fundamental structure von Neumann and Morgenstern had built. That structure was concerned with utility, not probability. Modern recognition of the personal nature of probability can be traced to L. J. Savage (see below).

Economists have in a sense turned their backs on the intellectual consequences of cardinally measureable utility. Welfare economists of the present day, for example, debate with decision analysts about how to assess the value of some socially important development, like a public park or clean air. Welfare economists want to measure that value in dollars, using observed willingness to pay as a basis for the measurements. Decision analysts see numerous problems in this, primarily in that it ignores nonmarket effects. They would much prefer to measure value as utility, in just the contemporary version of the von Neumann–Morgenstern sense. This is the intellectual partition that divides cost–benefit analysis from decision analysis.

Psychology: behavioral decision theory

Quite early, psychologists came to recognize that von Neumann and Morgenstern had proposed a formal model of individual choice behavior and that experimental tests of it would be interesting. Preston and Baratta (1948) published the first attempt at a direct test, and Mosteller (a statistician who interacted a great deal with psychologists) and Nogee (1951) published the second and far more influential one.

Among those influenced by the Mosteller–Nogee work, on the basis of a prepublication colloquium, was Edwards, then a graduate student in psychology at Harvard. In standard brash graduate-student style, he became indignant at the idea inherent in the Mosteller–Nogee study that respondents did not understand the value of a dollar but did understand the (displayed) probability of beating a specified hand at poker dice. Mosteller agreed, and supported his doctoral thesis, which, along with subsequent work (Edwards, 1953, 1954a,b), more or less established the necessity of taking subjective modifications of what was then considered to be an objective probability scale, as well as subjective scales of value, into account in predicting the results of experiments on choices in risky situations. In 1954d, Edwards published a review both of the historical economic literature on the theory of choice and of the psychological contributions to it that had been made since von Neumann and Morgenstern's book had established risky choice as a topic of psychological study.

At the University of Michigan and at RAND Corporation, R. M. Thrall and C. H. Coombs had, since 1950, been leading efforts to stimulate sophisticated thought about decision making from a variety of points of view. In 1954, Thrall, Coombs, and Davis edited a book entitled *Decision Processes* that contained papers by many of the key thinkers in the field. It is probably fair to say that this book and Edwards's review article, appearing in the psychological literature in the same year, established human decision making as a significant topic of psychological study and thus gave birth to behavioral decision theory.

Statistics: L. J. Savage

L. J. Savage wrote only one book that is important for the history of decision analysis: *The Foundations of Statistics* (1954). But his ideas entered into the field in numerous quiet ways, so that the influence of his thought on decision analysis has innumerable facets, impossible to trace. This was because he was a willing, brilliant, and prolific consultant, both face to face and in letters. We doubt if there is a major figure in decision theory of the 1950s and 1960s who did not correspond or consult with Savage and modify his views as a result.

The Foundations of Statistics is two books within one cover, and only the first is important. The first half formally does little more than extend the von Neumann–Morgenstern axiomatization to cover probabilities, conceived of exactly as they are presented in this book, as well as utilities. The second half tries to justify conventional statistical procedures of that time from this new standpoint. Savage later repudiated that effort and indeed considered himself a founder of the statistical point of view called Bayesian (see, e.g., Phillips, 1973, for an exposition). The repudiation was visible in several of Savage's post-1954 papers and was quite explicit by 1962 (see Savage, 1962). *The Foundations of Statistics* was reprinted in 1972. In a new preface, Savage wrote, "The second part of the book is indeed devoted to personalistic discussion of frequentist devices but for one after another it reluctantly admits that justification has not been found. Freud alone could explain how the rash and unfulfilled promise (made early in the first edition, to show how frequentistic ideas can be justified by means of personal probabilities) went unamended through so many revisions of the manuscript" (Savage, 1972, p. iv).

Savage was very clear about his intellectual ancestry. He came to statistics, as virtually all statisticians did, trained in the British tradition associated with the names of Neyman, Pearson, and Fisher. But he acknowledged major intellectual debts to Ramsey and even more to de Finetti. The other key influence on Savage was Abraham Wald (1950), who had, as a consequence of von Neumann and Morgenstern's book, reformulated classical British statistical thinking into the idea that inference was a matter of decision and therefore dependent on utilities as well as probabilities.

Savage left us two major intellectual legacies. One, important to the history of decision analysis but not really a part of it, was the Bayesian movement in statistics; Chapter 5 presents a few of its basic ideas. The other was the notion of personal probability itself. Savage saw probabilities as orderly opinions to be inferred from betting behavior. He was rather unsympathetic to the idea that simply asking would do equally well – though, in his usual tolerant way, he readily admitted that it might.

Savage died too early, in 1969, before decision analysis had really been born. Had he lived longer, we believe that he would have been, not a decision analyst, but a sympathetic and helpful fellow traveler.

14.4. 1954–1963

Psychology: SEU maximization as a descriptive model

Much effort during the period from 1954 to 1963 was devoted to understanding and testing the SEU model and to some extent to reacting against it. This effort produced a substantial but rather forgettable literature. The key participants were Coombs, Edwards, and their students. A review is contained in Edwards (1961). It is perhaps a fair summary of that decade of experimentation to say that the SEU model does a very mediocre job of predicting choices among bets, but nothing else does much better. Edwards's (1962b) paper, which introduced the idea of subjective probabilities that do not have to sum to 1, was intended as a sign-off article; that line of experimentation had become too frustrating to pursue, and other more interesting ones had opened up. Nonadditive probabilities, by the way, are very much alive today in psychologists' descriptive models of decision making (see Kahneman and Tversky, 1979b).

Psychology: inference as a research topic

Edwards spent the period from 1954 to 1958 working for the U.S. Air Force. These valuable years made clear and dramatic the thoughts that decision making was an important and demanding human activity and that both decision theory and psychological research on decision making should be relevant to it. In effect, these years defined the agenda that Edwards's professional life has followed ever since.

In 1958 Edwards joined the faculty of the University of Michigan; by coincidence, so did L. J. Savage. This physical proximity gave Edwards an opportunity to be intensively tutored by Savage in the Bayesian point of view. One result was a paper by Edwards, Lindman, and Savage (1963) that summarized that point of view and brought it to the attention of psychologists. A second result was the idea that a system called PIP (Edwards, 1962a) could partition the task of making inferences from evidence into a judgmental part appropriately performed by experts and a computational part for which Bayes's theorem was appropriate.

But perhaps the most immediately influential effect was the emergence of the idea that experiments comparing Bayes's theorem, a formally optimal model of inference, with actual inferences could be carried out in the same way that the SEU model had been compared with actual risky choices. Such experiments were well under way by 1963, though they were not published until later. The results are reviewed in Chapter 13.

Immediate antecedents of decision analysis

The fundamentals of decision analysis emerged during the late 1950s and early 1960s at the Harvard Business School. In 1959, Robert Schlaifer published *Probability and Statistics for Business Decisions*. This text, intended for MBA students, can be called the first text in decision analysis, though it wasn't described as such. Its emphasis is on practical business examples and cases; statistical theory is presented from the standpoint of practical use and, by itself, is given very little mathematical exposition. Schlaifer clearly advocates utility (not multiattributed), personal probability, and SEU as the appropriate normative principle for putting them together. One gets the impression that Schlaifer read voraciously in statistics and from time to time found himself longing for answers to mathematical questions the literature could not then supply. He updated the book in 1951 and greatly expanded it in 1969.

Howard Raiffa, a statistician by training who while at Columbia had published with Luce a review of *Games and Decisions* (Luce and Raiffa, 1957) and who moved to Harvard in 1958, soon helped to remedy that. In 1961, Raiffa and Schlaifer published *Applied Statistical Decision Theory*. In spite of its title, this book is a mathematically demanding and rather complete treatment of the mathematics of distribution theory from a Bayesian point of view, with enough about how to combine distributions with utilities to make the word *decision* in the title make sense.

14.5. 1963–1971

The emergence of decision analysis

The period from 1963 to 1971 was clearly the time when decision analysis emerged as a viable applied activity. Its emergence seems to have occurred at Harvard, Stanford, and Michigan as a result of the activities of groups led by Raiffa, Ronald A. Howard, and Edwards, respectively.

In 1968, Raiffa published a fairly small paperback book called *Decision Analysis,* which contained relatively implementable treatments of most of the ideas presented here. It contrasted strongly in tone and in its orientation toward application with Raiffa and Schlaifer's 1961 book. Raiffa started working on it, in the form of lectures, in 1961 and kept updating and revising as he went along. He published a preliminary version as an article, with Schlaifer and John Pratt, in 1964 (Pratt, Raiffa, and Schlaifer, 1964). Though Raiffa did not coin the term *decision analysis* (R. A. Howard did that), we think it fair to say that his 1968 book gave the topic much of its visibility and academic interest.

In 1964 Ronald A. Howard published an article called "Bayesian Decision Models for Systems Engineering" and in 1966 he published one called "Decision Analysis: Applied Decision Theory." As far as we can tell, the latter was the first instance of a publication bearing the words *decision analysis.* Yet the two papers are not that different; Howard's thought had simply become more systematic about practical procedures for implementing the abstractions of Bayesian decision theory. A more mature version of those ideas appears in Howard (1968).

Perhaps the most important difference between Howard's approach and that of others, both during the 1960s and now, is that Howard places very strong emphasis on modeling the processes he is studying. Decision analysis, as Howard sees it, links various models together. Outcomes of actions should be modeled in detail; uncertainties should be modeled in as much detail as the sensitivity of the decision to the uncertainties justifies. Elicitation comes late in the process.

Another important difference is Howard's emphasis on the use of monetary variables as measures of value outcomes. This emphasis on money brings Howard's version of decision analysis nearer to the economist's tool of cost–benefit analysis than any other version. It is by no means identical with cost–benefit analysis, since it does not focus on such behavioral measures as observed willingness to pay. But Howard's ideas are probably closer to cost–benefit thinking than to the version of multiattribute utility proposed, for example, by Keeney and Raiffa (1976). Though the differences at the level of mathematics and conceptualization are relatively minor, the differences in both intellectual flavor and actual procedures are vast.

In 1965, Howard established a joint program between Stanford University and the Stanford Research Institute, which in 1967 grew into the Decision Analysis Group at SRI; Dr. James E. Matheson was its director, Dr. D. Warner North was a key figure, and Howard was its principal consultant. The SRI group was exceedingly active in a variety of public and private applied decision-analytic activities and gathered an extremely strong group of analysts. During the mid-1970s, the group started reproducing by fission. As a result, the San Francisco Bay Area is seeded with small consulting companies that apply decision-analytic ideas. Almost all of them can trace their origins directly or indirectly to Howard.

During the 1960s, Edwards and his colleagues and students maintained an active program of research on Bayesian ideas, focused mainly on Bayes's theorem as a descriptive model of inference and on the PIP idea. The former led to three theories about reasons for conservatism (see Edwards, 1968), which were briefly discussed in Chapter 13. The latter led to a major study (Edwards et al., 1968) showing that PIP worked better in a somewhat realistic laboratory setting than did purely intuitive systems intended to perform the same task. Though the PIP idea is obviously decision analytic in flavor, Edwards and his colleagues were not aware of the broader utility of decision analysis until they read Raiffa's 1968 book.

Multiattribute utility

Raiffa also originated the key ideas of multiattribute utility. They appeared both in his 1968 book and in a RAND Corporation publication (Raiffa, 1969), which made their usefulness considerably clearer. Edwards had long considered the problem of utility assessment to be more important than the problem of probability assessment and indeed had collaborated with L. W. Miller and R. J. Kaplan in applications of holistic utility assessment to military topics (see Miller, Kaplan, and Edwards, 1967, 1969). In 1971, Edwards published his first paper on SMART, an attempt to implement Raiffa's multiattribute utility idea using simple psychophysical tools.

14.6. 1971–1979

Development of appliers

The Decision Analysis Group established at SRI in 1967 seems to have been the first organized consulting group in decision analysis. The second, formed by some of Edwards's former colleagues and students in Washington, D.C., was called Decisions and Designs, Inc., and came into existence in 1971. Since then a number of others have developed, primarily either in the Washington, D.C., area or in the region around Stanford University.

A key stimulus to the development of these groups was a rapid growth of military receptivity to decision-analytic ideas and tools. One reason was the fact that the Advanced Research Projects Agency of the Department of Defense (DARPA) established a program concerned with the application of decision-analytic tools to military problems. This well-funded and very successful program supported both academics and consulting firms, and its projects ran the gamut from very basic to rather applied tasks. At least half the ideas presented in this book grew out of DARPA-funded work. An enormous virtue of DARPA work was that virtually all of it was unclassified. Much of the work on business applications that took place in the 1970s is unlikely ever to be published, since most corporations are reluctant to allow the publication of applied work done for them. In more recent times, the importance of military applications has escalated, and as a result the ease with which they can be published has diminished. A student reading today's literature might well be puzzled. The number of published applications has considerably decreased, and yet the demand for new PhDs trained in decision analysis has increased dramatically, in both business and governmental environments. The paradox simply reflects the difficulty of publishing papers about important applied topics.

Howard, Raiffa, and Edwards

Howard, though still a professor at Stanford, has been extremely active in a consulting firm of which he is a principal. Its major interest seems to be strategic planning for corporations.

Raiffa spent three years as director of the International Institute for Applied Systems Analysis in the early 1970s and then returned to Harvard. Ralph Keeney and Raiffa together published a very important book on multiattribute utility (Keeney and Raiffa, 1976). A significant amount of its technical content is presented in this book. On his return to Harvard, Raiffa got involved in the topic of bargaining and negotiation and has published a book on that topic (Raiffa, 1982).

Edwards moved from Michigan to the University of Southern California in 1973. His concerns about the effect of the cognitive illusions research paradigm on public perception of human cognitive capabilities, discussed at length in Chapter 13, profoundly affected his choice of research topics. He abandoned the cognitive illusions paradigm and instead studied technical issues having to do with elicitation techniques, validation of utility measurements, and the like.

The DARPA project ended in 1979, and we conclude our history there. Though much has happened since then, we cannot bring ourselves to see it as history.

14.7. A glimpse of the future: a research agenda for decision analysis

In the previous chapters we mentioned various issues that we consider unsatisfactorily developed in decision technology. In this final section we discuss a few of these in greater detail and hint at what we think can be done.

Research on problem structuring

Every working analyst we know agrees that good problem structuring is the key to successful analysis. We see four classes of structuring steps; research needs are inherent in each.

The first is option invention. We believe that options can be invented on the basis of preexisting value structures and, indeed, that an intuitive version of just this is what normally suggests options. But we know of only a few primitive efforts to turn that process from art to technology. We consider this a high-priority need, since we believe the "something must be done" kind of problem is much more common than the "which is better, A or B?" kind of problem. We believe that a highly computer facilitated technology for such problems could be developed.

The second is value structuring. The major technological discussion in the literature at the moment concerns whether values should be top-down or bottom-up. (*Top-down* means that abstract values should be defined first and more concrete values inferred from them, until a level sufficiently concrete to be susceptible to measurement and/or judgment is reached. *Bottom-up* means that specific value attributes that discriminate among options should be identified and classified into a tree structure if necessary.) Such little research as is available suggests that which approach is preferable depends on the problem. That dependence requires greater understanding than now exists. Top-down approaches are both more cumbersome and more common than bottom-up approaches. Under what circumstances can the easier approach be effective?

The third is inference structuring. This topic is so new that almost anything one might do would be of value. The little evidence that is now available, reviewed in Chapter 6, suggests that full decomposition of an inference problem into an inference structure results in better inferences – but the evidence is extremely feeble. We are not aware of much systematic thought about how to turn the ideas of inference structuring from a set of mathematical abstractions into a technology. The beginnings of work on that problem occurred in the 1960s and early 1970s. More recently the topic has been dropped – except by the students of artificial intelligence, many of whom seem to have ignored the formal mathematics relevant to the problem. Almost anything one could do about inference structuring would most likely be exciting. In particular, we see enormous promise in combining the kind of real-world Bayesian inference processes discussed in Chapter 6 with other kinds of inference processes based on scenarios. The reason for the distinction is that scenario-based inferences refer as easily to the future as to the past, while the more familiar kinds of inference processes with which Chapters 5 and 6 were concerned deal with the future only indirectly, if at all.

The fourth topic is decision tree structuring. In this area we see few if any interesting research needs, though that more likely reflects our parochial views than a consensus of the field.

Research on number elicitation

A major step in any analysis is the elicitation of the numbers that describe the likely impacts of the alternative courses of action in the form of point estimates, time series, probability distributions, and the like. To us the key issue in this step is not the specific method of elicitation, but rather the means of integrating the *different* kinds of inputs, for example, from systems modeling, human judgment, and statistics. Consider, for example, three estimates of the probable health impacts of a pollutant emitted by a coal-fired power plant. The first comes from a deterministic dispersion model coupled with a relatively simple dose–response model of human health effects. The second comes from many observations around one specific power plant. The last comes from the direct assessment of the probabilistic dose–response relations by four medical doctors. Useful research might address the question of how these three kinds of estimates might be related.

In more general terms, linking human judgment and what we earlier called environmental models, and linking both with models of decision making, seems to be a promising research avenue.

Of much less interest are the methods of eliciting human judgments. Although a variety of procedures have been proposed and a great deal of research has been done on their merits, the major conclusion to which that research has led is that virtually any method, carried out with care and including many internal consistency checks, will most likely do fairly well. Computerization of these methods, however, is an important technological topic.

Research on the validation of structures and numbers

If the procedures about which we write are ever to become more than art, they must be validated. The validation of structures is hard even to think about. What makes one structure more valid than another? The few publications on the topic offer an answer that is little more than a sophisticated translation of the familiar thought of user satisfaction. Perhaps that is the best we can do. But any form of research, especially empirical research, that can lead to greater confidence in decision-analytic structures would be very important indeed.

The validation of subjectively assessed decision-analytic numbers has been studied extensively. Indeed, the validity of judged probabilities has been a major research topic in psychology for two decades. Although the topic is controversial, we believe that suitable methodological precautions can lead to very satisfactory numbers. The validation of utilities has been studied much less extensively. Again, the data are encouraging, though not at this point definitive. This topic requires much more work, and research paradigms are readily available.

In any work on the validation of decision-analytic numbers, it is important to recognize that the method of assessment rather than the numbers assessed must be validated. Decision analysis is a technology; its important claim must be that it will come up with useful structures and numbers in new problem situations.

Validation of the output of decision analyses by comparing such outputs with intuitive decisions is often done, but is, we believe, unusually inappropriate. The whole point of decision analysis is to produce decisions that are wiser than, and therefore sometimes different from, those that would be produced by naked intuition. We consider such attempts to compare the two procedures useful only in demonstrating that they do indeed lead to different results – which we already knew.

Research on the use of decision-analytic tools for social conflict reduction

Evidence has existed in the literature for at least a decade that decision-analytic tools can reduce the extent of social conflict over public decisions. The reason for this seems simple enough. People argue about what they disagree about, while multiattribute utility procedures compel them to pay attention to the agreements as well as the disagreements. Moreover, the careful delineation of objectives often leads to the invention of new and perhaps Pareto-optimal options – that is, options that help all contenders to get more of what they really want.

This topic, which shades into research on bargaining and negotiation, is just emerging as a lively one in decision analysis. It is in its infancy primarily because it cannot be very well studied in laboratory settings; it requires real conflicts. Some of the case histories of real work are very suggestive. Indeed, even more dramatic examples of success exist but are not available because they are classified.

It is a challenge to the imaginations of researchers to design problems real enough to engage angry passions and yet open enough to permit participant–observer studies of the way in which agreement is reached. We ourselves consider this to be perhaps the most exciting prospect for decision-analytic work in the years immediately ahead. The challenge lies not only in spelling out a technology, but also in thinking about how to fit the technology into existing institutions designed for dispute resolution.

It is evidence of the force of decision-analytic ideas that they have progressed as far as they have in the face of institutions not designed to accommodate them comfortably. This is true not only in dispute resolution, but also in much simpler problems, such as program evaluation.

Research on computerization

The computer has so far had two rather uninteresting roles in decision-analytic practice. One has been that of a computational and display aid to the decision analyst interacting with a group. This function has been indispensable but has made little intellectual contribution to decision analysis itself. The other has been the development of decision-analytic stand-alone programs. The ones we have seen are, in our view, gallant failures; they require too much prior knowledge from the user to be successful on a stand-alone basis.

We believe that the full computerization of at least some decision analyses, so that a human analyst interacting with the decision maker(s) is unnecessary, is a difficult but probably attainable goal. Elicitation of numbers by unaided computer techniques is possible now. Computation is trivial. The explanation of outputs is not that hard a problem. But structuring is still an art, not an algorithm.

The key to computerization of structuring is the use of generic structures. The expert in performing decision analyses on plant-siting problems soon finds that most such problems have basically the same structure. Many medical problems are generic. Schum and Martin (1981, 1982) have identified various inference structures in criminal cases; there is some reason to think that the list may be nearly exhaustive, at least for criminal law.

Those interested in generic structures have for the most part not been interested in computerization. Consequently, we know of only one attempt to computerize generic structures. That one happens to be concerned with very complex hierarchical inference. It necessarily uses techniques borrowed from artificial intelligence, since the human operators of the system being developed cannot be expected to have more than about 3 months of training in its use.

An attempt has already been made to computerize the task of option invention from value structures. Though the merit of that attempt is debatable, we are confident that the approach will succeed.

As computer technology develops and penetrates virtually every context in which decisions are made, we can expect the slogan "decision support systems" to become increasingly important and to stimulate much interest. At present, the slogan seems to refer only to ways of organizing and presenting information, but as such systems develop, the integration of methods of information processing and use into them is almost inevitable. Consequently, we think it entirely possible that the rather clinical tradition of decision analysis and the inevitably algorithmic tradition of decision support systems will eventually merge.

But the heavy dependence of decision analysis on expertise implies considerable potential synergy between these two approaches to intellectual technology. Decision analysts, many from behavioral science traditions, should be able to help expert-system designers improve the structures and elicitation procedures they use. Expert-system designers should be able to help decision analysts embody more of their technology in computer programs.

At a minimum, the availability of decision-analytic programs that could do more than crunch numbers would be of enormous help. At a maximum, that availability could solve the problem that now most severely detracts from the usefulness of decision analysis. The problem is simply that, as presented in this book, decision analysis requires a competent analyst for almost every new application. The fact makes the technology expensive, esoteric, and likely to be used only if the stakes are high and the user knowledgeable. As long as decision analysis depends on the intervention of high priests, it will be costly and rarely used. If the high priests could be replaced by computer programs, the high priests could spend their time either working on problems too new or difficult or important to be handled by programs, or developing new programs. We hope that this kind of synergy will eventually evolve from the increasingly frequent interactions between decision analysts and computer scientists. But we do not expect to see it soon.

Disciplinary and organizational implications

By now it should be clear that the research agenda we propose lies at the intersection of psychology, operations research, statistics, and computer science. But in a physical sense, where do these disciplines intersect?

In academia, they don't. Psychology is part of the College of Letters, Arts, and Sciences at the University of Southern California and is similarly located in most other universities. Operations research is usually a part of industrial engineering, occasionally of a school of business. Statistics is often part of a department of mathematics, occasionally a separate department. Computer science is often a very independent part of a school of engineering. The ecumenical bent of schools of business can bring such groupings of interests together, and indeed most decision-analytic teaching is done in these schools. But neither psychologists nor computer scientists are particularly comfortable in such environments.

In principle, an interdisciplinary institute would be the natural home for such a collection of people. While such interdisciplinary organizations do exist, they have not yet played any major role in the development of decision analysis, though this book was written in one. The combination of talents we write of occurs naturally in consulting firms and has been fruitful in such settings. But consulting firms do little research.

Some day, a major donor will found an institute for research on intellectual technology that is well enough endowed to hire the needed mixture of top-quality people. When that happens, we will be camping in its director's outer office, research agenda in hand.

References

Aczel, J., & Pfanzagl, J. (1966). Remarks on the measurement of subjective probability and information. *Metrika, 11,* 91–105.

Adams, E. W. (1954). *A survey of Bernoullian utilities and application.* (Behavioral Models Project, Tech. Rep. No. 9). New York: Columbia University.

Adams, E. W. (1960). Bernoullian utility theory. In H. Solomon (Ed.), *Mathematical thinking in the measurement of behavior* (pp. 151–268). Glencoe, IL: Free Press.

Adams, E. W., & Fagot, R. F. (1959). A model of riskless choice. *Behavioral Science, 4,* 1–10.

Allais, M. (1953). Le comportement de l'homme rationnel devant le risque: Critique des postulats et axiomes de l'ecole americaine. *Econometrica, 21,* 503–46.

Allais, M., & Hagen, J. (Eds.). (1979). *Expected utility hypotheses and the Allais paradox.* Dordrecht, The Netherlands: Reidel.

Alpert, M., & Raiffa, H. (1982). A progress report on the training of probability assessors. In D. Kahneman, P. Slovic, & A. Tversky (Eds.), *Judgment under uncertainty: Heuristics and biases* (pp. 294–305). Cambridge University Press.

Arrow, K. J. (1951). *Social choice and individual values* (Cowles Commission Monograph 12). New York: Wiley.

Aschenbrenner, K. M., & Kasubek, W. (1978). Challenging the Cushing syndrome: Multiattribute evaluation of cortisone drugs. *Organizational Behavior and Human Performance, 22,* 216–34.

Aschenbrenner, K., & Wendt, D. (1978). Expectation versus ambition motivation in probability estimation. *Organizational Behavior and Human Performance, 22,* 146–70.

Baird, J. C., & Noma, E. (1978). *Fundamentals of scaling and psychophysics.* New York: Wiley.

Barclay, S., Brown, R. V., Kelly, C. W., III, Peterson, C. R., Phillips, L. D., & Selvidge, J. (1977). *Handbook for decision analysis.* McLean, VA: Decisions & Designs.

Bar-Hillel, M. (1973). On the subjective probability of compound events. *Organizational Behavior and Human Performance, 9,* 396–406.

Bar-Hillel, M. (1980). The base rate fallacy in probability judgements. *Acta Psychologica, 44,* 211–33.

Barnard, G. A. (1947). A review of *Sequential Analysis* by Abraham Wald. *Journal of the American Statistical Association, 42,* 658–64.

Barron, H. F., von Winterfeldt, D., & Fischer, G. W. (1984). Theoretical and empirical relationships between risky and riskless utility functions. *Acta Psychologica, 56,* 233–44.

Beach, L. R., Wise, J. A., & Barclay, S. (1970). Sample proportion and subjective probability revisions. *Organizational Behavior and Human Performance, 5,* 183–90.

Beck, J. R., Kassirer, J. P., & Pauker, S. G. (1982). A convenient approximation of life expectancy (the "DEALE"). I. Validation of the method. *American Journal of Medicine, 73,* 883–8.

Beck, J. R., Pauker, S. G., & Gottlieb, J. E. (1982). A convenient approximation of life expectancy (the "DEALE"). II. Use in medical decision making. *American Journal of Medicine, 73,* 889–97.

575

Becker, G. M., DeGroot, M. H., & Marschak, J. (1963). An experimental study of some stochastic models for wagers. *Behavioral Science, 8,* 199–202.

Becker, G. M., & McClintock, G. C. (1967). Value: Behavioral decision theory. *Annual Review of Psychology, 18,* 239–86.

Beckwith, N. E., & Lehmann, D. R. (1973). The importance of differential weights in multiple attribute models of consumer attitude. *Journal of Marketing Research, 10,* 141–5.

Behn, R. D., & Vaupel, J. W. (1982). *Quick analysis for busy decision makers.* New York: Basic Books.

Bell, D. E. (1981). Components of risk aversion. In J. P. Brans (Ed.), *Proceedings of the Ninth IFORS Conference* (pp. 235–42). Amsterdam: North Holland.

Bell, D. E. (1982). Regret in decision making under uncertainty. *Operations Research, 30,* 961–81.

Bell, D. E., Keeney, R. L., & Raiffa, H. (1977). *Conflicting objectives in decisions.* New York: Wiley.

Bell, D. E., & Raiffa, H. (1979). *Marginal value and intrinsic risk aversion.* Unpublished manuscript, Harvard Business School, Cambridge, MA.

Bell, D. E., & Raiffa, H. (1980). *Decision regret: A component of risk aversion.* Unpublished manuscript, Harvard Business School, Cambridge, MA.

Bell, R. S., & Loop, J. W. (1971). The utility and futility of radiographic skull examinations for trauma. *New England Journal of Medicine, 284,* 236–9.

Bernoulli, D. (1738). Specimen theoriae novae de mensura sortis. *Comentarii Academiae Scientiarum Imperiales Petropolitanae, 5,* 175–92.

Beyth-Marom, R. (1981). *The subjective probability of conjunctions* (Decision Research Rep. No. 81-12). Eugene, OR: Decision Research.

Beyth-Marom, R. (1982). How probable is probable? Numerical translations of verbal probability expressions. *Journal of Forecasting, 1,* 257–69.

Blackwell, D., & Dubins, L. (1962). Merging of opinions with increasing information. *Annals of Mathematical Statistics, 33,* 882–6.

Borel, E. (1924a). A propos d'un traite des probabilites. *Revue Philosophique, 1924, 98,* 321–36. Reprinted in E. Borel (1939). *Valeur pratique et philosophie des probabilites* (pp. 134–46) Paris: Gautier-Villars.

Borel, E. (1924b). Sur les jeux ou interviennent l'hazard et l'habilite des joueurs. In *Theorie des probabilites* (pp. 204–44). Paris: Librairie Scientifique, J. Hermann. Translated by L. J. Savage (1953). *Econometrica, 21,* 101–15.

Brier, G. W. (1950). Verification of forecasts expressed in terms of probability. *Monthly Weather Review, 75,* 1–3.

Brown, R. S. (1973). *An experiment in probabilistic forecasting* (Report No. R-944-ARPA). Santa Monica, CA: Rand Corporation.

Brown, R.V. (1970). Do managers find decision theory useful? *Harvard Business Review, 48,* 78–89.

Brown, R.V., Kahr, A.S., & Peterson, E. (1974). *Decision analysis for the manager.* New York: Holt, Rinehart, & Winston.

Calfee, R. (1970). Effects of payoff on detection in a symmetric auditory detection task. *Perceptual and Motor Skills, 31,* 895–901.

Caramazza, A., McCloskey, N., & Green, B. (1981). Naive beliefs in "sophisticated" subjects: Misconceptions about trajectories of objects. *Cognition, 9,* 117–23.

Carroll, J. S., & Siegler, R. S. (1977). Strategies for the use of base rate information. *Organizational Behavior and Human Performance, 19,* 392–402.

Central Unit on Environmental Pollution. (1976a). *Accidental oil pollution of the sea* (Pollution Paper No. 8, Department of Environment). London: HMSO.

Central Unit on Environmental Pollution. (1976b). *The separation of oil from water for North Sea oil operations* (Pollution Paper No. 6, Department of Environment). London: HMSO.

Chapman, L. J., & Chapman, J. P. (1967). Genesis of popular but erroneous psychodiagnostic observations. *Journal of Abnormal Psychology, 73,* 193–204.

Chapman, L. J., & Chapman, J. P. (1969). Illusory correlation as an obstacle to the use of valid psychodiagnostic signs. *Journal of Abnormal Psychology, 74,* 271–80.

Chinnis, J. O., Kelly, C. W., Minckler, R. D., & O'Connor, M. F. (1975). *Single Channel Ground and Airborne Radio Systems (SINGCARS) evaluation model* (Tech. Rep. No. DT/TR 75-2). McLean, VA: Decisions & Designs.

Cohen, J. J. (1972). A case for benefit–risk analysis. In H. J. Otway (Ed.), *Risk vs. benefit: Solution or dream* (Report No. LA-4860-MS). Los Alamos, CA: Los Alamos Scientific Laboratory.

Cohen, J., & Hansel, C. E. M. (1957). The nature of decisions in gambling. *Acta Psychologica, 13,* 357–70.

Cohen, L. J. (1977). *The probable and the provable.* Oxford: Clarendon.

Cook, R. L., & Stuart, K. R. (1975). A comparison of seven methods for obtaining subjective descriptions of judgmental policy. *Organizational Behavior and Human Performance, 13,* 31–45.

Coombs, C. H. (1964). *A theory of data.* New York: Wiley.

Coombs, C. H., Bezembinder, T. C. G., & Goode, F. M. (1967). Testing expectation theories of decision making without measuring utility and subjective probability. *Journal of Mathematical Psychology, 4,* 72–103.

Coombs, C. H., & Huang, L. C. (1976). Tests of the betweenness property of expected utility. *Journal of Mathematical Psychology, 13,* 323–37.

Council for Environmental Quality. (1974). *OCS oil and gas developments: An environmental assessment: Vol. 5. Analysis of oil spill statistics.* Washington, DC: NTIS.

Dalkey, N. C. (1969). The Delphi method: An experimental study of group opinion (Report No. RM-5888-PR). Santa Monica, CA: Rand Corporation.

Dalkey, N. C. (1975). Toward a theory of group estimation. In H. A. Linstone & M. Turoff (Eds.), *The Delphi method: Techniques and applications* (pp. 236–61). Reading, MA: Addison-Wesley.

Dalkey, N. C., & Helmer, O. (1963). An experimental application of the Delphi method to the use of experts. *Management Science, 3,* 458.

Davidson, D., Suppes, P., & Siegel, S. (1957). *Decision making: An experimental approach.* Stanford, CA: Stanford University Press.

Dawes, R. M., & Corrigan, B. (1974). Linear models in decision making. *Psychological Bulletin, 81,* 95–106.

de Finetti, B. (1937). La prevision: Ses lois logiques, ses sources subjectives. *Annales de l'Institut Henri Poincare, 7,* 1–68. Translated by H. E. Kyburg in H. E. Kyburg, Jr., & H. E. Smokler (Eds.). (1964). *Studies in subjective probability.* New York: Wiley.

de Finetti, B. (1959). La probabilita e la statistica nei rapporti con l'induzione, secondo i diversi punti da vista. *Induzione e Statistica.* Rome: Instituto Matematico dell' Universita.

DeGroot, M. H. (1970). *Optimal statistical decisions.* New York: McGraw-Hill.

DeGroot, M. H. (1974). Reaching a concensus. *Journal of the American Statistical Association, 69,* 118–21.

Delbecq, A., Van de Ven, A., & Gustafson, D. (1975). *Group techniques for program planning* Glenview, IL: Scott Foresman.

Delbeke, L., & Fauville, J. (1974). An empirical test of Fishburn's additivity axiom. *Acta Psychologica, 38,* 1–20.

de Neufville, R., & Keeney, R. L. (1972). Use of decision analysis in airport development for Mexico City. In A. W. Drake, R. L. Keeney, & P. M. Morse (Eds.), *Analysis of public systems* (pp. 497–519). Cambridge, MA: MIT Press.

Dershowitz, A. (1971). Imprisonment by judicial hunch. *American Bar Association Journal, 57,* 560–4.

deSmet, A. A., Fryback, D., & Thornbury, J. R. (1979). A second look at the utility of radiographic skull examination for trauma. *American Journal of Radiology, 132,* 75–99.

Doyle, A. C. The adventure of Silver Blaze. From *The memoirs of Sherlock Holmes.* London: The Strand Magazine, 1892.

Dyer, J. S., & Miles, D. (1976). An actual application of collective choice theory to the selection of trajectories for the Mariner Jupiter/Saturn Project. *Operations Research, 24,* 220–43.

Dyer, J. S., & Sarin, R. A. (1979). Measurable multiattribute value functions. *Operations Research, 22,* 810–22.

Eckenrode, R. J. (1965). Weighting multiple criteria. *Management Science, 12* (3), 180–91.

Eddy, D. M. (1982). Probabilistic reasoning in clinical medicine: Problems and opportunities. In D. Kahneman, P. Slovic, & A. Tversky (Eds.), *Judgment under uncertainty: Heuristics and biases* (pp. 3–23). Cambridge University Press.

Edgeworth, F. Y. (1881). *Mathematical psychics.* London: Kegan Paul.

Edwards, W. (1953). Probability-preferences in gambling. *American Journal of Psychology, 66,* 349–64.

Edwards, W. (1954a). Probability-preferences among bets with differing expected values. *American Journal of Psychology, 67,* 56–7.

Edwards, W. (1954b). The reliability of probability-preferences. *American Journal of Psychology, 67,* 68–95.

Edwards, W. (1954c). Variance preferences in gambling. *American Journal of Psychology, 67,* 441–52.

Edwards, W. (1954d). The theory of decision making. *Psychological Bulletin, 41,* 380–417.

Edwards, W. (1961). Behavioral decision theory. *Annual Review of Psychology, 12,* 473–98.

Edwards, W. (1962a). Dynamic decision theory and probilistic information processing. *Human Factors, 4,* 59–73.

Edwards, W. (1962a). Dynamic decision theory and probabilistic information processing. *Human Factors, 4,* 59–73.

Edwards, W. (1968). Conservatism in human information processing. In B. Kleinmuntz (Ed.), *Formal representation of human judgment* (pp. 17–52). New York: Wiley.

Edwards, W. (1971). Social utilities. *Engineering Economist,* Summer Symposium Series, *6,* 119–29.

Edwards, W. (1977). How to use multiattribute utility measurement for social decision making. *IEEE Transactions on Systems, Man and Cybernetics, SMC-7,* 326–40.

Edwards, W. (1979). Multiattribute utility measurement: Evaluating desegregation plans in a highly political context. In R. Perloff (Ed.), *Evaluator interventions: Pros and cons* (pp. 13–54). Beverly Hills, CA: Sage.

Edwards, W. (1980). Reflections on and criticism of a highly political multiattribute utility analysis. In L. Cobb & R. M. Thrall (Eds.), *Mathematical frontiers of behavioral and policy sciences* (pp. 157–68). Boulder, CO: Westview Press.

Edwards, W., Guttentag, M., & Snapper, K. (1975). Effective evaluation: A decision theoretic approach. In E. L. Streuning & M. Guttentag (Eds.), *Handbook of evaluation research* (Vol. 1, pp. 137–81). Beverly Hills, CA: Sage.

Edwards, W., Lindman, H., & Savage, L. J. (1963). Bayesian statistical inference for psychological research. *Psychological Review, 70,* 193–242.

Edwards, W., & Newman, J. R. (1982). *Multiattribute evaluation.* Beverly Hills, CA: Sage.

Edwards, W., Phillips, L. D., Hays, W. L., & Goodman, B. C. (1968). Probabilistic information processing systems: Design and evaluation. *IEEE Transactions on Systems Science and Cybernetics, SSC-4,* 248–65.

Edwards, W., & Tversky, A. (1967). *Decision making: Selected readings.* Harmondsworth, Middlesex, England: Penguin Books.

Edwards, W., von Winterfeldt, D., & Moody, D. L. (in press). Simplicity in decision analysis: An example and a discussion. In D. Bell (Ed.), *Decision making: Descriptive, normative, and prescriptive interactions.* Cambridge, MA: Harvard Business School.

Eils, L., & John, R. S. (1980). A criterion validation of multiattribute utility analysis and of group communication strategy. *Organizational Behavior and Human Performance, 25,* 268–88.

Eils, L., Seaver, D., & Edwards, W. (1977, August). *Developing the technology of probabilistic inference: Aggregating by averaging reduces conservatism* (Research Rep. No. 77-3). Los Angeles: University of Southern California, Social Science Research Institute.

Einhorn, H., & Hogarth, R. M. (1975). Unit weighting schemes for decision making. *Organizational Behavior and Human Performance, 13,* 171–92.

Einhorn, H., & Hogarth, R. (1981). Behavioral decision theory: Processes of judgment and choice. *Annual Review of Psychology, 32,* 53–88.

Ekman, G., & Sjoberg, L. (1965). Scaling. *Annual Review of Psychology, 16,* 451–74.

Ellsberg, D. (1961). Risk, ambiguity, and the Savage axioms. *Quarterly Journal of Economics, 75,* 643–69.

Environmental Protection Agency. (1975). *Development document for interim final effluent limitation guidelines and new source performance standards for the offshore segment of the Oil and Gas Extraction Point Source Category* (EPA-440/1-75/055). Washington, DC: Author.

Epstein, E. S. (1969). A scoring system for probability forecasts of ranked probability scores. *Journal of Applied Meteorology, 18,* 985–7.

Fechner, G. T. (1860). *Elemente der Psychophysik* (Vols. 1 & 2). Leipzig, Germany: Breithopf & Hartel.

Feller, W. (1968). *An introduction to probability theory and its application* (Vol. 1). New York: Wiley.

Ferguson, T. S. (1967). *Mathematical statistics: A decision theoretic approach.* New York: Academic Press.

Fischer, G. W. (1972). *Four methods for assessing multiattribute utilities: An experimental validation* (Tech. Rep.). Ann Arbor: University of Michigan, Engineering Psychology Laboratory.

Fischer, G. W. (1975). Experimental applications of multiattribute utility models. In D. Wendt & C. Vlek (Eds.), *Utility, probability, and human decision making* (pp. 7–46). Dordrecht, The Netherlands: Reidel.

Fischer, G. W. (1976). Multi-dimensional utility models for risky and riskless choice. *Organizational Behavior and Human Performance, 17,* 127–46.

Fischer, G. W. (1977). Convergent validation of decomposed multi-attribute utility assessment procedures for risky and riskless decisions. *Organizational Behavior and Human Performance, 18,* 295–315.

Fischer, G. W. (1979). Utility models for multiple objective decisions: Do they accurately represent human preferences? *Decision Sciences, 10,* 451–79.

Fischer, G. W. (1982). Scoring rule feedback and the overconfidence syndrome in subjective probability forecasting. *Organizational Behavior and Human Performance, 29,* 357–69.

Fischer, G. W., & Peterson, C. (1973). *Ratio vs. magnitude estimation of importance weights* (Tech. Rep.). Ann Arbor: University of Michigan, Engineering Psychology Laboratory.

Fischhoff, B. (1975). Hindsight ≠ foresight: The effect of outcome knowledge on judgment under uncertainty. *Journal of Experimental Psychology: Human Perception and Performance, 1,* 288–99.

Fischhoff, B. (1976). Attribution theory and judgment under uncertainty. In N. H. Harvey, W. J. Ickes, & R. F. Kidd (Eds.), *New directions in attribution research* (pp. 421–52). Hillsdale, NJ: Erlbaum.

Fischhoff, B. (1980). For those condemned to study the past: Reflections on historical judgment. In R. A. Schweder & D. W. Fiske (Eds.), *New directions for methodology of behavioral science: Fallible judgment in behavioral research* (pp. 79–93). San Francisco: Jossey-Bass.

Fischhoff, B. (1982). Debiasing. In D. Kahneman, P. Slovic, & A. Tversky (Eds.), *Judgments under uncertainty: Heuristics and biases* (pp. 422–44). Cambridge University Press.

Fischhoff, B., & Beyth, R. (1975). "I knew it would happen": Remembered probabilities of once-future things. *Organizational Behavior and Human Performance, 13,* 1–16.

Fischhoff, B., Goitein, B., & Shapira, Z. (1980). *The experienced utility of expected utility approaches* (Tech. Rep. No. PTR-1091-80-4). Eugene, OR: Decision Research.

Fischhoff, B., & Slovic, P. (1980). A little learning . . . Confidence in multicue judgment. In R. Nickerson (Ed.) *Attention and performance* (Vol. 8, pp. 779–800). Hillsdale, NJ: Erlbaum.

Fischhoff, B., Slovic, P., & Lichtenstein, S. (1978). Fault trees: Sensitivity of estimated failure probabilities to problem representation. *Journal of Experimental Psychology: Human Perception and Performance, 4,* 330–4.

Fischhoff, B., Slovic, P., & Lichtenstein, S. (1980). Knowing what you want: Measuring labile values. In T. Wallsten (Ed.), *Cognitive processes in choice and decision behavior* (pp. 64–85). Hillsdale, NJ: Erlbaum.

Fischhoff, B., Lichtenstein, S., Slovic, P., Derby, S. L., & Keeney, R. L. (1981). *Acceptable risk.* Cambridge University Press.

Fishburn, P. C. (1965). Independence in utility theory with whole product sets. *Operation Research, 13,* 28–45.

Fishburn, P. C. (1967). Methods of estimating additive utilities. *Management Science, 13,* 435–53.

Fishburn, P. C., & Kochenberger, G. A. (1971). Two-piece von Neumann and Morgenstern functions. *Decision Sciences, 10,* 503–18.

Fisher, R. A. (1956). *Statistical methods and scientific inference* (2nd ed.). Edinburgh: Oliver & Boyd.

Flavell, J. H. (1977). *Cognitive development.* Englewood Cliffs, NJ: Prentice-Hall.

Friedman, M., & Savage, L. J. (1948). The utility analysis of choices involving risk. *Journal of Political Economy, 56,* 279–304.

Friedman, M., & Savage, L. J. (1952). The expected utility hypothesis and the measurability of utility. *Journal of Political Economy, 60,* 463–75.

Fryback, D. G. (1974). *Bayes' theorem and conditional non-independence of data in a medical diagnosis task* (Michigan Mathematical Psychology Program Rep. No. MMPP 1974-7). Ann Arbor: University of Michigan.

Fryback, D. G., Goodman, B. C., & Edwards, W. (1973). Choices among bets by Las Vegas gamblers: Absolute and contextual effects. *Journal of Experimental Psychology, 98,* 271–8.

Fuchs, L. (1963). *Partially ordered algebraic systems.* Reading, MA: Addison-Wesley.

Fujii, T. (1967). Conservatism and discriminability in probability estimation as a function of response model. *Japanese Psychological Research, 9,* 42–47.

Gabrielli, W., & von Winterfeldt, D. (1978). *Are importance weights sensitive to the range of alternatives in multiattribute utility measurement?* (Research Rep. No. 78-6) Los Angeles: University of Southern California, Social Science Research Institute.

Galanter, E., & Holman, G. L. (1967). Some invariances of the iso-sensitivity function and their implications for the utility function of money. *Journal of Experimental Psychology, 75,* 333–9.

Gardiner, P. (1974). *The application of decision technology and Monte Carlo simulation to multiple objective public policy decision making: A case study in California coastal zone management.* Unpublished doctoral dissertation, University of Southern California, Los Angeles.

Gardiner, P., & Edwards, W. (1975). Public values: Multiattribute utility measurement for social decision making. In M. F. Kaplan & S. Schwartz (Eds.), *Human judgment and decision processes.* New York: Academic Press.

Gettys, C. F., Fisher, S. D., & Mehle, T. (1978). *Hypothesis generation and plausibility assessments* (Tech. Rep. No. 15-10-78). Norman: University of Oklahoma, Decision Process Laboratory.

Gettys, C. F., Kelly, C. W., III, & Peterson, C. R. (1973). The best guess hypothesis in multistage inference. *Organizational Behavior and Human Performance, 10,* 363–73.

Gettys, C. F., Mehle, T., Baca, S., Fisher, S., & Manning, C. (1979). *A memory retrieval aid for hypothesis generation* (Tech. Rep. No. 27-7-79). Norman: University of Oklahoma, Decision Process Laboratory.

Gettys, C. F., & Willke, T. A. (1969). The application of Bayes' theorem when the true data state is uncertain. *Organizational Behavior and Human Performance, 4,* 125–41.

Ghiselli, E. E. (1964). *Theory of psychological measurement.* New York: McGraw-Hill.

Goldsmith, R. W. (1978). Assessing probabilities of compound events in a judicial context. *Scandinavian Journal of Psychology, 19,* 103–10.

Goodman, B. (1972). Action selection and likelihood estimation by individuals and groups. *Organizational Behavior and Human Performance, 7,* 121–41.

Goodman, B., Saltzman, M., Edwards, W., & Krantz, D. H. (1979). Prediction of bids for two outcome gambles in a casino setting. *Organizational Behavior and Human Performance, 29,* 382–99.

Gough, R. (1975). *The effect of group format on aggregate subjective probability distributions.* Paper presented at the 13th conference on Bayesian Research, Los Angeles.

Green, A. E., & Bourne, A. J. (1972). *Reliability technology.* New York: Wiley-Interscience.

Green, D. M. (1960). Psychoacoustics and detection theory. *Journal of the Acoustical Society of America, 32,* 1189–1203.

Green, D. M., & Swets, J. A. (1966). *Signal detection theory and psychophysics.* New York: Wiley.

Grether, D. M. (1979). Bayes' rule as a descriptive model: The representativeness heuristic. *Quarterly Journal of Economics, 95,* 535–57.

Grether, D. M., & Plott, C. R. (1979). Economic theory of choice and the preference reversal phenomenon. *American Economic Review, 69,* 623–38.

Griffin, G., & von Winterfeldt, D. (1984). *On the behavioral distinction between riskless value and risky utility.* Unpublished manuscript, University of Southern California, Social Science Research Institute, Los Angeles.

Gulliksen, H. (1950). *Theory of mental tests.* New York: Wiley.

Gustafson, D. H., Grest, J. H., Stauss, F. F., Erdman, H., & Laughren, T. (1977). A probabilistic system for identifying suicide attemptors. *Computers and Biomedical Research, 10,* 83–9.

Gustafson, D. H., & Holloway, D. C. (1975). A decision theory approach to measuring severity in illness. *Health Services Research,* Spring, 97–106.

Gustafson, D. H., Shukla, R. U., Delbecq, A., & Walster, G. W. (1973). A comparative study of differences in subjective likelihood estimates made by individuals, interacting groups, Delphi groups, and nominal groups. *Organizational Behavior and Human Performance, 9,* 280–91.

Hammerton, M. (1970). An investigation into changes in decision criteria and other details of a decision-making task. *Psychonomic Science, 21,* 203–4.

Hammerton, M. (1973). A case of radical probability estimation. *Journal of Experimental Psychology, 101,* 252–4.

Hammond, K., Hamm, R. M., Grassia, J., & Pearson, T. (1983, June). *Direct comparison of intuitive, quasi-rational, and analytical cognition* (Report No. 248). Boulder: University of Colorado, Center for Research on Judgment and Policy.

Hammond, K. R., McClelland, G. H., & Mumpower, J. (1980). *Human judgment and decision making: Theories, methods, and procedures.* New York: Praeger.

Hammond, K. R., Stewart, T. R., Brehmer, B., & Steinmann, D. O. (1975). Social judgment theory. In M. F. Kaplan & S. Schwartz (Eds.), *Human judgment and decision processes* (pp. 272–312). New York: Academic Press.

Hax, A. C., & Wiig, K. M. (1977). The use of decision analysis in a capital investment problem. In D. Bell, R. L. Keeney, & H. Raiffa (Eds.), *Conflicting objectives in decisions* (pp. 277–97). New York: Wiley.

Healy, A. F., & Kubovy, M. (1977). A comparison of recognition memory numerical decisions: How prior probabilities affect cutoff location. *Memory and Cognition, 5,* 3–9.

Healy, A. F., & Kubovy, M. (1978). The effect of payoffs and prior probabilities as indices of performance and cutoff location in recognition memory. *Memory and Cognition, 6,* 544–53.

Helson, H. (1964). *Adaptation-level theory.* New York: Harper & Row.

Hershey, J. C., Kunreuther, H. C., & Schoemaker, P. J. H. (1982). Sources of bias in assessment procedures for utility functions. *Management Science, 8,* 931–54.

Hershey, J. C., & Schoemaker, P. J. H. (1980). Risk taking and problem context in the domain of losses: An expected utility analysis. *Journal of Risk and Insurance, 47,* 111–32.

Hershey, J. D., & Schoemaker, P. J. H. (1983). *Equivalence judgments that are not equivalent: Probability vs. certainty equivalence methods in utility measurement* (Tech. Rep.). University of Chicago, Graduate School of Business.

Hicks, J. R., & Allen, R. G. D. (1934). A reconsideration of the theory of value. *Economica, 14,* 52–76, 197–219.

Hoepfl, R. T., & Huber, G. P. (1970). A study of self-explicated utility models. *Behavioral Science, 5,* 408–14.

Hoffman, P. J. (1960). The paramorphic representation of clinical judgment. *Psychological Bulletin, 47,* 116–31.

Hogarth, R. M. (1977). Methods for aggregating opinions. In H. Jungermann & G. de Zeeuw (Eds.), *Decision making and change in human affairs* (pp. 231–55). Dordrecht, The Netherlands: Reidel.

Hogarth, R. (1980). *Judgment and choice: The psychology of decisions.* Chichester, England: Wiley.

Holloway, C. A. (1979). *Decision making under uncertainty: Models and choices.* Englewood Cliffs, NJ: Prentice-Hall.

Höpfinger, E., & von Winterfeldt, D. (1979). A dynamic model for setting railway noise standards. In O. Moeschling & D. Pallaschke (Eds.), *Game theory and related topics* (pp. 59–69). Amsterdam: North Holland.

Howard, R. A. (1964). Bayesian decision models for systems engineering. *IEEE Transactions on Systems Science and Cybernetics, SSC-1,* 36–40.

Howard, R. A. (1966). Decision analysis: Applied decision theory. In D. B. Hertz & J. Melese (Eds.), *Proceedings of the Fourth International Conference on Operational Research* (pp. 55–71). New York: Wiley-Interscience.

Howard, R. A. (1968). The foundations of decision analysis. *IEEE Transactions on Systems Science and Cybernetics, SSC-4,* 211–19.

Howard, R. A., & Matheson, J. E. (1980). *Influence diagrams* (Tech. Rep.). Menlo Park, CA: Stanford Research Institute International.

Howard, R. A., Matheson, J. E., & Miller, R. L. (Eds.). (1976). *Readings in decision analysis.* Menlo Park, CA: Stanford Research Institute.

Huber, G. P., Daneshgar, R., & Ford, D. L. (1971). An empirical comparison of five utility models for predicting job preferences. *Organizational Behavior and Human Performance, 6,* 276–82.

Humphreys, P. C. (1983). Decision aids: Aiding decisions. In L. Sjöberg, T. Tyszka, & J. A. Wise (Eds.), *Human decision making* (pp. 14–44). Bodafors, Sweden: Doxa.

Humphreys, P. C., & Humphreys, A. R. (1975). An investigation of subjective orderings for multiattributed alternatives. In D. Wendt & C. Vlek (Eds.), *Utility, probability, and human decision making* (pp. 119–33). Dordrecht, The Netherlands: Reidel.

Humphreys, P. C., & McFadden, W. (1980). Experiences with MAUD: Aiding decision structuring versus bootstrapping the decision maker. *Acta Psychologica, 45,* 51–69.

Humphreys, P. C., & Wishuda, A. (1980). Multiattribute utility decomposition (Tech. Rep. No. 72-2/2). Uxbridge, Middlesex, England: Brunel University, Brunel Institute of Organization and Social Studies, Decision Analysis Unit.

Inhelder, B., & Piaget, J. (1958). *The growth of logical thinking from childhood to adolescence.* New York: Basic Books.

Isaacs, G. L., & Novick, M. R. (1974). A Bayesian computer assisted data analysis (CADA) monitor (Tech. Rep.). University of Iowa, Department of Measurement and Statistics, Iowa City.

Jennings, D. L., Amabile, T. M., & Ross, L. (1982). Informal covariation assessment: Data-based versus theory-based judgments. In D. Kahneman, P. Slovic, & A. Tversky (Eds.), *Judgments under uncertainty: Heuristics and biases* (pp. 211–35). Cambridge University Press.

John, R. S. (1984). *Value tree analysis of social conflicts about risky technologies.* Unpublished doctoral dissertation, University of Southern California, Los Angeles.

John, R. S., & Edwards, W. (1978). *Importance weight assessment for additive riskless preference functions: A review* (Research Rep. No. 78-3). Los Angeles: University of Southern California, Social Science Research Institute.

John, R. S., Edwards, W., & Collins, L. (in press). Learning and recovering importance weights in a multiattribute evaluation context. *Organizational Behavior and Human Performance.*

John, R. S., Edwards, W., von Winterfeldt, D., & Barron, F. H. (1980). *Equal weights, flat maxima, and trivial decisions* (Research Rep. No. 80-2). Los Angeles: University of Southern California, Social Science Research Institute.

John, R. S., von Winterfeldt, D., & Edwards, W. (1983). The quality and user acceptance of decision analysis performed by computer vs. analyst. In P. Humphreys, O. Svenson, & A. Vari (Eds.), *Analysing and aiding decision processes* (pp. 301–29). Budapest: Hungarian Academy of Sciences.

Kahneman, D., Slovic, P., & Tversky, A. (1982). *Judgment under uncertainty: Heuristics and biases.* Cambridge University Press.

Kahneman, D., & Tversky, A. (1972a). On prediction and judgment. *Oregon Research Institute Research Monograph, 12* (4).

Kahneman, D., & Tversky, A. (1972b). Subjective probability: A judgment of representativeness. *Cognitive Psychology, 3,* 430–54.

Kahneman, D., & Tversky, A. (1973). On the psychology of prediction. *Psychological Review, 80,* 237–51.

Kahneman, D., & Tversky, A. (1979a). Intuitive prediction: Biases and corrective procedures. *TIMS studies in Management Science, 12,* 313–27.

Kahneman, D., & Tversky, A. (1979b). Prospect theory: An analysis of decision under risk. *Econometrica, 47,* 263–91.

Kahneman, D., & Tversky, A. (1982). On the study of statistical intuitions. *Cognition, 11,* 123–41. Reprinted in D. Kahneman, P. Slovic, & A. Tversky (Eds.). (1982). *Judgments under uncertainty: Heuristics and biases.* Cambridge University Press.

Keeney, R. L. (1968). Quasi-separable utility functions. *Naval Research Logistics Quarterly, 15,* 551–65.

Keeney, R. L. (1973). A decision analysis with multiple objectives: The Mexico City airport. *Bell Journal of Economics and Management Science, 4,* 101–17.

Keeney, R. L. (1979). Evaluation of proposed pumped storage sites. *Operations Research, 17,* 48–64.

Keeney, R. L. (1980). *Siting energy facilities.* New York: Academic Press.

Keeney, R. L. (1981). Analysis of preference dependencies among objectives. *Operations Research, 29,* 1105–20.

Keeney, R. L., & Lamont, A. (1979, August). *A probabilistic analysis of landslide potential.* Paper presented at the Second Annual Conference on Earthquake Engineering, Stanford University, Stanford, CA.

Keeney, R. L., & Raiffa, H. (1976). *Decisions with multiple objectives: Preferences and value tradeoffs.* New York: Wiley.

Keeney, R. L., Renn, O., & von Winterfeldt, D. (1985). *Structuring Germany's energy objectives.* Unpublished manuscript, University of Southern California, Institute of Safety and Systems Management, Los Angeles.

Keeney, R. L., & Sicherman, A. (1976). An interactive computer program for assessing and using multiattribute utility functions. *Behavioral Science, 21,* 173–82.

Kelly, C. W., III. (1978). *Decision aids: Engineering science and clinical art* (Tech. Rep.). McLean, VA: Decisions & Designs.

Kelly, C. W., III, & Barclay, S. (1973). A general Bayesian model for hierarchical inference. *Organizational Behavior and Human Performance, 10,* 388–403.

Kelly, C. W., III, & Peterson, C. R. (1971). *Probability estimates and probabilistic procedures in current-intelligence analysis* (Report No. FSC-71-5047). Gaithersburg, MD: IBM, Federal Systems Division.

Keller, L. R. (1985). The effects of problem representation on the sure-thing and substitution principles. *Management Science, 31,* 738–51.

Kent, S. (1964). Words of estimated probability. *Studies in Intelligence, 8,* 49–65.

Knop, H. (1979). *The Tennessee Valley Authority: A field study* (Report No. IIASA-RR-79-2). Laxenburg, Austria: International Institute of Applied Systems Analysis.

Koriat, A., Lichtenstein, S., & Fischhoff, B. (1980). Reasons for confidence. *Journal of Experimental Psychology: Human Learning and Memory, 6,* 107–18.

Krantz, D. H. (1964). Conjoint measurement: The Luce–Tukey axiomatization and some extensions. *Journal of Mathematical Psychology, 1,* 248–77.

Krantz, D. H., Luce, R. D., Suppes, P., & Tversky, A. (1971). *Foundations of Measurement* (Vol. 1). New York: Academic Press.

Krischer, J. P. (1980). An annotated bibliography of decision analytic applications to health care. *Operations Research, 20,* 97–113.

Kubovy, M., & Healy, A. F. (1977). The decision rule in probabilistic categorization: What it is and how it is learned. *Journal of Experimental Psychology: General, 106,* 427–46.

Kubovy, M., & Healy, A. F. (1980). Process models of probabilistic categorization. In T. S. Wallsten (Ed.), *Cognitive processes in choice and decision behavior* (pp. 239–62). Hillsdale, NJ: Erlbaum.

Kyburg, H. E., Jr., & Smokler, H. E. (Eds.). (1964). *Studies in subjective probability.* New York: Wiley.

Lathrop, R. G., & Peters, B. E. (1969). *Subjective cue weighting and decisions in a familiar task.* Paper presented at the 77th Annual Convention of the American Psychological Association, Washington, DC.

Leon, M., & Anderson, N. H. (1974). A ratio-rule from integration theory applied to inference judgments. *Journal of Experimental Psychology, 102,* 27–36.

Lichtenstein, S., & Fischhoff, B. (1977). Do those who know more also know more about how much they know? The calibration of probability judgments. *Organizational Behavior and Human Performance, 20,* 159–183.

Lichtenstein, S., & Fischhoff, B. (1980). Training for calibration. *Organizational Behavior and Human Performance, 26,* 149–71.

Lichstenstein, S., Fischhoff, B., & Phillips, L. D. (1977). Calibration of probabilities: The state of the art. In H. Jungermann and G. de Zeeuw (Eds.), *Decision making and change in human affairs* (pp. 275–324). Dordrecht, Holland: Reidel.

Lichtenstein, S., Fischhoff, B., & Phillips, L. D. (1982). Calibration of probabilities: The state of the art to 1980. In D. Kahneman, P. Slovic, & A. Tversky (Eds.), *Judgment under uncertainty: Heuristics and biases* (pp. 306–34). Cambridge University Press.

Lichtenstein, S., & Slovic, P. (1971). Reversals of preferences between bids and choices in gambling decisions. *Journal of Experimental Psychology, 89,* 46–55.

Lichtenstein, S., & Slovic, P. (1973). Response induced reversals of preferences in gambling: An extended replication in Las Vegas. *Journal of Experimental Psychology, 101,* 16–20.

Lieblich, A., & Lieblich, I. (1969). Arithmetical estimation under conditions of different payoff matrices. *Psychonomic Science, 14,* 87–8.

Lieblich, I., & Lieblich, A. (1969). Effects of cost and payoff matrices on arithmetic estimation tasks: An attempt to produce rationality. *Perceptual and Motor Skills, 29,* 467–73.

Lindley, D. V. (1961). The use of prior probability distributions in statistical inferences and decision. In *Proceedings of the Fourth Berkeley Symposium on Mathematics and Probability* (Vol. 1, pp. 453–68). Berkeley and Los Angeles: University of California Press.

Linstone, H. A., & Turoff, M. (Eds.). (1975). *The Delphi method: Techniques and applications.* Reading, MA: Addison-Wesley.

Luce, R. D. (1959). *Individual choice behavior.* New York: Wiley.

Luce, R. D., & Krantz, D. H. (1971). Conditional expected utility. *Econometrica, 39,* 253–71.

Luce, R. D., & Raiffa, H. (1957). *Games and decisions: Introduction and critical survey.* New York: Wiley.

Luce, R. D., & Suppes, P. (1965). Preference, utility, and subjective probability. In R. D. Luce, R. R. Bush, & E. Galanter (Eds.), *Handbook of Mathematical Psychology,* (Vol. 3, pp. 249–410). New York: Wiley.

Luce, R. D., & Tukey, J. W. (1964). Simultaneous conjoint measurement: A new type of fundamental measurement. *Journal of Mathematical Psychology, 1,* 1–27.

Ludke, R. L., Stauss, F. Y., & Gustafson, D. H. (1977). Comparison of five methods for estimating subjective probability distributions. *Organizational Behavior and Human Performance, 19,* 162–79.

Lukaszewski, J. S., & Elliot, P. N. (1962). Auditory threshold as a function of forced choice techniques, feedback and motivation. *Journal of the Acoustical Society of America, 34,* 223–8.

Lusted, L. B. (1977). *A study of the efficacy of diagnostic radiologic procedures: Final report on diagnostic efficacy.* American College of Radiology, Chicago.

Lusted, L. B., Roberts, H. V., Edwards, W., Wallace, P. L., Lahiff, M., Loop, J. W., Bell., R. S., Thornbury, J. R., Seale, D. L., Steele, J. P., & Fryback, D. G. (1980). *Efficacy of diagnostic X-ray procedures.* American College of Radiology, Chicago.

Lykken, D. T. (1975). The right way to use a lie detector. *Psychology Today, 8,* 56–60.

Lyon, D., & Slovic, P. (1976). Dominance of accuracy information and neglect of base rates in probability estimation. *Acta Psychologica, 40,* 287–98.

MacCrimmon, K. R. (1968). Descriptive and normative implications of the decision theory postulates. In K. Borch & J. Mossin (Eds.), *Risk and uncertainty* (pp. 3–32). New York: Macmillan.

MacCrimmon, K. R., & Larsson, S. (1979). Utility theory: Axioms or "paradoxes." In M. Allais & O. Hagen (Eds.), *Expected utility and the Allais Paradox* (pp. 333–409). Dordrecht, The Netherlands: Reidel.

MacCrimmon, K. R., & Toda, M. (1968). *The experimental determination of indifference curves* (Working Paper No. 124). Los Angeles: University of California, Western Management Science Institute.

MacCrimmon, K. R., & Toda, M. (1969). The experimental determination of indifference curves. *Review of Economic Studies, 36,* 433–51.

MacCrimmon, K. R., & Wehrung, D. A. (1977). Trade-off analysis: The indifference and preferred proportions approaches. In D. F. Bell, R. L. Keeney, & H. Raiffa (Eds.), *Conflicting objectives in decisions.* (pp. 123–47). New York: Wiley.

Mannheim, M. L., & Hall, F. (1968). Abstract representation of goals: A method for making decisions in complex problems. In *Transportation: A Science Service. Proceedings of the Sequisentennial Forum.* New York: New York Academy of Sciences.

Markowitz, J. (1959). *Portfolio selection.* New York: Wiley.

Marks, D. F., & Clarkson, J. K. (1972). An explanation of conservatism in the bookbag-and-pokerchips situation. *Acta Psychologica, 36,* 145–60.

Marks, G., & von Winterfeldt, D. (1984). Not in my backyard: The effect of motivational concerns on judgments about a risky technology. *Journal of Applied Psychology, 69,* 408–15.

Martin, A. W. (1980). *A general algorithm for determining likelihood ratios in cascaded inference* (Research Rep. No. 80-03). Houston, TX: Rice University, Department of Psychology.

Matheson, J. E., & Winkler, R. L. (1976). Scoring rules for continuous probability distributions. *Management Science, 22,* 1087–90.

Mazur, A. (1980). Societal and scientific causes of the historical development of risk assessment. In J. Conrad (Ed.), *Society, technology and risk assessment* (pp. 151–57). New York: Academic Press.

McClelland, G. (1978). *Equal versus differential weighting for multiattribute decision: There are no free lunches* (Center Rep. No. 207). Boulder: University of Colorado, Institute of Behavioral Science.

McCloskey, M., Caramazza, A., & Green, B. (1980). Curvilinear motion in the absence of external forces: Naive beliefs about the motion of objects. *Science, 210,* 1139–41.

McCormick, N. J. (1981). *Reliability and risk analysis.* New York: Academic Press.

McGargee, E. I. (1976). The prediction of dangerous behavior. *Criminal Justice and Behavior, 3,* 3–22.

McNeil, B. J., Pauker, S., Sox, H. C., Jr., & Tversky, A. (1982). On the elicitation of preferences for alternative therapies. *New England Journal of Medicine, 306,* 1259–62.

Meehl, P. E., & Rosen, A. (1955). Antecedent probability and the efficacy of psychometric signs, patterns, or cutting scores. *Psychological Bulletin, 52,* 194–216.

Meyer, R. F., & Pratt, J. W. (1968). The consistent assessment and fairing of preference functions. *IEEE Transactions on Systems Science and Cybernetics, SSC-4,* 270–8.

Miller, A. C., Merkhofer, M. W., Howard, R. A., Matheson, J. E., & Rice, T. R. (1976). Development of automated aids for decision analysis (Tech. Rep.). Menlo Park, CA: Stanford Research Institute.

Miller, J. R., III. (1969). *Assessing alternative transportation systems.* (Report No. RM-5865-DOT). Santa Monica, CA: Rand Corporation.

Miller, J. R., III. (1970). *Professional decision making: A procedure for evaluating complex alternatives.* New York: Praeger.

Miller, L. W., Kaplan, R. S., & Edwards, W. (1967). JUDGE: A value-judgment based tactical command system. *Organizational Behavior and Human Performance, 2,* 329–74.

Miller, L. W., Kaplan, R. S., & Edwards, W. (1969). JUDGE: A laboratory evaluation. *Organizational Behavior and Human Performance, 4,* 97–111.

Morgan, J. J. B., & Morton, J. T. (1944). The distortion of syllogistic reasoning produced by personal convictions. *Journal of Social Psychology, 20,* 39–59.

Moroff, S. V., & Pauker, S. G. (1983). What to do when the patient outlives the literature, or DEALE-ing with a full deck. *Medical Decision Making, 3,* 313–38.

Morris, P. A. (1974). Decision analysis expert use. *Management Science, 20,* 1233–41.

Morris, P. A. (1977). Combining expert judgments: A Bayesian approach. *Management Science, 23,* 679–93.

Moskowitz, H. (1974). Effects of problem representation and feedback on rational behavior in Allais and Morlat-type problems. *Decision Science, 5,* 225–42.

Mosteller, F., & Nogee, P. (1951). An experimental measurement of utility. *Journal of Political Economy, 59,* 371–404.

Murphy, A. H. (1973). A new vector partition of the probability score. *Journal of Applied Meteorology, 12,* 595–600.

Murphy, A. H., & Winkler, R. L. (1970). Scoring rules in probability assessment and evalua-tion. *Acta Psychologica, 34,* 273–86.

Murphy, A. H., & Winkler, R. L. (1974). Probability forecasts: A survey of National Weather Service forecasters. *Bulletin of the American Meteorological Society, 55,* 1449–53.

Murphy, A. H., & Winkler, R. L. (1977a). Can weather forecasters formulate reliable forecasts of precipitation and temperature? *National Weather Digest, 2,* 2–9.

Murphy, A. H., & Winkler, R. L. (1977b). The use of credible intervals in temperature fore-casting: Some experimental results. In H. Jungermann & G. de Zeeuw (Eds.), *Decision making and change in human affairs.* (pp. 45–56). Dordrecht, The Netherlands: Reidel.

National Research Council. (1977). *Implications of environmental regulation for energy pro-duction and consumption.* Washington, DC: National Academy of Science.

Navon, D. (1978). The importance of being conservative: Some reflections on human Bayesian behavior. *British Journal of Mathematical and Statistical Psychology, 31,* 33–48.

Nisbett, R. E., & Borgida, E. (1975). Attribution and the psychology of prediction. *Journal of Personality and Social Psychology, 32,* 932–43.

Nisbett, R. E., Bordiga, E., Crandall, R., & Reed, H. (1976). Popular induction: Information is not always informative. In J. S. Carroll & J. W. Payne (Eds.), *Cognition and Social Behavior, 2,* 227–36.

Nisbett, R. E., Krantz, D. H., Jepson, C., & Kunda, Z. (1983). The use of statistical heuristics in everyday inductive reasoning. *Psychological Review, 90,* 339–63.

Nisbett, R. E., & Ross, L. (1980). *Human inference: Strategies and shortcomings of social judg-ment.* Englewood Cliffs, NJ: Prentice-Hall.

Novick, M. R. (1973). High school attainment: An example of a computer assisted Bayesian approach to data analysis. *International Statistical Review, 41,* 264–71.

O'Connor, M. F. (1972). *The application of multiattribute scaling techniques to the development of indices of water quality.* Unpublished doctoral dissertation, University of Michigan, Ann Arbor.

O'Connor, M. F. (1973). *The application of multiattribute scaling procedures to the development of indices of water quality* (Report No. 73-39). University of Chicago, Center for Math-ematical Studies in Business and Economics.

Oskamp, S. (1965). Overconfidence in case-study judgments. *Journal of Consulting Psychology, 29,* 261–5.

Pai, G. K., Gustafson, D. H., & Kiner, G. W. (1971). *Comparison of three non-risk methods for determining a preference function.* Unpublished manuscript, University of Wisconsin, Madison.

Pareto, V. (1906). *Manuale di economia politia, con une introduzione ulla scienza sociale.* Milan, Italy: Societa Editrice Libraria. The 1927 edition of the book was translated and republished as V. Pareto, *Manual of political economy.* New York: Kelley.

Pauker, S. G. (1976). Coronary artery surgery: The use of decision analysis. *Annals of Internal Medicine, 85,* 8–18.

Pearl, J. (1977). A framework for processing value judgments. *IEEE Transactions on Systems, Man, and Cybernetics, SMC-7,* 349–54.

Pearl, J. (1978). A goal-directed approach to structuring decision problems. (Report No. UCLA-ENG-7811). Los Angeles: University of California.

Pearl, J., Leal, A., & Saleh, J. (1980). GODDESS: A goal directed decision structuring system (Report No. UCLA-ENG-8034). Los Angeles: University of California.

Peterson, C. R. (Ed.). (1973). Cascaded inference [Special issue]. *Organizational Behavior and Human Performance, 10,* 315–432.

Peterson, C. R., & Beach, L. R. (1967). Man as an intuitive statistician. *Psychological Bulletin, 68,* 29–46.

Pfanzagl, J. (1968). *Theory of measurement.* New York: Wiley.

Phillips, L. D. (1973). *Bayesian statistics for social scientists.* New York: Crowell.

Phillips, L. D., & Edwards, W. (1966). Conservatism in a simple probability inference task. *Journal of Experimental Psychology, 72,* 346–57.

Phillips, L. D., Hays, W. L., & Edwards, W. (1966). Conservatism in complex probabilistic inference. *IEEE Transactions on Human Factors in Electronics, 7,* 7–18.

Piaget, J., & Inhelder, B. (1975). *The origin of the idea of chance in children.* New York: Norton. (Original work published 1951.)

Pitz, G. F. (1974). Subjective probability distributions for imperfectly known quantities. In L. W. Gregg (Ed.), *Knowledge and cognition.* New York: Wiley.

Pitz, G. F., Sachs, N. J., & Heerboth, J. (1980). Procedures for eliciting choices in the analysis of individual decisions. *Organizational Behavior and Human Performance, 26,* 396–408.

Pitz, G. F., & Sachs, N. J. (1984). Judgment and decision: Theory and application. *Annual Review of Psychology, 35,* 139–63.

Pollack, I. (1964). Action selection and the Yntema–Torgerson worth function. In *Information System Science and Engineering: Proceedings of the First Congress on the Information System Sciences.* New York: McGraw-Hill.

Pollak, R. A. (1967). Additive von Neumann and Morgenstern utility functions. *Econometrica, 35,* 485–94.

Pommerehne, W. W., Schneider, F., & Zweifel, P. (1982). Economic theory of choice and the preference reversal phenomenon: A reexamination. *American Economic Review, 72,* 569–74.

Poulton, E. C. (1979). Models of biases in judging sensory magnitude. *Psychological Bulletin, 86,* 777–803.

Pratt, J. W., Raiffa, H., & Schlaifer, R. (1964). The foundations of decisions under uncertainty: An elementary exposition. *Journal of the American Statistical Association, 59,* 353–75.

Preston, M. G., & Baratta, P. (1948). An experimental study of the auction-value of an uncertain outcome. *American Journal of Psychology, 61,* 183–93.

Quattrone, G. A., & Jones, E. E. 1980. The perception of variability within in-groups and out-groups: Implications for the law of large numbers. *Journal of Personality and Social Psychology, 38,* 141–52.

Raiffa, H. (1968). *Decision analysis.* Reading, MA: Addison-Wesley.

Raiffa, H. (1969). Preferences for multiattributed alternatives (Report No. RM-5868-DOT/RC). Santa Monica, CA: Rand Corporation.

Raiffa, H. (1982). *The art and science of negotiation.* Cambridge, MA: Belknap Press/Harvard University Press.

Raiffa, H., & Schlaifer, R. (1961). *Applied statistical decision theory.* Cambridge, MA: Harvard University Press, 1961.

Ramsey, F. P. (1931). Truth and probability. In R. B. Braithwaite (Ed.), *The foundations of mathematics and other logical essays.* New York: Harcourt Brace. Book republished as F. P. Ramsey, *The foundations of mathematics and other logical essays.* London: Littlefield, Adams. London: International Library of Psychology, Philosophy, and Scientific Methods. Series No. 214, 1960.

Rapoport, A., & Burkheimer, G. J. (1971). Models for deferred decision making. *Journal of Mathematical Psychology, 8,* 508–38.

Rapoport, A., & Wallsten, T. S. (1972). Individual decision behavior. *Annual Review of Psychology, 23,* 131–76.

Reilly, R. J. (1982). Preference reversal: Further evidence and some suggested modifications in experimental design. *American Economic Review, 72,* 576–84.

Rouanet, H. (1961). Etudes de decisions experimentales et calcul de probabilites. In *La Decision* (pp. 33–43). Rapport du Colloque Internationale du C. N. R. S., Paris.

Rowse, G. L., Gustafson, D. H., & Ludke, R. L. (1978). Comparison of rules for aggregating subjective likelihood ratios. *Organizational Behavior and Human Performance, 21,* 189–208.

Saaty, T. L. (1980). *The analytic hierarchy process.* New York: McGraw-Hill.

Sackman, H. (1974). *Delphi assessment: Expert opinion, forecasting, and group process* (Report No. R-1283-PR). Santa Monica, CA: Rand Corporation.

Sarin, R. K. (1982). Strength of preference and risky choice. *Operations Research, 30,* 982–97.

Savage, L. J. (1954). *The foundations of statistics.* New York: Wiley.

Savage, L. J. (1962). *The foundations of statistical inference: A symposium.* New York: Wiley.

Savage, L. J. (1972). *The foundations of statistics* (2nd rev. ed.). New York: Dover.

Schaefer, R. E., & Borcherding, K. (1973a). The assessment of subjective probability distributions: A training experiment. *Acta Psychologica, 37,* 117–29.

Schaefer, R. E., & Borcherding, K. (1973b). A note on the consistency between two approaches to incorporate data from unreliable sources in Bayesian analysis. *Organizational Behavior and Human Performance, 9,* 504–8.

Schlaifer, R. (1959). *Probability and statistics for business decisions: An introduction to managerial economics under uncertainty.* New York: McGraw-Hill.

Schlaifer, R. (1961). *Introduction to statistics for business decisions.* New York: McGraw-Hill.

Schlaifer, R. (1969). *Analysis of decisions under uncertainty.* New York: McGraw-Hill.

Schmitt, N. (1978). Comparison of subjective and objective weighting strategies in changing task situations. *Organizational Behavior and Human Performance, 21,* 171–88.

Schoemaker, P. J. H. (1980). *Experiments on decision under risk: The expected utility hypothesis.* Boston: Nijhoff.

Schoemaker, P. J. H., & Waid, C. D. (1982). An experimental comparison of different approaches to determining weights in additive utility models. *Management Science, 28,* 182–96.

Schum, D. A. (1977a). Contrast effects in inference: On the conditioning of current evidence by prior evidence. *Organizational Behavior and Human Performance, 18,* 217–53.

Schum, D. A. (1977b). The behavioral richness of cascaded inference models: Examples in jurisprudence. In N. J. Castellan, Jr., D. B. Pisoni, & G. R. Potts (Eds.), *Cognitive Theory* (Vol. 2, pp. 149–73). Hillsdale, NJ: Erlbaum.

Schum, D. A. (1979a). *On factors which influence the redundancy of cumulative and corroborative testimonial evidence* (Tech. Rep. No. 79-02). Houston, TX: Rice University, Department of Psychology.

Schum, D. A. (1979b). *A Bayesian account of transitivity and other order-related effects in chains of inferential reasoning* (Tech. Rep. No. 79-04). Houston, TX: Rice University, Department of Psychology.

Schum, D. A. (1980). Current development in research on cascaded inference. In T. S. Wallsten (Ed.), *Cognitive processes in decision and choice behavior* (pp. 179–215). Hillsdale, NJ: Erlbaum.

Schum, D. A. (1981a). *Assessing the probative value of equivocal testimony or no testimony on a relevant issue at trial* (Tech. Rep. No. 81-04). Houston, TX: Rice University, Department of Psychology.

Schum, D. A. (1981b). *Formalizing the process of assessing the probative value of alibi testimony* (Tech. Rep. No. 81-05). Houston, TX: Rice University, Department of Psychology.

Schum, D. A., & DuCharme, W. M. (1971). Comments on the relationship between the impact and the reliability of evidence. *Organizational Behavior and Human Performance, 6,* 111–31.

Schum, D. A., DuCharme, W., & dePitts, K. (1973). Research on human multistage probabilistic inference processes. *Organizational Behavior and Human Performance, 10,* 404–423.

Schum, D. A., & Martin, A. W. (1980). *Empirical studies of cascaded inference in jurisprudence: Methodological considerations* (Tech. Rep. No. 80-01). Houston, TX: Rice University, Department of Psychology.

Schum, D. A., & Martin, A. W. (1981). *Assessing the probative value of evidence in various inference structures* (Tech Rep. No. 81-02). Houston, TX: Rice University, Department of Psychology.

Schum, D. A., & Martin, A. W. (1982). Formal and empirical research on cascaded inference in jurisprudence. *Law and Society Review, 17,* 105–57.

Seaver, D. A. (1973). *Correlational analysis of approximations and sensitivity for multiattribute utility.* Unpublished manuscript.

Seaver, D. A. (1978). *Assessing probability with multiple individuals: Group interaction versus mathematical aggregation* (Research Rep. No. 78-3). Los Angeles: University of Southern California, Social Science Research Institute.

Seaver, D. A., von Winterfeldt, D., & Edwards, W. (1978). Eliciting subjective probability distributions on continuous variables. *Organizational Behavior and Human Performance, 21,* 379–91.

Selvidge, J. (1975). *Experimental comparison of different methods for assessing the extremes of probability distributions by the fractile method* (Tech. Rep.). Boulder: University of Colorado, Graduate School of Business Administration.

Shafer, G. (1976). *A mathematical theory of evidence.* Princeton, NJ: Princeton University Press.

Shanteau, J. C. (1970). An additive model for sequential decision making. *Journal of Experimental Psychology, 85,* 181–91.

Sieber, J. E. (1974). Effects of decision importance on the ability to generate warranted subjective uncertainty. *Journal of Personality and Social Psychology, 30,* 688–94.

Slovic, P. (1969). Analyzing the expert judge: A descriptive study of stockbrokers' decision processes. *Journal of Applied Psychology, 53,* 255–63.

Slovic, P., Fischhoff, B., & Lichtenstein, S. (1977). Behavioral decision theory. *Annual Review of Psychology, 28,* 1–39.

Slovic, P., & Lichtenstein, S. (1968). Relative importance of probabilities and payoffs in risk taking. *Journal of Experimental Psychology, 78,* 1–18.

Slovic, P., & Lichtenstein, S. (1971). Comparison of Bayesian and regression approaches to the study of information processing in judgment. *Organizational Behavior and Human Performance, 6,* 649–744.

Slovic, P., & Lichtenstein, S. (1983). Preference reversals: A broader perspective. *American Economic Review, 73,* 596–605.

Slovic, P., & Tversky, A. (1974). Who accepts Savage's axiom? *Behavioral Science, 19,* 368–73.

Snapper, K. J., & Fryback, D. G. (1971). Inferences based on unreliable reports. *Journal of Experimental Psychology, 87,* 401–4.

Snapper, K. J., & Seaver, D. A. (1980a). *The irrelevance of evaluation research for decision making: Case studies from the community anti-crime program* (Tech. Rep. No. 80-12). Falls Church, VA: Decision Science Consortium.

Snapper, K. J., & Seaver, D. A. (1978). *Application of decision analysis to program planning and evaluation* (Tech. Rep. No. 78-1). Washington, DC: Decision Science Consortium.

Spetzler, C. S., & Staël von Holstein, C.-A. (1975). Probability encoding in decision analysis. *Management Science, 22,* 340–52.

Staël von Holstein, C.-A. (1971). The techniques for assessment of subjective probability distributions: An experimental study. *Acta Psychologica, 35,* 478–94.

Staël von Holstein, C.-A. (1972). Probabilistic forecasting: An experiment related to the stock market. *Organizational Behavior and Human Performance, 8,* 139–58.

Stevens, S. S. (1935). The operational definition of psychological concepts. *Psychological Review, 42,* 517–27.

Stevens, S. S. (1936). A scale of measurement of a psychological magnitude: Loudness. *Psychological Review, 43,* 405–16.

Stevens, S. S. (1951). Mathematics, measurement and psychophysics. In S. S. Stevens (Ed.), *Handbook of experimental psychology* (pp. 1–49). New York: Wiley.

Stigler, G. J. (1950). The development of utility theory. *Journal of Political Economy, 58,* 307–27, 373–96.

Stillwell, W., Barron, F. H., & Edwards, W. (1980). *Evaluating credit applications: A validation of multiattribute utility techniques against a real world criterion* (Research Rep. No. 80-1). Los Angeles: University of Southern California, Social Science Research Institute.

Stillwell, W., Barron, F. H., & Edwards, W. (1983). Evaluating credit applications: A validation of multiattribute utility weight elicitation techniques. *Organizational Behavior and Human Performance, 32,* 87–108.

Stillwell, W., & Edwards, W. (1979). *Rank weighting in multiattribute utility decision making: Avoiding the pitfalls of equal weights* (Research Rep. No. 79-2). Los Angeles: University of Southern California, Social Science Research Institute.

Stillwell, W. G., Seaver, D. A., & Edwards, W. (1981). A comparison of weight approximation techniques in multiattribute utility decision making. *Organizational Behavior and Human Performance, 28,* 62–77.

Stillwell, W. G., Seaver, D. A., & Schwartz, J. P. (1981). *Expert estimation of human error probabilities in nuclear power plant operations: A review of probability assessment and scaling* (Report No. NUREG/CR-2255). Washington, DC: Nuclear Regulatory Commission.

Stillwell, W. G., von Winterfeldt, D., & John, R. S. (1981). *Value tree analysis of energy alternatives* (Research Rep. No. 81-2). Los Angeles: University of Southern California, Social Science Research Institute.

Straughan, D. (Ed.). (1971). *Biological and oceanographic survey of the Santa Barbara oil spill, 1969-1970.* Los Angeles: University of Southern California, Los Angeles, Allan Hancock Foundation.

Summer, D. A., Taliaferro, J. D., & Fletcher, D. J. (1970). Subjective weights vs. objective descriptions of judgment policy. *Psychonomic Science, 18,* 249–50.

Suppes, P., & Winet, M. (1955). An axiomatization of utility based on the notion of utility differences. *Management Science, 1,* 259–70.

Suppes, P., & Zinnes, J. L. (1963). Basic measurement theory. In R. D. Luce, R. R. Bush & E. Galanter (Eds.), *Handbook of Mathematical Psychology* (Vol. 1, pp. 1–76). New York: Wiley.

Swensson, R. G., & Edwards, W. (1971). Response strategies in a two choice reaction task with a continuous cost for time. *Journal of Experimental Psychology, 88,* 67–81.

Swets, J. A., & Sewall, S. T. (1963). Invariance of signal detectability over stages of practice and levels of motivation. *Journal of Experimental Psychology, 66,* 170–6.

Swets, J. A., Tanner, W. P., Jr., & Birdsall, T. G. (1961). Decision processes in perception. *Psychological Review, 68,* 301–40.

Tanner, W. P., Jr., & Swets, J. A. (1954). A decision-making theory of visual detection. *Psychological Review, 61,* 401–9.

Thornbury, J. R., Fryback, D. G., & Edwards, W. (1975). Likelihood ratios as a measure of the diagnostic usefulness of excretory urogram information. *Radiology, 114,* 561–4.

Thrall, R. M., Coombs, C. H., & Davis, R. L. (Eds.). (1954). *Decision processes.* New York: Wiley.

Thurstone, L. L. (1927). A law of comparative judgment. *Psychological Review, 34,* 273–86.

Torgerson, W. S. (1958). *Theory and methods of scaling.* New York: Wiley.

Tversky, A. (1967). Additivity, utility, and subjective probability. *Journal of Mathematical Psychology, 4,* 175–201.

Tversky, A. (1969). Intransitivity of preferences. *Psychological Review, 76,* 31–48.

Tversky, A., & Kahneman, D. (1971). The belief in the "law of small numbers." *Psychological Bulletin, 76,* 105–10.

Tversky, A., & Kahneman, D. (1973). Availability: A heuristic for judging frequency and probability. *Cognitive Psychology, 5,* 207–32.

Tversky, A., & Kahneman, D. (1974). Judgment under uncertainty: Heuristics and biases. *Science, 185,* 1124–31.

Tversky, A., & Kahneman, D. (1981). The framing of decisions and the psychology of choice. *Science, 211,* 453–8.

Tversky, A., & Kahneman, D. (1983). Extensional versus intuitive reasoning: The conjunction fallacy in probability judgment. *Psychological Review, 90,* 293–315.

Uhlela, Z. J. (1966). Optimality of perceptual decision criteria. *Journal of Experimental Psychology, 71,* 564–9.

Ulvila, J., & Brown, R. V. (1981). *Development of decision analysis for non-proliferation safeguards: Project summary and characterization of the IAEA decision structure* (Tech. Rep. No. 81-7). Falls Church, VA: Decision Science Consortium.

Ulvila, J., & Brown, R. V. (1982). Decision analysis comes of age. *Harvard Business Review, 60,* 130–41.

U.S. Geological Survey. (1976). *Oil Spills, 1971–1975, Gulf of Mexico, OCS.* Washington, DC: U.S. Government Printing Office.

U.S. Nuclear Regulatory Commission. (1975). *Reactor safety study: An assessment of accident risks in U.S. commercial nuclear power plants* (Report No. NUREG-75/014). Washington, DC: National Research Council.

Van de Ven, A., & Delbecq, A. (1971). Nominal vs. interacting group processes for committee decision making effectiveness. *Academy of Management Journal, 14,* 203–12.

Van Meter, D., & Middleton, D. (1954). Modern statistical approaches to reception in communication theory. *Transactions of the IRE Professional Group on Information Theory, PGIT-4,* 119–41.

Vari, A., & Vecsenyi, J. (1983). Decision analysis of industrial R&D problems: Pitfalls and lessons. In P. Humphreys, O. Svenson, & A. Vari (Eds.), *Analyzing and aiding decision processes* (pp. 183–95). Budapest: Hungarian Academy of Sciences.

Vinogradov, A. A. (1969). Ordered algebraic systems. In R. U. Gamkrelidze (Ed.), *Progress in mathematics* (Vol. 2, pp. 77–126). New York: Plenum.

Vlek, C., & Wagenaar, W. A. (1979). Judgment and decision under uncertainty. In J. A. Michon, E. G. Eijkman, & L. F. W. DeKlerk (Eds.), *Handbook of Psychonomics II* (pp. 253–345). Amsterdam: North Holland.

von Neumann, J. (1928). Zur Theorie der Gesellschaftsspiele. *Mathematischen Annalen, 100,* 295–320.

von Neumann, J., & Morgenstern, O. (1947). *Theory of games and economic behavior.* Princeton, NJ: Princeton University Press.

von Winterfeldt, D. (1975). *An overview, integration, and evaluation of utility theory for decision analysis* (Research Rep. No. 75-9). Los Angeles: University of Southern California, Social Science Research Institute.

von Winterfeldt, D. (1978). A decision aiding system for improving the environmental standard setting process. In K. Chikocki & A. Straszak (Eds.), *Systems analysis applications to complex programs* (pp. 119–24). Oxford: Pergamon Press.

von Winterfeldt, D. (1979). *Functional relationships between risky and riskless multiattribute utility functions* (Research Rep. No. 79-3). Los Angeles: University of Southern California, Social Science Research Institute.

von Winterfeldt, D. (1980a). Additivity and expected utility in risky multiattribute preferences. *Journal of Mathematical Psychology, 121,* 66–82.

von Winterfeldt, D. (1980b). Structuring decision problems for decision analysis. *Acta Psychologica, 45,* 71–93.

von Winterfeldt, D. (1982). Setting standards for offshore oil discharges: A regulatory decision analysis. *Operations Research, 14,* 247–56.

von Winterfeldt, D. (1983). Pitfalls of decision analysis. In P. Humphreys, O. Svenson, & A. Vari (Eds.), *Analysing and aiding decisions* (pp. 167–81). Budapest: Hungarian Academy of Sciences.

von Winterfeldt, D., Barron, H. F., & Fischer, G. W. (1980). *Theoretical and empirical relationships between risky and riskless utility functions* (Research Rep. No. 80-3). Los Angeles: University of Southern California, Social Science Research Institute.

von Winterfeldt, D., & Edwards, W. (1973a). *Evaluation of complex stimuli using multiattribute utility procedures* (Report No. 011-313-2-T). Ann Arbor: University of Michigan, Engineering Psychology Laboratory.

von Winterfeldt, D., & Edwards, W. (1973b). *Flat maxima in linear optimization models* (Tech. Rep. No. 011-313-4-T). Ann Arbor: University of Michigan, Engineering Psychology Laboratory.

von Winterfeldt, D., & Edwards, W. (1975). *Error in decision analysis: How to create the possibility of large losses by using dominated strategies* (Research Rep. No. 75-4). Los Angeles: University of Southern California, Social Science Research Institute.

von Winterfeldt, D., & Edwards, W. (1982). Costs and payoffs in perceptual research. *Psychological Bulletin, 19,* 609–22.

von Winterfeldt, D., & Fischer, G. W. (1975). Multiattribute utility theory: Models and assessment procedures. In D. Wendt & C. Vlek (Eds.), *Utility, probability and human decision making* (pp. 47–66). Dordrecht, The Netherlands: Reidel.

von Winterfeldt, D., & Rios, J. (1980). Conflicts about nuclear power safety: A decision theoretic approach. In M. H. Fontana & D. R. Patterson (Eds.), *Proceedings of the ANS/ENS Topical Meeting on Thermal Reactor Safety* (pp. 696–709). Springfield, VA: NTIS.

Wagenaar, W. A., & Sagaria, S. D. (1975). Misperception of exponential growth. *Perception and Psychophysics, 18,* 416–22.

Wagenaar, W. A., & Timmers, H. (1978). Intuitive prediction of growth. In D. F. Burkhardt & W. H. Ittelson (Eds.), *Environmental assessment of socioeconomic systems.* New York: Plenum, 1978.

Wainer, H. (1976). Estimating coefficients in linear models: It don't make no nevermind. *Psychological Bulletin, 83,* 713–17.

Wald, A. (1950). *Statistical decision functions.* New York: Wiley.

Wallsten, T. S., & Budescu, D. V. (1983). Encoding subjective probabilities: A psychological and psychometric review. *Management Science, 29,* 151–73.

Ward, L. M. (1975). Heuristic use of information integration in the estimation of subjective likelihoods. *Bulletin of the Psychonomic Society, 6,* 43–46.

Watson, C. S., & Clopton, B. M. (1969). Motivational changes of auditory sensitivity in a simple detection task. *Perception and Psychophysics, 5,* 281–7.

Wheeler, G. E., & Edwards, W. (1975). *Misaggregation explains conservative inference about normally distributed populations* (Research Rep. No. 75-11). Los Angeles: University of Southern California, Social Science Research Institute.

Wigmore, J. H. (1937). *The science of judicial proof as given by logic, psychology, and general experience, and illustrated in judicial trials* (3rd ed.). Boston: Little, Brown.

Wilkins, M. C. (1928). The effect of changed material on ability to do formal syllogistic reasoning. *New York State Archives of Psychology,* No. 102.

Winkler, R. L. (1968). The consensus of subjective probability distributions. *Management Science, 15,* 61–75.

Winkler, R. L. (1971). Probabilistic prediction: Some experimental results. *Journal of the American Statistical Association, 66,* 675–85.

Winkler, R. L., & Murphy, A. H. (1973). Experiments in the laboratory and the real world. *Organizational Behavior and Human Performance, 10,* 252–70.

Woodworth, R. S. (1938). *Experimental psychology.* New York: Holt.

Woodworth, R. S., & Sells, S. B. (1935). An atmosphere effect in syllogistic reasoning. *Journal of Experimental Psychology, 18,* 451–60.

Wright, W. F. (1977). Financial information processing models: An empirical study. *Accounting Review, 52,* 676–89.

Wyer, R. S., Jr. (1970). The quantitative prediction of belief and opinion changes: A further test of subjective probability models. *Journal of Personality and Social Psychology, 16,* 559–71.

Yntema, D. B., & Klem, L. (1965). Telling a computer how to evaluate multi-dimensional situations. *IEEE Transactions on Human Factors in Electronics, HFE-6,* 3–13.

Yntema, D. B., & Torgerson, W. S. (1961). Man–computer cooperation in decision requiring common sense. *IRE Transactions on Human Factors in Electronics, HFE-2,* 20–6.

Zadeh, L. (1978). Fuzzy sets as a basis for a theory of possibility. *Fuzzy Sets and Systems, 1,* 3–28.

Zinnes, P. (1969). Scaling. *Annual Review of Psychology, 20,* 447–8.

Zlotnick, J. (1968). A theorem for prediction. *Foreign Service Journal, 45,* 20.

Author index

Aczel, J., 125
Adams, E. W., 127, 278, 560
Allais, M., 378–9
Allen, R. G. D., 561–2
Alpert, M., 128
Amabile, T. M., 539
Anderson, N. H., 534
Arrow, K. J., 560
Aschenbrenner, K. M., 23, 365–6, 369, 447

Baca, S., 56
Baird, J. C., 216, 231
Baratta, P., 563
Barclay, S., 23, 46, 51, 98–9, 533
Bar-Hillel, M., 534, 535, 536, 538, 541, 547
Barnard, G. A., 144
Barron, H. F., 213, 308, 340–1, 342, 358, 367, 368, 443
Beach, L. R., 533, 560
Beck, J. R., 409
Becker, G. M., 116, 371, 383, 560
Beckwith, N. E., 364
Behn, R. D., 64
Bell, D. E., 32, 225, 340, 357, 382–3
Bell, R. S., 115, 129, 448, 451–2, 521
Bernoulli, D., 372
Beyth, R., 98, 540, 547
Beyth-Marom, R., 98, 540, 547
Bezembinder, T. C. G., 374
Birdsall, T. G., 445
Blackwell, D., 141
Borcherding, K., 128, 180
Borel, E., 140, 561
Borgida, E., 537
Bourne, A. J., 542
Brehmer, B., 363
Brier, G. W., 126, 129
Brown, R. S., 134
Brown, R. V., 46, 51, 65, 98–9, 448, 517, 522
Budescu, D. V., 115
Burkheimer, G. J., 421

Calfee, R., 447
Caramazza, A., 545, 546

Carroll, J. S., 535
Central Unit on Environmental Pollution, 150, 460–2, 521
Chapman, J. P., 539
Chapman, L. J., 539
Chinnis, J. O., 491–9
Clarkson, J. K., 533
Clopton, B. M., 447
Cohen, J. J., 541
Cohen, L. J., 96, 164, 547
Collins, L., 362, 365, 367
Cook, R. L., 364
Coombs, C. H., 216, 374, 383, 563, 564
Corrigan, B., 439, 441, 443
Council for Environmental Quality, 174, 460–1
Crandall, R., 537

Dalkey, N. C., 134, 135
Daneshgar, R., 364, 366, 439
Davidson, D., 116, 374
Davis, R., 563
Dawes, R. M., 439, 441, 443
de Finetti, B., 144, 561, 564
DeGroot, M. H., 134, 187, 383
Delbecq, A., 135
Delbeke, L., 367
de Neufville, R., 298
DePitts, K., 200
Derby, S. L., 22
Dershowitz, A., 535
deSmet, A. A., 129
Doyle, A. C., 171, 172
Dubins, L., 141
DuCharme, W., 180, 196, 200
Dyer, J. S., 210, 213, 277, 287–8, 292, 327, 339, 340, 357, 517, 526–7

Eckenrode, R. J., 365
Eddy, D. M., 535
Edgeworth, F. Y., 561
Edwards, W., 21, 22, 23, 27, 61, 94, 96, 115, 116, 127, 128, 129, 137, 141, 143, 151, 153, 159, 160, 178, 200, 205–7, 224, 225,

595

Edwards, W. (*cont.*)
    251, 259, 260–3, 278, 284, 357, 359, 360,
    362, 364, 367, 371, 374–6, 377, 413–19,
    420, 421, 422, 436, 442, 443, 445, 448–
    52, 462–74, 475–82, 490, 521, 522, 524–
    6, 528, 529, 533, 534, 538, 554, 557, 560,
    563, 564, 565, 566, 567, 568
Eils, L., 367, 533
Einhorn, H., 21, 117, 371, 440–1, 560
Ekman, G., 218
Elliot, P. N., 447
Ellsberg, D., 382, 386
Environmental Protection Agency, 37, 504
Epstein, E. S., 126
Erdman, H., 452–5, 528

Fagot, R. F., 278
Fauville, J., 367
Fechner, G. T., 218
Feller, W., 21
Ferguson, T. S., 426
Fischer, G. W., 126, 135, 213, 241, 296, 308,
    334, 340–2, 356–7, 358, 363, 364, 365,
    367, 368, 443, 500
Fischhoff, B., 21, 22, 53–4, 55, 56, 114, 117,
    122, 127, 128, 131–3, 355–6, 362, 371,
    531, 532, 540, 541, 543, 560
Fishburn, P. C., 278, 295, 304, 361
Fisher, R. S., 144, 564
Fisher, S. D., 56
Flavell, J. H., 548
Fletcher, D. J., 366
Ford, D. L., 364, 366, 439
Friedman, M., 562
Fryback, D. G., 115, 129, 175, 200, 359, 360,
    448–52, 521
Fuchs, L., 315
Fujii, T., 115

Gabrielli, W., 285, 368
Galanter, E., 446
Gardiner, P., 23, 279, 280–2, 288, 356, 364,
    368, 370
Gettys, C. F., 50, 56, 180, 200
Ghiselli, E. E., 440
Goitein, B., 356
Goode, F. M., 374
Goodman, B. C., 21, 115, 134, 359, 445, 528,
    533, 557, 567
Gottlieb, J. E., 409
Gough, R., 134, 135, 200
Grassia, J., 550
Green, A. E., 542
Green, B., 545–6
Green, D. M., 157, 182, 421, 445, 447
Grest, J. H., 452–5, 528
Grether, D. M., 359, 380, 534
Griffin, G., 215

Gulliksen, H., 440
Gustafson, D. H., 23, 129, 134, 135, 364,
    452–5, 517, 528
Guttentag, M., 61

Hagen, J., 378
Hall, F., 38
Hamm, R. M., 550
Hammerton, M., 446, 535
Hammond, K. R., 363, 366, 550
Hansel, C. E. M., 547
Hax, A. C., 513, 515–19
Hays, W. L., 200, 528, 533, 557, 567
Healy, A. F., 446
Heerboth, J., 56
Helmer, O., 135
Helson, H., 352
Hershey, J. D., 215, 360, 361
Hicks, J. R., 561–2
Hoepfl, R. T., 364
Hoffman, P. J., 366
Hogarth, R. M., 21, 117, 134, 440–1, 530,
    560
Holloway, C. A., 23, 65
Holman, G. L., 446
Höpfinger, E., 35
Howard, R. A., 32, 56–8, 448, 566–7, 568
Huang, L. C., 374, 383
Huber, G. P., 364, 366, 439
Humphreys, A. R., 41
Humphreys, P. C., 41, 57, 517, 527

Inhelder, B., 543, 545, 549
Isaacs, G. L., 162

Jennings, D. L., 539
Jepson, C., 543–4
John, R. S., 355, 362, 365, 367, 369, 385,
    443, 522
Jones, E. E., 543

Kahneman, D., 109, 121, 361, 372–3, 376,
    378–9, 380–1, 382, 383–4, 386, 530–1,
    532, 533, 534–6, 537, 538, 539, 541, 542,
    543, 547, 548, 549, 552, 560, 565
Kahr, A. S., 65
Kaplan, R. S., 23, 205–7, 567
Kassirer, J. P., 409
Kasubek, W., 23, 365, 366, 369
Keeney, R. L., 22, 23, 32, 38, 43, 44, 45, 59,
    60, 203, 225, 238, 249, 253, 255, 256,
    277, 278, 285, 292, 295, 298, 299–302,
    304, 307, 308, 311, 332, 337, 339, 340,
    341, 346, 405, 448, 455–9, 482–90, 567,
    568
Keller, L. R., 379
Kelly, C. W., III, 22, 23, 46, 51, 58, 59, 60,
    98–9, 200, 491–9

Kent, S., 98–9
Kiner, G. W., 364
Klem, L., 364, 366
Knop, H., 524
Kochenburger, G. A., 361
Koriat, A., 128, 133
Krantz, D. H., 21, 210, 216, 232, 276, 278, 295, 315, 316, 318, 321, 322, 327, 340, 360, 445, 543–4
Krischer, J. P., 448
Kubovy, M., 446
Kunda, Z., 542, 544
Kunreuther, H. C., 360
Kyburg, H. E., 560

Lahiff, M., 115, 129, 448–52, 521
Lamont, A., 23, 455
Larsson, S., 355
Lathrop, R. G., 367
Laughren, T., 452–5, 528
Leal, A., 56
Lehmann, D. R., 364
Leon, M., 534
Lichtenstein, S., 22, 53–5, 56, 114, 117, 122, 127, 128, 131, 133, 200, 355–6, 357, 359, 362, 363, 371, 379, 533, 541, 543, 560
Lieblich, A., 446
Lieblich, I., 446
Lindley, D. V., 142
Lindman, H., 94, 137, 141, 143, 151, 153, 159–60, 534, 538, 565
Linstone, H. A., 135
Loop, J. W., 115, 129, 448, 452, 521
Luce, R. D., 210, 216, 218, 219, 232, 276, 278, 295, 315, 316, 318, 321, 322, 327, 332, 340, 560, 562
Ludke, R. L., 129, 134
Lukaszewski, J. S., 447
Lusted, L. B., 115, 129, 448–52, 533
Lykken, D. T., 535
Lyon, D., 535

McClelland, G., 363, 366, 441, 443
McClintock, G. C., 116, 371, 560
McCloskey, M., 545, 546
McCormick, N. J., 46
MacCrimmon, K. R., 298, 355, 379
McFadden, W., 527
McGargee, E. I., 535
McNeil, B. J., 382
Mannheim, M. L., 38
Manning, C., 56
Markowitz, J., 374
Marks, D. F., 533
Marks, G., 369
Marschak, J., 383
Martin, A. W., 23, 164, 166, 169–70, 178, 192–9, 201, 202, 204, 573

Matheson, J. E., 32, 56–8, 126, 448, 567
Mazur, A., 521
Meehl, P. E., 412, 535
Mehle, T., 56
Merkhofer, M. W., 56
Meyer, R. F., 255
Middleton, D., 156
Miles, D., 526–7
Miller, A. C., 56, 448
Miller, J. R., III, 22, 38
Miller, L. W., 23, 205–7, 567
Miller, R. W., 32
Minckler, R. D., 491–9
Moody, D. L., 474–82
Morgan, J. J. B., 548
Morgenstern, O., 209, 299, 317, 321, 335, 348, 561–4
Moroff, S. V., 408–11
Morris, P. A., 134
Morton, J. T., 548
Moskowitz, H., 355
Mosteller, F., 374, 563
Mumpower, J., 363, 366, 534
Murphy, A. H., 127, 129, 130, 421, 424, 425

National Research Council, 504
Navon, D., 534
Newman, J. R., 61, 260–6, 413–19
Neyman, J., 147, 564
Nisbett, R. E., 537, 539, 543–4, 560
Nogee, P., 374, 563
Noma, E., 216, 231
North, D. W., 567
Novick, M. R., 162

Occupational Safety and Health Administration, 37
O'Connor, M. F., 23, 232, 365, 491–9
Oskamp, S., 535

Pai, G. K., 364
Pareto, V., 561
Pauker, S. G., 382, 408–11, 509–13
Pearl, J., 56, 363
Pearson, E. S., 147, 564
Pearson, T., 550
Peters, B. E., 367
Peterson, C. R., 22, 23, 46, 51, 65, 98–9, 200, 365, 397, 560
Pfanzagl, J., 125, 235, 317
Phillips, L. D., 46, 48, 50, 51, 94, 98–9, 114, 115, 127–8, 131, 178, 200, 517, 528, 533, 557, 563, 567
Piaget, J., 543, 545, 549
Pitz, G. F., 21, 56, 117, 128, 371, 560
Plott, C. R., 359, 380
Pollack, I., 364, 366
Pollak, R. A., 278, 340

Pommerehne, W. W., 359
Poulton, E. C., 220, 352–3
Pratt, J. W., 255, 256, 566
Preston, M. G., 563

Quattrone, G. A., 543

Raiffa, H., 32, 38, 43–4, 59, 65, 128, 147,
    148, 152, 187, 225, 249, 253, 255, 256,
    277, 278, 285, 295, 298, 299–302, 304,
    307, 308, 311, 332, 337, 339, 340, 341,
    357, 382–3, 405, 448, 562, 566, 567, 568
Ramsey, F. P., 116, 561, 564
Rapoport, A., 117, 371, 421, 560
Reed, H., 537
Reilly, R. J., 359
Renn, O, 22, 203
Rice, T. R., 56
Rios, J., 22
Roberts, H. V., 115, 129, 448, 451–2, 521
Rosen, A., 412, 535
Ross, L., 539, 560
Rouanet, H., 533
Rowse, G. L., 134

Saaty, T. L., 58–9, 365
Sachs, N. J., 21, 56, 117, 371, 560
Sackman, H., 135
Sagaria, S. D., 549
Saleh, J., 56
Saltzman, M., 21, 360, 445
Sarin, R. K., 210, 213, 214, 277, 287–92,
    327, 339, 340, 357
Savage, L. J., 18, 94, 117, 137, 141, 143, 151,
    153, 158, 159–60, 213–14, 317, 321, 322,
    533, 534, 538, 560, 562, 563–4, 565
Schaefer, R. E., 128, 180
Schlaifer, R., 65, 147, 148, 152, 187, 565–6
Schmitt, N., 362, 367
Schneider, F., 359
Schoemaker, P. J. H., 215, 359–60, 364, 365,
    376, 382
Schum, D. A., 23, 51, 163, 166, 169, 170,
    178, 180, 192–9, 200, 201, 202, 204, 528,
    573
Schwartz, J. P., 115
Seale, D. L., 115, 129, 448, 451–2, 521
Seaver, D. A., 115, 128, 133, 135–6, 442,
    443, 517, 519–20, 533
Sells, S. B., 548
Selvidge, J., 46, 51, 98–9, 121
Sewall, S. T., 447
Shafer, G., 96, 164
Shanteau, J. C., 534
Shapira, Z., 356
Shukla, R. U., 135
Sicherman, A., 292, 302
Sieber, J. E., 128

Siegel, S., 116, 374
Siegler, R. S., 535
Sjoberg, L., 218
Slovic, P., 21–2, 53–5, 56, 114, 117, 122,
    133, 200, 355–6, 357, 359, 362, 363, 366,
    371, 379, 530, 533, 535, 540, 541, 543,
    560
Smokler, H. E., Jr., 560
Snapper, K. J., 61, 200, 519–20
Sox, H. C., Jr., 382
Spetzler, C. S., 113, 115
Staël von Holstein, C.-A., 113, 115, 134
Stauss, F. Y., 129, 452–5, 528
Steele, J. P., 115, 129, 448, 451–2, 521
Steinmann, D. O., 363
Stevens, S. S., 112, 218, 316, 352
Stewart, T. R., 363
Stigler, G. J., 560
Stillwell, W. G., 115, 284, 367, 369, 442
Straughan, D., 500
Stuart, K. R., 364
Summer, D. A., 366
Suppes, P., 116, 210, 216, 218, 219, 232, 276,
    295, 315, 316, 318, 321, 322, 327, 332,
    340, 374, 560
Swensson, R. G., 445
Swets, J. A., 156, 157, 182, 445, 447

Taliaferro, J. D., 366
Tanner, W. P., Jr., 156, 445
Thornbury, J. R., 115, 129, 448–52, 521
Thrall, R. M., 563
Thurstone, L. L., 217
Timmers, H., 549
Toda, M., 298
Torgerson, W. S., 216, 231, 235, 366
Tukey, J. W., 278, 321
Turoff, M., 135
Tversky, A., 109, 121, 210, 216, 232, 276,
    295, 315, 316, 318, 321, 327, 332, 340,
    355, 361, 367, 372–3, 376, 378–9, 379–
    83, 384, 386, 530–1, 533, 534–6, 537,
    538, 539, 541, 542, 543, 547, 548–9, 552,
    560, 565

Uhlela, Z. J., 446
Ulvila, J., 448, 522
U.S. Geological Survey, 152, 461
U.S. Nuclear Regulatory Commission, 37,
    48, 52, 55, 542

Van de Ven, A., 135
Van Meter, D., 156
Vari, A., 522
Vaupel, J. W., 64
Vecsenyi, J., 522
Vinogradov, A. A., 315
Vlek, C., 534

von Neumann, J., 209, 299, 317, 321, 335, 348, 561–4
von Winterfeldt, D., 22, 27–9, 32–5, 66, 72, 128, 203, 213, 214, 215, 251, 266, 285, 296, 308, 309, 335, 339, 340–1, 342, 347, 348, 357–8, 363, 364, 365, 368, 369, 377, 392, 420, 421, 422, 436, 443, 444, 474–82, 499–509, 517, 521–2, 555

Wagenaar, W. A., 534, 549
Waid, C. D., 364, 365
Wainer, H., 441
Wald, A., 564
Wallace, P. L., 115, 129, 448–52, 521
Wallsten, T. S., 115, 117, 371, 560
Walster, G. W., 135
Ward, L. M., 534
Watson, C. S., 447
Wehrung, D. A., 298, 379
Wendt, D., 447

Wheeler, G. E., 533
Wigmore, J. H., 164
Wiig, K. M., 513, 515–19
Wilkins, M. C., 548
Willke, T. A., 50, 180
Winet, M., 316
Winkler, R. L., 126, 129–30, 134, 421, 424–5, 534
Wise, J. A., 533
Wishuda, A., 41, 57
Woodworth, R. S., 548
Wright, W. F., 366
Wyer, R. S., Jr., 547

Yntema, D. B., 364, 366

Zadeh, L., 96
Zinnes, J. L., 218, 315, 318, 322
Zlotnick, J., 129
Zweitel, P., 359

Subject index

account, mental, 373
actor, *see* stakeholder
Addis Ababa, Ethiopia, 90, 91
additive difference independence (ADI), 288, 326–8, 339, 345, 350
additive expected utility independence (AEUI), 304, 335, 339, 346, 350, 367–8, 486
admissibility, 388, 391, 395, 418, 426; *see also* dominance
alibi, 167, 168, 189, 193, 199
Allais's paradox, 378, 379
almanac questions, 127, 135
American College of Radiology, 448–9, 521
analytic hierarchy process, 365
anchoring and adjustment, 541–2
Archimedean axioms, 320, 324–5, 334
artificial intelligence, 24, 56
assessment, *see* elicitation techniques
assets: current, 374–7; final, 372, 374, 376, 377; status quo, 374
atherosclerosis, 9–14
attitude toward risk, *see* qualitative properties of utility functions
attribute, 6; definition of, 38; *see also* value trees
availability, 542–3
averaging out and folding back: general procedure, 76–8, 81; for value of perfect information, 82–3; for value of sample information, 83–5
axiomatic validity of multiattribute utility models: concepts of, 363; experiments on, 367–8
axioms for conjoint measurement: Archimedean, 334; cancellation, 332; joint independence, 294, 331–2, 339, 367, 486; single independence, 294, 332, 339; Thomson condition, 332–3; unrestricted solvability, 334; weak order, 331
axioms for expected utility measurement: Archimedean, 324–5; connectedness, 322; equal standard sequences, 324;

solvability, 324–5; sure thing, 213, 214, 304, 323–4; transitivity, 322; weak order, 323
axioms for multiattribute utility measurement: additive expected utility independence, 304, 335, 339, 346, 350, 367–8, 486; marginality assumption, 304, 335; multilinear expected utility independence, 308, 337, 339, 358; multiplicative expected utility independence, 306–7, 337, 339, 349, 350, 486
axioms for multiattribute value measurement: additive difference independence, 288, 326–8, 339, 345, 350; multilinear difference independence, 293, 327, 339, 345, 358; multiplicative difference independence, 292, 329–30, 339, 345, 350; strong difference independence, 292; weak difference independence, 293
axioms for value measurement: Archimedean, 320; cancellation, 319; connectedness, 318–19; solvability, 320; summation, 319; transitivity, 319; weak order, 319

Baker Street Irregulars, 172
base rate, ignoring, 534–7
basic reference lottery tickets (brlts), *see* elicitation techniques for single-attribute utility measurement
behavioral decision theory, 16, 21, 563
bent-stick illusion, 531
biases and errors: in arithmetic, 548–9; in logic, 547–8; in physics, 545–6
biases in probability judgments: anchoring and adjustment, 541–2; availability, 542–3; base rate, ignoring, 534–7; conservatism, 200, 533–4; hindsight, 131–3, 540–1; motivational, 527; nonregressive prediction, 538–9; overconfidence, 127–9, 131–3, 539–40;

600

sample size, ignoring, 537–8; underconfidence, 128
break-even analysis, 399, 401, 402–3, 406–7, 410, 411, 417, 438
Brier score, 127–8, 129; *see also* scoring rules for probability assessments, proper
bronchoscopy, 409–12
budget allocation, 61, 474–82
bushy messes, 65–6, 525

CADA (computer assisted data analysis, a Bayesian statistics program package), 162
calibration of probability judgments, 114, 122–3, 127–31
cancellation axioms, 319, 332
capital investment, 513–19
Central Intelligence Agency (CIA), 31
Central Unit on Environmental Pollution (CUEP), 460–2, 500, 503–4, 507, 521–2
certainty effect, 378–9, 381
certainty equivalents, 246–9, 250, 254–5, 404
checking operations, 558
clairvoyant, 113, 427–8, 431
coastal zone management, 279–82, 369
Community Anticrime Program (CAC), 519–20
complementarity, 346
conditional expected utility theory, 322
conditional independence, 106–7
conditional values: of decision functions, 393–6; of gambles, 389–91
conjoint measurement theory, 287, 294–8
conjugate distributions, 148–52
conservatism in probability revision, 200, 533–4
Construction Engineering Research Laboratory (CERL), 474–82, 522
contenders, *see k* out of *N*
contingency planning, 60–1
convergent validity of multiattribute utility techniques (MAUT): concepts, 362; between groups, 369, 370; between response modes, 356, 357–8, 359; between utility and intuitive judgments, 362, 362–6; of utility and value, 358
convexity, 422–4
convex mixtures, 390–1, 394, 395
coronary bypass surgery, 509–13; *see also* surgery
cost–benefit analysis, 42, 419, 562
credibility of evidence, 196–7
crisis management, 31
curve fitting: utility functions, 247, 252–3; value functions, 237–9
debiasing techniques for probability assessments, 131–3

decision aids, computer program, 24–5; DESIGN, 397–9; EVAL, 58; EXPERT CHOICE, 58–9; MAUD, 58, 527; OPINT, 58; SURVAV, 59
decision analysis software, *see* decision aids
decision conferences, 397–8; *see also* decision aids
decision support systems (DSS), 24; *see also* decision aids
declining exponential approximation to life expectancy (DEALE), 409–12
Defense Advanced Research Projects Agency (DARPA), 568–9
Delphi procedure, 135
DESIGN, 397–9
diagnosticity, 448
dispatching problem, 205
dog in the nighttime, 171–2, 203
dominance: cardinal, 265, 388–92, 418; due to inferior information, 435–6; elimination of, 396–9; higher order, 88, 392–6, 400–1, 414, 435–6; among multiattributed options, 391–2; ordinal, 8, 18, 380, 388–92, 414; stochastic, 517
dual standard sequences, 267–72, 273–4, 295

earthquake, 455, 466–7
editing operations, 372–3; *see also* prospect theory
efficacy, diagnostic, 448
elicitation techniques for probabilities, continuous, 118–20; direct estimation, 118–19; fractile procedure, 119; parameter estimation, 119
elicitation techniques for probabilities, discrete, 114–18; certainty equivalent method, 116–18; direct estimation, 114–15; group, 133–6; log odds, 115, 121; reference events, 115; reference lotteries, 117–18
elicitation techniques for probabilities, extreme, 120–2
elicitation techniques for single-attribute utility measurement: variable certainty equivalent method, 217, 224, 226, 246–9, 253–5, 273–4, 299, 311, 321–3, 360, 361; variable probability method, 217, 224, 226, 241–4, 249–53, 273, 274, 311, 321–3, 360, 361, 486–8
elicitation techniques for single-attribute value measurement: bisection, 217, 224, 226, 274, 310, 318; category estimation, 224, 226, 231, 274; curve drawing, 224, 226, 231–2, 262, 274, 283, 310, 493; direct rating, 218, 224, 226–31, 262, 274, 282, 310; ratio estimation, 218, 224, 226, 231–2, 310; standard sequence, 217, 224, 226, 232–3, 274, 288, 310, 318, 320, 334

elicitation techniques for weights: cross-attribute indifference, 271, 272, 274, 275; direct rating, 284; importance ratios, 274, 281, 283, 470, 476; rank weighting, 284; strength of preference, 274–5, 289–91; swing, 274–5, 286–7, 493; trade-off, 488–90; variable probability method, 274, 275, 299–300, 305, 486–7
Ellsberg's paradox, 382
encoding, *see* elicitation techniques
equity, 44
European Community, 28–9
EVAL, 58
event trees, 26, 57, 121; construction techniques of, 52–3; examples of, 47, 52
evidence: ancillary, 117–18, 202; contradictory, 178, 194; corroboratively redundant, 178, 194, 198; cumulatively redundant, 168, 178, 195, 197; mainframe, 177–8, 202; negative, 171; *see also* inference trees
evidence structures, 164; *see also* inference trees
exchangeability, 106, 107, 173
EXPERT CHOICE, 58–9
expert systems, 24

face validity of value judgments, 211
fault trees, 26, 121; construction techniques of, 53–6; examples of, 48, 54
flat maxima: implications for behavioral studies, 445–7; in MAUT models, 437–9; principles of, 399; reasons for, 420–1; in scoring rules, 421–6; sensitivity to decisions, 434; sensitivity to information, 434–6; sensitivity to prior probabilities, 426–34
fractile method, 119
functional relationships between utility and value, 340–1, 342, 368
fuzzy set theory, 96

game theory, 35
gin, 110
grade point average, 51, 364

hedging, 26, 65
hidden agendas, 520
high priests, 573
hindsight, 131–3, 540–1
Holmes, Sherlock, 171–2, 203
homomorphism, 316
hypothesis invention, 31, 55–6

impact matrix, 10–12
independence: conditional, 53, 79, 154–5, 163, 172–5, 452; environmental, 44, 344;

and indifference curves, 158; judgmental, 42, 44, 51, 344
independence assumptions, *see* axioms
independence from irrelevant alternatives, 343–4
inference structures, *see* inference trees
inference trees, 26, 46, 48–52, 58–9, 169, 176–8, 184, 202–3
influence diagrams, 56, 58
International Atomic Energy Agency (IAEA), 532–3
International Institute for Applied Systems Analysis (IIASA), 28
interocular traumatic test, 161, 162
interval scale, 209, 353
intuition, 550, 552–5
investment decision, 244–9

joint independence (JI), 294, 331–2, 339, 367, 486
judged utility decision generator (JUDGE), 205

k out of N, 396, 442–3

labile values, 355–7
landslide risks, 455–9
Law Enforcement Assistance Administration (LEAA), 519–20
likelihood principle, 144–7, 173, 175–6, 203
linear programming, 27
location measures, 38
lock step procedure, *see* dual standard sequences
Los Angeles Unified School District (LAUSD), 464–9
losers, *see* k out of N

marginality assumption, 304, 335
marker events, 121–2
MAUD, 58, 527
meteorology, probability assessments in, 123, 126, 129; *see also* Brier score
minimax theorem, 562
modified Bayes's theorem, 180–1
multiattribute prioritization system (MAP), 474–82
multiattribute risk aversion, 304, 307, 309, 347–8, 489
multiattribute risk proneness, 348
multiattribute utility models: additive, 275–7, 303, 336; multilinear, 276, 307, 337; multiplicative, 276, 299, 306, 336–7, 486–9
multiattribute value models: additive, 287–92, 326–7; multilinear, 293, 326, 328; multiplicative, 292–3, 326, 330

multilinear difference independence (MLDI), 293, 327, 339, 345, 358
multilinear expected utility independence (MLEUI), 308, 337, 339, 358
multiple cue probability learning (MCPL), 366, 367
multiplicative difference independence (MDI), 292, 329–30, 339, 345, 350
multiplicative expected utility independence (MEUI), 306–7, 337, 339, 349, 350, 486
myocardial infarction, 10, 510

nominal group technique, 135
nonregressiveness, 538–9
null hypothesis testing, 158
numerical subjectivity, 20

objectives hierarchies, *see* value trees
odds, 5, 100–2; *see also* elicitation techniques for probabilities, discrete odds–likelihood ratio form of Bayes's theorem, 139–40
oil spills, 27–9, 33, 35, 150–3, 460–3
oily water emissions, 499–509
OPINT, 58
options: invention of, 8, 22, 26, 31, 55–6, 65, 398, 444–5, 569; packaging of, 377, 379–80; unpackaging of, 381
ordered algebraic structures, 315
ordinal utility, 561
orthosonority, 353
outcome by value matrix, 10, 11, 12, 27, 67
outcomes, instrumental, 65–6
overconfidence, 127–9, 131–3, 539–40

Pareto analysis, 34; *see also* dominance
Pareto frontier, 391, 397–9
partition, 92, 94, 139, 144, 145
personalistic view of probability, 93–4
Petroleum Production Division (PPD), 500–5
positive difference structures, 318, 326
predictive distributions, 152–3
predictive validity of multiattribute utility techniques (MAUT): concepts of, 362; experiments on, 366–7
preference reversals, 359–60, 385
preferential independence, *see* joint independence
principle of insufficient reason, 110
probabilistic choice models, 218–19
probabilistic information processing system (PIP), 200, 528, 567
prospect theory, 15, 372–3
proxy attributes, 45, 484
pruning: decision trees, 66, 71–2; value trees, 43–4

psychophysics, 112–13, 209, 216, 218, 351–2
pumped storage sites, 45, 482–90

qualitative properties of utility functions: concavity, 255–6; convexity, 255–6; monotonicity, 257; risk aversion, 212, 214, 223, 255–7; risk neutrality, 68, 212, 214, 255; risk proneness, 224–5
qualitative properties of value functions: concavity, 237, 248; convexity, 237, 240, 246, 251; linearity, 237–8; monotonicity, 237, 246; single peakedness, 237
qualitative scales, *see* scales, constructed
quality-adjusted life expectancy, 409

radicalism in probability revision, 200
radiotherapy, 409, 410–11, 412
RAND Corporation, 567
random sampling, 90, 91, 105–6, 137, 173
random variable, 90, 104, 105–6
range of scales: defining endpoints, 230–1, 285–6; weight sensitivity to, 285, 312, 368, 479–80
rationality, instrumental, 1, 6–15, 18, 19
receiver operating characteristic function (ROC), 156–7
reference point, 373; *see also* status quo
reflection effect, 376, 379, 382
regret, 214, 382
regulation, 34, 61, 499–509; *see also* standard setting
relational system: for expected utility measurement, 322; for value measurement, 318
relative expected loss (REL), 429, 432, 433
relative frequencies, 91–2, 97–8, 110–12
relative risk aversion, 342
risk analysis, 46
risk attitudes, *see* qualitative properties of utility functions
risk–benefit analysis, 42
r out of *N* (*r/N*) hypothesis, 534
ruin and quasi ruin, 21, 324–5

sample size, ignoring, 537–8
sandbagging, 199
saw tooth procedure, *see* dual standard sequence
scales: constructed, 221–3, 282, 477, 479, 484–5; natural, 221, 225; and psychological issues, 216–20
scenarios, 45, 64–5, 121, 163–5, 166–7, 171–2, 174, 184, 196
school desegregation, 402–5, 525, 529
scoring rules for probability assessments: Brier score, 126–7; proper, 114, 118, 123–7, 421, 423–4; strictly proper, 125, 422;

scoring rules for probability assessments (*cont.*)
   see also elicitation techniques for probabilities, discrete
seduction, 164
sensitivity analysis for the analyst: general principles, 387, 399–400; investment example, 402–7; medical example, 409–10; multiattribute example, 412–19
sensitivity analysis for the client: general principles, 397, 400–1; investment example, 407–8; medical example, 411–12; multiattribute example, 419
sequential trade-offs, 273–4
signal detectability theory (SDT), 156–8, 182, 445, 446
simple dichotomy, 153–61; see also signal detectability theory
simple multiattribute rating technique (SMART), 259, 260–5, 272, 273, 274, 277, 278–87, 465, 474
simulation, 27
single channel ground and airborne radio system (SINGCARS), 491–9
single independence (SI), 294, 332, 339
siting, 59–60, 298–304, 482–90
skull fractures, 448–9
stable estimation, principle of, 141–4, 150, 162
stakeholder, 28–9
stakeholders, multiple, 6, 22, 24, 465–70
standard setting, 27–9, 33, 35, 61, 499–509
stationarity, 111
statistical weights, 366–7
status quo: changes of, 374–5, 376, 377; definition of, 21, 374
stopping rules, 146–7; see also sufficiency, principle of
strength of preferences: in bisection, 235–6; in direct rating, 226–9; over lotteries, 343; as a relation, 217–18, 316–17, 318–21; in standard sequences, 232–5; in value measurement, 210–11, 288
subaggregation, 392; see also dominance, higher order
substitution, 346
substitution principle, 385–6
sufficiency, principle of, 106, 145–6, 173, 175–6, 203
suicide prediction, 452–5
sunk cost, 88
sure losers, 465; see also k out of N
sure thing axiom, 213, 214, 304, 323–4
sure winners, see k out of N
surgery, 8–14, 72, 100, 509–13
SURVAV, 59
symmetry as basis for probability assessments, 90, 92–3

task difficulty, 551
Tennessee Valley Authority (TVA), 524
Thomson condition, 332–3
time series analysis, 111
trade-offs: sequential, 297–8; in weak orders, 297
transaction streams, 374–7
transitivity, 319, 322
triangular matrix for weight assessments, 283
twig weights, 260–1

underconfidence, 128
unscratched itch, 31

value trees, 26, 58, 59, 205, 260–1, 262, 466–7, 468–9, 476–7, 483, 492
value–utility distinction: and functional relations, 222, 223; general considerations of, 211–15

weak order, 331